# B A S I C
# CIVIL
# LITIGATION

**Herbert G. Feuerhake**
Attorney-at-Law
Norwalk, Connecticut

**GLENCOE**
McGraw-Hill

New York, New York
Columbus, Ohio
Woodland Hills, California
Peoria, Illinois

**SHEPARD'S**
McGRAW-HILL

Colorado Springs, Colorado

Feuerhake, Herbert G.
    Basic civil litigation / Herbert G. Feuerhake.
        p.   cm. — (Legal studies series)
    Includes index.
    ISBN 0-02-800015-3 (text). — ISBN 0-02-800016-1 (IG)
    1. Civil procedure—United States.   2. Legal assistants—United
States   I. Title.   II. Series.
KF8841.F49 1993
347.73'5—dc20                                                    92-39629
[347.3075]                                                       CIP

Imprint 2000

Send all inquiries to:
Glencoe/McGraw-Hill
8787 Orion Place
Columbus, OH 43240

ISBN 0-02-800015-3

Printed in the United States of America.

5 6 7 8 9 10  066  02 01 00

# OTHER TITLES

# IN THE

# GLENCOE/SHEPARD'S

# LEGAL STUDIES SERIES

# ABOUT THE AUTHOR

**H** erbert G. Feuerhake is a litigation specialist with a focus on general commercial litigation, but with substantial experience in securities law, municipal law, and workers compensation defense. He has been a guest lecturer in legal studies at Norwalk Community College in Norwalk, Connecticut, and is contributing author of Basic Legal Writing (Glencoe, 1992). He has written, and continues to write extensively, in the area of federal civil procedure for Matthew Bender & Company, Inc. He is also a member of the Connecticut and Delaware Bars.

Herbert Feuerhake's educational background includes receiving a B.A., Cum Laude, in political science and economics from the University of Delaware and a J.D. from the University of Pennsylvania Law School.

# CONTENTS

_____

_____

_____

_____

_____

_____

## _GLENCOE_
McGraw-Hill

and

## SHEPARD'S
McGRAW-HILL

proudly announce their cooperative effort to publish
textbooks and other instructional material
of the highest quality and integrity
for paralegal education.

Shepard's/McGraw-Hill, located in Colorado Springs, Colorado, has been
long known for its legal citation services. It also publishes single- and
multi-volume practice sets, specialty newsletters and law reporters, legal
directories, demonstrative videos, and document drafting software. Shepard's
publications cover a wide range of legal practice at the state and federal levels.
Each publication is kept current by a series of periodic updates, revisions, or
supplements to keep pace with constantly evolving changes in the law and
legal procedures.

# PREFACE

This textbook has been written to provide you with the fundamentals necessary to begin a career as a litigation paralegal. It has been written taking into account the fact that most beginning students lack a great deal of familiarity with many of the concepts discussed, and hence require thorough explanation of the basics. While other textbooks sometimes lose the forest for the trees, this text has been structured to keep you on track from the first chapter. Case examples and sample forms are provided where necessary to give you a sense for a particular concept. Particular effort has been made to anticipate areas which may be confusing, then structure discussions which eliminate confusion before it begins. Emphasis has been placed on the Federal Rules of Civil Procedure (which apply throughout the United States), but the prospect of state court variations and peculiarities is referenced where appropriate.

## Organization of the Text

The text is broken up into twelve chapters. The first and second chapters will introduce the student to (1) a broad concept of civil litigation, (2) the American legal system, and (3) the structure of a typical private law firm.

Chapter 3 is brief, but its importance should not be underestimated; it performs three key functions. First, it identifies the focus of the whole process of litigation in the courts—namely the *trial*. Second, it introduces the foundation on which our whole system of justice in some sense rests— namely *legal ethics*. Third, it sets forth the facts of two fictional cases, which will be tracked throughout the remainder of the book in an effort to give the student some sense of the manner in which an actual case proceeds through the court system.

Chapters 4 and 5 relate to the interrelationship between the legal system and the identification and proof of facts. Chapter 4 focuses on how investigation leads to the uncovering of facts; Chapter 5 on how the rules of evidence affect the formal presentation of factual information at trial.

Chapters 6 through 11 form the "heart" of the book. Relying heavily on the Federal Rules of Civil Procedure, but with many references to possible alternative procedures in state court systems, these chapters follow the two sample cases from the filing of the complaints, through the pleading and discovery phases, through trial, and onward through the appellate process. Related topics, such as settlement or the formulation of litigation strategy, are discussed as well.

Finally, Chapter 12 discusses several processes which are closely related to litigation in the courts. Administrative procedure and arbitration are covered, as well as methods of alternative dispute resolution such as conciliation and mediation.

## Text Design

Each chapter begins with a topic outline, followed by a commentary in which the student is introduced to the information discussed in the chapter. Chapter objectives follow. In addition to the substantive discussion, each chapter includes a section entitled "Practical Considerations," intended to impart some useful "common sense" approaches to the student.

This text was designed to be user-friendly. The lined margins provide ample space for both instructors and students to make notes within each chapter. Key terms are boldfaced and defined at first use, with a list of such terms at the end of the chapter (in order of first appearance), and an extensive alphabetical glossary of all bold-faced terms is located at the back of the book. The unique "Paralegalert!" feature highlights potentially troublesome concepts or rules. A summary at the end of each chapter (keyed to the chapter sections) should be a useful tool for review of the material covered, and the "Questions for Review and Discussion" should challenge the student to recall what has been learned. Finally, activities are suggested for the student who wants to go beyond the confines of the text itself.

## Instructional Support

To facilitate the teaching and learning process, an *Instructor's Manual* accompanies this text. Included are model course syllabi for classes that meet on the quarter system and for those on semester schedules. In addition, there are answer keys to all "Questions for Review and Discussion" which appear in the text, and teaching suggestions keyed to each chapter. Finally, there are test questions (true/false; multiple choice; short-answer essay) provided for each chapter, along with an answer key.

## State-Specific Supplements

Although the basic concepts associated with civil litigation are common to virtually all jurisdictions, the student will soon learn that the rules applicable to each individual system often differ in the details. For example, while this text emphasizes the methods used in the *federal* courts, there are fifty *state* court systems with myriad variations on the basic themes. Since the details of specifically applicable rules are critical in litigation practice, supplements have been prepared which discuss the rules and procedures applicable in certain individual states. For more information about these supplements, contact the publisher.

## Acknowledgments

The author wishes to thank the contributions of the following reviewers, without whose efforts, suggestions, ideas, and insights this text would not be as valuable a tool as it is.

Frank A. Conner, Esq., Adjunct Instructor, Legal Assisting Program, Saddleback College, Mission Viejo, California

John B. Hayes, Esq., Adjunct Instructor, Paralegal Institute, Duquesne University, Pittsburgh, Pennsylvania

Kathleen Mercer Reed, Esq., Instructor, Paralegal Program, University of Toledo Community and Technical College, Toledo, Ohio

Dorothy B. Moore, M.A.T., Dean/Instructor, Paralegal Studies, Fort Lauderdale College, Fort Lauderdale, Florida

The author also wishes to acknowledge the assistance, support, and guidance of editor Rick Adams, who never failed to lend his cheerful encouragement to a sometimes arduous task.

Last but foremost, the author wishes to provide special and heartfelt thanks to his wife, Laurel, for her patience and support throughout the many months during which the author was working full-time to complete this text.

# CHAPTER 1  Introduction to Civil Litigation

## OUTLINE

## COMMENTARY

You recently mailed a batch of letters to law firms throughout your region. Each day since, you've been checking your mailbox, hoping for that first break you'll need to begin your paralegal career.

It looks like today's the day! In your mail is a letter from a nearby law firm in need of a well-trained litigation paralegal, to begin as soon as possible. They'd like to schedule you for an interview!

But what does a litigation paralegal do? You must be ready to impress this law firm with your knowledge of the job requirements, your enthusiasm in the interview, and ultimately, your performance on the job. And in order to do that, you'll need to learn the essentials of litigation.

## OBJECTIVES

Knowledge of the institutions and workings of the American court system is the foundation of your education in civil litigation. After completing Chapter 1, you will be able to:

1. Define litigation.
2. Distinguish between criminal litigation and civil litigation.
3. Describe the structure of a typical court system.
4. Explain the function of an intermediate appellate court.

5. Differentiate subject matter jurisdiction from personal jurisdiction.
6. Explain what is meant by *venue*.
7. Identify the trial courts in the federal court system.
8. Explain the concept of *judicial review*.
9. Explain the difference between procedural rules and substantive law.
10. Explain the difference between legal remedies and equitable remedies.

## 1−1  Civil Litigation Defined

**Litigation** is the process by which the disputes of opposing parties are administered by a neutral third party, where the neutral third party has the power to render a resolution of the dispute binding upon the disputants.

There are a lot of implications to those few words. Let's address a few of the more important ones.

First, take the term "disputes of opposing parties." Generally, the dispute must relate to a real (as opposed to a hypothetical) situation: the disputants must be truly at odds over the matter in question, rather than simply curious about it. Some real interest must be at stake.

Next consider the phrase, "administered by a neutral third party." Resort to litigation occurs because at least one of the disputants has decided that the dispute cannot be resolved without outside intervention; the dispute is thus brought before an outside third party, who provides a forum in which the dispute can be considered, or "administered." It would be unfair if this outside third party were biased, since that would give one of the disputants an edge. Hence the third party must be neutral, which is to say, without *vested interest* in the subject matter of the dispute and without a *relationship* to any of the disputants.

Our definition of litigation next provides that the neutral third party must have "the power to render a resolution of the dispute." This means that the third party must have the authority to choose between the competing positions of the disputants—in other words, that the process of litigation must lead toward an ultimate decision. The process itself might not actually resolve the dispute (for example, the disputants might decide to settle the dispute themselves after the litigation has commenced, ending the process without a decision from the neutral third party), but it must be designed so that, if followed to its conclusion, it will result in a resolution.

Finally, we come to the phrase "binding upon the disputants." This phrase implies that the disputants are compelled to accept the decision of the neutral third party. Does this mean that the term "litigation" does not apply to a court trial where the disputants retain the right to appeal the decision? The answer to that is *no*, for two reasons. First, if there is no appeal, the decision is, in fact, final and binding. Second, if there is an appeal, the appellate court is considered to be merely a subsequent step in the same system, at the pinnacle of which will come an ultimate resolution that cannot be appealed further. You'll understand more about the nature of trials and appeals after reading the next section, which discusses the structure of a typical court system.

Our definition of litigation has been drafted broadly enough to encompass more than just the court system. Such processes as private arbitration and administrative adjudication, for example, can also lead to binding dispute resolution by neutral third parties, and hence also fit our definition (and we will discuss these processes further in Chapter 12). In a practical sense, such processes can also be considered part of the world of litigation. In most law firms, for example, the same attorneys who litigate in the courts also handle arbitrations and administrative hearings. You should be aware, however, that the term "litigation" is often deemed to refer only to the formal dispute resolution that takes place in the court system. For the most part, this book will be concerned with the process of litigation in the courts.

Now we are ready to differentiate between "civil" and "criminal" litigation. One way of stating the difference is to say that all litigation which is not "criminal" is "civil." You might not be very satisfied with this definition, but it is probably the best we can do, at least until we define what we mean by "criminal litigation." **Criminal litigation** involves the prosecution and punishment of crimes; **crimes** are actions or forms of behavior considered to be offenses against the public at large (even if only a small number of people are actually affected) and prohibited by the government. It is the government that prosecutes crimes; hence it can be said that the driving force behind criminal litigation is virtually always the government.

Although "litigation" as we have defined it includes some forms of alternative dispute resolution as well as courtroom practice, the term is often understood to refer only to that dispute resolution which takes place in the courts.

In civil litigation, the prosecution of a crime is not at issue. At issue, rather, are certain alleged rights, privileges, and obligations of the disputants, who are seeking an accurate determination of the bounds of those rights, privileges, and obligations. In the great majority of civil litigation matters, the disputants are private individuals, organizations, or business entities (although governments are sometimes involved as well, where government rights or obligations are at issue). Thus, the driving force behind civil litigation is not government prosecution, but simply the inclination of individuals or entities to resolve their noncriminal dispute through the litigation process.

Putting all these factors together, and keeping in mind our definition of "criminal litigation," we can offer this definition, then, for **civil litigation:** it is the process by which the *noncriminal* disputes of opposing parties are administered by a neutral third party, where the neutral third party has the power to render a resolution of the dispute binding upon the disputants, *and where the dispute centers upon the determination of the bounds of certain alleged rights, privileges, and/or obligations of the disputants.* As you can see, we have added the italicized words to refine our original definition of "litigation" (see Figure 1–1).

**Figure 1–1    Litigation and Civil Litigation Defined**

*Litigation:* The process by which the disputes of opposing parties are administered by a neutral third party, where the neutral third party has the power to render a resolution of the dispute binding upon the disputants.

*Civil Litigation:* The process by which the *non-criminal* disputes of opposing parties are administered by a neutral third party, where the neutral third party has the power to render a resolution of the dispute binding upon the disputants, *and where the dispute centers upon the determination of the bounds of certain alleged rights, privileges, and/or obligations of the disputants.*

Now that we have defined civil litigation, let's take a look at the forum in which most litigation takes place—the court system. The courts, as you will recall from high school civics, form one of the three branches of government—the **judicial branch** (the other two are the executive branch and the legislative branch). The first point to note in any consideration of the judicial branch of the federal and state governments (and it is an important point) is that there is no one format of court organization that is universally followed. Each state has its own individual court system, as does the federal government, and each system has its own means of allocating judicial power. Often, two courts in different states with the same name or title (for example, "Superior Court") will exercise entirely different powers. Thus, in conducting research or in performing any of your responsibilities as a paralegal, you must never assume anything about the powers of a given court, or the structure of a given court system. You must, rather, identify and analyze the statutes or constitutional provisions that establish the court or define the system to determine the precise nature of the court or system at issue.

> **PARALEGALERT!**
>
> The name or title of a court cannot be relied upon as an indicator of its function. For example, two courts with the same name or title, but in different states, might exercise completely different authority or powers. If you seek to determine the scope of jurisdiction or authority of a court, check the statute or constitutional provision that defines the court. Never assume anything!

That being said with regard to specific courts in specific situations, it is nevertheless safe to sketch out a sample court structure that is typical to most court systems. The details may differ from one jurisdiction to the next, but the general approach is fairly uniform. In our typical court system, there are three courts: the trial court; the intermediate appellate court; and the high court. Let's take a look at each.

The **trial court** is a court of **original jurisdiction**. We will discuss the concept of *jurisdiction* in more detail in the next section, but for now you should simply understand that (1) "jurisdiction" applies to the authority of a court to administer and decide a particular case (or, using the language of our definition of *civil litigation*, the "power to render a resolution of the dispute"); and (2) a court of "original jurisdiction" is the court to which disputants first bring their competing claims, the forum in which a lawsuit is initiated.

The role of the trial court is significantly different from that of the appellate court. A **lawsuit** (also called a **civil action**) begins in the trial court when one of the disputants, called a **plaintiff,** files a document called a **complaint** with the court, formally setting forth his or her claim. The individual or entity against whom the plaintiff is making the claim is called the **defendant.** The defendant receives a copy of the complaint and responds to the claims made by filing with the court a document called an **answer.** The defendant and the plaintiff, who are also referred to as **litigants** or **parties,** often file **motions** (which are requests to the court for an order of some sort) attacking the opposing party's complaint or answer, or seeking some other judicial directive. The complaint and the answer (as well as certain other, similar filings that identify claims or defenses) are referred to as **pleadings.** We will study pleadings in great detail in future chapters. Prior to trial, the parties are also entitled to request disclosure of factual information in the possession of the other side (including the taking of pretrial testimony in an official proceeding called a **deposition**) through a formal process known as **discovery.** We will study this process in great detail in Chapter 9.

After the pleading and discovery phases of the lawsuit have been concluded, and any pretrial motions have been resolved, a **trial** takes place. In a trial, evidence is presented by the parties, with rulings as to the admissibility of contested evidence made by the judge. At the conclusion of the presentation of evidence, a decision based upon this evidence is rendered. The decision may require rulings on questions of law and questions of fact. Questions of law (relating to the interpretation of legal rules and precedents) are always decided by the judge. Questions of fact (relating to disputed aspects of the events leading up to, or in some way affecting, the dispute) may be decided by the judge or a jury. If the questions of fact are decided by a judge, the trial is referred to as a **bench trial, court trial,** or **nonjury trial,** and no jury is present. If the questions of fact are decided by a jury (whose decision regarding those questions of fact is called a **verdict**), the trial is referred to as a **jury trial.** The final decision of the court, whether in a jury trial or a bench trial, resolving the disputed issues of law and fact, is called the **judgment.**

We will refer at times in this text to the **trier-of-fact.** This is a generic term referring to the decisionmaker with regard to questions of fact: the judge in a bench trial, or the jury in a jury trial.

For disputes that are brought to the court system, it is only in the trial court that witnesses are questioned and documents and exhibits entered into evidence for the purpose of obtaining a favorable decision—in other words, only in the trial court can a trial take place. Many people unfamiliar with the judicial process mistakenly assume that, when a case is on **appeal,** another full-scale trial takes place, with witness testimony, cross-examination, and even another jury. Don't make this mistake; it is absolutely wrong.

What happens, then, when a party dissatisfied with the decision of the trial court files an appeal? If not a trial, then what?

The answer is found in studying the role of the **intermediate appellate court.** First, let's define what we mean by this term. An intermediate appellate court is one that has the authority to render a decision overruling or upholding the decision of a trial court, but whose decision may itself be appealed to a still higher court. Well, that makes *some* sense, you're saying, but how can such a court reverse ("reverse" means the same thing as "overrule" in this context) or uphold the decision of the trial court if it doesn't hear evidence?

The answer is simple: the intermediate appellate court is charged with reviewing the **record** of the trial court and deciding whether the preliminary rulings and ultimate decision of the trial court were proper and led to a fair result. The record includes the **transcript** of the trial, which is a verbatim recitation of the questions asked, testimony given, judicial rulings made, and indeed, every word spoken "on the record" while court was in session during the trial. The record also includes the exhibits presented to the court (both those admitted into evidence and those excluded). The intermediate appellate court itself usually consists of three or more judges (as opposed to the single judge in the trial court), who together make up what is called a **panel** of judges. There is never a jury in an appellate court; juries only exist at the trial level.

Does the panel of judges simply review the record, then, and render a decision? The answer to that is *no.* Rather, the party that appeals must state the grounds on which the appeal is taken—in other words, the specific reasons it contends that the actions or decision of the trial court were wrong, and hence

---

**PARALEGALERT!**

Only in the trial court does a trial take place. The appellate court does not conduct a new trial of the case appealed, but rather reviews the record of the proceedings in the trial court to determine whether the issues on which the appeal has been based merit reversal of the original decision.

justify a reversal. The intermediate appellate court then reviews the points raised by the appealing party, reviews the record, hears the arguments of both sides on the issues presented, and renders its decision.

Based on this analysis, can there ever be a second trial in a given situation? The answer is *yes*—if the intermediate appellate court finds that the errors were sufficient to justify it (for example, if the trial court excluded certain evidence that should have been admitted), the case can be sent back to the trial court for another trial. This "sending back" is called a **remand.** During the appeal phase, a second trial would only be conducted after a remand to the trial court; it would never occur in the appellate court itself. You should note that the trial court itself might order a new trial prior to appeal, a possibility we'll address further in Chapter 11.

What happens after the intermediate appellate court has rendered its decision? There is one more potential step in the process: appeal to the **high court,** often called the "supreme court." (Often but not always: in New York, the trial court is called the "Supreme Court," a good example of why you can never assume a court's function based upon its name.) The high court is exactly that: the highest court in a given court system. A party dissatisfied with the decision of the intermediate appellate court may appeal that decision to the high court. The role of the high court is similar to that of the intermediate appellate court: it reviews the record, as well as the decision of the intermediate court, but never conducts a trial. It too, is made up of a panel of judges, often known as **justices.** It is different in one important respect, however: its decision is final, and cannot be appealed to a higher court—at least not to a higher court in that system. There are circumstances in which the decision of a state's highest court can be appealed to the United States Supreme Court, which we will discuss in Section 1–5; under most circumstances, however, the high court provides the final word on a matter.

You should understand that the pursuit of an appeal is never automatic. The losing party at trial may decide to appeal, but may also decide that, for economic reasons, or lack of justifiable appealable issues, or for some other reason, appeal is simply not worthwhile. Similarly, a losing party at the intermediate appellate level may decide not to appeal to the high court. Furthermore, depending on the provisions of the governing statutes, the appellate or high court may exercise discretion to refuse to consider the appeal. Under these circumstances, the decision of the court at the level at which the case concluded is thereafter final and binding upon the parties.

So there you have it, a typical court system: trial court, intermediate appellate court, high court. Remember, of course, that it is typical, but not universal. Some states have only a trial court and a high court; some states have more than one intermediate appellate court; many states have more than one type of trial court. For example, there may be a *family court* for domestic disputes, a *small claims court* for disputes involving a monetary amount below a certain maximum level, and a *probate court* for disputes involving wills and estates; see, for example, Figure 1–2. Furthermore, the lines as to responsibilities are sometimes blurred. Some trial courts, for instance, have appellate jurisdiction over the decisions of certain administrative agencies or lower trial courts (for example, a general trial court may handle appeals from small claims courts). Sometimes high courts (even the United States Supreme Court) have original jurisdiction over certain specified types of cases. But if you do two

## PARALEGALERT!

In our typical court system, there is a trial court, an intermediate appellate court, and a high court. But not all states are typical; there may be more than one type of trial court in a given state, or no intermediate appellate court, or some other configuration which deviates from the typical system. Check the rules and statutes in the jurisdiction in which your case is pending to determine the structure of the court system.

**Figure 1–2  Structure of a Typical Court System**

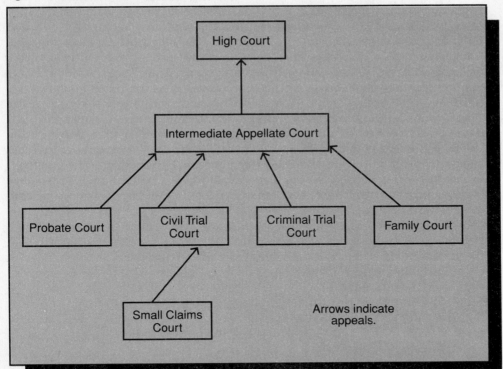

things—first, study and understand the role of each type of court in our typical court system; second, always check the statutes and constitutional provisions that define the courts with which you are specifically dealing—you will begin to develop a useful and meaningful understanding of the workings of the judicial branch in the United States.

# 1–3   Jurisdiction

Now that you have an understanding of a typical court system, let's take a closer look at a concept we've already introduced, and which we promised to define in more detail: **jurisdiction**, the authority of a court to administer and decide cases.

## Personal Jurisdiction and Subject Matter Jurisdiction

For a court to be legally authorized to administer a case and render a binding decision, the requirements of two specialized categories of jurisdiction—personal jurisdiction and subject matter jurisdiction—must be satisfied.

**Personal jurisdiction** is the authority of a court to exercise its powers over the specific parties involved in the case. Personal jurisdiction over the plaintiff in a lawsuit is never at issue, because the plaintiff initiated the lawsuit, and hence is deemed to have specifically submitted to the authority of the court. The existence of personal jurisdiction over the defendants, however, is not so easily determined. Its presence or absence is established by an analysis (1) of the residency and citizenship of the defendants, (2) of the geographic reach of their actions, and (3) of the manner in which they have been given notice of the pendency of the lawsuit. In particular, for the court to have personal jurisdiction over a defendant, he or she must be either a resident or a citizen of the locality in which the court exercises power, or have acted in some manner that has taken effect within that locality (i.e., the defendant's actions must have established some "minimum contact" with the locality, to use a phrase often invoked). Personal jurisdiction requirements also mandate that defendants receive adequate notice from the plaintiff of the filing of the lawsuit (it would be unfair for a court to render a decision or enter any orders against a defendant who was not given reasonable opportunity to defend, under the "due process" requirements of the U.S. Constitution). This notice is provided through a procedure called **service of process,** which we discuss in detail in Chapter 6.

In addition to having personal jurisdiction over the parties, a court must also have the authority to administer the category of dispute existing between the parties. This authority is called **subject matter jurisdiction.** The presence or absence of subject matter jurisdiction is determined by analyzing the statute or constitutional provision that establishes and defines the role of the court. The statute or constitutional provision will spell out the types of cases that the court is empowered to handle: perhaps only criminal cases, or only divorce cases, or only cases in which less than $2000 is at stake, or perhaps a wider spectrum of disputes.

An example might help you gain a clearer understanding of the impact and importance of these two basic forms of jurisdiction. Consider a probate court situated in Houston, Texas. Such a court does *not* have jurisdiction to decide a contract dispute brought by one California resident against another California resident, relating to a contract entered into and performed in Los Angeles, since (1) a contract dispute is not a probate matter (hence the subject matter jurisdiction requirement is not satisfied), and (2) the defendant is neither a citizen nor a resident of Texas, nor has he or she performed the contract in such a way that his or her actions constitute "minimum contact" with Texas (hence the personal jurisdiction requirement is not satisfied). Suppose the contract entered into by the two California residents related to the sale of building materials to be delivered to Houston and used in the construction of a Houston office building. Would a Texas trial court with general civil jurisdiction have the authority to administer this case? The answer is probably *yes*, even though the defendant is neither a Texas resident nor citizen, because (1) a contract dispute probably falls within the court's subject matter jurisdiction, and (2) the defendant's actions probably constitute the necessary "minimum contact" with Texas (see discussion of "long arm" jurisdiction, pg. 10) so that if the "service of process" requirement is satisfied then the court also has personal jurisdiction over the defendant.

## Venue

In addition to the personal jurisdiction and subject matter jurisdiction requirements, one final requirement must be satisfied to justify the exercise of jurisdiction by a particular court: the **venue** requirement. Venue is, essentially, the geographical location in which a lawsuit proceeds. For example, if the issue in a particular case involves a federal statute, the United States District Courts have subject matter jurisdiction over the matter, but not every

**Figure 1–3 United States District Courts, Arranged by Circuit**

**First Circuit**
District of Maine
District of Massachusetts
District of New Hampshire
District of Puerto Rico
District of Rhode Island

**Second Circuit**
District of Connecticut
District of Vermont
Northern District of
 New York
Southern District of
 New York
Eastern District of New York
Western District of
 New York

**Third Circuit**
District of Delaware
District of New Jersey
Eastern District of
 Pennsylvania
Middle District of
 Pennsylvania
Western District of
 Pennsylvania
District of the Virgin Islands

**Fourth Circuit**
District of Maryland
Eastern District of
 North Carolina
Middle District of
 North Carolina
Western District of
 North Carolina
District of South Carolina
Eastern District of Virginia
Western District of Virginia
Northern District of
 West Virginia
Southern District of
 West Virginia

**Fifth Circuit**
District of the Canal Zone
Eastern District of
 Louisiana
Middle District of Louisiana

Western District of
 Louisiana
Northern District of
 Mississippi
Southern District of
 Mississippi
Northern District of Texas
Eastern District of Texas
Southern District of Texas
Western District of Texas

**Sixth Circuit**
Eastern District of Kentucky
Western District of
 Kentucky
Eastern District of Michigan
Western District of Michigan
Northern District of Ohio
Southern District of Ohio
Eastern District of
 Tennessee
Middle District of
 Tennessee
Western District of
 Tennessee

**Seventh Circuit**
Northern District of Illinois
Central District of Illinois
Southern District of Illinois
Northern District of Indiana
Southern District of Indiana
Eastern District of
 Wisconsin
Western District of
 Wisconsin

**Eighth Circuit**
Eastern District of Arkansas
Western District of
 Arkansas
Northern District of Iowa
Southern District of Iowa
District of Minnesota
Eastern District of Missouri
Western District of Missouri
District of Nebraska
District of North Dakota
District of South Dakota

**Ninth Circuit**
District of Alaska
District of Arizona
Northern District of
 California
Eastern District of California
Central District of California
Southern District of
 California
District of Idaho
District of Montana
District of Nevada
District of Oregon
Eastern District of
 Washington
Western District of
 Washington
District of Guam
District of Hawaii

**Tenth Circuit**
District of Colorado
District of Kansas
District of New Mexico
Northern District of
 Oklahoma
Eastern District of
 Oklahoma
Western District of
 Oklahoma
District of Utah
District of Wyoming

**Eleventh Circuit**
Northern District of
 Alabama
Middle District of Alabama
Southern District of
 Alabama
Northern District of Florida
Middle District of Florida
Southern District of Florida
Northern District of Georgia
Middle District of Georgia
Southern District of Georgia

**D.C. Circuit**
District of the District of
 Columbia

one of the numerous U.S. District Courts (see Figure 1–3) would satisfy the venue requirement. Venue requirements are usually spelled out by statute (for example, section 1391 of Title 28 of the United States Code, discussed further in Chapter 6), and are designed to ensure that lawsuits proceed in a convenient and efficient location rationally related to the events and parties involved in the case—for example, near the residence of one or more of the parties, or near the location where principal incidents in the lawsuit occurred, or some other suitable location. As you might have surmised, there is some correlation between the factors that serve to justify the exercise of personal jurisdiction and the factors that establish appropriate venue, but the concepts are nevertheless different. A court that has personal jurisdiction over all the parties might nevertheless be an improper venue, based on the statutory venue requirements. We discuss venue again in Chapter 6, when we turn to a consideration of the factors that influence the filing of a complaint, but for now you should simply understand venue to be, as we stated, the geographical location of the court in which a lawsuit proceeds.

## Concurrent Jurisdiction and Choice of Forum

Sometimes two or more courts might be in a position to exercise personal and subject matter jurisdiction over a given case, and at the same time also satisfy applicable venue requirements. For example, a contract dispute in an amount over $50,000 between a citizen of New York and a citizen of Illinois who was doing business in New York could conceivably be filed in the New York federal court, or the New York state court, or the Illinois federal court, or the Illinois state court (more about the distinction between state and federal courts in Section 1–4). These courts are therefore said to have **concurrent jurisdiction.** However, a lawsuit can only be filed in one court at a time, and the losing party cannot get a second chance in another court with concurrent jurisdiction. The second court will, almost without exception, recognize the judgment of the first (giving "full faith and credit" to the first court's decision, as required by the U.S. Constitution)

**PARALEGALERT!**

Even when concurrent jurisdiction exists, a lawsuit can be filed *in only one court* at a time. Furthermore, after a lawsuit goes to judgment, the losing party cannot get a second chance in another court with concurrent jurisdiction; the case is over.

The choice of the court in which to file a lawsuit, when concurrent jurisdiction exists, is called a **choice of forum,** the forum of a case being the particular court in which the case is brought. The choice of forum might well involve a tactical decision on the part of the plaintiff's lawyers, depending on many factors including the differing approaches of the competing forums with regard to the questions of substantive law involved, the nature of differing procedural rules (see Section 1–6 about the difference between substantive law and procedural rules), and the attendant costs of out-of-state litigation. Sometimes the parties to a contract will actually specify in the terms of the contract the forum to be used should a dispute develop.

In addition to *personal*, *subject matter*, and *concurrent jurisdiction*, there are many other (sometimes conceptually overlapping) categories of jurisdiction. Some of the more significant include original jurisdiction (which we've already discussed), which empowers a court to adjudicate a lawsuit from the filing of the complaint through trial; **appellate jurisdiction,** which empowers a court to hear a given appeal; **exclusive jurisdiction,** which is present when there is only one court empowered to hear a given case (i.e,. no other court has concurrent jurisdiction); **general jurisdiction,** which applies to a court empowered to hear many different types of cases; **limited jurisdiction,** which applies to a court empowered to hear only specified types of cases (for example, only criminal cases, or only divorce cases); *in rem* **jurisdiction,** which relates to a court's jurisdiction over a *thing*, such as land; **long-arm jurisdiction,** a colorful term relating to the ability of a court to make the "long arm of the law" reach into another state and establish personal jurisdiction over an out-of-state defendant (because the geographic reach of the defendant's actions constitutes at least the "minimum contact" with the forum state); and **diversity jurisdiction,** which is a special kind of federal court jurisdiction that we discuss in Section 1–4.

## 1–4   Federal Courts and State Courts

In section 1–2 you learned about the three types of courts in a typical court system, each of which has different powers and responsibilities. In this section, you'll learn about the two major categories of court systems: federal and state.

The existence of the federal court system is authorized under Article III of the Constitution of the United States. That article expressly creates the United States Supreme Court, and authorizes "such inferior Courts as the Congress may from time to time ordain and establish." Pursuant to this constitutional power, the Congress has established a system that mirrors our "typical" system. The main trial courts in the federal system are the **United States District Courts.** There is at least one district court in each of the states; in some of the larger states, there are as many as four. As you can see from Figure 1–3, in states with more than one district court, the different courts are identified by their geographic location within the state (for example, the "United States District Court for the Southern District of New York").

Most federal cases are initiated in these U.S. District Courts, which have jurisdiction (granted by Congress; see Title 28 of the United States Code, sections 1330 et seq.) over cases involving federal constitutional principles, federal statutes, and foreign treaties, as well as cases in which the United States is a party. In addition, certain other cases can be adjudicated in the U.S. District Courts based upon the diversity of citizenship of the parties involved. Diversity jurisdiction exists when no two opposing parties reside in the same state, and the amount in controversy is in excess of $50,000. The theory that led to the creation (again, by act of Congress) of diversity jurisdiction was that state courts might be biased against out-of-state parties, hence some recourse to the federal courts for such parties was desirable and justifiable. We discuss diversity jurisdiction further in Chapter 6.

In addition to trial courts, the federal system also has intermediate appellate courts, known as the **United States Courts of Appeal.** There are 13 of these intermediate courts. Twelve of them exercise jurisdiction over appeals taken from the decisions of the multiple U.S. District Courts within a specified region, called a "circuit." For example, the United States Court of Appeals for the Second Circuit handles all appeals from the district courts in Vermont, Connecticut, and New York (see Figure 1–3). Ten other numbered circuits are identified in Figure 1–3; as for the other two Courts of Appeal, one (the United States Court of Appeals for the District of Columbia Circuit) has jurisdiction only over appeals from the D.C. District whereas the other (the United States Court of Appeals for the Federal Circuit) has jurisdiction over some of the more specialized federal trial courts (such as the United States Claims Court and the United States Court of International Trade) and also hears other specified appeals, regardless of the District Court in which they originated.

The high court in the federal system is, of course, the **United States Supreme Court.** The U.S. Supreme Court reviews certain decisions of the lower federal courts, as well as certain decisions of the state court systems. Most of the cases heard by the U.S. Supreme Court are not mandatory appeals that the court *must* hear and decide but, rather, cases presented by one or more of the involved parties for review and thereafter heard (or rejected) at the discretion of the Justices of the U.S. Supreme Court. We discuss the U.S. Supreme Court further in the next section.

There are other courts in the federal system (see Figure 1–4), including the bankruptcy courts (which are technically units of the United States District Courts under section 151 of Title 28 of the United States Code), and the more specialized courts already mentioned (the United States Claims Court and the United States Court of International Trade). For now, however, it is most important that you simply remember the basic structure of the federal system: the trial courts are the U.S. District Courts; the intermediate appellate courts are the U.S. Courts of Appeal for the various circuits; and the high court is the U.S. Supreme Court.

In addition to its U.S. District Court, each state also has its own state court system. The state courts handle disputes that do not meet the jurisdictional requirements of the federal courts; they also handle cases where jurisdiction is concurrent between the federal and state courts and the litigants have chosen to litigate in the state court. As we noted, among the 50 state court systems there is great diversity as to structure. The names of the courts vary, as does the scope of their jurisdictions. Some states have a trial court level with a broad jurisdiction, such that most cases commence in that court. An example of such a state is Connecticut, where the Superior Court has original jurisdiction over virtually all cases other than probate matters. In other states, there are a great number of courts of original jurisdiction. In Delaware, for example, there is a Family Court handling domestic matters, a Court of Chancery handling many corporate and other matters, a Justice of the Peace Court handling small matters, and a Superior Court handling certain criminal and most other civil matters. Many states have an intermediate appellate level between the trial courts and the highest court; some do not. Finally,

**Figure 1–4  Basic Structure of the Federal Court System**

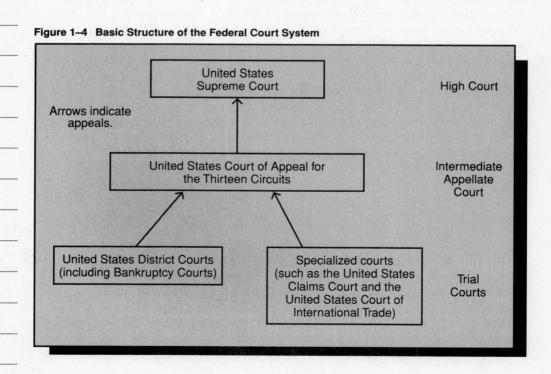

many states also include municipal and county courts within their judicial structure.

Most cases in which you are involved will be brought in the state in which you are located, and you should obviously know the procedures and structure of your own state's judicial system in detail. Although you do not need to have a thorough understanding of the judicial systems existing in every state, you must have a thorough understanding of the court structure of any state in which you have (or anticipate having) a case pending. You cannot make assumptions about that structure; you must research the statutes and master the specifics.

## 1–5  The United States Supreme Court

At the pinnacle of the American court system is the United States Supreme Court. It consists of nine judges, the **Chief Justice** and the other eight **Associate Justices,** appointed for lifetime terms by the President and approved by the Senate.

The jurisdiction of the Supreme Court is defined by the U.S. Constitution and sections 1251 et seq. of Title 28 of the United States Code. It has original jurisdiction over cases involving ambassadors and foreign officials, and cases in which a state is a party; these types of cases, however, arise infrequently. The great majority of cases heard by the Supreme Court involve a review of the decision of some lower court.

The Supreme Court is the highest appellate court in the United States, empowered to review the decisions of the federal courts and the "highest court of a State in which a decision could be had" (section 1257(a) of Title 28 of the United States Code).

As noted, the specific jurisdiction of the U.S. Supreme Court is defined in the United States Code. Cases brought to the Supreme Court are generally heard (or rejected) at the discretion of the Justices. A party desiring to have the Supreme Court review a lower court decision must file with the Supreme Court a **petition for *certiorari.*** This petition provides the justices with a summary of the issues presented for review. If the justices decide to hear the case, they grant a **writ of *certiorari,*** which authorizes the appeal. A writ of *certiorari* is usually granted only when a significant constitutional issue is presented, when the issue involved has widespread application, or when there exists a split in reasoning among the federal circuits; even in these situations, however, the court still retains the right to reject the petition.

An important concept associated with the U.S. Supreme Court, and indeed with the court system in general, is the concept of **judicial review.** In the celebrated case of *Marbury v. Madison,* 1 Cranch, 5 U.S. 137, 2 L.Ed. 60 (1803), the great Chief Justice John Marshall established the principle of judicial review, which, as it has developed, grants two significant rights to the courts: first, the right to determine the meaning of the language used in the Constitution, statutes, and regulations; and second, the right to determine whether the activities of the executive and legislative branches of government (including the substantive content and effect of statutes and administrative regulations passed or sought to be enforced) is in accord with the requirements and prohibitions of the Constitution. It is thus the courts that determine the meaning and constitutionality of statutes and regulations.

## 1–6 Procedural Rules and Substantive Law

The court systems in the United States deal with an enormous volume of lawsuits. In order to process this heavy caseload efficiently, the courts must operate according to clearly specified and strictly applied rules. The rules that establish the manner in which lawsuits are administered are called **procedural rules.** The procedural rules in use in the federal court system are called the **Federal Rules of Civil Procedure** (abbreviated FRCP; we refer to the FRCP often throughout this book). These rules establish such things as: (1) the manner of filing a lawsuit; (2) the manner of notifying all opposing parties that an action has been filed; (3) deadlines for filing various documents and motions; (4) the means of obtaining factual information from opposing parties through the discovery process; and (5) the manner in which a party requests a jury trial (among many other things). Each state court system has its own set of procedural rules (some patterned closely after the federal rules, others differing significantly).

Procedural rules appear, at first glance, to present a maze of interrelated and complex concepts. As you become more familiar with the rules, however, you will begin to recognize that they actually work in a comprehensible and rational manner to ensure that litigation practice is both fair and efficient. You will also recognize that it is in the details that procedural rules become most important, because each court expects—indeed, demands—that its own rules be followed to the letter. Hence a few cautionary words are in order here, and they are words we will repeat over and over throughout this text: *There is no substitute for a thorough knowledge of the specific procedural rules that apply to a given lawsuit!* Failure to follow precisely the procedural rules specifically applicable to your matter may be fatal to your cause.

In addition to rules of procedure (such as the FRCP), which are standard throughout a particular court system, many individual courts establish **local rules** and practices that must be followed, often relating to such seemingly minor details as acceptable margins and spacing on pleadings, or numbers of copies of pleadings to be filed with the court. Do not make the mistake of assuming that these minor details can be overlooked. Nothing is more disturbing to an attorney or paralegal than finding that a document filed just before a deadline is thereafter rejected by the court for some technical defect. Under such circumstances you would be at the mercy of the court's indulgence in letting you file the document after the deadline has passed. Although some of the negative repercussions of technical defects have been alleviated in federal practice by a 1991 amendment to Rule 5(e) of the FRCP (limiting the right of a clerk's office to reject pleadings not in "proper form"), the consideration still applies to many state court actions. Even in federal court it is important to remain vigilant; for example, although the clerk can no longer reject a motion not in proper form, a judge might refuse to grant it. Indeed, the best way to avoid the "litigation nightmare" that a defective pleading or motion can create is simply to master the rules applicable to all your pending cases, and become meticulous (almost obsessive!) in following them.

In contrast to procedural rules, which establish the manner in which a lawsuit proceeds, **substantive law** provides the rules that govern the nonprocedural issues presented to the court for decision. Was a contract violated? Is the deed valid? Is the homeowner responsible for the injuries suffered by the delivery-

---

**PARALEGALERT!**

There is no substitute for a thorough knowledge of the specific procedural rules, including the local rules, that apply to the cases on which you will be working. Never make assumptions about procedural details. KNOW THE RULES!

---

person who tripped while dropping off a package? The answers to these sorts of questions involve the application of substantive law.

As you can imagine, there is an enormous body of substantive law, covering virtually every aspect of human behavior and interaction. Most of the civil cases that are litigated, however, fall into one or more of several major areas of the law. **Contract law** relates to disputes arising over the performance, or lack of performance, of agreements. **Tort law** relates to disputes arising when one party accuses another party of wrongfully causing an injury or damage to person or property. **Domestic relations law** governs marital status, child custody, and other circumstances associated with family relations. **Property law** concerns interests relating to land (known as "real property") and other tangible things (generally known as "personal property"). The list could go on and on—the law of agency, the law of partnerships, admiralty law, general commercial law, securities law, product liability law, zoning and planning, debtor/creditor relations, and more. But most civil disputes, and most other areas of the civil law, are directly or indirectly related to one of the four major areas identified.

As we explore the world of civil litigation in this book, we touch on certain aspects of the substantive law. But as you will see as we proceed, the study of civil litigation is in large measure the study of the procedural rules—knowing how to proceed in the courts, knowing how and when to take certain steps in a lawsuit, and learning the steps by which formal resolution of disputes is achieved.

## 1–7  Remedies

When litigants go to court, they have a purpose in mind: to obtain a legal resolution to a problem. The resolution sought is called a **remedy.** There are two broad categories of remedies: **legal remedies** and **equitable remedies.**

### Legal Remedies

In the typical civil action, one party is suing another party with the goal of obtaining money damages. The recovery of damages in the form of money is referred to as a *legal remedy*. There are several categories of legal remedies, including compensatory damages and punitive damages.

**Compensatory damages** are awarded to a party who has proved that the other side is at fault, and that damage has been sustained in a quantifiable amount. The damages awarded to compensate that party, to the extent of the quantifiable amount, are known as *compensatory damages*. The purpose of compensatory damages is to place the prevailing party in as good a position as he or she would have been had the losing party not committed the wrong that led to the lawsuit.

Compensatory damages can be further broken down into two additional categories: **special damages** and **general damages.** Special damages relate to those items of compensatory damages that are precisely calculable. In a personal injury case, for example, special damages would include such things as bills for the plaintiff's medical treatment, or the dollar-value of time the plaintiff actually lost from employment, or the bills for repair of plaintiff's vehicle (if the injuries were sustained in an automobile accident). Special damages are often evidenced by bills or invoices, although this is not always the case (the value of time lost from employment, for example, must generally be calculated).

General damages, on the other hand, relate to those items of compensatory damages *not* precisely calculable. Examples of general damages (again considering a personal injury case) include compensation for pain and suffering, or for future physical disabilities. Such items are never supported by a bill or invoice, nor can they be calculated with certainty. Judges and juries have great discretion in determining the amount of general damages; hence awards for similar situations may vary significantly. A good way to remember the difference between special and general damages is: special damages can be *calculated with precision*; general damages must be *estimated* (although the estimate may be based on a speculative calculation of some sort).

If the plaintiff proves that the actions of the wrongdoer were intentional or excessively reckless, **punitive damages** are sometimes awarded in an amount in excess of the actual, quantifiable injury sustained by the party bringing the lawsuit. The justification for awarding such excess damages might be to punish the wrongdoer, or to discourage other parties from engaging in such wrongful behavior in the future, or to provide an incentive to encourage future plaintiffs to pursue certain types of cases that are of potential benefit to the public.

## Equitable Remedies

An *equitable remedy*, in contrast to the legal remedies just discussed, resolves a dispute not by the imposition of money damages, but rather, by directing the wrongdoer to perform a certain specified act, or to refrain from performing a certain specified act. For example, let's say the neighbor of one of your firm's clients insists on mowing his lawn with a loud power mower in the middle of the night, making it impossible for the client to sleep. Your firm could bring a lawsuit against the neighbor, seeking an equitable remedy. In this particular case, the equitable remedy might be a court order forbidding the neighbor from cutting his lawn between the hours of 8:00 P.M. and 7:00 A.M. Such a court order, directing a party to perform or not perform a certain specified act, is referred to as an **injunction.**

A second type of equitable remedy is referred to as **specific performance,** and relates to contract law. If your client enters into a contract to purchase a famous painting, for example, but when the time comes to close the deal the current owner refuses to go through with it because the value has suddenly skyrocketed, by seeking the remedy of specific performance your supervising attorney will be seeking an order of the court not for money damages, but rather, to force the owner of the painting to perform as he had agreed to under the terms of the contract, i.e., to sell the painting at the original contract price. If the court so orders the defendant to perform, that is called an "order of specific performance." A showing that the object of the contract is "unique" is often a prerequisite to such an order.

## Distinction Between Legal and Equitable Remedies

The distinction between legal and equitable remedies should be clear: the former relating to money damages and the latter to some less quantifiable result. Because we use the word *legal* to describe *anything* related to the law,

**Figure 1–5   Legal and Equitable Remedies**

---

*Legal Remedies*

*Money Damages:* Damages expressed in dollars and cents; all legal remedies involve money damages.

*Compensatory Damages:* Awarded to a party who has proven that the other side is at fault and that damages were thereby sustained; designed to place the party receiving the damages in as good a position as he would have been in had the wrong not taken place.

*Special Damages:* Compensatory damages which are precisely calculable (and which are often evidenced by bills or invoices).

*General Damages:* Compensatory damages which are not capable of precise calculation but must rather be estimated, such as the value of pain and suffering or future disability.

*Punitive Damages:* Designed to punish the wrongdoer, to discourage future parties from engaging in wrongful behavior, or to provide an incentive to future plaintiffs to risk bringing an otherwise expensive or difficult lawsuit.

*Equitable Remedies*

*Injunction:* Directs a wrongdoer to perform a certain act, or conversely *not* to perform a certain act.

*Specific Performance:* Requires a breaching party to perform the obligations of a breached contract; generally requires that the object of the contract be "unique."

---

however, it might seem to you that an equitable remedy could in this broader sense be described as a "legal" remedy. Perhaps that is true, but don't allow this to confuse you. The more restrictive distinction, identifying a *legal remedy* as money damages and an *equitable remedy* as some nonmonetary resolution, dates back to the old English court system, where "courts of law" handled cases involving money damages and "courts of equity" handled cases where resolution required something other than money damages. The terminology of "legal remedies" and "equitable remedies" flowing out of this system has stayed with us to this day, even though most courts are now authorized to handle cases involving either type of remedy, and even though we now often use the word *legal* in the broader sense. When discussing remedies, remember to use the more restrictive definition of the term *legal*.

A chart summarizing the various legal and equitable remedies we have discussed appears as Figure 1–5.

> **PARALEGALERT!**
>
> Don't let the word "legal" in the term "legal remedies" confuse you. A legal remedy is one involving money damages; an injunction or other equitable remedy, even though obtained through what we generally refer to as the *"legal* system," is *not* a "legal remedy."

## 1–8   Practical Considerations

The preceding pages have contained a lot of material, and probably more than a few concepts that are new to you. Many of these concepts are interrelated, and it is often difficult to understand each new concept fully until you've grasped the meaning of still other concepts. Thus, you shouldn't be frustrated if, after a single reading, you're a bit overwhelmed. Particularly in the beginning of your study of civil litigation, you'll need to reread earlier sections of this book with an eye to applying more recently obtained knowledge. You'll need to study concepts carefully, and you'll probably have questions. But if you take the time to find the answers and expend the effort necessary to understand the basics of the amazing American court system, you'll have a solid foundation on which to build your detailed understanding of civil litigation.

# SUMMARY

## 1–1

Litigation is the process by which the disputes of opposing parties are administered by a neutral third party, where the neutral third party has the power to render a resolution of the dispute binding upon the disputants. Criminal litigation involves the prosecution and punishment of crimes. Civil litigation is noncriminal litigation involving a determination of the bounds of certain alleged rights, privileges, and/or obligations of the disputants.

## 1–2

A typical court system has three levels of courts: the trial court; the intermediate appellate court; and the high court. In the trial court the lawsuit is commenced by a plaintiff, who files a complaint; the complaint is followed by an answer from a defendant, and possibly motions and discovery as well. After trial, there may be an appeal to the intermediate appellate court, and, ultimately, another appeal to the high court. The case is not retried in the intermediate appellate court and high court; rather, these courts review the record of the case on appeal. If, on appeal, it is determined that a new trial is necessary, the case is remanded to the trial court.

## 1–3

Jurisdiction is the authority of a court to administer cases. Personal jurisdiction is the authority of a court to exercise its powers over the specific parties involved in the case; subject matter jurisdiction is the authority of a court to administer and decide a particular category of dispute. Venue is the geographical location in which a lawsuit proceeds. If concurrent jurisdiction exists, the plaintiff must make a choice of forum. There are many (sometimes overlapping) categories of jurisdiction, including personal, subject matter, original, appellate, exclusive, general, limited, in rem, long-arm, and diversity.

## 1–4

In the federal court system, the trial courts are the United States District Courts; the intermediate appellate courts are the United States Courts of Appeal for the various circuits; and the high court is the United States Supreme Court. The U.S. District Courts have jurisdiction over cases involving federal constitutional principles, federal statutes, and foreign treaties, as well as cases in which the United States is a party. They also have diversity jurisdiction over certain cases that qualify based on the citizenship of the parties and the amount in controversy. The 50 state court systems handle disputes that do not meet the jurisdictional requirements of the federal courts, and disputes where federal and state jurisdiction is concurrent and the parties have chosen to litigate in state court. There is great diversity in the structure of the state court systems.

## 1–5

The United States Supreme Court consists of one Chief Justice and eight Associate Justices. It reviews decisions of the lower federal courts and certain decisions of state courts as well. Most appeals to the U.S. Supreme Court are discretionary, requiring an involved party to file a petition for *certiorari* with the court (which can be granted or denied by the Justices). Judicial review grants to the courts (1) the right to determine the meaning of statutory and constitutional language, and (2) the right to determine whether the activities of the legislative and executive branches are in conformity with the requirements and prohibitions of the Constitution.

## 1–6

The laws that establish the manner in which lawsuits are administered are called procedural rules. These rules, including the local rules, are very important. There is no substitute for a thorough knowledge of the specific procedural rules that apply to a given lawsuit. Substantive law provides the rules that govern the nonprocedural issues presented to the court for decision, covering such areas as contract law, tort law, domestic relations law, and property law.

## 1–7

Legal remedies involve money damages, and include such subcategories as compensatory damages, special damages, general damages, and punitive damages. Equitable remedies resolve disputes not by the imposition of money damages but, rather, by directing the wrongdoer to perform or refrain from performing a certain specified act. An injunction is such an equitable remedy, as is an order of specific performance (requiring a party to perform its specific contractual obligations).

## 1–8

Particularly in the beginning of your study of civil litigation, you'll need to reread material studied earlier as you gain familiarity with various topics. Many of the concepts are interrelated, and it is hard to grasp each new concept until you've fully grasped the meaning of still other concepts. But if you expend the effort to understand the basics, you'll have a solid foundation on which to build your detailed understanding of civil litigation.

## REVIEW

### Key Terms

Before proceeding, review the key terms listed below to be sure you understand each one. If necessary, read over the corresponding section of the chapter. When you are ready to test your understanding, answer the Review Questions.

litigation
criminal litigation
crimes
civil litigation
judicial branch
trial court
original jurisdiction
lawsuit
civil action
plaintiff
complaint
defendant
answer
litigants
parties
motions
pleadings
deposition
discovery
trial
bench trial
court trial
nonjury trial

verdict
jury trial
judgment
trier-of-fact
appeal
intermediate appellate court
record
transcript
panel
remand
high court
justices
jurisdiction
personal jurisdiction
service of process
subject matter jurisdiction
venue
concurrent jurisdiction
choice of forum
appellate jurisdiction
exclusive jurisdiction
general jurisdiction
limited jurisdiction
*in rem* jurisdiction
long-arm jurisdiction
diversity jurisdiction
United States District Courts
United States Courts of Appeal
United States Supreme Court
Chief Justice
Associate Justices

petition for *certiorari*
writ of *certiorari*
judicial review
procedural rules
Federal Rules of Civil Procedure
local rules
substantive law
contract law
tort law
domestic relations law
property law
remedy
legal remedy
equitable remedy
compensatory damages
special damages
general damages
punitive damages
injunction
specific performance

## Questions for Review and Discussion

1. Define the term *litigation.*
2. What is the difference between civil litigation and criminal litigation?
3. How is a typical court system structured?
4. What is the function of an intermediate appellate court?
5. Explain the difference between subject matter jurisdiction and personal jurisdiction.
6. What is meant by *venue?*
7. What is the name given to the principal trial courts in the federal court system?
8. Define the concept of *judicial review.*
9. What is the difference between procedural rules and substantive law?
10. How do legal remedies differ from equitable remedies?

## Activities

1. Determine the structure of your state's court system by researching the applicable statutes.
2. Determine whether your state has a long-arm statute, and if so, review its provisions.
3. Review the federal statute establishing the United States District Court in your state. It will be found in Title 28 of the United States Code, between sections 81 and 131.

# CHAPTER 2    Basic Law Office Structure and Procedure

## OUTLINE

## COMMENTARY

You're in the office of a senior partner in a prestigious local law firm, interviewing for a position as a litigation paralegal. You've been answering her questions, focusing on your knowledge of the litigation process and your poise under the pressure of an interview. Now she's turned the interview back to you; she wants to know if you have any questions about her firm. What do you say?

In order to ask intelligent questions, you'll need to know something about the workings of a private law firm. Private law firms remain the largest employers of litigation paralegals; thus, learning about typical law firm structure and procedures is an important part of your education as a litigation paralegal. Even if you are eventually employed in a corporation or government agency, you will likely have significant contact with outside law firms.

## OBJECTIVES

In the last chapter you learned the basics of civil litigation and the American court system. In this chapter, you'll begin to understand the structure and workings of a typical private law firm. After completing Chapter 2, you will be able to:

1. Differentiate a law firm partner from an associate.
2. Explain what an of-counsel attorney is.
3. List several categories of law firm staff personnel.

4. Explain the role of an office manager.
5. Define the term *billable hour*.
6. Draft a simple retainer letter.
7. Identify the eight subfiles in the typical litigation case file.
8. Perform a conflicts check.
9. Explain the importance of a statute of limitations.
10. Identify some important considerations when closing a case file.

## 2–1 The Structure of a Typical Law Firm

Who works at a law firm? Lawyers, of course—but it is not enough for you to know that someone is a lawyer. Lawyers or attorneys (the two terms are interchangeable) can be further differentiated by their status in the firm.

**Partners** are the most senior lawyers in a law firm. By virtue of their status as a founder, years of service, the high quality of their work, and/or their ability to attract new clients, they have achieved ownership status and a voice in firm management. They share in the firm's profits and share responsibility for the firm's liabilities; in a sense they *are* the firm. In large firms, some partners may reach a still higher level, called **senior partner,** where they are accorded additional rights and privileges (for example, a more powerful voice in management issues or a larger share of the profits).

In smaller firms, every lawyer may be a partner, which is to say that every lawyer has a say in management. As firms get larger, however, they begin to hire lawyers who do not immediately become partners. For example, many large firms hire new law school graduates each year, none of whom yet has the experience to justify partner status. Such nonpartner lawyers are called **associates.** Associates do not have a voice (at least not a decisive voice) in firm management and do not share in the profits of the firm. They are, rather, salaried employees.

The partner/associate distinction (see Figure 2–1) is the most important categorization of lawyers in the majority of law firms. As a general rule, associates work a set number of years (usually between three and eight), during which their work, contributions, and personal characteristics are evaluated by the firm's partnership. If, after the allotted time, their performance measures up to the standards established by the partnership, they will be elevated from associate to partner.

Another category of lawyer seen in some firms is called **of counsel.** A lawyer who is "of counsel" is generally affiliated with a firm in some way other than as a full-time employee, either as an occasional advisor or as a retired (but still somewhat active) partner.

A law firm often has many nonlawyer employees, collectively referred to as the staff. The staff of a large firm might be made up of paralegals, legal secretaries and receptionists, word-processing personnel, title searchers (who research and verify ownership rights in, and liens upon, real estate), messengers, private investigators, one or more law librarians, billing and accounting personnel, computer specialists, and possibly even a marketing consultant. The hiring and management of staff is usually coordinated by an **office manager** or **office administrator,** although the hiring of some of the more specialized

> ## ᴘARALEGALERT!
>
> A well-informed paralegal should know not only the *names* of all the lawyers in the firm, but also which lawyers are the *partners* and which lawyers are *associates*.

**Figure 2–1    Partners and Associates**

> *The distinction between* partners *and* associates *is the most important categorization of lawyers in the vast majority of firms:*
>
> **Partner:** A senior lawyer with ownership status and a voice in firm management. Some firms also have *senior partners*, who have a more powerful voice in management issues and retain a larger share of the firm's profits than other partners.
>
> **Associate:** A junior lawyer without ownership status and without a decisive voice in firm management. Associates are salaried employees who may, after a several-year tenure, be elevated to partner status.

positions (such as paralegals or law librarians) is usually handled exclusively by, or with significant input from, the firm's attorneys. Smaller firms have less elaborate personnel structures; a **sole practioner** (that is, a lawyer practicing without any partners), for example, might get by with one staff person who performs the multiple functions of a secretary, receptionist, word processor, and even paralegal. A large firm, on the other hand, might have hundreds of lawyers supported by hundreds of staff personnel. For a schematic view of a typical law firm, see Figure 2–2.

Another category of law firm employee is the **law clerk.** Law clerks are law students, not yet admitted to the bar, hired to perform certain research and writing functions. Many firms hire one or more law clerks in order to evaluate their performance before deciding whether a permanent position will be offered upon graduation from law school. Indeed, many firms have established formal summer programs in which the law clerks are referred to as "summer associates" and paid (and to a large extent treated) as if they were actual associates.

In addition to categories of personnel, firms are also broken down into departments, with the division being made along substantive lines. For example, there may be a real estate department, a tax department, a litigation department, and/or a corporate department. Large firms have departments that cover virtually every area of the law; smaller firms may specialize in one area, or may try to handle different types of cases without establishing individual departments (since there are not enough attorneys in the firm to justify departmentalization).

Since we are concerned with civil litigation, it is worthwhile to spend a moment discussing litigation departments. In some firms, the litigation department is further broken down into practice areas, including personal injury litigation, insurance defense litigation, domestic relations litigation, criminal litigation, and corporate litigation, with different lawyers engaging in distinct specialties. In other firms, there is no breakdown by practice area, and the litigators are all "generalists." Sometimes a given lawyer in a large, specialized firm nevertheless manages to remain a generalist. A litigation paralegal may likewise specialize in a specific litigation practice area, or, conversely, may act as a litigation generalist.

Meetings are often an important part of a litigation department's agenda. Except for being a bit more dramatic, the litigation meetings seen on *L.A. Law* are not far from the reality. Most litigation departments need to meet at regularly scheduled intervals to review the status of pending cases and to ensure deadline control. Indeed, scheduling and deadlines are among the most important practical concerns of a litigation department.

**Figure 2–2  Structure of a Typical Large Law Firm**

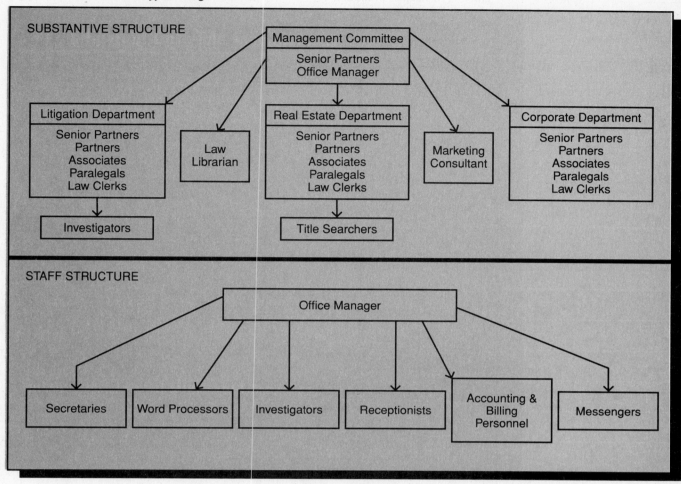

## 2–2  Time Sheets and Billing

How does a law firm generate income? It doesn't sell a tangible product, as does a manufacturing company. Law firms are, rather, providers of professional services. The "product" lawyers sell (in addition to their knowledge and expertise) is their *time*. Keeping track of this time is critically important to the economic health of a law firm; thus, each firm must develop a system of timekeeping.

At the foundation of every firm's timekeeping system is the concept of the **billable hour.** A billable hour is an hour during which tasks are performed on behalf of a specific client; the value of this time is ultimately billed to that client (except in contingent fee cases, which we discuss later) at the current rate for that lawyer or paralegal. Rates vary with experience and ability.

Lawyers and paralegals record all their work-related activities on forms called **time sheets.** A typical time sheet is shown in Figure 2–3. Spaces are provided to identify the lawyer or paralegal performing the service; the type of service provided (with common tasks addressed in shorthand code, and a space allowed for additional comments); the client, matter, and internal file number;

Figure 2–3   Example of Time Sheet

**TIME SHEET**

*Paula Paralegal*                              *9/10/93*
Name                                           Date

**Record**

| Code | Comments | Client and Matter | File Number | Hours | Tenths |
|------|----------|-------------------|-------------|-------|--------|
| 09 | on trespass issue | Jones v. Smith | J129 | 3 | 5 |
| 03 | .complaint | Gizmo Inc. v. Johnson | G356 | 4 | 0 |
| 08 | with Mr. Jones | Jones v. Smith | J129 | | 3 |
| | | | | | |
| | | | | | |
| | | | | | |
| | | | | | |
| | | | | | |

**Expenses and Disbursements**

| Description | Client and Matter | File Number | Amount |
|-------------|-------------------|-------------|--------|
| Long distance phone call Mr. Jones | Jones v. Smith | J129 | 4.00 |
| | | | |
| | | | |
| | | | |
| | | | |

**Explanation of Codes**

| | | | | | |
|---|---|---|---|---|---|
| 01 | Review | 04 | Office Conference | 07 | Letter |
| 02 | Revise | 05 | Court Appearance | 08 | Phone Conference |
| 03 | Draft | 06 | Prepare | 09 | Legal Research |

the amount of time spent on the task; and the date of service. Provision is also made for expenses (such as long-distance telephone calls) and disbursements (such as payment for case-related photographs).

By tabulating the cumulative totals of all the time sheets of all the lawyers and paralegals in a firm, bills can be generated for services rendered. In the past, the records kept on individual time sheets were carefully transferred to ledgers for each case or client, and the bills were ultimately generated from these ledgers. Today, for most firms, the process has been computerized.

What about time spent by legal secretaries, or messengers, or the office manager? Is this time recorded and billed to the client? The answer to that is *no*. Although the billing practices of law firms have evolved in response to increased market pressures and competition, for the most part it is still only lawyers' and paralegal time and out-of-pocket expenses and disbursements that are billed to the client. All other expenses of the firm are considered *overhead*, which must be covered by the fees generated under this system.

Earlier we mentioned the contingent fee case as an exception to the rule that clients are billed for the value of the time expended by lawyers and paralegals. A **contingent fee case** is one in which the fee charged by the lawyers depends on the result in the case. The best example of such a case is the personal injury matter, where the client has been injured in an accident and comes to the law firm seeking representation in a lawsuit against the person who allegedly caused the accident. Firms generally take this kind of case on a contingent basis; the fee charged will be a percentage of the amount ultimately won by the injured party. If the injured party loses at trial, the law firm gets nothing from the client (except reimbursement of out-of-pocket expenses and disbursements). You should note, however, that certain types of contingent fees are prohibited by the rules of ethics. A lawyer cannot, for example, charge a different fee depending on whether he or she wins or loses a criminal trial. We discuss other ethical considerations that relate to paralegals in chapter 3.

Although the time spent on contingent cases is not billed directly to the client, it nevertheless remains necessary to record accurately on time sheets all tasks performed. The most obvious justification for this is an economic

**Figure 2–4  Simple Retainer Letter**

# Lincoln & Hoover
## Attorneys at Law

February 1, 1993

Mr. Kevin Client
123 Main Street
Anytown, U.S.A. 54321

Dear Mr. Client:

The purpose of this letter is to set forth the substance of our meeting of this date with regard to our attorney/client relationship.

You have agreed to retain this firm to represent you in your dispute with Mr. Peter Piper. Mr. Piper has alleged that you removed a peck of pickled peppers from his premises, and has brought suit against you for money damages and to recover his pickled peppers. We will enter an appearance in that lawsuit and defend your interests.

As a partner in this firm, I will be in charge of the case and will bill my time at the rate of $200.00 per hour. My associate, Lisa Lawyer, will also work on the case, with her time billed at the rate of $100.00 per hour. Finally, Paula Paralegal will also work on the case, with her time billed at the rate of $50.00 per hour. You will also be charged for all out-of-pocket expenses and disbursements.

Billing will be done monthly. You have paid a $5000.00 retainer which will be drawn down as fees are earned. When the retainer is exhausted, future billings should be paid within thirty days.

If you agree to the terms presented herein, please sign in the space provided at the bottom of the letter, and return the original letter to us in the enclosed envelope.

Very truly yours,

Sam Superlawyer, Esq.

_____
Kevin Client

one: by comparing the value of the time spent on contingent cases with the ultimate contingent fee earned, the firm can determine which types of cases are the most profitable, and which of the firm's lawyers and paralegals are the most efficient.

How is a specified fee arrangement established with a client? By the use of a **retainer letter,** which sets forth both the fact of representation and the manner of billing (contingent or hourly). Sometimes, in cases billed on an hourly basis, a specified amount is paid to the law firm in advance. This amount, called a **retainer,** is kept by the firm in a special account that is drawn down as fees are earned. A brief example of a retainer letter is shown in Figure 2–4, and a typical bill that might be sent to the client is shown in Figure 2–5.

For many lawyers and paralegals, timekeeping is as annoying as it is important. A certain amount of discipline is required to record each and every act performed, as it is being performed. The importance of immediate recording must be emphasized, how-

**PARALEGALERT!**

If you let too much time pass before you fill out your time sheets, you will inevitably forget what you've done, and/or how long it took to do it. Fill out your time sheets *as the work is performed!*

**Figure 2–5  Example of a Bill**

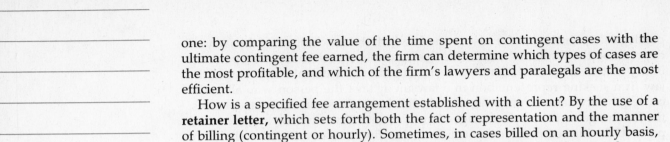

# Lincoln & Hoover
## Attorneys at Law

Billing Statement of August 1, 1993

Note: More complete itemization appears on the enclosed computer printout.

To:   Mr. Kevin Client
      123 Main Street
      Anytown, U.S.A. 54321

| Atty. or Para. | Description | Date | Rate | Time | Amount |
|---|---|---|---|---|---|
| Lisa Lawyer | Preparing answer | 5/12/93 to 5/15/93 | 100 | 12.2 hrs | $1220.00 |
| S. Superlawyer | Prepare for Deposition | 7/09/93 | 200 | 3 hrs | 600.00 |
| | Deposition of Client | 7/10/93 | 200 | 3.5 hrs | 700.00 |
| P. Paralegal | Prepare discovery | 7/11/93 to 7/15/93 | 50 | 12 hrs | 600.00 |
| Total | | | | | $3120.00 |

| | |
|---|---|
| Amount of retainer | $5000.00 |
| Previously billed | 4200.00 |
| Balance of retainer | 800.00 |
| | |
| Current amount due | 3120.00 |
| Retainer balance | 800.00 |
| Total amount now due | $2320.00 |

ever: ask any lawyer or paralegal who lets a few days pass without filling in a time sheet, and then tries to remember all the tasks and services he or she has performed. It is inevitable under such circumstances that items will be forgotten and time incorrectly estimated. Time sheets should be filled out as tasks are performed.

## 2–3 Litigation Case-File Management

Terminology can get a little confusing in the practice of law—take, for example, the word *case*. It can mean the formal, published opinion of a court deciding one or more issues in a pending lawsuit; it can mean the lawsuit itself (as where one lawyer asks another, "Did you win that dog-bite case?"); it is sometimes used to refer to a matter on which a firm has opened a file, whether or not a lawsuit has been started. For the purposes of this section, we will use the word *case* in the latter sense, as a matter on which a firm has opened a file, and we will define an **internal litigation case file** as the folder and contents of the file for any client matter assigned to or handled by the litigation department. This would include matters in which a lawsuit is pending; matters in which a lawsuit will be pending, but has not yet been filed; matters in which a decision must be made whether or not to initiate a lawsuit; matters that are in the process of settlement without a lawsuit; and, in general, any matter assigned or handled by the litigation department for which a file is opened.

In the subsections that follow, we first consider the contents of a typical litigation case file, then discuss several aspects of the management of such files.

### Contents of a Typical Litigation Case File

A litigation case file is typically divided further into several subfiles. The overall file is often stored in an expandable folder, with the subfiles found in legal-size manila folders (see Figure 2–6) maintained inside the expandable folder. The subfiles for a typical litigation case file include correspondence; pleadings; motions and other court filings; exhibits and original documents; discovery materials; legal research; investigation; and billing (see Figure 2–7).

The **correspondence subfile** contains letters that have been written between your firm and the client, the court, opposing counsel, or investigatory sources; basically, any and all correspondence generated during the course of the case. It generally includes the original letters that you have received, and copies of those that you have sent. These letters are not evidence in the case, but rather, are written in the ordinary course of business in order to advance the case. The correspondence file might also include internal "to-do" memos and informational memos (recounting the events during a motion argument or a settlement conference, for instance), telephone messages, handwritten memos, business cards, or other miscellaneous materials; the precise content varies depending on the firm and the nature and size of the case. One important distinction to keep in mind if you are charged with responsibility for filing documents in the litigation case file: letters that will be used in evidence (for example, those exchanged between your client and the opposing party) should be kept not in the correspondence subfile, but rather in the subfile containing exhibits and original documents.

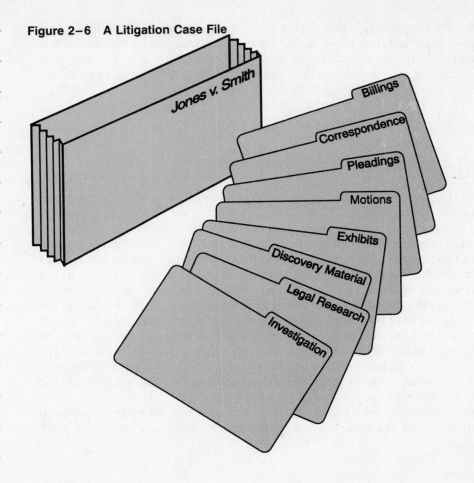

Figure 2–6   A Litigation Case File

The **pleadings subfile** contains the complaint, the answer, special defenses, any counterclaims or cross-claims, replies or answers to counterclaims and cross-claims, and any other court filing that is defined by the relevant jurisdiction to be a *pleading* (usually those filings that set forth claims or defenses). This file thus remains empty until a lawsuit is commenced. In complicated lawsuits with large numbers of pleadings, the pleadings subfile is often indexed (see Figure 2–8 for an example of a pleadings index), with numbered tabs separating the pleadings so that each is easily located.

The **motions and other court filings subfile** includes copies of motions and any other documents (except pleadings and discovery requests and responses filed with the court by any party, as well as documents generated by the court itself (such as scheduling orders or rulings on contested motions). Thus, this file also remains empty until a lawsuit is commenced. In a relatively uncomplicated case, this subfile might be combined with the pleadings subfile.

In the **exhibits and original documents subfile** are found all original documents supplied by the client (or obtained from any other source) that are relevant to the substantive dispute, as well as photographs and other potential exhibits that are capable of file storage (oversize exhibits must be stored elsewhere). Reports of experts, relevant medical bills or other original documents relating to the damages

**PARALEGALERT!**

When filing letters, be sure to separate original letters that have evidentiary impact from those that merely pertain to the case in the ordinary course of business. Letters with evidentiary impact should NOT be filed in the correspondence subfile, but rather with the exhibits and original documents.

**Figure 2–7   The Eight Subfiles of a Litigation Case-File**

*Correspondence*

Letters written to advance the case in the ordinary course of business; possibly informational or "to-do" memos; possibly original retainer letter.

*Pleadings*

Any court filing defined by the relevant jurisdiction as a pleading (usually the complaint, the answer, and certain other documents setting forth claims or defenses).

*Motions and Other Court Filings*

Copies of motions and any other documents filed with or by the court, with the exception of pleadings and documents relating to discovery.

*Exhibits and Original Documents*

All evidentiary materials, including such correspondence as has evidentiary value.

*Investigation*

Memos and materials related to investigation, including notes on witness statements; there may be some overlap between this subfile and the *Exhibits and Original Documents* subfile.

*Discovery*

Discovery requests, responses, and objections; deposition transcripts and exhibits.

*Legal Research*

Research memos; copies of relevant statutes and judicial opinions.

*Billing*

Computer printouts on billing and payment status; copies of bills and payments received; information as to disbursements and expenses; possibly original retainer letter.

suffered—in general, any documents that you anticipate will be entered into evidence at trial—are kept in this subfile. Finally, we reiterate the distinction pointed out previously: correspondence generated in the ordinary course of business to move the case along goes into the *correspondence* subfile; correspondence with potential evidentiary value goes into the *exhibits and original documents* subfile.

The **investigation subfile** contains the materials uncovered during the investigatory stage of the case (which we discuss further in Chapter 4). Included would be such things as notes taken during conferences with potential witnesses, lists of names of potential witnesses or experts, or useful phone numbers and addresses that have been developed. There is some overlap between this subfile and the exhibits and original documents subfile. For example, if a signed statement is taken during the investigatory stage from a potential witness, the original of the statement should be placed in the exhibits and original documents subfile, with a copy in the investigation subfile.

The **discovery subfile** contains the discovery requests, responses, and objections filed by each party, as well as deposition transcripts and deposition exhibits. As we noted in Chapter 1, *discovery* is the formal process by which the parties obtain factual information in the possession of the other side. One word of caution about the discovery subfile: be sure to maintain an accurate record of the source of all documents. Your firm will often obtain through the discovery

**Figure 2–8 Pleadings Index**

| # | Description | Date |
|---|---|---|
| 1 | Complaint | 3/1/93 |
| 2 | Answer of Defendant Jones | 4/7/93 |
| 3 | Answer and Counterclaim of Defendant Wilson | 6/26/93 |
| 4 | Plaintiff's Reply to Wilson Counterclaim | 7/7/93 |
| | | |
| | | |
| | | |
| | | |
| | | |
| | | |
| | | |
| | | |
| | | |
| | | |

process a significant number of copies of original documents in the possession of the other side; in a complex case, there is a danger that documents produced in discovery will be confused with documents obtained from another source. We discuss document control in more detail in Chapter 9, but for now simply keep in mind that the discovery subfile should be carefully organized, well labeled, and handled with care to avoid disrupting the tracking system for document control that your firm employs.

The **legal research subfile** contains all legal research and memos relating to the matter. This includes copies of relevant judicial opinions and statutes.

The **billing subfile** contains computer printouts on billing and payment status, copies of actual billings, copies of payments, and other information relevant to billing, such as expense reports, receipts, and disbursement records. The original retainer letter may also be kept here, or it may be kept in the correspondence subfile.

These eight subfiles—correspondence, pleadings, motions and other court filings, exhibits and original documents, discovery, investigation, legal research, and billing—are the main subdivisions of a litigation case file. For individual cases the subfiles may differ; for example, in extremely complex cases there may be separate subfiles for different categories of correspondence, of legal research, or for discovery responses received from each individual opposing party. Different law firms may also employ slightly different case-file formats. But for the most part, if you understand these eight categories of subfiles you will be able to analyze most litigation case files.

## Opening a Litigation Case File

Every law firm has its own procedure for opening case files, so the information in this section should be considered advisory only, not taken as universally accepted procedure. With that qualification in mind, several useful points can nevertheless be raised (see Figure 2–9 for a summary).

Most firms delegate the file-opening role to a single person, or to a centralized and coordinated group of persons. The reason for this is simple—with fewer people involved, mistakes (such as accidentally assigning the same internal file number to two different files) are less likely. Thus, the first step to follow when you've been asked by your supervising attorney to open a new litigation case file is to find out who in your firm performs the file-opening function (we'll call this person the "file opener").

The file opener will likely request certain basic information from you (perhaps to be entered on a standard form). This information would include the name of the client, together with addresses and phone numbers for both business and residence. If the client is a business, the name of the responsible employee would be provided. All opposing parties, as well as opposing counsel, are identified (if known). The attorney in your firm who generated the case (which is to say, the attorney who brought the client to the firm) would likely be identified, as would the senior attorney responsible for the legal work to be done and the "billing" attorney responsible for seeing that the client is regularly billed. Other attorneys and paralegals assigned to assist might also be identified. Finally, the subject matter of the case may be slotted into the applicable category.

After the necessary background information is provided, the file opener will assign an internal file number. Once a number is assigned, the litigation case-file format we've discussed (with the eight categories of subfile) can be set up, and the information and materials already held can be filed in the appropriate subfiles.

## Conflicts Check

Simultaneous with the opening of a file, the firm must conduct a **conflicts check.** A conflicts check is an inquiry designed to determine whether the firm is

**Figure 2–9   Summary of File-Opening Procedure**

| *Information provided:* | *Personnel issues:* |
| --- | --- |
| Client name | Generating attorney |
| Business address | Billing attorney |
| Business phone # | Responsible attorney |
| Residence address | Other attorneys assigned |
| Residence phone # | Paralegals assigned |
| If client is a corporation or business, the responsible employees | |
| Opposing parties | *Procedural matters:* |
| Opposing counsel | Conflicts check |
| | Statute of limitations safeguards |

prevented, for any reason, from representing the client in the new matter—if, for example, the firm already represents one of the opposing parties. Again, different firms have different methods for determining the existence of conflicts. Some firms circulate sheets identifying the parties involved in all newly opened files, with all attorneys reviewing and signing off on the sheet. Other firms maintain centralized files containing the names of all clients and opposing parties, with the file opener responsible for comparing the parties involved in the new matter to those identified in the central file. Some firms do both; some firms use another system, such as a computerized conflicts check. Whatever the system, the conflict check is obviously an important part of the file-management process, because it would be costly and wasteful (and possibly an ethical violation) to commence representation of a new client, only to find that a conflict makes further representation impossible.

## Statute of Limitations Safeguards

When a client or potential client comes to a law firm with a claim against another party, there is almost certain to be a statutory time limit within which the claim must be raised. If a lawsuit based on the claim is not filed within that time limit, the right to pursue the claim in the courts is lost forever. The statute that establishes such a time limit is called a **statute of limitations.** Keeping track of statutes of limitations is a critically important task for a law firm. If a lawsuit is not filed before time runs out, the firm may well find itself involved in a legal malpractice suit.

Firms have several methods of tracking limitation dates. When a file is opened, or very shortly thereafter, the date on which the statute runs out may be posted on a master calendar (on which important items are recorded in the space allotted to the relevant dates). In the alternative, the date may be entered into a computerized calendaring system (which prints out a daily calendar showing impending deadlines), or in a tickler system (discussed further in the next section). Whatever the method used, someone (often an experienced paralegal) will be responsible for regularly reviewing the calendar or computer system and notifying responsible attorneys of the impending statute of limitations deadline. Such notification will likely be made at several points prior to the deadline (perhaps a year, six months, and 30 days ahead of time, and with extreme urgency if the time left until the deadline is less than 30 days).

Statutes of limitations are so important that most firms have several overlapping systems to ensure that even if one tracking system breaks down, another system will alert the responsible attorneys in time. At least one system will probably be devoted exclusively to statutes of limitations, with the others possibly including other deadlines as well.

## Tickler System

Many important dates and deadlines, in addition to the date on which the statute of limitations runs out, arise during the course of a lawsuit. Motions attacking the other side's pleadings must be filed within specified deadlines, for example, as must responses to such motions. Dates of court hearings, dates of motion arguments, deadlines for demanding a jury trial, and deadlines for filing objections to oppressive discovery requests are examples of other significant dates that must be tracked. In addition to using master calendars and computerized systems to track these dates, many firms have also found the **tickler system** to be a useful method.

A tickler system utilizes a folder or other receptacle in which individual empty slots represent future dates. A deadline is entered onto a small form, showing the name of the applicable case, the responsible attorney, the action required, and the ultimate deadline. Several copies of the form are then placed into the slots corresponding to several key dates (for the statute of limitations reminders, for example, a year, six months, and 30 days prior to the deadline) as reminders.

## Regular Filing, Ongoing Adjustments, and Maintenance

No system of management of litigation case files, however ingenious, is of any use if it is not followed meticulously. If documents are not regularly filed, for example, the eight subfiles become outdated, and loose documents may disappear. Similarly, if deadlines are not entered into the applicable tracking system, the tracking system will fail to alert the responsible attorneys and paralegals. Thus, it is not enough to have file-management systems; attorneys and paralegals must discipline themselves to keep the files up-to-date.

Sometimes over the course of a case it may be wise to adjust the composition of subfiles. For example, as discovery responses are received the discovery subfile may become too large or confusing. New subfiles should then be set up that better organize the materials, segregating them by party, for example, or by type of response. A correspondence or pleadings subfile can similarly grow to enormous size; one solution is to create new subfiles for separate chronological periods, or for different categories of document.

Files can even develop, after months or years of continuous use, physical weaknesses. Manila folders fray; expandable folders tear. A file that is falling apart not only looks sloppy to the client and to the court, it may lead to lost documents and missing exhibits. Keep an eye on the files under your control, and replace or repair them as needed.

## Storage of Files

A case file should never be left lying around in a random location, but should be returned to its permanent location after each use. Some firms maintain all their files in one central location, with strict sign-out rules for lawyers and paralegals who need to work on the file; other firms have less formalized, but no less important, systems for on-site storage of active files. By returning a file to its "home" location after each use, you minimize the risk of losing all or part of the file. This is particularly important with regard to large, multifolder files, where separation of the folders can often lead to misplaced materials. Finally, if you have removed a particular file from its customary storage location in order to work on it, it is a good idea to let the responsible attorney know that you have it. Something more important may come up so that he or she needs it, and it is your responsibility not to hinder his or her ability to respond.

## Closing a Case File

At the conclusion of a matter, a file cannot simply be discarded. It may become necessary or desirable to consult the correspondence or pleadings at some later date; the client may need to refer to some aspect of the file; documents or research prepared for this case might become useful in another case. For all these reasons, and for the unpredictable eventualities that lawyers habitually fear and prepare for, files are maintained by firms after—even *long* after—the matters have reached their conclusion. Sometimes they are maintained on premises, sometimes in warehouses, sometimes on microfilm. Firms must have a system for (1) closing files, (2) indicating "closed" status on billing or client-list records, and (3) storing and retrieving closed files. You should develop familiarity with whatever system your firm employs, so that you will be ready both to assist in the closing of the file on a newly completed matter, and to locate information needed from a closed file.

When closing a file, certain procedures should be followed. Extraneous matter, if any, such as multiple copies of the same document, should be removed from the file to minimize the amount of storage space it requires. Special care should be taken to ensure that everything is filed properly; often, in the late stages of a case, there is a great deal of activity (a trial, for example, or extensive settlement discussions) and items have a tendency to end up loose in the file. By taking the time to reorganize the file prior to closing it (when you still have some familiarity with the subfiles and the nature of the case), you can facilitate future searches for specific items.

Litigation case-file management is obviously essential to a successful litigation practice. Just how essential it is will become clearer to you as you read the chapters that follow, and develop a clearer understanding of the full civil litigation process.

## 2−4  Practical Considerations

One of the most important practical considerations for a litigation paralegal working in a private law firm (or any other employer, for that matter) is *time management*. At any given time you will likely be involved with several different assignments on several different files, and it is important that you manage your time so that all tasks are accomplished in a prompt and efficient manner. With that in mind, here are a few tips to help you with time management.

First, you should *set priorities*. Preparing lists of things to do will be helpful. At the start of each day, you should identify those tasks that you want to complete by the end of the day, perhaps numbering them in order of importance. You might also want to maintain another list of longer-range projects as well, fitting them in when time allows.

Second, do *one task at a time*. Often, the requirements of civil litigation become burdensome, and you will have the feeling that everything on your to-do list needs to be done immediately. The tendency in such a situation is to try to do everything at once—and the result, if you respond in such a fashion, is that nothing gets done. If you have six projects on your desk, a ringing telephone, a client waiting in the conference room, and a stack of phone messages to be returned, don't panic—do one thing at a time. Eventually, all tasks will be completed and things will settle down.

Third, *finish tasks!* Much time is wasted by a worker who starts a project, fails to complete it, then abandons it to work on something else. When he or she eventually returns to the original project, he or she must spend precious time refamiliarizing him or

**PARALEGALERT!**

Good time management is essential for success as a paralegal. Remember to:

(1) set priorities;

(2) do only one thing at a time;

(3) finish jobs that you start;

(4) be flexible.

herself with the project, often necessitating repetition of research or other tasks. If you reach a difficult stage in a project, rest assured that it won't be any easier tomorrow than it is today. If you have questions, ask your supervising attorney, but don't abandon it out of frustration.

Fourth, be flexible when applying the first three rules. For example, if a big assignment appears to require 40 or more hours of work, it will probably be impossible to work exclusively on that project to completion, because other important things will arise. The "finish tasks" rule cannot be precisely applied here, but it can be modified. Break the larger task down into segments, for example, and make sure to finish each segment once you start it.

So far in this book, you've been introduced to the court system, and to the structure and procedures of a private law firm. Now it's time for your first cases.

## SUMMARY

### 2–1

The lawyers in a law firm include the partners (senior lawyers having ownership status, a voice in management, and a share in the profits); the associates (less experienced lawyers who do not have a decisive voice in firm management and who are salaried); and *of-counsel* attorneys (who are affiliated with the firm in some less than full-time capacity). Other law firm personnel include paralegals, legal secretaries and receptionists, word processing personnel, law clerks, title searchers, messengers, private investigators, law librarians, billing and accounting personnel, computer specialists, a marketing consultant, and an office manager. Law firms are often divided into departments corresponding to the substantive work performed; the litigation department may be further broken down into practice areas corresponding to the various types of litigation.

### 2–2

A billable hour is an hour during which tasks are performed on behalf of a specific client; the value of this time is ultimately billed to that client (except in contingent fee cases). Lawyers and paralegals keep track of their time by recording on time sheets the tasks they have performed. A contingent fee case is one in which the fee charged depends on the result in the case. A retainer letter sets forth the fact of representation and the manner of billing the client; a retainer is an amount paid in advance by the client, and drawn against as fees are earned. Time sheets should be filled out as the work is being performed.

### 2–3

An internal litigation case file consists of the folder and contents of the file for any client matter assigned or handled by the litigation department, whether or not suit has been commenced. There are eight subfiles in the typical litigation case file. They include *correspondence* (letters that advance the case in the ordinary course of business, and possibly other items); *pleadings* (documents filed with the court identifying the claims and defenses of the parties); *motions and other court filings* (those documents, other than pleadings and discovery requests and responses, filed with or by the court); *exhibits and original documents* (items with some potential evidentiary value); *investigation* (materials uncovered during the investigatory stage, the contents of which may overlap somewhat with the exhibits and original documents subfile); *discovery* (discovery requests, responses, and objections, as well as deposition transcripts and exhibits); *legal research* (research memos and copies of relevant judicial opinions and statutes); and *billing* (computer printouts on billing status, copies of bills, records of payments, and sometimes the original retainer letter). Opening a file requires that certain information be provided to the file opener (such as names of the client and opposing parties). It is also the time to (1) perform a conflicts check to ensure that the firm can represent the client in the new matter, and (2) establish statute of limitations safeguards, if there is a statute of limitations applicable to the new matter. A tickler system, in which forms are deposited into slots for future key dates, is a common system of deadline control. Regular filing and ongoing adjustments and maintenance serve to keep files up-to-date and in good shape. Correctly storing files (which includes returning them to their proper place when your task is finished) is important to prevent loss of file materials. When closing a case file, extraneous materials should be removed to minimize the amount of storage space required.

### 2–4

Time management is an important consideration for a paralegal. Be sure to: (1) set priorities; (2) do one thing at a time; (3) finish tasks; and (4) be somewhat flexible in applying the first three rules (apply common sense).

# REVIEW

## Key Terms

Before proceeding, review the key terms listed below to be sure you understand each one. If necessary, read over the corresponding section of the chapter. When you are ready to test your understanding, answer the Review Questions.

partners
senior partner
associates
of counsel
office manager
office administrator
sole practioner
law clerk
billable hour
time sheets
contingent fee case
retainer letter
retainer
internal litigation case file
correspondence subfile
pleadings subfile
motions and other court filings subfile
exhibits and original documents subfile
investigation subfile
discovery subfile
legal research subfile
billing subfile
conflicts check
statute of limitations
tickler system

## Questions for Review and Discussion

1. What is the difference between a partner and an associate in a law firm?
2. What is an of-counsel attorney?
3. List several categories of law firm staff personnel.
4. Explain the role of the office manager in a law firm.
5. Define the term *billable hour*.
6. What items should be included in a simple retainer letter?
7. What are the eight subfiles in a typical litigation case file?
8. How is a conflicts check performed?
9. Why is a statute of limitations important?
10. What are some of the important considerations when closing a case file?

## Activities

1. Go to your local law library and ask to see the *Martindale-Hubbell Law Directory* for your state. Review the listings for some of the firms in your region, noting distinctions between partners, associates, and of counsel.
2. Spend a day recording all tasks you perform for school or work, just to get some sense of the discipline needed to fill in time sheets.
3. Review the statute of limitations in your state that governs tort actions based on an allegation of negligence. Also try to find the statute of limitations that relates to actions based on a contract claim.

# CHAPTER 3   The Paralegal and the Case

## OUTLINE

## COMMENTARY

It's your first day on the job as a litigation paralegal. You're accustomed to textbooks and professors, but now you're dealing with clients and courts, partners and judges, ringing phones and mail to be answered. The "hypothetical" situations you've discussed in class are suddenly real. "Plaintiff" and "defendant" are no longer abstract concepts; they're living human beings whom your firm represents.

The dry doctrines of the law come to life in the practice of a law firm. Real people, real problems, and the need for real solutions—this is what litigation personnel face every day.

## OBJECTIVES

In this chapter we discuss the focus of litigation, introduce you to some ethical considerations, explore the factors that influence a firm in accepting or refusing a given case, and introduce you to the facts in two sample cases. After completing Chapter 3, you will be able to:

1. Identify the focus of litigation.
2. Explain the importance of maintaining confidentiality with regard to a client's case.
3. Identify a growing trend in paralegal ethics.
4. Explain what a *pro bono* case is.
5. Explain what a law firm should do if a client wants to pursue a frivolous claim.

## 3-1 The Focus of Litigation

In Chapter 1 we defined litigation as a *process,* and as you may already know (or will soon find out), it can be a lengthy process. From the first moment when the course of events leads the parties involved to contemplate a lawsuit, to the final moment when all appeals are exhausted and the decision of the neutral third party is absolutely final, *years* can elapse. During this extended interval, is there any one aspect of the process that can be identified as the continuing focus of litigation?

Yes. The focus of litigation in the courts is the *trial.* Someday, if the lawsuit is pursued and settlement fails, there will be a trial of the various claims raised. Because of the backlog of cases handicapping so many of our court systems, and for a variety of other reasons, in the early stages of a case the trial may lurk several years in the future. It is easy to lose sight of an eventuality so remote, but you *must not* do so! From the moment you put pencil to paper to begin drafting a complaint or answer—indeed, from the first moment you even become aware of a new situation that may result in the involvement of a client in litigation, you should be thinking about that future moment when the judge instructs counsel to ''call the first witness.''

Why is this so? Why should you be thinking about the trial when you are, say, drafting a complaint or answer? The reason is that every step, every restriction, and every requirement of the litigation process, from pleading guidelines to discovery rights to motion practice to appellate procedure, has been crafted to lead to the fairest possible result at trial.

**PARALEGALERT!**

The focus of litigation is the trial that will eventually occur if the underlying claims and contentions are not resolved.

Consider, for example, the complaint and answer to which we just referred. A complaint is not drafted in a vacuum. It must take into account the knowledge that certain facts will have to be proved at trial; it is drafted with the recognition that the plaintiff's recovery at trial is limited to those claims raised in the complaint. Similarly, an answer is prepared with the knowledge that denials will have to stand up at trial, as will the facts supporting special defenses.

As we noted, the trial continues as the focus of litigation even during the appellate stage of a lawsuit. But how is that possible, since the trial is always completed (except for the rare interlocutory appeal situation, addressed in Chapter 11) before the appellate stage begins? Think back for a moment about what we identified, in Chapter 1, as the role of appellate courts. Appellate courts are charged with reviewing the record of the trial court to determine whether the trial court was fair regarding the finding of facts and accurate regarding the application of legal principles. Thus, even after the trial has been completed, it still remains the focus of the litigation process.

Cases often settle. It is frequently in everyone's best interest when they do. However, until settlement (or some other resolution) occurs, all litigation personnel, including litigation paralegals, must always remember: the focus of litigation practice is the trial.

## 3-2 Legal Ethics for the Paralegal

In addition to the focus on the trial, there is one other aspect of litigation practice that permeates the process from start to finish: the importance of ethical conduct.

Attorneys are bound by **professional codes of ethics.** The rules and provisions of these codes require attorneys to represent their clients zealously, but with respect for the system and for the rights of others. Attorneys are expected to pursue their practice in a forthright and honorable manner.

Although they virtually always work closely with attorneys, paralegals are not directly bound by the rules and provisions of these codes of ethics. (But see Canon 12 in Figure 3–2.) Despite this fact, paralegals are nevertheless *affected* by these rules and provisions; indeed, attorneys are required to take necessary steps to ensure that their staff members do not engage in unethical activity. Thus, paralegals are, in a sense, *indirectly* regulated by attorney codes of ethics. Therefore, you must understand certain basic ethical principles in order to properly assist your supervising attorney. Let's look at a few of the more important ethical considerations facing a paralegal, then consider briefly a growing trend in the paralegal community.

Perhaps most important among the ethical considerations that a paralegal should keep in mind is the restriction against practicing law. Only lawyers may practice law; paralegals merely assist lawyers in their practice. As you are surely beginning to recognize through your studies, to be able to assist an attorney properly requires a great deal of training and knowledge on your part; paralegals clearly earn the title of paraprofessionals. Nevertheless, the line between an assistant and one who actually practices law must not be crossed. If you have not graduated from a law school and passed the state bar examination, any services performed that cross this line constitute the unauthorized practice of law—which is a crime.

Happily for your career, this restriction does not prevent you from performing a wide variety of services on behalf of the firm's clients. You may do many of the things a lawyer does, as long as your work is performed under a lawyer's supervision. You may not represent a client in court, however, nor in any other forum except for certain administrative hearings discussed in Chapter 12. You may not sign papers to be filed with a court, but you may prepare drafts of such papers for an attorney to review and sign (one of the goals of this book is to prepare you to draft such papers in an accomplished manner). You may not accept fees directly from the client, nor set fees, nor may you enter into a fee-splitting or other partnership arrangement with attorneys. We refer often in this book to "the client"; you must remember that this client is your supervising attorney's or firm's client, *never* your client.

A good strategy for avoiding the inadvertent appearance of practicing law is to make clear to outsiders your status as a paralegal. This status should be directly and unambiguously indicated to all clients with whom you have contact. Clients must be made to recognize and understand that your role is to assist the attorneys responsible for the case, and that you are not yourself authorized to provide legal advice. Indeed, in every initial client contact (whether in a phone conversation, an interview, or simply as an observer in a lawyer-client conference) your first statement to the client should be to identify yourself as a paralegal. If necessary, you should explain to the client the meaning and implications of that status.

Another key ethical consideration for paralegals is the importance of maintaining **confidentiality** with regard to information about legal matters, whether

**P**ARALEGALERT!

"The client" is your *firm's* client or your *supervising attorney's* client—not *yours!*

**P**ARALEGALERT!

When establishing contact with a client for the first time, whether in person, over the phone, or in correspondence, you must identify yourself as a paralegal. If the client does not fully understand the difference between the role of a paralegal and that of an attorney, you must explain the distinction.

pending or closed cases. In your work as a paralegal, you will be exposed not only to the private thoughts and positions of the client, but also to the strategies of your supervising attorney and, in many instances, to candid internal appraisals of the weaknesses of your client's position. None of these things should be talked about with anyone outside the firm—not even with friends or family members. To do so might jeopardize your client's ability to achieve his or her goals.

Finally, you should be concerned with personal **conflicts of interest.** You owe the client and firm a duty of complete loyalty, and if you have some vested interest in an opposing party, you will not be able to live up to that duty. Let's say, for example, that your supervising attorney asks you to work on an antitrust lawsuit against XYZ Corporation, but you have invested all your savings in XYZ Corp. stock. Under these circumstances, you shouldn't be working on the case because your loyalties will be divided between the desire to assist the firm and the client, and your personal interest in seeing the value of the stock go up. You should either ask to be reassigned, or immediately sell your stock. You might even have to verify with your supervising attorney that the sale of your stock would not violate the insider-trading provisions of the securities laws.

Earlier in this section we promised to tell you about a growing ethical trend in the paralegal community. That trend is toward separate codes of ethics specifically applicable to paralegals. For example, the National Federation of Paralegal Associations has issued its "Affirmation of Professional Responsibility," which appears in Figure 3–1; the National Association of Legal Assistants, Inc. has likewise issued its "Code of Ethics and Professional Responsibility," which appears in Figure 3–2. This promising trend is indicative of the importance attached to ethical conduct in the legal profession. You should review both figures carefully.

Ethical issues present themselves in so many different contexts, and with so many twists and peculiarities, that we cannot fully discuss the subject within the bounds of this text. In general, however, if you approach your work with three factors always in mind—loyalty to your firm and the client; integrity in all your outside dealings; and faithfulness to the requirements of the legal profession, as established in both attorney canons of ethnics and the new paralegal codes of conduct—you will be able to avoid most ethical dilemmas. Equally important, you will be able to recognize, analyze, and ethically deal with those dilemmas that are unavoidable (see Figure 3–3).

## 3–3  The Case

The study of civil litigation necessarily involves many abstract concepts. But abstract though these concepts may be, litigation itself (as we noted when discussing the drafting of a complaint) never occurs in a vacuum: there must be competing parties and interests; there must be controversy; there must be a real issue and a factual foundation. You must prepare for that day when the abstractions of the classroom are replaced by the realities of active practice: real supervising attorneys, real documents and exhibits, real courtrooms, real witnesses—and real clients with real problems. Random, hypothetical contexts will no longer shift at the whim of a professor; your actions and strategy will be guided by the specific facts of your case.

If civil litigation is practiced with the facts always in mind, why not learn it that way? Why not try to make the abstractions of the classroom come to life?

**Figure 3–1** The "Affirmation of Professional Responsibility" of the National Federation of Paralegal Associations

## Preamble

The National Federation of Paralegal Associations recognizes and accepts its commitment to the realization of the most basic right of a free society, equal justice under the law.

In examining contemporary legal institutions and systems, the members of the paralegal profession recognize that a redefinition of the traditional delivery of legal services is essential in order to meet the needs of the general public. The paralegal profession is committed to increasing the availability and quality of legal services.

The National Federation of Paralegal Associations has adopted this Affirmation of Professional Responsibility to delineate the principles of purpose and conduct toward which paralegals should aspire. Through this Affirmation, the National Federation of Paralegal Associations places upon each paralegal the responsibility to adhere to these standards and encourages dedication to the development of the profession.

### I. Professional Responsibility

A paralegal shall demonstrate initiative in performing and expanding the paralegal role in the delivery of legal services within the parameters of the unauthorized practice of law statutes.

*Discussion:* Recognizing the professional and legal responsibility to abide by the unauthorized practice of law statutes, the Federation supports and encourages new interpretations as to what constitutes the practice of law.

### II. Professional Conduct

A paralegal shall maintain the highest standards of ethical conduct.

*Discussion:* It is the responsibility of a paralegal to avoid conduct which is unethical or appears to be unethical. Ethical principles are aspirational in character and embody the fundamental rules of conduct by which every paralegal should abide. Observance of these standards is essential to uphold respect for the legal system.

### III. Competence and Integrity

A paralegal shall maintain a high level of competence and shall contribute to the integrity of the paralegal profession.

*Discussion:* The integrity of the paralegal profession is predicated upon individual competence. Professional competence is each paralegal's responsibility and is achieved through continuing education, awareness of developments in the field of law, and aspiring to the highest standards of personal performance.

### IV. Client Confidences

A paralegal shall preserve client confidences and privileged communications.

*Discussion:* Confidential information and privileged communications are a vital part of the attorney, paralegal, and client relationship. The importance of preserving confidential and privileged information is understood to be an uncompromising obligation of every paralegal.

### V. Support of Public Interests

A paralegal shall serve the public interests by contributing to the availability and delivery of quality legal services.

*Discussion:* It is the responsibility of each paralegal to promote the development and implementation of programs that address the legal needs of the public. A paralegal shall strive to maintain a sensitivity to public needs and educate the public as to the services that paralegals may render.

### VI. Professional Development

A paralegal shall promote the development of the paralegal profession.

*Discussion:* This Affirmation of Professional Responsibility promulgates a positive attitude through which a paralegal may recognize the importance, responsibility, and potential of the paralegal contribution to the delivery of legal services. Participation in professional associations enhances the ability of the individual paralegal to contribute to the quality and growth of the paralegal profession.

*Source:* National Federation of Paralegal Associations, P.O. Box 33108, Kansas City, MO. Reprinted by permission.

**Figure 3–2  The "Code of Ethics and Professional Responsibility" of the National Association of Legal Assistants, Inc.**

### Code of Ethics and Professional Responsibility

It is the responsibility of every legal assistant to adhere strictly to the accepted standards of legal ethics and to live by general principles of proper conduct. The performance of the duties of the legal assistant shall be governed by specific canons as defined herein in order that justice will be served and the goals of the profession attained. The canons of ethics set forth hereafter are adopted by the National Association of Legal Assistants, Inc., as a general guide and the enumeration of these rules does not mean there are not others of equal importance although not specifically mentioned.

*Canon 1.* A legal assistant shall not perform any of the duties that lawyers only may perform nor do things that lawyers themselves may not do.

*Canon 2.* A legal assistant may perform any task delegated and supervised by a lawyer so long as the lawyer is responsible to the client, maintains a direct relationship with the client, and assumes full professional responsibility for the work product.

*Canon 3.* A legal assistant shall not engage in the practice of law by accepting cases, setting fees, giving legal advice, or appearing in court (unless otherwise authorized by court or agency rules).

*Canon 4.* A legal assistant shall not act in matters involving professional legal judgment as the services of a lawyer are essential in the public interest whenever the exercise of such judgment is required.

*Canon 5.* A legal assistant must act prudently in determining the extent to which a client may be assisted without the presence of a lawyer.

*Canon 6.* A legal assistant shall not engage in the unauthorized practice of law.

*Canon 7.* A legal assistant must protect the confidences of a client, and it shall be unethical for a legal assistant to violate any statute now in effect or hereafter to be enacted controlling privileged communications.

*Canon 8.* It is the obligation of the legal assistant to avoid conduct which would cause the lawyer to be unethical or even appear to be unethical, and loyalty to the employer is incumbent upon the legal assistant.

*Canon 9.* A legal assistant shall work continually to maintain integrity and a high degree of competency throughout the legal profession.

*Canon 10.* A legal assistant shall strive for perfection through education in order to better assist the legal profession in fulfilling its duty of making legal services available to clients and the public.

*Canon 11.* A legal assistant shall do all things incidental, necessary, or expedient for the attainment of the ethics and responsibilities imposed by statute or rule of court.

*Canon 12.* A legal assistant is governed by the American Bar Association Model Code of Professional Responsibility and the American Bar Association Model Rules of Professional Conduct.

*Source:* National Association of Legal Assistants, Inc., 1601 S. Main St., Tulsa, OK. Reprinted by permission.

Why not, indeed? In this section, we present you with the facts of two hypothetical cases. Then, in the remainder of the book, we analyze litigation concepts using examples drawn from these hypothetical cases. The goal is to create, to the extent possible, some of the feel of actual litigation practice.

By first introducing you to clients with legal problems, then formulating strategy, drafting documents, preparing for trial, and performing all the tasks of a civil litigation paralegal with these clients and problems in mind, we hope to minimize the sterility of civil litigation in the abstract. Litigation is a fascinating subject, with elements of psychology, research and writing, strategizing, negotiation, empathy for the client's plight, and goal setting. Dynamic thinking

**Figure 3–3   Summary of Key Ethical Issues for a Paralegal**

- A paralegal may not engage in the practice of law, but rather may only assist a lawyer in the practice of law.

- A paralegal must maintain confidentiality with regard to information learned about pending matters, and even closed files.

- A paralegal owes a duty of loyalty to the firm and to clients, and must not allow conflicts to impinge upon this duty.

- A paralegal should demonstrate integrity in all outside dealings and faithfulness to the requirements of the legal profession.

is essential. By analyzing underlying concepts in the context of a "real" case, you will come to understand not only those individual components which together make up civil litigation, but also the manner in which they are integrated into the whole. You will learn not only the "nuts and bolts," but an approach to litigation.

Our hypothetical cases have been designed to reflect the diverse elements of civil litigation. The first case involves personal injuries suffered in an automobile accident, which will lead to litigation in a state court. The second involves a business dispute which will lead to litigation in federal court.

### The Hampton Case

If Harry Hampton had known what was about to happen to him, he would never have taken the shortcut.

It all began on the afternoon of April 14, 1992. After getting off the bus on his way home from work, Harry walked over to Bud's Auto Service, a white clapboard garage and filling station that had served motorists of Milltown, in the state of Exurbia, for over a generation. Buddy Lindquist gestured from Bay 1 for Harry to meet him in the tiny office.

"You had a problem with the electrical system," said Buddy as he slipped behind the counter. "I had to do some work on the wiring. Little Buddy finished it up this morning. Should be fine now." Little Buddy was Buddy's teenage son.

"Thanks, Buddy," said Harry. "Can I put it on my credit card? I've got to do my taxes tonight, so I'd rather not write a check."

Buddy laughed. "No problem, Harry."

Harry paid the bill, thanked Buddy again, then drove the half mile to his house. His wife was away with the children, visiting her mother in Los Angeles, so Harry fixed himself a frozen pizza for dinner, then sat down at his desk with a year's worth of receipts, bills, statements, and other assorted records, and waded into his Form 1040. It was a marathon session, and several times Harry thought that the evil piece of paper had beaten him, but finally, at 3:30 A.M. on April 15, he filled in the last number and signed at the bottom. It was a weary taxpayer who trudged up the stairs to bed.

At 6:30 his alarm buzzed him awake. Harry groaned, reached over to shut it off, then lay back on the pillow to steal another five minutes of sleep.

When he next awoke it was 7:45. He had to be at work at 8:30; he was going to be late! He charged through his shower, jumped into his clothes, then dashed out the door without even a cup of coffee.

As he drove toward the Metro Parkway, his intention was to make a quick stop at the Milltown Post Office to mail his tax return. As he approached the post office, he flicked on his right turn signal to indicate a turn into the 10-minute parking zone. To Harry's great frustration, the dashboard indicator failed to indicate that the signal was on. Harry parked and mailed his letter. As he got back into his car, he slammed the door with frustration: Buddy hadn't fixed anything!

Meanwhile, on the other side of Milltown, Judith Johnson handed a lunch bag to her youngest son, Billy, who bounced out the door to catch his school bus. Judith then finished the breakfast dishes, checked her make-up, and headed out for her car. She had plenty of time to reach her job as a dental hygienist in Metro City, where her work day began at 10:00. She planned to use her extra time to visit at a travel agent before work, to start on plans for an upcoming vacation.

Harry pulled onto Metro Parkway and proceeded for about a mile until the traffic stopped dead in front of him. He flipped on WMET and learned from the traffic report that a tractor-trailer had jackknifed in the other direction, but "rubberneckers" heading into Metro City were slowing commuter traffic. He was tired, he was annoyed at Buddy, and this back-up was the last straw. He decided to take the next exit, at Higgins Lane, and use a back-road shortcut to Metro City that was longer in miles, but, in light of the traffic, would be quicker than staying on Metro Parkway.

Judith, meanwhile, was listening to a symphony on her car's sophisticated audio system, blissfully unaware of the traffic conditions on Metro Parkway as she navigated Pruitt Street in the direction of the nearest parkway entrance, and equally unaware of her impending encounter with Harry.

The intersection of Pruitt Street and Higgins Lane was regulated by four-way stop signs. The pole of the stop sign on Pruitt Street was completely bent over, so that approaching cars could not see that it was a stop sign. Judith, however, was familiar with this intersection, having crossed it almost every day for several years, and was familiar with the stop sign. She had even written a letter to the Milltown traffic department, asking them to fix it.

As Judith approached the intersection, at a moment when she was enraptured by the strains of Mozart's Symphony #40, she sneezed. The sneeze caught her off guard, and forced her to close her eyes momentarily. When she opened them, she realized she was zooming toward the intersection, and might not be able to stop. She had to make a snap decision—should she slam on the brakes, which might succeed in stopping her in time but might also leave her stranded in the middle of the intersection, or should she accelerate to get through the intersection before the next car came through?

At that moment, Harry had just come to a stop at the intersection. He was to Judith's left, on Higgins Lane heading west. He had every intention of continuing straight on Higgins Lane, right through the intersection, and there was no indication on his dashboard that he would be proceeding in any other fashion. His right turn signal, however, blinked a different intention—a right turn! Little Buddy had accidentally crossed the wires, so that when Harry activated the signal there was *no* signal; when he stopped signaling there was a *continuous right turn* signal—and there was no response of *any* kind at *any* time on the signal-indicator light on the dashboard!

Judith had to make her decision *now*. She saw Harry's car, saw that it was the only other car at the intersection, saw that the right turn signal was on, and decided that her safest course was to accelerate through the intersection, since Harry was intending to make a right turn. Harry, expecting her to stop, had no intention of turning, of course, but rather proceeded forward.

Suddenly there was an enormous crash of metal against metal as the two cars collided. Brakes screeched, tires swerved, metal twisted, and there was general chaos in the morning air.

At first, Harry was too stunned to move. Then he felt the numbness in his fingers, realized his arm was broken, and it hit him—he'd had an accident, maybe even a serious one! He looked over at the other car and saw Judith slumped over the steering wheel, apparently unconscious. He had to do something fast! He forced his door open with his good arm and struggled out of his car. As he took his first step toward her car to see how she was, he felt a sharp pain as his knee buckled under him.

Louella Williams, an elderly woman who lived in the house on the southeast corner of Higgins and Pruitt, had been watering her flowers when the accident occurred. She had seen the whole thing. At the initial impact she shuddered, then raced inside and called the police.

Within seven minutes the authorities were on the scene. Both Harry and Judith were taken away by ambulance. Officer Skip Evans took statements from Harry, Judith (who had regained consciousness), and Louella Williams.

## Widgets and Gizmos, Inc.

Edgar Ellison is the President and Chief Operating Officer of Widgets and Gizmos, Inc., a corporation specializing in supplying components to manufacturers of personal computers incorporated in the state of Exurbia and with a principal place of business in Metro City, Exurbia. The corporation recently realized the fruits of a lengthy and expensive research and development project: their new widgenometer had reached the marketing stage. The widgenometer, a microscopic circuit etched into aluminum chips by a newly patented process, multiplies the speed of a computer's CPU (central processing unit) by as much as tenfold, a revolutionary development in computer technology. Ellison was ecstatic at the news.

He was not so ecstatic, however, about a memo written by Hans Hoobermann, the longtime head of research at Widgets and Gizmos, Inc. and inventor of the widgenometer. Despite the success of every test and trial to which the widgenometer had been subjected, Hans noted in the memo (written to the vice-president in charge of operations) his concern that additional tests were needed before releasing the widgenometer into the market, and that the composition of the alloy used to manufacture the chip might be suspect.

Ellison was more concerned about showing the shareholders a return on the sixteen million dollars that had been invested in the widgenometer's development than he was in extending the testing period. There had been frustration expressed by a powerful block of shareholders at the last annual meeting; Ellison knew he and his management team had a limited time to produce before the patience of this group was exhausted. He punched two holes at the top of the memo from Hoobermann and placed it in his personal widgenometer file, then picked up his dictation microphone.

"Memo to Rodriguez," he intoned into the machine, referring to Maximilian Rodriguez, the Vice-President of Operations. "Date: February 17, 1992. I have read the memo to you from Hoobermann. I have also read, and frankly studied in detail, the prior test results. As you know, my background in electrical engineering prior to focusing on the business aspects of this company enables me to analyze these results with an informed eye. It is my opinion that Hoobermann's excessive caution is not consistent with the positive nature of the tests and trials. Taking these results into account, and in consideration of the current needs of this corporation in the present business climate, it is my opinion that the widgenometer is ready for production and sale. Hence it is my decision that you commence manufacture, and we will conclude negotiations with TapTapTap, Inc. for exclusive rights to the first 50,000 widgenometers we produce. End of memo."

TapTapTap, Inc. is a corporation that had, over the last few years, established itself as the dominant keyboard manufacturer in the computer industry, and was known to Widgets and Gizmos, Inc. to be looking to expand into other computer hardware components. TapTapTap, Inc. is incorporated, and maintains its principal place of business, in California. Its key executives had been introduced to the potential of the widgenometer in a series of secret meetings, and they had been excited at the prospect of bursting onto the hardware market with such a potentially novel improvement. Their strategy was to aim not for the home computer market, but for the business market; they estimated that the power and speed implied by the new widgenometers was beyond that needed by home users, but would justify a highly profitable pricing pattern within the financial reach of most businesses.

Negotiations between Widgets and Gizmos, Inc. and TapTapTap, Inc. were soon in full swing. The technical requirements were negotiated for Widgets and Gizmos, Inc. by Rodriguez, who was not as well versed as Hoobermann but who Ellison knew to be a tough negotiator. Certain important specifications were requested by TapTapTap, Inc., and Widgets and Gizmos, Inc. agreed to modify the widgenometer to conform to these specifications. There was some discussion over the specification of the alloy used for the chips, but nothing definite appeared in the contract. Agreement was eventually reached and production begun. Units were soon being shipped to TapTapTap, Inc.

If only Ellison had listened to Hoobermann! The widgenometer was indeed a miracle device, and in the early going TapTapTap, Inc. was excited at the prospect of a dominant entry into the business computer market. Initial sales were exceptional, and the stock prices of both Widgets and Gizmos, Inc. and TapTapTap, Inc. soared. But then a curious phenomenon arose. About one of every fifteen widgenometers began failing long before the anticipated "mean time between failures" (also known as the "MTBF"). TapTapTap, Inc.'s customers began frantically requesting warranty service and replacement. The repair costs mounted, and some companies began clamoring for damages beyond mere repair—they claimed their businesses had been damaged by the defective computers, and they wanted compensation!

Hans Hoobermann, meanwhile, had continued his testing on the new, modified widgenometers produced according to the altered specifications requested by TapTapTap, Inc. He discovered that the new composition of the alloy used for the chip on which the widgenometer circuit was etched seemed to demonstrate a tendency to become magnetized if exposed to an electrical current for extended periods of time—and that, once magnetized, its effectiveness was negated. Indeed, once magnetized, it actually developed a tendency to scramble or destroy data processed by the CPU.

A series of bitter correspondence has been transmitted between Edgar Ellison and Emily Tapman, the President of TapTapTap, Inc. It has centered on the failure of the widgenometers to meet the specifications agreed upon in the contract between the two corporations. Tapman has asserted that Widgets and Gizmos, Inc. is responsible to TapTapTap, Inc. for hundreds of thousands of dollars (or more) of damages as a result of allegedly defective widgenometers. It is becoming clear, however, that the contract is vague on the specifications that seem to be at issue between the parties, and it is unclear as to exactly *which* specifications may have led to the failures.

The business press has begun to report the numerous claims of defects and the growing dispute; stock prices of both corporations are down; and customers of TapTapTap, Inc. are very upset. It is becoming ominously clear that trouble is on the horizon.

There you have it—the basic facts of your first two cases. Of course, in the real world, the facts are not so easily obtained. In the real world, litigation personnel must uncover the relevant facts through interviews, fact gathering, and research. In the next chapter, we introduce you to the investigatory aspect of litigation. But first, let's turn to a common issue facing attorneys—whether to accept or reject a new case.

## 3—4   Accepting and Rejecting Cases

Although it will virtually always be the attorneys who decide which cases to accept and which to reject, it will be useful to your understanding of litigation practice to explore briefly some of the factors that influence these decisions.

Economic factors certainly play a role in deciding which cases to handle. Consider, for example, a personal injury case (such as the Harry Hampton matter) in which the fee for plaintiff's counsel will be contingent upon victory. If the injuries and other damages are slight, and if establishing the liability of potential defendants promises to be difficult, a firm may decide that the risks in representing the plaintiff are too great, and the potential rewards too meager, to justify taking the case. Similarly, if a potential client comes to the firm needing an attorney to defend a lawsuit, but is unable to pay the substantial fees that the defense will engender, the firm may also view this as a case they cannot accept. Economics is not always a decisive factor, however; lawyers recognize a duty to the community to provide some legal services in situations where the client is unable to pay the going rate, and most firms have a *pro bono* policy by which certain cases are handled at a reduced fee, or even for free.

A second consideration that enters into the calculation is expertise. Certain cases require certain types of expertise. If a lawyer has spent an entire career in a real estate practice, for example, he or she probably should not take a personal injury case in which a lawsuit will likely be filed. He or she simply lacks the necessary experience to handle the case properly. Similarly, a litigator probably lacks the expertise necessary to draft a complicated will with associated trusts and extensive tax considerations.

Although individual lawyers cannot be experts in every area of practice, many law firms are large enough to cover most commonly arising problems.

Thus, once a case is accepted, it is simply assigned to the attorney or department with the necessary expertise.

Another important issue involved in accepting or rejecting cases is the issue of conflicts, which we discussed in our discussion of legal ethics. A law firm cannot accept a case that is to be brought against one of its present clients, or that is adverse to the interests of any of its present clients. Avoiding such conflicts is not always easy; in large firms with many lawyers and clients, for example, complicated procedures to ensure the avoidance of conflicts must be established. In addition, it is sometimes a close call whether the interests at stake in a potential new case are adverse to the interests of a present client. The important point to remember is the necessity of spotting potential conflict situations and doing the necessary investigation and research to determine whether a conflict exists (and, of course, working closely with your supervising attorneys, who make the final decision).

Sometimes the issue in accepting or rejecting a case comes down to the client's motive. For example, if a client is raising a frivolous claim for the purpose of harassing the potential defendant, it would be inappropriate (and unethical) for any attorney to take the case. There are sometimes close judgment calls in this area as well. For example, suppose a claim raised by the potential client is adverse to existing law, but nevertheless represents a situation in which it might reasonably be argued that existing law should be modified to allow such a claim. The client may not, then, be acting frivolously by requesting that an attorney make a good-faith effort to change the existing law. Each situation has to be judged on its own individual merits.

## 3–5   A Typical Day for a Litigation Paralegal

One of the factors that makes litigation enjoyable (and sometimes a little maddening) is that every day is different and presents a new challenge. Despite this, it will be useful and fun for you to take a brief glimpse into your future, as we follow you during a fairly typical day as a litigation paralegal at a private law firm.

You arrive at the office at 8:15 A.M., a little early so that you can enjoy a cup of coffee before you start your day. At 8:30 the mail arrives on your desk—both mail addressed to you and mail addressed to your supervising attorney, who has assigned you the task of screening the "junk mail" from the important mail. You separate the pleadings and client letters from the sales flyers and other low-priority items, attaching notes to those pleadings that appear to require immediate attention. You also set up your time sheet and begin recording tasks performed and time expended.

At 9:00 you meet with your supervising attorney to review the mail and to go over a complaint you drafted the day before for a new personal injury case. He likes the job you've done on the complaint, but he has a new legal theory about the case that he wants you to research and include in your second draft. From 9:30 to 11:00, you're in the library researching and drafting.

From 11:00 to 12:00, you organize and review a large volume of documents that are to be provided to opposing counsel in a securities fraud lawsuit, in response to a production request he recently filed. Organizing discovery responses is an important task often performed by paralegals.

After you get back from lunch at 1:00, you pull the file on a contract dispute over the behind-schedule construction of an office building. Another attorney to whom you are assigned is taking the deposition of the construction foreman at

2:00, and she has asked you to prepare copies of all relevant invoices so that she can use them as exhibits in the deposition. You make the copies, meet with her to discuss the case, and then sit in on the deposition from 2:00 to 4:00, listening carefully and taking notes on the testimony.

At 4:00 you dictate your deposition notes onto a tape so they can be transcribed by a secretary. After completing the dictation, you begin reviewing a new file on a products liability case. Tomorrow morning you're going to interview the client, who was injured when a soft drink bottle exploded in a supermarket.

At 4:45 you review your time sheet for completeness, then review your phone messages and return several calls.

At 5:00 you go home. It's been another interesting day, and you've learned still more about the substance and methods of civil litigation practice. Tomorrow will be a fascinating day as well—you'll be receiving a memo about two new cases: one involving Harry Hampton, the other involving Widgets and Gizmos, Inc.

## 3–6 Practical Considerations

Cases are complicated creatures; no two are alike. In every new case there will be an odd twist, a subtle consideration, an unusual factor that you've never faced before.

As a result, you must remember an important practical consideration: *study*, and *master*, the facts of your cases. You may be anxious at the outset to begin legal research, but you can't properly address legal issues until you understand the facts that have led to the underlying dispute. If you begin researching before you've mastered the facts, you may waste time researching the wrong legal issues.

At this point, you've probably read the facts of our two sample cases once. Once is never enough. Go back, right now, and read them again—and be prepared to refer back to them, time and again, as you go through the chapters that follow.

Sometimes the least likely aspects of a case turn out to be the most important; analyzing facts often amounts to solving a mystery. Before you can rely on your analysis of the facts, however, you must satisfy yourself that you *have* all the facts. Thus, we turn in our next chapter to the fact-gathering process: investigation.

# SUMMARY

## 3–1

The focus of litigation in the courts is the trial. This is true for every step of the litigation process, through and including the appellate stage.

## 3–2

Attorneys are bound by professional codes of ethics. Although not directly bound by these codes, paralegals are affected by them and must understand their requirements. Paralegals can only assist attorneys; they cannot practice law. Paralegals may not represent a client in a court or other forum (except for certain administrative hearings). They may not sign papers to be filed with a court, but they can draft such documents under an attorney's supervision. They may not accept fees directly from a client. Paralegals should directly and unambiguously indicate their status to all clients with whom they have contact. Client matters must be kept confidential. Paralegals must avoid personal conflicts of interest that might impinge on their duty of complete loyalty to the client. There is a growing trend toward separate codes of ethics specifically for the conduct of paralegals. Paralegals should approach their work with three factors always in mind: loyalty to the firm and the client; integrity in all outside dealings; and faithfulness to the requirements of the legal profession.

## 3–3

The study of civil litigation involves many abstract concepts. But litigation doesn't occur in a vacuum, and it is valuable to consider the abstract concepts in the context of sample cases. The Hampton case and the Widgets and Gizmos, Inc. case will be referred to throughout this book; go back now and read them again!

## 3–4

Economic factors can play a role in the decision of an attorney to accept or reject a case, although sometimes a sense of duty to the community will induce an attorney to accept a case on a *pro bono* (i.e., reduced-fee or free) basis. Attorneys should not accept cases for which they lack adequate expertise, nor should they handle matters in which a conflict exists. If a client wants to raise a frivolous claim for the purpose of harassment, the attorney should decline to handle the case.

## 3–5

In a typical day, a litigation paralegal might review and process the mail for his or her supervising attorney; do library research for a complaint; organize a discovery response; prepare copies of relevant documents for a deposition; attend a deposition and thereafter prepare a memo from notes taken; review a file preliminary to a client interview; and perform many other tasks as well.

## 3-6

No two cases are alike, and the nuances can be very important. Study the facts of our sample cases, and in your career always strive to master the facts of every case with which you are involved.

# REVIEW

## Key Terms

Before proceeding, review the key terms listed below to be sure you understand each one. If necessary, read over the corresponding section of the chapter. When you are ready to test your understanding, answer the Review Questions.

professional codes of ethics
confidentiality
conflicts of interest
*pro bono*

## Questions for Review and Discussion

1. What is the focus of litigation?
2. Why is it important to maintain confidentiality with regard to a client's case?
3. Identify a growing trend in paralegal ethics.
4. What is meant by a *pro bono* case?
5. What should a law firm do if a client wants to pursue a frivolous claim?

## Activities

1. Review the attorney code of ethics applicable in your state.
2. Read the sample cases again—you can never be too familiar with the facts of your cases!
3. Call your state's bar association, and determine whether there are any *pro bono* requirements or guidelines placed upon the attorneys of your state.

# CHAPTER 4   Investigation

## OUTLINE

## COMMENTARY

It's only Tuesday, and already you're having a busy week at your firm. Your supervising attorney is involved in a trial, and the uproar surrounding a recent explosion at a manufacturing facility operated by an important client has monopolized the time of many others in the litigation department. You've been pressed into service on some important matters this week, and it's been an exciting time for you. When you sit down at your desk to catch up on your mail, you find the following memo.

To: Paula Paralegal
From: Sam Superlawyer
Re: New client interviews
Date: September 10, 1993

    I have been contacted by two individuals who have brought to my attention two potential litigation matters. I would like you to set up interviews with these individuals THIS WEEK to obtain more detais.

    The first interview will be with Mr. Harry Hampton, who was involved in a motor vehicle accident on April 15, 1992. I do not have any additional information on this matter at this time. You should contact Hampton and set up a conference at your convenience (as long as it is *this* week). His telephone number is 555-5555. Also, please open a file for this matter.

    The second interview will be with Mr. Edgar Ellison, President and Chief Operating Officer of Widgets and Gizmos, Inc., the well-known manufacturer of computer components. Widgets is a long-time client, and has become involved in a dispute with TapTapTap, Inc. I suggest that you review the *Wall Street Journal* article of August 21, 1993, as well as the litigation case file that we have already opened. You should also ask my secretary, Ms Taylor, for a copy of the file compiled to date by lawyers in our corporate department. After completing this preliminary review, please schedule an interview with Mr. Ellison for Friday afternoon, then let's meet to discuss your role in the interview.

    The Calvin Client trial is, as you know, keeping me busy. However, I expect to be available at 8:15 Wednesday morning. Let's meet in my office at that time.

After you finish reading the memo, you jot down a few notes to yourself. These will be your first client interviews, and you want to be prepared.

## OBJECTIVES

In Chapter 3 you were introduced to our two sample cases. In this chapter we discuss investigatory strategies designed to uncover the facts of such cases. After completing Chapter 4, you will be able to:

1. Identify items for the client to bring to the initial client interview.
2. Explain the importance of an interview checklist.
3. Utilize several basic interviewing techniques and tips.
4. Prepare a postinterview memorandum.
5. Follow the four cardinal rules of investigation.
6. Identify a source for much basic corporate information.
7. Explain how a medical report is requested and obtained.
8. Explain what is meant by *physical evidence*.
9. Identify some important considerations when interviewing a witness.
10. Locate and retain an expert witness.

## 4–1  Investigation in General

Perhaps no distinction is more fundamental to litigation practice than the distinction between *facts* and *law*. All persons involved in the litigation process—attorneys, litigation paralegals, even on occasion litigation secretaries—must understand this crucial distinction.

A litigator wears two hats: that of scholar and that of detective. The scholar develops theories of law after long hours of study in the law library. The detective, with whom we will be concerned in this chapter, ferrets out the facts that will provide the context in which the legal theories come to life.

**Investigation** is the term we apply to the gathering of facts—the "detective" role of litigation. Ultimately, it is something more than the mere gathering of facts: it is the gathering of facts that will be admissible in evidence (we will discuss the meaning and impact of the rules of evidence in the next chapter). Initially, the investigation process involves simply digging out the factual information necessary to the formulation of a meaningful response to the legal issues presented.

Where should you start? A good starting point is found in a concept called a **cause of action,** which we discuss in more detail in Chapter 6 but that we can address briefly now. Simply stated, a cause of action is a legal theory that, if proved, will lead to judgment if no successful defense is raised. Such a legal theory consists of component elements, each of which must be proved by admissible evidence. For example, in one cause of action in the Harry Hampton matter, Hampton will be trying to prove that Judith Johnson was negligent, and that her negligence was the proximate cause of the accident in which he was injured. Hampton may also seek to prove, in another cause of action, that Bud's Auto Service was negligent in its repair effort. Your investigation will be seeking the factual information

**Figure 4–1    Preliminary Investigation List for Harry Hampton Case**

> ### Cause of Action I: Versus Judith Johnson, Alleging Negligence
>
> Judith Johnson ran stop sign
>
> Judith Johnson traveling at excessive rate of speed
>
> Judith Johnson failed to keep a proper lookout for other cars
>
> Judith Johnson's negligent actions were the proximate cause of the accident
>
> Harry Hampton was *not* contributorily negligent
>
> ### Cause of Action II: Versus Bud's Auto Service
>
> Turn signal assembly negligently serviced
>
> Problem with turn signal caused, or contributed to the cause of, the accident
>
> ### Damages
>
> Physical injuries, including pain and suffering, medical bills, and future disability
>
> Damage to vehicle
>
> Lost time from work
>
> Effect on Harry's enjoyment of life: activities his injuries prevent him from enjoying

needed to prove each of the elements of these causes of action. If you represented the defendant, your investigation would seek information needed to counter these causes of action.

In addition to proving his cause of action, Harry Hampton must also prove that he suffered damages. He will need to introduce evidence of damage to his car and of physical injuries suffered, including medical bills and the evaluation of a physician about the future effect of his injuries; he may also try to prove that he lost time from work, with an eye to recovering for lost wages.

An important early step in planning your investigation process is to make a list of all the facts you believe are necessary to prove your causes of action (or, if your firm represents the defendant, necessary to counter the plaintiff's causes of action) at trial. This list may grow as the case develops, or it may shrink. An example of a preliminary investigation list for the Harry Hampton matter is found in Figure 4–1.

Even before you will be able to analyze potential causes of action and damages, however, you will have to develop some understanding of the basic facts of the case. Thus, another step in the investigatory process actually precedes the preparation of your preliminary list. Let's turn to that step now.

## 4–2    The Initial Client Interview

The first significant exposure of a law firm to a new matter is generally the **initial client interview,** usually preceded only by the client's first phone call to an attorney or legal secretary, and perhaps some preliminary correspondence. It is during the initial client interview that the investigation process really begins, and the potential for asserting various causes of action begins to appear.

Attorneys often conduct the initial client interview, but since your supervising attorney, Sam Superlawyer, is busy with a trial, you have been asked to step in for the interviews of Harry Hampton and Edgar Ellison. In preparing for these interviews, you should first take note of an important distinction between the situations presented by these two clients. In the case of Harry Hampton, he is an entirely new client with whom the firm has never dealt before. Thus your interview will be preceded by only a minimal preliminary background review (since there may not yet be anything to review beyond Sam Superlawyer's notes of the initial phone conversation); the interview itself will require significant background questioning.

In the case of Edgar Ellison, a long association exists between his corporation and your firm. In addition, there have been recent consultations on this specific matter between Ellison and your firm's corporate department. Thus, while your interview with Ellison may be the first in-person contact of the litigation department on this matter, much has gone before (indeed, a litigation file has already been opened based on the course of events to date). Hence your interview will be preceded by extensive background review, and will be characterized by a more focused approach (see Figure 4–2).

Let's turn now to a consideration of three key aspects of the interview process: the preliminaries; techniques associated with the interview itself; and postinterview procedures. As we do so, keep in mind the differing considerations of the Hampton and Ellison interviews.

## Interview Preliminaries

A successful interview requires advance planning. The preliminaries can be divided into four steps: selecting the location of the interview; conducting background review and research; identifying those items that the client should bring to the interview; and preparing those items that *you* should bring to the interview.

**Interview Location**   You will need to select a suitable location to conduct your interview, then ensure its availability for the scheduled time. A conference room is often a good choice. Your firm is likely to have an established procedure for reserving a conference room—be sure to follow it, so that no surprises interfere with your interview. If you have your own office, that is a good location as well; but if you share an office, make arrangements to ensure that you will not be disturbed during the interview. If you are stationed in a cubicle in an open area of the office, you should make arrangements for a more private location. No client wants to discuss important and sensitive matters within earshot of others, however professional and discreet they might be, and this hesitancy may adversely influence the accuracy and candor of the information provided (as

**Figure 4–2   Comparison of Preliminary Background Review for the Hampton and Ellison Interviews**

> ***Interview of Hampton:***
>
> Minimum of background review (because the firm had no prior contact with Hampton before this case)
>
> Maximum of broad, basic fact-gathering during interview itself
>
> ***Interview of Ellison:***
>
> Extensive background review (including the corporate department's file; press clippings; the newly opened litigation file; and possibly other files involving *Widgets and Gizmos, Inc.*)
>
> The interview itself will be more focused and involve less basic fact-gathering

well as create a negative impression of your firm). Another concern is the need to maintain the confidentiality of the interview in order to preserve attorney-client privilege, an issue we discuss further in the next chapter.

Whatever location you select, make sure it is neat. Minimizing clutter will maximize client attention, leading to a more focused interview. A disorganized, messy office can only distract the client (and you) from the important task at hand. You should also be sure to put away the files of any other clients, so no breach of confidence occurs with regard to those matters. Finally, you should arrange for the availability of water, coffee, or other refreshment.

**Background Review and Research**   As we noted earlier, the Hampton and Ellison interviews will differ as a result of their differing circumstances: Hampton is a new client, Ellison one of long standing and with a legal problem already familiar to your firm's corporate department. These differing circumstances will affect the extent of the background review and research necessary to prepare for each interview.

With regard to the case of Mr. Hampton, no file yet exists, and you have only the barest understanding of his situation. In the phone conversation scheduling his interview, you should elicit enough information to enable you to do some brief legal research on the issues involved. For example, a brief summary by Mr. Hampton will enable you to begin researching such issues as driver negligence, liability of a repair shop, and basic damages (see Figure 4–3). The research should focus on only the broad, basic issues presented. More precise and in-depth research should wait until the information obtained during the interview enables you to fill in gaps in your knowledge and accurately target your research.

With regard to Mr. Ellison, your approach will be quite different. Here, background research is essential to bring you up-to-date. Few things make a paying client more uneasy than repeating previously provided information to a new attorney or paralegal; it leaves the impression that one hand doesn't know what the other is doing at your firm. With this in mind, you will certainly want to read the *Wall Street Journal* article mentioned in your supervising attorney's memo, as well as the litigation file that has been opened. In addition, you should look into the corporate department's related file, reviewing the course of the matter to date (with particular attention to any earlier interviews conducted with Ellison) and probably consulting directly with the responsible corporate attorneys.

These steps are essential, but for Ellison your review may go even further. You may want to look at the files on other Widgets and Gizmos, Inc.

> ## PARALEGALERT!
>
> When interviewing a client, be sure to do adequate background review so that you don't ask questions to which the client has already provided answers in an earlier interview (unless you are confirming or seeking clarification). Similarly, don't carelessly request a document already in your file. These kinds of mistakes create a bad impression of your firm in the client's mind.

matters that your firm has handled, in order to develop a sense for how the relationship between your firm and the client has unfolded over time. You may want to do further research on how the TapTapTap, Inc. matter has been reported in the press. Finally, you may want to look into any legal research that has already been done on such issues as the interpretation of specifications in manufacturing contracts, although, as with the Hampton matter, you should not go too far, since you may not have all the relevant facts until after your interview is complete.

**Items for the Client to Bring to the Interview**   An interview often falters as a result of the unavailability of a key document or other item. As a result, it is important to anticipate the items that will be needed. This can be facilitated by

**Figure 4–3    Legal Research Issues to Consider Prior to Hampton Interview**

- Duty of Judith Johnson to drive in a safe manner

- Issue of Judith Johnson's negligence as the proximate cause of the accident

- Applicable standards regarding contributory negligence of Harry Hampton

- Duty of an automobile repair shop to perform services with due care

- Issue of negligent repair as the proximate cause of the accident

- Damages allowable if causes of action are proven

discussing the issue with the client when setting up the interview, and instructing the client to bring necessary items. In general, the client should bring any documents or other materials that pertain to the matter in controversy, including those that establish (or refute, if your firm represents the defendant) the basic claims in question and those that serve to establish (or refute) claims of damages.

For the Hampton interview, the items for the client to bring are readily identifiable. Your list would include medical bills and reports; insurance information; the police report (if he doesn't have a copy, you should obtain this before the interview); photographs of the accident scene, the damage to his vehicle, and his injuries (again, if he doesn't have such photos, you should arrange for them to be taken, particularly if his injuries are healing or the accident scene is being altered or the vehicle destroyed); copies of any correspondence he has received or sent (from or to the other driver, an insurance company or any other involved person) with regard to the accident; a recent pay stub or other information concerning his lost wage claim; estimates or other information with regard to vehicle damage; and any other relevant documents or materials in his possession (see Figure 4–4).

For the Ellison interview, the list of documents that he should bring will be less straightforward than in the Hampton situation—you will have to develop a more "customized" list, based upon your file review. Probable items on the list

**Figure 4–4    Items for Harry Hampton to Bring to Initial Client Interview**

- Medical bills

- Medical reports, if any

- Insurance information

- Police report, if he has it

- Relevant photographs (of accident scene; of damages to vehicle; and/or of his injuries)

- Relevant correspondence (from or to the other driver; from or to an insurance company; or any other relevant correspondence in his possession)

- Recent pay stub or other records relevant to lost wage claim

- Invoices or estimates on vehicle damage

- Catch-all request: any other relevant documents in his possession would include all correspondence between Widgets and Gizmos, Inc. and TapTapTap, Inc. pertaining to this matter; a copy of the contract; internal memoranda (such as the Hoobermann memo) that are relevant; and any documentation relating to potential damages. As with a repetitive question, a redundant document request leaves a bad impression with a client, so you should review the file with care to make sure that it does not already contain the documents you are requesting the client to bring (although you may want to request that he bring originals of documents for which you only have copies). For example, your request directed to Ellison may ultimately be limited to *recent* correspondence between Widgets and Gizmos, Inc. and TapTapTap, Inc. not already in your file.

After discussing the various items to bring in your phone conversations with Hampton and Ellison, it is important to send each a follow-up letter listing all the items again (see Figure 4–5). By putting the list in writing, two objectives are served: first, the client is more likely to bring the items; second, confusion is avoided over the scope of the original oral request. Indeed, in every area of your practice it is always important to follow up oral conversations with confirmation letters. Until an understanding is placed in writing, the potential for misunderstanding is always present.

**P**ARALEGALERT!

Always confirm in writing any significant portion of an oral conversation. Reducing an oral understanding to written form prevents a misunderstanding!

**Items for the Paralegal to Bring to the Interview**  Your preparation is not limited to reviewing the file, finding an interview location, then informing the client what he or she must bring—you must also prepare certain materials in advance of the interview. In the case of Hampton, for example, you should obtain authorizations for the release of medical information, employment information, school records, and possibly other information as well. These **authorization forms** enable you to obtain confidential information from those doctors, employers, or schools identified by the client as having relevant information in their files. The forms should be prepared by you prior to the interview, so that the client can execute them while in your office. Care should be taken to execute these in conformity with statutory requirements; this may require obtaining the client's permission to leave the date blank (unless prohibited by statute) and to fill it in at the time of use so that statutory requirements regarding duration of validity are met. Examples of medical and employment authorization forms appear in Figure 4–6.

**P**ARALEGALERT!

In some states, a medical or other authorization form is only good for a specified period of time from the date of its execution. In addition, some doctors and hospitals have established their own internal guidelines regarding "stale" authorizations. It is a good idea, then, to obtain the client's agreement to leave the date section *blank* at the time of signing. Then, when the authorization is actually used, you can fill in the then-current date.

Another document that will probably be necessary for the Hampton interview is the client retainer or fee agreement, which we discussed in Chapter 2. Make sure you consult with your supervising attorney before having a client execute such an agreement.

In addition to authorization forms and fee agreements, a third category of document to bring to the Hampton interview is your outline or checklist of substantive areas to cover during the interview. Such a document can be as detailed as a list of the specific questions you intend to ask, or as brief as a list of broad topics—it will vary with your level of experience and comfort as an interviewer. The purpose of such outlines or checklists is to ensure that your

# Lincoln & Hoover
## Attorneys at Law

September 10, 1993

Mr. Edgar Ellison
Widgets and Gizmos, Inc.
888 Widget Street
Metro City, Exurbia 12345

Re: Dispute with TapTapTap, Inc.

Dear Mr. Ellison:

The purpose of this letter is to confirm our office interview scheduled for September 14, 1993, at 10:00 a.m. at the offices of Lincoln and Hoover, 123 Lincoln Street in Metro City. Upon your arrival, please check in with the receptionist on the twelfth floor, and I will see you immediately thereafter.

As we discussed in our phone conversation of September 10, please bring with you the following items:

1. all recent correspondence between Widgets and Gizmos, Inc. and TapTapTap, Inc. not already in our file;

2. the original Hoobermann memo, which as we discussed is not yet in our file;

3. the invoices presented to you by TapTapTap, Inc. representing damages suffered by their customers; and

4. any other relevant materials not yet in our file.

If you have any questions about the interview or the items to bring, please do not hesitate to call me at any time.

Very truly yours,

Paula Paralegal
Legal Assistant

interview is thorough—that you inquire into all appropriate areas. For the Hampton case, the inquiry will fall into a standard "car accident/negligence" format. An example of a checklist for such a case is found in Figure 4–7. Similar checklists, some quite detailed, can be found in various trial manuals or other volumes designed to help lawyers prepare their cases, such as *American Jurisprudence Proof of Facts, 3rd Series* (published by Lawyers Cooperative Publishing).

For the Ellison interview, you will not need authorization forms because there is no need to write to doctors, schools, or employers for confidential information. You may, however, need a new fee agreement, depending on the arrangements the firm has historically followed with this client. For example, litigation matters may be billed differently from general corporate matters, and require different documentation. You should check with your supervising attorney on this point.

**Figure 4–6  Samples of Authorization Forms**

---

### Authorization of Release of Medical Records

To:  [Fill in name and address of doctor or medical facility]

re:  Medical records of  [Fill in name of client/patient, together with any necessary identifying information such as social security number or patient ID number]

To whom it may concern [or fill in name of specific person]:
I, the undersigned _____, hereby authorize the release of all medical records pertaining to my treatment to my attorneys, Lincoln & Hoover, of 123 Lincoln Street, Metro City, Exurbia. Such records include but are not limited to: office notes; charts; X-rays; billing information; hospital records including operative reports, discharge summaries, nurses' reports, and laboratory reports; all other laboratory reports; records or summaries regarding my medical history; and any and all medical records of any kind within your possession which relate to my medical treatment.

_____
[Signature]
Date:

---

### Authorization of Release of Employment Records

To:  [Fill in name of employer]

re:  Employment records of _____.

  Dates of employment: _____ to _____.

To whom it may concern [or fill in name of specific person]:
I, the undersigned _____, hereby authorize the release of all records relating to my employment with your company during the time period indicated to my attorneys, Lincoln & Hoover, of 123 Lincoln Street, Metro City, Exurbia. Such records include but are not limited to: personnel files; performance reviews; payroll records; and any and all other records which relate to my employment at your company.

_____
[Signature]
Date:

---

With regard to the outline or checklist for the Ellison interview, the purpose is identical to that of the outline or checklist for the Hampton interview, but the method of developing it will likely differ. As with the list of documents to be brought by Ellison, the questions to ask will be more "customized" than with Hampton, since the facts of his matter do not easily fall into a "standard" category of case type. The dispute with TapTapTap, Inc. is relatively unique, and preparing a good outline will take some original thought. Outlines of basic contract questions from one or more of the commercial trial manuals will not be as helpful here, although they are not without some usefulness. An example of notes for the interview of Ellison is found in Figure 4–8.

Note the standard background information requested in both Figures 4–7 and 4–8, including such things as home and business addresses and phone numbers. You should generally obtain, or take the opportunity to confirm, this information in an interview. With Ellison, emphasize that you are merely confirming; then you will not fall into the "repetitive request" trap discussed earlier.

**Figure 4–7   Checklist for Auto Accident Case, Modified for Hampton Matter**

_____ Background information; Hampton's date of birth; address and phone number; spouse and children; business address and residence address

_____ Date and time of accident

_____ Identity of any passengers with Hampton

_____ Location of accident

_____ Weather conditions at time of accident

_____ Road conditions

_____ Traffic conditions

_____ Witnesses who may have observed faulty turn signal

_____ Witnesses to accident

_____ Witnesses who can testify as to his physical condition or limitations

_____ Identity of other involved drivers

_____ Owners of other involved vehicles

_____ Nature of injuries

_____ Names, addresses, and phone numbers of all doctors and hospitals

_____ Potential witnesses at Bud's Auto Service

_____ Hampton's insurance carrier

_____ Insurance carrier of other driver

_____ Hampton's version of accident events

_____ Review police report

_____ Review any statements given by client

_____ Review any statements given by other drivers or witnesses

_____ Name, address, and phone number of employer

_____ Dates out-of-work

_____ Lost wages

_____ All identifiable damages to date

_____ Any pre-existing medical conditions

_____ Relevant photos of which Hampton is aware

_____ Have Hampton draw a diagram of the accident

**PARALEGALERT!**

If a client will be marking on relevant documents during an interview or at any other time, make sure the marking is done on a copy. _Never_ make marks on an _original_ document!

Some materials are of such a nature that you will bring them to every interview, whether of the Hampton variety or of the Ellison variety. For example, any relevant materials found in your preliminary review should be at your fingertips for easy reference. If your firm has developed a file of any sort, it should be readily available. If the file is large, as it might well be in a case similar to the Ellison matter, you might not want to bring the whole file with you to the interview site, but you would certainly want to know where it is in case something is needed. In addition to originals, copies of relevant

**Figure 4–8   Sample Notes for Interview of Edgar Ellison**

_____ Background information: _Confirm_ phone numbers, addresses, and other basic information

_____ Step-by-step chronology

_____ Review relevant correspondence

_____ Discuss Ellison's reasoning for overruling Hoobermann and producing widgenometers

_____ Nature and content of all oral conversations with Emily Tapman

_____ Potential witnesses: identity of his employees most familiar with the product

_____ Potential witnesses: identity of his employees most familiar with the negotiations

_____ Potential witnesses: list of all _Widgets and Gizmos, Inc._ employees involved in any way

_____ Potential witnesses: names and phone numbers of key people in the technical departments of _Widgets and Gizmos, Inc._

_____ Potential witnesses: identity of _Tap Tap Tap, Inc._ personnel involved in the negotiations

_____ Potential witnesses: identity of _Tap Tap Tap, Inc._ technical personnel

_____ Discuss past dealings with _Tap Tap Tap, Inc._

_____ Review nature and content of Ellison's dealings with Hoobermann both before and after problems arose

_____ Review the expertise of Rodriguez in the area of widgenometer specifications

_____ Identify potential damages which _Widgets and Gizmos, Inc._ may incur

_____ Identify potential damages which _Tap Tap Tap, Inc._ may claim

_____ Identify the goals of _Widgets and Gizmos, Inc._ in both the short term and the long term with regard to this dispute (for example, do they seek to maintain _Tap Tap Tap, Inc._ as a future customer, or is this dispute to constitute "all-out war"?)

documents might also be useful, and, if they are to be marked on by the client, essential. An original document should NEVER be marked on. Finally, you should always bring with you adequate supplies of pens, pencils, and legal pads.

## Interviewing Techniques

Preparation is important, but of course the most important part of an interview is—the interview! After your preparation for your first interview is complete, there will come a moment when you are face-to-face with a client who expects you to act like a confident and professional legal assistant. And you may feel that you are doing exactly that—_acting_.

Interviewing can be intimidating at first, but it is a skill that you can and will master over time. Experience will provide you with confidence, enabling you to develop and perfect your own style. Still, knowing the value of experience will not be very comforting as you prepare for your interviews with Harry Hampton and Edgar Ellison, because at this early stage of your career, experience is the one thing you don't have. There's no need to panic, however, because even for the inexperienced interviewer there are tips and guidelines that can take you through the interview, step by step, and lead to a positive result (see Figure 4–9).

**Figure 4–9    Interviewing Tips**

- Identify yourself as a paralegal, and explain what that means.

- Establish a rapport with the client.

- Work from an outline or checklist. Don't be afraid to allow the client to vary the order in which you cover the various subjects on your checklist, but make sure you ultimately cover *all* necessary areas.

- Start with broad questions: allow the client to tell his or her own story before you begin a more focused inquiry.

- Avoid leading questions; the client may give you the answers he or she thinks you *want*, rather than honest and accurate answers.

- Don't be afraid of tough questions—explain that they will be asked by the other side, and that your firm must know the answers in order to establish strategy.

- Work from the general to the specific, and when gaps and inconsistencies present themselves, use focused questions to clarify the issue.

- Obtain background information regarding client's source or sources for the information provided. This will impact on your supervising attorney's ability at trial to "lay a foundation" for the testimony (to be discussed further in Chapter 5).

- Take careful notes, but keep in mind the next tip as well.

- *Listen!* And equally as important: *Observe!* Don't get so caught up in your notes or questions that you miss a key response. And remember that it is often the nuances of a response—the tone of voice, hesitancy, posture—which tell as much as the content.

- Be sure to review the client's story and statements more than once; you may have misunderstood his or her meaning, or he or she may have misspoken. The time to get the facts straight is *before* the interview is terminated.

Just prior to launching into the substantive areas of the interview, remember that you must explain to the client that you are not an attorney, but rather a paralegal. If the client is unsure what that means, take the time to explain the role of the paralegal in the litigation process (Harry Hampton, for example, is probably less familiar with law firms and litigation than is Edgar Ellison). You should reassure the client that the interview is protected by the attorney/client privilege (which we discuss further in Chapter 5), particularly if you are recording the interview on audiotape or videotape. You may even want to answer any questions the client has about the litigation process itself, although this can be difficult until you have a better understanding of the precise nature of the client's problem.

You should also be mindful of the need to make the client feel at ease, and to begin to establish real rapport with the client. A strong professional relationship contributes to an atmosphere of teamwork in which lawyers, paralegals, and the client will all be working toward one end—obtaining for the client the best possible result. Establishing rapport is important, particularly when dealing with a client who is scared by his or her dilemma and intimidated by the system (including even his or her own lawyers and paralegals). The client's emotional state must be factored into your approach—you must work to calm the client's fears, though not by minimizing the scope of the problem (see the discussion about "asking tough questions" later in this section).

After the client has been informed of your paralegal status, it is useful to begin the substantive interview by developing with the client a general picture of the problem. Ask the client to summarize the problem in a couple of sentences, so that you have a good, solid idea of the broad parameters of the situation. The client may not have analyzed the "big picture" perfectly, but you will at least understand the client's perception of the problem, and such understanding can be valuable as you refine your own analysis and begin to ask more focused questions that shed light on the legal ramifications of the situation.

Once you have the big picture, start your focused inquiry with broad questions. The goal is to encourage the client to provide as much information as possible without prodding. Only after you are satisfied that the client has finished describing the general should you begin to probe the particular.

As the client's story begins to develop broad outlines, you will need to sharpen your focus still further. You may want to ask questions with "yes" or "no" answers. In other words, after the client has been allowed the freedom to present the facts as he or she sees them, there will undoubtedly be inconsistencies, discrepancies, or gaps that need to be explained. You may at this point be able to ask direct questions to elicit explanation: "Did Hoobermann ever say to you directly, Mr. Ellison, that the widgenometer might be defective?" Or: "Mr. Hampton, was there ever an indication on your dashboard, at any time that morning, that your signal was on?" Depending on the answer, you would then follow up with questions that allow the interviewee to explain further the "yes" or "no" answer.

You should avoid **leading questions,** i.e., questions that suggest an answer, until absolutely necessary. An inappropriate question posed to Mr. Hampton, for example, is: "Wasn't the Johnson car speeding as it approached the stop sign?" A better question would be: "Can you describe for me the manner in which the Johnson car approached the stop sign?" The danger in the first question is that Mr. Hampton is likely to give the answer that he thinks you want to hear, rather than an accurate answer. As with the "big picture" aspect, and the movement from broad to specific questions, the goal here is to get the client's candid version of events, as opposed to a version colored by external influences.

Don't be afraid to ask the client tough questions that require exploring areas that might place the client, or his or her position, in an unpleasant light. For example, you should ask Ellison why he didn't expend more effort in investigating Hoobermann's reservations regarding the readiness of the widgenometer. Clients are often resistant to such questions; they may even take offense at extended probing. Such questions are important, however— you need to know the downside of the client's position as well as its strong points. Tough questions can be asked without damaging the rapport we talked about if they are preceded by something like the following: "The next few questions concern some sensitive issues. You may not like answering these questions. But you can be sure that someday, in a deposition or at trial, the other side will be asking you these very questions. And if we're going to prepare you for depositions and trial, and properly prepare our legal arguments and strategy, we must know your responses to these questions." Another approach is to ask the client what positions he or she suspects the opposing side will take with regard to disputed factual issues. This encourages the client to think about the negative side of his or her situation.

As we discussed in the previous section, you should work from a checklist or outline. Don't be afraid to allow the client to vary the order in which you cover the subjects on your checklist, but make sure you cover all necessary areas. A client should be allowed to run with a thought (since this may be the best chance to get detailed information), but it is up to you to get the interview back on track eventually—be flexible, in other words, but be thorough.

# PARALEGALERT!

Don't be afraid to ask the client tough questions! You need to know the weaknesses of the client's case, as well as the strengths. To soften the impact, explain to the client that, since the other side will certainly be asking the same questions, proper preparation requires that you know the answers to these questions *now*.

Another important consideration is to obtain from the client background information regarding how he or she came to have the information that he or she is relating. The source of knowledge affects the ability of your supervising attorney to lay a foundation for the testimony, a prerequisite to admissibility at trial. We discuss further the concept of *foundation* in Chapter 5.

You should take notes throughout the interview. You might want to leave space to insert answers or comments on your checklist, outline, or list of questions. Your notes should be thorough, but you shouldn't let your note taking interfere with the interview process itself.

The next point might seem obvious, but it is often honored in the breach: *Listen!* Equally important: *Observe!* This is why you must be careful not to get too caught up in making notes or referring to your checklist—because you might miss a key response. If you want the client to pause for a moment while you write something down, say so; don't let him or her continue speaking if you are absorbed in recording prior comments. Remember also that it is often nuances—tone of voice, hesitancy, posture—that reveal as much as the content of a response. A client may make statements that he or she only *thinks* are true; if you can spot such statements, you can ask follow-up questions that explore the uncertainty and yield a more nearly accurate picture of the client's ultimate ability to testify on a given point.

**PARALEGALERT!**

During the interview, *listen* to the client and *observe* the client's demeanor. This advice might seem obvious, but unless you consciously work at following it, you may lose sight of the client's answers (as well as nuances such as posture or tone of voice) as you focus on your next question.

As the interview nears its conclusion, make sure you review with the client all the information you have received. This will give you the opportunity to clarify discrepancies, both in the client's statements, and in your notes. If you misunderstood the client, or if the client misspoke, you can correct the error before it causes any damage. The best time to get the story straight is during the interview, while the client is present. Don't be hesitant to review your notes orally from beginning to end; it will help both you and the client to focus.

Finally, don't allow the interview to extend too long. Clients (and paralegals) get tired after a while, and the quality of the information transmitted (and your ability to interpret it) may deteriorate. An hour is probably a good general time limit. If you must extend beyond that time, and you feel the quality of the interview slipping, you should take a break or possibly even adjourn and reschedule at a later date (although the latter alternative should only be exercised if authorized by your supervising attorney). In any event, you should always make it clear to the client that a break is acceptable at any time he or she thinks it necessary.

**Figure 4–10   The Benefit of the Immediate Postinterview Memo**

> ***What your notes say:***
>
> Hampton—turn signal—malfunction—serviced by Bud's Auto Service
>
> ***What your memo should say:***
>
> Hampton's turn signal continued to malfunction even after Bud's Auto Service claimed, on 4/14/92 immediately prior to the accident, to have fixed it. We should investigate whether the malfunction contributed to the accident.
>
> ***What your memo might mistakenly say if you wait too long to interpret your notes:***
>
> Hampton's malfunctioning turn signal was fixed by Bud's Auto Service.

## Postinterview Procedures

Your job has not ended when the client walks out the door. Indeed, perhaps the most important part of your interview assignment lies ahead: the **postinterview memorandum.** It is in the postinterview memo that you transmit to your supervising attorney the substance of your interview; thus, it is extremely important that the memorandum be accurate and thorough.

The postinterview memorandum should be done immediately after the conclusion of the interview. Few things are more frustrating than sitting down a few days after an interview to write a memo, only to find that your notes are incomplete and your memory has fogged (see Figure 4–10 for a brief example of what can go wrong). If you write the memo immediately after the interview, your impressions will still be fresh, your ability to decipher what may later become cryptic references in your notes will still be sharp, and your memory will easily fill in gaps. You will also be able to forward the memo to your supervising attorney in a timely manner, and if he or she has questions you will be better able to address them. See Figure 4–11 for an example of a portion of the postinterview memo relating to your interview with Harry Hampton.

**P**ARALEGALERT!

Do your postinterview memorandum immediately after the interview, when impressions are fresh, memory is adequate, and ability to decipher notes is as a maximum.

**Figure 4–11    Portion of Postinterview Memorandum for Hampton Interview**

### Memorandum

From: Paula Paralegal
To: Sam Superlawyer
Date: September 12, 1993
re: Interview of Harry Hampton on this date

Harry Hampton is a forty-four year old (Date of Birth: July 10, 1949) married individual with two children. His wife's name is Diana (Date of Birth: August 16, 1951). Their marriage took place on June 5, 1974. His children: William (Date of Birth: August 21, 1977) and Jennifer (Date of Birth: November 20, 1979).

The Hamptons live at 1001 Elm Street, Milltown, in the state of Exurbia. Their home phone number is 555-5555.

Harry Hampton works for the Ace Appliance Company, at 774 Winchester Street in Metro City. He is a marketing executive. His business phone number is 777-7777.

On April 15, 1992, at approximately 8:20 a.m., Hampton was in an auto accident at the intersection of Higgins Lane and Pruitt Street in Milltown. According to both Hampton and the police report, there were two cars involved. The other driver was Judith Johnson, of 143 Wingate Street in Milltown.

According to an eyewitness to the accident, Louella Williams (Age: 79 years), the Johnson vehicle ran a stop sign. Mrs. Williams lives at 35 Higgins Lane, on the corner of Higgins and Pruitt. Her telephone number is 987-6543.

Mrs. Johnson claims, in a statement provided to the investigating police officer and included with the police report, that Hampton's turn signal was indicating a right turn, although he proceeded straight through the intersection. Hampton confirmed that this was in fact the case, but that it was due to a negligent repair performed at Bud's Auto Service. Hampton was aware at the time of the accident that the turn signal was malfunctioning, but he was not aware of the exact nature of the malfunction, and did not know that his signal indicated a turn.

After completing the postinterview memo (and consulting with your supervising attorney), you should send a follow-up letter to the client, reviewing the facts discussed in the interview and identifying tasks to be performed. For example, Harry Hampton may have agreed to send you photographs of the intersection taken the day after the accident occurred. You should remind Harry of this in the letter. If you agreed to do the necessary paperwork to obtain the police report (and you should have; more about that in the next section on the cardinal rules of investigation), you should note that fact in the letter as well. The purpose of the follow-up letter is threefold: (1) to allow the client the opportunity to correct any factual confusion; (2) to remind the client to complete the tasks discussed in the interview; and (3) to create a record of both the facts discussed and the tasks assigned.

Finally, you should prepare for yourself a list of all tasks that need to be performed on the new file: a "to do" list. This should be done in consultation with your supervising attorney, and would certainly include all the tasks discussed in the follow-up letter to the client (those assigned to the client would appear on your list as items to check on to ensure completion; those assigned to you would appear as ordinary "to do" items). The list should include technical tasks (which thus weren't discussed with the client). For example, you may want to remind yourself to read a certain case that you know to be relevant. Finally, add tasks that you identified only after the interview.

## 4–3   The Cardinal Rules of Investigation

Investigation entails diverse tasks: making phone calls, drafting letters, conducting interviews, taking photographs, performing on-site inspections, consulting experts, reviewing records. The list is long and the procedures varied. Despite this great variety, four cardinal rules apply to virtually all your investigatory pursuits. Before we discuss the specifics further, let's consider these generally applicable rules.

Rule #1: Perform your investigatory tasks *at the earliest possible date*. This consideration applies to all elements of investigation, including the initial client interview. You need information *today*, not tomorrow! Unfortunately for those with a tendency to procrastinate, general investigation (as opposed to formal discovery, which we discuss in Chapter 9) is one aspect of the litigation process that does not carry a court-imposed deadline; it can, theoretically, be done at your convenience. Hence, there is always the temptation to handle more pressing matters before turning to investigatory tasks. Avoid this temptation! It is impossible to evaluate a case and formulate a litigation strategy until all the facts are known.

But facts don't change, do they? Why, then, is it so important to pin down facts right away? There are three reasons (see Figure 4–12). First, some "facts" actually might change, in a sense. Witnesses' recollections may fade; documents may be destroyed before their relevance is recognized. By moving quickly, these problems are minimized. Second, pinning down certain facts may take significantly longer than you might have expected. For example, certain government agencies may take weeks, or even months, to supply certified copies of relevant filings; some witnesses may have to be tracked down before

**Figure 4–12 Three Reasons to Perform Investigatory Tasks at the Earliest Possible Date**

> ***Reason #1:*** Facts might, in a sense, "change": witness recollections may fade; important documents might be inadvertently destroyed before their importance is recognized.
>
> ***Reason #2:*** It may take significantly longer to complete investigatory tasks than anticipated. By starting early, the impact of delays is minimized.
>
> ***Reason #3:*** Once facts become known, they often tend to raise *new* questions in *other* areas, necessitating further inquiry and investigation.

an interview is even possible. By starting early, the impact of such delays is minimized, and if they do become a problem you can appeal to the court for extra time, arguing that you made a good-faith effort to obtain the information in a timely manner. Third, once facts become known they often tend to raise new questions in other areas, necessitating further inquiry and investigation. A document may point to potential witnesses of whose existence you had been unaware; a witness interview may lead you to additional documents not previously considered. By getting the process moving quickly, follow-up can be started quickly.

In addition to performing investigatory tasks at the earliest possible date, you must also follow cardinal rule #2: Accept responsibility to perform investigatory tasks *yourself!* Never assume that the task will be performed merely because the responsibility to perform it has been assigned to someone else (the client, for example). Make it your responsibility to see that the investigatory objective has been accomplished—either by performing the task yourself, or, at a minimum, by carefully following up with the person to whom performance of the task has been assigned.

**P**ARALEGALERT!

Always accept for yourself the responsibility to perform investigatory tasks. Never assume that someone else (for example, the client) will perform the task, even if that person has agreed to accept the responsibility. Either do it yourself, or verify that the person to whom the task was assigned actually did it.

An example on this point is enlightening. Assume Harry Hampton offers to obtain the police report relating to his accident. You may be busy with several matters pending, and his offer is tempting. Once again, *avoid the temptation!* It is better for you to perform the task (and thereby remain in control of the situation) than to delegate it and end up waiting for, or relying on, someone else. Nothing is worse for a litigator than to find him- or herself on the eve of trial without a crucial piece of evidence or information, because everyone assumed that obtaining it was someone else's responsibility. Even if the paper trail of assignments points to someone other than yourself as the prime culprit in such a situation, you have still let down the client. In litigation, everyone must take responsibility. In that way, oversights can be discovered before they create problems.

Next, we come to cardinal rule #3: If an investigatory request is made over the phone (as they often are), always *confirm it* in two ways: (1) by a memo to the file identifying the date and time of the call, the nature of the request, and the person to whom you spoke; and (2) by a letter to the person to whom you spoke, reiterating the conversation and confirming the agreement to fulfill the request. Further, the initial conversation should establish, and the file memo and confirmation letter should identify, the date by which you can expect the request to be fulfilled; and this date should be entered on your calendar or in your firm's tickler system. Then, if the materials have not been received by the date anticipated, you can immediately follow up to determine why not.

**Figure 4–13 The Four Cardinal Rules of Investigation**

> **Rule #1:** Perform your investigatory tasks *at the earliest possible date!*
>
> **Rule #2:** Accept responsibility for the completion of investigatory tasks *yourself.* Either perform the task personally, or verify that the person to whom the task was assigned actually completed it.
>
> **Rule #3:** Confirm telephone requests by a memo to the file and by a letter to the party upon whom the request was made. The memo and letter should both identify: the date and time of the call; the nature of the request; the person to whom you spoke; and the date by which compliance with the request is to be expected. The compliance date should then be entered into your firm's tickler system.
>
> **Rule #4:** Be *thorough* and *creative* in your approach to investigation! You must not, of course, "make things up," but you *must* use your ingenuity and imagination to determine all possible sources of useful information or evidence.

Finally, we come to cardinal rule #4: Be *thorough* and *creative*. You must approach the challenge of proving necessary facts with ingenuity, tenacity, and imagination. To be creative, of course, does not imply that you will be making things up but that you will be drawing upon all your intellectual resources in identifying possible sources for useful evidence. For example, an inquiry to the Milltown traffic department regarding complaints about the bent stop sign at the intersection of Higgins and Pruitt might seem somewhat peripheral—but in the Hampton case, it would turn up a letter written by Judith Johnson herself (look back at the facts of the Hampton matter in Chapter 3).

These four rules are so important that they bear repeating (see Figure 4–13). To summarize: (1) perform investigatory tasks at the earliest possible date; (2) perform investigatory tasks yourself or, at a minimum, keep careful track to make sure the investigatory objective has been accomplished; (3) for investigatory requests made by phone, record the details of the request in a file memo, confirm the request by a letter, and assign to the request a deadline that is recorded on the case calendar (and, if the request is not honored by the deadline, follow up immediately); and (4) be thorough and creative.

## 4–4 Obtaining Necessary Documents

Much of what occurs in a courtroom, and hence much of what is relevant to the litigation process, flows from the contents of, and the interpretation placed upon, various documents. Obtaining these documents is thus a critically important element of the investigation stage. Let us take a moment to consider the detective function of litigation as it applies to obtaining documents, identifying a few likely sources. You should note before we start that there is a certain element of randomness to our survey, in that every case will have its own unique twists leading to unusual but nevertheless important sources of documents. We cannot hope to cover every potential source, nor is that our aim. Rather, we wish to point out several sources of frequent usefulness that merit attention, and to provide you with a sense of how to approach the unique twists of your own case.

Much litigation involves corporations, and it is often necessary to obtain basic corporate information early on in the litigation process, even before a lawsuit is commenced. Such basic corporate information is maintained at the office of the

Secretary of the State (or some equivalent state agency) for the states in which the corporation is incorporated or authorized to conduct business (see Figure 4–14). (By the way, do not confuse the state office known as the "Secretary of the State" with the federal government's Secretary of State; the two offices are entirely unrelated, except for the unfortunate similarity of names.) By supplying the correct name of a corporation to the appropriate Secretary of the State, you can determine: (1) whether the corporation is incorporated in your state; (2) if not incorporated, whether it is authorized or registered to do business in your state; and (3) if it is incorporated or authorized to do business, such information as the address of the principal place of business, the identities of the officers of the corporation, and the identity of the **agent for service of process** (also sometimes called a *registered agent*; the identity of this person may have to be determined in order to serve the corporation with a lawsuit). When making an inquiry of the office of the Secretary of the State by phone or letter, keep in mind that these offices are swamped with similar requests, and thus there are often relatively extensive delays in obtaining information. Thus, it is most important that you follow our first cardinal rule of investigation: make your request as early as possible.

**P**ARALEGALERT!

Do not confuse the state government office known as the "Secretary of the State" with the federal cabinet-level position known as "Secretary of State." The former maintains much basic information about corporations; the latter is a completely unrelated *federal* office.

Many cases, including personal injury cases and medical malpractice cases, involve medical records. Obtaining and reviewing these records is often very important in establishing your case. The actions of medical professionals must be carefully reviewed in a malpractice action; in a personal injury case, the amount of medical bills is an important element of damages. Records can be obtained by requesting them from the medical professional or facility, and enclosing the authorization form we discussed earlier (see Figure 4–6). The letter requesting the documents should be specific, including the patient's name, file number, if known (the client may have the file number attached to copies of bills in his or her possession), and the precise items sought (such as emergency room records, laboratory reports, X-rays, or nurse's charts, to name just a few possibilities) to the extent known. There should also be a catch-all request to include any documents of which you are not yet aware. A typical letter requesting information for the Harry Hampton matter is shown in Figure 4–15.

Another document that will be needed in cases presenting medical issues is the **medical report.** A medical report is an evaluation of the medical situation prepared by the treating physician. Such reports are not always prepared in the

**Figure 4–14   Basic Corporate Information**

> ***Corporate information maintained at the office of the Secretary of the State***
>
> ● Whether the corporation is incorporated in your state
>
> ● If not incorporated, whether the corporation is authorized to do business in your state
>
> ● If it is incorporated or authorized to do business:
>
>   address of the principal place of business
>
>   identity of the officers, often with addresses
>
>   identity of the agent for service of process

**Figure 4–15**  Typical Letter Requesting Medical Information

# Lincoln & Hoover
## Attorneys at Law

September 14, 1993

Dr. William Healer
Healer Building
165 Maple Street
Metro City, Exurbia 12345

Re: Treatment of Harry Hampton, your patient file #92-0358

Dear Dr. Healer:

This law firm represents your patient, Harry Hampton, with regard to injuries which he suffered in a motor vehicle accident occurring on April 15, 1992. Accompanying this letter is a form signed by Hampton authorizing you to release to us medical information relating to Mr. Hampton's injuries and treatment. In particular, we request the following information:

- your office notes and chart

- any correspondence with, or instructions provided to, Hampton

- x-ray reports and, if possible, copies of actual x-rays

- laboratory records

- hospital records or reports in your possession

- information as to Hampton's prior physical history

- invoices or other billing records

- any other relevant materials

If there is a fee for photocopying or other expenses, or if you have any questions regarding this request, please contact me immediately.

Very truly yours,

Paula Paralegal
Legal Assistant

ordinary course of business of a physician or other medical professional, so such a report must often be specifically requested by the patient (or an attorney or paralegal acting on behalf of the patient). The letter making the request should be carefully prepared, explaining to the doctor exactly what is needed. It will likely request a description of the injuries, a conclusion as to the cause of the injuries, and the doctor's best estimate of future expenses and disabilities. An example of a letter requesting a medical report is shown in Figure 4–16. You should note that doctors generally charge a fee for these reports; you should determine the fee and include with your request a check in that amount, so that the report can be obtained as quickly as possible.

Some states have statutes with regard to access to, and the method of obtaining, medical records and reports. You should make sure to check the procedures applicable in your state.

**Figure 4–16  Typical Letter Requesting Medical Report**

# Lincoln & Hoover
## Attorneys at Law

October 2, 1993

Dr. William Healer
Healer Building
165 Maple Street
Metro City, Exurbia 12345

Re: Harry Hampton, your patient file #92-0358

Dear Dr. Healer:

As you recall, this firm represents Harry Hampton. Your file should contain a medical authorization form signed by Hampton, and sent to you with our earlier letter of September 14, 1993.

Thank you for supplying us with the requested medical records and billing information. At this time we are requesting that you prepare a medical report describing the injuries suffered by Hampton in the automobile accident of April 15, 1992. In particular, we would appreciate coverage of the following topics:

- the cause of Hampton's injuries

- detailed description of his fractured arm

- detailed description of his fractured patella (kneecap)

- detailed description of any other injuries suffered by Hampton

- your estimate of any permanent disability associated with these injuries, including the effect on Hampton's ability to work

- your estimate as to potential future medical expenses which Hampton may need to incur as a result of these injuries

Enclosed is this firm's check in the amount of $150.00, which your office personnel indicated was the required fee for a medical report.

Thank you for your cooperation. If you have any question, please feel free to call me, or Sam Superlawyer, at any time.

Very truly yours,

Paula Paralegal
Legal Assistant

Personal injury cases often arise out of automobile accidents. It is likely that the underlying accident was investigated by the state or local police; you should be sure to obtain any **police report** filed with regard to the accident. A request must be placed with the relevant police authority; a small processing fee may apply. As with all other documents, you should move to obtain these quickly; the police investigation will go a long way toward determining liability for an auto accident.

Obtaining documents from the client is also important. When discussing this issue with the client, you should remember that the client is not as familiar with

**Figure 4–17    Post-Interview Follow-Up Letter to Edgar Ellison**

# Lincoln & Hoover
## Attorneys at Law

September 18, 1993

Mr. Edgar Ellison
Widgets and Gizmos, Inc.
888 Widget Street
Metro City, Exurbia 12345

Re: Dispute with TapTapTap, Inc.

Dear Mr. Ellison:

Enclosed is a copy of my post-interview memorandum detailing the areas covered in our interview of September 14, 1993. Please review the memo carefully, and contact me immediately if any fact has either been incorrectly stated or omitted.

As you recall, at the conclusion of the interview we discussed several documents which you were to obtain and forward to me. As a reminder, that list included the following:

- the letter from Emily Tapman dated September 12, 1993

- Hoobermann's office notes, which we discussed at length

- a list of all of Hoobermann's research assistants, with phone numbers

- any other relevant materials which you uncover

If you have any questions about the contents of this letter, or any aspect of your case, please do not hesitate to contact me at any time.

Very truly yours,


Paula Paralegal
Legal Assistant

the litigation process as are lawyers and paralegals. Thus, if you tell the client to supply you with "all relevant documents," the client may not fully understand the "relevance" of certain types of documents. It is important to make your request specific. Your request may be made initially in a letter; if made orally, it should be confirmed in a letter. The letter should spell out the specific categories of materials that you are able to identify; for example, correspondence and internal memoranda. Only after identifying these specific materials should you resort to the general request of a catch-all provision (see the follow-up letter sent to Edgar Ellison after his interview, Figure 4–17).

There may even be situations in which you want the client to create relevant documents. For example, in a personal injury case, the plaintiff may be experiencing daily inconveniences and physical discomforts as a result of injuries suffered. You will want to have such a plaintiff maintain a diary for the purpose of recording all such inconveniences and discomforts. This will provide a valuable means of preserving what might otherwise be fleeting, or repressed, memories of difficult experiences.

**Figure 4–18   Basic Rules for Determining Potential Document Sources**

- Do a thorough analysis of your file, making notes and coming up with your *own* basic ideas.

- Ask other attorneys and paralegals for their thoughts and suggestions.

- Consult the many secondary sources of checklists and investigative aids which contain exhaustive analyses of numerous factual contexts.

There are many other sources of documents, far too numerous to discuss in detail. There may be relevant records from the Department of Motor Vehicles; if road conditions are at issue, you may need records of the U.S. Weather Bureau; bank records, phone records, or newspaper accounts may be relevant. In identifying other potential sources for relevant documents, you should: (1) do a thorough analysis of your file, making notes and coming up with your own basic ideas; (2) ask other attorneys and paralegals for their thoughts and suggestions; and (3) consult the many secondary sources of checklists and investigative aids that contain exhaustive analyses of all sorts of potential factual situations (see Figure 4–18).

One final note on documents: in complex cases, the number of relevant documents can run into the thousands or more. Maintaining organization and control of such documents, including the development of a system identifying the source of each document, is absolutely essential. We'll address the problem of such document control in complex cases in Chapter 9, on discovery.

## 4–5   Obtaining Physical Evidence

Much of the advice just discussed with regard to locating documents also applies to obtaining physical evidence. Thorough file analysis; asking experienced coworkers for their ideas; using secondary sources—all these things are necessary for tracking down and obtaining **physical evidence** as well. Let's look at some of the tangible items that might constitute useful evidence in the trials of our two cases.

Physical evidence is best described by telling what it is *not:* it is not testimony. Physical evidence consists, rather, of tangible items that play a role in the dispute. Relevant documents certainly constitute physical evidence, although they are usually analyzed separately. In general, physical evidence includes such things as the murder weapon in a criminal trial, or the defective product in a product liability trial, or a neck brace in a personal injury trial.

In the Harry Hampton matter, Harry's damaged car is certainly a highly relevant piece of physical evidence. Of course, he will probably wish to have it repaired as soon as possible, or, if "totaled," dispose of it rather than incur heavy storage costs. So photographs should be taken of the vehicle before it is repaired or destroyed. This illustrates why it is important to perform your investigative tasks early—if you hesitate too long before arranging for photographs of the Hampton car, for example, it might be repaired or destroyed in the interim.

Harry himself is relevant evidence—or, more precisely, his physical condition is relevant evidence. In this regard, remember that bruises and abrasions heal—thus, once again, you must move quickly to have photographs taken of relevant injuries.

What other things might be relevant to the Harry Hampton matter? Defendant Judith Johnson might want to photograph the corner with the missing stop sign. Hampton might want to photograph the "Four-Way Stop" notice attached to the stop sign on his corner of the intersection. What about other things besides photographs? Both parties may be interested in preserving the turn signal assembly, on which Little Buddy crossed the wires. Hampton may have been on crutches for several weeks after the accident; you may want to show these to the jury. Judith Johnson may have worn a neck brace following the accident; her attorneys may want to introduce it as an exhibit.

The Widgets and Gizmos, Inc. matter will also feature physical evidence. TapTapTap, Inc. will want to introduce into evidence the allegedly defective widgenometers. TapTapTap, Inc. may also want to offer a large-scale model of a widgenometer, or a detailed flowchart for the purpose of demonstrating more clearly the manner in which the widgenometer failed. Widgets and Gizmos, Inc. may also want to offer into evidence a widgenometer, in order to prove that the product in fact met the specifications established by TapTapTap, Inc., and as proof that it was in fact such specifications, and not negligence or incompetence by Widgets and Gizmos, Inc., that caused the widgenometers to fail.

As with documents, the list of items that might potentially constitute physical evidence is as varied as the number of factual situations that lead to lawsuits. Defective toasters spouting sparks; photographs of a toxic waste spill; models of a proposed building; pants shredded by a dog bite; a torn rug that caused a fall; we could go on indefinitely. The key points to remember in locating physical evidence: Be thorough, be prompt, and use your ingenuity and imagination!

## 4–6   Witness Investigation

In addition to interviewing the client and obtaining necessary documents and physical evidence, you also have to determine both the identity of relevant witnesses and the substance of their testimony. Let us first discuss how to identify and locate witnesses, then discuss the witness interview; finally, we will say a few words about expert witnesses.

### Identifying and Locating Witnesses

The first step in witness investigation is obvious: you must determine who the potential witnesses are. Taking your list of elements and damages as a starting point, you must proceed to identify those individuals who possess information needed to establish the facts that support such elements and damages (see Figure 4–19).

The first and best source for the identification of potential witnesses is, of course, the client; included in our checklists in Figures 4–7 and 4–8 are basic questions as to witness identity. Note that you will not merely ask the client to list potential witnesses; you must, in addition, carefully guide the client through each factual area, explaining what needs to be proved and how such proof might best be accomplished. Only then can you be sure that the client will accurately

**Figure 4–19  Sources for Identifying Possible Witnesses**

- The client, who should be informed of the factual areas on which witness testimony might be needed.

- Relevant documents, such as police reports, medical records, news articles, internal memoranda, or other such materials.

- Witnesses themselves, who are often good sources for *other* witnesses of whom you had no prior knowledge.

- The discovery process.

and exhaustively convey to you the identities of those potential witnesses of whom he or she is aware. Hampton, for example, might not realize that the testimony of his coworkers is useful to demonstrate how his job performance was affected by his injuries, but your guidance will prompt him.

Having exhausted the client's ideas, you next turn to the documents you have uncovered. The police report in the Harry Hampton matter, for example, will identify Louella Williams as an eyewitness to the collision. The police report will also identify the investigating officer and possibly the other emergency personnel on the scene (who can testify about Hampton's physical condition immediately after the accident). The hospital report may identify treating or consulting physicians of whose identity Hampton was unaware—for example, those in the emergency room. In the Widgets and Gizmos, Inc. matter, news articles might identify the other businesses (customers of TapTapTap, Inc.) that are claiming damages blamed on defective widgenometers. They might also identify independent experts who have examined the widgenometers for defects.

Witnesses themselves are sources for other witnesses. Hoobermann, for example, will be able to provide the names of others in the research department of Widgets and Gizmos, Inc. who worked on the widgenometer project. Emergency personnel identified in Hampton's police report may be able to identify other emergency personnel *not* identified in the report, who can also provide information about the circumstances surrounding the accident.

A final method of uncovering witness identities is through the discovery process. You can inquire of the other side as to those witnesses of which they are aware. We discuss this source later, in our chapter on discovery.

If partial identities are uncovered, such as a name on a police report but not an address, you will have to get more creative in your investigative efforts—for example, searching through phone books or checking with the U.S. Postal Service. You may even need to hire a professional investigator. Extended searches can get complicated and expensive. You should certainly consult with your supervising attorney before you spend excessive amounts of time and money pursuing what might be unnecessary information.

Locating witnesses is an important part of the investigation process, and it is often part of the role of the litigation paralegal to assist in the search. Your supervising attorney will provide significant guidance; as you get more experienced, you may be given added (and more independent) responsibilities. In general, you should keep the same factors in mind when locating witnesses as with locating documents or physical evidence: be imaginative; be thorough; and, when you're having problems, don't hesitate to ask other litigation personnel for assistance.

## Interviewing Witnesses

In addition to locating witnesses, you will, of course, have to contact them and obtain their stories. Such interviews have much in common with your client interview—you should follow a checklist, identify the foundation for the witness's testimony, seek to establish rapport, progress from generalized opening questions to a more focused follow-up, take careful notes, and review the facts with the witness to verify accuracy. There are, however, some other factors that must be considered (see Figure 4–20).

First and foremost, you must remember that a witness may be far more reluctant to talk to you than was the client. A witness may not want to get involved; if you believe such a witness has testimony helpful to your client, you must work to convince him or her that, in the interest of justice, it is important that the full story be told.

A witness may be personally hostile to your client, even though his or her testimony is important (and helpful) to your client. Such a witness should be informed that you will not hesitate to serve him or her with a subpoena for a formal deposition, hence voluntary cooperation would be easier for everyone. This should not be presented as a threat, but rather as a simple fact of the litigation process.

**Figure 4–20   Factors to Consider When Interviewing a Witness**

| Same as for Client Interview | Different for Witness Interview |
|---|---|
| (1) Follow a checklist. | (1) The witness may be reluctant; if he or she has useful information, appeal to his or her sense of justice. |
| (2) Take careful notes. | (2) If the witness is hostile, indicate that you will not hesitate to resort to a subpoena and deposition if that becomes necessary. (Present this not as a threat, but as a simple fact of the litigation process.) |
| (3) Identify the "foundation" for the testimony. | |
| (4) Review the facts with the witness to verify for accuracy. | |
| (5) Establish a rapport. | (3) You may have to work hard to accommodate the witness on scheduling. Be flexible. |
| (6) Progress from generalized questions to more focused follow-up. | (4) Get to a potentially "neutral" witness *first.* |
| | (5) Don't share information about the case which the witness doesn't need to know. |
| | (6) Time may be limited, so ask important questions right away. |
| | (7) If the witness is represented by an attorney for this matter, you must communicate through the attorney, and not with the witness directly. |
| | (8) Obtain a signed statement if the witness's testimony appears to be helpful (and possibly even if it is not in order to pin down the witness on details). |
| | (9) Obtain address information, in the event a subpoena is necessary for a deposition. |

Even if the witness is relatively cooperative, you will probably have to work hard to accommodate witnesses on such factors as location and time of the interview. This may involve working around a witness's schedule, which may take you beyond your ordinary work hours. It may also involve conducting the interview outside the office. These circumstances should be discussed with your supervising attorney, but as a "team player" you should be prepared to do what it takes to get the job done, even if extended hours are necessary.

Particularly where a presumably "neutral" witness is involved, you should make every effort to contact the witness as soon as possible. Theoretically, the witness's story should be identical regardless of which side makes the first contact; but human nature being what it is, witnesses often lean toward the position of the first participant to whom they speak. Get there *first*.

When interviewing witnesses, you should be careful not to influence their stories. You want their version of events; and you do not want their credibility eroded in court someday by their indication that they are testifying based upon what you told them. In general, you should tell witnesses as little as is required to get an accurate story; there is no need for you to divulge other aspects of your investigation beyond what each witness needs to know.

The time available for a witness interview may well be limited. The witness may become impatient, or even refuse to answer additional questions. Thus, it is important that you cover the most critical areas early in the interview—it may be your only chance.

A witness may be represented by an attorney with regard to his or her testimony on the matter in question. If such representation is known to you, you must not contact the witness directly. Rather, you should arrange any proposed contact through the witness's attorney.

Particularly if a witness's version of events is helpful to your client, it is useful (and probably wise) to obtain a signed statement. By obtaining such a statement, you will be able to preserve the story if the witness becomes unavailable. Even if the statement hurts your client's position, it can be used to discredit the witness at trial should the details of the trial testimony differ from the earlier statement. A witness statement can be taken in several ways: the witness might write it in his or her own handwriting to establish authenticity; the witness might sign a typed statement; the witness might sign and verify a letter from you setting forth the facts.

With important witnesses, a deposition (see our discussion of the formal discovery process in Chapter 9) may be necessary, even if an interview is conducted and a signed statement obtained. Since a subpoena may be necessary to compel the attendance of the witness at such a deposition, the background information you obtain with regard to the witness (particularly place of residence and place of employment) is very important, since the official who serves the subpoena must be able to find the witness. We speak more about subpoenas and service of subpoenas in the chapters on discovery and trial preparation, but for now remember that it is important to obtain full background information.

## Expert Witnesses

Many cases involve the opinions and analyses of independent experts with regard to certain relevant facts. Real estate appraisers, handwriting analysts, product safety experts, medical professionals, accident reconstruction specialists—the list of potential experts is long and varied. In the Harry Hampton case, there will certainly be testimony from doctors (who will evaluate the medical condition of the injured parties) and possibly from expert auto mechanics (who

**Figure 4–21  Some Considerations When Retaining an Expert**

- Familiarize yourself with the relevant field.

- Contact obvious experts, such as treating physicians who have already been consulted by the client.

- Contact directly a prestigious company, research facility, or university department in the relevant field and inquire as to the identity of experts.

- Utilize a technical expert service.

- Review the classified section of relevant legal publications, where experts frequently advertise their services.

- Ask for advice from other attorneys or paralegals in your firm who have worked on similar types of cases.

- Once you find a potential expert, be sure to obtain a resumé or curriculum vitae, so that you can assure yourself of the expert's qualifications.

- Beware of so-called "professional experts."

will evaluate the repairs performed by Bud's Auto Service). In the Widgets and Gizmos, Inc. matter, there will likely be technical computer experts who will evaluate both the specifications set forth in the relevant contract and the performance characteristics of the widgenometer. Cases often turn on the testimony of such experts (see Figure 4–21).

How are experts identified? In the case of Harry Hampton, it will certainly be necessary for his treating physicians to testify. Additional physicians, perhaps those with superior credentials (hence superior credibility as witnesses) may also be asked (by either the plaintiff or the defendant) to examine Hampton and review his medical records, then testify as to their conclusions. (In Chapter 9 we discuss the method by which a party can compel an opposing party whose physical condition is at issue to submit to a medical examination.)

What about locating experts in other areas? There are several sources. Direct contact with individuals in a relevant field or industry is one possibility—what might be termed "cold calling," in which you simply contact a prestigious company, research facility, or university department in the appropriate field. Another source would be one of the many technical services that advertise to the legal profession, and which maintain large rosters of potential experts in diverse specialties all across the country. These services are well known to litigators; you should discuss their usefulness with your supervising attorney. Yet another source is the classified section of various legal publications, which often contain the advertisements of experts offering their services. Finally, you might simply ask other attorneys or paralegals in your firm who have handled a case requiring an expert in the same field.

You and your supervising attorney should be cautious before retaining a so-called "professional expert witness." Some experts make a career of testifying; if such a background is revealed, and the expert appears to specialize in representing certain types of parties (injured plaintiffs, for example, or insurance companies defending injury claims), his or her impartiality may be questioned and credibility undermined.

If you are asked to interview an expert, certain considerations are important. First, you should obtain the resume or *curriculum vitae* of the expert, so that you and your supervising attorney are satisfied that the expert's credentials justify further contact. Next, the expert should be fully informed of the facts surrounding the technical question on which he or she is expected to provide an opinion. Unless he or she has all the facts, the expert cannot provide a meaningful analysis. Third, you should indicate whether you want the expert to prepare a report, or whether you simply want to discuss the situation with the expert after his or her review. Remember that a report may be discoverable by the other side; we discuss this issue further in the chapter on discovery). Fourth, you should make every effort to educate yourself on the technical area in question, so that when you interview the expert you will have some understanding of the subject area (the expert may be able to suggest some good sources for you, as a layman, to review). Finally, you should conduct the interview in a professional manner, using many of the suggestions we've discussed earlier (establish rapport; use a checklist; work from the general to the particular, if that seems useful considering the technical subject matter).

One final consideration on the issue of expert witnesses is cost. Experts will not testify, or even evaluate your case, for free. Indeed, some well-credentialed experts in complex and difficult fields charge extremely high fees for their work. Even if expensive, the consultation may be justified, but your supervising attorney should always be consulted before the expense is incurred.

## 4-7 Practical Considerations

The detective function is a very important element of litigation practice. As we have noted, you must apply ingenuity and imagination in completing your investigatory tasks. You must be thorough and prompt. You should consider the impact of the rules of evidence, which we discuss in the next chapter. You should also be sure to work closely with your supervising attorney, proceeding only as authorized.

Keeping in mind these considerations, you should also let yourself have a little fun. Investigation involves talking to people, viewing locations, working with experts, obtaining scale models—all of which can be enjoyable, if pursued with the right attitude. There will, of course, be the occasional belligerent witness or overcharging expert or agonizingly slow government agency to remind you that investigation is not *all* fun. Indeed, you have a serious responsibility to the client that must never be taken lightly. Still, there is no reason you can't enjoy your investigatory responsibilities even as you're working harder than you've ever worked before!

## SUMMARY

### 4-1

*Investigation* is the term applied to the gathering of litigation-related facts. When performing an investigation, begin by identifying the facts needed to prove the relevant cause of action and associated damages.

### 4-2

The initial client interview involves three key aspects: the preliminaries; interviewing techniques; and postinterview procedure. Preliminaries include such factors as selecting a proper location; performing necessary background review and research; and identifying those items which you and the client should bring to the interview. Interviewing techniques include establishing rapport with the client; working from the general to the particular; asking tough questions in a diplomatic manner; and listening to (and observing) the client. A postinterview memorandum, follow-up letter, and "to do" list should be prepared immediately after the interview.

### 4-3

There are four cardinal rules of investigation. First, perform investigatory tasks at the earliest possible date. Second, accept responsibility to see that necessary investigatory tasks are accomplished. Third, confirm phone requests in writing, establish a date by which the request should be answered, and enter the date on your firm's master calendar or tickler system. Fourth, be thorough and creative—use your ingenuity and imagination.

### 4-4

Corporate documents and information can generally be found at the office of the Secretary of the State of each state. Medical records and invoices can be obtained from those physicians and facilities that provided treatment; medical reports may not be prepared by medical personnel in the ordinary course of business, hence must often be specifically requested. Accident cases often involve a police report, which often has significant impact on the issue of liability. When requesting documents from the client, be as specific as possible. The client may not be as knowledgeable as you about the kinds of documents that may be relevant.

### 4-5

As with obtaining documents, locating and obtaining physical evidence involves thorough file analysis, asking experienced coworkers for their ideas, and referring to secondary sources for further ideas. Photographs, models and exhibits, or other items that play a significant role in a factual dispute are likely to be useful physical evidence. As with other areas of factual investigation, you should be thorough and prompt, and should use your ingenuity and imagination.

### 4-6

The first and best source for identifying potential witnesses is the client. After inquiring of the client, next examine relevant documents for clues to other potential witnesses. Witnesses, too, may be able to identify other witnesses of whom you had previously been unaware. Finally, the discovery process may provide you with the names of still other potential witnesses. Interviewing witnesses is similar, in some ways, to interviewing clients, but remember that witnesses may not be anxious to testify. Thus, you will have to be flexible in scheduling, and you should ask the most important questions first, in case the witness refuses to answer any more questions. You may want to obtain a signed statement; you should also obtain background information, such as residence address, in case a subpoena is needed at some later date. Experts can be found by "cold calling" companies, universities, or research facilities in the relevant field, by using one of the technical expert services, or by searching in the classified sections of legal journals and publications. You should obtain an expert's resume or other list of qualifications, and you should educate yourself to some extent on the relevant subject matter prior to your interview with an expert. Be prepared to pay a substantial fee for a qualified expert; make sure any such payment is approved by your supervising attorney.

**4–7**
Work hard at your investigatory tasks— but be sure to have some fun with them, too!

# REVIEW

## Key Terms

Before proceeding, review the key terms listed below to be sure you understand each one. If necessary, read over the corresponding section of the chapter. When you are ready to test your understanding, answer the Review Questions.

investigation
cause of action
initial client interview
authorization forms
leading questions
postinterview memorandum
agent for service of process
medical report
police report
physical evidence

## Questions for Review and Discussion

1. What items should the client be instructed to bring to the initial client interview?
2. What is the importance of an interview checklist?
3. List several interviewing tips.
4. Why is a postinterview memorandum important?
5. What are the four cardinal rules of investigation?
6. Identify a good source for obtaining basic corporate information.
7. How is a medical report obtained?
8. What is meant by the term *physical evidence?*

9. What are some important considerations when interviewing witnesses?
10. How are expert witnesses located?

## Activities

1. Go to your local police department and determine the office in which requests for police reports are administered. Ask the person in charge for a copy of a police report relating to a recent automobile accident (there is usually a small fee for copies).
2. Call the Office of the Secretary of the State for your state (you may have to obtain the phone number for the "Corporations Division" or some other specific department; being resourceful in obtaining the correct phone number may be your first taste of the challenges of investigation). Ask the representative to identify the types of information available and the procedure for obtaining such information. Inquire about the proper procedure for both (1) obtaining basic corporate information over the phone, and (2) obtaining certified copies of relevant corporate filings.
3. Ask a doctor (possibly your own personal physician) if you can look at a medical report he or she has prepared. Unless names and all identifying information have been deleted, this will almost certainly require the consent of the patient described in the report. If consent is required, it may be difficult to obtain.

# CHAPTER 5  Evidence

## OUTLINE

## COMMENTARY

You're sitting in a courtroom, in the first row of seats behind the counsel table. It is the trial of the Widgets and Gizmos, Inc. matter, and the judge has just ordered a recess for lunch. Everyone rises as the jury files out and the judge returns to his chambers. Your supervising attorney, Sam Superlawyer, motions for you to come over to the counsel table.

Taking a seat next to the client, you listen carefully as Sam Superlawyer tells you of his suspicion that opposing counsel is going to try to introduce a certain document into evidence after the recess, and that such introduction may be objectionable based on the requirements of the "Best Evidence Rule." He would like you to help him do some quick research on the issue, then grab a sandwich and discuss your findings.

The rules of evidence determine what forms of proof are acceptable for presentation in a trial. Developing an understanding of these rules will contribute substantially to your growth as a litigation paralegal.

## OBJECTIVES

In Chapter 4 you learned how to gather facts. In this chapter you'll learn some of the basic rules regulating your supervising attorney's ability to bring those facts to the attention of the trier-of-fact at trial. After completing Chapter 5, you will be able to:

1. Distinguish direct evidence from circumstantial evidence.
2. Explain the distinction between relevance, materiality, and probative value.
3. Explain how a foundation is laid for witness testimony.
4. Identify the circumstances under which leading questions are acceptable.

5. Explain how witness testimony can be impeached.
6. Identify some important characteristics of the attorney-client privilege.
7. Identify some important exceptions to the Hearsay Rule.
8. Differentiate real evidence from demonstative evidence.
9. Explain what is meant by a chain of custody.
10. Explain the importance of the Best Evidence Rule.

## 5–1  Background Considerations

Evidence is a complicated subject on which volumes have been written, and this chapter presents only a brief glimpse at a few selected highlights. Further study is highly recommended. Fully understanding the rules of evidence, and, most important, the reasoning that justifies each rule, is extremely useful in promoting full comprehension of the principles that guide, and the purposes behind, the U.S. system of justice. We hope that you will have, after completing this chapter, some sense of the value of understanding the rules of evidence.

The rules of evidence apply to lawsuits in which the facts are in dispute. Thus, in some lawsuits the rules of evidence play no specific role; these would be lawsuits in which there is no dispute over the facts, but only over how the law should interpret, or be applied to, such facts. An example of such a situation might be a will contest, where everyone agrees (1) that the testator is dead; (2) that he or she left a valid will; and (3) that a certain document is, in fact, the valid will. The disagreement in such a situation might arise over the legal effect of certain unambiguous words used by the testator. Under the rules of will construction applicable in many jurisdictions, where the words of the will are unambiguous, further extrinsic evidence of the testator's intent is not allowed. Thus if the competing parties differ in their assertions about the proper interpretation of these words under the relevant case law and other applicable principles of testamentary construction, they will file competing legal briefs arguing their respective positions. As to the words themselves, however (which is to say, the *facts*), there is no dispute, hence there will be no need to apply the rules of evidence in this lawsuit. The parties can agree beforehand, in a **stipulation of facts,** on all relevant facts.

> **P**ARALEGALERT!
>
> The rules of evidence apply only to lawsuits in which the *facts* are in dispute. Of course, this includes most lawsuits!

In most cases, however, there *is* some dispute over the facts. One side says the stoplight was red; the other says it was green. One side claims that injuries suffered are disabling for life; the other side claims that they are not serious, or are unrelated to the accident in question. One side says a house was built incorrectly; the other side claims that the plans were open to more than one interpretation. One side says goods ordered were never delivered; the other side says they were delivered, but never paid for.

If the parties to such factual disputes cannot resolve their differences and subsequently go to court, the trier-of-fact (who, you will recall from Chapter 1, is the judge in a bench trial and the jury in a jury trial) must decide what the facts are. The trier-of-fact will hear the respective positions of the two sides and reach a conclusion as to the true state of affairs.

Unfortunately, a trier-of-fact cannot travel back in time to determine conclusively whether the light was red or green; nor can a trier-of-fact peer into the future to determine whether injuries are disabling for life. In both cases, the trier-of-fact must do its best to render a fair and impartial decision as to the facts now, in the present, after trial.

This is where the rules of evidence come into play. Over the hundreds of years that our system of courts and trials has existed, much intellectual effort has been expended attempting to formulate certain rules that "secure fairness" in resolving disputes so that "the truth may be ascertained and proceedings justly determined" (Rule 101 of the Federal Rules of Evidence; these federal rules will henceforth be referred to as FRE). The rules of evidence are designed to ensure that courts will hear only such evidence as experience has determined to be appropriate. Evidence that is appropriate is **admissible,** which means that it may be presented to the trier-of-fact by a party in support of that party's factual position, and may be considered by the trier-of-fact in reaching a decision; evidence that is not appropriate is **inadmissible,** which means that it may not be presented to, nor considered by, the trier-of-fact.

The rules of evidence, then, exist for the purpose of distinguishing appropriate (hence admissible) evidence from inappropriate (hence inadmissible) evidence. You should note further that the determination of admissibility is not made in a vacuum; evidence must be evaluated in light of the fact for which it is offered as proof. This last consideration is very important: certain evidence may actually be admissible to prove one specific fact, but inadmissible to prove a different fact. This may seem odd, but it will become clearer in our discussion of hearsay.

Who decides whether evidence is admissible? The judge. Although evidence is offered to resolve disputed issues of fact, whether certain evidence is admissible is actually an issue of law, and, as you learned in Chapter 1, it is always the judge who decides disputed issues of law.

Before we launch into our discussion of the rules, let's take a moment to discuss a broad distinction between two forms of evidence that you've probably seen discussed in crime films or courtroom dramas—direct and circumstantial evidence. **Direct evidence** is offered to prove a fact in dispute without requiring the trier-of-fact to draw an inference. **Circumstantial evidence** is offered to prove a secondary fact that relates to the primary fact in dispute; the trier-of-fact must then infer a conclusion on the primary fact based upon its relationship to the secondary fact. Those are a lot of words that might seem confusing; an example should make the difference clear. Suppose the issue in dispute is whether John Doe was at work on April 1, 1993. If Jane Smith testifies that she was at work that day and specifically remembers going into John Doe's office and playing an "April Fool's" joke on him as he sat at his desk, her testimony is direct evidence that John Doe was, in fact, at work that day (because the trier-of-fact need not draw an inference, but must only believe Smith's testimony). On the other hand, if the parking lot attendant testifies that he saw John Doe's car in the parking lot that day, but doesn't remember seeing John Doe himself, that would be

**P**ARALEGALERT!

You cannot determine whether a particular piece of evidence is admissible or not until you know the disputed fact for which it is being offered as evidence. Certain evidence may actually be admissible to prove *one* fact, but for some reason inadmissible to prove *another* fact.

**P**ARALEGALERT!

The determination of the admissibility of evidence is a question of law, and is decided by the judge.

**P**ARALEGALERT!

*Direct evidence* is offered to prove a fact in dispute *without* requiring the trier-of-fact to draw an inference; *circumstantial evidence* is offered to prove a secondary fact, from which the trier-of-fact must infer a conclusion as to the primary fact.

circumstantial evidence that John Doe was at work that day. The latter evidence is circumstantial because, in order to find the primary fact, the trier-of-fact must first believe that the attendant saw John's car, then in addition draw the logical inference that, since John's car was in the lot, John must have been at work.

The law does not necessarily favor direct evidence over circumstantial evidence; both may be admissible. You should also note that direct evidence is not necessarily better than circumstantial evidence; for example, if a witness with a reputation for lying provides direct testimony while sweating, blushing, and hesitating often, such direct evidence may have less influence on the trier-of-fact than strong circumstantial evidence from an impeccable witness. The testimony of the impeccable witness may well have more credibility with the trier-of-fact.

Now we turn to a consideration of the rules themselves. For lawsuits pending in the federal courts, the rules of evidence are found in the Federal Rules of Evidence. Some states have similar codified rules of evidence (found in state statutes or rules of procedure) that apply to state court cases. Other states have common-law rules of evidence, which can be located by researching the opinions handed down by the courts of these states. The rules of evidence are obviously a critically important area of litigation practice, because they directly affect the ability of an attorney to prove his or her case in court. You should develop a thorough understanding of the rules applicable in your jurisdiction. In the following pages, we discuss only general principles; eventually you will need to go further and learn the specific rules that apply to the cases on which you will be working.

The first test in determining whether evidence is admissible under the rules, whether the FRE or state rules, is to determine whether the evidence is relevant. **Relevancy** is the "tendency to make the existence of any fact that is of consequence to the determination of the action more probable or less probable than it would be without the evidence" (Rule 401 of the FRE); to be relevant, in other words, evidence must logically affect one's analysis of a disputed factual issue. Relevancy is often broken down into two basic elements—materiality and probative value. **Materiality** requires that the fact to be proved "be of consequence to the determination of the action." In other words, evidence offered to prove some extraneous fact would be *immaterial,* hence irrelevant. **Probative value** is the "tendency" of the proffered evidence to make a material fact "more or less probable"; in other words, it relates to the impact of the evidence on the trier-of-fact's analysis.

Evidence that is irrelevant, either because it is immaterial or because it has no probative value, is not admissible. Relevant evidence, on the other hand, is admissible except as otherwise provided by (1) the Constitution (example: privilege against self-incrimination), (2) statutes, or (3) the rules of evidence (see Rule 402 of the FRE).

Let's look at a few examples to clarify the concepts of relevancy, materiality, and probative value. Suppose in a murder case the issue is whether a particular witness could possibly have seen a murder that took place at midnight, outdoors, in an area with no artificial lighting. Testimony by the witness that, at the time of the murder, there was a full moon would be relevant; the fact to be proved (presence of adequate light) is material and the evidence offered (testimony regarding full moon) has probative value as to the existence of that fact. So would testimony that the sky was clear, since this fact implies that the available moonlight was not obscured. Evidence that the witness had a valid driver's license, however, would likely be irrelevant in this case, either because

**P**ARALEGALERT!

Direct evidence is not necessarily "better" than circumstantial evidence. For example, direct evidence from a suspect source would probably be less helpful to proving a given fact than circumstantial evidence from an impeccable source.

(1) it has no probative value affecting one's conclusion on the material issue of light, or (2) it only serves to prove an immaterial fact, namely, that the witness was licensed (a fact that has no bearing on the case).

Let's look at an example of a situation where evidence that is relevant might nevertheless be held inadmissible. Suppose that, in our "midnight murder" case, evidence is offered to show that a certain variable star in the constellation Orion was in the brightest phase of its luminosity cycle on the night in question. This evidence might be thought of as relevant, since it is probative on the material issue of the amount of light at the crime scene (since at some scientifically measurable level this star did, in fact, contribute to the total amount of light present). The contribution is so infinitesimal, however, that the minimal probative value of the evidence is outweighed by the "confusion" and "waste of time" it would cause (Rule 403 of the FRE); hence, it would likely be deemed inadmissible, even though technically relevant.

It is instructive for you to consider the manner in which the requirements of relevancy are applied, first to direct evidence, second, to circumstantial evidence. In the case of direct evidence, the analysis is straightforward: the evidence offered must itself meet the test of relevancy. In the case of circumstantial evidence, there is a slightly more complicated, two-step process: first, the evidence offered must be relevant to prove the circumstantial fact; second, the circumstantial fact itself must be relevant to justify an inference regarding the primary fact.

As noted, a positive demonstration of relevancy is a prerequisite to the admissibility of evidence, but such a demonstration is not conclusive on the issue. There are situations where evidence that is both relevant and material is nevertheless inadmissible, because it can be shown to be inappropriate based upon some other consideration, such as the minimal probative value of the evidence in our starlight example. The remaining rules of evidence might be thought of as identifying those situations in which relevant evidence is deemed inadmissible. In the sections that follow, we will consider the impact of the rules of evidence on three broad categories of evidence: testimony, physical evidence, and documents.

One final preliminary point: most of the issues we discuss in the remainder of this chapter relate primarily to the actions of attorneys in presenting evidence to the trial court. This may raise two questions in your mind: first, if the rules of evidence relate primarily to the actions of attorneys, why does a paralegal need to learn them? Second, if the rules relate primarily to presentations made at trial, why consider them at this early stage of the text?

Concerning the first question, the reason is simple: since the rules of evidence relate to factual matters, and since paralegals are often involved in the investigation of factual matters, mastering the rules of evidence sharpens basic investigatory skills. Your investigations can be refined, in other words, to generate not merely information, but information that will be admissible at trial. The answer to the second question should now also be clear: because the rules of evidence have an effect on your investigatory methodology, and since investigation begins at an early stage of the litigation process, we are addressing the subject of evidence at this stage of the text.

## 5−2    Testimony

When you think of evidence, perhaps the first thing that comes to your mind is the sight of a witness on the stand, answering questions posed by an attorney. Witness testimony is, indeed, an important form of evidence. We discuss in this section six aspects of testimonial evidence: foundation; proper questioning techniques; impeachment; opinion testimony; privileges; and the hearsay rule.

## Foundation

When an attorney begins questioning a witness, he or she is not allowed to launch directly into questions that bear on the factual issues in dispute. To allow such questioning might allow the witness to voice statements or opinions that are not necessarily appropriate or reliable. The witness must first be shown to have some knowledge that is relevant to the factual issues in dispute (see Rule 602 of the FRE). The attorney establishes that the witness has such knowledge by asking the witness background questions that, when answered, demonstrate that the witness indeed has some relevant information. By employing such preliminary questioning, an attorney is said to be "laying a **foundation**" for further inquiry, a concept we touched on in Chapter 4.

An example will serve to make this concept clearer. Assume your supervising attorney is questioning Louella Williams at the Harry Hampton trial. His first question would *not* be: "Did the car driven by Judith Johnson stop or fail to stop on April 15, 1992, before entering the intersection of Higgins and Pruitt?" At this point, the court has not been made aware of any special knowledge that Mrs. Williams has about the facts surrounding the accident. For all the court knows, Mrs. Williams might be answering this question based on the fact that Mr. Hampton *told* her that Judith Johnson failed to stop (which would be inappropriate hearsay testimony), rather than based upon her own knowledge. The court must be given the opportunity to determine whether Mrs. Johnson's knowledge is sufficient to establish that her answer to the question is independently reliable.

Thus, your supervising attorney must first lay a foundation. He asks Mrs. Williams to state her name and address, and follows up with something like this: "Do you recall your whereabouts on the morning of April 15, 1992, at approximately 8:30 A.M.?" She replies, "Yes, I was out in my front yard, at the corner of Pruitt and Higgins." The attorney then asks, "Did you see anything happen at the intersection of Pruitt and Higgins at about that time?" She replies, "Yes, an auto accident involving two cars." Attorney: "Did you see who was driving each car?" Mrs. Williams: "Yes, the plaintiff was driving one and the defendant was driving the other." Attorney: "Did you observe the Johnson vehicle as it approached the intersection?" Mrs. Williams: "Yes, I observed it from just before it reached the intersection until the time it collided with the other car." The attorney may then follow with additional questions further establishing her opportunity to observe the collision and her capacity to testify about what she observed. Now the attorney has established a foundation. It is clear that Mrs. Williams has firsthand knowledge of the situation, so now it is appropriate to ask the question we set forth before: "Did the car driven by Judith Johnson stop or fail to stop on April 15, 1992, before entering the intersection of Higgins and Pruitt?"

It is always important for you, as an investigating paralegal, to determine exactly *how* a potential witness came to know those facts of which the witness claims knowledge. By probing during your

**PARALEGALERT!**

An attorney must begin the examination of a witness by asking background questions that demonstrate the witness's knowledge of the matters to which the testimony is addressed. This process is called *laying a foundation*.

**PARALEGALERT!**

When interviewing a witness or client, you should always ask how the witness came to know those facts for which knowledge is claimed. This will enable you or your supervising attorney to determine whether a successful foundation can be laid for the witness's testimony.

interview with the witness, you can determine whether the knowledge asserted is the sort of firsthand knowledge for which a successful foundation can be laid. If it is not firsthand knowledge, testimony as to those facts is likely to be inadmissible.

## Proper Questioning Techniques

Our analysis of proper questioning techniques begins at a point even before the witness takes the stand. The first factor to consider is which side called the witness. The side that called the witness asks questions *first*, in what is known as **direct examination.** After the direct examination is completed, the other side is entitled to ask questions, in what is known as **cross-examination.** Certain types of questions that are allowable on cross-examination are not allowable on direct examination; hence, even before the witness takes the stand it is important to consider who called the witness.

Let's consider direct examination first. After the witness has been sworn to tell the truth, the attorney who called him or her begins the questioning. First, the questioner must avoid asking any leading questions. **Leading questions** are those that suggest the answer in their phrasing, as we discussed in our section on interviewing. Such questions are, in general, unacceptable during direct examination (but they *are* acceptable on cross-examination, as we will discuss further; see Rule 611(c) of the FRE). Here are two examples of a leading question: "The defendant was driving about fifty miles per hour in a twenty mile per hour zone, wasn't he?" "Was the defendant driving fifty miles an hour?" A nonleading question would be: "How fast was the defendant driving?"

There are a few exceptions to the rule against leading questions on direct examination. For example, leading questions might be acceptable for background questions ("Do you live at 123 Main Street?") or to refresh the recollection of a witness who is drawing a temporary blank on matters of which he or she has knowledge. In addition, if a witness is called in expectation that his or her testimony will be helpful, and then surprises the direct examiner by giving hostile testimony, the direct examiner is entitled to ask leading questions. A judge has wide discretion to allow or disallow questions, leading or otherwise; as a general rule, however, attorneys should avoid leading questions on direct examination.

Certain questions are unacceptable whether they are asked on direct or cross-examination. For example, a question that is unclear or ambiguous is objectionable. Questions based on assumptions about facts not in evidence will probably be held objectionable. Questions that call for a legal conclusion are also generally objectionable; for example, asking a witness whether a contract is void. The witness can testify as to the facts that allegedly render the contract void; but it is up to the court to determine whether the facts indeed render the contract void *as a matter of law.*

As we noted, leading questions are acceptable on cross-examination. Are there any other restrictions on cross-examination questions, beyond those (such as ambiguity) that we've already mentioned? Yes, there is one major restriction: questions asked on cross-examination are limited to the areas covered on direct examination. If the cross-examiner wants to explore an unrelated area, he or she will have to wait until it is his or her turn to call witnesses, then re-call the witness and ask the question on direct examination. If an attorney improperly addresses such a new area in cross-examination, the opposing side can object to the question on the grounds that it is beyond the **scope,** or subject matter, of the direct examination (see Rule 611(b) of the FRE).

Suppose that after cross-examination the original questioner wants to explore additional questions with the witness? He or she may then conduct redirect examination. Such redirect examination cannot involve new areas of questioning, however; it is limited to those subjects discussed during cross-examination. The process can conceivably go even further: recross-examination, and so on. Each stage is limited to the scope of the previous stage, however.

As noted, judges have wide discretion in allowing or disallowing questions; they tend, however, to follow the guidelines of the rules fairly closely. It is thus critically important for an attorney to understand the bounds of appropriate questioning, and important for you to understand it as part of your general understanding of the litigation process (see Figure 5–1).

## Impeachment

Suppose a witness for the other side has been questioned by the opposing attorney on a sensitive point, and the witness's testimony has hurt your client's case. What can your supervising attorney do to minimize the damage?

One option, of course, is to produce another witness who testifies to a different version of events. Another option is to **impeach** the testimony of the other side's witness. To impeach testimony means to discredit it (see Figure 5–2).

Impeachment can be accomplished by several methods. Evidence may be offered that brings into question, simply and directly, the tendency of a witness to tell the truth. For example, other witnesses may be brought in to testify as to the first witness's reputation for lack of truthfulness. Once his or her reputation is so questioned, the original witness is then entitled to counter the impeachment with evidence of his or her honesty (Rule 608 of the FRE).

Another method of impeaching a witness is to demonstrate that prior statements made by that witness are inconsistent with the current testimony. Witness statements provided to investigators or insurance companies are examples of possible sources of prior inconsistent statements. Another source of prior inconsistent statements might be deposition testimony.

There are other methods of impeaching credibility as well (see, for example, Rules 608, 609, and 613 of the FRE). Evidence of certain types of prior criminal conviction, demonstration of a vested interest that implies a lack of objectivity on the part of the witness, or even a direct attack on the foundation originally laid to support the testimony are all possible methods of impeachment.

**Figure 5–1    Summary of Appropriate and Inappropriate Questioning Techniques**

- On direct examination, avoid leading questions, unless they are (1) related to simple background information, (2) used to refresh the witness's recollection, or (3) used if the witness turns hostile.

- On all examinations other than direct (for example cross, re-direct, etc.), limit your questions to the scope of the questioning of the previous examination.

- Avoid ambiguous questions.

- Avoid questions based on assumptions as to facts not in evidence.

- Avoid questions which call for the witness to draw a legal conclusion.

**Figure 5–2   Some Methods of Impeachment**

- Introduce evidence which brings into question the witness's reputation for honesty.

- Demonstrate that the witness has made prior inconsistent statements which contradict his current testimony.

- Demonstrate that the witness has a vested interest in the subject matter of the testimony which implies a lack of objectivity.

- Attack the foundation originally laid by opposing counsel.

- Introduce evidence that the witness has been convicted of certain felonies involving dishonesty.

## PARALEGALERT!

In order to assist your supervising attorney should impeachment become necessary, you should develop a thorough knowledge of the background of potential witnesses, as well as of the content of their prior statements and deposition testimony.

As a paralegal, your role will be to investigate possible grounds for impeachment. You should develop a thorough knowledge of the background of potential witnesses (for example, prior convictions or reputation for truthfulness), and you should be intimately familiar with the content of their prior statements and their deposition testimony. In this way you will be prepared to offer suggestions to your supervising attorney should impeachment become necessary at the trial.

### Opinion Testimony

There are two types of **opinion testimony** that are admissible at trial. The first involves the opinion of an expert on a subject related to his or her area of expertise. The second involves certain opinions of nonexpert lay witnesses.

In a previous section we discussed locating, retaining, and interviewing **expert witnesses.** In this section, we simply add a few words about how the testimony of an expert is admitted into evidence (see Rules 702 to 706 of the FRE). The basic requirement for the admission of expert testimony is to lay a proper foundation—in other words, to identify and present the necessary preliminary facts that justify the admission into evidence of the expert's testimony. Two elements are required. First, it must be established to the satisfaction of the court that the issue on which the expert is to testify is relevant. This may be apparent from the nature of the case, such as the need for expert medical testimony in a personal injury suit. Second, it must be established to the satisfaction of the court that the qualifications of the witness are sufficient to justify a finding of expert status. This should not be a close call; your experts should have excellent credentials, because even if the court were willing to accept as an expert someone with mediocre credentials, the opinions of such an expert might not be given much weight by the trier-of-fact.

Experts may testify on a wide range of issues. The testimony need only be based on *reasonable* (not *absolute*) certainty, but for the testimony to have any influence on the trier-of-fact, the expert's belief in his or her opinion should be strong. An important issue in a case may come down to a "battle of the experts"

## PARALEGALERT!

To lay the foundation for expert testimony requires two steps: (1) establishing to the satisfaction of the court that the issue on which the expert is to testify is relevant; and (2) establishing to the satisfaction of the court that the witness's credentials justify the finding that he or she is an expert.

testifying for the opposing sides; if one expert expresses near certainty and the other is on the fence, the trier-of-fact will probably be more influenced by the more confident expert.

**Lay witnesses** are nonexpert witnesses. Opinion testimony of lay witnesses is more limited than that of expert witnesses. This is because, as a general principle, lay witnesses should testify as to facts, and the judge or jury should decide what the facts mean. In other words, it is generally for the judge or jury, and not for the witness, to form opinions based on the facts. Nevertheless, the opinions of nonexperts can be admissible under certain circumstances. Two conditions must be satisfied: the opinion must be "rationally based on the perception of the witness," and it must be "helpful to a clear understanding of the witness's testimony or the determination of a fact in issue" (Rule 701 of the FRE). Subjects on which lay witnesses' opinions might be found admissible include such issues as the speed of a car prior to an accident, or whether a person was exhibiting signs of intoxication, or whether someone was of "sound mind" to make a will. In questioning the witness on his or her opinion, of course, the attorney should explore the concrete facts that support the lay witness's opinion.

**P**ARALEGALERT!

As a general rule, lay witnesses should testify as to *facts*, not their opinions. Nevertheless, the opinions of lay witnesses can be admissible if the opinion is "rationally based on the perception of the witness," and if it is "helpful to a clear understanding of the witness's testimony or the determination of a fact in issue" (Rule 701 of the FRE).

## Privileges

Certain questions that relate to relevant matters, and for which a proper foundation has been laid, are nevertheless objectionable based upon a **privilege.** A privilege is a right to prevent testimony as to certain past communications between those individuals who have a relationship that falls into a special category recognized by the court. Examples of privileges include the attorney-client privilege, the priest-penitent privilege, the physician-patient privilege, and the husband-wife privilege. Confidential communications between these individuals are protected; questions at trial (or during discovery) that infringe on this confidentiality are considered objectionable.

An important consideration with regard to privileges is identifying the specific party who holds, hence who can *waive*, the privilege. For example, the attorney-client privilege protects communications between a client and his or her attorney, so that the client can be candid with the attorney without fear that candid statements will be used against him or her at a later time. Can an attorney waive this privilege? No—the privilege is held by the client. Can the client waive the privilege? Yes. If the client waives the privilege, the attorney can be compelled to testify about confidential communications.

The husband-wife privilege is generally found to be held by the spouse who offered the communication, since the purpose is to encourage marital communication. In other words, if the husband tells something to the wife, the wife cannot waive the privilege and reveal what her husband told her, but if the husband waives the privilege then the wife *could* testify about the communication.

It is important for a paralegal to understand a few key aspects of the attorney-client privilege (see Figure 5–3). First, employees of the attorney are

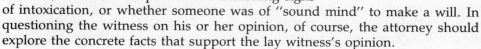

**P**ARALEGALERT!

Only the person who *holds* a privilege can *waive* it; for example, only the client can waive the attorney-client privilege.

**Figure 5–3   Key Aspects of the Attorney-Client Privilege**

- Employees of the attorney are included within the privilege, so that communications between a client and a paralegal are protected.

- To qualify under the privilege, a communication must be confidential. Thus, when communicating with a client on sensitive matters, there should be no third parties present who would destroy the confidentiality.

- Documents are included within the privilege, so that you should take care that correspondence between the client and the law firm is neither turned over to the other side during discovery, nor shown to outside third parties (thereby destroying the confidentiality).

included within the privilege, so that communications between the client and a paralegal fall within the privilege. Second, to qualify under the privilege a communication must be confidential; in other words, no one should be able to hear the communication except the client, his or her attorney, and employees of the attorney. This is important for you, as a paralegal, to take into consideration when communicating with a client—there should be no third parties present who would destroy the confidentiality. Third, documents are included within the privilege. Thus, you should take care that correspondence between the client and the law firm is neither turned over to the other side during discovery, nor shown to outside parties; to do these things would destroy the confidentiality and hence vitiate the privilege.

## The Hearsay Rule

The Hearsay Rule is often thought of as a confusing area of the law. Don't be scared by this. The Hearsay Rule is actually quite logical, and the logic of the rule underscores the basic purpose of all the rules of evidence—that they lead to a fair and just ascertainment of the truth.

Let's start our consideration of the Hearsay Rule by defining what we mean by *hearsay*. **Hearsay** is any statement made out of court but offered in the court to establish the truth of the facts contained in the statement.

Now let's clarify our definition with an example. Suppose at the scene of an accident six months ago, John Doe had said, "The stoplight was red." Assume Mary Jones heard this, and she is later called as a witness at a trial relating to the auto accident that occurred immediately before John Doe made his observation. With regard to the specific issue of whether the light was red, the statement made by John Doe as reported by Mary Jones is hearsay. This is because John Doe's statement was made out of the court, but would be offered in the court to establish the truth of the facts contained in the statement, namely that the light was red.

Suppose, however, that the trial did not relate to a traffic accident. Suppose, instead, that the trial related to a will, with the plaintiff claiming that John Doe, who had just died, was a Russian immigrant who never understood English; hence his will should be declared invalid and a fraud. Suppose Mary Jones is called to testify now. Is John Doe's statement still hearsay? No! The fact at issue is not whether the light was red; and thus the out-of-court statement is not being offered to establish the truth of the facts contained in the statement. The issue is, rather, whether John Doe could speak English. If Mary Jones heard him exclaim, "The stoplight was red", clearly he could speak *some* English, and thus the statement is not hearsay if offered as proof on this issue.

Thus, depending on the context, the same out-of-court statement may be deemed hearsay if offered to prove one fact, *not* hearsay if offered to prove another. The point of this exercise is to emphasize to you that, if you wish to determine whether a certain out-of-court statement represents hearsay, you must know both the content of the statement and the purpose for which it is being offered in evidence.

Now that you know what hearsay is, what do the rules of evidence say about it? In general, the **Hearsay Rule** holds that hearsay is not admissible in court (see Rule 802 of the FRE). This is because, since the person who made the hearsay statement is not testifying, hence is not available for cross-examination, to admit the statement into evidence for the purpose of establishing the truth of the facts contained in the statement would be unfair.

Despite this general rule, there are a large number of exceptions to the Hearsay Rule. Some apply only when the person who made the out-of-court statement (the **declarant**) is, for some reason, unavailable to testify at trial; others are applicable regardless of the availability of the declarant. Each exception

## PARALEGALERT!

In order to determine whether a particular out-of-court statement is hearsay, it is not enough simply to analyze the content of the statement. You must know both the *content* of the statement and the *purpose* for which the statement is being offered in evidence. If the statement is not being used to establish in court the truth of the content of the statement, then it is not hearsay.

exists for the same reason: because the circumstances present in the exception somehow raise the level of reliability of the statement. Rule 803 of the FRE (which applies regardless of the availability of the declarant), for example, lists

**Figure 5–4　Some Important Hearsay Exceptions**

*Some hearsay exceptions apply only if the person making the out-of-court statement, called the "declarant," is unavailable to testify. Others apply regardless of the availability of the declarant. Some of the more important hearsay exceptions appear below, each with a brief explanation for the rationale justifying its trustworthiness.*

**The Following Statements Are *Not* Excluded by the Hearsay Rule Regardless of the Availability of the Declarant**

(1) A statement providing a description or explanation of an event made while the declarant was actually perceiving the event, or immediately thereafter (referred to as the "present sense impression" exception). Trustworthy because the statement is a contemporaneous description, with no time to fabricate details.

(2) A statement or exclamation relating to a startling event or condition and made by the declarant while under unusual stress or excitement caused by the event or condition (referred to as the "excited utterance" exception). Trustworthy because, as with the "present sense impression" exception, it is a statement made contemporaneously with an event or condition, with no time to fabricate details.

**The Following Statements Are *Not* Excluded by the Hearsay Rule if the Declarant is *Unavailable***

(1) Testimony at a prior hearing or deposition, if the party against whom the testimony is now offered had an opportunity to examine the declarant on the point for which the evidence is offered. Trustworthy because of the requirement of prior opportunity to examine.

(2) A statement made by a declarant under the belief that his or her death was imminent. Trustworthy because it is likely that a person facing imminent death would not lie.

(3) A statement made by a declarant which is against his own personal interest, either proprietary or such that it would subject the declarant to civil or criminal liability. Trustworthy because it is unlikely that a person would make such a detrimental statement unless it was true.

23 specifically enumerated exceptions and includes a twenty-fourth, "catch-all" provision that, in essence, authorizes the admissibility of any hearsay that can be shown to be sufficiently trustworthy. Rule 804 similarly identifies exceptions that apply only when the declarant is unavailable.

Some of the more important hearsay exceptions are shown in Figure 5–4, with a brief explanation of both the exception and the grounds that justify the trustworthiness. You should review these carefully, as well as Article VIII of the Federal Rules of Evidence and your own state's rules, for further guidance.

## 5–3  Physical Evidence

In this section we discuss physical evidence other than documents. **Physical evidence** can be thought of as nontestimonial evidence, coming in two varieties: **real evidence,** involving actual "things" that played a role in the matter at issue; and **demonstrative evidence,** involving items that are illustrative or explanatory of the matter at issue, but which did not themselves play an actual role.

Real evidence can be just about anything. In the Harry Hampton matter, for example, the real evidence might include such things as the crutches that Hampton was forced to use for the first six weeks after the accident, or the turn signal assembly from his car, showing crossed wires. In the Widgets and Gizmos, Inc. matter, real evidence might include an allegedly failed widgenometer, retrieved from one of the clients of TapTapTap, Inc.

If documents such as contracts or invoices played a role in the matter at issue, these documents might be thought of as "real evidence." There are special considerations with regard to documents, however; we consider them further in Section 5–4.

One of the key evidentiary issues with regard to real evidence is called the **chain of custody.** Simply stated, a chain of custody is a thorough accounting of the whereabouts of a piece of evidence from the time it was obtained until the time it is offered at trial. The reason for the requirement of a chain of custody is to establish to the satisfaction of the court that evidence is, in fact, what it purports to be, and not a recently fabricated substitute.

The chain of custody issue is thus a *foundation* issue—in other words, in order to establish an adequate foundation for the introduction of a piece of real evidence, the court must be satisfied that the object is indeed what the offering attorney asserts it to be. This is accomplished through a process known as **authentication.** Authentication is a process in which the evidence is shown actually to be what the party offering it into evidence claims it to be (see Rule 901 of the FRE).

To establish an adequate foundation for a piece of real evidence, it is not necessary that every person who had contact with the evidence be called to testify, nor does it even require that every person who has had possession of the object testify. It does, however, require adequate testimony to satisfy the court that the object or item is, in fact, what it purports to be. If the evidence in question is an item with highly distinctive, even unique, characteristics, the court might determine that the foundation requirement has been satisfied if the object is simply identified as authentic by a witness in a position to know (see Rule 901(b)(1) of the FRE). If it is a mass-produced item easily mistaken or substituted for another, the requirement will be more difficult to satisfy. Some positive showing (for example, a detailed chain of custody) must then be made that verifies that this *specific* object being offered into evidence is, in fact, the actual object that played a role in the case.

Along with demonstrating that the evidence is actually what it purports to be, a showing should be made that it is in essentially the same condition as it was at the relevant time (an irrelevant change does not affect the admissibility of the object). Consider, for example, an attorney in a construction dispute who offers into evidence an aluminum two-by-four (removed from the relevant construction project) for the purpose of proving that aluminum two-by-fours were used, rather than the wooden two-by-fours required by the contract. The fact that the aluminum two-by-four was accidentally bent and disfigured while in storage during the pendency of the case would not affect its admissibility, since the issue for which it is being offered is whether the two-by-fours used were aluminum or wood. Suppose, however, that although aluminum two-by-fours were authorized by the contract, the issue in dispute was whether the builder had been using *damaged* aluminum two-by-fours. Since the condition of the two-by-four would then be the relevant issue, and since the condition had changed between the time the two-by-four was removed from the project and the time of trial, the two-by-four would now probably be held inadmissible.

As a paralegal, part of your role may be to maintain the inventory of real evidence in various pending cases. You should consult with your supervising attorney with regard to how best to maintain an adequate chain of custody for such evidence, and how to maintain the evidence in satisfactory condition so that it will remain admissible at trial.

Let's turn now to demonstrative evidence. Demonstrative evidence is used to illustrate, demonstrate, or explain something relevant to the case, even though such evidence did not itself play a role in the events at issue. A plastic model of a human spine used to illustrate a slipped disc suffered by Harry Hampton, for example, would constitute demonstrative evidence, as would a large, four-color graph showing the rate of failure of the widgenometers. Demonstrative evidence can also be a duplicate or model of a piece of real evidence that is unavailable. For example, if Harry Hampton's car was totaled in the accident, and was destroyed between the time his automobile expert investigated the turn signal assembly and the time of trial, your supervising attorney might ask the expert to obtain a duplicate of the turn signal assembly and demonstrate how he determined the wires had been crossed.

As with real evidence, the key issue with demonstrative evidence is laying a proper foundation. The court must be satisfied that the demonstrative evidence is a valid representation of whatever it is offered to illustrate—that the spine model is anatomically accurate, for example, and similar to Hampton's own spine; that the graph is a fair and accurate representation of the failure rate of widgenometers (see Rule 1006 of the FRE); and that the model of the turn signal assembly is identical to the original. This can be done with the testimony of expert witnesses, or those lay witnesses with special knowledge of the issue in question.

Physical exhibits, both real and demonstrative, come in an enormous number of varieties. We can't discuss them all, but we can discuss one type of evidence that straddles the line between real and demonstrative evidence—namely, photographs—to point up some of the problems that can arise.

Are photographs *real* or *demonstrative* evidence? Generally speaking, photographs are demonstrative, but consider how the value of the "illustration" of the photograph differs under the following circumstances. First, consider an auto accident scene on a July night. A newspaper photographer is on the scene, taking photographs of the cars, the injured parties, and the condition of the surrounding area, including the obscured view of one of the cars as it approached the intersection. These photos are very close to real evidence, since they were taken on the scene, at the time of the accident. After being verified by a witness as representing the accident scene on the night in question, they basically speak for themselves. Next, consider the situation where no pictures were taken at the time of the accident, but a photographer was dispatched by the plaintiff later. Photos taken at this later date are more demonstrative than real, since they do not speak for themselves but must be accompanied by some further corroboration, such as testimony that they were taken at the same time of year as the accident occurred (so that seasonal fluctuations in foliage are accounted for), that they were taken at the same time of day (for fluctuations in lighting), and that other substantive changes have not occurred in the intervening time.

As with the other physical exhibits we've discussed, the key problem with having photographs admitted into evidence is laying a proper foundation. Taking our two examples of differing contexts in which photographs are taken, it is clear that different methods must be followed in establishing a proper foundation. It is important to analyze the nature of relevant photographs, and indeed all relevant physical exhibits, and carefully determine what foundation the court is likely to require before allowing the physical exhibit into evidence.

## 5–4  Documents

Documents, as we have noted, play a central role in many lawsuits. How are documents entered into evidence? To answer that question, we must analyze two issues: first, how to establish an adequate foundation for the document; second, how to satisfy the requirements of the Best Evidence Rule. Let's look at these two areas.

Suppose you want to enter a certain document into evidence. The document cannot testify—so how can you establish a foundation? Establishing a foundation for a document, as with physical evidence, is accomplished through the authentication process (see Rules 901 and 902 of the FRE). There are several methods of authenticating documents. First, a pretrial agreement may be reached between the two sides stipulating to the document's authenticity, perhaps during a pretrial conference (we discuss pretrial conferences in Chapter 11). Second, a witness in a position to know can testify that the document is authentic. For example, someone familiar with the signature of the person who signed the document can verify the signature's authenticity, or, in the case of an unsigned document, someone can testify that he or she has special knowledge of the specific document in question, and that the document offered into evidence is, in fact, that specific document. Third, a handwriting expert might verify the signature's authenticity. Fourth, certain documents are considered to be self-authenticating: for example, certified copies of government documents are often presumed to be authentic. Fifth, certain so-called "ancient documents" are presumed to be authentic. These ancient documents must generally be: (1) 20 or more years old; (2) in such condition as would not arouse suspicion of tampering; and (3) originally found in a place where they would be expected to be. An example of such a qualifying ancient document might be a will found in a decedent's safe-deposit box or safe. Refer to Rules 901 and 902 of the FRE for other possible methods of authentication.

Once authenticated, a document must satisfy the second evidentiary requirement we have identified—the **Best Evidence Rule.** The Best Evidence Rule requires that, if available, the *original* of a certain document must be offered into evidence, rather than a copy (see Rule 1002 of the FRE). A good way to remember this rule is to note that the "best evidence" of the contents of a certain document would, in fact, be the original document itself—since copies might be illegible, or, worse yet, may have been tampered with in a fraudulent manner. The Best Evidence Rule also requires that, rather than merely having a witness testify about the contents of a document, the original document itself should be offered into evidence. Thus, a question to a witness about a document not in evidence may lead to an objection that raises the best evidence issue.

The Best Evidence Rule does not absolutely forbid the introduction of copies into evidence, nor does it absolutely forbid testimony as to the contents of documents not in evidence. Rather, it establishes the principle that the original document is required if available. For example, if the original document has been destroyed, or if it is held by some party beyond the reach of the court's *subpoena* authority (see Chapter 19), the party desiring to enter the contents of the document into evidence can proceed by some alternative method (such as introducing a copy).

A side issue in this area involves the distinction between **duplicates** and **copies.** Suppose a contract is finalized and, before signatures are added, two photocopies are made. The parties to the agreement are then brought in to sign the original contract and the two blank photocopies. After signing, several additional photocopies are made of the signed contracts. Under these circumstances, all three documents containing original signatures are considered to be original documents; they are *duplicate originals*. The duplicates thus satisfy the Best Evidence Rule, unless a showing can be made of some inconsistency or fraudulent alteration. The photocopies of the originals are *not*, however, considered to be originals; they would *not* satisfy the requirements of the Best Evidence Rule if any of the duplicate originals were available.

## PARALEGALERT!

The Best Evidence Rule relates to documents, and holds that an original document is the "best evidence" of the contents of that document—better than copies. Thus, if the original document exists and is available, copies are generally not admissible as evidence. Furthermore, if an original document is available, no testimony concerning the contents of the document is admissible until the document *itself* has been admitted as an exhibit.

## 5–5   Practical Considerations

The rules of evidence are quite complex; we have merely scratched the surface to give you an introduction to some basic concepts. Further independent study is advised.

Perhaps the most obvious practical consideration with regard to the rules of evidence is something we've already mentioned—namely, the fact that you, as a paralegal, will never have the primary responsibility to be sure that your client's courtroom proof is in conformity with the applicable rules of evidence. It is your supervising attorney who must worry about bringing your client's story to the attention of the court with admissible evidence.

We mention this again not because we seek to minimize the importance, to a litigation paralegal, of understanding the rules of evidence. Quite the opposite. We mention it because you must not use this lack of ultimate courtroom responsibility as a justification for shoddy study of the rules of evidence. This is true for at least two reasons.

First, analyzing the rationale behind the various rules we have discussed provides a thumbnail sketch of the purposes behind our system of courts and trials. The system is dedicated to the search for truth. The rules of evidence are based on an assumption that, by considering only admissible evidence, the search for truth will yield a just result. By understanding the rules of evidence, you will come to understand how just results are achieved in practice.

Second, since the role of the paralegal is to assist the attorney, it is important that paralegals have a full understanding of the issues, choices, and challenges faced by attorneys. By gaining an understanding of the rules of evidence, a litigation paralegal will develop a deeper insight into the investigation process and a more useful approach to trial preparation, and even someday offer a helpful suggestion in the midst of a trial that assists an attorney to convince a court of a crucial evidentiary question. There are few feelings as fulfilling as knowing that your hard work and acquired knowledge have contributed directly to victory for your client.

# SUMMARY

## 5–1

The rules of evidence apply when facts are in dispute, and are designed to secure fairness so that the truth will be ascertained and proceedings justly determined. To establish admissibility, you must know the fact for which the evidence is offered as proof. Direct evidence does not require the trier-of-fact to draw an inference; circumstantial evidence is offered to prove a secondary fact, from which the trier-of-fact must infer the primary fact. Relevancy is the requirement that the evidence have a tendency to make a material fact more or less probable. A material fact is one that is of consequence to the determination of the action. Probative value is the tendency of evidence to make the existence of a certain fact more or less probable.

## 5–2

A foundation must be laid for witness testimony, demonstrating that the witness has some relevant knowledge about the matters to which he or she is testifying. Direct examination, which is performed by the attorney who called the witness, should generally not include leading questions. Leading questions are, however, acceptable on cross-examination. Questions that are ambiguous, or call for a legal conclusion, or that are based on assumptions as to facts not already in evidence, are improper. Impeachment is accomplished by offering evidence on such things as prior inconsistent statements or a reputation for dishonesty. Opinion testimony of experts requires that a proper foundation be laid, establishing the expert's credentials. Lay witnesses can testify to their opinions if the opinions are rationally based on their perceptions, and helpful to a clear understanding of the testimony or a fact in dispute. Privileged communications are those that can be shielded from inquiry during trial, and include communications between a husband and wife, a physician and patient, and an attorney and client. Communications between a paralegal and a client are included within the attorney-client privilege. Hearsay is a statement made out of court but offered in the court to establish the truth of the facts contained in the statement. As a general rule, hearsay is inadmissible, but there are many exceptions.

## 5–3

Real evidence involves actual objects that played a role in the matter at issue. Demonstrative evidence involves items that are illustrative or explanatory of the matter at issue but which did not themselves play an actual role. A chain of custody is a thorough accounting of the whereabouts of a piece of evidence from the time it was obtained until the time it is offered into evidence. The key issue with regard to the admissibility of real and demonstrative evidence is in laying the proper foundation (accomplished through authentication), which is to say, demonstrating to the satisfaction of the court that the item at issue actually *is* what it purports to be, or is a valid representation of the issue it is offered to illustrate.

## 5–4

Authentication of documents is necessary to establish a valid foundation. The Best Evidence Rule requires that, if available, the original of a document must be offered into evidence, rather than a copy.

## 5–5

Learning the rules of evidence is important to paralegals for at least two reasons. First, it provides insight into the purposes behind our system of courts and trials. Second, it enables a paralegal to offer greater assistance in the areas of investigation and trial preparation.

# REVIEW

## Key Terms

Before proceeding, review the key terms listed below to be sure you understand each one. If necessary, read over the corresponding section of the chapter. When you are ready to test your understanding, answer the Review Questions.

stipulation of facts
admissible
inadmissible
direct evidence
circumstantial evidence
relevancy
materiality
probative value
foundation
direct examination
cross-examination
leading question
scope
impeach
opinion testimony
expert witnesses
lay witnesses
privilege
hearsay
hearsay rule
declarant
physical evidence
real evidence
demonstrative evidence
chain of custody
authentication
best evidence rule
duplicates
copies

## Questions for Review and Discussion

1. What is the difference between direct evidence and circumstantial evidence?

2. Explain how the concepts of *relevancy, materiality,* and *probative value* apply to evidence law.

3. How does an attorney establish a foundation for witness testimony?

4. Under what circumstances are leading questions acceptable?

5. How can witness testimony be impeached?

6. Identify some important characteristics of the attorney-client privilege.

7. What are some of the important exceptions to the hearsay rule?

8. Compare real evidence with demonstrative evidence.

9. Explain what is meant by a chain of custody.

10. What is the significance of the best evidence rule?

## Activities

1. Identify the rules of evidence applicable in your state's courts, then spend some time studying the rules regarding hearsay.

2. Call the clerk's office of the nearest state or federal courthouse to determine the date and time of an upcoming trial, then make plans to attend at least an hour of the trial so as to observe the manner in which evidence is presented.

3. Go to your local land records (probably in the local town hall or county offices) and find out the procedure for obtaining a certified copy of a deed. If certified copies are available, ask to see one and note the manner in which the certification is made.

# CHAPTER 6 The Complaint

## OUTLINE

## COMMENTARY

Your interview with Edgar Ellison has revealed that TapTapTap, Inc. has failed to make timely payment for the most recent shipment of widgenometers (the amount currently due is over $750,000). Thus, TapTapTap, Inc. is technically in breach of its contract with Widgets and Gizmos, Inc., although the correspondence and swirling controversy have made it clear that TapTapTap, Inc. believes it has a right to withhold payment based on the contention that the widgenometers are defective.

Meanwhile, you have received a copy of the police report for Harry Hampton's accident. Mrs. Williams, the witness, has given a statement to the police indicating that Judith Johnson's car failed to stop at the intersection.

You meet with Sam Superlawyer to discuss the two situations. He asks you to prepare draft complaints. A complaint, when filed with the court, begins a lawsuit.

## OBJECTIVES

In this chapter you'll learn how to use the factual information you've gathered and the legal theories you'll develop to draft a complaint and commence a lawsuit. After completing this chapter, you'll be able to:

1. Explain what is meant by a cause of action.
2. Explain why pleadings have numbered paragraphs.
3. Identify the requirements for federal diversity jurisdiction.
4. Determine appropriate venue for a lawsuit.
5. Differentiate fact-pleading from notice-pleading.
6. Explain the usefulness of form books.

7. Ensure that your client's case is tried by a jury.
8. Explain what a *TRO* is.
9. Identify the two key purposes of a summons.
10. Explain the difference between in-hand service and abode service.

## 6–1    The Cause of Action

In Chapter 1 we defined the **complaint** as the document in which the plaintiff formally states his or her claim to the court. We're going to expand on that definition and take you step-by-step through the complaint-drafting process, but first we need to introduce some important background concepts.

First, consider the following: when a client brings to you a problem and sketches out for you the framework of his or her claim, how do you decide whether the claim even justifies a lawsuit? For the moment, disregard the amount of the claim, or the difficulty and expense of proving it—we simply want to ask how you decide whether the facts as stated by the client are sufficient to provide the basis for a viable lawsuit.

The answer is to determine whether the facts of the claim establish a valid **cause of action.** As discussed in Chapter 4, a cause of action is a legal claim that, if proved and if no successful defenses are raised, is sufficient to justify the entry of judgment in favor of the party asserting the claim. Causes of action can range from contract claims to personal injury claims to product liability claims to will contests. These causes of action and others are all found and defined in one (or both) of two places: (1) judicial opinions, and (2) statutes.

A cause of action, you may recall from Chapter 4, is made up of components, called **elements,** which are those essential allegations necessary to be proved if the cause of action is to be established. Elements are determined by reviewing those cases and/or statutes that define the cause of action. With thorough research, careful reading, and well-developed analytical skills, you will be able to draw from these cases and statutes all the elements that must be proved to establish your cause of action. If you analyze the facts ascertained during your factual investigation in conjunction with the required elements, you should be able to determine whether a valid cause of action exists in your client's situation. If it does, you have established a basis for your lawsuit. We will talk further about elements in Section 6–4, where we discuss the drafting of complaints for the Harry Hampton and Widgets and Gizmos, Inc. matters.

We should mention here that the allegations of a complaint are intended to assert the *facts* that establish the plaintiff's cause (or causes) of action; generally speaking, the underlying legal doctrines are not included. "Plead the facts, not the law" is a common maxim; you will virtually never, for example, see cited in a complaint a judicial opinion (even one that has a direct impact on the issues raised). There are a few exceptions to this maxim: applicable statutes, for example, are often referenced; words with legal effect (such as "negligence" or "breach of contract") are often employed for the sake of clarity and convenience. Furthermore, you must keep in mind that the form in which the factual allegations will be stated is directly influenced by the applicable legal doctrines, even though these doctrines are not

## PARALEGALERT!

As a general proposition, the allegations of a complaint should relate to facts, not law. Of course, the form in which these factual allegations are stated is directly influenced by the applicable legal doctrines, and words with legal effect (such as "negligence" or "breach of contract") are often employed for the sake of clarity and convenience. Applicable statutes are often cited as well; judicial opinions, however, are virtually never cited in a complaint.

specifically mentioned in the complaint. For example, the facts establishing each element required by the applicable statutes and judicial opinions must be adequately alleged, or the complaint will be open to attack by the defendant (we discuss such attacks on the complaint in Chapter 7). Despite these exceptions, however, as a rule your allegations should relate to facts, not law.

In conjunction with analyzing whether the elements of the plaintiff's proposed cause of action can be supported by the facts, you must also determine the identity of the party against whom the cause of action will be asserted. This party will be the *defendant* in the lawsuit started by the complaint.

Sometimes the factual context indicates that causes of action exist against several potential defendants. Does this mean that there must be several different lawsuits? No; under Rule 20 of the FRCP (and under the analogous rule applicable in state courts) the concept of **joinder of parties** holds that multiple defendants may be sued in one lawsuit if the plaintiff asserts a right to relief against such defendants "arising out of the same transaction, occurrence, or series of transactions or occurrences and if any question of law or fact common to all defendants will arise in the action" (Rule 20 of the FRCP). Multiple plaintiffs sometimes also join together in one lawsuit, a possibility we discuss further in Chapter 8.

The identity of the potential defendants is often fairly obvious, but not always. Let's look at the Harry Hampton case to see why. In drafting a complaint on behalf of Hampton, there are two potential defendants, both of whom are obvious. The first is Judith Johnson; from Hampton's perspective, her negligence in running the stop sign caused the accident. The second obvious defendant is Bud's Auto Service; it failed to correct the signal problem and may be liable to Hampton as a result.

Consider the Hampton case from Judith Johnson's perspective, however. She may have gone to a lawyer as well, on the theory that Hampton was negligent because, though his signal indicated an intention to turn, he nevertheless went straight through the intersection. She may decide to try to "get the jump" on Hampton and start a lawsuit herself, with her own complaint stating a claim for negligence against him. If she does, and if, in fact, Bud's Auto Service was negligent in repairing the turn signal, the negligence of Bud's Auto Service may also have been a contributing cause of her injuries. Yet at this stage of the case, she is not in a position to have any knowledge of the involvement of Bud's Auto Service; therefore, the identity of a potential defendant will not be immediately obvious to her attorney. This potential defendant (i.e., Bud's Auto Service) will only become known to Johnson and her attorney later in the process, when investigation or discovery requests reveal that Bud's Auto Service was involved and may have been negligent—at which time Johnson can amend her pleadings to include this claim.

So that you're not misled even before you start, we'll get ahead of ourselves just a bit here, and explain to you what happens when each party in a dispute believes that it has a valid claim against the other party. Such a situation does not imply that there will be two lawsuits, each started by a separate complaint. Rather, one party strikes first with a complaint; the other party will then assert its cause of action in the same lawsuit by filing a **counterclaim** (see, for example, Rule 13 of the FRCP). Thus, if Hampton filed his suit first, with Judith Johnson as a defendant, she would assert *her* claim against *him* in a counterclaim in the same lawsuit. We discuss counterclaims further in Chapter 8.

Situations often arise in which a plaintiff has several claims against a single defendant; in other words, there may be several legal theories or causes of action (arising out of the same set of facts or an entirely different set of facts) on which a judgment against that defendant might be justified. These multiple claims can all be joined together in one lawsuit: under Rule 18 of the FRCP, a party asserting a claim against another party "may join, either as independent or as

**Figure 6–1  Defining a "Complaint"**

> **Complaint:** The formal statement of a plaintiff's cause or causes of action seeking a legal or equitable remedy against one or more defendants which, when filed with the court and served upon the defendants in the required manner, successfully commences a lawsuit.

alternate claims, as many claims . . . as the party has against an opposing party." The governing concept is known as **joinder of claims.** Such multiple causes of action may be in the *alternative* (which is to say, they may be competing or inconsistent theories, only one of which can eventually prove true; see Rule 18 and also Rule 8(e)(2) of the FRCP) or *cumulative* (that is, independent and possibly all valid). We discuss further in Section 6–4 how multiple causes of action are incorporated into one complaint.

Once you've identified all potentially viable causes of action and defendants, do you then have all the information you need to begin drafting your complaint? No, you must identify two more items—the **damages** suffered by your client as a result of the wrongful behavior alleged in the cause of action, and the **relief** from these damages that your client seeks. Your client may be seeking a legal remedy, such as money damages, or an equitable remedy, such as an injunction. If the complaint fails to specify the damages suffered and relief sought, then even if the court finds that the plaintiff proved the cause of action at trial, and is thus entitled to judgment in its favor, there will be no foundation on which to base the terms of the judgment.

At the beginning of this section, we promised to expand on our definition of the complaint. Now that we've introduced you to the important background concepts of *cause of action, defendants, damages,* and *relief,* here's the expanded version: the *complaint* is the formal statement of the plaintiff's cause or causes of action seeking a legal or equitable remedy against one or more defendants, which, when filed with the court and served upon the defendants in the required manner, successfully commences the lawsuit (see Figure 6–1).

## 6–2   A Few Preliminary Items

Before we examine how to present the plaintiff's causes of action in the proper format for a complaint, let's discuss a few preliminary items applicable to all pleadings: the *caption,* the *designation,* the *numbered paragraphs,* and the *signature block.* We'll also discuss an item applicable to all pleadings *except* the complaint— namely, the *certificate of service* (also called a proof of service or certification)—and we'll explain how the function of the certificate of service is performed for a complaint by a far more elaborate substitute.

First, let's reiterate what we mean by a pleading. As we noted in Chapter 1, **pleadings** are certain documents filed with the court that identify the claims or defenses of the parties. Rule 7 of the FRCP indicates that, in a federal civil action, the pleadings include the complaint (filed by the plaintiff) and the answer (filed in response to the complaint by the defendant). Also included are certain other documents that identify claims and defenses; we discuss these in future chapters. We refine our definition of "pleadings" further in Chapter 7; for now, you should review Rule 7 of the FRCP, and also check to see how pleadings are defined in your state court system.

**Figure 6–2  Hampton Caption**

| | | |
|---|---|---|
| HARRY HAMPTON, | : | Superior Court |
| Plaintiff | : | State of Exurbia |
| v. | : | Judicial District of |
| JUDITH JOHNSON and BUD'S | : | Metro County |
| AUTO SERVICE, | : | |
| Defendants | : | October 10, 1993 |

Next, we'll consider the **caption** of a pleading. As we discussed in Chapter 1, litigation practice is dominated by rules; among the rules are requirements as to format of pleadings. The format requirements dictate that every pleading have a caption at the top of the first page, providing certain key information. An example of a caption for the complaint we're about to draft in the Harry Hampton matter is shown in Figure 6–2. Let's analyze it, starting with the left side. The parties are identified here (first the plaintiff, then the defendants); this is called the **title of the action** (see Rule 10(a) of the FRCP). Under Rule 10(a), the caption for the complaint should include the names of all the parties; we'll assume the rules of Exurbia's state courts (applicable to the Hampton complaint) have the same requirement. Under the FRCP, pleadings, motions, and other papers subsequent to the complaint need identify only the first named plaintiff and defendant (again, see Rule 10(a)), indicating the existence of the other parties by the Latin phrase *et al.*, meaning "and others." The names of the parties are usually capitalized, whereas their status (i.e., "plaintiff" or "defendant") is usually not (although with this, as with all aspects of litigation, you must check the specific rules applicable in the appropriate jurisdiction). Between the parties is "v." or "vs.," signifying "versus." The left side of the caption is separated from the right side by a series of dots (often typed by using colons) or some other dividing mark. On the right side is found the state (in our case, the imaginary state of Exurbia), the name and location of the court, and the date.

Something is missing from the caption in Figure 6–2 that you will find on all captions other than the complaint: the **docket number.** The docket number (also called a **civil action number**) is assigned by the court to the case, for the purpose of differentiating it from all other cases. It cannot appear on a draft complaint, because the case hasn't yet been filed, hence there isn't yet a docket number to which you can refer. Once the complaint is filed, however, the docket number is immediately assigned by the court, and all subsequent filings in that case must show the same docket number in their caption (in federal court and many state courts, the docket number is always placed on the complaint as well, not by the drafter but by the court clerk; you'll learn how this occurs in Section 6–6). The docket number helps the court to manage the thousands of documents filed in the pending cases under its authority. In Figure 6–3, where we show several alternative caption styles, each has a docket number included.

> **PARALEGALERT!**
>
> A docket number will always appear on a federal court complaint, but will sometimes not appear on a state court complaint (depending on the applicable state court rules). All pleadings subsequent to the complaint, however, in both federal court and state court, must contain the docket number.

**Figure 6–3   Alternative Caption Formats**

**(a)**            UNITED STATES DISTRICT COURT FOR THE SOUTHERN
                             DISTRICT OF CALIFORNIA

                    Civil Action, File Number 94-LQZ-0135

MICHAEL BUFFETT, et al.               §
            Plaintiffs                §
                                      §        ANSWER
vs.                                   §
                                      §        June 5, 1994
CARMEN BROWN, et al.                  §
            Defendants                §

---

**(b)**                UNITED STATES DISTRICT COURT FOR THE
                             DISTRICT OF NEW JERSEY

XTC CORPORATION, Plaintiff             :
            vs.
SMITH, INC., Defendant                 :        ANSWER AND SPECIAL DEFENSE

                                       :        CIVIL ACTION NO. 135-OUH-94

                                       :        February 15, 1994

---

**(c)**         UNITED STATES DISTRICT COURT FOR THE NORTHERN
                    DISTRICT OF ILLINOIS, CHICAGO DIVISION

                    Civil Action, File Number LQQ-00185-94

XTC CORPORATION, Plaintiff             *
            vs.                        *        ANSWER AND COUNTERCLAIM
SMITH, INC., Defendant                 *        October 10, 1995
                                       *

---

**(d)**                                         NO. 89-7786-J

XTC CORPORATION,                       )        IN THE DISTRICT COURT OF
                                       )
            Plaintiff                  )
                                       )
vs.                                    )        DALLAS COUNTY, TEXAS
                                       )
SMITH, INC.,                           )
                                       )
Defendant                             )        191st JUDICIAL DISTRICT

Just below the caption we find the **designation** of the pleading (see Figure 6–4; note that in federal court cases, the designation is considered to be part of the caption). The designation identifies the purpose of the pleading; that is to say, whether it is a complaint, an answer, or some other type of pleading (see Rule 10(a) of the FRCP, which references the possible designations set forth in Rule 7(a)). In some complex cases, it is useful to provide, as part of the designation, additional information that more specifically identifies the precise purpose. For example, in a case with multiple defendants, one defendant might file a pleading with the following designation: "Second Amended Answer of

**Figure 6–4 Hampton Caption with Designation**

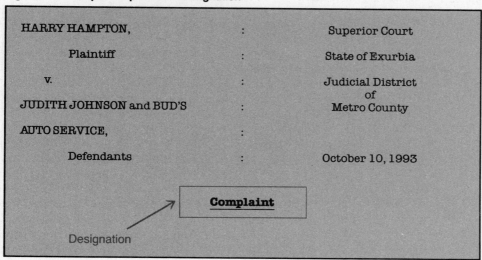

| | | |
|---|---|---|
| HARRY HAMPTON, | : | Superior Court |
| Plaintiff | : | State of Exurbia |
| v. | : | Judicial District of |
| JUDITH JOHNSON and BUD'S | : | Metro County |
| AUTO SERVICE, | : | |
| Defendants | : | October 10, 1993 |

**Complaint**

Designation

Defendant Ajax Machinery Co., Inc." By identifying itself by name in the designation (i.e., "Ajax Machinery Co., Inc."), this defendant has clarified from which defendant the answer has come; by further noting that it is the "second amended answer," the pleading is differentiated from earlier versions filed by the same defendant. Obviously, if this pleading had simply been labeled "Answer," the designation would not have been very useful; determining the pleading's purpose would have required considerable effort (both in reading the pleading itself and in reviewing prior pleadings) to place it in its proper context.

The information contained in pleadings is set forth in **numbered paragraphs** (see Rule 10(b) of the FRCP). Each separate allegation of a complaint is usually stated in a single sentence, which is made a separate numbered paragraph; Rule 10(b) notes that each numbered paragraph should be "limited as far as practicable to a statement of a single set of circumstances . . . ." The reason for this is to facilitate clarity in both the pleading itself and the responses thereto. A single allegation set forth in a numbered paragraph can be answered in a crisp fashion: "The allegation of paragraph 6 is admitted," for example, or, "The allegation of paragraph 6 is denied." If the allegations were to be set forth in a long, complex narrative, it would be impossible to respond concisely concerning exactly which portions of the original narrative's allegations were admitted and which denied. The potential for confusion would be high; the litigation process is designed to eliminate, not encourage, confusion.

Every pleading filed with a court must be signed. The place where the signature is found, at the end of the substantive portion of the pleading, is called the **signature block.** If a party is not represented by an attorney, the party must sign his or her own name to each pleading; if represented by an attorney, the attorney must sign the pleading. The signer must, in addition, include an address, and generally also a phone number. Some states or local federal rules require even further information in a signature block, such as an identifying registration number assigned by the court system to the signing attorney or law firm. An example of a signature block is shown in Figure 6–5. You should keep in mind that a paralegal can never sign a pleading; to do so would violate the ethical and statutory constraints against the unauthorized practice of law.

The signature requirement is not a mere formality that can be taken lightly by the signing party or attorney. Rule 11 of the FRCP, for example, holds that the signature constitutes a "certification by the signer that the signer has read" the document, has made "reasonable inquiry," and is satisfied that the contents are

**Figure 6–5   Sample Signature Block**

THE PLAINTIFF, HARRY HAMPTON

By: _____

Samuel Superlawyer, Esq.
His attorney
Lincoln & Hoover
123 Lincoln Street
Metro City, Exurbia 12345
Atty. Reg. #: 87654
Phone: (901) 222-2222

## PARALEGALERT!

Signing a pleading is not a mere formality: the signer must make reasonable inquiry that the pleading is accurate, and may be subject to sanctions if it is not. Remember that a paralegal can *never* sign a complaint or other pleading; to do so would constitute the unauthorized practice of law.

"well grounded in fact" and either in conformity with the law or in conformity with a "good faith" argument to modify the law, and that the document is not being used for wrongful purposes such as unnecessary delay or harassment. If the requirements of Rule 11 are violated, the court is authorized to impose a sanction against the party and attorney involved.

Occasionally, a complaint must have a verified signature, also called a **verification;** such requirements are far more common in state courts than in federal court. The verified signature is always that of the party making the allegation; a complaint with such a verified signature is referred to as a **verified complaint.** Verification is accomplished by having the signing party swear, before a person authorized by statute to administer an oath, to the truth of the allegations contained in the complaint. An example of a verification clause appears in Figure 6–6. The requirement for a verified signature often arises where the allegations of the complaint impugn the character of the defendant; for example, if the complaint alleges that the defendant committed a fraudulent act. The verification is just one more layer of protection against a frivolous charge.

**Figure 6–6   Sample of Verified Signature Clause**

The plaintiff, Harry Hampton, hereby swears and affirms that the contents of the foregoing complaint are true and correct to the best of his knowledge and belief.

_____
Harry Hampton

Subscribed and sworn to before me, the undersigned _____,
notary public in and for the state of Exurbia, on this the _____ day of
_____, 1993.

_____
Notary Public

My commission expires:
_____

**Figure 6–7  Sample Certificate of Service**

---

### Certificate of Service

The undersigned certifies that a copy of the foregoing document was mailed, postage prepaid, this _____ day of _____, 1993, to all counsel of record.

_____
Samuel Superlawyer, Esq.

*[Note: Many jurisdictions require that each lawyer to whom a copy was sent be identified, by name and address, in the Certificate of Service.]*

---

The next preliminary matter we will touch upon is the **certificate of service.** A sample certificate of service is shown in Figure 6–7. The purpose of a certificate of service is simple: to certify to the court that a copy of the attached pleading has been sent, usually by first-class mail, to the other side. The opposing parties each need to know the positions asserted by the other; the court needs assurance that every party is fully informed; and it would be expensive and extraordinarily inefficient if each side had to check the court file every day at the courthouse to determine whether the opposition had filed a responsive pleading, motion, or other document. Thus, the rules create an obligation upon the parties to provide each other with copies of all pleadings filed (see, for example, Rule 5 of the FRCP).

As we mentioned at the beginning of this section, the complaint is the only pleading that need not contain a certificate of service. This is not because the other side is not supplied with a copy of the complaint, but rather because the requirement is actually much stricter with regard to the certification of delivery of a complaint. We discuss this stricter requirement, called "service of process," in Section 6–6.

Finally, we'll consider the concept of "filing." Briefly stated, the court can only resolve a dispute if it is made aware of the claims and defenses asserted by the parties. Thus, under Rule 5(d) of the FRCP, most official documents (orders of the court, pleadings, motions, and the like) generated to move the lawsuit forward under the rules of procedure must be "filed with the court within a reasonable time . . . ." These requirements are satisfied, under Rule 5(e), by filing such documents "with the clerk of the court . . . ." This means that these documents must be filed in the **clerk's office** of the applicable courthouse. "Filing" usually means delivering (in person or by mail) the *original* document (with *original* signature) to the clerk's office; you should note, however, that in 1991 Rule 5(e) was modified to allow filing by "facsimile transmission" (commonly referred to as "FAXing") where the local federal rules permit.

Just as the service requirements with regard to the complaint differ from those that apply to other documents, so, too, do the filing requirements. We discuss in detail in Section 6–6 the procedures that apply to complaints.

## 6–3  Choosing a Court

An important initial consideration prior to drafting a complaint is choosing the court in which to file the complaint. This involves analyzing at least three factors: the presence or absence of concurrent jurisdiction; the requirements of venue; and the impact of conflicting laws. Let's look at each of these factors in turn.

The presence or absence of concurrent jurisdiction is obviously the first factor to consider. If there is no concurrent jurisdiction, there will be no choice between court systems. In the Harry Hampton matter, there does not appear to be any ground for federal court jurisdiction. Why is this? Consider our discussion of federal court jurisdiction in Chapter 1. Such jurisdiction is generally based on one or more of three specific situations: the applicability of a federal statute; the applicability of a federal constitutional principle; or the existence of diversity of citizenship among the parties. None of these situations exists in the Harry Hampton matter. Opposing parties Hampton and Judith Johnson are both citizens of the same state, Exurbia, so diversity is not present. Furthermore, since negligence is the legal issue forming the basis of the potential causes of action, and since negligence is generally a state law issue involving no federal statutes or federal constitutional principles, those potential grounds for federal court jurisdiction are similarly inapplicable. The Hampton matter will thus be filed in state court.

The Widgets and Gizmos, Inc. matter leads to a different analysis. Diversity of citizenship is, in fact, present here. The federal diversity statute, 28 U.S.C. §1332, reads in pertinent part as follows:

§1332. Diversity of citizenship . . .

(a) The district courts shall have original jurisdiction of all civil actions where the matter in controversy exceeds the sum or value of $50,000.00, exclusive of interest and costs, and is between:

(1) citizens of different states;

* * *

(c) For the purposes of this section . . .

(1) a corporation shall be deemed to be a citizen of any State by which it has been incorporated and of the State where it has its principal place of business . . . .

As you recall from the basic facts set forth in Chapter 3, the state of incorporation and the principal place of business of Widgets and Gizmos, Inc. is the state of Exurbia, whereas the state of incorporation and the principal place of business of TapTapTap, Inc. is California. In addition, TapTapTap, Inc. is late on a payment in excess of $750,000, easily exceeding the minimum jurisdictional amount. Thus, federal diversity jurisdictional requirements have been satisfied.

Suppose that TapTapTap, Inc. filed the complaint in a lawsuit against Widgets and Gizmos, Inc., alleging defective widgenometers, and also alleged an additional cause of action against the Conner Corporation of California, alleging that Conner had provided defective microchips that contributed to TapTapTap, Inc.'s damages. Would diversity jurisdiction remain? The answer to that is *no*. Assuming that the Conner Corporation is incorporated in California and has its principal place of business in California, diversity is destroyed because two parties on opposite sides of the lawsuit would be citizens of the same state (that is, both TapTapTap, Inc. and Conner Corporation would be California citizens). Diversity jurisdiction is only established where diversity is *complete*—where no two parties on opposite sides are from the same state.

When, after examining a situation, you determine that diversity doesn't exist, that doesn't necessarily mean that the case cannot be filed in federal court. Remember that there are other possible grounds for

---

**PARALEGALERT!**

Federal diversity jurisdiction requires *complete* diversity. If any two parties on opposite sides of a proposed federal lawsuit are from the same state, diversity of citizenship does not exist and hence cannot supply the basis for the federal jurisdiction.

federal jurisdiction, which we discussed in Chapter 1. If a federal statute has been violated, for example, or if a federal constitutional principle is at issue, you might be able to make these the basis for a cause of action, thereby giving the federal court jurisdiction even if all the parties are from the same state (and with no jurisdictional requirement as to the minimum amount of damages alleged).

Suppose you have two causes of action against a nondiverse defendant. Suppose further that one of these causes of action justifies federal jurisdiction, but the other does not. What happens then? Do you have to file two lawsuits, one in federal court on the federal cause of action and another in state court on the state cause of action? The answer to that is, generally speaking, *no*. Under the principle of **pendent jurisdiction** (embodied since 1990 in section 1367 of Title 28 of the United States Code, and referenced therein as "supplemental jurisdiction"), the federal court is generally empowered to hear all causes of action between the parties as long as one of them is a valid federal cause of action, and they arise from a common factual situation and would ordinarily be tried in the same lawsuit.

You should be aware that the concept of pendent jurisdiction, and a close cousin called "ancillary jurisdiction" (which relates to the federal court's authority to decide state-law issues on matters that, although they do not necessarily arise out of a common factual situation, are nevertheless subordinate and related to the federal cause of action that brought the matter at hand before the federal court; it is also now embodied in section 1367 of Title 28 as "supplemental jurisdiction") can sometimes lead to quite complicated analysis.

We have provided you with only a brief explanation of the principles of pendent and ancillary jurisdiction; if you see such issues developing in your case, it would be wise to discuss with your supervising attorney the possibility that additional research might be necessary. In this chapter, we'll avoid such complications, focusing instead on the basics to provide you with a solid foundation.

The next issue to address is proper venue. As you recall from Chapter 1, *venue* is the geographical location in which a lawsuit proceeds. As a general matter, venue is determined by a specific statute or court rule. Having identified your cause of action, and determined the court (state or federal) in which the lawsuit will be filed, you will need to find the statute that establishes the proper venue for your lawsuit. Sometimes there is a specific statute that relates only to your specific cause of action; sometimes you will have to resort to a "general" venue statute that applies to all causes of action that don't have such specific venue guidelines. The venue statutes generally take into account the residences of the involved parties, as well as the location where the events underlying the cause of action took place, and are designed to lead to venues that are as convenient and economically efficient for all involved parties as possible. You should review the general federal venue statute, 28 U.S.C. §1391, pertinent parts of which are set forth in Figure 6–8, to see how venue is determined in the federal court.

Sometimes, even after choosing a court (state or federal) and applying the requirements of the venue statute, you may still have a choice remaining. For example, let's say you've decided to file the action in the Widgets and Gizmos, Inc. matter in federal court. Both California and Exurbia would be proper venues, since both arguably satisfy the requirements of 28 U.S.C. §1391. The defendant resides in California, justifying venue in the United States District

**Figure 6–8   Pertinent Portions of General Federal Venue Statute, 28 U.S.C. § 1391**

---

**§ 1391.   Venue generally**

(a)   A civil action wherein jurisdiction is founded only on diversity of citizenship may, except as otherwise provided by law, be brought only in (1) a judicial district where any defendant resides, if all defendants reside in the same State, (2) a judicial district in which a substantial part of the events or omissions giving rise to the claim occurred, or a substantial part of property that is the subject of the action is situated, or (3) a judicial district in which the defendants are subject to personal jurisdiction at the time the action is commenced.

(b)   A civil action wherein jurisdiction is not founded solely on diversity of citizenship may, except as otherwise provided by law, be brought only in (1) a judicial district where any defendant resides, if all defendants reside in the same State, (2) a judicial district in which a substantial part of the events or omissions giving rise to the claim occurred, or a substantial part of property that is the subject of the action is situated, or (3) a judicial district in which any defendant may be found, if there is no district in which the action may otherwise be brought.

(c)   For purposes of venue under this chapter, a defendant that is a corporation shall be deemed to reside in any judicial district in which it is subject to personal jurisdiction at the time the action is commenced. In a State which has more than one judicial district and in which a defendant that is a corporation is subject to personal jurisdiction at the time an action is commenced, such corporation shall be deemed to reside in any district in that State within which its contacts would be sufficient to subject it to personal jurisdiction if that district were a separate State, and, if there is no such district, the corporation shall be deemed to reside in the district within which it has the most significant contacts.

---

Court in California; and a substantial part of the events giving rise to the claim (i.e., the negotiation and execution of the contract) occurred in Exurbia, justifying venue in the United States District Court in Exurbia. Thus, you still have a choice of where to file the action. You may simply choose to file the case in the court closest to your home, namely, the Exurbia court. But the choice may be more complicated than that—it may come down to an analysis of **conflict of laws.** "Conflict of laws" refers to a situation where it is not absolutely clear which state's laws govern a matter.

For example, in the Widgets and Gizmos, Inc. matter, the contract was probably signed in both states, and negotiations were probably conducted in both states. It is entirely possible that the California federal court might decide that, under its conflict-of-laws guidelines, California contract law controls the case. The Exurbia federal court may decide that it is Exurbia contract law that controls. And your research may show that your chances of winning are better under Exurbia law than under California law. If that were the case, your decision would finally be clear—you would choose to file the matter in Exurbia federal court.

Identifying the proper court is a complicated matter. This section merely introduces you to some of the important considerations. However, it will be your supervising attorney who decides where to file. After the appropriate court has been chosen, you would then be asked to draft the complaint. Let's turn now to the actual drafting process.

## 6–4   Drafting the Complaint

In Figures 6–9 and 6–10, we show you completed draft complaints in the Harry Hampton and Widgets and Gizmos, Inc. matters. You should read these complaints carefully before going any further. In the remainder of this section,

**Figure 6–9  Hampton Complaint, Page 1**

HARRY HAMPTON,          :         Superior Court

      Plaintiff         :         State of Exurbia

      v.         :         Judicial District
                           of

JUDITH JOHNSON and BUD'S    :         Metro County

AUTO SERVICE,         :

      Defendants        :         October 10, 1993

## Complaint

**First Count** (against defendant Judith Johnson)

1. The plaintiff, Harry Hampton, resides at 1001 Elm Street, Milltown, in the State of Exurbia.
2. The defendant, Judith Johnson, resides at 143 Wingate Street, Milltown, in the State of Exurbia.
3. On April 15, 1992, at approximately 8:20 a.m., Harry Hampton was proceeding in a westerly direction on Higgins Lane in Milltown, in his 1990 Pontiac Grand Am.
4. As he arrived at the intersection of Higgins Lane and Pruitt Street, Hampton came to a complete stop, as required by the stop sign.
5. The stop sign facing Hampton contained a smaller sign, immediately below the red "Stop" sign, which indicated that this intersection was a "Four-Way Stop" intersection.
6. At or about the same time, defendant Judith Johnson was proceeding in a southerly direction on Pruitt Street, approaching the intersection with Higgins Lane, in her 1992 Ford Taurus station wagon.
7. As defendant Judith Johnson approached the intersection, Harry Hampton had already come to a complete stop at the stop sign, as described in Paragraph 4 above.
8. Although required to stop before entering the intersection, defendant Judith Johnson's vehicle failed to stop.
9. As Harry Hampton's vehicle proceeded to enter the intersection after completing his full stop, defendant Judith Johnson's vehicle shot into the intersection and crashed into Hampton's vehicle in a violent collision.
10. The collision was the result of the negligence of the defendant Judith Johnson, in that she:
    - (a) failed to stop although required to do so;
    - (b) failed to keep a proper lookout for, and avoid colliding with, other vehicles; and
    - (c) under all of the circumstances then and there existing, failed to use that degree of care which would be expected of an ordinarily prudent person.
11. As a result of the collision and the negligence of defendant Judith Johnson, Harry Hampton suffered the following injuries, all of which were accompanied by great pain and suffering, and the effects of some or all of which are likely to be permanent:
    - (a) injuries to his arm, including a fractured tibia;
    - (b) injuries to his knee, including a fractured patella; and
    - (c) contusions and abrasions on his arms, legs, upper body, head, and face.
12. As a further result of the collision and the negligence of defendant Judith Johnson, Harry Hampton was unable to perform the duties of his employment for a period in excess of four weeks, causing him to lose substantial wages, in an amount in excess of $5000.00.
13. As a further result of the collision and the negligence of defendant Judith Johnson, Harry Hampton has lost the future ability to perform many of life's enjoyable activities.
14. As a further result of the collision and the negligence of defendant Judith Johnson, Harry Hampton suffered damage to his 1990 Pontiac Grand Am automobile in the amount of at least $3550.00.

Figure 6–9  Hampton Complaint continued, Page 2

15. As a further result of the collision and negligence of defendant Judith Johnson, Harry Hampton has incurred significant expenses for medical treatment, currently totaling in excess of $8500.00 and continuing to accrue.

16. Defendant Judith Johnson is liable to Harry Hampton for the injuries and damages described above.

**Second Count** (as to defendant Bud's Auto Service)

1. Paragraphs 1-9 of the First Count are hereby repeated and made paragraphs 1-9 of this, the Second Count.

10. The defendant, Bud's Auto Service is a sole proprietorship owned by Bernard Lindquist of 714 Ruth Street, Milltown, in the State of Exurbia.

11. Defendant Bud's Auto Service is engaged in the business of repairing automobiles, and has a principal place of business at 142 Franklin Turnpike, Milltown, in the State of Exurbia.

12. On April 14, 1992, at approximately 7:15 a.m., while starting his 1990 Pontiac Grand Am in his driveway at home, Harry Hampton noticed a warning light flash on his dashboard, indicating an engine problem of some sort.

13. Despite the warning light, Hampton was able to start the car without any difficulty.

14. After starting his car, Harry Hampton proceeded to bring the car directly to defendant Bud's Auto Service, in order to determine the reason for the flashing warning light.

15. Bernard Lindquist, acting in his capacity as owner of defendant Bud's Auto Service, suggested to Hampton that he leave the car there for the day, whereupon Hampton turned the keys over to Lindquist.

16. At approximately 6:15 p.m. that same day of April 14, 1992, Harry Hampton returned to defendant Bud's Auto Service and was informed by Bernard Lindquist, who was still acting in his capacity as owner of Bud's Auto Service, that there had been a wiring problem with Hampton's 1990 Pontiac Grand Am, and that defendant Bud's Auto Service had corrected and repaired the problem.

17. Defendant Bud's Auto Service owed a duty to Harry Hampton to use reasonable care in performing repair work on Hampton's automobile.

18. Defendant Bud's Auto Service was in fact negligent in the performance of its repair work on Harry Hampton's vehicle, in that:
    (a) certain wires were crossed by one or more of the employees of defendant Bud's Auto Service, such that the turn signal on the vehicle was caused to thereafter malfunction;
    (b) Hampton was not alerted to the malfunctioning turn signal;
    (c) a reasonably prudent and careful repair shop would have discovered and corrected the malfunctioning turn signal before returning the vehicle to its owner; and
    (d) under all of the circumstances then and there existing, defendant Bud's Auto Service failed to perform its repair services with that degree of care owed to its customer, Harry Hampton.

19. The malfunctioning turn signal was a proximate cause of the collision described in paragraph 9.

20. As a result of the negligence of defendant Bud's Auto Service, Harry Hampton suffered the injuries and damages described in paragraphs 11-15 of the First Count, which injuries and damages are restated herein by reference.

21. Defendant Bud's Auto Service is liable to Harry Hampton for the injuries and damages described above.

WHEREFORE, the plaintiff Harry Hampton claims judgment against the defendants, Judith Johnson and Bud's Auto Service, in an amount in excess of $50,000.00.

A jury trial is hereby demanded.

THE PLAINTIFF, HARRY HAMPTON

By: _____
Samuel Superlawyer, Esq.
Lincoln & Hoover
123 Lincoln Street
Metro City, Exurbia 12345

**Figure 6–10  Complaint of *Widgets and Gizmos, Inc.***

United States District Court
for the
District of Exurbia

WIDGETS AND GIZMOS, INC.     :

    Plaintiff     :     Civil Action No. _____

    vs.     :     October 21, 1993

TAPTAPTAP, INC.     :     JURY TRIAL DEMANDED

    Defendant     :

### Complaint

### Jurisdictional Statement

1. This court has jurisdiction of this matter under 28 U.S.C. §1332, based upon the diversity of citizenship of the parties and the fact that the amount in controversy is in excess of $50,000.00, exclusive of interest and costs.

### Plaintiff's Allegations

2. The plaintiff, Widgets and Gizmos, Inc. (hereinafter identified as "Widgets"), is incorporated in the State of Exurbia with a principal place of business in Metro City, Exurbia.

3. The defendant, TapTapTap, Inc. (hereinafter identified as "Taps"), is a California corporation with a principal place of business in San Jose, California.

4. Widgets manufactures, among other items, a product called a "widgenometer," which is a computer circuit etched into an aluminum chip with the capability of enhancing the speed of a computer's central processing unit by a factor of up to ten.

5. On or about January 27, 1992, Widgets and Taps entered into a contract, under the terms of which Widgets was to manufacture 50,000 widgenometers, and Taps was to purchase these widgenometers at a price of $250.00 per widgenometer. A copy of this contract is made Exhibit A hereto.

6. At the time of the filing of this complaint, Widgets had manufactured and shipped to Taps a total of 3000 widgenometers, in compliance with the terms of the contract.

7. Taps has failed and refused to make payment for any of the widgenometers, despite the fact that payment is due under the terms of the contract and despite the fact that Widgets has made demand for such payment.

8. As a result of the actions described in paragraph 7, Taps is in breach of the contract.

9. The amount outstanding as of the date of the filing of this complaint was $750,000.00, exclusive of interest, costs, and attorney's fees allowable under the terms of the contract.

10. Taps is liable to Widgets for breach of contract.

WHEREFORE, the plaintiff Widgets and Gizmos, Inc. demands that judgment be entered against the defendant, TapTapTap, Inc., in the full amount due and owing, plus interest, costs, and allowable attorney's fees, and for such other and further relief as the court may deem appropriate, just, and equitable.

THE PLAINTIFF, WIDGETS AND GIZMOS, INC.

By: _____
    Samuel Superlawyer, Esq.
    Its attorney
    Lincoln & Hoover
    123 Lincoln Street
    Metro City, Exurbia 12345
    Atty. Reg. #: 87654
    Phone: (901) 222-2222

as we discuss the concepts behind, and considerations surrounding, complaint drafting, we will make reference to the corresponding segments of our sample complaints.

Before we begin dissecting our sample complaints, let's address for a moment a distinction that applies to the burden of pleading requirements—that between fact-pleading and notice-pleading. As traditionally understood, **fact-pleading** jurisdictions require more detail in the complaint as to the facts surrounding each cause of action, whereas **notice-pleading** jurisdictions require only such detail as is adequate to put the defendant on notice of the cause of action.

As a practical matter, you will generally be pleading all the significant facts that underlie your claim; to do otherwise leads to vague or ambiguous allegations that can only serve to slow the litigation process. What, then, does the distinction really mean? To some extent, the concept of notice-pleading is designed to make it easier for a plaintiff to start a lawsuit; the theory is that the defendant can develop detailed information about the plaintiff's claim through the discovery process, so that only the basic allegations necessary to identify the relevant cause of action need be pleaded in the complaint. In fact-pleading jurisdictions, more detail is required in the complaint; but, oddly enough, if it is determined by the court that a complaint filed in a fact-pleading jurisdiction lacks adequate detail, the court will generally give the plaintiff a chance to amend the complaint to bring it into conformity with the fact-pleading requirements. So you may be thinking—what's the point?

A comparison of an actual notice-pleading requirement with a fact-pleading requirement may help to make the distinction a little clearer. Consider Rule 8 of the FRCP, which governs complaints filed in federal court, and which requires a "short and plain statement of the claim showing that the pleader is entitled to relief." This is a notice-pleading requirement; no elaborate details are required. In general, however, you will nevertheless plead all those significant facts that together comprise your cause of action; such an approach might well satisfy a fact-pleading requirement anyway. As to claims alleging fraud (which might do great harm to a defendant's reputation), Rule 9 of the FRCP requires that the circumstances allegedly establishing the fraud be stated in the complaint with "particularity." This is a fact-pleading exception to the generally applicable notice-pleading requirement of the federal rules. Thus, when alleging fraud in a federal lawsuit, you must be sure to include adequate detail, alleging all those facts that together comprise the fraud. Yet even when alleging fraud, it is not necessary to identify in the complaint each piece of evidence that underlies the fraud. Rather, the plaintiff must simply make it clear exactly what conduct on the part of the defendant allegedly constitutes fraud.

This analysis has probably still left you confused. You want to know the answer to one question: what does all this mean for me, as the drafter of a complaint? It means, quite simply, that your draft complaint should always contain the *significant* facts that you intend to prove at trial, regardless of whether you are in a fact-pleading or a notice-pleading jurisdiction. This should include, at a minimum, those facts that serve to establish the component elements of your causes of action. If you are in a fact-pleading jurisdiction, or if a fact-pleading rule (such as Rule 9 of the FRCP) applies,

## PARALEGALERT!

When drafting a complaint, allege all significant facts that you intend to prove at trial. If you are in a fact-pleading jurisdiction, or if a fact-pleading rule applies, you must do further research to determine how much additional detail may be required.

you will have to do further research to determine precisely how much additional detail is required. Finally, and most important, you should work closely with your supervising attorney to identify those additional facts to include, or those facts included that should be deleted; attorneys will often have tactical reasons for including more or less detail, depending on the circumstances of the particular case.

Once you've researched your cause of action, and identified the facts you need to plead, you're ready to draft your complaint—but where do you start? Let's turn for a moment to one final topic before our analysis of drafting begins—the usefulness of form books as a place to start. **Form books** are extensive collections of sample or model pleadings relating to all sorts of different circumstances. Sometimes form books are the product of a commercial publisher; some law firms maintain their own internal collections of sample and model pleadings; sometimes the official rules themselves contain forms (see, for example, the official forms that follow the FRCP). A form book might have sample complaints for automobile negligence cases, icy-sidewalk slip-and-fall negligence cases, contract breach cases, and so on. A form book may also have pages of specific paragraphs that might apply to different situations—for example, 50 or more paragraphs, each identifying a different way in which an automobile driver might be negligent (only two or three of which might apply to a given case). These paragraphs can be inserted into the appropriate location of your complaint.

Why are form books useful? In the case of official forms, they carry with them official approval; in the case of commercial or other form collections, they often reflect formats and language that have been tested in court and found to be adequate. They give you a place to start; they get you thinking about the considerations that you must keep in mind in successfully stating your causes of action. Should form books be trusted blindly? Absolutely not! You must still be mindful of court decisions and statutes that apply to and define the requirements relating to your particular cause of action. Nevertheless, form books are often a useful starting point in drafting a complaint, or any pleading.

**PARALEGALERT!**

Form books provide a good place to start your drafting, but they must never be trusted blindly.

Now you're ready to begin the actual drafting of a complaint. As we go through the Harry Hampton and Widgets and Gizmos, Inc. complaints step by step, we begin with a word of caution. To identify and establish causes of action is a very important, and sometimes difficult, task. Certain statutory causes of action, as defined and refined by years of court decisions, carry with them complicated pleading requirements, even in notice-pleading jurisdictions. Identifying applicable causes of action, and the necessary elements of each, can be quite complicated. These complications relate to the substantive law behind the cause of action. Our selected causes of action will give you a taste of these potential complications below but, in general, our purpose in this book is to introduce you to the procedural process of litigation, as opposed to the substantive law behind the many potential causes of action. We will try to keep the substantive analysis simple; substantive law will be addressed elsewhere in the course of your paralegal education. That being said, let's begin our analysis with the Harry Hampton complaint.

**The Hampton Complaint**  Let us first consider the possible causes of action. As you read the case yet again, there are two that are immediately apparent—a cause of action against Judith Johnson, alleging negligence; and a cause of action against Bud's Auto Service, also alleging negligence. What are the elements of these causes of action? Let's take the cause of action against Judith Johnson first (and remember that, since determining elements is a substantive law question, you'll learn more about negligence elements in your course on tort law). The elements of a negligence cause of action against Johnson are as follows:

1. That Johnson had a duty, owed to Hampton, to operate her automobile in a reasonable manner;
2. That she breached this duty;
3. That her breach of this duty was the proximate cause of the accident with Harry Hampton; and
4. That as a result of the accident caused by the breach, Harry Hampton has suffered damage.

Now let's turn to the complaint in Figure 6–9 (pp. 117–118) to see how these elements are incorporated into the text.

The starting point is the identifying heading "First Count" in Figure 6–9. When a complaint contains more than one cause of action, each cause of action is stated in a separate **count.** "Count" is simply the word applied to each separate cause of action. If your complaint has two causes of action against a single defendant, it would have two counts. If it has one separate cause of action against each of two defendants, it would similarly have two counts. The parenthetical showing that the First Count is "against defendant Judith Johnson" is not generally required, although in complicated cases such clarifying information is often helpful.

The next section of Figure 6–9 to consider consists of the first two numbered paragraphs of the First Count. These paragraphs contain basic background information about the parties involved. The court must know the identity of the parties it is dealing with for two reasons: first, to establish the basis for jurisdiction; and second, obviously, to establish against or in favor of whom the court will render its judgment.

Paragraphs 3 to 9 of the First Count set forth the facts of the Hampton situation. There are a few points to make with regard to these facts. First, you must remember that, if you allege a fact, you will be expected to prove that fact at trial. If you have neither adequate proof of a fact nor a reasonable expectation that you will be able to obtain such proof, it is probably unwise to allege it; if you fail to prove it at trial, the trier-of-fact may then become skeptical about even those facts on which adequate evidence was introduced. For example, suppose Harry Hampton thinks that Johnson not only failed to stop but actually accelerated into the intersection, but he can't remember for sure. Your interview with eyewitness Louella Williams indicates that she doesn't remember seeing an acceleration. You should consult with your supervising attorney before alleging in the complaint that Johnson accelerated. He may not want to allege such an acceleration until Johnson is questioned in her deposition; if she admits accelerating, he would then amend the complaint to include the allegation.

**P**ARALEGALERT!

Don't include in your complaint allegations regarding facts you can't prove. Failure to introduce, at trial, persuasive evidence on these facts, even if they are not essential to establishing your cause of action, may cause the trier-of-fact to look with greater skepticism at your basic claims.

Keep in mind, of course, that the minimum facts necessary to establish a cause of action must be alleged in the complaint; otherwise it will be subject to attack by motion (which we discuss in Chapter 7). Presumably your supervising attorney will have been satisfied, after preliminary research and investigation, that he either has sufficient evidence to prove such minimum facts, or at least has a reasonable expectation that he will be able to obtain such evidence; otherwise the decision to file the lawsuit might be open to question under Rule 11 of the FRCP (or a similar state court rule).

Our next comment on paragraphs 3 to 9 relates to the way in which Harry Hampton and Judith Johnson are identified. Hampton is always identified simply as "Harry Hampton," or just "Hampton." Judith Johnson is always identified as "defendant Judith Johnson." The reason for this is simple. This case, if it is tried, will likely be a jury trial. In some jurisdictions the pleadings are read to the jury. The continuing use of the word "defendant" is designed to create in the minds of the jurors a negative impression of Judith Johnson, as compared with Harry Hampton: Hampton is portrayed as just an ordinary person to whom a wrong has been done; Judith Johnson is, on the other hand, a defendant, with the jurors perhaps taking away a negative connotation. Judith Johnson's attorney would take the same approach in drafting an answer, by resorting to language that paints Hampton in a negative light. This might seem a minor consideration; indeed, the issue is really a matter of style, and every attorney has his or her own style and preferences with regard to suitable draftsmanship. But the larger point must be kept in mind—namely, that when you are drafting a complaint, or any pleading, you are not an objective observer but rather an advocate, whose responsibility is to present the issues not only accurately, but also in a light that is most favorable to the client. Therefore, be forceful; be persuasive.

**PARALEGALERT!**

When drafting a complaint, remember that you are not an objective observer, but rather an advocate. Your job is to present the facts in a light most favorable to the client's position. Be forceful; be persuasive. This consideration applies to the preparation of all pleadings.

Another example of the manner in which language can be used to advocate the client's cause is found in paragraph 9. In particular, note how Johnson's car is described as having "shot" into the intersection, and that it "crashed" into Hampton's car in a "violent" collision. This is your chance to tell the client's story vividly and persuasively. Don't be afraid to choose colorful language, particularly if the pleadings will be read to the jury. The client, whether the plaintiff or the defendant, is counting on you to be a strong partisan.

Take a look back at the first of our four elements relating to this complaint: "that Johnson had a duty, owed to Hampton, to operate her automobile in a reasonable manner." In which paragraph of the complaint is that element alleged? The answer is: none of them, exactly. But doesn't that fly in the face of what we've been saying—that the elements must all be alleged? Yes, in a sense—but not really. In general, operating an automobile implies a well-known and generally accepted legal duty to drive it in a reasonably safe manner, the duty to do so being owed to all other drivers and pedestrians encountered. So in a sense, implicit in paragraph 6 (which alleges that Judith Johnson was driving her car) is an allegation that she had a duty owed to Hampton to drive the car in a reasonably safe manner. Furthermore, specifically alleging the existence of a "legal duty" actually amounts to pleading law rather than facts; and you will

**PARALEGALERT!**

Until you are an experienced complaint drafter, include a specific paragraph alleging each element of your cause of action, even those elements that might be implied from the context. Your supervising attorney will make the decision whether to leave such paragraphs out.

recall our basic maxim that the drafter should plead facts, not law. Nevertheless, a paragraph such as the following is generally considered acceptable:

> 7.    Judith Johnson owed a duty to Harry Hampton to drive her motor vehicle with reasonable care.

Generally speaking, until you are experienced in drafting complaints you may want to include something like our suggested paragraph 7, immediately above, making the existence of the necessary element explicit. By including such allegations, you ensure that you have adequately covered the necessary elements of your cause of action, and your supervising attorney can thereafter make the decision to leave it out. In any event, you should discuss the options with your supervising attorney, and review the pleading practices of your jurisdiction.

Another point to note about paragraphs 3 to 9 (and, indeed, all numbered paragraphs in any complaint or other pleading you draft) is that there is basically one point, and hence one sentence, in each paragraph. As we noted in our discussion of numbered paragraphs in Section 6–2, the purpose of limiting the number of points per numbered paragraph is to facilitate responding to the allegations stated. If a complicated series of allegations was made in just one paragraph, the response might itself be so complicated that readers would be uncertain which allegations were admitted and which denied. We will cover responses in more depth in Chapter 8.

A few other comments are in order with regard to the details of paragraphs 3 to 9. Note that, in paragraph 8, it does not say, "Judith Johnson proceeded through the stop sign without stopping." This is because, as you recall from the facts set forth in Chapter 3, the stop sign facing Judith Johnson was bent down, so that it couldn't be seen by approaching drivers. Rather than raise the issue of the bent stop sign, the complaint simply pleads (1) that it was a four-way-stop intersection (see paragraph 5), and (2) that Judith Johnson was required to stop and didn't. If you alleged, "Judith Johnson proceeded through the stop sign without stopping," you would have violated a rule we just mentioned: alleging something you cannot prove. She didn't proceed through a readily visible stop sign, but she was aware that it was a four-way-stop intersection (look back at the facts set forth in Chapter 3 and note the reference to a letter that Judith Johnson had written to the Milltown traffic department). Thus, the allegations you've made accurately reflect Harry Hampton's knowledge of events at this stage of the case, and the more specific facts (for example, about Judith Johnson's preexisting knowledge of the problem with the stop sign) will be developed through discovery and further investigation as the lawsuit proceeds.

Next consider paragraph 10. This paragraph corresponds to the second and third elements identified above previously—it alleges that Johnson was negligent, and that this negligence was the cause of the collision. Subparagraphs (a) and (b) identify the specific reasons why Hampton asserts that Johnson was negligent. These are the sorts of subparagraphs that might be pulled out of a form book. Subparagraph (c) is a general, catchall paragraph designed to incorporate any other negligent acts committed by Judith Johnson that contributed to the collision (and the proper language for this might also have been found in a form book). Some jurisdictions may find such an allegation excessively vague, hence improper, whereas other jurisdictions will allow it.

Paragraphs 11 to 15 identify the damages suffered by Hampton, and allege that these damages resulted from the negligence of Judith Johnson. These allegations represent the fourth element of your cause of action. You should be reasonably specific when setting forth damages. You will recall that in Chapter 1 we identified two categories of compensatory damages, special damages (which are precisely calculable) and general damages (which are not). For federal actions, Rule 9(g) of the FRCP requires that "items of special damage . . . be specifically stated."

This practice should generally be followed in state court complaints as well, and in an injury case such as the Hampton matter will often involve a careful examination of the relevant medical bills, as well as auto repair invoices and wage or salary records for time lost from work. Specificity may be difficult, of course, with regard to items such as ongoing medical expenses or future disability. Where precision is impossible (as, for example, with such categories of damages as pain and suffering), be sure to identify at least the applicable *category* of damages, and possibly provide a rough estimate as well. The point of the damages paragraphs is to establish a clear picture of the results of the defendant's wrongdoing, both to ensure that the court has a basis for a damages award, and to place the wrongful actions of the defendant in perspective for the judge and jury.

Paragraph 16 of the First Count is an allegation on an ultimate issue—the liability of Judith Johnson for her negligence. Some drafters leave out such an allegation on the theory that the other allegations, taken as a whole, establish the negligence and the liability anyway. You can also include a demand for a finding of liability in the prayer for relief (which we discuss further in this section). Some courts find an allegation on an ultimate issue to be improper, and will grant a motion that requests that it be revised out of a complaint. You should research your local standards, and identify your supervising attorney's preference.

We'll turn now to the Second Count of Hampton's complaint, also shown in Figure 6–9, pages 117–118, and directed against defendant Bud's Auto Service. Let's first consider the elements of a negligence cause of action by Hampton against Bud's Auto Service. They are virtually identical to the elements of the First Count:

1. That Bud's Auto Service had a duty owed to Hampton to repair his car in a reasonable manner;
2. That Bud's Auto Service breached this duty;
3. That the breach of this duty was the proximate cause of the accident of Harry Hampton; and
4. That as a result of the accident caused by the breach, Harry Hampton has suffered damage.

Let's analyze the Second Count to see how these elements are incorporated into the text.

First, consider paragraph 1 of the Second Count. This paragraph states that the first nine numbered paragraphs of the First Count should be considered to be the first nine numbered paragraphs of the Second Count. The allegations contained in those paragraphs are all necessary to the cause of action against Bud's Auto Service; they identify the participants and the important background facts. The language used in paragraph 1 of the Second Count is fairly standard, and enables you to eliminate what would otherwise be redundant allegations. Take a look at paragraph 20 of the Second Count to see another way in which allegations made in the First Count can be incorporated into the Second Count.

The next numbered paragraph of the Second Count is number 10. It is designated number 10 rather than number 2 because paragraph 1 actually represents nine paragraphs from the First Count; this paragraph thus becomes the tenth paragraph of the Second Count. In some courts, rules or common practice dictate that this paragraph should be identified as paragraph 2 anyway, despite the fact that paragraph 1 actually represents nine paragraphs. In other courts, paragraph numbering continues in a consecutive fashion from the First Count; in other words, the first paragraph of the Second Count would be numbered 15 (the next consecutive number after the last numbered paragraph of the First Count) and the second paragraph would be either number 16 or number 24, depending on how the court treats the fact that nine paragraphs are incorporated from the First Count. To determine the proper method for a given lawsuit, check the rules and discuss it with your supervising attorney.

What about the substance of paragraphs 10 and 11? As with paragraphs 1 and 2 of the First Count, paragraphs 10 and 11 of the Second Count provide basic background information about defendant Bud's Auto Service.

Paragraphs 12 to 16 allege those facts not already recited in the First Count which are pertinent to the Second Count. You should review these paragraphs, keeping in mind the various pointers we identified in our analysis of the First Count.

Paragraph 17 specifically alleges the duty owed by Bud's Auto Service to Harry Hampton. This might also be implicit in the relationship, as was the duty of Judith Johnson to Hampton to drive safely; the drafter of this complaint thought it best to include it as a separate and distinct allegation, in order to avoid any question.

Paragraph 18 contains the allegations of negligence with regard to the crossed wires. Note the specific allegations in subparagraphs (a), (b), and (c), followed by the catch-all allegation of subparagraph (d).

Paragraph 19 causally links the occurrence of the collision with the negligence of Bud's Auto Service. Note that the detail of this paragraph is minimal; at this stage, Hampton's knowledge of the effect of the faulty turn signal is probably limited to those statements or comments of Judith Johnson that are reflected in the police report. More information about the effect of the faulty turn signal on Judith Johnson's decision to accelerate will not be developed until later, in the discovery stage of the lawsuit.

As we noted previously, paragraph 20 shows another method by which paragraphs of the First Count can be incorporated into the Second Count. In this case, the damage allegations of the First Count are incorporated into the Second Count. You should be careful to determine whether there are different damage allegations associated with a different defendant; if there are, you must remember to identify all relevant damage claims.

Finally, paragraph 21 alleges the ultimate issue—that Bud's Auto Service is liable to Hampton. As noted in our discussion of the First Count, this type of allegation may or may not be required, and, if not required, may or may not be preferred, depending on the stylistic preferences of your supervising attorney.

Let us take a moment here to inject a comment about a possible third count to the Hampton complaint, which we have not, but possibly could have, included. Most states authorize a loss of consortium cause of action, by which the spouse of an injured party is entitled to join as a second plaintiff in the injured party's lawsuit and allege a separate count for damages the spouse has sustained as a result of the injuries to the injured party (for example, alleging the loss of companionship as a result of the injured party's chronic pain). Thus, Harry Hampton's wife might have brought a third count in this lawsuit. The inclusion of such a claim depends on the governing tort law—which is to say that it is a question of substantive law. We mention this now simply to reemphasize what we've said earlier—that our purpose in this book is to demonstrate the procedural considerations influencing civil litigation; hence our purpose in this chapter is to emphasize the procedural considerations influencing the drafting of a complaint. We are not seeking to analyze exhaustively the substantive issues that our sample cases might present; indeed, we want to keep those substantive issues as simple as possible so as not to obscure the procedural considerations. Thus, in the interest of simplifying the analysis we are excluding any examination of the loss of consortium aspect in the Hampton matter, and in general our analysis of the substantive issues presented by our sample cases should not in any way be interpreted as, nor does it purport to be, definitive.

There are two final points for us to address with regard to the Harry Hampton complaint, contained in the two unnumbered paragraphs that appear between paragraph 21 and the signature block of the Hampton complaint. The first point relates to the paragraph that reads as follows:

> WHEREFORE, the plaintiff respectfully demands that the court enter judgment against the defendants, Judith Johnson and Bud's Auto Service, in an amount in excess of $50,000.

This paragraph constitutes a **prayer for relief** (also sometimes called the "wherefore clause"). It explains in a simple and straightforward fashion exactly what the plaintiff is seeking from the court. If injunctive relief is sought, or if the relief sought in one count differs from that sought in another count, the prayer for relief would be lengthened to reflect this additional information. Requirements of state courts vary as to the prayer for relief, particularly with regard to the manner in which the amount of damages sought is stated. Some states require that the full amount sought be identified; others require only that certain categories be identified, for example "less than $15,000" or "more than $15,000." Rule 8(a) of the FRCP alludes simply to "a demand for judgment for the relief the pleader seeks." Check the rules of the jurisdiction in which you are filing the complaint to determine the applicable requirements.

The final paragraph before the signature block is known as the **jury demand.** Juries are not automatically assigned to cases; they must be demanded by a party who claims a right to a jury trial. The rules governing jury demands (see, for example, Rule 38(b) of the FRCP) often require, or at least allow, jury demands to be made in the complaint. Failure to follow proper procedure may lead to an inadvertent waiver of the right to a jury trial; thus, you must check the applicable rules at the time you are drafting your complaint, and include the jury demand in your complaint if desired and necessary. Sometimes the jury demand appears at the end of the complaint; sometimes it appears in the caption (see our discussion of the Widgets and Gizmos, Inc. complaint immediately following). The point is to *check the rules.* We discuss jury demands further in Chapter 8.

## PARALEGALERT!

Failure to follow proper procedures may lead to inadvertent waiver of the right to a jury trial. Be sure to check the applicable procedure for demanding a jury at the time you draft your complaint!

**The Widgets and Gizmos, Inc. Complaint**   We turn now to an analysis of the Widgets and Gizmos, Inc. complaint, to be filed in the United States District Court for the District of Exurbia (and which appears in Figure 6–10, p. 119). The claim of Widgets and Gizmos, Inc. is fairly straightforward, hence our analysis with regard to the elements of the cause of action will be straightforward as well. We will also indicate several considerations that apply to federal complaints in general, and make a few comments that apply to this complaint specifically.

First, let's consider the caption. The fact that the name of the court is now in a different location in the caption than the name of the court in the Hampton caption is nothing more than a reflection of the applicable rules. Once again, you must check the specifically applicable rules in order to determine that you have set up your caption correctly.

Note that the jury demand appears in the caption here. This is simply an alternative method of setting forth a jury demand, allowable under the FRCP and the local rules for the United States District Court for the District of Exurbia. To reiterate, the important points to remember about jury demands are (1) that they may be required to accompany the complaint, and (2) that in any event, the means of demanding a jury will be specified by the rules and must be checked at the time of drafting the complaint to determine applicable deadlines and requirements.

Note also that a space is provided in the caption for a civil action number (which, as we noted in Section 6–2, is another term meaning the same thing as a docket number). A question that may now come to mind is: how can you place a civil action number on a draft complaint that hasn't yet been assigned such a number by the court? The answer is that you can't, but your leaving a space for it means the number can be filled in by the court at the time of filing. The significance of this for a federal court complaint will become clearer in Section 6–6, on service of process. For now, simply remember that your draft federal complaint caption must provide a space for the civil action number; the same consideration applies for complaints filed in many state courts as well.

We turn now to the substantive portion of the complaint. First consider the heading, "Jurisdictional Statement." Rule 8 of the FRCP requires that a complaint include "a short and plain statement of the grounds upon which the court's jurisdiction depends . . . . " Such a **jurisdictional statement** is not generally required in state court complaints, although you must always check the applicable rules to be sure. In any event, paragraph 1 of the Widgets and Gizmos, Inc. complaint establishes that jurisdiction is claimed under the diversity statute. The paragraph includes an allegation that the claim is "in excess of $50,000, exclusive of interest and costs," tracking the requirements of the language of §1332 that we discussed in Section 6–3.

Sometimes the jurisdictional statement is set forth under a separate heading, as we have done in Figure 6–10. Sometimes it appears only as a numbered paragraph, with no special heading. Once again, the style depends on the preferences of the drafter in conjunction with the requirements of the applicable rules.

This brings us to a consideration of the second heading that appears in Figure 6–10, "Plaintiff's Allegations." Since there is only one count here, it is unnecessary to divide the allegations into separate counts; the whole complaint represents one count. Both the headings that we currently have, namely, "Jurisdictional Statement" and "Plaintiff's Allegations," probably could have been eliminated here; including them is, as noted with regard to the jurisdictional statement heading, a decision based on stylistic preferences and applicable local rules.

Now let's turn to a substantive analysis of the allegations themselves. The elements for this contract cause of action are, in essence, the following:

1. That a contract existed between Widgets and Gizmos, Inc. and TapTapTap, Inc.;
2. That Widgets and Gizmos, Inc. performed its obligations under the contract;
3. That TapTapTap, Inc. breached the contract; and
4. That Widgets and Gizmos, Inc. has suffered damages as a result of the breach.

Keeping in mind these elements, let's see how our complaint satisfies these requirements.

First, look at paragraphs 2 and 3. These paragraphs identify the parties, and are needed for the same reasons as those that identified the parties in the Hampton matter: to establish jurisdiction and to establish against or in favor of whom the court will be rendering its judgment. By including the state of incorporation and principal place of business as part of the identification, these paragraphs bolster the assertion of diversity jurisdiction.

Paragraph 4 provides some background information about the widgenometer. Under the federal notice-pleading rules, this paragraph probably could have been left out, at the option of the plaintiff.

Paragraph 5 alleges the first element of the cause of action: that a contract existed between the parties. Note the reference in paragraph 5 to a "copy of this contract" that "is made Exhibit A hereto." When certain key documents are central to the claims raised, copies of the documents are generally made **exhibits** to the complaint, and referenced in this manner. This is true for complaints filed in state court as well as for those filed in federal court.

Paragraph 6 alleges the second element of the cause of action: that Widgets and Gizmos, Inc. performed its obligation under the contract, shipping 3000 widgenometers.

Paragraphs 7 and 8 allege that TapTapTap, Inc. breached the contract by failing to pay for the widgenometers shipped by Widgets and Gizmos, Inc.

Paragraph 9 identifies the damages allegedly suffered by Widgets and Gizmos, Inc., and paragraph 10 states the legal conclusion that TapTapTap, Inc. is liable for these damages.

The prayer for relief in the Widgets and Gizmos, Inc. complaint is somewhat more detailed than that in the Hampton complaint. It requests interest, which is reasonable to expect in this situation since the amount in question was a clearly identifiable amount due at a specific point in time, namely, when TapTapTap, Inc. received the shipment of widgenometers. The prayer also calls for an allowance of attorney's fees, which may be authorized under the terms of the contract, and *costs*, which refers to the official costs associated with the lawsuit. Official costs include such things as the original filing fee paid to the court at the commencement of the lawsuit. A request for costs could have been included in the Hampton prayer for relief as well, although failure to include it probably does not affect the right to recover such costs; as always, check the applicable rules of your courts, and include it if necessary.

The prayer for relief in the Widgets and Gizmos, Inc. complaint also contains a request for "such other and further relief as the court may deem appropriate, just, and equitable." The purpose of this is to leave the prayer somewhat open-ended, in the event that the proceedings lead the court to fashion some unusual form of relief (which doesn't happen often, making this commonly seen clause somewhat superfluous).

Your job is not completed when you finish drafting a complaint, however, even if your supervising attorney accepts your draft word for word. We must discuss two other critical considerations. First, in the next section on preliminary injunctions, we'll address the possibility that you may be requesting the court to grant to your client some special, preliminary relief. Second, in Section 6–6 on service of process, we'll explain how defendants are notified of a pending lawsuit.

## 6–5 Preliminary Injunctive Relief

When a plaintiff is commencing a lawsuit, he or she sometimes seeks to accomplish more than simply stating the causes of action in a complaint. The plaintiff may seek, under certain circumstances, immediate equitable relief from some continuing wrongful action allegedly being perpetrated by the defendant.

Equitable relief from wrongful action, you will recall from Chapter 1, requires an injunction. Let's consider a few important points regarding injunctions.

As we noted in Chapter 1, an **injunction** is an order of the court that a party perform a certain act, or refrain from performing a certain act. There are three broad categories of injunction: the **permanent injunction;** the **preliminary injunction;** and the **temporary restraining order** (TRO). You should note that the precise labels or names applied to these injunctions may vary somewhat from one jurisdiction to the next; the labels just identified are used in the federal courts. The *permanent injunction* is a remedy sought in a complaint in conjunction with an ordinary cause of action, and to be granted only after a full-scale trial. If ordered by the court, it amounts to a final judgment on the issue. But a plaintiff may want injunctive relief before the trial is concluded, during the pendency of the case, because he or she claims to be suffering additional damages with each day that passes; hence the other two types of injunction.

The key to understanding preliminary injunctions and TROs is to understand the concept of "immediate and irreparable injury, loss, or damage" (Rule 65 of the FRCP), often called simply **irreparable harm.** Irreparable harm is some damage suffered by a party that cannot later be compensated by money damages easily calculable. For example, suppose the failure of a supplier to live up to the terms of a contract threatens to put a manufacturer out of business. The potential damage to the manufacturer in this situation would not be limited to easily calculable money damages, but would rather constitute the sort of irreparable harm (i.e., destruction of the business) that might justify a preliminary injunction or TRO. By compelling the supplier to continue to perform under the contract, the court can prevent further damage prior to the full-scale trial.

The difference between the preliminary injunction and the TRO relates to the circumstances under which each is granted, and the duration of the relief imposed. If the application for a TRO is found by the court to be justified, the relief requested can be ordered by a court instantly, in an *ex parte* manner, to prevent imminent irreparable harm. Under Rule 65(b) of the FRCP, however, the party seeking the TRO must certify to the court its efforts to give notice to the other side, and the reasons supporting the claim that the TRO should enter without notice. Once ordered, the TRO immediately affects the behavior of the enjoined party, even before that party has been able to tell its side of the story. Because it is such a drastic measure, TROs are only valid for a short period (usually no more than ten days; see, for example, Rule 65(b) of the FRCP), until a preliminary hearing can be scheduled; indeed, in the federal courts, the party against whom the TRO operates can request a hearing to dissolve the TRO on two days' notice (Rule 65(b)). If the court then determines, after the preliminary hearing (at which both sides present evidence), that the danger of irreparable harm will continue to exist during the pendency of the lawsuit, and further, that the party seeking the injunctive relief has a reasonable likelihood of prevailing after a full-scale trial, the court will then grant a preliminary injunction that enjoins the referenced behavior until the full-scale trial.

The key difference between the TRO, the preliminary injunction, and the permanent injunction, then, has to do with timing. The TRO is granted immediately, without a hearing, but lasts only a short time; the preliminary injunction is granted after a preliminary hearing and lasts during the pendency of the lawsuit; and the permanent injunction is granted after a full-scale trial and lasts, theoretically, forever (see Figure 6–11). Because the TRO and preliminary injunctions are drastic remedies, and, if granted wrongfully, can cause significant damage to the party enjoined, the court often requires that the party in whose favor the injunction runs post a **bond** securing the enjoined party against any damages suffered if the injunction

**Figure 6–11    The Three Types of Injunctions**

> **Permanent Injuntion:** A permanent injunction is a form of relief requested in a complaint, and granted only after a full-scale trial. It lasts, theoretically, forever.
>
> **Temporary Restraining Order:** A temporary restraining order, or TRO, is granted instantly by a court, in an *ex parte* manner. It is designed to prevent immediate irreparable harm. It lasts only a very short time, usually only a few days, until a preliminary hearing can be scheduled.
>
> **Preliminary Injunction:** A preliminary injunction is designed to prevent irreparable harm occurring during the pendency of a lawsuit. It is granted only after a preliminary hearing.

turns out to have been wrongfully entered (see, for example, Rule 65(b) and Rule 65.1 of the FRCP).

The most important thing to note about temporary restraining orders and preliminary injunctions in the context of the complaint-drafting process is that you must determine the documents that are needed to make your request. In general, you will need to file a *motion* or *application* for the injunctive relief you seek; a *proposed order* for the TRO or preliminary injunction hearing; and an *affidavit* supporting the client's position. Under the FRCP, a verified complaint can substitute for an affidavit. Keep in mind that details about these documents can differ in different state court systems; you should research the injunction procedure that applies in your state.

Having now drafted your complaint, and prepared (if desired) materials necessary to request preliminary injunctive relief, you are still not finished. You must get the materials you've prepared to the defendant, putting him or her on notice that a lawsuit has been commenced. It is time to turn our attention to the summons, civil cover sheet, and the procedure for completing service of process.

## 6–6   Service of Process

In Chapter 1 we told you that, for a court to exercise personal jurisdiction over the defendant in a lawsuit, the court must be satisfied that the defendant has been given adequate notice that the lawsuit had been filed. This is because, under the due process requirements of the federal and state constitutions, it is unconstitutional to render a judgment depriving a party of property unless that party has been given sufficient opportunity to defend the lawsuit. As noted earlier in this chapter, the manner in which a defendant is notified of the pendency of a lawsuit is through a procedure known as **service of process.**

There are essentially two things you must know about service of process. First, you must know the documents that are included in the "package" which will give the defendant notification of the pending lawsuit. This package constitutes what is called the **process.** Take a moment and consider this usage of the word *process.* Ordinarily, we think of a "process" as a series of actions or occurrences that lead to a result. For example, we have referred in this book to the litigation process; or consider the constitutional principle of which we just spoke, "due process," which refers to the adequacy of the litigation process. In the context of "service of process," however, the word "process" refers not to a series of actions or occurrences but to a thing, namely, the package constituting the documents by which the lawsuit is commenced and the defendant notified. We will, in the interest of clarity, continue to refer to a "package" of documents to be served; but you should remember that this package is actually the thing called legal *process*.

The second essential thing you must know about service of process is the procedure by which the package is delivered to the defendant. This procedure is known as the **service**. Service, in this context, should be thought of as *delivery*. We address both the documents and the procedure of service of process in the subsections that follow, but first let's address one final preliminary note: the possibility of a difference between service of process under the federal system and that of your state.

## Possible Difference Between State and Federal Procedures

**PARALEGALERT!**

Be sure to pay careful attention to the specific rules relating to service of process, and keep in mind that there may be substantial differences between federal procedure and that of a particular state court. For example, under the federal procedure, the complaint is *first* filed in the court, *then* served on the defendants; but under the procedure of a few states, the sequence of these two key events is reversed.

Our discussion of service of process will focus on the practices prescribed under the Federal Rules of Civil Procedure for lawsuits filed in federal court (set forth in Rule 4 of the FRCP, which appears in pertinent part in Figure 6–12).

You must note, however, that when starting a lawsuit in state court, it is state procedure that applies. The differences are not often conceptual, in that the same purpose (notifying the defendant) is being furthered under both systems, and the documents in question perform the same basic functions. But as we have said many times before and will continue to emphasize, specific details contained in specifically applicable rules are extremely important and must be given the highest consideration. The rules of the federal courts can sometimes differ markedly from those of a given state, even though designed to further the same purpose. For example, in a few states a copy of the package of documents is delivered to the defendant *before* the original is filed with the court; under the federal system (and that of most states), however, the delivery takes place *after* the filing.

In addition, different states may have different terms for documents that represent, by function and basic content, identical aspects of the document package: for example, one state may refer to a "writ" with formal instructions to the sheriff or other process server as to the delivery procedure, or a *praecipe* constituting a request to the court that your complaint and summons be delivered to the defendant. These terms are holdovers from centuries of court procedure, and the functions of such documents are accounted for in the framework established under the FRCP (even though the terminology may differ). In any event, when preparing your service of process materials, make sure you learn and follow the details of the applicable rules and procedure.

## Documents for Service of Process

As we have already noted, the documents used to alert the defendant of the pendency of a lawsuit can be thought of as a package. Each component of the package is essential; if any component is left out, the service of process may be defective, and the court may find that it cannot decide the case because it does not have personal jurisdiction over the defendant. The following discussion thus

**Figure 6–12    Pertinent Portions of Rule 4 of the FRCP**

**Rule 4. Process.**

(a) SUMMONS: ISSUANCE. Upon the filing of the complaint the clerk shall forthwith issue a summons and deliver the summons to the plaintiff or the plaintiff's attorney, who shall be responsible for prompt service of the summons and a copy of the complaint. Upon request of the plaintiff separate or additional summons shall issue against any defendants.

(b) SAME: FORM. The summons shall be signed by the clerk, be under the seal of the court, contain the name of the court and the names of the parties, be directed to the defendant, state the name and address of the plaintiff's attorney, if any, otherwise the plaintiff's address, and the time within which these rules require the defendant to appear and defend, and shall notify the defendant that in case of the defendant's failure to do so judgment by default will be rendered against the defendant for the relief demanded in the complaint. When, under Rule 4(e), service is made pursuant to a statute or rule of court of a state, the summons, or notice, or order in lieu of summons shall correspond as nearly as may be to that required by the statute or rule.

(c) SERVICE.

(1) Process, other than a subpoena or a summons and complaint, shall be served by a United States marshal or deputy United States marshal, or by a person specially appointed for that purpose.

(2)(A) A summons and complaint shall, except as provided in subparagraphs (B) and (C) of this paragraph, be served by any person who is not a party and is not less than 18 years of age.

(B) A summons and complaint shall, at the request of the party seeking service or such party's attorney, be served by a United States marshal or deputy United States marshal, or by a person specially appointed by the court for that purpose, only—

(i) on behalf of a party authorized to proceed in forma pauperis pursuant to Title 28, U.S.C. § 1915, or of a seaman authorized to proceed under Title 28, U.S.C. § 1916,

(ii) on behalf of the United States or an officer or agency of the United States, or

(iii) pursuant to an order issued by the court stating that a United States marshal or deputy United States marshal, or a person specially appointed for that purpose, is required to serve the summons and complaint in order that service be properly effected in that particular action.

(C) A summons and complaint may be served upon a defendant of any class referred to in paragraph (I) or (3) of subdivision (d) of this rule—

(i) pursuant to the law of the State in which the district court is held for the service of summons or other like process upon such defendant in an action brought in the courts of general jurisdiction of that State, or

(ii) by mailing a copy of the summons and of the complaint (by first-class mail, postage prepaid) to the person to be served, together with two copies of a notice and acknowledgment conforming substantially to form 18-A and a return envelope, postage prepaid, addressed to the sender. If no acknowledgment of service under this subdivision of this rule is received by the sender within 20 days after the date of mailing, service of such summons and complaint shall be made under subparagraph (A) or (B) of this paragraph in the manner prescribed by subdivision (d)(1) or (d)(3).

(D) Unless good cause is shown for not doing so the court shall order the payment of the costs of personal service by the person served if such person does not complete and return within 20 days after mailing, the notice and acknowledgment of receipt of summons.

(E) The notice and acknowledgment of receipt of summons and complaint shall be executed under oath or affirmation.

(3) The court shall freely make special appointments to serve summonses and complaints under paragraph (2)(B) of this subdivision of this rule and all other process under paragraph (I) of this subdivision of this rule.

Figure 6–12  Pertinent Portions of Rule 4 of the FRCP, continued

(d) SUMMONS AND COMPLAINT: PERSON TO BE SERVED. The summons and complaint shall be served together. The plaintiff shall furnish the person making service with such copies as are necessary. Service shall be made as follows:

(1) Upon an individual other than an infant or an incompetent person, by delivering a copy of the summons and of the complaint to the individual personally or by leaving copies thereof at the individual's dwelling house or usual place of abode with some person of suitable age and discretion then residing therein or by delivering a copy of the summons and of the complaint to an agent authorized by appointment or by law to receive service of process.

(2) Upon an infant or an incompetent person, by serving the summons and complaint in the manner prescribed by the law of the state in which the service is made for the service of summons or other like process upon any such defendant in an action brought in the courts of general jurisdiction of that state.

(3) Upon a domestic or foreign corporation or upon a partnership or other unincorporated association which is subject to suit under a common name, by delivering a copy of the summons and of the complaint to an officer, a managing or general agent, or to any other agent authorized by appointment or by law to receive service of process and, if the agent is one authorized by statute to receive service and the statute so requires, by also mailing a copy to the defendant.

(4) * * *

(5) * * *

(6) * * *

(e) SUMMONS: SERVICE UPON PARTY NOT INHABITANT OF OR FOUND WITHIN STATE. Whenever a statute of the United States or an order of court thereunder provides for service of a summons, or of a notice, or of an order in lieu of summons upon a party not an inhabitant of or found within the state in which the district court is held, service may be made under the circumstances and in the manner prescribed by the statute or order, or, if there is no provision therein prescribing the manner of service, in a manner stated in this rule. Whenever a statute or rule of court of the state in which the district court is held provides (1) for service of a summons, or of a notice, or of an order in lieu of summons upon a party not an inhabitant of or found within the state, or (2) for service upon or notice to such a party to appear and respond or defend in an action by reason of the attachment or garnishment or similar seizure of the party's property located within the state, service may in either case be made under the circumstances and in the manner prescribed in the statute or rule.

(f) TERRITORIAL LIMITS OF EFFECTIVE SERVICE. All process other than a subpoena may be served anywhere within the territorial limits of the state in which the district court is held, and, when authorized by a statute of the United States or by these rules, beyond the territorial limits of that state...

(g) RETURN. The person serving the process shall make proof of service thereof to the court promptly and in any event within the time during which the person served must respond to the process. If service is made by a person other than a United States marshal or deputy United States marshal, such person shall make affidavit thereof. If service is made under subdivision (c)(2)(C)(ii) of this rule, return shall be made by the sender's filing with the court the acknowledgment received pursuant to such subdivision. Failure to make proof of service does not affect the validity of the service.

(h) * * *

(i) * * *

(j) SUMMONS: TIME LIMIT FOR SERVICE. If a service of the summons and complaint is not made upon a defendant within 120 days after the filing of the complaint and the party on whose behalf such service was required cannot show good cause why such service was not made within that period, the action shall be dismissed as to that defendant without prejudice upon the court's own initiative with notice to such party or upon motion. This subdivision shall not apply to service in a foreign country pursuant to subdivision (i) of this rule.

provides information essential to beginning a lawsuit, and should be studied with care.

**Complaint**   Included with the package is, of course, the complaint you've just drafted. The complaint alerts the defendant to the nature of the plaintiff's underlying claims: it tells the defendant why he or she is being sued.

**Summons**   The **summons** serves two purposes: first, to summon the defendant to appear in court at a certain day and time in order to answer the claim of the plaintiff; second, to alert the defendant to the fact that, if he or she fails to appear, **judgment by default** may be entered against him or her. Judgment by default amounts to the defendant losing not on the merits of the dispute, but based only upon his or her failure to appear in court. We discuss the procedure relating to defaults in Chapter 7.

An example of a summons form for a lawsuit in federal court is shown in Figure 6–13; the form is designed to comply with the requirements of Rule 4(b) of the FRCP, and can be obtained from the federal court clerk's office. (Someone in your firm, probably a senior litigation paralegal, will likely be responsible for seeing that a supply of such forms is available in the office.) We have filled in the information that would appear on the summons prepared on behalf of Widgets and Gizmos, Inc., summoning TapTapTap, Inc. to the United States District Court for the District of Exurbia. As you can see, the summons in Figure 6–13 accomplishes both purposes we have identified: it summons TapTapTap, Inc. to court, and it identifies the possibility of a default judgment if TapTapTap, Inc. fails to appear in court. If there are multiple defendants in a case, the summons forms for each will differ somewhat (since each defendant must be individually summoned to court).

> **P**ARALEGALERT!
>
> When you are preparing summons forms for multiple defendants in a federal court lawsuit, keep in mind that the summons form for each will differ slightly (since each defendant must be individually summoned to court).

State court summonses are similar in content, but not always in format. Sometimes the summons is made part of the complaint, as a separate paragraph or page; sometimes it is combined with one of the other documents to be discussed, such as the basic civil cover sheet. Sometimes appear the words: "You are being sued" (see, for example, Figure 6–14, which shows a combined summons and civil cover sheet used in the courts of Connecticut). Check your state's rules to determine the format for a state court summons, and be aware that summons forms, as well as some of the other forms we will discuss, are generally obtained from the clerk's office of the applicable court.

The back side of the federal summons sheet, also shown in Figure 6–13, contains space for information about "return of service." We will discuss this concept further in our discussion of procedures associated with service of process.

**Civil Cover Sheet**   An example of a **civil cover sheet** for a federal court case is shown in Figure 6–15. The civil cover sheet requires you to provide basic background information about the case to assist the clerk's office personnel in setting up the court file and tracking case types. As you can see, the information requested includes such things as the full names and places of residence of the parties, their attorneys, if known, the basis for jurisdiction, citizenship of the two listed parties, the amount in demand, and whether a jury is demanded.

**Figure 6–13   Federal Summons Form**

# United States District Court

_____  **DISTRICT OF**  Exurbia  _____

Widgets and Gizmos, Inc.

V.

TapTapTap, Inc.

**SUMMONS IN A CIVIL ACTION**

CASE NUMBER:

[ Filled in by clerk ]

TO: (Name and Address of Defendant)
   TapTapTap, Inc.
   123 Goldenstate Street
   San Jose, California 98765

**YOU ARE HEREBY SUMMONED** and required to file with the Clerk of this Court
and serve upon

PLAINTIFF'S ATTORNEY (name and address)
   Samuel Superlawyer, Esq.
   Lincoln & Hoover
   123 Lincoln Street
   Metro City, Exurbia 12345

an answer to the complaint which is herewith served upon you, within _____ 20 _____
days after service of this summons upon you, exclusive of the day of service. If you fail to
do so, judgment by default will be taken against you for the relief demanded in the
complaint.

_____[Filled in by clerk]_____          _____[Filled in by clerk]_____
CLERK                                            DATE

_____[Filled in by clerk]_____
BY DEPUTY CLERK

Much of the same information is requested in the combination summons/cover sheet in Figure 6–14.

You should also note that, for federal court lawsuits, the civil cover sheet, although filed with the court to commence the lawsuit, need not be served upon the defendant.

**Mail Acknowledgement Form**   The federal rules provide for service by mail. If your service is to be made by mail, the form shown in Figure 6–16 (which is an official form drawn from Title 28 of the United States Code) must be included with your package. Service by mail will be discussed further in the section on procedure.

**Figure 6–13   Federal Summons Form, continued**

| RETURN OF SERVICE | |
|---|---|
| Service of the Summons and Complaint was made by me[1] | DATE |
| NAME OF SERVER (PRINT) | TITLE |

*Check one box below to indicate appropriate method of service*

☐ Served personally upon the defendant. Place where served: _____

☐ Left copies thereof at the defendant's dwelling house or usual place of abode with a person of suitable age and discretion then residing therein.
  Name of person with whom the summons and complaint were left: _____

☐ Returned unexecuted: _____
_____
_____

☐ Other (specify): _____
_____
_____
_____

| STATEMENT OF SERVICE FEES | | |
|---|---|---|
| TRAVEL | SERVICES | TOTAL |

**DECLARATION OF SERVER**

I declare under penalty of perjury under the laws of the United States of America that the foregoing information contained in the Return of Service and Statement of Service Fees is true and correct.

Executed on _____        _____
              *Date*                                 *Signature of Server*

_____
*Address of Server*

**Other Documents in the Package**   There are a few other documents that may be necessary to complete your package. Filing a lawsuit requires that you pay a filing fee to the court (the amount can be ascertained by reviewing the rules or calling the clerk's office); hence you will have to requisition a check from your firm's accounting department, and include it with the papers filed with the court.

If you are seeking a preliminary injunction or a TRO, you will need to include the documents we discussed in Section 6–5, such as your application to the court, and the proposed order for the judge to sign if he or she grants the injunctive relief. Also useful to include are cover letters to both the process server and the clerk's office, spelling out exactly what you are trying to accomplish with your package. In the case of the clerk's office, the cover letter should reference the documents you are filing and the number of the check you are using to pay the filing fee. For the process server, you should spell out the exact procedure the process server is to follow (examples of such cover letters appear in Figures 6–17 and 6–18). These letters assist the relevant personnel in processing your package, and create a record verifying that certain procedures

**Figure 6–14 Combined Summons and Civil Cover Sheet Used in Connecticut**

**SUMMONS**
**CIVIL** *(except family actions)*
**JD-CV-1 Rev. 3-91**
GEN. STAT. 51-346, 51-347, 51-349, 51-350, 52-45a,
52-48, 52-259
PR. BK. 49, 63, 66

**SUPERIOR COURT**

**"X" ONE OF THE FOLLOWING:**
*Amount, legal interest or property in demand, exclusive of interest and costs is*
a. ☐ less than $2,500
b. ☐ $2,500 through $14,999.99
c. ☐ $15,000 or more

d. ☐ *Claiming other relief in addition to or in lieu of money damages.*

**INSTRUCTIONS**
1. *Prepare on typewriter: sign original summons (top sheet) and conform copies of the summons (sheets 3 and 4).*
2. *If there is more than one defendant, prepare or photocopy conformed summons for each additional defendant.*
3. *Attach the original summons, with computer sheet attached (page 2), to the original complaint, and attach a copy of the summons to each copy of the complaint. Also, if there are more than 2 plaintiffs or 4 defendants prepare form JD-CV-2 and attach it to the original and all copies of the complaint.*
4. *After service has been made by officer, file original papers and officer's return with the clerk of the court.*
5. *The party recognized to pay costs must appear personally before the authority taking the recognizance.*
6. *Do not use this form for actions in which an attachment, garnishment or replevy is being sought. See Practice Book Section 49 for other exceptions.*

**TO: Any proper officer; BY AUTHORITY OF THE STATE OF CONNECTICUT, you are hereby commanded to make due and legal service of this Summons and attached Complaint.**

| ☐ JUDICIAL DISTRICT ☐ HOUSING SESSION ☐ G.A. _____ | AT *(Town in which writ is returnable) (Gen. Stat. 51-346, 51-349)* | RETURN DATE *(Mo., day, yr.)* |
|---|---|---|
| ADDRESS OF CLERK OF COURT WHERE WRIT AND OTHER PAPERS SHALL BE FILED *(Gen. Stat. 51-347, 51-350)* | | CASE TYPE *(From Judicial Dept. code list)* Major    Minor |

| PARTIES | NOTE: *Individual's Names: Last, First, Middle Initial*    NAME AND ADDRESS OF EACH PARTY | ☐ Form JD-CV-2 *attached* |
|---|---|---|
| **FIRST NAMED PLAINTIFF ▶** | | |
| Additional Plaintiff | | |
| **FIRST NAMED DEFENDANT ▶** | | |
| Additional Defendant | | |
| Additional Defendant | | |
| Additional Defendant | | |

**NOTICE to each DEFENDANT**

1. You are being sued.
2. This paper is a Summons in a lawsuit.
3. The Complaint attached to these papers states the claims that each Plaintiff is making against you in this lawsuit.
4. To respond to this summons, or to be informed of further proceedings, you or your attorney must file a form called an "Appearance" with the Clerk of the above named Court at the above Court address on or before the second day after the above Return Date.
5. If you or your attorney do not file a written "Appearance" form on time, a judgment may be entered against you by default.

6. The "Appearance" form may be obtained at the above Court address.

7. If you believe that you have insurance that may cover the claim that is being made against you in this lawsuit, you should immediately take the Summons and Complaint to your insurance representative.

8. If you have questions about the Summons and Complaint, you should consult an attorney promptly. The Clerk of Court is not permitted to give advice on legal questions.

| DATE | SIGNED *(sign and "X" proper box)* | ☐ Commissioner of Superior Court ☐ Assistant Clerk | TYPE IN NAME OF PERSON SIGNING AT LEFT |
|---|---|---|---|

**FOR THE PLAINTIFF(S) ENTER THE APPEARANCE OF:**

| NAME AND ADDRESS OF ATTORNEY, LAW FIRM OR PLAINTIFF IF PRO SE | TELEPHONE NO. | JURIS NO. *(If atty. or law firm)* |
|---|---|---|
| NAME AND ADDRESS OF PERSON RECOGNIZED TO PROSECUTE IN THE AMOUNT OF $250 | | SIGNATURE OF PLAINTIFF IF PRO SE |

| NO. PLFS. | NO. DEFS. | NO. CNTS. | SIGNED *(Official taking recognizance; "X" proper box)* | ☐ Commissioner of Superior Court ☐ Assistant Clerk | *For Court Use* |
|---|---|---|---|---|---|
| | | | | | RECEIPT NO.    ☐ No Fee |

**IF THIS SUMMONS IS SIGNED by a CLERK:**

a. The signing has been done so that the Plaintiff(s) will not be denied access to the courts.

b. It is the responsibility of the Plaintiff(s) to see that service is made in the manner provided by law.

c. The Clerk is not permitted to give any legal advice in connection with any lawsuit.

d. The Clerk signing this Summons at the request of the Plaintiff(s) is not responsible in any way for any errors or omissions in the Summons, any allegations contained in the Complaint, or the service thereof.

FILE DATE

| I hereby certify I have read and understand the above: | SIGNED *(Pro se plaintiff)* | DATE SIGNED | DOCKET NO. |
|---|---|---|---|

**SUMMONS, Civil**

**Figure 6–15  Federal Civil Cover Sheet**

# CIVIL COVER SHEET

The JS-44 civil cover sheet and the information contained herein neither replace nor supplement the filing and service of pleadings or other papers as required by law, except as provided by local rules of court. This form, approved by the Judicial Conference of the United States in September 1974, is required for the use of the Clerk of Court for the purpose of initiating the civil docket sheet. **(SEE INSTRUCTIONS ON THE REVERSE OF THE FORM.)**

## I (a) PLAINTIFFS

Widgets & Gizmos, Inc.
888 Widget Street
Metro City, Exurbia 12345

## DEFENDANTS

TapTapTap, Inc.
123 Goldenstate Street
San Jose, California 98765

**(b)** COUNTY OF RESIDENCE OF FIRST LISTED PLAINTIFF  Metro County
(EXCEPT IN U.S. PLAINTIFF CASES)

COUNTY OF RESIDENCE OF FIRST LISTED DEFENDANT  Santa Clara County
(IN U.S. PLAINTIFF CASES ONLY)
NOTE:  IN LAND CONDEMNATION CASES, USE THE LOCATION OF THE TRACT OF LAND INVOLVED

**(c)** ATTORNEYS (FIRM NAME, ADDRESS, AND TELEPHONE NUMBER)

Lincoln & Hoover
123 Lincoln Street
Metro City, Exurbia 12345

## ATTORNEYS (IF KNOWN)

Unknown

## II. BASIS OF JURISDICTION
(PLACE AN x IN ONE BOX ONLY)

- ☐ 1 U.S. Government Plaintiff
- ☐ 2 U.S. Government Defendant
- ☐ 3 Federal Question (U.S. Government Not a Party)
- ☒ 4 Diversity (Indicate Citizenship of Parties in Item III)

## III. CITIZENSHIP OF PRINCIPAL PARTIES
(For Diversity Cases Only)  PLACE AN x IN ONE BOX FOR PLAINTIFF AND ONE BOX FOR DEFENDANT

| | PTF | DEF | | PTF | DEF |
|---|---|---|---|---|---|
| Citizen of This State | ☐ 1 | ☐ 1 | Incorporated *or* Principal Place of Business in This State | ☒ 4 | ☐ 4 |
| Citizen of Another State | ☐ 2 | ☐ 2 | Incorporated *and* Principal Place of Business in Another State | ☐ 5 | ☒ 5 |
| Citizen or Subject of a Foreign Country | ☐ 3 | ☐ 3 | Foreign Nation | ☐ 6 | ☐ 6 |

## IV. CAUSE OF ACTION
(CITE THE U.S. CIVIL STATUTE UNDER WHICH YOU ARE FILING AND WRITE A BRIEF STATEMENT OF CAUSE.
DO NOT SITE JURISDICTIONAL STATUTES UNLESS DIVERSITY)

28 U.S.C. §1332

## V. NATURE OF SUIT (PLACE AN x IN ONE BOX ONLY)

### CONTRACT
- ☐ 110 Insurance
- ☐ 120 Marine
- ☐ 130 Miller Act
- ☐ 140 Negotiable Instrument
- ☐ 150 Recovery of Overpayment & Enforcement of Judgment
- ☐ 151 Medicare Act
- ☐ 152 Recovery of Defaulted Student Loans (Excl. Veterans)
- ☐ 153 Recovery of Overpayment of Veteran's Benefits
- ☐ 160 Stockholders' Suits
- ☒ 190 Other Contract
- ☐ 195 Contract Product Liability

### REAL PROPERTY
- ☐ 210 Land Condemnation
- ☐ 220 Foreclosure
- ☐ 230 Rent Lease & Ejectment
- ☐ 240 Torts to Land
- ☐ 245 Tort Product Liability
- ☐ 290 All Other Real Property

### TORTS

**PERSONAL INJURY**
- ☐ 310 Airplane
- ☐ 315 Airplane Product Liability
- ☐ 320 Assault, Libel & Slander
- ☐ 330 Federal Employers' Liability
- ☐ 340 Marine
- ☐ 345 Marine Product Liability
- ☐ 350 Motor Vehicle
- ☐ 355 Motor Vehicle Product Liability
- ☐ 360 Other Personal Injury

**PERSONAL INJURY**
- ☐ 362 Personal Injury—Med Malpractice
- ☐ 365 Personal Injury—Product Liability
- ☐ 368 Asbestos Personal Injury Product Liability

**PERSONAL PROPERTY**
- ☐ 370 Other Fraud
- ☐ 371 Truth in Lending
- ☐ 380 Other Personal Property Damage
- ☐ 385 Property Damage Product Liability

### CIVIL RIGHTS
- ☐ 441 Voting
- ☐ 442 Employment
- ☐ 443 Housing/ Accommodations
- ☐ 444 Welfare
- ☐ 440 Other Civil Rights

### PRISONER PETITIONS
- ☐ 510 Motions to Vacate Sentence Habeas Corpus:
- ☐ 530 General
- ☐ 535 Death Penalty
- ☐ 540 Mandamus & Other
- ☐ 550 Civil Rights

### FORFEITURE/PENALTY
- ☐ 610 Agriculture
- ☐ 620 Other Food & Drug
- ☐ 625 Drug Related Seizure of Property 21 USC 881
- ☐ 630 Liquor Laws
- ☐ 640 R.R. & Truck
- ☐ 650 Airline Regs
- ☐ 660 Occupational Safety/Health
- ☐ 690 Other

### LABOR
- ☐ 710 Fair Labor Standards Act
- ☐ 720 Labor/Mgmt. Relations
- ☐ 730 Labor/Mgmt. Reporting & Disclosure Act
- ☐ 740 Railway Labor Act
- ☐ 790 Other Labor Litigation
- ☐ 791 Empl. Ret. Inc. Security Act

### BANKRUPTCY
- ☐ 422 Appeal 28 USC 158
- ☐ 423 Withdrawal 28 USC 157

### PROPERTY RIGHTS
- ☐ 820 Copyrights
- ☐ 830 Patent
- ☐ 840 Trademark

### SOCIAL SECURITY
- ☐ 861 HIA (1395ff)
- ☐ 862 Black Lung (923)
- ☐ 863 DIWC/DIWW (405(g))
- ☐ 864 SSID Title XVI
- ☐ 865 RSI (405(g))

### FEDERAL TAX SUITS
- ☐ 870 Taxes (U.S. Plaintiff or Defendant)
- ☐ 871 IRS—Third Party 26 USC 7609

### OTHER STATUTES
- ☐ 400 State Reapportionment
- ☐ 410 Antitrust
- ☐ 430 Banks and Banking
- ☐ 450 Commerce/ICC Rates/etc.
- ☐ 460 Deportation
- ☐ 470 Racketeer Influenced and Corrupt Organizations
- ☐ 810 Selective Service
- ☐ 850 Securities/ Commodities/ Exchange
- ☐ 875 Customer Challenge 12 USC 3410
- ☐ 891 Agricultural Acts
- ☐ 892 Economic Stabilization Act
- ☐ 893 Environmental Matters
- ☐ 894 Energy Allocation Act
- ☐ 895 Freedom of Information Act
- ☐ 900 Appeal of Fee Determination Under Equal Access to Justice
- ☐ 950 Constitutionality of State Statutes
- ☐ 890 Other Statutory Acts

## VI. ORIGIN (PLACE AN x IN ONE BOX ONLY)

- ☒ 1 Original Proceeding
- ☐ 2 Removed from State Court
- ☐ 3 Remanded from Appellate Court
- ☐ 4 Reinstated or Reopened
- ☐ 5 Transferred from another district (specify)
- ☐ 6 Multidistrict Litigation
- ☐ 7 Appeal to District Judge from Magistrate Judgment

## VII. REQUESTED IN COMPLAINT:

CHECK IF THIS IS A **CLASS ACTION**
☐ UNDER F.R.C.P. 23

**DEMAND $** $750,000 +

Check YES only if demanded in complaint:
**JURY DEMAND:** ☒ YES ☐ NO

## VIII. RELATED CASE(S) IF ANY
(See instructions):
JUDGE _____  DOCKET NUMBER _____

DATE _____  SIGNATURE OF ATTORNEY OF RECORD

United States District Court

**Figure 6–16   Notice and Acknowledgment For Service by Mail**

# United States District Court

_____ DISTRICT OF _____

V.

## NOTICE AND ACKNOWLEDGMENT
## FOR SERVICE BY MAIL

CASE NUMBER:

## NOTICE

To: _____

Name and Address of Person to be Served

The enclosed summons and complaint are served pursuant to the Rule 4(c)(2)(C)(ii) of the Federal Rules of Civil Procedure.

You must complete the acknowledgment part of this form and return one copy of the completed form to the sender **to be received by the sender within 20 days of the date of mailing indicated below.**

You must sign and date the acknowledgment. If you are served on behalf of a corporation, unincorporated association (including a partnership), or other entity, you must indicate under your signature your relationship to that entity. If you are served on behalf of another person and you are authorized to receive process, you must indicate under your signature your authority.

**If you do not complete and return the form to the sender within the period indicated above,** you (or the party on whose behalf you are being served) may be required to pay any expenses incurred in serving the summons and complaint in any other manner permitted by law.

**THIS FORM IS NOT AN ANSWER TO THE COMPLAINT.** You must answer the complaint within the period of time indicated on the summons. If you fail to do so, judgment by default may be taken against you for the relief demanded in the complaint.

I declare under penalty of perjury that this Notice and Acknowledgment of Receipt of Summons and Complaint will have been mailed on _____.

Date

_____

Signature of Sender

_____          _____

Name of Sender                              Address of Sender

### ACKNOWLEDGMENT OF RECEIPT OF SUMMONS AND COMPLAINT

I declare under penalty of perjury that I received a copy of the summons and of the complaint in this case on _____ at _____

Date of Receipt                                              Address

_____          _____

Date of Signature                                            Signature

_____          _____

Name (Please Type or Print)          Relationship of Entity Served or Authority
                                                       to Receive Service of Process

_____

Current Address

**Figure 6–17** **Cover Letter to Court Clerk**

# Lincoln & Hoover
## Attorneys at Law

October 22, 1993

Ray Doe, Esq.
Clerk of the Court
U.S. District Court
101 Court Street
Metro City, Exurbia 12345

Dear Mr. Doe:

Enclosed you will find an original and 4 copies of the complaint in the matter of *Widgets and Gizmos, Inc. v. TapTapTap, Inc.*, as well as associated summons forms. Also enclosed is this firm's check #57649 in the amount of $125.00 in payment of the filing fee to initiate a civil action.

Please enter this case on your docket and assign a civil action number. Also, please complete and issue the summons forms, and return them to us with the copies of the complaint.

If you have any questions, please contact me immediately.

Very truly yours,

Paula Paralegal

were to be followed at your direction. (Note that copies of the filing fee check and the cover letters need not be served upon the defendant.)

## Procedure for Service of Process

The basic purpose of service of process, as we have noted, is to notify the defendant that he or she has been sued; and, to be more specific, to get the "package" we've discussed into the hands of the defendant. Now that you know the documents that comprise the package, let's turn our analysis to the manner of delivery.

It is useful to think of the service of process procedure as having three separate components: (1) filing the package with the court; (2) serving the package on the defendant; and (3) notifying the court that the package has been served upon the defendant. We will consider these three components as they are fulfilled under the federal procedure, in which the package is filed first with the court, then a copy served upon the defendant. Keep in mind the alternative procedure that we identified earlier, which applies to some state court lawsuits, where a copy of the package is first served on the defendant and then the original is filed with the court (see Figure 6–19). Make sure you identify and follow the applicable rules.

**Filing the Package with the Court**   To start a lawsuit in federal court, first complete your package of documents and have it reviewed and signed in the

**Figure 6–18 Cover Letter to Process Server**

# Lincoln & Hoover
## Attorneys at Law

October 12, 1993

Sheriff John Juris
Metro County Sheriff's Office
7631 Nottingham Road
Metro City, Exurbia 12345

Dear Sheriff Juris:

Enclosed you will find two copies of the summons and complaint in the matter of Hampton v. Johnson. As we discussed over the phone, you are to serve one copy of this complaint on Judith Johnson, and one copy on Bernard Lindquist in his capacity as owner of defendant Bud's Auto Service. Please serve these defendants in the following manner:

*Judith Johnson:* Serve her in-hand if possible. If that is not possible, make abode service at her home, 143 Wingate Street, Milltown. For your information, and in the interest of assisting your attempt at in-hand service, note that Ms. Johnson works for Dr. Samuel Teedy, a dentist practicing at 77 Incisor Street, Metro City.

*Bud's Auto Service:* Serve Bernard Lindquist in-hand. He will be easy to find at Bud's Auto Service at 142 Franklin Turnpike in Milltown. For your information, his residence is 714 Ruth Street, Milltown.

After service has been made, please prepare your sheriff's return of service and deliver it to this office. We would like all service to be completed no later than November 5, 1993.

If you have any questions, please call me immediately.

Very truly yours,

Paula Paralegal

relevant places by your supervising attorney. Then, make sufficient copies of the package to enable you to serve copies on all defendants. The number of copies can be calculated beforehand, depending on the manner in which you and your supervising attorney choose to serve the package (see the next subsection). You should note that, in some state systems, the copies must be certified as "true and

**Figure 6–19 Two Alternative Sequences for Service of Process**

| *Sequence in Federal (and most State) Courts:* | *Sequence in Some States:* |
|---|---|
| | Have summons and copies of complaint served upon defendants |
| File original complaint with court | |
| Have summons and copies of complaint served upon defendants | File summons, original complaint, and "return of service" with the court |
| After service, file "return of service" with the court | |

attested" (which is to say, *exact*) copies of the original documents. This certification is often supplied by the process server (who will be discussed further in the next subsection). The copies must also be exact copies under the federal system, although there is no corresponding requirement that they be so certified.

The original package and all the summons forms are then taken to the clerk's office of the applicable United States District Court. Technically, the clerk is required to issue each summons "under the seal of the court" under Rules 4(a) and 4(b) of the FRCP; practically speaking, you will prepare all necessary summonses in advance, and the clerk will sign them, apply the court seal, assign the case a docket number (and often, a specific judge as well), and stamp the docket number on all the summons forms. The clerk will also stamp the docket number on the original complaint (this is why you need to leave a space for a civil action number in the caption of a federal court complaint), and other original documents in your package (such as a request for a hearing for a preliminary injunction). If you bring the additional copies of the package, the clerk will often stamp the docket number on them as well, as a courtesy.

The clerk will keep the original package (with original signatures) to start the court file, and return to you all summons forms, which you will need for service on the defendants, and any copies of the package that were stamped as a courtesy.

If you have made a request for a preliminary injunction, the clerk will also have to schedule a date for the pretrial hearing, and a notice of this hearing will be included with your package.

If the package includes a request for a temporary restraining order, the package will have to be presented to a judge, who will determine whether the relief requested is justified. If he or she does find it to be justified, the judge will sign the appropriate order, which will be included with your package and be served on the defendants. The order will also generally identify a hearing date on which the continuance of the TRO will be considered.

**Serving the Package on the Defendant** At this stage of your lawsuit, you have now drafted your complaint and associated documents, filed the original with the court, and obtained sufficient copies of the summons forms and other components of the package to serve the defendants. The next step is to actually deliver copies of the package to the defendants. As we noted, this delivery is referred to as the *service*. Three factors need to be considered in analyzing service: *by whom* it is made; *upon whom* it is made; and, taking into account the first two factors, *how* it is made.

Our first task is identifying *by whom* service is made. Service has traditionally been made by a person known generically as a **process server.** Prior to 1983, the process server for a federal court complaint had to be a United States Marshal. Since 1983, however, Rule 4 of the FRCP has been amended to allow, for the most common types of defendants, service "by any person who is not a party and is not less than 18 years of age" (Rule 4(c)(2)(A)). Many state court systems authorize service by local sheriffs, or, as with the federal system, by any "indifferent person" who is without interest in the matters raised by the complaint.

Not only did the 1983 amendments to the FRCP do away with the need to use U.S. Marshals as process servers, they also made it possible to do away entirely with process servers by allowing for **mail notice.** We'll talk more about mail notice, but first let's address the second factor in our analysis of service: *upon whom* service is made.

Service is made upon the defendant. That perhaps seems simple and obvious, and if the defendant is an individual person, such as Judith Johnson, it *is*—you simply serve a copy on Judith Johnson. But what about Bud's Auto Service? And, in the Widgets and Gizmos, Inc. matter, how do you serve TapTapTap, Inc.? In short, upon whom is service made when the defendant is a corporation or other organization?

Rule 4(d) of the FRCP identifies the person upon whom service of process is made. Subdivision (3) of Rule 4(d) states that in the context of a corporation or other business, service shall be made upon "an officer, a managing or general agent, or to any agent authorized by appointment or by law to receive service of process . . . ." This would include the "agent for service of process" (or "registered agent" in some areas) to whom we referred in our discussion in Chapter 4 relating to corporate information maintained at the state Office of the Secretary of the State.

This brings us to the third factor affecting our service of process analysis: namely, *how* the service is made. The first and most obvious method is for the process server to find the defendant and give him or her a copy of the summons and complaint. This is often called **in-hand service.** Another method is for the process server to leave a copy with some competent person at the defendant's usual place of residence; this is often referred to as **abode service.** Both in-hand and abode service are addressed (and approved) for service on individuals, in Rule 4(d)(1) of the FRCP. Under some state systems, abode service is completed simply by leaving a copy of the package at the usual place of residence, regardless of whether any person is there to accept it.

In-hand and abode service relate not only to individual defendants such as Judith Johnson, but often to the business principals, corporate officers, and agents for service of process who are served on behalf of corporate or business defendants.

What about lawsuits filed against out-of-state defendants? In Chapter 1 we talked about something called "long-arm jurisdiction," where the "long arm of the law" reaches into another state and establishes personal jurisdiction over a defendant. Many states have a so-called **long-arm statute,** which identifies the procedure for notifying such out-of-state defendants that they have been named as defendant in a lawsuit. Long-arm statutes usually require such things as sending out-of-state defendants copies of the summons and complaint by certified mail, or serving a copy upon the Secretary of State of your state, who then mails it to the out-of-state defendant. You should find and review the procedure in your own state's long-arm statute. The federal procedure for service upon an out-of-state party is set forth in Rule 4(e) of the FRCP, and can incorporate the provisions of a state long-arm statute.

What about a defendant who, despite your best efforts, cannot be located? How can you serve documents on a defendant you can't find? The procedure can get complicated in such a situation, but you should be aware of a "last recourse": an **order of notice.** An order of notice is an order of the court, upon request of a plaintiff, that a certain specified defendant cannot be located and may be "served" in some alternative fashion, usually by mail to a last known address and/or by placing a notice in a prominent newspaper of the town of that last known address. After the plaintiff has completed all the steps required by the order of notice, the court assumes personal jurisdiction over the defendant on the theory that he or she has *constructive notice* of the lawsuit. Actual notice is preferable to constructive notice, of course, and one of your investigatory tasks as a paralegal may be to track down a missing defendant.

This brings us, finally, to federal mail notice. Figure 6–16 (page 140), as we noted earlier, is the official form used for federal mail notice. By analyzing this form, in conjunction with Rule 4(c)(2)(C), (D), and (E), you will come to understand the procedure behind federal mail notice. In short, that procedure requires that the plaintiff or the plaintiff's attorney mail a copy of the summons and complaint to the defendant, along with the official mail notice form with the

**Figure 6–20   Summary Table of Documents and Procedures Associated with Service of Process**

**Complaint:** Identifies parties; sets forth facts, including elements of causes of action; identifies damages and relief sought. In federal court and most state courts, original is *first* filed with court *then* copies are served on defendants; in some state courts, copies are *first* served on defendants *then* original is filed with court.

**Summons:** Alerts defendants of the need to appear in court by a certain date, and of the possibility of judgment by default if they do not so appear. Must be served along with the complaint.

**Civil Cover Sheet:** Provides court with background information which assists in the file-opening process. Not served upon the defendants, unless part of a combined civil cover sheet and summons.

**Combined Civil Cover Sheet and Summons:** In some state courts, the functions of the summons and civil cover sheets have been combined in one document. This document must be served on the defendants along with the complaint.

**Mail Notice and Acknowledgment Form:** In federal court, the rules allow for service of process by mail. In such case, the plaintiff must arrange for a copy of the complaint and summons to be mailed to the defendants, along with a copy of the mail notice and acknowledgment form. The mail notice and acknowledgment form does not need to be filed with the court at the time of filing of the complaint, but see further discussion of the mail acknowledgment form below.

**Mail Acknowledgment Form:** Upon receipt of the summons, complaint, and mail notice and acknowledgment form, the defendant must return the acknowledgment form to the sender, or risk paying the plaintiff's costs for alternative service of process. When the sender receives the acknowledgment form *back* from a defendant, the acknowledgment form must *then* be filed with the court as part of the return of service.

**Proposed Injunction Order, with Supporting Affidavit and Motion or Application:** When seeking a preliminary injunction or temporary restraining order ("TRO") at the commencement of a lawsuit, a proposed order must be submitted to the judge, along with a supporting affidavit and a motion or application requesting that the preliminary injunction or TRO be entered. If the judge signs the order, then the order, affidavit, and motion or application all must be served upon the defendants, along with the summons and complaint.

**Cover Letter to Court Clerk:** It is useful to include a cover letter to the court clerk at the time of filing the complaint, identifying what is being filed (i.e. the complaint and associated documents) and referencing the check for the filing fee. The letter itself need not be served on the defendants.

**Cover Letter to Process Server:** A letter should be provided to the process server setting forth detailed instructions as to how the service of process is to be performed. This should be done even if the process server is experienced, so as to create a record of the instructions. The letter itself need not be served on the defendants.

**Filing Fee Check:** Since there is a filing fee associated with the commencement of a lawsuit, a check for this fee must accompany the documents filed with the court to commence the lawsuit.

**Return of Service:** The court must be made aware of the manner in which service of process was completed against defendants. Thus the return of service must be filed with the court, after service of process is completed. Return of service includes the mail acknowledgment form described earlier, if mail notice procedure is used.

appropriate information filled in, and with a return envelope (with postage) addressed to the sender. The defendant, upon receipt of the mail notice, must thereafter execute the acknowledgment portion of the form, acknowledging receipt of the complaint and summons. If the defendant fails to return this acknowledgment form to the sender within 20 days, he or she becomes subject to payment of the costs that the plaintiff is thereafter forced to incur for the personal service of the summons and complaint. The requirement of such payment is justified by the fact that this personal service was only made necessary as a result of the failure of the defendant to return the acknowledgment form.

One final point must be emphasized with regard to service of process procedure: applicable deadlines. The deadline for service appears in Rule 4(j) of the FRCP. It requires that service be made within 120 days of the filing of the complaint, unless the party who filed the complaint can show "good cause why such service was not made within that period . . . . " If service is not so made and no good cause can be shown, the lawsuit is dismissed (without prejudice to the claims being raised again).

You should be sure to check your state deadlines regarding service of process.

**Notifying the Court that the Package Has Been Served**  The court must be notified that a defendant has been served with a summons and complaint. This is done by a procedure known as **return of service.** Rule 4(g) of the FRCP establishes the requirements for proving that service has been made. In general, two types of return are seen in federal court. If the service is made by a process server, the back of the summons form (see Figure 6–13) is executed by the process server and filed with the court. If the service is made by mail notice, then, when the acknowledgment is received back by the sender, it is filed with the court. You should review your state's procedure for return of service in the state courts.

**PARALEGALERT!**

Service of process involves complicated rules, as a brief review of all the sections and subsections of Rule 4 of the FRCP will demonstrate. Take the time to study and master the rules applicable in your jurisdiction.

Service of process can be a very complicated issue, and it is not uncommon for defendants to challenge the adequacy of the service and the existence of personal jurisdiction. We have, in this section, merely scratched the surface of the subject area, and introduced you to a few key concepts; it would be worthwhile for you to pursue further study. Figure 6–20 lists the basic service of process documents and summarizes what is generally done with each during the service of process procedure.

## 6–7  Practical Considerations

We need to address two practical considerations in this section. First, we'll briefly examine the interrelationship between complaints and the statute of limitations; then we'll consider the clerk's office.

A statute of limitations, as you recall from Chapter 2, identifies the time frame within which a claim must be raised in a lawsuit; if not so raised, the claim is lost forever. In other words, the statute of limitations provides the deadline for initiating a lawsuit. When the deadline is approaching, a critically important issue is: what action does a plaintiff have to complete in order to satisfy the statute of limitations? Is it enough to file the complaint with the court before the deadline? Must the complaint be both filed and served? Must it be filed, served, and returned to court? And does it matter whether the system is the federal system (where filing takes place before service) or one of the alternative state systems (where service takes place before filing)?

The answer to this question is so important that we're not going to try to answer it. Why not? Because we don't want to mislead you with a generalization. If your deadline under the statute of limitations is approaching, you must be absolutely sure that you have determined the precise requirements applicable in your type of case, in your court, and regarding the specific defendants against whom your claim is being raised. You must do all necessary research to determine the appropriate procedure. In fact, you should do some research on your own now about statutes of limitations procedures in your state. But if the issue ever comes up in any of your cases, you should do the research again, to be absolutely sure.

Next, we turn to a topic we have spoken about often, the clerk's office at the courthouse. Perhaps you have visited a clerk's office already; but even if you have, you do not yet have a well-defined sense of its importance.

The clerk's office is the nerve center of the litigation process. From the day you file a complaint to the day, probably years later, when the trial is completed and you stop by to retrieve your original exhibits from the official files, the clerk's office is the filter through which every official document flows, and the hub around which attorneys, judges, witnesses, jurors, and clients revolve.

Clerk's office personnel are often extraordinarily knowledgeable about the details of the litigation process. They understand the administrative minutiae that occasionally confound even the most competent attorneys, and fortunately they are often willing and able to help litigation personnel, particularly young attorneys or paralegals, through the minefield that the procedural rules can sometimes present. You should get to know the personnel at your local clerk's offices. A friend there can be more valuable than just about any other "connection" you can make.

**Recent Developments**  Between the first and second printing of this book, the Supreme Court of the United States submitted to Congress amendments to the Federal Rules of Civil Procedure. Pursuant to Section 2074 of Title 28 of the United States Code, these amendments took effect on December 1, 1993.

The amendments include significant changes to Rules 4 and 11, and the addition of a new Rule 4.1 (derived from certain provisions of the pre-existing Rule 4). Rule 11 has been modified to allow, among other things, an allegedly offensive pleading (or other document or contention) to be withdrawn or corrected, and by such withdrawal or correction avoid susceptibility to sanction. Rule 4 has been modified to clarify the procedures related to service of the summons and complaint, including an expansion of the procedure for obtaining waiver of service by the party sued (replacing the pre-existing "mail notice" procedure). Rule 4.1 includes former provisions of Rule 4 relating to service of process other than a summons or subpoena. Several official forms reflecting these changes have also been added, deleted, or modified to reflect the new rules.

# SUMMARY

## 6—1

A cause of action is a legal claim that, if proved and if no successful defenses are raised, is sufficient to justify the entry of judgment in favor of the plaintiff. A cause of action consists of essential allegations called "elements." Elements are found in judicial opinions and statutes. In order to draft a complaint, you must identify the cause of action and the related elements, identify the defendant or defendants, and determine the damages that have been suffered and the relief sought. A complaint is the formal statement of the plaintiff's cause or causes of action seeking a legal or equitable remedy against one or more defendants that, when filed with the court and served upon the defendants in the required manner, successfully commences the lawsuit.

## 6—2

The caption appears at the beginning of every pleading, and identifies the parties, the court, the designation of the pleading, and the date. Every pleading after the complaint will also have the docket number in its caption; in the federal courts and some state courts, the complaint will also have the docket number. The designation identifies the purpose of the pleading; in complex cases, a detailed designation helps to distinguish similar pleadings. The information contained in pleadings is set forth in numbered paragraphs, which facilitate clarity and eliminate confusion both in the pleading itself and in responses thereto. All pleadings are signed in the signature block; such signatures are not mere formalities, but constitute certifications by the signer as to the reliability of the contents of the pleading. Certain serious allegations require that a party provide a verified signature, swearing to the truth of the allegations. The certificate of service is designed to ensure that copies of the pleading have been sent to all parties.

## 6—3

Choosing a court requires that the plaintiff consider the existence of concurrent jurisdiction, the requirements of venue, and the effect of conflict of laws. Diversity of citizenship jurisdiction, which enables a lawsuit to be brought in federal court, is present where no two parties on opposite sides of a lawsuit are from the same state, and the amount in controversy is in excess of $50,000, exclusive of interest and costs. Even if diversity jurisdiction cannot be established, the parties may still be able to file their lawsuit in federal court if a federal statute or federal constitutional principle is at issue. Pendent jurisdiction enables a party to bring all suitably related causes of action in the same federal lawsuit, even if only one of the causes of action justifies federal jurisdiction. Venue is determined by statute. If the venue statute allows more than one location for a lawsuit, conflict of laws analysis may be required to determine the best location for a lawsuit to proceed.

## 6—4

Fact-pleading jurisdictions or rules require more detail in the allegations than notice-pleading jurisdictions. Form books are useful, although they should never be relied upon absolutely. A complaint must contain allegations as to all the elements of each cause of action, although some may be implied by the context. Each separate cause of action requires a separate count. The parties must be identified in a complaint, both to establish the basis for jurisdiction and to establish against or in favor of whom judgment will enter. Don't allege facts in a complaint that you can't prove. Because you are an advocate, your complaint should be drafted both accurately and in a light most favorable to the client; be forceful and persuasive. Be reasonably specific when alleging damages. Federal court complaints require a jurisdictional statement. Be sure to include a jury demand if desired and required.

## 6—5

Permanent injunctions are granted after a full-scale trial; preliminary injunctions are granted after a preliminary hearing and are in force during the pendency of a lawsuit; temporary restraining orders are granted instantly, in an *ex parte* manner, and last only until a preliminary hearing can be arranged. For the complaint-drafting process, the key factor with regard to preliminary injunctive relief is to determine the documents that must be drafted to accompany the complaint. These documents include motions or applications, affidavits, and proposed orders.

## 6–6

Service of process is the name given to the procedure by which a defendant is notified of the pendency of a lawsuit. The package of documents that make up the "process" includes the complaint, the summons, a civil cover sheet, a check for the filing fee, documents related to re-quested injunctions, and possibly a mail acknowledgment form. In federal court, after copies of the complaint are filed with the court, service is made by a process server or by mail notice. If made by a process server, service might be made in-hand or at the defendant's abode. After service of process is completed, the court is notified of the completion by the return of service.

## 6–7

If a statute of limitations is approaching as you commence a lawsuit, be sure to determine the exact steps that you must complete in order to satisfy the statute of limitations. Get to know the procedures and personnel at your local clerk's offices.

## REVIEW

### Key Terms

Before proceeding, review the key terms listed below to be sure you understand each one. If necessary, read over the corresponding section of the chapter. When you are ready to test your understanding, answer the Review Questions.

complaint
cause of action
elements
joinder of parties
counterclaim
joinder of claims
damages
relief
pleadings
caption
title of the action
docket number
civil action number
designation
numbered paragraphs
signature block
verification
verified complaint
certificate of service
clerk's office
pendent jurisdiction
conflict of laws

fact-pleading
notice-pleading
form books
count
prayer for relief
jury demand
jurisdictional statement
exhibits
injunction
permanent injunction
preliminary injunction
temporary restraining order
irreparable harm
bond
service of process
process
service
summons
judgment by default
civil cover sheet
process server
mail notice
in-hand service
abode service
long-arm statute
order of notice
return of service

### Questions for Review and Discussion

1. What is a cause of action?

2. Why do pleadings have numbered paragraphs?
3. What are the requirements for federal diversity jurisdiction?
4. How is the appropriate venue of a lawsuit determined?
5. What is the difference between fact-pleading and notice-pleading, and how does this difference affect the drafter of a complaint in practical terms?
6. How are form books useful?
7. How does a plaintiff's attorney ensure that the case will be tried by a jury?
8. What is a TRO, and how is it obtained?
9. What are the two key purposes of a summons?
10. What is the difference between in-hand service and abode service?

## Activities

1. Research your state's negligence standards, and compile a list of the elements needed to allege a negligence cause of action.
2. Ask at your local state court clerk's office whether you can have a blank summons form that would be used to start a negligence lawsuit involving an automobile accident. Then research your state court rules and/or statutes to locate the provisions authorizing the format of the form.
3. Go to your federal court clerk's office, and ask to see the file for a pending case. Look through the file, identify the complaint and the return of service, and study the manner in which they comply with the rules and guidelines we've discussed. Be sure to return the file to the clerk in exactly the same condition in which you received it.

# CHAPTER 7 Motion Practice and Other Subsequent Activity

## OUTLINE

## COMMENTARY

Sam Superlawyer was impressed with your drafting job on the complaints we prepared in the last chapter; he signed both without a single change! The Hampton complaint has been filed with the court and served in-hand by a Metro County sheriff on defendant Judith Johnson, and also in-hand on Bernard Lindquist as the owner of Bud's Auto Service. After completing his service, the sheriff supplied you with his "return of service," which was thereafter filed with the court, in accord with the procedural requirements of the State of Exurbia.

The Widgets and Gizmos, Inc. complaint has been filed with the U.S. District Court for the District of Exurbia, and a copy of the summons and complaint mailed to the agent for service of process of TapTapTap, Inc. (whose name was registered with the Secretary of the State of Exurbia). The defendant TapTapTap, Inc. has sent back the mail acknowledgment form, fully executed by its president, Emily Tapman, and you've now filed that with the court as well.

And so the first lawsuits with which you have been associated have begun! But preparing, filing, and serving a lawsuit is only the initial step—there's much more to learn as we dig deeper into the litigation process.

## OBJECTIVES

In the last chapter you learned how a cause of action is transformed into a complaint. In this chapter, you'll examine the manner in which the lawsuit started by the complaint moves toward resolution. After completing Chapter 7, you'll be able to:

1. State the three key objectives that the rules of procedure seek to foster during the pretrial process.
2. Precisely define the term *pleading*.
3. Differentiate a pleading from a motion.
4. Describe the basic federal procedure for computing time intervals.
5. Explain what a default is.
6. State what is meant by *removal*.
7. List five ways in which the assertions in a pleading might be found lacking.
8. Identify the motion filed to attack a vague or ambiguous pleading.
9. Explain what is meant by "failure to state a claim on which relief can be granted."
10. Identify the purpose of a motion *in limine*.

## 7–1   The Pretrial Process

We start this chapter with a broad question: What is the pretrial process all about? A complaint states a claim, after all, and the trial provides the means by which the court resolves the issues presented by the claim; what else do we need? Why bother with all this pretrial manuevering? Why not get right to the trial?

The *pretrial process* (a term we're using to refer to the forward progression of the lawsuit, under the rules, during the period between the filing of the complaint and the commencement of trial) can vary substantially, depending on the nature of the particular case and the approach of the involved attorneys. Generally speaking, there are three key objectives that the rules seek to foster during the pretrial period: first, that the contested issues be clearly defined and legitimate; second, that the lawsuit ultimately constitute an inclusive and efficient determination of all reasonably related issues; and third, that the parties have an opportunity to uncover and analyze virtually all information relevant to the issues (see Figure 7–1).

In order to explain fully how these three objectives are advanced, let's analyze the pretrial process in three segments. One of these segments is the discovery process, which enables the parties to develop a full picture of the facts behind

**Figure 7–1   Three Key Objectives of the Pretrial Process**

> *The pretrial process is designed to:*
>
> (1) ensure that the contested issues will be clearly defined and legitimate (accomplished through *pleadings* and *pretrial motions*);
>
> (2) ensure that the trial will be an inclusive and efficient determination of all reasonably related issues (accomplished through *pleadings* and *pretrial motions*); and
>
> (3) provide the parties with the opportunity to uncover and analyze virtually all information relevant to the contested issues (accomplished through the *discovery* process).

the dispute. Discovery minimizes the potential for surprise at trial and accomplishes our third pretrial objective, namely, that the parties have the opportunity to uncover and analyze virtually all available information. (We study this process in detail in Chapter 9.)

The other two segments of the pretrial process are pretrial motions and pleadings. These segments work together to accomplish the first and second objectives of the pretrial process: that the issues presented for resolution at trial be clearly defined and legitimate, and that the lawsuit constitute an inclusive and efficient determination of all outstanding issues. In this chapter we discuss how pretrial motions aid in accomplishing these objectives; in Chapter 8 we discuss how the answer, and other pleadings, contribute to the process.

It would be wonderful, for the purposes of analysis, if we could stop our introduction right here and launch directly into a discussion of motion practice. But there is a problem. Although our introduction has just divided the pretrial process into three neat, clearly denominated segments (discovery; pretrial motions; pleadings), in the real world the divisions are not so neat. The problem is this: there is a close relationship between certain pretrial motions and the pleadings, making it difficult to discuss one without considering the other. The interrelationship is so close, in fact, that in a moment we're going to start our discussion by carefully reexamining exactly what we mean by a pleading and by a motion. But first we'll reiterate something we noted in our "Practical Considerations" in Section 1–8: that the study of civil litigation can become confusing and difficult not because the underlying concepts themselves are complicated, but rather because of just this sort of interrelationship between the concepts. It is possible to face a situation, for example, where it will be difficult to understand fully Concept *A* until you have mastered Concept *B*, while at the same time you cannot fully understand Concept *B* itself until you've mastered Concept *A*! Our advice: read, reread, and study. It will all fall into place, and when it does you will marvel that you ever had trouble with the concepts. But in the beginning you simply have to work hard and persist. Enough said. Let's move on to our reexamination of the terms *pleadings* and *motions*.

**PARALEGALERT!**

In studying civil litigation, you will sometimes be frustrated by the seeming circularity that arises out of the need to master new, interrelated concepts in a near-simultaneous fashion. The best thing to do in such situations: *read, reread,* and *study*. Perseverance will pay off!

## Pleadings

We have defined the *pleadings* to be the complaint, the answer, and certain other documents that assert claims and defenses. As set forth in Rule 7(a) of the FRCP, the pleadings include the complaint, the answer, a reply to a counterclaim (a counterclaim states a claim in a manner analogous to a complaint), an answer to a cross-claim (a cross-claim also states a claim in a manner analogous to a complaint), and third-party complaints and answers thereto. We discuss many of these pleadings in detail in the next chapter.

You should note that, because there are several defenses that can be raised by motion, our definition of a pleading can't include all documents that assert claims and defenses; hence we've said that pleadings include only certain documents that constitute claims or defenses. We'll turn to a discussion of motions in just a moment, but for now we'll clarify our basic definition of a pleading. A **pleading** will be defined to be any one of the documents listed in Rule 7(a), each of which represents an assertion by a party as to that party's legal and factual positions on matters at issue, made in anticipation of trial, requiring

**Figure 7–2    Precise Definition of the Term "Pleading"**

> A *pleading* is any one of the documents listed in Rule 7(a) of the FRCP, each of which represents an *assertion* by a party as to that party's legal and factual positions on matters at issue, made in anticipation of trial, requiring resolution at trial, and immediately operative for the purpose of defining the matters at issue without any need of further court order.

resolution at trial, and immediately operative for the purpose of defining the matters at issue without any need of further court order (see Figure 7–2).

The complaints we prepared in the last chapter, then, were assertions by Harry Hampton and Widgets and Gizmos, Inc. as to certain alleged causes of action, made in anticipation of trial, requiring resolution at trial, and requiring no further order of the court to become operative. The party filing a complaint is simply stating, "This is the way I think the facts and law line up, this is the relief to which I think I am entitled, and I shall prove it at trial and win." An answer (which is another pleading, to be discussed in detail in the next chapter) is similarly an assertion in anticipation of trial. In the answer, the defendant is stating, "This is the way *I* see the facts and law lining up, and I shall prove it at trial and win."

## Motions Attacking the Pleadings

What if some aspect of the assertions in a complaint or answer appears to be legally deficient in some way? What then? Does the opposing party have to go through the time and expense of a trial before getting the opportunity to address the alleged deficiencies? Or is there some way to attack allegedly deficient assertions before trial? The answer is: alleged deficiencies can be attacked in the pretrial motion process.

An example is helpful here. Assume the defendant believes that the manner in which the plaintiff has asserted his or her causes of action in the complaint violates certain rules of pleading. The complaint may be unacceptably vague, for example, or may contain language that is inflammatory; or the plaintiff may have failed to allege all the necessary elements of the cause of action asserted. Under such circumstances, the defendant is authorized by the rules of procedure to file a motion that (1) points out the alleged deficiencies to the court, and (2) requests a court order that either requires the plaintiff to modify the complaint to bring it into compliance with proper procedures, or dismisses the complaint or certain deficient portions of it.

We just defined a pleading as an assertion requiring no further court order to become operative. Our discussion reveals that a motion *does* require a court order to become operative; indeed, as we noted in Chapter 1, a **motion** is, by definition, a request to a court for an order of some sort. This is a key distinction to remember: a pleading is an *assertion*; a motion is a *request* requiring an *order* (see Figure 7–3).

**Figure 7–3    Key Distinction Between a "Pleading" and a "Motion"**

> A pleading is an *assertion* requiring no further court order to become operative; a motion is a *request* requiring an *order* to become operative.

The motion attacking a pleading is a powerful and important weapon. It provides an opportunity (if the court can be convinced that the motion should be granted) to influence the content of an opposing party's pleadings. Used properly, pretrial motions lead to pleadings that unambiguously and fairly state legitimate contentions, thereby paving the way for an efficient and equitable trial. We'll explore the details of motions attacking the pleadings in Section 7–4.

Not all motions attack the pleadings. Many motions seek an order of the court on some other aspect of the case. We discuss motions in general in Section 7–3, but first let's examine the initial steps and considerations that immediately follow the filing and service of a complaint, even before motions are filed.

## 7–2 The Appearance, Deadlines, Defaults, and Removal

Harry Hampton and Widgets and Gizmos, Inc. have taken the leap—lawsuits have been filed.

Somewhere sit Judith Johnson and Bernard Lindquist, and also President Emily Tapman of TapTapTap, Inc., each staring at a pile of papers—the summons and complaint. You now know that motions and other pleadings are likely to follow. But what, exactly, comes next?

### The Appearance

Think back to our discussion of the summons form. One of the purposes of the summons form was to summon the defendant to appear in court at a certain day or time to respond to the claims of the plaintiff. Does this mean that the defendant must literally show up at the courthouse? Generally speaking, no. The defendant must generally first file with the court a document called an **appearance**. An appearance might be a preprinted form, such as the form in Figure 7–4, or it might look similar to a pleading, such as the appearance in Figure 7–5. If the party is not represented by an attorney, he or she would generally fill out and file the appearance personally; such an appearance is called a *pro se* **appearance**, because a party who represents himself or herself without an attorney is called a *pro se* **party**.

The defendant, however, will in most cases be represented by an attorney. In such situations, the attorney fills out and files the appearance, thereby officially establishing the representation in the eyes of the court.

It is not always necessary to file a separate appearance form. Appearances are usually automatically entered for the attorney signing a complaint; look closely, for example, at Figure 6–14 (p. 138). Under the rules of some courts, appearances are also automatically entered for a defendant when a responsive pleading or motion is filed, so that no formal appearance form need be prepared. Under the rules of other courts, however, attorneys are not authorized to sign or file documents with the court unless and until a separate appearance form is filed. The applicable rules can even vary between different U.S. District Courts; you and your supervising attorney must learn and follow the specific provisions that apply to your cases.

Where appearance forms are required, sometimes an entire firm can file a single appearance; any attorney in that firm is thereafter authorized to sign and file documents with the court relating to that case. Sometimes each attorney, even from the same firm, must file a separate appearance form. Again, you must check the specific rules that apply to each case.

**Figure 7–4 Preprinted State Court Appearance Form**

---

**APPEARANCE**　　　　STATE OF EXURBIA
**SUPERIOR COURT**

**INSTRUCTIONS**

1. **Judicial District Court Locations:** *In any action returnable to a Judicial District court location, file only the original with the clerk.*
2. **Geographical Area or Juvenile Matters Court Locations:** *In any action returnable to a Geographical Area or Juvenile Matters court location, except criminal actions, file original and sufficient copies for each party to the action with the clerk.*
3. *If a party who has been defaulted for failure to appear files an appearance prior to the entry of judgment after default, the default shall automatically be set aside by the clerk.*

| DOCKET NO. |
| --- |
| RETURN DATE |

**TO: The Superior Court**

NAME OF CASE *(FIRST-NAMED PLAINTIFF VS. FIRST-NAMED DEFENDANT)*

☐ Judicial District　☐ Housing Session　☐ G.A. No. _____

ADDRESS OF COURT *(No., street, town and zip code)*

**PLEASE ENTER THE APPEARANCE OF ▶**

NAME OF OFFICIAL, FIRM, PROFESSIONAL CORP., INDIVIDUAL ATTY., OR PRO SE PARTY

**MAILING ADDRESS** *(No., street, P.O. Box)*　　ATTY. REG. NO. *(If applicable)*

CITY/TOWN　　STATE　　ZIP CODE　　TELEPHONE NO.

**in the above-entitled case for:** *("X" appropriate box)*
☐ The Plaintiff.
☐ All Plaintiffs.
☐ The following Plaintiff(s) only: _____
☐ The Defendant.
☐ All Defendants.
☐ The following Defendant(s) only: _____

NOTE: *If other counsel have already appeared for the party or parties indicated above, state whether this appearance is:*
☐ *In lieu of appearance of attorney or firm* _____ *already on file (Pr. Bk. 65) OR*
　　　　　　　　　　　　　　　　　　*(Name)*
☐ *In addition to appearance already on file.*

SIGNED *(Individual attorney or pro se party)*　　PRINT OR TYPE NAME OF PERSON SIGNING AT LEFT　　DATE SIGNED
**X**

---

**CERTIFICATION**　　　　*FOR COURT USE ONLY*

*This certification must be completed in summary process cases (Pr. Bk. § 64 (c)); for "in-lieu-of" appearances (Pr. Bk. § 65); and in criminal cases (Pr. Bk. § 630).*

**I hereby certify that a copy of the above was mailed/delivered to:**
　☐ All counsel and pro se parties of record.
　　*(For summary process and criminal actions)*
　☐ Counsel or the party whose appearance is to be replaced.
　　*(For "in-lieu-of" appearances)*

SIGNED *(Individual attorney or pro se party)*　　DATE COPY(IES) MAILED/DELIVERED

**APPEARANCE**

*Source:* Adapted from Official Connecticut State Superior Court forms.

Appearances once were commonly divided into two categories, general appearances and special appearances. When a **general appearance** was filed, it was held to constitute an admission by the defendant that the court had personal jurisdiction over him or her. If the defendant wanted to contest the existence of personal jurisdiction, he or she had to file a **special appearance,** which enabled him or her to appear before the court for the sole purpose of contesting jurisdiction. Most courts have done away with this distinction,

**Figure 7–5  Appearance with Caption**

United States District Court
for the
District of Exurbia

WIDGETS AND GIZMOS, INC.

Plaintiff

    vs.

TAPTAPTAP, INC.

Defendant

Civil Action No. 93-OWH-00543

October 29, 1993

#### Appearance

Please enter the appearance of attorney Tim Tiptop of the law firm of Tiptop and Towe, 71 Ferguson Street, Metro City, Exurbia, on behalf of defendant *TapTapTap, Inc.*

THE DEFENDANT, *TapTapTap, Inc.*

By: _____
    Tim Tiptop, Esq.
    Its attorney
    Tiptop and Towe
    71 Ferguson Street
    Metro City, Exurbia 12345
    Atty. Reg. #: 65488
    Phone: (901) 333-3333

#### Certificate of Service

This is to certify that a copy of the foregoing Appearance was mailed, postage prepaid, this 29th day of October, 1993, to Sam Superlawyer, Esq., Lincoln & Hoover, 123 Lincoln Street, Metro City, Exurbia, 12345.

_____
       Tim Tiptop, Esq.

allowing for only one category of appearance and eliminating the admission as to personal jurisdiction. Such modern practice allows the appearing defendant to contest personal jurisdiction even after filing the appearance form. Again, check the specific rules of the court system in which your case is pending.

There is no provision of the FRCP that directly regulates procedure for appearances; the issue is usually covered by the local rules of the particular U.S. District Court. You should review both your local federal rule regarding appearances and your state court procedure.

## Deadlines

There are few things more important to a litigation practitioner than **deadlines.** The rules establish clear time periods by which certain steps after the filing of the

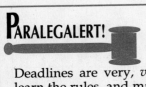

## PARALEGALERT!

Deadlines are very, *very* important! You must learn the rules, and master the manner in which they are applied by the courts.

complaint are to be taken. You must learn these rules, and master the manner in which they are applied by the courts.

The first relevant deadline is that associated with the appearance form; in some courts, the rules hold that an appearance must be filed within a certain specified number of days of the service of the complaint. As noted already, in some courts the requirement for entering an appearance is satisfied by the filing of a responsive pleading.

Federal Rule 12(a) establishes a basic deadline of 20 days from service to file a responsive pleading to a previous pleading stating a claim. As we discuss further in section 7–4, this deadline is modified if a motion attacking the previous pleading is filed within the same deadline. For the moment, however, let us briefly address an issue that arises once a deadline is identified, be it a deadline associated with the pleadings, or a deadline associated with some other aspect of the litigation process, such as discovery: how does one compute the exact day on which a deadline expires?

The answer is found in Rule 6(a) of the FRCP, relating to computation of time and quoted in pertinent part in Figure 7–6. The basic rules established by Rule 6(a) are:

1. Don't count the day of the action from which the period starts to run.
2. The last day is included, unless it is a Saturday, Sunday, legal holiday, or a day on which weather has made the clerk's office inaccessible.
3. If the deadline allows for fewer than 11 days, Saturdays, Sundays, and legal holidays that fall within the period are excluded.

Examples of this rule in actual use are provided in Figure 7–7.

Rules and cases that establish deadlines, and the means of computing deadlines, are obviously very important, and you should be sure to master the specifics. We've provided a brief discussion of the applicable federal provision; be sure to review your corresponding state provision. It's also useful to apply "worst-case analysis" when calculating deadlines, a method we discuss further in Section 7–7 on "Practical Considerations."

### Defaults

Suppose 20 days pass after the service of a federal court complaint prepared by your firm, and your opponent fails to file a responsive pleading. Is there anything you can do to press the issue? Yes, you can seek a default.

**Figure 7–6  Rule 6(a) of the FRCP in Pertinent Part**

> **Rule 6. Time.**
> (a) COMPUTATION. In computing any period of time...the day of the act, event, or default from which the designated period of time begins to run shall not be included. The last day of the period so computed shall be included, unless it is a Saturday, a Sunday, or a legal holiday, or, when the act to be done is the filing of a paper in court, a day on which weather or other conditions have made the office of the clerk of the district court inaccessible, in which event the period runs until the end of the next day which is not one of the aforementioned days. When the period of time prescribed or allowed is less than 11 days, intermediate Saturdays, Sundays, and legal holidays shall be excluded in the computation...

**Figure 7–7    Examples of Deadline Computation Applying Rule 6(a) of the FRCP**

| | |
|---|---|
| *Action taken:* | Wednesday, November 4, 1992 |
| *Time limit:* | 20 days |
| *Special considerations:* | Wednesday, November 11, 1992 is Veterans Day |
| *Deadline:* | Tuesday, November 24, 1992 |

*Analysis:* The day of the act is not counted. Thus beginning with November 5 as "Day 1," the twentieth day counted is November 24. Since, under the rule, the "last day of the period so computed shall be included," the deadline falls at the end of the day on November 24, the twentieth day. Although there are Saturdays, Sundays, and Veterans Day falling during the period in question, since the time limit is not "less than 11 days" such intermediate "off" days are *not* excluded when making the calculation.

| | |
|---|---|
| *Action taken:* | Monday, November 2, 1992 |
| *Time limit:* | 20 days |
| *Special considerations:* | November 11 is Veterans Day |
| *Deadline:* | November 23, 1992 |

*Analysis:* Applying the same method used in the preceding example, the twentieth day is computed to be Sunday, November 22. If the last day of the period is on a Sunday, even if the time limit is 20 days, the deadline does not expire until the end of the next day which is not a Saturday, Sunday, holiday, or bad-weather day.

| | |
|---|---|
| *Action taken:* | Monday, November 2, 1992 |
| *Time limit:* | 10 days |
| *Special considerations:* | November 11 is Veterans Day |
| *Deadline:* | Tuesday, November 17, 1992 |

*Analysis:* Because the time limit is less than 11 days, five days will be excluded in our calculation: Saturday, November 7; Sunday, November 8; the holiday, Wednesday, November 11; Saturday, November 14; Sunday, November 15. Omitting these days, counting from November 3 as "Day 1," the tenth day counted is November 17. The deadline in this case expires at the end of the day on November 17, 1992.

| | |
|---|---|
| *Action taken:* | Monday, November 2, 1992 |
| *Time limit:* | 10 days |
| *Special considerations:* | November 11 is Veterans Day; November 12 a blizzard closed the courthouse |
| *Deadline:* | Tuesday, November 17, 1992 |

*Analysis:* Exactly the same as the preceding example. Weather conditions creating an inaccessible courthouse are only relevant if the courthouse is closed on the day the deadline expires; under such circumstances the deadline would fall at the end of the next day which is not a Saturday, Sunday, holiday, or bad weather day. If the blizzard had occurred on Tuesday, November 17, 1992, for example, the deadline would have expired at the end of the day on Wednesday, November 18, 1992.

| NOVEMBER 1992 | | | | | | |
|---|---|---|---|---|---|---|
| **SUN** | **MON** | **TUES** | **WED** | **THURS** | **FRI** | **SAT** |
| 1 | 2 | 3 | 4 | 5 | 6 | 7 |
| 8 | 9 | 10 | 11 | 12 | 13 | 14 |
| 15 | 16 | 17 | 18 | 19 | 20 | 21 |
| 22 | 23 | 24 | 25 | 26 | 27 | 28 |
| 29 | 30 | | | | | |

Let's first address what is meant, substantively, by the term *default*. A **default** is an official recognition by the court of a failure by a party against whom a claim has been asserted to "plead or otherwise defend" in response to the claim (see Rule 55 of the FRCP). Examples of situations that justify the entry of a default would include: (1) the failure of a defendant to file either an appearance or a responsive pleading within 20 days after receipt of the complaint; (2) the failure of a defendant who has filed an appearance to file a responsive pleading (or a Rule 12 motion, as we'll discuss in Section 7–4) within 20 days of receipt of the complaint; and (3) the failure of a plaintiff to file a responsive pleading within 20 days of receipt of a counterclaim asserted by a defendant. We discuss counterclaims further in Chapter 8.

How does one obtain a default against an opposing party in federal court? The circumstances justifying the entry of the default must be brought to the attention of the court "by affidavit or otherwise," after which "the clerk shall enter the party's default" (see Rule 55). This is usually done by filing a document called a Request to the Clerk for Entry of Default (see Figure 7–8), often accompanied by an affidavit of counsel as to the circumstances justifying the default (see Figure 7–9, indicating that defendant TapTapTap, Inc. has filed neither an appearance nor a responsive pleading).

What does the entry of a default mean? As we noted previously, it represents an official recognition by the court that the party against whom it has been entered is culpable for the failure "to plead or otherwise defend." If a default is entered by the clerk, and the party against whom the default was entered takes no action to correct the deficiency, the next procedural step is usually for the original party to seek a judgment based upon the default, which would end the need for a trial (see Rule 55(b)). Defaults can thus be serious problems for the party against whom they are granted; we discuss default judgments further in Chapter 10.

Default procedures in state courts may differ from the federal procedure. Sometimes the default is requested by a motion for an order from a judge, rather than by a request addressed to the clerk; sometimes the scope of wrongful behavior that justifies the entry of default is broader (extending to failures to respond in a timely manner to the opposing party's discovery requests, for example). Be sure to review your state's procedure with regard to defaults.

## Removal

In our discussion of federal courts in Section 1–4, we noted that one of the justifications for federal diversity jurisdiction was the danger that the more parochial state courts might be biased against an out-of-state party; hence some recourse to the federal courts, with their national perspective, was desirable. That's fine for protecting the interests of the plaintiff, since the plaintiff initially decides in what court to file the complaint. But what about the defendant? Suppose a defendant who is sued by a plaintiff in a state court would rather have the issues decided in a federal court? Does the defendant have any recourse?

Yes. The **removal** procedure provides the vehicle by which a defendant can have the entire lawsuit transferred from the state court to the federal court for the district in which the state court is located. Removal to federal court is not, however, available in every case filed in state court. The federal court must have concurrent jurisdiction over the dispute. In other words, there must be a jurisdictional basis for the removal, such as the presence of diversity of citizenship or a controversy over a federal statutory or constitutional issue, which would have justified the plaintiff's starting the lawsuit in the federal court in the first place.

**Figure 7–8   Request to the Clerk for Entry of Default in *Widgets and Gizmos, Inc.* Case**

United States District Court
for the
District of Exurbia

WIDGETS AND GIZMOS, INC.          :

    Plaintiff          :

                        Civil Action No. 93-OWH-00543

    vs.          :

                        November 20, 1993

TAPTAPTAP, INC.          :

    Defendant          :

                        :

### Request to the Clerk
### for Entry of Default

TO THE CLERK:

    More than 20 days having expired since service of the summons and complaint upon the defendant *TapTapTap, Inc.*, and said defendant having filed neither an appearance nor a pleading, nor having otherwise made effort to defend this action, the plaintiff *Widgets and Gizmos, Inc.* hereby requests that a default be entered against said defendant *TapTapTap, Inc.* under Rule 55 of the Federal Rules of Civil Procedure. The Affidavit of Sam Superlawyer accompanies this Request.

                    THE PLAINTIFF, *Widgets and Gizmos, Inc.*

        By: _____
               Samuel Superlawyer, Esq.
               Its attorney
               Lincoln & Hoover
               123 Lincoln Street
               Metro City, Exurbia 12345
               Atty. Reg. #: 87654
               Phone: (901) 222-2222

### Entry of Default

    The foregoing Request for Entry of Default having been presented to this Court, and it appearing to the Clerk that defendant *TapTapTap, Inc.* has failed to appear, plead, or otherwise defend, DEFAULT is hereby entered against the defendant *TapTapTap, Inc.*

                        THE COURT

        By: _____
             Clerk

        Date: _____

 

The basic procedure relating to removal is set forth in 28 U.S.C. §1446. Removal is accomplished by filing a Notice of Removal with the federal court, containing a "short and plain statement of the grounds for removal . . . ." Accompanying the Notice of Removal should be "a copy of all process, pleadings, and orders served upon such defendant or defendants in such action." Opposing parties, as well as the original state court, must be notified.

United States District Court
for the
District of Exurbia

WIDGETS AND GIZMOS, INC.                    :

    Plaintiff                                        :

    vs.                                              Civil Action No. 93-OWH-00543

                                                     November 20, 1993

TAPTAPTAP, INC.                             :

    Defendant                                        :

                                                     :

### Affidavit of Samuel Superlawyer

The affiant, Samuel Superlawyer, being duly sworn, hereby deposes and says as follows:

1.  I am the attorney for *Widgets and Gizmos, Inc.*, the plaintiff in the above-captioned matter.

2.  I am over the age of eighteen years and understand the obligation of an oath.

3.  By summons and complaint dated October 21, 1993, the plaintiff *Widgets and Gizmos, Inc.* commenced the above-captioned action against the defendant, *TapTapTap, Inc.*

4.  The defendant returned the "Acknowledgment of Receipt of Summons and Complaint" pursuant to Rule 4 of the Federal Rules of Civil Procedure, with a signature of the President of the defendant *TapTapTap, Inc.* and a date of October 25, 1993.

5.  The defendant has to date filed neither an appearance nor a pleading, and has failed to make any effort to defend this action.

6.  The defendant, *TapTapTap, Inc.*, is a corporation and hence is not in the military service of the United States. As a corporation, defendant *TapTapTap, Inc.* is neither an incompetent person nor an infant.

                    _____
                    Samuel Superlawyer, Esq.
                    Attorney for
                    *Widgets and Gizmos, Inc.*

Subscribed and sworn to before me, this the _____
day of _____, 1994.

_____
Ms. Nadine Nemeth
Notary Public of the State of Exurbia
Commission expires: _____

Most aspects of a case in which removal is indicated will be closely monitored by your supervising attorney. You should be generally aware of the removal option, however, as well as deadlines associated with it. There is one basic deadline, and one exception to this basic deadline, to keep in mind. The basic deadline requires that the Notice for Removal be filed within 30 days of the

**Figure 7–10   Summary of Removal Deadlines**

> (1) Where the basis for federal jurisdiction is present in the original complaint, the Notice of Removal must be filed within thirty days of the receipt of the complaint.
>
> (2) Where the initial pleading creating the concurrent federal jurisdiction is filed subsequent to the original complaint, and the basis for the federal jurisdiction is something other than diversity, the Notice of Removal must be filed within thirty days of the receipt of that pleading.
>
> (3) Where the initial pleading creating the concurrent federal jurisdiction is filed subsequent to the original complaint, and the basis for the federal jurisdiction is diversity, the Notice of Removal must be filed within *both* thirty days of the receipt of that pleading and one year of the commencement of the underlying lawsuit. If more than one year has passed since the commencement of the lawsuit, removal is no longer available.

receipt by the defendant of the "initial pleading" that justified removal. The "initial pleading" would usually be the complaint filed at the beginning of a lawsuit. But if a plaintiff who commenced a lawsuit in state court originally alleged only a state cause of action, then later filed an amended complaint alleging a new cause of action based upon a federal statute, the removal deadline would be within 30 days after receipt by the defendant of the amended complaint, since the amended complaint was the "initial pleading" that established the right of removal.

Thus, the basic deadline associated with removal is 30 days after the party seeking removal receives the initial pleading establishing the right of removal. The exception to this basic deadline arises in a situation in which an amended complaint creates a right to remove based only upon newly established diversity jurisdiction. Such a situation would arise when an amended complaint drops a cause of action against a former defendant who spoiled complete diversity. The remaining defendant has the right, under such circumstances, to remove the case to federal court within 30 days of receipt of the initial pleading that established the right to remove, unless (here's the exception) more than one year has passed since commencement of the original action. Thus, if an amended complaint drops the "spoiling" defendant 12½ months after the original complaint, removal is impossible. You should note that the exception applies only to diversity situations; thus, if an amended complaint filed 12½ months after commencement of the original action includes a new cause of action based on a federal statute, removal is allowed if the notice is filed within 30 days. These situations are summarized in Figure 7–10.

Removal can be complicated; we've given you only a sample of the most important points. You should review sections 1441–1452 of Title 28 of the United States Code (which establish the detailed application of the removal option), and be sure to work only under the close guidance of your supervising attorney if a removal question arises.

## 7–3   Motions in General

We noted in Section 7–1 that not all motions attack the pleadings. Let's turn for a moment to a general consideration of this creature called a "motion," and discuss some characteristics that apply both to motions that attack the pleadings and all other motions as well.

**Figure 7-11    Rule 7(b) of the FRCP Concerning Motions**

> **Rule 7. Pleadings Allowed; Form of Motions.**
>
> (a) * * *
>
> (b) MOTIONS AND OTHER PAPERS
>    (1) An application to the court for an order shall be by motion which, unless made during a hearing or trial, shall be made in writing, shall state with particularity the grounds therefor, and shall set forth the relief or order sought. The requirement of writing is fulfilled if the motion is stated in a written notice of the hearing of the motion.
>    (2) The rules applicable to captions and other matters of form of pleadings apply to all motions and other papers provided for by these rules.
>    (3) All motions shall be signed in accordance with Rule 11.

First of all, what does a motion look like? There is no absolute answer to that question. The format for motions in the federal courts is determined in part by Rule 7 of the FRCP, and in part by the local rules established in each district, so there is some minor variance from one district to the next. In Figure 7-11 we show Rule 7(b) of the FRCP. In Figure 7-12, we show a sample local rule from the U.S. District Court for the District of Exurbia; subsection (a) of that rule discusses format. State rules as to motion format, of course, vary from state to state. Generally speaking, motions are similar in appearance to pleadings, containing a caption, a designation, numbered paragraphs, a signature block, and a certification. But a motion may also contain, or be accompanied by, several other items that a pleading doesn't have: a proposed order; a request for oral argument; a notice of hearing or notice of motion; and a supporting memorandum or brief.

In the remainder of this section, we discuss these general characteristics of motions in the context of a simple, commonly seen motion: the Motion for Extension of Time. Our choice of this motion as the means for exploring the general characteristics of motions is not made randomly; it often becomes relevant early in the litigation process, when a responsive pleading will soon be due under Rule 12, and thus fits logically into our factual chronology as well.

Assume that the current status of the Widgets and Gizmos, Inc. case is as follows: the complaint has been filed and served, and the appearance form seen in Figure 7-5 has been filed by TapTapTap, Inc.'s attorney. The federal procedural rules require that a response to the complaint must be filed by the defendant within 20 days after the complaint was served; let's further assume, however, that the attorneys for TapTapTap, Inc. recognize that they cannot analyze the complicated issues presented by this matter and prepare a proper response before the deadline expires. Is there anything they can do to avoid the entry of a default? The answer is yes, they can file the **Motion for Extension of Time** seen in Figure 7-13.

Let's take a look at the general characteristics of this motion. As we have noted, it resembles a pleading in basic format, with such components as a caption, designation, signature block, and certification (see Rule 7(b)(2) of the FRCP). Although the single paragraph that makes up the body of the motion is not numbered, that is because there is only one paragraph; if there were more than one paragraph, the rules of the federal courts, as those of most jurisdictions, would have required that the paragraphs be numbered (again, see Rule 7(b)(2) of the FRCP).

There are other characteristics of the motion in Figure 7-13, however, that differentiate it from a pleading. Consider, for example, the notation at the bottom of the first page of the motion: "No oral argument is requested." The rules generally allow the opposing parties on a pending motion to come to

**Figure 7–12   Sample Local Rule Regarding Motion Practice**

---

*The following appears in the local rules of the United States District Court for the District of Exurbia:*

**Rule 9.   Motion Procedures.**

(a) FORMAT. All motions shall be double-spaced on 8.5" x 11" paper, with a left margin of at least 1" free from all typewritten or printed material and shall have legibly typed at the end of the motion, directly beneath the signature of the attorney or party filing the motion, the name of the counsel or party, along with address, phone number, and Exurbia attorney registration number. Each motion shall have a caption including all the information required on pleadings.

(b) PROCEDURES. All motions should indicate on the bottom left-hand corner of the first page whether oral argument is requested, and should contain a proposed order. Any motion which involves disputed issues of law and which is not uncontested shall be accompanied by a written memorandum of law. Such memorandum shall include a separate caption and signature line, containing the same information specified in paragraph (a) of this rule, and shall not exceed forty pages without permission of the court.

(c) OPPOSITION TO MOTION. If there is opposition to the granting of a motion, other than a motion for extension of time, a written memorandum of law in opposition shall be filed within 21 days of the filing of the original motion. The memorandum in opposition shall indicate on the bottom left-hand corner of the first page whether oral argument is requested. Any memorandum in opposition which fails to so indicate shall be rejected and returned to the filing party or counsel forthwith by the clerk. If oral argument was not requested by the party filing the motion but is desired by the party opposing the motion, then in addition to so indicating on the memorandum in opposition the party opposing the motion shall also file, within five days of the receipt of the motion, a Notice of Intent to Argue.

(d) MOTIONS FOR EXTENSION. All motions for extension of time shall include a statement of the moving counsel that he or she has inquired of opposing counsel whether there is agreement or objection to the motion, or that, despite diligent effort, he or she cannot ascertain opposing counsel's position. Agreement of counsel as to any extension of time does not require that the motion be granted. Motions for extension of time may be granted in an *ex parte* fashion. Memorandums in opposition to a motion for extension of time must be filed within five days of the filing of the motion for extension. If a motion for extension is granted prior to the filing of the memorandum in opposition, opposing counsel may move to set aside the order within five days of the signing of the order.

(e) PROOF OF SERVICE. Proof of service of motions, supporting memorandums, and memorandums in opposition may be made by written acknowledgment of such service by the attorney or party filing the motion by a certificate of service identifying the person or persons who were served with a copy, the manner in which service was made, and the date of service.

---

court and argue, in front of the judge, their respective positions on the merits of the motion. The rules often further require that the motion must indicate on its face whether or not *oral argument* is desired by the party filing the motion (see section (b) of the rule in Figure 7–12). This indication is made by including on the motion a notation called a **request for oral argument.** If the motion fails to indicate whether or not oral argument is desired, the clerk's office in a state court case might actually reject the motion, sending it back to the party that prepared it, on the grounds that it fails to comply with the strict requirements of the motion rules. The clerk in a federal court can no longer reject a motion or other

**P**ARALEGALERT!

Details as to motion format requirements, such as placement of oral argument requests, are important. Failure to satisfy precisely the requirements of the rules can lead to rejection of your motion by a state court clerk's office, which can be devastating if a deadline has passed before the omission is remedied. You must be meticulous about details!

**Figure 7–13 Motion for Extension of Time in *Widgets and Gizmos, Inc.* Case**

United States District Court
for the
District of Exurbia

WIDGETS AND GIZMOS, INC.     :

    Plaintiff          :

    vs.              :

TAPTAPTAP, INC.         :

    Defendant     :

                    :

Civil Action No. 93-OWH-00543

November 9, 1993

### Motion for Extension of Time

The undersigned counsel for the defendant *TapTapTap, Inc.* hereby moves the court for an order extending the time for filing a response to the complaint to November 20, 1993. The undersigned counsel was not retained by the defendant until November 8, 1993, and thus additional time is needed in order to prepare an appropriate response. Counsel for the plaintiff has been contacted with regard to the subject matter of this motion, and has no objection to its being granted.

THE DEFENDANT, *TapTapTap, Inc.*

By: _____
    Tim Tiptop, Esq.
    Its attorney
    Tiptop and Towe
    71 Ferguson Street
    Metro City, Exurbia 12345
    Atty. Reg. #: 65488
    Phone: (901) 333-3333

### Order

The foregoing Motion for Extension having been heard by this Court, it is hereby ORDERED:        Granted / Denied

THE COURT

By: _____
    Judge

### Certificate of Service

This is to certify that a copy of the foregoing Motion for Extension was mailed, postage prepaid, this 9th day of November, 1993, to attorney Sam Superlawyer, 123 Lincoln Street, Metro City, Exurbia, 12345.

NO ORAL ARGUMENT    _____
    IS REQUESTED        Tim Tiptop, Esq.

document based on failure to follow proper format requirements (see the 1991 amendment to Rule 5(e) of the FRCP), but the judge might refuse to grant such a motion if the format is improper. Thus, you should remain vigilant as to the details surrounding federal court motions as well. With regard to our sample motion, since the issue posed (namely, the request for an extension of time to file a responsive pleading) is quite simple, oral argument has not been requested.

Sometimes the opposing party may desire oral argument on a motion to which the original filing party did not request oral argument. The applicable procedural rules include a provision by which an opposing party can make a request for oral argument; usually there are strict deadlines associated with making such a request, and, as with every other deadline, you must be careful to identify the requirements and comply with them (see section (c) of Figure 7–12).

As we've defined a motion, it cannot become operative without a court order. An **order** is a ruling of the court either granting or denying the motion, or granting it in part and denying it in part. Many jurisdictions require that the parties file, along with their motion, a **proposed order,** identifying the relief sought and leaving space for the court either to grant or deny the motion. For some simple motions, such as our Motion for Extension, the proposed order is extremely brief. All that is required in such cases is a short reference to the order sought (e.g., "The foregoing motion is ordered: granted/denied," with the judge having the authority to grant it or deny it) and a space for the judge's signature and the date. As you will see in Sections 7–4 and 7–5, certain motions are quite complicated; for more complicated motions, the proposed orders that accompany them may be complicated as well. Under the rules of some courts, a proposed order is not required; all that is needed is a reference in the motion itself to the relief sought (see, for example, Rule 7(b)(1) of the FRCP, which allows a party either to identify the relief sought or to set forth the order sought).

Another consideration that applies to motions is whether they are contested or uncontested. A **contested** motion is one in which the parties disagree about whether the motion should be granted; an **uncontested** motion is one in which there is no opposition to the granting of the motion. Motions for extension are often uncontested; opposing parties, as a courtesy to each other and in recognition of the difficulties inherent in the litigation process, often agree beforehand, in phone conversations or letters exchanged between counsel, not to oppose each other's reasonable requests for additional time to complete required steps. The courts will sometimes automatically grant motions for extensions where there is no objection, but not always; look carefully at section (d) of our Exurbia local federal rule in Figure 7–12 to see how such motions are handled in Exurbia.

Let's assume that TapTapTap, Inc.'s attorney has called you or your supervising attorney seeking agreement to a Motion for Extension. Let's also assume that you find the request for additional time to be, for some reason, unjustifiable. Perhaps previous extensions have already been granted, and circumstances do not demonstrate any justification for further delay. You refuse to agree to the granting of the motion; thus, this will now be a contested motion. What happens next?

Look again at section (b) of our local rule for Exurbia. It contains the following provision: "Any motion that involves disputed issues of law and that is not uncontested shall be accompanied by a written memorandum of law." Thus, TapTapTap, Inc.'s attorney must file a **memorandum of law** (also called a **brief**) in support of the position taken in the motion. In order to do this, research will have to be conducted to find relevant judicial opinions, statutes, or other applicable law. After the motion and brief are filed, your supervising attorney will be

# PARALEGALERT!

Contested motions are usually accompanied by a written memorandum of law, and are responded to by a memorandum of law in opposition.

given the opportunity to file a memorandum or brief in opposition to that filed by TapTapTap, Inc.'s attorney.

The format for a brief or memorandum of law is similar to that of pleadings and motions: caption, designation, signature block, and certificate of service will generally be included.

Briefs or memoranda relating to issues raised by pending motions can be extensive. As you can see, the Exurbia local rule limits such briefs to 40 pages; but if the circumstances justify it, the court will allow longer briefs. In addition, supporting materials are often filed to accompany the brief; for example, there may be relevant documents, transcripts, or affidavits that bolster or illuminate the contentions raised by the motion and the brief. The motion for extension that we have been discussing would be unlikely to engender lengthy briefs; but as you will see, many of the more complicated motions may require lengthy and significant supporting briefs and materials.

Suppose a motion is filed and oral argument requested. Two actions must follow: oral argument must be scheduled, and all parties notified of the time and place of the hearing. These two actions are accomplished in different ways by different courts. Let's discuss a few possibilities.

Many court systems handle motion arguments by scheduling arguments in many pending cases to be heard at the same time, or on the same day (see, for example, Rule 78 of the FRCP). These so-called **motion days** or **motion calendars** are designed to handle the greatest number of oral arguments in the least amount of time, thereby maximizing efficiency. Several judges and courtrooms may be assigned, and the arguments may be prescreened by the judges or other court personnel in order to process them expeditiously. Sometimes the results are positive; on other occasions, the attorneys involved may wait in court for long periods of time for an argument to be heard by the court. In the federal courts, where cases are generally assigned to individual judges from start to finish, there may be a shorter motion calendar, unlike the unwieldy versions sometimes seen in state courts.

Other methods of scheduling oral argument are also seen. The judge may notify the party who filed the motion of the time and place for oral argument, and instruct that party to serve a **Notice of Hearing** on the other parties a certain number of days before the argument. The court may also schedule the argument so that it will be heard individually (rather than as part of a large calendar), after sending notices to all the parties. Because there is such a variety of possibilities, we end our discussion of the generalities by simply warning you that it is very important to learn the specific procedures used by the courts in which your cases are pending.

**PARALEGALERT!**

You must check the applicable local rules and inquire of your supervising attorney about local practices with regard to the scheduling of motions. Scheduling procedures vary from one court system to the next, and even sometimes among individual judges within the same court system. You must be aware of the specific methods affecting pending cases.

## 7–4   Motions Attacking the Pleadings

We now turn to that special and very important group of motions, those attacking the pleadings. The rules that establish these motions enable the parties to challenge legally deficient pleadings, so that the assertions that ultimately remain in the pleadings (i.e., after the issues presented by the motions are decided by the court) relate to clearly defined and legitimate issues.

In order to understand motions attacking the pleadings, you must first understand the ways in which pleadings might fail to be clearly defined and legitimate. There are five ways in which a pleading might so fail:

1. The language employed is lacking, such that it leads to vagueness and ambiguity.
2. The language employed is excessive in a manner that requires modification or a deletion.
3. The court lacks the authority to render a decision on the issues presented.
4. The claim stated does not constitute a cause of action for which the legal system provides a remedy.
5. The claim cannot legitimately be evaluated unless other, indispensable parties are also brought into the lawsuit.

In the next several subsections, we address the manner in which Rule 12 of the FRCP provides a means for addressing each of these irregularities in federal court lawsuits. We will then add a few words about related state court procedures.

Before we begin with our discussion of these five specific areas, let's first discuss a few general considerations with regard to Rule 12 of the FRCP. The full text of the rule is reprinted in Figure 7–14. You should read Rule 12, from start to finish, before going any further, then refer back to it as we discuss various subparts of the rule.

In Rule 12(a), the basic pleading deadlines are established. An answer to the complaint must be made by a defendant "within 20 days after the service of the summons and complaint upon that defendant . . . ." Other deadlines with regard to counterclaims and cross-claims are identified as well; you will understand these more fully after reading Chapter 8. But take careful note of the last sentence of section (a), which establishes that a motion filed under the provisions of Rule 12 "alters these periods of time . . . ." If such a motion is filed, the requirement that an answer be filed is, in effect, suspended until the court takes some action on the motion. This makes sense, since it would be unfair to require a party to respond to a pleading that it alleges to be defective in some manner. Thus, as long as either an answer or a Rule 12 Motion is filed within 20 days after the service of the summons and complaint, the defendant can avoid the entry of a default.

Let's now begin our consideration of the five grounds for attacking a pleading (summarized in the chart in Figure 7–15).

> **P**ARALEGALERT!
>
> Although Rule 12 of the FRCP requires that an answer be filed "within 20 days after the service of the summons and complaint," the filing of a motion under Rule 12 suspends the deadline until the court takes some action on the motion.

## Vague or Ambiguous Pleadings

Rule 12(e) provides a procedure by which a party can attack an opposing pleading that is "so vague or ambiguous that a party cannot reasonably be required to frame a responsive pleading . . . ." The solution is to file a **Motion for More Definite Statement.** The motion "shall point out the defects complained of and the details desired." In other words, the motion must specify the ambiguity or vagueness, and suggest how it might be remedied. If such a motion is granted, and the defect not remedied within 10 days (or such other time as the court may fix) after notice of the granting, the court can "strike the pleading . . . or make such order as it deems just."

Figure 7–14    Rule 12 of the FRCP

**Rule 12.  Defenses and Objections—When and How Presented—By Pleadings or Motion—Motion for Judgment on Pleadings.**

(a)  WHEN PRESENTED. A defendant shall serve an answer within 20 days after the service of the summons and complaint upon that defendant, except when service is made under Rule 4(e) and a different time is prescribed in the order of court under the statute of the United States or in the statute or rule of court of the state. A party served with a pleading stating a cross-claim against that party shall serve an answer thereto within 20 days after the service upon that party. The plaintiff shall serve a reply to a counterclaim in the answer within 20 days after service of the answer or, if a reply is ordered by the court, within 20 days after service of the order, unless the order otherwise directs. The United States or an officer or agency thereof shall serve an answer to the complaint or to a cross-claim, or a reply to a counterclaim, within 60 days after the service upon the United States attorney of the pleading in which the claim is asserted. The service of a motion permitted under this rule alters these periods of time as follows, unless a different time is fixed by order of the court: (1) if the court denies the motion or postpones its disposition until the trial on the merits, the responsive pleading shall be served within 10 days after notice of the court's action; (2) if the court grants a motion for a more definite statement the responsive pleading shall be served within 10 days after the service of the more definite statement.

(b)  HOW PRESENTED. Every defense, in law or fact, to a claim for relief in any pleading, whether a claim, counterclaim, cross-claim, or third-party claim, shall be asserted in the responsive pleading thereto if one is required, except that the following defenses may at the option of the pleader be made by motion: (1) lack of jurisdiction over the subject matter, (2) lack of jurisdiction over the person, (3) improper venue, (4) insufficiency of process, (5) insufficiency of service of process, (6) failure to state a claim upon which relief can be granted, (7) failure to join a party under Rule 19. A motion making any of these defenses shall be made before pleading if a further pleading is permitted. No defense or objection is waived by being joined with one or more other defenses or objections in a responsive pleading or motion. If a pleading sets forth a claim for relief to which the adverse party is not required to serve a responsive pleading, the adverse party may assert at the trial any defense in law or fact to that claim for relief. If, on a motion asserting the defense numbered (6) to dismiss for failure of the pleading to state a claim upon which relief can be granted, matters outside the pleading are presented to and not excluded by the court, the motion shall be treated as one for summary judgment and disposed of as provided in Rule 56, and all parties shall be given reasonable opportunity to present all material made pertinent to such a motion by Rule 56.

(c)  MOTION FOR JUDGMENT ON THE PLEADINGS. After the pleadings are closed but within such time as not to delay the trial, any party may move for judgment on the pleadings. If, on a motion for judgment on the pleadings, matters outside the pleadings are presented to and not excluded by the court, the motion shall be treated as one for summary judgment and disposed of as provided in Rule 56, and all parties shall be given reasonable opportunity to present all material made pertinent to such a motion by Rule 56.

(d)  PRELIMINARY HEARINGS. The defenses specifically enumerated (1)–(7) in subdivision (b) of this rule, whether made in a pleading or by motion, and the motion for judgment mentioned in subdivision (c) of this rule shall be heard and determined before trial on application of any party, unless the court orders that the hearing and determination thereof be deferred until the trial.

(e)  MOTION FOR MORE DEFINITE STATEMENT. If a pleading to which a responsive pleading is permitted is so vague or ambiguous that a party cannot reasonably be required to frame a responsive pleading, the party may move for a more definite statement before interposing a responsive pleading. The motion shall point out the defects complained of and the details desired. If the motion is granted and the order of the court is not obeyed within 10 days after notice of the order or within such other time as the court may fix, the court may strike the pleading to which the motion was directed or make such order as it deems just.

(f)  MOTION TO STRIKE. Upon motion made by a party before responding to a pleading or, if no responsive pleading is permitted by these rules, upon motion made by a party within 20 days after the service of the pleading upon the party or upon the court's own initiative at any time, the court may order stricken from any pleading any insufficient defense or any redundant, immaterial, impertinent, or scandalous matter.

**Figure 7–14  Rule 12 of the FRCP, continued**

(g) CONSOLIDATION OF DEFENSES IN MOTION. A party who makes a motion under this rule may join with it any other motions herein provided for and then available to the party. If a party makes a motion under this rule but omits therefrom any defense or objection then available to the party which this rule permits to be raised by motion, the party shall not thereafter make a motion based on the defense or objection so omitted, except a motion as provided in subdivision (h)(2) hereof on any of the grounds there stated.

(h) WAIVER OR PRESERVATION OF CERTAIN DEFENSES.

(1)  A defense of lack of jurisdiction over the person, improper venue, insufficiency of process, or insufficiency of service of process is waived (A) if omitted from a motion in the circumstances described in subdivision (g), or (B) if it is neither made by motion under this rule nor included in a responsive pleading or an amendment thereof permitted by Rule 15(a) to be made as a matter of course.

(2)  A defense of failure to state a claim upon which relief can be granted, a defense of failure to join a party indispensable under Rule 19, and an objection of failure to state a legal defense to a claim may be made in any pleading permitted or ordered under Rule 7(a), or by motion for judgment on the pleadings, or at the trial on the merits.

(3)  Whenever it appears by suggestion of the parties or otherwise that the court lacks jurisdiction of the subject matter, the court shall dismiss the action.

Evaluating "vagueness" or "ambiguity" has some interrelation with our earlier discussion of fact-pleading versus notice-pleading. The FRCP generally requires only notice-pleading; hence a cause of action is not necessarily "vague" merely because it states the claim in a broad fashion. If a defendant is faced with a complaint that is broadly stated, but nevertheless sufficient to satisfy the notice-pleading requirement, further details may be sought through the discovery process. However, if the pleading or a portion of it is so vague or ambiguous that a response cannot be framed, then the Motion for More Definite Statement is justified.

A Motion for More Definite Statement can be used to attack any pleading "to which a responsive pleading is permitted . . . ." Look back at Rule 7, which identifies the pleadings permitted. No response to an answer is permitted unless

**Figure 7–15  Chart of Key Rule 12 Motions**

| Weakness in Pleading | Federal Motion Attacking Weakness | Corresponding Provision of FRCP |
|---|---|---|
| Vague or ambiguous claim for relief | Motion for More Definite Statement | Rule 12(e) |
| Excessive language: redundant, immaterial, impertinent, or scandalous | Motion to Strike | Rule 12(f) |
| Lack of judicial authority to decide issues | Motion to Dismiss | Rules 12(b)(1) through 12(b)(5) |
| Failure to allege a valid cause of action (i.e., "failure to state a claim on which relief can be granted") | Motion to Dismiss | Rule 12(b)(6) |
| Failure to name an indispensable party | Motion to Dismiss | Rule 12(b)(7) |

ordered by the court; thus, an answer cannot be attacked with a Motion for More Definite Statement. But suppose a plaintiff is faced with an answer that is so vague or ambiguous as to be unresponsive to the complaint? Is such a plaintiff left without a remedy?

No. Such a plaintiff could file a Request to the Clerk for Entry of Default, claiming that the defendant has failed to file a proper answer as required. The plaintiff might also file a Rule 12(f) Motion to Strike, asking the court to order stricken from the answer any defense of the defendant deemed "insufficient." Rule 12(f) motions are usually employed for a different purpose, however; let's turn to that purpose now.

## Excessive Language in Pleadings

Suppose, in the Widgets and Gizmos, Inc. complaint against TapTapTap, Inc., the complaint alleged that the "evil robber barons operating the foul corporation known as TapTapTap, Inc. have failed to honor their contract with Widgets and Gizmos, Inc." Or suppose the complaint repeated, far more often than was necessary, that the defendant TapTapTap, Inc. had breached its contract. Do the rules afford to TapTapTap, Inc. a means to insist that the issues be framed in less inflammatory or redundant language?

Yes, by filing a Rule 12(f) **Motion to Strike,** which allows a party to attack an opposing pleading (whether a responsive pleading is required or not) that is alleged to contain any "redundant, immaterial, impertinent, or scandalous matter." If granted, such a motion allows the party to eliminate repetitious, unimportant, irrelevant, or inflammatory language from the pleadings of an opposing party. You should note that, if the subject matter of the allegedly offensive pleading is itself arguably "scandalous," such would be acceptable; only if some extraneous "scandalous" language is inserted does the rule come into play.

## Lack of Judicial Authority

Suppose in a nondiversity matter filed in federal court, no federal statute or constitutional principle is at issue? Or suppose the plaintiff has filed the complaint in a federal court that does not have personal jurisdiction over the defendant (for example, if the defendant is an out-of-state corporation over which the applicable long-arm statute is insufficient to confer jurisdiction)? Or suppose that, although there is clearly federal court jurisdiction, the venue chosen doesn't satisfy the requirements of the applicable venue statute? What recourse does a defendant have in these situations?

The answer is found in one of the most important passages of the FRCP, Rule 12(b). Rule 12(b) relates to defenses to a "claim for relief." The term "claim for relief" is used because the rule is meant to apply not only to defenses to the complaint, but also to defenses to any of the three close cousins of a complaint (counterclaim; cross-claim; third-party complaint), which we will be discussing in more detail in Chapter 8, and which also contain claims for relief. A defense to a "claim for relief" is actually a defense to the entire cause of action underlying the claim for relief, whether that cause of action is stated in a complaint or in one of the three "close cousins."

In order to foster your understanding of Rule 12(b), we will discuss it in the context of the simplest situation, in which a defendant who has been served with a complaint is preparing to respond.

The basic principle established by Rule 12(b) is that all defenses are to be asserted in a responsive pleading (presumably the answer); but there is an exception to this basic principle, and it is the exception that is the key to understanding the importance of Rule 12(b). The exception relates to seven specifically identified defenses that may be asserted, either in a responsive pleading or in a motion, at the option of the pleader. We consider two of these seven in the next two subsections; here we consider the first five, which relate to defenses attacking the alleged authority of the court to administer the lawsuit, as follows:

1. Lack of jurisdiction over the subject matter;
2. Lack of jurisdiction over the person;
3. Improper venue;
4. Insufficiency of process; and
5. Insufficiency of service of process.

The first three of these defenses, relating to subject matter jurisdiction, personal jurisdiction, and venue, should be familiar to you by this point in your studies. They correspond to the three situations we posed at the beginning of this subsection. The next two, relating to process and service of process, cover situations where the summons and complaint, or the service of the summons and complaint, are alleged to have failed to comply with the required procedures that we identified in the last chapter. Because of the important exception identified by Rule 12(b), these defenses can be asserted not only in an answer, but also by motion.

This **Rule 12(b) Motion,** commonly called a **Motion to Dismiss,** is perhaps the most important of the motions attacking the pleadings. It goes beyond the Motion for More Definite Statement and Motion to Strike, which assert that the allegations of the complaint are a little vague, or that the language is somewhat excessive. The Motion to Dismiss asserts that some aspect of the summons and complaint (or the service of process) is defective to such an extent that the court should dismiss the case entirely. In the case of the first five defenses just identified, the allegation of the Motion to Dismiss is that the court either does not have jurisdiction to decide the claim asserted in the complaint, or does not satisfy the applicable venue requirement, hence the court must dismiss the case (or enter some other appropriate order, such as a transfer to a proper venue).

It is worthwhile here to consider, just for a moment, what we mean by a "dismissal." Dismissal of actions is treated in Rule 41 of the FRCP, and discussed in more detail in Chapter 10. For now, you should understand a **dismissal** to be an order of the court disallowing further litigation of the assertions made in the complaint, or some cause of action raised in the complaint. Dismissal can thus apply to an entire lawsuit, or to one or more pending counts in a lawsuit. When issuing an order that grants a Motion to Dismiss, judges often give to plaintiffs the right to amend the offending complaint to correct the defects that caused the dismissal. Such correction is not always possible when the defect is jurisdictional, but is more likely to be successful for some of the other situations that lead to a motion to dismiss.

Let's turn now to the sixth defense that can be asserted in a Motion to Dismiss, and investigate further the specifics of a Rule 12(b) motion.

## Failure to Allege Valid Cause of Action

The first five Rule 12(b) defenses we've just discussed (as to venue, jurisdiction, or service of process) do not arise very frequently. A Motion to Dismiss under Rule 12(b)(6), however, is often filed and is perhaps one of the two most important pretrial battlegrounds in a lawsuit (the other being the Motion for Summary Judgment, which we discuss in Chapter 10).

To what, exactly, does a Rule 12(b)(6) motion apply? It applies to a situation where the defendant alleges that some aspect of the underlying cause of action asserted by the plaintiff is so defective that, even if the plaintiff proves all the facts alleged, he or she will still fail to prevail at trial. In other words, even if everything the plaintiff has alleged were true, plaintiff still has no valid cause of action. To use the specific language of Rule 12(b)(6), the plaintiff in such a situation has failed "to state a claim on which relief can be granted . . . ."

The motion to dismiss for failure to state a claim on which relief can be granted was historically called a "demurrer." Although the FRCP, and the rules of most states, have done away with this term, you will still come across it in older judicial opinions, some of which retain precedential value; hence it is useful to recognize the term.

What sort of situations might justify a Rule 12(b)(6) motion? A plaintiff may have failed to allege all the essential elements of a cause of action; or the complaint may not have been filed before the applicable statute of limitations expired. In the first case, an amendment to the complaint, if allowed, might correct the defect, and the court may be willing to vacate the dismissal if such amendment is made in a timely fashion; in the second case, the plaintiff is probably out of luck.

Motions to dismiss under Rule 12(b)(6) can be complex, since the underlying causes of action, and their associated elements, may themselves be complex. The specifics of pleading requirements for various causes of action is beyond the scope of this book; but a sample Motion to Dismiss in a complicated matter appears in Figure 7–16. The memorandum or brief filed in support of this motion will probably be quite lengthy, as will the memorandum or brief filed in opposition.

## Failure to Name an Indispensable Party

We come now to the seventh and final defense that can be made by motion. Under Rule 12(b)(7), the defense that the complaint has failed "to join a party under Rule 19" can also be asserted in a Rule 12(b) Motion to Dismiss. This corresponds to the fifth potential manner in which a pleading might be defective: because the claims raised cannot be legitimately evaluated until some additional, indispensable parties are brought into the lawsuit. The subject of involving additional parties in a lawsuit is called **joinder** (which we discussed briefly in the last chapter); Rule 19 of the FRCP is entitled "Joinder of Persons Needed for Just Adjudication." Joinder issues and requirements relate to the desirability, or even necessity, of bringing all related claims and parties before the court in order to ensure a fair, as well as judicially efficient, resolution of pending issues.

It is unlikely that resolving joinder questions would be left to you, as a paralegal, since the legal issues involved are often complicated. You should, however, be able at least to identify a situation where joinder analysis is necessary. An example might be a case involving a three-party contract, where only two of the parties are currently before the court. We talk further about joinder in Chapter 8.

## Consolidation and/or Waiver of Rule 12 Defenses

Now that you've been introduced to all the various Rule 12 defenses and motions, we're going to ask you to make several assumptions. Assume first that

**Figure 7–16 Example of a More Complicated Motion to Dismiss in a Complex Case**

United States District Court
for the
District of Exurbia

JOHN Q. PUBLIC,             :

    Plaintiff              :

                              Civil Action No. 93-OWH-00112

      v.                 :

                              October 21, 1993

ABLE BROKERS, INC.      :
and SANDRA SANTIAGO,
    Defendants       :

### Motion to Dismiss

The defendants, Able Brokers, Inc. and Sandra Santiago, hereby move the court for an order dismissing the claims of the plaintiff, John Q. Public, on the following grounds:

1. as to each of the four counts of the complaint, the allegations fail to state a claim on which relief can be granted under rule 12(b)(6) of the Federal Rules of Civil Procedure (FRCP) in that the details of the alleged fraud have not been stated with the particularity required by Rule 9(b) of the FRCP;
2. as to the First Count, alleging common law fraud, the allegations have failed to assert that the plaintiff relied upon the alleged misrepresentations of the defendant;
3. as to the Second Count, alleging violation of the federal securities laws, 15 U.S.C. 78t(a), the plaintiff has failed to adequately allege that defendant Able Brokers, Inc. controlled the activities of Sandra Santiago; and
4. as to the Fourth Count, alleging racketeering activity under 18 U.S.C. 1962(c), the plaintiff has failed to adequately allege the existence of an enterprise.

                       THE DEFENDANT,
                       ABLE BROKERS, INC.

    By: _____
            Susan Muldoon, Esq.
            Muldoon and Maverick
            35 Park Street
            Milltown, Exurbia 12344
            Atty. Reg. # 86205
            (901) 111-0000

### Order

The foregoing motion having been heard, it is hereby ORDERED that the following counts of the complaint are hereby dismissed:

First Count    _____        Third Count    _____
Second Count  _____        Fourth Count  _____

    By: _____
         Judge

### Certification

This is to certify that a copy of the foregoing Motion to Dismiss was mailed, postage prepaid, to attorney John Dominguez, 175 Wilson Street, Metro City, Exurbia, this the 21st day of October, 1993.

ORAL ARGUMENT    _____
    REQUESTED        Susan Muldoon, Esq.

your firm represents the defendant in a pending federal court lawsuit. Assume further that your review of the complaint filed by the plaintiff indicates that it can be attacked on three separate grounds: (1) parts of it are vague, justifying a Motion for More Definite Statement; (2) parts of it are inflammatory, justifying a Motion to Strike; and (3) the allegations in one cause of action fail to include a necessary element, justifying a Motion to Dismiss for Failure to State a Claim on which Relief Can Be Granted.

With these assumptions in mind, let's address two questions. First, may these three separate motions, and any other possible Rule 12 defenses or motions, be set forth in one motion? Second, if the answer to the first question is yes, then must all available Rule 12 defenses be set forth in one motion, at the risk of being waived if omitted?

The answer to our first question is, indeed, yes. Look at subsection (g) of Rule 12, regarding **consolidation**. That provision allows a motion made under Rule 12 to include "any other motions herein provided for and then available to the party." In other words, the three grounds for attacking the complaint discussed at the beginning of this subsection could be consolidated into one motion. Such a motion would probably be entitled simply a "Rule 12 Motion," rather than some tortured combination such as a "Motion for More Definite Statement, to Strike, and to Dismiss for Failure to State a Claim on which Relief Can Be Granted."

The answer to our second question is a bit more complicated. Reading sections (g) and (h) of Rule 12 together, we are left with the following basic rules as to **waiver**:

1.  Failure to raise the defense of a lack of subject matter jurisdiction (Rule 12(b)(1)) in a Rule 12 motion does not waive the right to raise it later, at any time and in any manner.
2.  Failure to raise the defenses identified in Rule 12(b)(6) and/or Rule 12(b)(7) in a Rule 12 motion does not waive the right to make these defenses in any subsequent pleading permitted under Rule 7(a), by a motion for judgment on the pleadings, or at the trial.
3.  The defenses of lack of jurisdiction over the person, improper venue, insufficiency of process, or insufficiency of service of process (Rules 12(b)(2) through 12(b)(5)) must be included if a Rule 12 motion is filed, or they are waived forever.
4.  If any other "motion or objection" provided for under Rule 12 (for example, a Motion for More Definite Statement or a Motion to Strike) is not included when any Rule 12 motion is filed, further presentation by motion is waived.

Thus, applying this rule to the assumptions we made at the beginning of this subsection, any Rule 12 motion filed would have to raise the objections based upon allegedly vague or inflammatory language or otherwise waive the right to raise these issues by motion, but the failure to state a claim on which relief can be granted, even if omitted in a Rule 12 motion, could nevertheless be asserted later in a subsequent pleading, by a motion for judgment on the pleadings, or at trial.

The language of Rule 12(g) limits the effect of the waiver rules to defenses "then available." This language would affect a situation in which the possibility of raising certain defenses becomes apparent only after a previous Rule 12 motion, such as a Motion for More Definite Statement, engenders a clarified pleading that makes the possibility of such

**PARALEGALERT!**

Rules as to consolidation and waiver of Rule 12 defenses and objections are both complicated and important. The failure to follow them precisely can result in a waiver of certain of your client's rights. If such an issue presents itself, be sure to alert your supervising attorney.

new defenses apparent. Such newly available defenses would not be waived by virtue of the earlier Rule 12 motion, because they were not "then available." They could thereafter be asserted in another Rule 12 motion, or in a responsive pleading.

You should note that if no Rule 12 motion is filed, the seven Rule 12(b) defenses can all be raised in a responsive pleading; none would be waived. Keep in mind, however, that Rule 12(h)(1) also has some ramifications relating to waiver of certain defenses that are also omitted from the subsequent responsive pleading (or an amended version permitted as a matter of course). We discuss these situations in the next chapter, in the section covering amendments to pleadings.

## Related State Court Procedures

One of the problems you will inevitably face in translating the theories of this textbook into useful "real world" knowledge flows out of a basic fact to which we have often made reference: namely, that there is great variety in the procedures employed in the various state court systems. Perhaps nowhere can the differences become more confusing than in analyzing motions attacking the pleadings. The problem is not conceptual, in that the five potential weaknesses of a pleading identified at the beginning of this section are universal, applying to lawsuits in state courts as well as federal courts. The problem is, rather, one of nomenclature: state systems sometimes attach different names to the motions used to attack the same weaknesses as do the federal Rule 12 motions, and sometimes it takes several state rules to accomplish the same objectives accomplished by the one federal rule, namely Rule 12. Furthermore, the details of the application of the state rules often differ from the details of the application of the federal rules.

Just to give you a few examples of the problematic possibilities, consider some of the following motions that state court procedure might provide for. A motion designed to perform the function of a Motion for More Definite Statement might be called a Request to Revise; and the rules defining the Request to Revise might include in it the function of the federal Motion to Strike or delineate different procedures with regard to orders or objections (see Figure 7–17). The same state's procedure might include something called a Motion to Strike, but the function of this Motion to Strike might be analogous to the federal Motion to Dismiss for failure to state a claim on which relief can be granted, rather than its federal namesake. The possibilities are really extensive: a federal Motion to Strike might be called a Motion to Expunge under analogous state rules; a federal Motion to Dismiss might be called a demurrer; and rules as to consolidation and waiver might differ in the state context.

**PARALEGALERT!**

Although conceptually similar to those used in the federal system, motions attacking the pleadings in state courts can have different names and be characterized by different procedures. The differences can get confusing; sometimes a motion with the same name (for example, a Motion to Strike) will have an entirely different function in state court than in federal court. As always, check the specifically applicable state court rules!

Many states have adopted rules of procedure patterned after the FRCP, which is helpful. But even in these states, procedural issues can arise requiring research in fairly old judicial opinions that predate the adoption of the federal-type system and incorporate ancient names for various types of pleadings and motions. When researching in such opinions, you will have to develop an understanding of the old concepts, in order to analogize the old (but still applicable and useful) precedents to current practices.

**Figure 7–17   Example of a State Procedure for Attacking a Pleading which Differs from the Federal Procedure**

> *Problem:* One portion of a pleading is vague; another portion is redundant.
>
> *Federal solution:* Combine a Motion for More Definite Statement to attack the vagueness, with a Motion to Strike to attack the redundancy in *one* "Rule 12 Motion."
>
> *Possible state court rule which creates a solution deviating from the federal procedure:*
>
> > **Request to Revise.**
> > Whenever a party desires to obtain (1) a more complete or particular statement of the allegations of an adverse party's pleading, or (2) the deletion of any scandalous, impertinent, redundant, immaterial, or otherwise improper material, the party desiring any such amendment in an adverse party's pleading may file a timely request to revise that pleading. The request to revise shall be deemed to be automatically granted unless objected to within thirty days of filing.
>
> The Request to Revise created by the above hypothetical state rule fulfills the function of both subparts of the federal Rule 12 motion. In addition, it is automatically granted unless objected to, another departure from federal practice.

Because of the potential for confusion in this area, we recommend that you follow a three-step process (see Figure 7–18). First, master the concepts that stand behind the federal motions attacking the pleadings. In particular, this means mastering and understanding the five weaknesses that a pleading might contain.

Second, study and master the way in which Rule 12 of the FRCP regulates the means of attacking these weaknesses. Since the FRCP applies in every federal court nationwide, you must understand the FRCP wherever your litigation practice takes you.

Third, identify the way your particular state system regulates the means of attacking these five weaknesses. If your state uses a system patterned after the FRCP, you are lucky, and will probably have a fairly easy time with this objective. If your state uses some other system, you will have to spend more time identifying the names of the motions or pleadings that are used to attack each of the five weaknesses, as well as any special procedural considerations with which they are associated.

**Figure 7–18   Motions Attacking the Pleadings: A Three-Step Process for Avoiding Confusion between State and Federal Court Practice**

> *Step One:* Master the five potential weaknesses of a pleading:
> (1) vagueness or ambiguity;
> (2) language which is excessive, redundant, immaterial, impertinent, or scandalous;
> (3) lack of judicial authority to consider issues presented;
> (4) failure to state a valid claim for which the legal system provides a remedy; and
> (5) lack of an indispensable party.
>
> *Step Two:* Study and master the manner in which Rule 12 of the FRCP regulates the means of attacking these weaknesses in federal court lawsuits.
>
> *Step Three:* Identify the way your particular state system regulates the means of attacking these weaknesses in state court lawsuits.

## 7–5 Other Motions

In this chapter we have differentiated motions from pleadings, given you some background information as to motion format and characteristics, and discussed a significant category of motions, namely, motions attacking the pleadings. All these items are important for you to explore and understand.

What we have failed to do, to this point, is to give some sense of the variety of motions that can arise during the course of a lawsuit. We shall attempt to remedy that failure in this section.

There are only two practical limits on the scope of motion practice: (1) the number and diversity of legal questions that might arise in a pending case (which sometimes seem almost infinite); and (2) the creativity of counsel in crafting motions that address these questions.

In this section we address several common types of motions. Some we'll merely introduce, with further exposition postponed to later chapters, but at least you'll gain insight into the multifarious nature of motion practice.

Let's first talk about another specific category of motions—**dispositive motions.** If granted, dispositive motions constitute a final resolution of some aspect of the case, possibly even the entire case. Such motions "dispose" of the need for further consideration of the issues resolved, hence the name *dispositive*. Motions to Dismiss, which we discussed above, are dispositive motions, since, if granted (and the decision to grant the motion is not appealed), they dispose of an entire count, or possibly an entire lawsuit. There are other types of dispositive motions as well, including the **Motion for Summary Judgment** and the **Motion for Judgment on the Pleadings** (which are identified in Rule 12(b) and (c) and Rule 56). We discuss all these dispositive motions further in Chapter 10.

A **Motion** *in Limine* is an important motion that can have enormous impact on a trial. Simply stated, this motion poses to the court an evidentiary question, seeking a preliminary judicial ruling on the admissibility of certain evidence. For example, suppose a dispute seems certain to develop at trial over the chain of custody established for a certain piece of physical evidence. In order to prepare a strategy for trial, one or both parties may want to determine beforehand whether the court will admit the evidence. By filing a Motion *in Limine,* counsel ensures that the issue will be resolved before trial, so that the parties can properly prepare.

Another type of motion relates to enforcement of Rule 11 of the FRCP, or a corresponding state court rule. Suppose a party signs a federal court pleading without checking the facts and legal arguments contained in the pleading, and those alleged facts and arguments turn out to be false, inaccurate, or unjustified. This can lead to a significant waste of time and effort on the part of all involved parties. You will recall from the last chapter that Rule 11 authorizes the court to impose a sanction against the offending party in such a situation. The court can order a sanction on its own, but sometimes the victimized party wants to force the issue. This can be done by filing a **Motion for Sanctions,** which identifies the offending issues and requests reasonable relief, for example an order that the offending party pay any costs incurred as a result of the improper pleading.

Finally, there are two important motions associated with discovery practice. The first, called a **Motion for Protective Order,** is filed by a party who believes the discovery requests of the other side are excessive; it seeks an order of the court that the filing party be excused from complying with these requests. The second, called a **Motion to Compel,** is filed by a party who seeks an order of the court forcing or compelling the other party to comply with a discovery request that is being ignored, avoided, or sidestepped. We discuss these two motions further in Chapter 9.

This is just the tip of the iceberg with regard to motions. For a broader picture of the potential motion options available, consult one of the commercial form books that list pages upon pages, and even multiple volumes, of sample motions.

## 7–6 Offer of Judgment

Another option available to a party defending against a claim is the **Offer of Judgment,** authorized by Rule 68 of the FRCP. As established by the rules, the offer of judgment is an "official" offer to resolve the case, which, if refused, has certain repercussions for the parties.

The offer of judgment device gives to the defendant (or other party defending a claim) the right to identify for the consideration of the plaintiff (or other party asserting the claim) the specific amount of money or property (or the specific "effect") to which it will agree to allow a judgment to be entered. If the offer of judgment is accepted by the party asserting the claim within 10 days, the clerk enters judgment; if not, the offer is withdrawn.

The potential repercussions arise when the plaintiff (or other party asserting a claim) refuses to accept the terms identified in the offer of judgment. If the ultimate judgment thereafter recovered is "not more favorable than the offer," then the refusing party will have to pay to the party making the offer "the costs incurred after the making of the offer" (Rule 68 of the FRCP).

The key issue with regard to the strategic usefulness of the offer of judgment is the manner in which the "costs incurred," as defined in Rule 68, are determined. Under certain statutory causes of action these costs may include attorney's fees, which might be substantial. If that is the case, the plaintiff will have to measure the size of the judgment offered against not only the likelihood of a greater recovery at trial but also against the danger of paying substantial "costs" (including these attorney's fees) should the recovery at trial be a lower figure. Where attorney's fees are not part of costs, the potential costs that the defendant will incur (including only such things as subpoena fees or deposition costs) are often relatively negligible, compared to the amount at stake in the lawsuit, and the offer of judgment will be evaluated by the plaintiff in a manner not significantly different from any other settlement.

An offer of judgment is served upon the adverse party in accord with the provisions of Rule 5 of the FRCP. The format resembles that of a motion or pleading, with a caption, designation, signature block, and certificate of service, as in Figure 7–19. It may be served at "any time more than 10 days before the trial begins," and the fact that one such offer "is made but not accepted does not preclude a subsequent offer" (Rule 68 of the FRCP). If the trial determines a liability issue but does not resolve the amount of damages, an offer of judgment can be raised after such trial if "not less than 10 days prior to the commencement of hearings to determine the amount or extent of liability."

Under the rules of some state courts, a plaintiff can also file an offer of judgment. If the plaintiff's offer of judgment is not accepted by the defendant within the specified deadline, and the plaintiff ultimately recovers an amount greater than the offer, the defendant becomes responsible for interest on the judgment from the date the offer of judgment was filed. Check your state's rules to see whether such a provision applies in your state courts.

**Figure 7-19   Offer of Judgment**

United States District Court
for the
District of Exurbia

WIDGETS AND GIZMOS, INC.                        :

    Plaintiff                                            :

                                                   :            Civil Action No. 93-OWH-00543

     vs.                                                  :
                                                   December 9, 1993

TAPTAPTAP, INC.                                  :

    Defendant                                            :

                                                      :

**Offer of Judgment**

To: Widgets & Gizmos, Inc. and its attorneys, Lincoln and Hoover

PLEASE TAKE NOTICE that *TapTapTap, Inc.*, defendant in the above-captioned action, hereby offers to allow judgment to be taken against it in the amount of $275,000.00, with costs accrued to this date, pursuant to Rule 68 of the Federal Rules of Civil Procedure. Evidence of this offer shall not be admissible in evidence except in a proceeding to determine costs. Plaintiff shall have ten (10) days after the service of this offer to accept it in writing; if not so accepted it shall be deemed withdrawn, pursuant to Rule 68.

                         THE DEFENDANT, *TapTapTap, Inc.*

          By: _____
               Tim Tiptop, Esq.
               Its attorney
               Tiptop and Towe
               71 Ferguson Street
               Metro City, Exurbia 12345
               Atty. Reg. #: 65488
               Phone: (901) 333-3333

**Certification**

    This is to certify that a copy of the foregoing Offer of Judgment was mailed, postage prepaid, this 9th day of November, 1993, to attorney Sam Superlawyer, 123 Lincoln Street, Metro City, Exurbia, 12345.

                      _____
                      Tim Tiptop, Esq.

## 7-7   Practical Considerations

As mentioned earlier in this chapter, we're going to discuss an important practical consideration with regard to computing deadlines: the usefulness of "worst-case analysis." By calculating your deadlines based on the assumption that every interpretation of the rules might ultimately work against you, you will

## PARALEGALERT!

Always calculate deadlines using a "worst-case" scenario. By calculating the earliest possible deadline that could be imposed based on a narrow interpretation of the rules, and then setting your *personal* deadline even two or three days before that to give yourself a margin of error, you will avoid the need to convince a skeptical court that days have been counted correctly and an important deadline met.

come up with the "worst case" yielding the earliest possible deadline. Once you've calculated this date, you should then make sure that the necessary action is taken at least a couple of days before that worst-case date. By always operating in this manner, making your personal deadlines fall safely within the deadlines established by the rules, you will never place your supervising attorney in a situation where he or she is straining to convince a court that a document was filed, or other action was taken, before an important deadline had expired.

**Recent Developments**   Between the first and second printing of this book, the Supreme Court of the United States submitted to Congress amendments to the Federal Rules of Civil Procedure. Pursuant to Section 2074 of Title 28 of the United States Code, these amendments took effect on December 1, 1993.

The amendments include substantive changes to Rules 11 and 12. Rule 11 has been modified to allow, among other things, an allegedly offensive pleading (or other document or contention) to be withdrawn or corrected, and by such withdrawal or correction avoid susceptibility to sanction. Rule 12 has been amended to account for new provisions of Rule 4 relating to waiver of service by a defendant; certain new deadlines have also been established.

# SUMMARY

**7–1**

During the pretrial process, the rules seek to foster three key objectives: (1) that the issues presented will be clearly defined and legitimate, (2) that the lawsuit will be an inclusive and efficient determination of all outstanding issues, and (3) that the parties have an opportunity to uncover relevant information through the discovery process. A pleading is an assertion; a motion (including a motion attacking the pleadings) represents a request for the court to enter an order.

**7–2**

An appearance is often the first document filed by a defendant with the court. If the defendant is represented by an attorney, the appearance officially establishes that relationship in the eyes of the court. Sometimes, however, the filing of a responsive pleading accomplishes the same objective, making the filing of an appearance unnecessary. Deadlines are extremely important to litigation personnel, as are the methods for computing the precise deadlines established by applicable rules. A request for entry of default seeks an acknowledgment by the court officially recognizing the failure of another party to file a responsive pleading. Removal is the procedure by which a defendant can have a case that was originally filed in state court transferred to a federal court with concurrent jurisdiction.

**7–3**

Motions are similar in appearance to pleadings, containing captions, designations, numbered paragraphs, signature blocks, and certifications. They may also contain proposed orders, requests for oral argument, and notices of hearings, and be accompanied by supporting memoranda of law or briefs. Motions for Extension of Time can be filed if a party needs more time to complete a required step in the litigation process; they are often uncontested, but even so are not always granted. Contested motions are generally accompanied by memoranda of law, and the opposing party will often file a memoranda of law in opposition. Motions are often scheduled on motion days or motion calendars, or by a Notice of Hearing.

**7–4**

There are five ways in which a pleading might be found lacking and hence subject to attack: (1) because the language employed is vague or ambiguous; (2) because excessive language requires a modification or deletion; (3) because the court lacks judicial authority; (4) because the cause of action is not one for which the legal system provides a remedy; and (5) because other, indispensable parties have not been brought into the suit. The filing of a motion attacking the pleadings in federal court suspends the deadline for responding to the pleading. A Motion for More Definite Statement is filed to attack a vague or ambiguous pleading in federal court; a Motion to Strike is filed to attack excessive (i.e., redundant, immaterial, impertinent, or scandalous) language in a federal court pleading. Lack of judicial authority, failure to state a claim on which relief can be granted, or failure to name an indispensable party are attacked in federal court by filing a Motion to Dismiss. Rules as to consolidation and waiver are both complicated and important; if a potential issue arises, be sure to discuss it with your supervising attorney. State court procedures with regard to motions attacking an opposing party's pleadings are conceptually similar to the federal rules, but often differ in the names assigned to the motions or other significant details. This can become very confusing; the way to avoid confusion is first to master the basic concepts, then study and learn both the federal procedure and your corresponding state procedure for applying these concepts.

**7–5**

There are many different kinds of motions besides those that attack pleadings. The dispositive motions represent final resolutions on some aspect of a case (or even the entire case). Motions to Dismiss are dispositive motions, as are Motions for Summary Judgment and Motions for Judgment on the Pleadings. Other important motions include the Motion *in Limine;* the Motion for Sanctions; the Motion for Protective Order; and the Motion to Compel.

### 7–6

An offer of judgment gives to a party defending a claim the right to make an

"official" offer to resolve the case. If the offer is refused by the other party, and if the ultimate judgment recovered is not more favorable than the offer, the party that made the offer can recover the costs incurred subsequent to the date of the offer.

### 7–7

When calculating deadlines, use "worst-case" analysis and a conservative approach. That way, you will avoid any questions as to whether your documents have been filed on time.

## REVIEW

### Key Terms

Before proceeding, review the key terms listed below to be sure you understand each one. If necessary, read over the corresponding section of the chapter. When you are ready to test your understanding, answer the Review Questions.

pleading
motion
appearance
*pro se* appearance
*pro se* party
general appearance
special appearance
deadlines
default
removal
Motion for Extension of Time
request for oral argument
order
proposed order
contested
uncontested
memorandum of law
brief
motion days
motion calendars
Notice of Hearing
Motion for More Definite Statement
Motion to Strike
Rule 12(b) Motion
Motion to Dismiss
dismissal

joinder
consolidation
waiver
dispositive motions
Motion for Summary Judgment
Motion for Judgment on the Pleadings
Motion *in Limine*
Motion for Sanctions
Motion for Protective Order
Motion to Compel
Offer of Judgment

### Questions for Review and Discussion

1. What are the three key objectives that the rules of procedure seek to foster during the pretrial process?
2. Provide a precise definition of a pleading.
3. What is the key distinction between a pleading and a motion?
4. Explain how time intervals are computed under the FRCP.
5. What is a default?
6. What is meant by removal?
7. List the five ways in which the assertions in a pleading might be found lacking.
8. What is the name, under the FRCP, of the motion used to attack a vague or ambiguous pleading?
9. What is meant by the "failure to state a claim on which relief can be granted?"

**10.** What is the purpose of a Motion *in Limine?*

## Activities

**1.** Find the case of *Luckett v. Harris Hospital-Fort Worth*, 764 F. Supp. 436 (N.D. Tex., 1991) in your local law library, and read it to learn how one court resolved a removal controversy.

**2.** Contact your state court clerk's office to learn the procedure for scheduling motions, and arrange to attend a motion day, motion calendar, or other scheduled hearing in which oral arguments are heard by the court.

**3.** Assuming that the Widgets and Gizmos, Inc. lawsuit was filed in your U.S. District Court, prepare a simple Request to the Clerk for Entry of Default, in conformity with the FRCP and your applicable local federal rules, on behalf of Widgets and Gizmos, Inc., asserting that TapTapTap, Inc. has failed to plead within the required deadline.

# CHAPTER 8   The Answer, Additional Claims, and Multiparty Practice

## OUTLINE

## COMMENTARY

Sam Superlawyer has left documents on your desk, with a note instructing you to review the documents, then meet with him. You sort through the pile and soon recognize that the two lawsuits you've filed are getting more complicated. In the Hampton case, the defendants have denied your claims, but their responses do not stop there. Judith Johnson is claiming that negligence on the part of both Hampton and Bud's Auto Service was the cause of her injuries. She is seeking to collect damages against both.

You dig a little deeper and find the responsive pleading filed by TapTapTap, Inc. It denies liability for contract breach, claiming that the widgenometers with which it has been supplied are defective. As with Judith Johnson's, this response goes further, stating a claim for contract breach against Widgets and Gizmos, Inc. that seeks recovery for damages caused by allegedly faulty widgenometers.

The rules of pleading require that the defendant must file a responsive pleading, called an "answer," to the complaint. The rules also afford to the parties a variety of options as to other related claims that might exist, enabling the parties to combine many claims in the same lawsuit. In this chapter we explore not only the answer to the complaint, but also the manner in which these other claims are stated.

## OBJECTIVES

In Chapter 7 you learned about the pretrial motion process. In this chapter you'll learn about the pleadings filed subsequent to the complaint, as well as some other complications involving multiparty practice. After completing this chapter, you'll be able to:

1. Admit, deny, or plead insufficient knowledge to the allegations of a complaint.
2. Define an affirmative defense.
3. Explain why it is important to consider the filing of a jury demand at or about the time an answer is filed.
4. Differentiate between a permissive counterclaim and a compulsory counterclaim.
5. Explain what an answer, a reply to counterclaim, and an answer to cross-claim have in common.
6. Explain how counterclaims, cross-claims, and complaints are similar.
7. Explain what a class action is.
8. Define the term *impleader*.
9. Describe circumstances that would justify intervention.
10. Explain the difference between an amended pleading and a supplemental pleading.

## 8–1   The Answer

The complaint generally sets forth a wide range of facts, from allegations seemingly objective (such as the street address of a party) to allegations teeming with controversy (such as an assertion of negligence or contract breach). As to certain minor allegations, there may actually be agreement between the parties; as to other, more serious allegations, there will likely be fundamental disagreement.

It is essential that, during the pretrial process, areas of disagreement be identified, since these areas constitute the contested issues that will have to be resolved at trial. Indeed, as you learned in the last chapter, clearly defining the contested issues is one of the three key objectives of the pretrial process (see Section 7–1). As you also learned in the last chapter, motions attacking the complaint assist in achieving this objective. Although these motions do serve to clarify the allegations of the complaint and to eliminate illegitimate causes of action, they nevertheless leave a critical question unanswered: what is the position of the defendant on those properly stated claims and allegations that remain after the motion is decided? Or, put another way: which proper allegations made by the plaintiff does the defendant dispute? Where, in other words, are the areas of disagreement that will have to be resolved at trial?

In order to answer these critical questions, the pleading process must provide a mechanism by which the areas of disagreement are identified. The mechanism provided is called an **answer.** Under the FRCP, the *answer* is the pleading in which the defendant responds to the allegations of the complaint, identifies defenses, and states any relevant additional claims.

The answer, you will recall, is among the pleadings authorized by Rule 7 of the FRCP; it will thus have a caption, numbered paragraphs, and the other characteristics identified in our discussion of pleadings in Section 6–2. Under the requirements of Rule 12 of the FRCP, the answer must be filed, generally speaking, within 20 days after service of the summons and complaint, unless a motion attacking the complaint is filed (review Rule 12) or a Motion for Extension granted. You should check your state rules of procedure to determine your analogous state court guidelines and deadlines.

The defendant uses the answer to respond to the allegations of the complaint by either (1) admitting them, (2) denying them, or (3) indicating an inability to admit or deny them (see Figure 8–1, which fully defines the answer). In the subsection that follows, we consider each of these three possibilities. There is a fourth possibility as well: namely, that the allegations stated in the complaint don't tell the whole story, there being some basis for a defense independent of the ability to admit or deny those allegations. We consider this fourth possibility in the subsections on affirmative defenses and Rule 12 defenses.

In Figures 8–2 and 8–3 we have set forth the answers filed by defendants TapTapTap, Inc. and Judith Johnson in your two pending lawsuits. You should read the documents in both figures now. As you can see, they include not only admissions, denials, and defenses, but also counterclaims and, in the case of Judith Johnson, a cross-claim against another defendant. We address counter-claims and cross-claims in the next section; in this section, we begin our basic investigation of the answer.

## Admitting, Denying, or Pleading Insufficient Knowledge

Rule 8 of the FRCP begins to define the manner in which the answer confronts the allegations raised in the complaint. Rule 8 is shown in pertinent part in Figure 8–4. Under the provisions of Rule 8(b), a party responding to a claim "shall admit or deny the averments upon which the adverse party relies." "Averment" is simply another word for *allegation*. The rule goes on: "If a party is without knowledge or information sufficient to form a belief as to the truth of an averment, the party shall so state and this has the effect of a denial." Taking these two provisions together, Rule 8 authorizes the three basic responses to a pleading that we've identified. Let's talk about each.

First let's take the **admission.** The analysis of an admission is straightforward: by admitting that one of the allegations of a complaint is true, the defendant in effect relinquishes the right to question further whether that allegation is accurate. The allegation is, in plain English, admitted.

Next let's take the **denial.** By denying an allegation set forth in the complaint, the defendant has indicated that a disagreement exists between the plaintiff and the defendant on the points raised by the allegation. By denying the allegation

**Figure 8–1  Definition of the Answer**

> ***ANSWER:*** Under the FRCP, the answer is the pleading in which the defendant responds to each allegation of the complaint by either (1) admitting it, (2) denying it, or (3) indicating an inability to admit or deny it. The answer should also include affirmative defenses and Rule 12 defenses which the defendant wishes to assert, as well as any applicable counterclaim or cross-claim.

**Figure 8–2** Answer, Affirmative Defense, and Counterclaim of Defendant *TapTapTap, Inc.*

United States District Court
for the
District of Exurbia

WIDGETS AND GIZMOS, INC.                    :

    Plaintiff                    :

    vs.                    :                    Civil Action No. 93-OWH-00543

                                      January 21, 1994

TAPTAPTAP, INC.                    :

    Defendant                    :

                                            :

### Answer, Affirmative Defense, and Counterclaim
### of Defendant *TapTapTap, Inc.*

*Answer*

1. Paragraphs 1, 2, and 3 of the complaint are admitted.
2. Paragraphs 8, 9, and 10 are denied.
3. As to paragraph 4, defendant *TapTapTap, Inc.* (hereinafter "Taps") admits that the plaintiff *Widgets and Gizmos, Inc.* (hereinafter "Widgets") manufactures a product called a "widgenometer" but denies that the widgenometer has performed as called for in the specifications of the contract which is Exhibit A to the complaint.
4. As to paragraph 5, the defendant admits that the contract which appears as Exhibit A to the complaint was executed by the parties to this lawsuit, and asserts that the contract speaks for itself as to its terms.
5. As to paragraph 6, the defendant admits that 3000 units identified as "widgenometers" have been shipped, but denies that these units satisfy the requirements of the contract.
6. As to paragraph 7, the defendant admits that it has refused to make payment for the defective widgenometers, but denies that payment is due and owing.

### Affirmative Defense

The defendant Taps has no obligation to pay for any of the widgenometers shipped by the plaintiff Widgets because said widgenometers are defective and fail to meet the requirements of the contract which is Exhibit A to the complaint.

### Counterclaim

1. Paragraphs 1, 2, and 3 of the complaint are hereby restated and set forth as paragraphs 1, 2, and 3 of this counterclaim.
2. On or about January 27, 1992, Widgets and Taps entered into the contract which is Exhibit A to the complaint.
3. Widgenometer units shipped by Widgets have failed to satisfy the terms and requirements of the contract specifications.
4. The defective widgenometer units were installed in computers sold to customers by Taps.
5. As a result of the failure of the widgenometer units to satisfy the terms and requirements of the contract specifications, the computers supplied by defendant Taps to its customers have caused substantial injury to the customers.
6. Taps has suffered damages in that it is or may become liable to its customers for damages caused by the defective widgenometers.
7. In particular, and as a result of the defective nature of the widgenometer units, Taps has been presented with claims for damages from its customers totaling an amount in excess of $215,000.00, and anticipates that additional claims will be made which will increase this amount.

8. As a further result of the failure of the widgenometer units to satisfy the terms and requirements of the contract specifications, Taps has suffered damage to its business reputation.
9. Widgets is liable to Taps for the aforesaid damages based upon its breach of contract.

WHEREFORE, the defendant *TapTapTap, Inc.* demands that judgment be entered in its favor and against the plaintiff *Widgets and Gizmos, Inc.* on the claims stated in the complaint. Defendant also demands that judgment on the counterclaim be entered in its favor for the full amount of the damages suffered (in excess of $215,000.00), plus interest, costs, and allowable attorney's fees, and for such other and further relief as the court may deem appropriate, just, and equitable. A JURY TRIAL is demanded on the counterclaim.

THE DEFENDANT, TAPTAPTAP, INC.

By: _____
          Tim Tiptop, Esq.
          Its attorney
          Tiptop and Towe
          71 Ferguson Street
          Metro City, Exurbia 12345
          Atty. Reg. #: 65488
          Phone: (901) 333-3333

**Certificate of Service**

This is to certify that a copy of the foregoing Answer, Affirmative Defense, and Counterclaim was mailed, postage prepaid, this 21st day of January, 1994, to attorney Sam Superlawyer, Esq., 123 Lincoln Street, Metro City, Exurbia, 12345.

_____
Tim Tiptop, Esq.

the defendant has defined an issue that will need to be resolved at trial; evidence will have to be introduced, and a decision made by the trier-of-fact.

Suppose the complaint filed by Widgets and Gizmos, Inc. made a slight typographical error in one of its numbered paragraphs, alleging, for example, that the contract in question was entered into by "defendant *Rap*TapTap, Inc.," after correctly identifying "TapTapTap, Inc." in every previous reference (see Figure 8–5). Could defendant TapTapTap, Inc. deny the allegation simply on the grounds that the misspelling makes it inaccurate? The answer to that is *no*; Rule 8(b) requires that a denial "shall fairly meet the substance of the averments denied." This means that the answer must respond in good faith to the allegations raised by the complaint (a requirement supported by Rule 11); an obvious typo thus would not justify a denial. Would the proper response be an admission? See Figure 8–5 for the answer (an admission that points out the typo); if uncovered earlier in the process, the defendant might also have filed a Motion for More Definite Statement pointing out the problem and seeking a clarification.

---

**PARALEGALERT!**

If an allegation in the complaint is inaccurate for some minor technical reason, such as a typographical error, it is not acceptable to deny the allegation based on the minor error. The answer must respond in good faith to the substance of the allegation.

---

**Figure 8–3  Answer, Affirmative Defenses, Counterclaim, and Cross-Claim of Defendant Judith Johnson**

| | | |
|---|---|---|
| HARRY HAMPTON, | : | Superior Court |
| Plaintiff | : | State of Exurbia |
| vs. | : | Judicial District of |
| JUDITH JOHNSON and BUD'S AUTO SERVICE | : | Metro County |
| Defendants | : | |
| | | January 15, 1994 |
| | : | |

### Answer, Affirmative Defenses, Counterclaim, and Cross-Claim of Defendant Judith Johnson

*Answer*

1. Judith Johnson (hereinafter "Johnson") hereby admits paragraphs 1, 2, 3, 5, 6, and 8 of the First Count of the Complaint.
2. Paragraphs 4, 7, 10, 11, 12, 13, 14, 15, and 16 of the First Count are denied.
3. As to paragraph 9 of the First Count, Johnson admits that there was a collision but otherwise denies the allegations.
4. As the Second Count is directed against another defendant, Johnson has no response to the allegations contained therein.

*First Affirmative Defense*

The plaintiff, Harry Hampton, was contributorily negligent, leading to his injuries.

*Second Affirmative Defense*

There was no visible stop sign regulating the progress of Judith Johnson as she advanced through the intersection of Pruitt Street and Higgins Lane, and hence no legal obligation to stop.

*Counterclaim (against Harry Hampton)*

1. Paragraphs 1, 2, and 3 of the First Count of the Complaint are hereby made paragraphs 1, 2, and 3 of this Counterclaim.
4. As Hampton's vehicle approached the intersection of Higgins Lane and Pruitt Street, its turn signal indicated an intention to turn right.
5. Despite the aforementioned indication of an apparent intention to turn right, Hampton's vehicle in fact proceeded straight through the intersection, colliding violently with Johnson's vehicle.
6. The collision was the result of the negligence of the plaintiff Harry Hampton, in that he:
    (a) proceeded straight through the intersection, although his turn signal indicated an intention to turn right;
    (b) failed to keep a proper lookout for, and avoid colliding with, other vehicles; and
    (c) under all of the circumstances then and there existing, failed to use that degree of care which would be expected of an ordinarily prudent person.
7. As a result of the collision and the negligence of plaintiff Harry Hampton, Judith Johnson suffered the following injuries, all of which were accompanied by great pain and suffering and the effects of some or all of which are likely to be permanent:
    (a) concussion;
    (b) chronic headaches and nausea;
    (c) contusions and abrasions about the head and face; and
    (d) dislocation of the shoulder.
8. As a further result of the collision and the negligence of plaintiff Hampton, Judith Johnson incurred substantial bills and expenses for medical treatment, currently totaling an amount in excess of $4300.00, and continuing to accrue.
9. As a further result of the collision and the negligence of plaintiff Hampton, Judith Johnson's 1992 Ford Taurus motor vehicle was severely damaged, necessitating repair expense in the amount of $3175.00.

10. As a further result of the collision and the negligence of plaintiff Hampton, Judith Johnson was unable to perform the duties of her employment for a period of nine days, causing her to lose substantial wages.

11. As a further result of the collision and the negligence of plaintiff Hampton, Judith Johnson has lost the future ability to perform many of life's enjoyable activities.

12. Plaintiff Hampton is liable to Judith Johnson for the injuries and damages described above.

*Cross-Claim (against defendant Bud's Auto Service)*

1. Paragraphs 1 to 5 of the Counterclaim are hereby made paragraphs 1 to 5 of this Cross-Claim.

6. Shortly before the collision, defendant Bud's Auto Service was engaged by plaintiff Harry Hampton to perform certain repair work on Hampton's Pontiac Grand Am vehicle.

7. Defendant Bud's Auto Service was negligent in its performance of its repair work on Harry Hampton's vehicle, in that:

   (a) certain wires were crossed by one or more of the employees of defendant Bud's Auto Service, such that the turn signal on the vehicle was caused to thereafter malfunction;

   (b) Hampton was not alerted to the malfunctioning turn signal;

   (c) a reasonably prudent and careful repair shop would have discovered and corrected the malfunctioning turn signal before returning the vehicle to its owner; and

   (d) under all of the circumstances then and there existing, defendant Bud's Auto Service failed to perform its repair services with that degree of care owed to its customer, Harry Hampton.

8. The malfunctioning turn signal was a proximate cause of the collision described in paragraph 5.

9. As a result of the negligence of the defendant, Bud's Auto Service, Judith Johnson suffered the injuries and damages described in paragraphs 7 to 11 of the Counterclaim, which injuries and damages are restated herein by reference.

10. Defendant Bud's Auto Service is liable to Judith Johnson in that the damages she suffered were a reasonably foreseeable consequence of the negligence of Bud's Auto Service.

WHEREFORE, Judith Johnson claims:

(1) judgment in her favor and against the plaintiff on the claims raised in the complaint;

(2) judgment on the Counterclaim against the plaintiff Harry Hampton, in an amount in excess of $50,000.00, plus costs and allowable attorney's fees, and such other and further relief as the court may deem appropriate;

(3) judgment on the Cross-Claim against Bud's Auto Service in an amount in excess of $50,000.00, plus costs and attorney's fees, and such other and further relief as the court may deem appropriate; and

(4) a jury trial on all issues presented by the Counterclaim and Cross-Claim hereinabove stated.

THE DEFENDANT, JUDITH JOHNSON

By: _____

Shawn Schmidt, Esq.
Benson & Arnold
985 Cook Lane
Metro City, Exurbia 12345

**Certificate of Service**

This is to certify that a copy of the foregoing was mailed, postage prepaid, this 15th day of January, 1994, to attorney Sam Superlawyer, Esq., Lincoln & Hoover, 123 Lincoln Street, Metro City, Exurbia, 12345.

_____

Shawn Schmidt, Esq.

**Figure 8–4    Portions of Rule 8 of the FRCP Relating to the Answer**

*The following are the major provisions of Rule 8 of the FRCP relating to the preparation of an answer. Review the rule itself for the full text.*

**Rule 8. General Rules of Pleading.**

(a) [omitted]

(b) DEFENSES; FORM OF DENIALS. A party shall state in short and plain terms the party's defenses to each claim asserted and shall admit or deny the averments upon which the adverse party relies. If a party is without knowledge or information sufficient to form a belief as to the truth of an averment, the party shall so state and this has the effect of a denial. Denials shall fairly meet the substance of the averments denied. When a pleader intends in good faith to deny only a part or a qualification of an averment, the pleader shall specify so much of it as is true and material and shall deny only the remainder.
\* \* \*

(c) AFFIRMATIVE DEFENSES. In pleading to a preceding pleading, a party shall set forth affirmatively accord and satisfaction, arbitration and award, assumption of risk, contributory negligence, discharge in bankruptcy, duress, estoppel, failure of consideration, fraud, illegality, injury by fellow servant, laches, license, payment, release, res judicata, statute of frauds, statute of limitations, waiver, and any other matter constituting an avoidance or affirmative defense.
\* \* \*

(d) EFFECT OF FAILURE TO DENY. Averments in a pleading to which a responsive pleading is required, other than those as to the amount of damage, are admitted when not denied in the responsive pleading. Averments in a pleading to which no responsive pleading is required or permitted shall be taken as denied or avoided.

(e) [omitted]

(f) [omitted]

Suppose the defendant finds that part of an allegation is true, but disputes the balance. To admit such an allegation would be inaccurate; to deny it would also be inaccurate. How should the defendant plead? Turn to the text of Rule 8(b): "When a pleader intends in good faith to deny only a part or a qualification of an averment, the pleader shall specify so much of it as is true and material and

**Figure 8–5    How to Respond to an Allegation which has a Slight Typographical Error**

*Allegation:*

"5.   On or about January 27, 1992, *Widgets and Gizmos, Inc.* and *RapTapTap, Inc.* entered into the contract which is attached hereto as Exhibit A."

*Analysis of allegation:*

It is a valid allegation except for the incorrect spelling of *TapTapTap, Inc.*

*Proper response:*

"3.   The defendant admits that the contract which appears as Exhibit A to the Complaint was entered into on January 27, 1992, by *Widgets and Gizmos, Inc.*, and *TapTapTap, Inc.* (but not *RapTapTap, Inc.*, as identified in paragraph 5 of the complaint)."

*Note:* The defendant might also have filed a Motion for More Definite Statement pointing out the problem and seeking a clarification.

shall deny only the remainder." For an example of this rule in action, see paragraph 3 of the Answer in Figure 8–3.

There may be allegations in the complaint that the defendant is unable, in good faith, either to admit or deny. The defendant may simply not know the answer or may simply lack "knowledge or information sufficient to form a belief" as to the truth or falsity of the allegation. For example, suppose in a fraud case the plaintiff includes an allegation that he or she relied upon the allegedly fraudulent misrepresentations of the defendant. The defendant in such a case cannot know what was in the mind of the plaintiff, and thus cannot admit or deny with certainty what factors the plaintiff relied upon in the internal decision-making process. In such a situation, the defendant can plead "insufficient knowledge" to be able to respond. The effect of an assertion of insufficient knowledge is identical to that of a denial (see Rule 8(b)); in other words, the allegation is viewed by the court as if it had been denied, requiring resolution of the issue at trial. You should note that the defendant in this situation might have denied the allegation of reliance, despite the lack of knowledge, based upon a good faith belief or reasonable conclusion that the plaintiff did not in fact rely upon the alleged misrepresentation.

Suppose the defendant neither admits an allegation, nor denies it, nor pleads insufficient knowledge; in other words, suppose the defendant does nothing. Rule 8(d) holds that any "averment" to which a responsive pleading is required is considered admitted if not denied.

In preparing the answer, neither the paralegal nor the supervising attorney is acting in a vacuum. Just as the complaint is prepared with the close cooperation of the plaintiff-client, so the answer will also be prepared with the close cooperation of the defendant-client. By reviewing your firm's file, referring to form books and model pleadings, and conferring over the phone and in person with the client, you will gradually gather the information needed to respond to the allegations of the complaint.

The specific rules we have discussed in this section apply in federal court lawsuits. The procedures that apply in your state court are likely to track closely the federal rules; deadlines may vary, as well as other details, but the basic principles will be similar. You should review your state's rules with regard to admitting, denying, and pleading insufficient knowledge in response to the allegations of a complaint.

## Affirmative Defenses

Assume, for the purposes of this subsection, that the plaintiff has properly fashioned the complaint: that the allegations are sufficient to establish a valid claim for relief, or, to say it another way, that each count of the complaint alleges all the essential elements of the underlying cause of action.

Now also assume that as the defendant reviews the complaint, going through the allegations one by one, he or she recognizes that every single allegation of the complaint is true—he or she must admit them all.

Is that the end of the lawsuit? Has the defendant lost? Since there is no basis on which to deny any of the allegations, must he or she simply concede defeat?

Not necessarily. There may be some set of facts, or some legal restriction, that goes beyond the allegations identified in the complaint, and which, if established to the satisfaction of the court, would constitute a valid defense even if all the allegations of the complaint are true. Such a set of facts is called an **affirmative defense** or **special defense.** The most commonly cited example of an affirmative defense is the statute of limitations defense, which provides a useful

**Figure 8–6  Statute of Limitations as an Affirmative Defense**

---

***Framework for the Assertion of the Statute of Limitations as an Affirmative Defense***

(1) Assume the allegations in a Complaint filed in federal court on October 15, 1993, are, in their entirety, as follows:

    1. Plaintiff is Smith Corp. of Los Angeles, California.
    2. Defendant is Jones Corp. of New York, New York.
    3. Smith Corp. and Jones Corp. entered into a contract (attached as Exhibit A hereto) on January 2, 1985.
    4. Smith Corp. performed all its obligations as required under the terms of the contract.
    5. Jones Corp.'s only obligation under the contract was to deliver certain goods to Smith Corp.'s headquarters on or before February 10, 1985.
    6. Jones Corp. failed to fulfill its obligation, and is in breach of the contract.

(2) Assume further that, upon reviewing the allegations of the complaint, Jones Corp. realizes that the allegations are true, and will have to be admitted.

(3) Assume further that the statute of limitations which applies to the breach of contract claim asserted in the Complaint is six years.

(4) More than six years elapsed between the date of the breach (February 10, 1985) and the date on which suit was commenced (October 15, 1993).

(5) Thus, despite the fact that all of the allegations of the Complaint are true, there exists a defense under the statute of limitations.

(6) The answer filed by the defendant would read, in pertinent part, as follows:

**Answer**
    1. Paragraphs 1-6 of the Complaint are admitted.

    *Affirmative Defense*
    The action filed by plaintiff is void since it was not filed in a timely manner within the time limit established by the applicable statute of limitations. [The specific statute would be identified]

---

framework for showing the actual application of an affirmative defense in practice (see Figure 8–6).

You should note one important point, so that you're not misled by our definition. Although affirmative defenses constitute valid defenses even when all the allegations of the complaint are true, that does not mean that the only time to include an affirmative defense is when the allegations of the complaint are all true. Indeed, most affirmative defenses will accompany answers that admit some allegations and deny others (as in Figures 8–2 and 8–3).

Affirmative defenses are authorized by Rule 8(c) of the FRCP, which lists several specific examples (including the statute of limitations) and also incorporates "any other matter constituting an avoidance or affirmative defense." Some of the most frequently seen affirmative defenses are listed in Figure 8–7, with a brief explanation of the application of each. As for identifying other possible affirmative defenses,

**PARALEGALERT!**

Affirmative defenses constitute valid defenses even if all the allegations of the complaint are true. But that does not mean that the *only* time affirmative defenses are included is when the allegations of the complaint are all true. Indeed, they generally accompany answers that admit some allegations and deny others.

**Figure 8–7    Some Common Affirmative Defenses Explained**

*Accord and satisfaction:* Asserts that the involved parties have previously agreed to some compromise or settlement of the claim at issue.

*Assumption of risk:* Asserts that the plaintiff knowingly accepted the danger of incurring the injury of which he now complains, and hence defendant is not liable.

*Contributory negligence:* Asserts that the plaintiff's own negligence contributed to the incident on which the claim is based, negating defendant's liability.

*Duress:* A defense to a contract claim, asserting that any agreements made or actions taken by defendant were improperly coerced.

*Estoppel:* A broad defense, in which the defendant asserts that some one or more of the plaintiff's own actions serve to negate the claims made in the complaint.

*Failure of consideration:* For a contract to be enforceable under basic contract law, each side must receive something of value, called "consideration." This defense asserts that the consideration contemplated in the contract has in some manner failed to satisfy the requirement.

*Fraud:* Asserts (1) that the plaintiff intentionally distorted the truth in order to induce that action of the defendant on which the claim is based, and (2) that the defendant relied on the distortion to his detriment.

*Res judicata:* Asserts that the dispute at issue has already been resolved in another legal action.

*Statute of limitations:* Asserts that the plaintiff failed to enforce its claim within the time limits provided by law (see Figure 8–6).

just keep in mind the general governing principle: an affirmative defense consists of a set of facts, beyond those facts alleged in the complaint, that establishes a defense even if all the facts alleged in the complaint are true. The existence of such potential defenses is determined through review of procedural rules such as Rule 8(c) of the FRCP, as well as through legal research in judicial opinions and statutes and discussion with the client as to the facts of the case; just as a plaintiff must research potential causes of action, so a defendant must perform research on potential affirmative defenses.

Beyond learning to identify specific affirmative defenses, there is another very important consideration to keep in mind: avoiding waiver of an affirmative defense. Simply stated, when an affirmative defense exists, it *must* be set forth in the answer. Failure to plead an affirmative defense as part of the answer generally prevents the defendant from raising the defense at trial.

It is acceptable to set forth alternative affirmative defenses even if they are inconsistent (see Rule 8(e)(2) of the FRCP). For example, it would be acceptable to plead two affirmative defenses, one of which asserts that an obligation established by a contract was satisfied, and the other of which asserts that no obligation was ever established by the contract because there was a failure of consideration (see Figure 8–7 for an explanation of "failure of consideration").

You should locate and review your state rules of procedure regarding affirmative defenses. In general, most jurisdictions recognize most (if not all) of

**PARALEGALERT!**

When an affirmative defense exists, it generally *must* be set forth in the answer; otherwise it will be waived.

the same substantive affirmative defenses that are listed in Rule 8 of the FRCP, but there may be differing requirements as to the procedural details. One important difference applicable in some jurisdictions is a requirement that the plaintiff file a response to any affirmative defenses alleged by the defendant. Such a response constitutes a separate pleading called a **Reply to Affirmative Defenses.** The FRCP does not require such a reply, unless the court specifically orders it (see Rule 7(a)); under the FRCP, the "averments" in an affirmative defense are "taken as denied" (see the last sentence of Rule 8(d)).

Finally, we need to say a few things about the format of an affirmative defense. Under the FRCP, affirmative defenses are a segment of the answer. Thus, a pleading that includes the admissions, denials, and indications of insufficient knowledge we discussed in the last subsection, along with at least one of the affirmative defenses we are discussing in this subsection, could be designated simply "Answer." Such a pleading is often, however, designated "Answer and Affirmative Defenses," and since this is more descriptive, it is generally preferred. The affirmative defenses themselves should be specifically identified as such, with each individual affirmative defense stated separately (see, for example, the format shown in Figure 8–3).

**PARALEGALERT!**

If an answer includes affirmative defenses, the title should probably so indicate (i.e., "Answer and Affirmative Defenses of Defendant X"). This consideration applies to counterclaims and cross-claims as well.

## Rule 12 Defenses

Suppose that, even if all the allegations in the complaint are true, taken together they fail to state a valid cause of action. What then? Your initial reaction to this should be: file a Motion to Dismiss, under Rule 12(b)(6), alleging a failure to state a claim on which relief can be granted. Indeed, that is an option. But remember, each of the seven specific defenses identified in Rule 12(b) can be made either by motion or in a responsive pleading. If not waived (see the subsection on consolidation and waiver in section 7–4; see also the discussion of Rule 12(h) of the FRCP in section 8–4), each of these seven defenses may be asserted in the answer, as a **Rule 12 defense.**

If one of these defenses is applicable, it would be set forth in a manner similar to the way affirmative defenses are set forth, although eliminating the word "affirmative."

You should also note that, although the format used in Figures 8–2 and 8–3 for setting forth admissions, denials, and assertions of insufficient knowledge is commonly seen, an alternative exists (based on Form 20 of the FRCP) in which admissions and denials are set forth as what might be described as a "defense" under Rule 12 (although not one of the seven Rule 12(b) defenses). In Figure 8–8 we have set forth a format in which the "First Defense" contains the admissions, denials, and assertions of insufficient knowledge; the "Second Defense" is a Rule 12(b) defense; and these two defenses are followed by an "Affirmative Defense."

## Jury Demand

In Section 6–4, we introduced the concept of a **jury demand,** and directed your attention to Rule 38(b) of the FRCP. That rule reads in pertinent part as follows:

> Any party may demand a trial by jury of any issue triable of right by a jury by serving upon the other parties a demand therefor in writing at any time after the commencement of the action and *not later than 10 days after the service*

**Figure 8–8 Sample Alternative Format for Answer and Defenses**

> *[Caption and Designation]*
>
> *First Defense*
> The defendant admits the allegations of paragraphs 1, 2, 3, 7, and 9 of the Complaint; denies the allegations of paragraphs 5, 6, 8, 10, and 11; and is without knowledge or information sufficient to form a belief as to the allegations of paragraph 4.
>
> *Second Defense*
> Under Rule 12(b)(6) of the Federal Rules of Civil Procedure, the defendant asserts that the plaintiff has failed to state a claim on which relief can be granted.
>
> *Affirmative Defense*
> The contract on which the plaintiff bases his claim is void because its execution was induced by the fraud of the plaintiff.
>
> *["Wherefore" clause, signatures and Certificate of Service]*

*of the last pleading* directed to such issue. Such demand may be *indorsed upon a pleading* of the party. [emphasis supplied]

If the plaintiff has not already demanded a jury trial, each defendant must decide whether or not to do so. The demand may be placed in the caption of the answer (as was done in the caption of the complaint in Figure 6–10, p. 119) or requested in some other manner (see, for example, the next subsection). It is very important to note the time limit: "not later than 10 days after the service of the last pleading directed to such issue." Since the answer is the "last pleading" directed to the issues raised in the complaint, the deadline under the FRCP for demanding a jury on the issues raised in the complaint expires ten days after the answer is served. Thus, for both defendants and plaintiffs, this is the last chance to demand a jury by right, and one of the considerations that should always be kept in mind when preparing (or, if you represent the plaintiff, after receiving) an answer is whether a jury demand has yet been filed, and, if not, whether a jury trial is desired. Keep in mind that Rule 39(b) of the FRCP allows for a jury request by motion after the "by right" period expires (which the court may or may not grant); check to see if your state has a similar provision.

State court procedural rules in this area, as with every other area we've discussed, may differ from the federal procedural rules. Thus, you should be aware of your state's specific procedure and deadlines for demanding a jury.

**PARALEGALERT!**

Deadlines for demanding a jury trial often fall within a specified number of days after an answer is filed. Whether you represent the plaintiff or a defendant, you must keep in mind this important consideration at the time an answer is filed; if the demand for jury is not filed in a timely manner, the right to a jury trial may be waived.

## Concluding Paragraph: The "Wherefore Clause"

As with the complaint, an answer is completed by including a general statement that requests the court to return a judgment in the defendant's favor. Because it, too, generally begins with the word *wherefore*, it is sometimes called the "wherefore clause." Jury demands, if desired and necessary, are often placed in the "wherefore clause." Examples of such a clause can be seen in Figures 8–2 and 8–3.

## 8–2  Counterclaims and Cross-Claims

Think back for a moment to our second objective of the pretrial process: that the trial be an inclusive and efficient determination of all outstanding issues. We haven't addressed this objective at any great length; you may be wondering what, exactly, we mean by these words.

We mean that the rules of litigation should be (and are) designed to foster the fullest possible resolution of related disputes with the minimum expenditure of judicial resources. Once a dispute has resulted in a lawsuit, the lawsuit should include all involved parties and should resolve all reasonably related claims between and among those parties. In this section, we talk about additional claims between and among the parties already involved in the lawsuit, which are raised in counterclaims and cross-claims. In the next section, we talk about situations involving additional parties.

### Counterclaims

Although Widgets and Gizmos, Inc. struck first in its dispute with TapTapTap, Inc. by filing a lawsuit alleging breach of contract for failure to make payment, it has been apparent from the start that TapTapTap, Inc. has anticipated making its own claim for breach of contract against Widgets and Gizmos, Inc., based upon alleged defects in the widgenometers. As we pointed out in Section 6–1, TapTapTap, Inc. is not required to start a separate lawsuit, with its own complaint, in order to pursue this claim. The rules of procedure allow TapTapTap, Inc. to assert its claim in the original lawsuit filed by Widgets and Gizmos, Inc. through the filing of a **counterclaim.**

A counterclaim is best thought of as a claim for relief (essentially a "complaint") filed in a pending case by a defendant against the plaintiff (as defined in Rule 13 of the FRCP, a counterclaim is brought by one party against an "opposing party," rather than specifically by a defendant against a plaintiff, but it is usually the defendant who files a counterclaim against the plaintiff). The considerations that go into drafting a counterclaim are virtually identical to those that underlie the complaint (see our discussion in Section 6–4). The elements of the cause of action must be identified and alleged, as well as other salient facts that are judged necessary. Damages must be identified and a prayer for relief (i.e., the "wherefore clause") included. All these various items can be seen in Figures 8–2 and 8–3.

There are two broad types of counterclaim as defined by Rule 13 of the FRCP, compulsory and permissive. Rule 13(a) holds that a pleading "shall" state a *compulsory counterclaim*; in other words, a compulsory counterclaim *must* be asserted, or it is waived. Rule 13(b) holds that a pleading "may" state a *permissive counterclaim*; failure to state such a permissive counterclaim does not, however, waive the right to raise it at a later date in a separate lawsuit. Let's address further the distinction between compulsory and permissive counterclaims (see Figure 8–9).

A **compulsory counterclaim** is one that "arises out of the transaction or occurrence that is the subject matter of the opposing party's claim and does not require for its adjudication the presence of third parties of whom the court cannot acquire jurisdiction" (see Rule 13(a) of the FRCP). An example of such a compulsory counterclaim is that filed by TapTapTap, Inc. against Widgets and Gizmos, Inc. It

**P**ARALEGALERT!

A compulsory counterclaim *must* be asserted by a party, or it is waived and cannot be raised again in the future.

Figure 8–9   Compulsory and Permissive Counterclaims

*Compulsory Counterclaim:* A compulsory counterclaim is defined by Rule 13(a) of the FRCP to be one which "arises out of the transaction or occurrence that is the subject matter of the opposing party's claim and does not require for its adjudication the presence of third parties of whom the court cannot acquire jurisdiction."

A compulsory counterclaim *must* be asserted, or it is waived.

*Permissive Counterclaim:* A permissive counterclaim is one which does *not* arise out of the same transaction as the subject matter of the opposing party's claim (see Rule 13(b) of the FRCP).

A permissive counterclaim which is not asserted is *not* waived; it can be raised in a separate future lawsuit.

Permissive counterclaims must have an independent jurisdictional basis.

---

arises out of the same transaction as that identified in the complaint (namely, the widgenometer contract between the parties), and requires for its adjudication the presence of no additional parties. Hence if TapTapTap, Inc. ever intends to pursue this claim, it must be stated as a counterclaim *now* or is thereafter waived.

**Permissive counterclaims** are those claims against an opposing party that do *not* arise out of the same transaction (see Rule 13(b) of the FRCP). For example, suppose that there was another, entirely separate, contract between TapTapTap, Inc. and Widgets and Gizmos, Inc., under which TapTapTap, Inc. had paid Widgets and Gizmos, Inc. for delivery of some other components (i.e., *not* widgenometers), which Widgets and Gizmos, Inc. had failed to deliver. TapTapTap, Inc. could raise this breach of contract claim in the pending "widgenometer" lawsuit as a permissive counterclaim; however, if it failed to do so, the right to raise it later, in another lawsuit, would not be waived.

You should note that the courts generally require an independent jurisdictional basis for a permissive counterclaim. Consider, for example, the hypothetical contract claim of TapTapTap, Inc. that we have just discussed. To qualify as a permissive counterclaim, this claim must independently satisfy the requirements of federal jurisdiction; in other words, it must involve either a federal statutory or constitutional principle, or satisfy the diversity requirements. If diversity jurisdiction is asserted, the parties in this particular case obviously satisfy the citizenship requirements (since jurisdiction over the original complaint itself was based upon diversity of citizenship); the remaining question would be whether the minimum jurisdictional amount required for diversity cases ($50,000) is also satisfied independently by the permissive counterclaim.

An important issue to consider with regard to counterclaims, whether compulsory or permissive, is the possible need to demand a jury. No jury demand may yet have been filed in the case. Furthermore, under Rule 38 of the FRCP, a jury demand might be limited to certain specified issues. For example, the plaintiff's original jury demand might be specifically limited to, for example, the "issues presented by the complaint" (see Figure 8–10); such a limited jury demand would not apply to issues raised in the counterclaim. Thus, an additional jury demand would have to be filed if the defendant desires a jury trial on the issues raised in the counterclaim. Review again Rule 38(c) of the FRCP, which discusses the rights and requirements regarding jury demands.

**P**ARALEGALERT!

To be valid under the FRCP, a permissive counterclaim generally must have an independent jurisdictional basis.

**Figure 8–10 Example of a Limited Jury Demand**

> *The following is an example of a limited jury demand which might have been endorsed on the caption of the complaint in the* Widgets and Gizmos, Inc. *matter. Compare this to the caption which appears in Figure 6–10.*

United States District Court
for the
District of Exurbia

WIDGETS AND GIZMOS, INC.

    Plaintiff

    vs.

TAPTAPTAP, INC.

    Defendant

Civil Action No. _____

October 21, 1993

> A JURY TRIAL IS DEMANDED ON
> THE ISSUES PRESENTED BY THE
> COMPLAINT.

**Complaint**

Limited Jury Demand

You should also note that, as defined by Rules 7 and 13 of the FRCP, there is no separate pleading called a "counterclaim"; there is, rather, a right to state a counterclaim as a segment of another pleading. The "deadline" for filing a counterclaim might be thought of, then, as the deadline for filing your client's next required pleading; in other words, in the typical case, the defendant's deadline for filing an answer (20 days). But Rule 13(f) gives the court some discretion in allowing later counterclaims if they were omitted "through oversight, inadvertence, or excusable neglect, or when justice requires . . . ." See also Rule 13(e), which allows a counterclaim maturing after the filing of a responsive pleading to be included in a later supplemental pleading (more about supplemental pleadings in Section 8–4).

Because, under the FRCP, a counterclaim is not technically a pleading but rather a segment of another pleading, the designation of a pleading that includes a counterclaim need not identify the inclusion of a counterclaim; but as with affirmative defenses, the better and more common practice is probably to identify it in the designation anyway (for example, "Answer and Counterclaim of Defendant TapTapTap, Inc."). In terms of format, the counterclaim should be set forth in a manner that clearly distinguishes it from other components of the pleading, as can be seen in Figures 8–2 and 8–3. It is not necessary to specify whether the counterclaim is permissive or compulsory.

Finally, look back at Rule 7(a) of the FRCP for a moment. Among the pleadings listed is a "reply to a counterclaim denominated as such." If a defendant files a counterclaim, then, the plaintiff must respond with a **Reply to Counterclaim.** Just as a counterclaim is drafted to resemble a complaint, so a Reply to Counterclaim is drafted to resemble an answer: with a caption, designation, admissions, denials, assertions of insufficient knowledge, and affirmative and Rule 12 defenses. Rule 12 motions can also be filed in response to a counterclaim—look again at the opening sentence of Rule 12(b) to see the authorizing language.

Counterclaims, we have noted, are asserted against "opposing parties," usually by a defendant against a plaintiff. Suppose, however, there are two parties on the same side of a lawsuit, one of whom has a claim against another. Can such a claim be asserted in the pending lawsuit?

You may be thinking: how can they have a claim against each other if they're on the same side? Wouldn't they be on different sides if they had opposing claims?

The answer to this apparent logical conundrum is that, after the cross-claim is asserted, they *will* be on opposing sides for the purposes of resolving that claim; as for the initial claim that started the lawsuit, they remain on the same side. Before you get totally confused (and we wouldn't be surprised if you're a little confused right now), let's look at an example that should make everything clearer.

Consider the facts of the Harry Hampton matter. Hampton has filed suit against Judith Johnson and Bud's Auto Service. Thus, there are two defendants in this case; they are, obviously, Johnson and Bud's Auto Service. As the lawsuit stands, Johnson and Bud's Auto Service are "on the same side."

As we have seen, however, Johnson has her own claims that she wishes to assert in this matter. She clearly has a counterclaim against Hampton, seen in Figure 8–3. But, having reviewed the police report and the claims made by Hampton against Bud's Auto Service in the original complaint, Johnson believes that negligence on the part of Bud's Auto Service also contributed to her injuries, and she wants to assert a claim against it as well.

She will assert this claim in a **cross-claim,** which is a claim for relief asserted against a coparty in a pending lawsuit (see, for example, Rule 13(g) of the FRCP). Johnson's cross-claim can also be seen in Figure 8–3.

The cross-claim, like the counterclaim, is drafted in a manner similar to the complaint. Again, causes of action, prayer for relief, and a jury demand are all necessary considerations. As with the counterclaim, the opposing party will have to file a response to the cross-claim. The name of the responsive pleading is an **Answer to Cross-Claim** (see Rule 7(a) of the FRCP), which responds using the admissions, denials, affirmative defenses, and so on, which we discussed in the context of the Answer (and the Reply to Counterclaim). Once again, if any Rule 12 defenses are applicable, they may be asserted by motion or in the Answer to Cross-Claim.

You will recall that we earlier identified two types of counterclaim, compulsory and permissive. There is no compulsory cross-claim; if a party has the right to bring a cross-claim but fails to do so, the cross-claim is not waived, but can be brought in a later action. The very right to assert a cross-claim is more limited than the right to assert a counterclaim, however. Only claims that "arise out of the transaction or occurrence that is the subject matter either of the original action or of a counterclaim therein," or that relate "to any property that is the subject of the original action," may be stated as cross-claims.

The chart in Figure 8–11 compares the types of claims that may be brought as cross-claims with those claims brought as counterclaims.

## Counterclaims and Cross-Claims in Perspective

In the simplest configuration of claims in a lawsuit, there is a claim for relief stated by a single plaintiff in a document called a *complaint,* to which a response is made by a single defendant in a document called an *answer.*

**Figure 8–11  Chart Comparing Counterclaims and Cross-Claims Authorized by Rule 13 of the FRCP**

|  | Arising out of same transaction or occurrence as the Complaint | Arising out of same transaction or occurrence as the Complaint or a Counterclaim | Arising out of a different transaction or occurrence |
|---|---|---|---|
| **Claim Against "Opposing Party"** | Counterclaim *must* be asserted (i.e., it is compulsory); if not asserted, it is waived. | Not applicable | Counterclaim *may* be asserted (i.e., it is permissive) if there is an independent jurisdictional basis; if not asserted, it is not waived. |
| **Claim Against "Co-Party"** | → | Cross-Claim *may* be asserted, but is not waived if not asserted. | Can be joined under Rule 18 with a valid Cross-Claim if there is an independent jurisdictional basis; cannot stand independently as a Cross-Claim under Rule 13. |

As we move from this simple situation to the more complex, perspective becomes important. As it turns out, and as we have taken pains to emphasize, complaints, counterclaims, and cross-claims can all be considered "complaints" (or, more properly, "claims for relief") that are simply filed at different stages of the lawsuit between parties with differing status in the lawsuit. Thus, although it is important to understand the differences between a complaint, counterclaim, and cross-claim, it is equally important to recognize the many similarities that we have discussed.

In a case with multiple claims between and among the parties, the ultimate determination as to which claims will be asserted in the complaint, which in a counterclaim, and which in a cross-claim depends, in essence, on which party files suit first. For example, if Judith Johnson had filed a complaint alleging negligence against Harry Hampton and Bud's Auto Service, then Hampton would have filed a counterclaim against Johnson (in which the claims would have been virtually identical to the First Count of his complaint) and a cross-claim against Bud's Auto Service (which would have been virtually identical to the Second Count of his complaint). For a schematic comparison of the situation where Hampton files the complaint versus the situation where Johnson files the complaint, see Figure 8–12. By keeping in mind the close relationship between complaints, counterclaims, and cross-claims, your ability to understand these concepts fully will be greatly enhanced.

**PARALEGALERT!**

Where there are multiple claims between and among multiple parties to a lawsuit, the determination as to which claims will be stated in the complaint, which in counterclaims, and which in cross-claims depends, basically, on which party happens to strike first by filing a complaint.

The cross-claim is an example of the sort of complications that can arise when there are more than two parties involved in a lawsuit. Let's now turn to further consideration of the complexities of multiparty practice.

**Figure 8–12  Schematic Comparison of Claims in the Hampton Case**

> *Where Hampton files complaint first:*
>
> | | | |
> |---|---|---|
> | Hampton claim against Johnson | = | Complaint |
> | Hampton claim against Bud's | = | Complaint |
> | Johnson claim against Hampton | = | Counterclaim |
> | Johnson claim against Bud's | = | Cross-Claim |
>
> *Where Johnson files complaint first:*
>
> | | | |
> |---|---|---|
> | Hampton claim against Johnson | = | Counterclaim |
> | Hampton claim against Bud's | = | Cross-Claim |
> | Johnson claim against Hampton | = | Complaint |
> | Johnson claim against Bud's | = | Complaint |

## 8–3  Multiparty Practice

In many disputes, more than two parties are involved. Sometimes multiple parties participate in a pending lawsuit from its inception; in other situations, the participation of additional parties begins only after the lawsuit has commenced.

In the Harry Hampton case, multiple parties have been involved from the outset, since Hampton sued both Judith Johnson and Bud's Auto Service. Hampton was authorized to sue these two defendants in one lawsuit by virtue of the principles of joinder; in our discussion in Section 6–1, we noted that joinder of multiple defendants was permitted under Rule 20 of the FRCP, and similar state law provisions.

Joinder of plaintiffs is also authorized by Rule 20. We discuss this concept and that of *class action*, a concept somewhat analogous to joinder, further in the following subsections. These concepts might have been discussed in Chapter 6, since they relate to multiple plaintiffs filing an original complaint, but we wanted to keep that chapter simple and straightforward so that you would develop a clear understanding of the basics of the complaint. Thus, we're including them at this juncture, as part of our discussion of multiparty practice.

We'll also discuss several other situations involving multiple parties, including situations in which parties are brought into the lawsuit after it is already underway, and a special kind of multiparty lawsuit called an "interpleader action."

### Permissive Joinder of Plaintiffs in an Original Complaint

Rule 20(a) of the FRCP relates to **permissive joinder** of parties. In Chapter 6 we talked about permissive joinder of defendants. Given appropriate circumstances, Rule 20(a) also authorizes the presentation of the claims of multiple plaintiffs in a single complaint. The key language of the rule provides as follows:

> All persons may join in one action as plaintiffs if they assert any right to relief jointly, severally, or in the alternative in respect of or arising out of the same transaction, occurrence, or series of transactions or occurrences and if any question of law or fact common to all these persons will arise in the action.

Thus, there are two broad requirements to the joinder of plaintiffs—that the respective claims of each plaintiff be tied to some common "transaction or occurrence," and that there exist some common "question of law or fact."

An example may be helpful to make the concept clearer. Recall our discussion in Chapter 6 of the loss of consortium claim that might have been filed by Mrs. Hampton in Harry Hampton's lawsuit. She would be authorized to join her claim in her husband's lawsuit because, although her injuries and other damages are not identical to her husband's, the claims arise out of the same "occurrence" (the collision) and involve common questions of law and fact (the details of the collision, and the questions of negligence and liability).

Another example might involve the sale of shares in a limited partnership based upon a fraudulent offering statement. The purchasers having been defrauded in the same manner and their claims sharing common issues of fact and law (namely, the content and fraudulent nature of the offering statement), they would have the option of joining their claims in one complaint.

Consider another example that will help you understand the *limits* on joinder of plaintiffs. Suppose the same purchasers of shares in a limited partnership were deceived into making their purchases not by identical fraudulent offering statements but by a variety of fraudulent oral statements made by different salespeople. The details of each individual claim might differ substantially from the other claims, since the content and circumstances of the oral statements would vary, and these differences might well predominate over the common characteristics applicable to all. Under such circumstances, the court might find that the requirements of commonality have not been satisfied, and hence find joinder to be inappropriate.

Decisions on the appropriateness of joinder of plaintiffs are thus typically made on a case-by-case basis. The court must weigh the relative impact of the characteristics *common* to the claims of the proposed plaintiffs against those characteristics that *differ* between and among the claims, and determine whether joinder is justified.

Another practical limit on joinder is the sheer number of proposed plaintiffs. Large numbers of individual parties with claims that would otherwise justify joinder are sometimes simply too numerous to join as multiple plaintiffs; the ensuing lawsuit would become too unwieldy. But there is another option in such a situation: the class action.

## Class Actions

Assume the existence of an enormous number of parties with virtually identical claims against the same defendant. A certain company, for example, may have sold a product that has turned out to be defective; it doesn't perform as it was warranted to perform. Perhaps ten thousand units of the defective product were sold to consumers, and now, despite clear evidence that the product is defective, the company refuses to repair or replace any units, or otherwise to honor its warrantee obligations.

All ten thousand purchasers of this product have virtually identical claims. Clearly, joinder of ten thousand claims is unrealistic; the resulting lawsuit would be an administrative nightmare. But rather than requiring that the ten thousand claims be brought in ten thousand separate lawsuits, it would be far more efficient to authorize the virtually identical claims to be combined in one lawsuit brought on behalf of all ten thousand plaintiffs. Is there some way the claims can be joined in one suit?

Yes, by employing the **class action** device. Class actions are similar to the joinder situations that we discussed in the previous subsection, in that they, too,

**P**ARALEGALERT!

Class actions involve multiple plaintiffs, but the pursuit of the lawsuit is handled primarily by one party (or small subgroup of parties) suing as the *representative* of all similarly situated plaintiffs.

involve multiple plaintiffs; they differ, however, in that the pursuit of a class action suit is handled primarily by one party (or possibly one small subgroup of parties) suing as the representative of all similarly situated plaintiffs. In situations involving joinder of plaintiffs, in contrast, each of the multiple plaintiffs is a full-fledged party to the suit, with all the rights and obligations that this implies.

The basic federal rule regarding class actions is Rule 23. Issues relating to certain specific classes (corporate shareholders; members of unincorporated associations) are further discussed in Rules 23.1 and 23.2, but the basic guidelines are set forth in Rule 23. Rule 23(a) sets forth a four-part test for determining whether a group of potential plaintiffs constitutes a "class" under the rule; Rule 23(b) then discusses the circumstances that justify the bringing of an action on behalf of such a class. The application of these provisions is described in Figure 8–13.

Class actions are complicated creatures. Questions often arise as to (1) whether the court should certify the group of plaintiffs as an appropriate class under the rules; (2) which individual members of a certified class should be the specific "representative parties" who actively pursue the litigation; (3) what constitutes an acceptable manner for notifying the various individual members of the class of progress in the case; and (4) how decisions are to be made as to the course of the litigation so as not to prejudice any members of the class. In-depth consideration of these issues is beyond the scope of this book; but you should at least be aware of these potential problems.

**Figure 8–13   The Basics of a Class Action**

**A.  Certifying a Class Under Rule 23(a) of the FRCP**

In order to have a class certified under Rule 23(a), those parties seeking to represent the entire class must be able to demonstrate to the satisfaction of the court that:

(1)  the class is so *numerous* that joinder of all members is impracticable;

(2)  there are *questions of law or fact common* to the class;

(3)  the claims or defenses of the representative parties are *typical* of the claims or defenses of the class; and

(4)  the *representative parties* will fairly and adequately *protect the interests* of the class.

**B.  Maintaining a Civil Action as a Class Under Rule 23(b) of the FRCP**

A class which satisfies the above requirements may be represented in a class action where:

(1)  the pursuit of separate actions by individual members of the class would create the risk of inconsistent results;

(2)  a separate action by an individual member would, as a practical matter, substantially impair or impede the ability of other individual members to protect their own interests;

(3)  the context implies that the matter relates to a question of injunctive relief involving the class as a whole; or

(4)  the court finds that issues of law or fact common to the class are much more significant than those issues affecting only individual members.

The rules relating to class actions are drafted so as to pertain to classes of defendants as well as classes of plaintiffs, so that a plaintiff can, if the requirements are met, sue certain specified individuals as representatives of an entire class of defendants. The device is more often used on behalf of classes of plaintiffs, however.

## Joinder of Indispensable Parties

In the last chapter, we touched briefly on Rule 19, regarding "joinder of persons needed for a just adjudication." In essence, Rule 19 requires the presence, as a party to the lawsuit, of a person who is subject to service of process (and whose presence in the lawsuit will not deprive the court of jurisdiction) if:

1. In the person's absence complete relief cannot be accorded among those already parties; or
2. The person claims an interest relating to the subject matter and, if *not* made a party, either (a) the person's ability to protect his or her interest will be impaired or impeded, or (b) the other parties to the lawsuit may face double or inconsistent obligations by virtue of the absent person's claimed interest.

Civil practice under Rule 19 (as well as under Rule 21, which relates to situations where the requirements and guidelines of Rule 19 and other joinder rules are violated) is often complicated. The purpose of the rule is to ensure that a lawsuit will not proceed in the absence of some party whose relationship to the events is so significant that, in the party's absence, there might be some miscarriage of justice. As a paralegal, you need to recognize situations in which Rule 19 joinder is an issue, and discuss these situations with your supervising attorney.

## Third-Party Complaints

You learned, earlier in this chapter, about the counterclaim, which is brought against an opposing party, and the cross-claim, brought against a co-party. Suppose a defendant has a claim related to the events of the lawsuit, but involving another individual or organization *not* a party to the lawsuit? Is there any way for the defendant to bring the third party into the lawsuit?

In order to make this question less abstract, consider the following example. Assume that Judith Johnson struck first in her dispute with Harry Hampton, filing a complaint against Hampton alleging negligence. Hampton is now a defendant, and brings the complaint to Sam Superlawyer, asking for his advice. Sam Superlawyer reviews the facts of the complaint and the story that Hampton relates. He recognizes that Hampton has a counterclaim against Johnson, since her automobile failed to stop before proceeding into the intersection. He also recognizes that Bud's Auto Service may be secondarily liable to Hampton as a contributor for any claim that Johnson successfully asserts against Hampton; but Bud's Auto Service was not sued by Johnson, and hence is not yet involved in the lawsuit.

The question is this: Can Hampton now bring Bud's Auto Service into the lawsuit? The answer is *yes*, through the filing of a **third-party complaint.** The act of bringing in a third-party defendant is referred to as **impleader;** to file a third-party complaint is thus to implead the third-party defendant. The Hampton case is in the state courts of Exurbia, so you would have to look at

Exurbia's state procedure to determine the details of the applicable procedure in Exurbia's courts. Let's look at how such a claim is handled under the FRCP.

The applicable rule is Rule 14. A third-party complaint may be brought against "a person not a party to the action who is or may be liable . . . for all or part" of the original plaintiff's claim. In order to bring in the third-party defendant, the defendant (who is also called a "third-party plaintiff") must draft a summons and complaint, and complete service of process of these documents against the third-party defendant, in essentially the same manner as the original summons and complaint described in Chapter 6 (filing fees may vary; check with your local clerk's office). Copies would also be sent to the other parties involved in the action, by mail or some other such ordinary method (see Rule 5 of the FRCP and the discussion of certification in Section 6–2).

A third-party complaint can be filed without permission of the court at any time, up to 10 days after the filing of the answer. If more than 10 days pass from the filing of the answer, then the third-party plaintiff can no longer simply file the third-party complaint, but must first file a motion with the court requesting permission (called "leave" of the court) to file the third-party complaint. A copy of the proposed third-party complaint would be made an exhibit to this motion.

Once the third-party complaint is served, the third-party defendant responds to it as if it were an original complaint, by attacking it with a motion or filing an answer that admits, denies, or pleads insufficient knowledge as to the allegations presented, and asserts any applicable defenses. In addition, other parties in the lawsuit "may move to strike the third-party claim, or for its severance or separate trial" (Rule 14(a)).

One last distinction should be pointed out, using our earlier example in which Judith Johnson was the plaintiff and Hampton the defendant. Let's assume that the rules in Exurbia's state courts on the issues presented are identical to the FRCP. Hampton has been shown to be authorized, under such rules, to bring in Bud's Auto Service as a third-party defendant on the grounds that Bud's may be liable for all or part of Johnson's claim against Hampton for her injuries. But Hampton also has an independent claim against Bud's Auto Service, alleging that Bud's negligence caused Hampton's own injuries. Although this claim could not have justified, by itself, a third-party complaint, it could nevertheless be joined with the third-party complaint (see Rule 18(a) of the FRCP) once that third-party complaint was legitimately filed based on the requirements of Rule 14. See also Rule 13(h) of the FRCP, allowing for claims against nonparties in accordance with the provisions of the joinder rules.

### Intervention

Suppose that after a lawsuit has been filed, an individual (or organization) that was not made a party to the lawsuit recognizes that its own interests may be affected by the manner in which the court resolves the issues presented by the lawsuit. For example, suppose two passengers are killed in an airplane crash and the survivors of one of the passengers commence a product liability suit against the manufacturer of the plane that crashed. The survivors of the second passenger would have an interest in the outcome of the litigation; indeed, their ability to collect on their own claim would be directly affected by the results of the pending litigation. Is there any way for the survivors of the second to become parties to the litigation?

Yes, if they can qualify under the requirements of the **intervention** procedure. Under the FRCP, the applicable rule is Rule 24. The provisions of Rule 24(c) require that the party seeking to intervene prepare a Motion to Intervene, serving a copy on all parties. If the interest claimed is such that the disposition of the action "may as a practical matter impair or impede the applicant's ability to protect that interest," then the intervention is *of right*, which is to say it *must* be allowed by the court, "unless the applicant's interest is adequately represented by existing parties." The intervention is also *of right* if a statute of the United States identifies the circumstances as conferring an unconditional right to intervene.

Under certain circumstances, resort to intervention may not be by right, but rather, at the discretion of the court. Such would be the case where a statute of the United States confers a conditional right to intervene, or where the interest of the outside party involves a common issue of law or fact with the main action, but does not satisfy the requirements just discussed regarding intervention of right.

Intervention is a relatively complicated procedural twist. The specifics are beyond the scope of this book, and should be saved for a more advanced study of civil litigation. For now, you should review the basic requirements and guidelines of Rule 24 of the FRCP, and research your state system to see, in general, how matters of intervention are handled in your state's courts.

## Interpleader

A unique procedural device that relates to a special kind of situation is the **interpleader.** In general, an interpleader situation exists where a person is facing the possibility of multiple inconsistent liability. Rule 22 of the FRCP authorizes a person in such a situation to join as defendants all those persons whose claims subject the person to the possibility of the inconsistent liability; the court will then resolve the inconsistency.

An interpleader action often involves a "stakeholder." A stakeholder is one who holds a fund of some sort on behalf of someone else, where at least two other parties assert conflicting ownership claims to the fund. For example, a bank might hold a savings account for the benefit of a partnership, but the identity of the individual partners who comprise the partnership may be disputed. The bank in such a situation faces the unpleasant prospect of accidentally paying, in good faith, the wrong party, then becoming liable to another, rightfully claiming party. Under these circumstances, the bank could file an interpleader action, naming as defendants all those parties who claim an interest in the savings account. The court would then resolve the conflicting claims of the defendants.

If federal jurisdictional requirements are met, it is Rule 22 of the FRCP that authorizes such an interpleader action. Check your state statutes for an analogous state rule.

## A Final Word on Multiparty Practice

The rules on multiparty practice that we have been discussing are complicated. Decisions as to the method and availability of joinder of parties and claims often involve complex analysis. Furthermore, the rules are interrelated. For example, as we discussed previously, Rule 14 of the FRCP limits third-party complaints to claims alleging that the third-party "is or may be liable" for the original claim; but, once such a claim has been made, Rule 18(a) then authorizes the joinder of other claims against the third party, and Rule 13(h) authorizes still other claims against nonparties. This illustrates how the interrelation of the rules is critical to determining the acceptability of joining potential claims (and parties) in the same lawsuit.

Or consider this: ordinarily, a third-party complaint is thought of as being brought by a defendant, but sometimes a plaintiff will want to bring in a third-party defendant to a counterclaim (because the "defending party" identified in the first sentence of Rule 14 could be a plaintiff defending a counterclaim). Thus, the same party could conceivably be both a plaintiff and a third-party plaintiff in the same lawsuit.

The many possible complications, combinations, and permutations under the rules are too numerous to explore fully in this text. A review of published judicial opinions decided under these rules will reveal some of the varied situations that arise.

We will leave you with the following advice. First, you should carefully study the rules and principles we have discussed in this section, and thereby develop a basic working knowledge of the application of these rules in practice. But second, and perhaps more important, you should work closely with your supervising attorney when any complicated multiparty questions arise.

**P**ARALEGALERT!

The rules and principles regulating multiparty practice are complicated. You should develop a basic working knowledge of these rules, but more important, you should work closely with your supervising attorney when multiparty questions arise.

## 8—4 Amended, Revised, and Supplemental Pleadings

After a pleading is filed, the party that filed it may seek to modify it in some way. The desire for the modification may be due to an earlier oversight; it may be the result of newly changed circumstances, recently occurring events, or newly uncovered information; or it may be mandated by order of the court (as, for example, where the court has granted a Motion for More Definite Statement that sought clarification of some vague or ambiguous segment of the complaint).

Under the federal rules, a pleading that modifies an earlier pleading based on something other than transactions or occurrences happening since the date of the earlier pleading is considered an **amended pleading;** a pleading that modifies an earlier pleading based on transactions or occurrences taking place subsequent to that earlier pleading is called a **supplemental pleading.** Under the rules of some states, one or both of these situations may lead to a pleading called a **revised pleading.**

Sometimes the party seeking modification has an absolute right to modify; sometimes the party must first obtain the permission of the court. Under the FRCP, a pleading to which a response is required may be amended without permission of the court once at any time before the responsive pleading is served (see Rule 15 of the FRCP). If the pleading is one to which no response is required (such as the answer), it may be amended without permission of

**P**ARALEGALERT!

Amendments made "as a matter of course" (see Rule 15 of the FRCP) can be a valuable means of remedying errors in a pleading; study the procedure and learn the deadlines.

the court within 20 days after service (with one minor exception identified in Rule 15). These are referred to as amendments made "as a matter of course," and can be an important means of remedying errors in a pleading. See, for example, Rule 12(h), which allows for certain Rule 12 defenses that were omitted from an original answer to be set forth in an amendment made "as a matter of course"; these omitted defenses would otherwise be waived.

What about amendments sought after these deadlines have expired? Such amendments are only allowed "by leave of court" (i.e., only with permission of the court; Rule 15(a)), or with the written consent of the adverse party. The court's permission is "freely given when justice so requires" (Rule 15(a)). In order to obtain the court's permission, a Motion for Leave to Amend [name of pleading] is filed. The motion should explain and describe the amendment desired, and will often include as an exhibit a copy of the pleading as it will appear with the proposed amendment incorporated into the text; the court then issues an order either granting or denying permission to amend.

If the amendment is by right (i.e., without the need to obtain prior court permission), the party amending simply files the amended pleading with the court. If permission is needed, then after such permission is obtained, the amended pleading is then filed with the court. Although it is acceptable to file an amendment that simply specifies the manner in which the original pleading should be changed, it is more effective to file a complete new pleading incorporating all original text that survives the amendment, as well as the new material from the amendment itself. This prevents any confusion about the precise wording of the pleading as amended. In addition, the designation of an amended pleading should clearly differentiate it from earlier versions, as in "Second Amended Answer of the Defendant TapTapTap, Inc."

Amended pleadings can have retroactive effect for newly discovered causes of action or defenses if they are based on the same facts as stated in the prior pleading; the amended pleading is considered filed as of the date of the original pleading (this can be important for purposes of analysis under the applicable statute of limitations). If a claim or defense made in the amended pleading is an entirely new one, however, based on different facts, statute of limitations considerations limit the retroactive effect (compare Rules 15(c)(1) and (2)). Where the wrong party was named as defendant and the correct party is not prejudiced, retroactive effect is also justified (see Rule 15(c)(3)). These rules as to retroactivity often lead to complicated analysis, indicating the need for close consultation with your supervising attorney when a question arises.

As noted, amendments may actually be ordered by the court, as where a Rule 12 motion is granted. If the Rule 12 motion is a Motion for More Definite Statement under Rule 12(e), the amended pleading must be filed "within 10 days after notice of the order or within such other time as the court may fix"; other potential deadlines (such as a dismissal subject to a right to amend within a certain number of days) are at the discretion of the court.

Supplementation of pleadings to include newly occurring events is authorized, "upon such terms as are just," where a motion requesting such supplementation is filed and an order to that effect is issued by the court. The supplementation may be allowed even where the "original pleading is defective in its statement of a claim for relief or defense" (Rule 15(d)). Supplementations can also be made that include a new claim "which either matured or was acquired by the pleader after serving a pleading" (see Rule 13(e)).

**PARALEGALERT!**

When filing an amended or supplemental pleading, it is acceptable to file a document that references only the changes made. However, the better practice is to file a new pleading that includes both the surviving text from the original pleading and the changes, so as to avoid any confusion over the precise wording of the pleading as amended or supplemented.

In a procedure similar to that for changes made by amendment, supplementary changes may be filed without including the unchanged text from the original, but the better practice is to file the full text of the pleading as supplemented, so as to avoid any confusion about the precise wording. And, as with amended pleadings, the designation should adequately differentiate the supplemental pleading from earlier versions (for example, "Second Supplemental Answer of Defendant Jones").

Finally, the filing of an amended or supplemented pleading often necessitates that the opposing party prepare a new response to the altered pleading. Rule 15(a) holds that a party "shall plead in response to an amended pleading within the time remaining for response to the original pleading or within 10 days after service of the amended pleading, whichever period may be the longer, unless the court otherwise orders." Rule 15(d) holds that if "the court deems it advisable that the adverse party plead to the supplemental pleading, it shall so order, specifying the time therefor."

Check your state rules regarding amending, supplementing, and/or revising pleadings, and see how they compare to these federal rules.

## 8–5   The Pretrial Process and Litigation Strategy

Litigation is a highly competitive activity. It involves adversaries with competing objectives; the mindset is often combative.

From the drafting of the complaint onward, litigation adversaries spar for advantage. There is often a need for contentious posturing by establishing a claim in the complaint; by attacking pleadings with motions; by responding to opposing assertions via the answer. If a lawsuit is played out to completion, victory for one side generally means defeat for the other; there may be "win-win" possibilities if a case is settled, but if the case is tried the court must decide between the competing positions.

The presence of these combative characteristics implies the need for yet another, very important, aspect of litigation practice: litigation strategy. Now that you've learned about pleadings and motions attacking pleadings, let's talk for a moment about strategy.

In Chapter 3 we noted that, by introducing litigation concepts in the context of sample cases, we hoped to provide you with not merely the "nuts and bolts" of litigation, but with an "approach" to litigation. Nowhere is the concept of "approach" more relevant than in the setting of litigation strategy. In discussing (albeit briefly) litigation strategy, however, we begin with two obstacles to overcome: first, the fact that the whole subject area of litigation is still new to you, making any consideration of complex strategy decisions difficult (which is why we haven't addressed the issue sooner); second, that it is ultimately attorneys, and not paralegals, who set litigation strategy. As to the first obstacle, we can say that our purpose in discussing litigation strategy is not to overwhelm you with detail, but rather to give you an introduction to the idea. As to the second obstacle, whether you ever have input into setting litigation strategy or not, it is still helpful to your understanding of the mechanics of litigation practice to have some comprehension of the larger context in which the mechanics operate.

**Litigation strategy,** then, is best thought of as the broad, "big picture" view of the dispute that drives the decision-making processes of the parties as they maneuver their way through the procedural mechanics of the lawsuit. For the plaintiff, it might be thought of as the **theory of the case;** for the defendant, the **theory of the defense.**

The plaintiff's theory of the case begins to develop as causes of action are chosen for inclusion in the complaint; proving these causes of action at trial is a litigation goal that must be kept in mind throughout the litigation process (recall our discussion in Chapter 3 identifying the trial as the continuing focus of litigation practice). In our analysis of the complaint in Chapter 6, we considered the concept of a "cause of action" in a somewhat sterile manner; we deemphasized the impact of the substantive law because we wanted you to focus on the mechanics of drafting a complaint. But the substantive law is, obviously, very important, and it often presents options to the involved attorneys. Evaluating these options and making choices based upon available evidence, credibility of witnesses, estimated chances for success, and goals of the client is a difficult and involved process. It goes far beyond basic legal research; it often requires the perspective provided by experience. Your supervising attorney may pass up apparently viable options based on a strategic rationale, such as the desire to maintain the trier-of-fact's focus on the single strongest option.

In the Hampton case, for example, your supervising attorney might have made a decision not to sue Bud's Auto Service, in order to keep the focus of the case on the fact that Judith Johnson failed to stop; by suing Bud's, the spotlight is also made to fall upon the failure of Hampton's own turn signal, and the manner in which that failure may have influenced Johnson's action. If Hampton had not sued Bud's, the theory of the case would have been to portray it as a straightforward negligence case between two parties; by involving Bud's Auto Service, a decision was made to risk a more complicated scenario, with the hope that the jury could sort out the various conflicting positions. For our purposes in introducing you to the mechanics of litigation, the more complicated choice was the better one; but in actual practice, after considering all the evidence, credibility of the witnesses, and such, the simplified route might well have been the better choice.

Similar strategic choices are made by a defendant. The substantive law is also likely to present options as to the thrust of the defense; and attorneys for defendants, just as attorneys for the plaintiff, must measure the credibility of potential witnesses, the goals of the client, and the chances for success. In the Hampton case, for example, Judith Johnson's attorney, in formulating a theory of the defense, may be comparing the wisdom of emphasizing Johnson's lack of negligence versus alleging Hampton's contributory negligence versus trying to emphasize both.

Theories of the case and theories of the defense go beyond merely evaluating and asserting various causes of action and defenses. Each party must define his or her ultimate goals in the lawsuit (for example, potential settlement ranges and acceptable litigation expenses), then determine how best to achieve those goals: through earnest negotiation leading to mutually beneficial settlement, through all-out confrontation, through some carefully measured synthesis of these two strategies, or through the application of some other strategic rationale.

As we have said, it is not our purpose to examine theories of the case and theories of the defense in detail. These are complicated matters, closely intertwined with the substantive law, difficult to address in hypothetical situations, and often involving a level of reliance on intangible variables that only long experience can justify. At this stage of your education, it is not important that you are able to formulate such theories; but you should at least be aware that the manner in which such theories are determined is an "art" as well as a "science." Both the art and the science are important parts of the decision-making process of your supervising attorneys; hence they are an important part of the pleading process, and indeed the whole litigation process.

## 8-6   Practical Considerations

Your caseload (i.e., the number of cases assigned to you) while reading this book has been quite low—two, to be exact (the Hampton matter and the Widgets and Gizmos, Inc. matter). In the real world, your caseload is likely to be much higher. Indeed, in some firms, one of the key responsibilities of a paralegal is to "track," or monitor, the status of a large number of cases.

Tracking case status often means monitoring the status of the pleadings. Before a case is ready to be tried, the pleadings must be "closed"—which is to say, the filing of all required pleadings and responses must be complete. It would be hard to lose track of this process if your caseload were only two cases; but if your caseload were 102 cases, you can see that the possibility of an oversight increases. Thus, you must be vigilant in managing your caseload and ensuring that the pleading process advances toward completion.

This consideration is particularly important if you represent plaintiffs. In such situations your opponents, the defendants, may recognize that there will likely be some ultimate liability in a matter, and thus they often use delay as a tactic; if you fail to stay abreast of pleading status, you will be playing into the hands of these opponents.

Defendants are not always benefited by delay, however; for example, in a case where the plaintiff's claim is questionable the defendant might want to resolve the issues as quickly as possible, in expectation of a victory. Thus, the status of the pleadings in all your pending cases must be monitored, regardless of which party you represent. Indeed, defendants must also be sure to file all pleadings necessary to avoid the entry of a default for failure to plead or otherwise defend; if a request for such a default is filed, the pleadings should be quickly reviewed and necessary responses taken.

Time passes more quickly than we sometimes realize. Particularly when you are heavily involved in an active case, it is easy to lose track of some of your other, less active cases. Don't allow this to happen; stay on top of the status of pleadings!

### PARALEGALERT!

You must be vigilant in tracking the status of pleadings in cases to which you have been assigned. Until the pleadings are closed, the case is not ready to go to trial.

# SUMMARY

## 8-1

During the pretrial process, the areas of disagreement between the parties (which will constitute the contested issues of fact to be resolved at trial) are identified in the answer. The defendant must respond to each allegation of the complaint by either (1) admitting it; (2) denying it; or (3) indicating insufficient knowledge either to admit or deny. The defendant may also assert affirmative defenses and Rule 12 defenses. An affirmative defense is one that, even if all the allegations of the complaint are true, still constitutes a valid defense. At the time the answer is filed, both the plaintiff and the defendant should determine whether a jury has been demanded and, if not, whether one is desired.

## 8-2

A counterclaim is, generally speaking, a claim for relief (essentially a complaint) filed by the defendant against the plaintiff in a pending case. A compulsory counterclaim arises out of the same transaction or occurrence as the subject matter of the complaint, and does not require for its adjudication the presence of third parties over whom the court cannot establish jurisdiction; such a counterclaim must be raised, or it is waived. A permissive counterclaim is one that does not arise out of the same transaction or occurrence as the complaint; it is not waived if omitted. There must be an independent jurisdictional basis for a permissive counterclaim. A cross-claim is a claim for relief asserted in a pending lawsuit against a coparty. A cross-claim is not waived if omitted. Keep in mind that complaints, counterclaims, and cross-claims are all closely related "claims for relief"; where multiple claims between and among multiple parties are at issue, the determination as to which claims will be stated in the complaint and which as counterclaims and cross-claims depends, in essence, on which party happens to file a complaint first.

## 8-3

Joinder of multiple plaintiffs in one action is authorized by Rule 20 of the FRCP if (1) the claims of the plaintiffs are tied to some common transaction or occurrence; and (2) there exists some common question of law or fact. Decisions on the appropriateness of joinder are typically made on a case-by-case basis, with the court weighing common characteristics against characteristics that differentiate the various proposed plaintiffs. A large group of plaintiffs with closely related claims may qualify as a class, such that their claim may be pursued by a representative party suing on behalf of all similarly situated plaintiffs in a class action. Rules regarding joinder of indispensable parties are designed to ensure that a lawsuit will not proceed without the presence of some party whose relationship to the events in question is highly significant, and whose absence might lead to a miscarriage of justice. Third-party complaints allow a party to bring a nonparty into a pending lawsuit; the third-party defendant will receive a summons and complaint through service of process, just as a standard defendant. Third-party actions are referred to as impleader actions. The intervention procedure is available for outside parties who can demonstrate the need to join in the litigation to protect their interests. Interpleader actions allow for a party facing multiple inconsistent liability to bring the matter before the court, which will resolve the issues so as to avoid the inconsistency. Multiparty practice is often complicated, and you should be sure to consult closely with your supervising attorney when any questions arise in this area.

## 8-4

A pleading that modifies an earlier pleading based on something other than transactions or occurrences happening since the date of the earlier pleading is considered to be an amended pleading; a pleading that modifies an earlier pleading based on subsequent transactions or occurrences is a supplemental pleading. Amendments made "as a matter of course" are often useful for correcting errors in earlier pleadings, but the deadlines are short, and hence the procedure (see Rule 15 of the FRCP) should be reviewed carefully. If you receive an amended or supplemented pleading, keep in mind that you may have to file a new responsive pleading that takes into account the changes.

## 8–5

Litigation is highly competitive, and requires strategy. Litigation strategy is the broad, "big picture" view of the dispute that drives the decision-making processes of the parties. For the plaintiff, it is often thought of as the "theory of the case"; for the defendant, the "theory of the defense." Setting strategy involves sifting among options and making choices based on available evidence, credibility of witnesses, estimated chances for success, and the goals of the client. It is a difficult process, going beyond legal research and often requiring the perspective provided by experience.

## 8–6

You should be vigilant in keeping track of the status of the pleadings in cases to which you are assigned. Until the pleadings are closed, the case is not ready to go to trial.

## REVIEW

### Key Terms

Before proceeding, review the key terms listed below to be sure you understand each one. If necessary, read over the corresponding section of the chapter. When you are ready to test your understanding, answer the Review Questions.

answer
admission
denial
affirmative defense
special defense
Reply to Affirmative Defenses
Rule 12 defense
jury demand
counterclaim
compulsory counterclaim
permissive counterclaim
Reply to Counterclaim
cross-claim
Answer to Cross-Claim
permissive joinder
class action
third-party complaint
impleader
intervention
interpleader
amended pleading
supplemental pleading

revised pleading
litigation strategy
theory of the case
theory of the defense

### Questions for Review and Discussion

1. Explain how the defendant admits, denies, or pleads insufficient knowledge in response to the allegations of the complaint.
2. What is an affirmative defense?
3. Why is it important to consider the filing of a jury demand at or about the time the answer is filed?
4. How does a compulsory counterclaim differ from a permissive counterclaim?
5. What does an answer have in common with a reply to a counterclaim and an answer to a cross-claim?
6. How are complaints, counterclaims, and cross-claims similar?
7. What is a class action?
8. What is meant by the term *impleader*?
9. What circumstances justify an intervention?
10. What is the difference between an amended pleading and a supplemental pleading?

## Activities

1. Locate and review your state rules and procedures regarding the manner in which parties to a lawsuit may demand a jury trial.

2. Find the case of *Lamar Haddox Contractor, Inc. v. Potashnick*, 552 F. Supp. 11 (M.D. Louisiana, 1982) in your local law library, and read it to learn how one court resolved a controversy regarding the issue of an indispensable party (as well as the impact of the presence of the party on diversity jurisdiction).

3. Call your federal court clerk's office, and ask for the name of a pending class action. If such a case is among their active files, go to the clerk's office and look at the complaint.

# CHAPTER 9  Discovery

## OUTLINE

## COMMENTARY

It's going to be another hectic week at your law firm; you've just received the following memorandum from Sam Superlawyer:

Memorandum

To: Paula Paralegal
From: Sam Superlawyer
Re: Discovery: Hampton; Widgets and Gizmos, Inc.
Date: January 16, 1994

*Widgets and Gizmos, Inc. case*
    I have just received a set of interrogatories from the attorneys for TapTapTap, Inc. They have also sent a Notice of Deposition of Edgar Ellison.
    Please prepare a first draft of proposed responses to the interrogatories, indicating those (if any) to which you feel an objection is in order. Also, send a copy of the interrogatories and a copy of the deposition notice to Edgar Ellison.
    In your cover letter to Ellison (which I will review before mailing), briefly describe the nature of the deposition process (he should be generally familiar, as he has been deposed before in other cases). I note that there is a production request associated with the deposition notice; please see to it that Ellison gathers together those responsive documents which he has not yet forwarded to this office.

*(continued)*

As to the deposition notice, also prepare a first draft of a Motion for Protective Order; in particular, we want to limit the ability of TapTapTap, Inc.'s attorneys to inquire into Ellison's knowledge of the trade secrets of Widgets and Gizmos, Inc.

*Hampton case*

I have received a production request from counsel for Judith Johnson. With regard to this production request, please make a photocopy for Harry Hampton, along with a draft letter explaining the meaning of a production request (which I will also review before mailing). After Hampton receives the copy of the production request and your letter, make arrangements to meet with him to discuss a timetable for organizing the necessary materials. Also, since much of the requested material is already in our file, please begin organizing the response.

Finally, begin preparing our own interrogatory requests to be served on Judith Johnson.

Discovery is an essential element of the litigation process. It requires imagination, organization, and diligence. This week you'll be applying all three of these characteristics as you learn how to prepare both discovery requests and discovery responses.

## OBJECTIVES

In this chapter you will be learning about the discovery process, in which the parties to a lawsuit are given an opportunity to inquire, under official court procedures and rules, about information in the hands of others. After completing Chapter 9, you will be able to:

1. Define *discovery*.
2. Explain why the scope of discovery is described as "liberal."
3. Explain why interrogatories are often the first discovery device utilized.
4. Explain how discovery regarding expert witnesses is conducted.
5. Identify methods of controlling large volumes of documents.
6. Explain what steps a paralegal follows when reviewing the client's documents in preparation for making a production response.
7. Identify several reasons why depositions are important.
8. Explain what is meant by a *subpoena duces tecum*.
9. Identify some tasks of a paralegal associated with a deposition.
10. Compare a Motion for Protective Order with a simple objection to a discovery request.

## 9–1  Discovery in General

There is much posturing between and among the parties in a lawsuit; much jockeying for position, maneuvering for advantage, strategizing to gain an edge. As we noted in Chapter 8, litigation is competitive in the extreme; indeed, the rules of ethical conduct actually require that an attorney be a "zealous advocate" of the positions of his or her client. Thus, partisanship is not merely authorized, it is essential; partiality toward one's client is not merely tolerated, it is expected.

What is not tolerated in litigation practice, however, is deception or concealment. If there ever was a day when a "surprise witness" could stride into a courtroom at the eleventh hour and, to the shock of all those assembled, turn the tables and alter the outcome of a hotly contested trial, that day has passed.

Disputes should be resolved, it has been decided, not by subterfuge but by reasoned and fully informed debate. The playing field, as it were, should be level; both sides should have full access to the same information. The rules of procedure provide a means by which the parties can fully explore the issues and evidence that may affect the outcome of the trial; only then will the resolution of the underlying dispute be fair.

In this chapter we'll explore that area of litigation practice that fulfills the third objective of the pretrial process: to provide the parties with the opportunity to uncover and analyze virtually all information relevant to the contested issues. **Discovery** is the term applied to the rules, methods, and procedure by which the parties to a lawsuit are authorized to request (and, by seeking a court order, ultimately to compel) the disclosure of factual information held by opposing parties (or, in some instances, nonparty witnesses). It is, in short, the official information-gathering mechanism associated with a lawsuit; it provides the means by which the initial, informal, and unofficial investigation of a party (see Chapter 4) can be enhanced to provide the most complete picture possible of the full range of factual evidence.

The **scope of discovery**, which is the extent to which the right of inquiry reaches, is frequently described as "liberal," meaning that broad inquiry is authorized. Understanding the scope of discovery is so important that we quote directly from Rule 26 of the FRCP, which establishes principles mirrored in state law provisions nationwide:

> Parties may obtain discovery regarding *any matter, not privileged, which is relevant* to the subject matter involved in the pending action, whether it relates to the claim or defense of the party seeking discovery or to the claim or defense of any other party, including the existence, description, nature, custody, condition and location of any books, documents, or other tangible things and the identity and location of persons having knowledge of any discoverable matter. It is not ground for objection that the information sought will be inadmissible at the trial *if the information sought appears reasonably calculated to lead to the discovery of admissible evidence*. [emphasis supplied]

Thus, even matters inadmissible in evidence may be obtained through discovery; the only test is that they be relevant, not privileged, and "reasonably calculated to lead to the discovery of admissible evidence."

In essence, what this scope implies is that every party to a lawsuit is authorized to compel every other party to reveal exactly what it knows about the facts of the case. This may seem amazing to you; it is, however, largely true (save for privileged matters, requests deemed excessive or unnecessary under Rule 26(b)(1), and something called "work-product," discussed in a moment; also see our discussion of expert testimony in Section 9–2). That's why discovery practice is described as *liberal*.

What is work-product? **Attorney work-product** is the term applied to materials "prepared in anticipation of litigation" as discussed in Rule 26(b)(3). Discovery of such material is limited, on the theory that it is unfair for one party to be allowed to take advantage of the work-product of another party's efforts in the lawsuit; hence this is an exception to the doctrine of liberal discovery. If, for example, a party's attorney (or paralegals working for the attorney) invested a great deal of time organizing, in newly created tables, the information contained in certain business records, the records themselves would be discoverable but the tables would constitute work-product "prepared in anticipation of litigation." Such work-product would be discoverable "only upon a showing that the party seeking discovery has substantial need of the materials in the preparation of the party's case and that the party is unable without undue hardship to obtain the substantial equivalent of the materials by other means" (Rule 26(b)(3)). Such a hardship might exist in our example if the underlying records had been inadvertently destroyed; otherwise, the work-product tables would not be discoverable. The rule also requires that the court, if it does, in fact, find such materials to be discoverable, "shall protect against disclosure of the mental impressions, conclusions, opinions, or legal theories of an attorney or other representative of a party concerning the litigation" (Rule 26(b)(3)).

An important consideration relevant to discovery practice is the close involvement of the client. In every step of the litigation process, of course, client input is always important, but much of what has been discussed in the last three chapters with regard to motions and pleadings involves complex legal concepts beyond the expertise of most clients; indeed, lawyers are hired by clients specifically for their ability to deal intelligently with these technicalities. The discovery process, however, involves facts, and your best source of factual information remains the client. The client will not be your only source of information, but for the purposes of both responding to the requests of the other side and identifying the proper subject matter of requests to be served on them, contacting your client is often a crucial step.

We should say a word here about the important role of the paralegal in discovery. Simply stated, the role of the paralegal is often central. In many lawsuits, the information exchanged in discovery is both complicated and voluminous; a great deal of processing and correlating of raw data is involved. This processing and correlating applies not only to the gathering of information necessary to respond (or object) to discovery requests, but also to the foundation work needed to draft your own requests and the organization and analysis necessary to begin evaluating discovery responses received from the other side. In all these tasks (see Figure 9–1), paralegals can be extraordinarily useful to a litigation attorney; thus, a large part of the work of a litigation paralegal often involves discovery matters. In this chapter, we'll be focusing on the first two tasks, namely, drafting requests and preparing responses. Evaluating responses is by and large a substantive matter, for which you'll develop a facility with experience.

## PARALEGALERT!

An exception to the basic liberality of discovery is attorney work-product, which is discoverable only upon a showing of substantial need and undue hardship.

## PARALEGALERT!

Paralegals often play a very important role in the discovery process; their assistance can be extraordinarily helpful to supervising attorneys. Be sure to master the concepts presented in this chapter!

**Figure 9–1    The Three Key Discovery Tasks of the Paralegal**

(1) Drafting discovery *requests.*

(2) Gathering information and preparing discovery *responses* (including objections).

(3) *Evaluating* and *organizing* discovery responses received from the other side.

**PARALEGALERT!**

As with every other area of litigation practice, in discovery it's vital *to know the specific rules that apply!*

Let us also emphasize in this preliminary section a factor we've mentioned often before—the importance of identifying and following applicable rules. Although state court discovery practice is often similar to federal practice, even minor differences can have significant impact. Such details as specific deadlines are very, very important; you must check the rules to make sure you know your deadlines for both filing discovery requests and preparing discovery responses. In the pages that follow, we will be focusing (as we have throughout the book) on the applicable provisions of the Federal Rules of Civil Procedure. But even in the federal courts, you must be sure to identify applicable *local* federal rules that expand on the coverage of the FRCP. An example of such a local rule is seen in Figure 9–2; we will be making reference to this rule throughout the remainder of this chapter.

Another relevant consideration with regard to discovery deadlines and procedures is the applicability of a court-mandated **scheduling order.** Rule 26(f) provides for an optional **discovery conference,** which can be scheduled by the court on its own initiative, or acting upon a motion of a party. Following such a conference a scheduling order will be entered "tentatively identifying the issues for discovery purposes, establishing a plan and schedule for discovery, setting limitations on discovery, if any; and determining such other matters . . . as are necessary for the proper management of discovery in the action." Rule 26(f)

**Figure 9–2   Sample Local Rule Regarding Discovery**

*The following appears in the local rules of the United States District Court for the District of Exurbia:*

**Rule 10.   Discovery Procedures.**

(a) Unless otherwise permitted by the Court for good cause shown, such permission being granted only upon written motion to the Court, no party shall serve upon any other party more than thirty (30) written interrogatories, including all parts and subparts. This limit may not be waived by stipulation of counsel.

(b) Written interrogatories and requests for production, pursuant to Rules 33 and 34 of the FRCP, shall be served on all parties in the normal manner but shall not be filed with the Court. In lieu of filing interrogatories and requests for production, a Notice (with standard caption and signature of filing party or attorney) shall be filed indicating the date on which the interrogatories and/or production requests were served on the parties.

(c) Answers and objections to interrogatories and production responses shall state immediately before each answer or objection the interrogatory or request for production to which a response is being made. These answers and objections should be served on all parties and filed with the Court. Materials produced in response to discovery requests, such as documents produced in response to a request for production, shall not be filed with the Court unless the Court so orders.

(d) No motion pursuant to Rules 26 through 37 of the FRCP shall be filed by any party unless the party making the motion has conferred with the opposing party or counsel and discussed the contested discovery issues in detail in an effort to resolve the differences. An affidavit shall accompany any motion filed, attesting to the effort to resolve, in good faith, the contested discovery issues, and that said effort was unsuccessful.

(e) Memoranda of law shall accompany any discovery motion filed with this Court, containing a concise statement of the nature of the case and a specific verbatim listing of the items of discovery sought or opposed, followed by a legal analysis of the reasons why discovery of each particular item should or should not be allowed.

allows for the combination of a discovery conference with a Rule 16 pretrial conference; we discuss such pretrial conferences in more detail in Chapter 11. For now you should simply be aware that, as a general matter, judges and attorneys often work together in the early stages of a case to establish some guidelines that assist in the orderly advancement of the lawsuit. These guidelines often contain provisions that regulate the discovery to be conducted, and hence must be kept in mind when identifying deadlines or determining the impact of other discovery rules.

Other than setting the aforementioned guidelines in a pretrial or discovery conference, the court's involvement in discovery practice is, ideally, minimal. The rules are designed to allow and encourage the parties to proceed on their own to work out their difficulties. Disputes do arise, however, and we will discuss discovery motions designed to involve the court in the resolution of these disputes in Section 9–7.

Now that we've addressed some of the generalities, let's turn to the specifics. There are five basic methods of discovery: *interrogatories*, which are written questions calling for written answers; the *request for production of documents and things*, which seeks access to actual documents, tangible items, or physical locations; the *deposition*, which involves questions posed to a party or witness (called the deponent), whose oral answers are then recorded and preserved in a transcript; the *request for a medical examination*, which allows for an inspection of a party's physical or mental condition, when that condition is an issue in the lawsuit; and the *request for admissions*, which involves statements posed to a party for the purpose of eliciting the party's admission or denial of the truth of the statement, or for an admission as to the genuineness of specified documents.

**PARALEGALERT!**

There are five basic methods of discovery, usually employed in the following order:

1. Interrogatories
2. Requests for production
3. Depositions
4. Requests for medical exam
5. Requests for admission

Although there is no requirement dictating the sequence in which these various discovery options may be utilized (unless the court orders otherwise under Rule 26(d) of the FRCP), it is important that the manner in which discovery is pursued be purposeful rather than random. The sequence chosen (as well as the decision whether or not to utilize a given option) will often turn on the nature of the specific issues presented by the case. In practice, a particular pattern is frequently seen: first, the serving of interrogatories; second, the serving of production requests; third, depositions; fourth, the request for a medical examination (if the physical or mental condition of a party is at issue); fifth, filing of requests for admission. The logic of this sequence will become clearer to you as you work your way through the chapter.

Not only is there no specified sequence of discovery, there is also no specific limit on the number of times each method of discovery can be utilized. For example, after an initial set of interrogatories has been filed, a second and even a third set might be filed at a later date. Rule 26(b)(1), however, does allow the court to limit discovery where it determines that (1) the discovery sought is unreasonably duplicative, or is obtainable from some other source that is more convenient, less burdensome, or less expensive; (2) the party seeking the discovery has already had ample opportunity to obtain the information; or (3) the discovery sought is unduly burdensome or expensive, taking into account various factors including the needs of the case, the amount in controversy, limitations on the parties' resources, and the importance of the issues at stake (see Figure 9–3). Among other things, these provisions can be used to prevent a wealthy client (such as a large corporation) from burying a less wealthy client under an avalanche of time-consuming, expensive, and relatively immaterial discovery requests.

Figure 9–3   Three Limitations on Discovery under Rule 26 of the FRCP

*Rule 26(b)(1) of the FRCP establishes the following three circumstances under which the court is authorized, upon its own initiative or pursuant to a motion, to limit the extent or use of discovery:*

(1) if the discovery sought is unreasonably cumulative or duplicative, or is obtainable from some other source that is more convenient, less burdensome, or less expensive;

(2) if the party seeking discovery has had ample opportunity by discovery in the action to obtain the information sought; or

(3) if the discovery is unduly burdensome or expensive, taking into account the needs of the case, the amount in controversy, limitations on the parties' resources, and the importance of the issues at stake in the litigation.

We address each of the five methods of discovery in detail in the sections that follow. We then consider the motions that can influence the course of discovery, and close with our customary discussion of practical considerations.

## 9–2   Interrogatories

**Interrogatories** are written questions posed by one party to another with regard to matters within the scope of allowable discovery, requiring written responses. They are authorized and governed by Rule 33 of the FRCP.

It is important to first note that interrogatories can only be served on other parties; they cannot be served, for example, on nonparty witnesses. As we will discuss further, the only discovery device in which questions can be posed to nonparties is the deposition (some medical examinations can also involve nonparty individuals who are under the control of a party; see Rule 35).

As we noted earlier, interrogatories are often the first discovery device utilized by a party (see Figure 9–4). The responses often set the stage for requests

**PARALEGALERT!**

Interrogatories can only be served on *parties*, not non-party witnesses. The only discovery method in which questions can be posed to non-parties is the deposition.

Figure 9–4   Why Interrogatories are Often the First Discovery Device Used

*Interrogatories are often the first discovery device used by a litigant. There are two essential reasons for this:*

(1) by identifying the existence of certain relevant documents, or categories of documents, interrogatories can be used to "set the stage" for an ensuing *request for production of documents;* and

(2) by identifying potential deponents, and also providing basic background information which can serve as a starting point for further inquiry, interrogatories can also be used to "set the stage" for a *deposition.*

*Note that production requests are often the second discovery device used, because they can be used to further "set the stage" for the deposition; the deponent is often questioned about documents which have been produced.*

for production (by identifying the existence of certain relevant documents) and depositions (by identifying possible deponents, and providing basic information that serves as a starting point for the more wide-ranging examination typical in a deposition).

As with other discovery methods, there are two broad aspects of interrogatories that we must address: (1) how to draft interrogatories to be served on an opponent; and (2) how to prepare answers to interrogatories that have been served upon your firm's client.

## Drafting Interrogatories

The first question that arises in drafting interrogatories is an obvious one: what, exactly, should you be asking about? This will vary, first of all, with whether you represent the plaintiff or the defendant. In general, perhaps the best place to start when drafting interrogatories is to review the pleadings. Interrogatories posed by a defendant to a plaintiff will often focus on information that affects the elements of the cause of action identified in the complaint, and the damages alleged (while also seeking information that might support the defenses). If posed by the plaintiff to the defendant, they will focus on the nature of the defenses identified in the answer (while also seeking information that might support the causes of action). In general, all the competing allegations of the parties, and the facts and evidence that stand behind them, are fair game for inquiry by any party.

As we noted in the introductory section, the client is an essential source of ideas. No one is more intimately familiar with the basic facts of the case than is the client (or employees of the client), and, although not experienced at drafting appropriate interrogatories, clients can nevertheless provide valuable insight into worthwhile areas of inquiry.

Certain background questions are generally always included. If the opposing party is an individual person, such things as date of birth, residence and business addresses and phone numbers, marital status, children, and level of education attained are pertinent topics. If the opposing party is a corporation (as with the interrogatories filed by TapTapTap, Inc. in Figure 9–5), interrogatories as to the identity of the person preparing the responses (including such things as relevant addresses and phone numbers and job title), state of incorporation and principal place of business, and precise corporate name and details of corporate structure (such as the existence of parent or subsidiary corporations) are commonly prepared.

Certain standard categories of questions are also common. Interrogatories that inquire, for example, into the existence of relevant documents, or the names, addresses, and phone numbers of witnesses or other persons having relevant information, are virtually always included, regardless of the type of case at issue. If the case seeks damages for personal injuries, interrogatories as to the nature of the injuries and the circumstances of the accident causing the injuries would be served by the defendant; the plaintiff would likewise inquire into the circumstances of the accident and applicable insurance coverage, and both sides would seek information about expert testimony. Figure 9–6 shows several typical interrogatories that might be sent by a personal injury defendant to the plaintiff.

We should inject a word here about insurance-related interrogatories. As just noted, interrogatories are often served requesting information as to insurance agreements covering any liability created as a

**PARALEGALERT!**

Although information regarding applicable insurance coverage constitutes neither admissible evidence nor information likely to lead to the discovery of admissible evidence, it is nevertheless made discoverable by Rule 26(b)(2) of the FRCP.

**Figure 9–5    Interrogatories of *TapTapTap, Inc.* to *Widgets and Gizmos, Inc.***

*[Note: Depending on the applicable rules, each interrogatory is often separated from the next interrogatory by an inch or more of space in order to leave room to provide the answer. In the interest of saving space in this text, such considerations have been ignored. When drafting your own interrogatories, however, you will have to follow applicable spacing rules.]*

United States District Court
for the
District of Exurbia

WIDGETS AND GIZMOS, INC.

    Plaintiff

       vs.

TAPTAPTAP, INC.

    Defendant

:
:
:
:
:
:
:
:
:

Civil Action No. 93-OWH-00543

January 15, 1994

### Interrogatories of *TapTapTap, Inc.* to *Widgets and Gizmos, Inc.*

Pursuant to Rules 26 and 33 of the Federal Rules of Civil Procedure, the defendant *TapTapTap, Inc.* hereby requests that the plaintiff, *Widgets and Gizmos, Inc.*, respond to the following interrogatories, under oath and within the deadline established by the rules.

*Definitions*

The following definitions shall apply to these interrogatories:

1. "Documents" shall refer to all writings or other media in which information is stored, including but not limited to correspondence, memorandums, invoices, charts, graphs, maps, specifications, technical drawings or illustrations, newspaper or other periodical articles, computer disks, audio or video tapes, any other electronic information storage or retrieval system, or any other source of written or stored information. Any copy of a document which has been altered or marked with notations or comments of any kind shall be considered to be a separate original.
2. "Taps" shall refer to the defendant, *TapTapTap, Inc.*
3. "Widgets" shall refer to the plaintiff, *Widgets and Gizmos, Inc.*
4. "Widgenometer" shall refer to the widgenometer product identified in paragraph 4 of the Complaint.
5. "Identify," when used in conjunction with a document, shall mean to specify the type of document, date of document, a brief summary of the information contained in the document, and the name and address of the person in custody or possession of the document.
6. "Identify," when used in conjunction with a person, shall mean to specify the person's name, current residence and business addresses, residence and business phone numbers, and, where applicable, title of position of employment held at *Widgets and Gizmos, Inc.*

*Interrogatories*

1. Identify the person supplying answers to these interrogatories.
2. State the full corporate name of Widgets, and provide the state of incorporation and address of the principal place of business.
3. Identify any corporation which owns more than 30% of the outstanding stock of Widgets.

4. Identify any corporations of which Widgets owns 30% or more of the outstanding stock.
5. Identify all employees of Widgets who were involved in the design and development of the widgenometer.
6. Identify all employees of Widgets who were involved in the negotiation of the contract with Taps identified in paragraph 5 of the Complaint.
7. Identify the exact chemical composition of the alloy referred to as an "aluminum chip" in paragraph 4 of the Complaint.
8. Identify all documents, including but not limited to internal memoranda, which relate in any way to the alloy used for the "aluminum chip" referred to in paragraph 4 of the Complaint.
9. Identify the document which Widgets claims establishes the specifications for the widgenometer.
10. Identify the document which Widgets claims is referenced by the passage "a certain preliminary letter of agreement between Emily Tapman and Edgar Ellison" referenced in paragraph 6 of the contract referred to in paragraph 5 of the Complaint.
11. Identify all documents which Widgets claims establish or support the contention that it "shipped to Taps a total of 3000 widgenometers," as set forth in paragraph 6 of the Complaint.
12. Identify all damages which Widgets claims to have suffered as a result of the allegations set forth in the Complaint, including but not limited to contract damages, consequential damages, interest, costs, and attorneys' fees.
13. Please describe all tests performed on the widgenometers which related in any way to the possibility that the alloy used in the widgenometers might become magnetized if exposed to electrical currents.
14. Please identify all other persons or businesses to whom Widgets has sold or supplied widgenometers.
15. Identify all outside testing facilities, laboratories, or research centers which assisted in the development, testing, or production of the widgenometers.
16. State the minimum "Mean Time Between Failure" rate which Widgets asserts the widgenometers would have to achieve in order to satisfy the terms of the contract identified in paragraph 5 of the Complaint.
17. Identify all expert witnesses whom you expect to testify at trial, and for each state:
     (a) the subject matter on which the expert is expected to testify;
     (b) the substance of the facts and opinions to which the expert is expected to testify; and
     (c) a summary of the grounds for each opinion.

THE DEFENDANT, TAPTAPTAP, INC.

By: _____

Tim Tiptop, Esq.
Its attorney
Tiptop & Towe
71 Ferguson Street
Metro City, Exurbia 12345
Atty. Reg. #: 65488
Phone: (901) 333-3333

**Certificate of Service**

This is to certify that a copy of the foregoing was mailed, postage prepaid, this 15th day of January, 1994, to attorney Sam Superlawyer, Esq., Lincoln & Hoover, 123 Lincoln Street, Metro City, Exurbia, 12345.

_____
Tim Tiptop, Esq.

**Figure 9–6 Some Typical Interrogatories Filed by a Defendant in a Personal Injury Case**

*The purpose of this figure is to provide you with an introduction to a few typical interrogatories often filed by the defendant in personal injury cases. For a more complete picture, refer to one of the commercially-published sets of sample interrogatories. In the future, any law firm for which you work will also likely have model interrogatories which they suggest as a starting point for drafting interrogatories in personal injury cases, and perhaps many other types of cases as well.*

(1) Identify all injuries which plaintiff claims are the result of the events described in the Complaint, by stating the portion of the body injured, the nature of the injury, and the extent of any permanent disability.

(2) Identify all physicians or medical professionals who have provided you with treatment or medical services for any of the injuries described in the previous interrogatory, including but not limited to physical therapists, x-ray technicians, or medical laboratory personnel. For each physician or medical professional identified, please state (a) the date of treatment; (b) the nature of treatment; and (c) the cost of the treatment.

(3) Identify every hospital, extended-care facility, or emergency facility at which you received treatment for the injuries described in your response to interrogatory #1 above, and for each identify (a) the dates of treatment; (b) the nature of treatment; and (c) the cost of treatment.

(4) Identify all witnesses to the accident described in paragraphs _____ to _____ of the Complaint.

(5) Identify all expert witnesses you intend to have testify at trial, including but not limited to medical experts, accident reconstruction experts, or product safety analysts, and for each identify:
    (a) the subject matter on which the expert is expected to testify;
    (b) the substance of the facts and opinions to which the expert is expected to testify; and
    (c) a summary of the grounds for each opinion.

(6) Have you ever suffered illness or injury to any of the body parts identified in interrogatory #1 above, either prior or subsequent to the events described in the Complaint?

(7) If the answer to interrogatory #6 is in the affirmative, please state (a) the body part affected; (b) the date or dates of the illness or injury; (c) the nature of the illness or injury; and (d) the cause, if known, of the illness or injury.

(8) With regard to your claim for lost wages in paragraph _____ of the Complaint, please identify: (a) the name of the employer for whom you worked; (b) the period during which you were employed by this employer; (c) the dates of your inability to work; (d) your job title during the time you were unable to work; and (e) the full amount you claim for lost wages.

(9) Identify all of life's activities which you claim an inability to enjoy or participate in, as alleged in paragraph _____ of your Complaint.

(10) Identify all damages alleged to be the result of the events described in the Complaint which you have not yet identified in any other of these interrogatories.

result of the decision in the pending lawsuit. Such information is not generally admissible at trial, and can probably not qualify as "reasonably calculated to lead to the discovery of admissible evidence"; thus, under ordinary circumstances, it would not be discoverable. However, the rules specifically hold that insurance coverage is a proper subject of discovery (Rule 26(b)(2)), and thus it constitutes an exception to the general rule.

We should also mention that addresses of potential witnesses are very important to obtain, because *subpoenas* may someday be required to compel these witnesses to testify, either at a deposition or at trial. We will discuss *subpoenas* further in Section 9–4 on depositions.

As with pleadings and motions, it is useful to begin drafting interrogatories (or any discovery request) by consulting models taken from the files of similar cases your firm has handled, or from the pages of commercial form books. There are several useful series of volumes with suggested interrogatories covering an amazingly wide range of factual situations. By reviewing these models and form books, you will develop a good idea of the type of interrogatories that have been used in cases similar to yours. Of course, you must not rely exclusively on such aids; each case has its own unique twists, and you must apply your own personal analytical abilities to ensure that all necessary inquiries have been made.

The key consideration in drafting an interrogatory is to be absolutely clear in identifying the information that you are requesting. If the question asked is ambiguous, hence open to interpretation, you can be sure that opposing counsel will interpret it in a way that is most beneficial to the opposing party, and least informative for you.

Many cases involve the testimony or participation of **expert witnesses.** Rule 26(b)(4) of the FRCP relates to discovery of "facts known and opinions held by experts." In general, under the FRCP a party may file an interrogatory that inquires into four issues about the experts whom the other side expects to call as witnesses at trial: (1) the identity of each expert; (2) the subject matter on which the expert is expected to testify; (3) the substance of the facts and opinions to which the expert is expected to testify; and (4) a summary of the grounds for each opinion. Further discovery regarding the expert (such as a deposition) is only permitted if the court so orders after request by motion (Rule 26(b)(4)(A)), and the court is authorized to assess the expert's fees and/or expenses upon the party seeking the further discovery. State court rules may vary.

Discovery regarding an expert who, although retained by an opposing party, is not expected to testify at trial is authorized only upon a showing of "exceptional circumstances," as where it is "impracticable for the party seeking the discovery" to obtain the information by other means. Such a situation might arise where the nontestifying expert examined a piece of evidence that has since been destroyed; only that expert would then have information about the evidence in question. Also, if a medical expert conducts a court-ordered physical or mental examination under Rule 35, then even if the examining physician is not expected to testify, the party examined is entitled to a copy of the examining physician's "detailed written report" (see Rule 26(b)(4)(B) and Rule 35; see also Section 9–5).

As we noted, interrogatories are often used to "set the stage" for a deposition. This means that you should use interrogatories to obtain information regarding the identity of any individual who has useful information about the case; once the identity of such an individual is known, he or she can be deposed. Other interrogatory responses can also provide a useful starting point for deposition questioning. The sort of facts best requested through interrogatories are what might be thought of as "hard" facts, which is to say, facts requiring little or no

**PARALEGALERT!**

It is critically important that the interrogatories you draft be absolutely unambiguous. Ambiguity defeats the purpose of an interrogatory; it will engender either an objection or an evasive answer.

**PARALEGALERT!**

Depositions of expert witnesses can only be taken if the court so orders after request by motion. Without such a court order, inquiry into the findings of experts can only be conducted by filing interrogatories; and even these interrogatories are limited to the four categories of information identified in Rule 26(b)(4) of the FRCP.

analysis or interpretation (for example, the date on which a document was signed, or the precise amount of a repair bill). Once known, the implications of such facts can then be explored further in the deposition. Opinions and other nuances, which might be called "soft" facts, are often best explored in a deposition, as we discuss in Section 9–4. Interrogatories seeking hard facts and soft facts are compared in Figure 9–7.

If there is no plan to take the deposition of the opposing party (perhaps for reasons of cost), then the interrogatories filed might range into the more problematic "soft" facts; such interrogatories are more likely, however, to open the door to evasive responses. In general, interrogatories are most useful when focused on obtaining "hard" information.

The FRCP establishes no definitive guideline as to the acceptable number of interrogatories. Local federal rules often do set limits, however. If such limits apply, read the applicable rule closely; subparts of an interrogatory often count toward the limit. Thus if the limit is 30 interrogatories, and a party files 10 numbered interrogatories, each with subparts (a), (b), and (c), that party would then have reached the limit of thirty total interrogatories. Where such limits are in place, there is usually a provision for filing a motion requesting the right to file additional interrogatories if circumstances and justice so require. Review section (a) of the local rule in Figure 9–2.

A few words should be said about format of interrogatories. As you can see from Figure 9–5, interrogatory requests are similar to pleadings and motions in that they have a caption, designation, signature block, and certification. There is usually an introductory paragraph and often a "Definitions" section, which clarifies certain terms in order to minimize potential confusion (both of which are also seen in Figure 9–5). Local rules often require that space be left between interrogatories to allow the responding party to fill in the answer.

Certification requirements are important to keep in mind. All parties receive a copy of the request for interrogatories, not just the party from whom responses are sought (review Rule 5 of the FRCP). This enables all parties to keep track of

**Figure 9–7  Interrogatories: Comparison of "Hard" Facts and "Soft" Facts**

*"Hard" facts are not subject to interpretation; "soft" facts are. In general, interrogatories which seek information as to "hard" facts are more useful than interrogatories which seek information as to "soft" facts, since the latter can often lead to evasive or self-serving responses.*

**Interrogatories seeking "hard" facts (*Judith Johnson to Harry Hampton*):**

(1)  Please identify each date on which Bud's Auto Service performed repair work on the 1990 Pontiac Grand Am owned by the plaintiff Harry Hampton and mentioned in paragraph 3 of the First Count of the Complaint, for the six-month period preceding the collision described in the Complaint.

(2)  Please identify every employee of Bud's Auto Service with whom Harry Hampton had an oral or written communication regarding the "wiring problem" described in paragraph 16 of the Second Count of the Complaint, prior to the collision described in the Complaint.

**Interrogatories seeking "soft" facts (*Judith Johnson to Harry Hampton*):**

(3)  Explain why plaintiff Hampton didn't personally check the functioning of the turn signal of his 1990 Pontiac Grand Am prior to the collision described in the Complaint.

(4)  Describe the nature of the "great pain and suffering" which plaintiff describes in paragraph 11 of the First Count of the Complaint.

the course of discovery in the case; it may, to some extent, assist in reducing the number of duplicative requests.

Although copies of discovery requests must be sent to all parties, filing with the court is not always necessary. Rules 5(a) and (d) of the FRCP provide the court with some flexibility on this issue. Because discovery items (including requests, but particularly responses) are often lengthy, the court is authorized to establish an alternative procedure. A very brief notice, for example, may be filed with the court in place of the actual discovery request (see section (b) of our sample local rule in Figure 9–2). Under the local rule of Exurbia, the interrogatory requests are not filed with the court, but the responses are; this makes sense, because the responses include the original request anyway (see section (c) of our local rule), so that the court ultimately has all relevant information but less paper taking up valuable file space.

**PARALEGALERT!**

Rules 5(a) and (d) of the FRCP give a court some flexibility with regard to the filing of discovery requests and responses. Be sure to check your local rules to determine the applicable requirements.

## Responding to Interrogatories

Sam Superlawyer has placed on your desk the set of interrogatories filed by TapTapTap, Inc., which are seen in Figure 9–5. He wants you to begin preparing responses. Now what do you do?

The first thing you should do is contact the client, perhaps first by telephone, but certainly by sending a copy of the interrogatories. In this case, the client contact is Edgar Ellison. You might want to send a copy to other employees of Widgets and Gizmos, Inc. as well, if they are in a better position to answer the questions than is Ellison. All this should be done only after consulting with your supervising attorney (and probably Ellison himself). A sample letter to Ellison, referencing both interrogatory requests and a deposition notice, appears in Figure 9–8.

You must also review the interrogatories to determine whether you can file any **objections.** Interrogatories can be objectionable if they seek privileged or irrelevant information, if they are ambiguous or unclear, or if any of the other reasons listed in Rule 26(b)(1) apply (for example, if they are unduly burdensome or duplicative). Under Rule 33, the "reasons for objection are stated in lieu of an answer." Examples of interrogatories with accompanying objections are shown in Figure 9–9. Under the FRCP, objections to interrogatories are not automatically resolved by the court; if the opposing party disagrees with your objection, he or she must file a Motion to Compel (see Section 9–7), which is then considered by the court along with the original objection. In some states, objections can be argued directly, without the need to file a Motion to Compel. You should check your state's procedure with regard to handling discovery objections.

If the information sought is confidential, but not otherwise objectionable, you may want to file a Motion for Protective Order, which limits, or perhaps even prevents, further inquiry. We discuss such protective orders in Section 9–7, and compare them with simple objections.

After Mr. Ellison has received a copy of the requests, he will begin formulating responses. You, too, will be reviewing your firm's file, seeking answers from the various subfiles of client documents and investigatory materials that you have gathered. There will probably be telephone contact between you and the client at this stage, and possibly even a preliminary

# Lincoln & Hoover

## Attorneys at Law

January 18, 1994

Mr. Edgar Ellison
Widgets and Gizmos, Inc.
888 Widget Street
Metro City, Exurbia 12345

Re: Discovery requests from TapTapTap, Inc.

Dear Mr. Ellison:

We have received from the attorneys for *TapTapTap, Inc.* both a request for interrogatory responses and a request to take your deposition. We will have to respond to each.

*As to the interrogatories:*
I would like you to prepare preliminary responses to the interrogatories by January 26. Be sure to read each question carefully, and prepare thorough and truthful answers. Please feel free to call me with any questions you have. In the meantime, we are preparing several objections, and have filed a Motion for Extension of Time to respond, since it appears that the work involved in obtaining answers may be substantial.

Some of these questions may involve information which goes beyond your personal knowledge. You must work together with other employees who have relevant information. Again, please call me if you have any questions.

I am also preparing draft answers, based upon information in our file. When we prepare the final version, it will be based upon all available information. In our final draft, we will want to avoid volunteering information beyond that requested; for now, however, gather together all information which you believe pertains to the issues presented.

*As to the deposition:*
The defendant *TapTapTap, Inc.* has also filed a Notice of Deposition (copy enclosed) to take your deposition on February 20, 1994, at the offices of Tiptop & Towe. Accompanying the Notice of Deposition is a document request (see schedule A of the Notice). Please begin gathering together the documents which are responsive to the request. I would like to meet with you within one week to discuss your progress in obtaining the responsive documents.

With regard to the deposition itself, we are preparing a Motion for Protective Order in which we will be seeking to limit the ability of *TapTapTap, Inc.* to inquire into the trade secrets of *Widgets and Gizmos, Inc.*

Sam Superlawyer has informed me that you have been deposed before, so that you are generally familiar with the process. I would like to schedule an office conference with you within two weeks so that we can begin to review the status of the case and prepare you for your deposition. Just as a reminder, I would bring to your attention the following important general considerations with regard to testifying at a deposition:

(1)  Tell the truth!

office conference to review progress and discuss any problems that have arisen.

When formulating responses, both you and the client must read the interrogatory carefully and keep in mind the duty to answer the questions accurately and fully. Remember, however, that to answer fully does not require that you volunteer information; answer only the question posed. An exception

(2) Answer only the question posed; don't volunteer information unless necessary to put a more "positive" spin on a "negative" response;

(3) Think carefully before you answer, and if there is anything about the question that you don't understand, don't answer until the confusion is eliminated.

Please call me after you've had a chance to review this letter and the enclosed materials. At that time we can discuss any questions, set up a reasonable schedule for completion of our responses, and also schedule an appointment for you to come in for an office conference with Sam Superlawyer and me.

Very truly yours,

Paula Paralegal

to this general principle might be presented by a situation in which the answer is detrimental to the client's position; in that case you might want to provide a brief explanation that casts the answer in a more positive light.

Sometimes an interrogatory will ask you to provide certain information that is obtainable from the business records of your client. Under Rule 33(c), if the "burden of deriving or ascertaining the answer is substantially the same for the party serving the interrogatory as for the party served," it is satisfactory to respond by providing access to the relevant records, rather than directly answering the interrogatory.

Preparing discovery responses is often time-consuming, which can make impending deadlines a troublesome issue. The basic rule under the FRCP for responding to interrogatories is found in Rule 33: 30 days after service of the interrogatories or 45 days after service of the summons and complaint, whichever is longer. Note that this is subject to modification by the court, based either on a Motion for Extension, a scheduling order, or the pertinent provisions of a local rule. Never assume that such an extension is in place simply because the other side has agreed to it; check the rules to see if some court approval is required.

You will eventually reach a point where the responses are properly drafted. At that point the client must make a final review of the responses. This review is critical, because the client must attest to the truth of the responses: note the signing requirements of Rule 33:

> Each interrogatory shall be answered separately and fully in writing under oath, unless it is objected to, in which event the reason for objection shall be stated in lieu of an answer. The answers are to be signed by the person making them, and the objections signed by the attorney making them.

Thus the client must sign under oath the interrogatory answers, and the attorney must sign the objections. This is usually accomplished by the standard signing format seen in Figure 9–10; note how the "under oath" requirement is satisfied by the acknowledgment block.

The certification requirement under Rule 5 of the FRCP must be kept in mind with regard to responses as well as requests. You should note that just as interrogatory requests are sent to all parties (not just the party from whom a

**P**ARALEGALERT!

When preparing a response to an interrogatory, be sure to read it carefully, answer it accurately and fully, and avoid volunteering information beyond that requested.

**Figure 9–9  Sample Objections to Interrogatories**

> *Assuming that the following interrogatories were filed by* TapTapTap, Inc. *requesting responses from* Widgets and Gizmos, Inc., *they might be met by the following objections:*
>
> 1.  Identify every document contained in the files of *Widgets and Gizmos, Inc.* which in any way relates to the widgenometer, or any person involved in the development of the widgenometer.
>
> Objection: The interrogatory is overbroad and irrelevant in that there are many documents in the files of *Widgets and Gizmos, Inc.* which relate to persons involved with the widgenometer project and yet have nothing to do with the issues of this lawsuit. The interrogatory is also unduly burdensome under Rule 26 of the FRCP in that the number of documents which is responsive is quite large, and conducting a full search to locate every such document would be extremely time-consuming and expensive.
>
> 2.  For each expert witness whom you have retained but do not expect to testify, identify the facts known and opinions held with regard to the issues of this case.
>
> Objection: The defendant *TapTapTap, Inc.* has failed to make the showing of "exceptional circumstances" required by Rule 26(b)(4)(B) to justify the discovery requested.
>
> 3.  With regard to the preparation of the contract referenced in the Complaint, state the contents of any communication in which Widgets and Gizmos, Inc. was advised by any outside party to delete references to the composition of the alloy used in the manufacture of the widgenometer.
>
> Objection: This interrogatory is objected to insofar as it requests information with regard to communications protected by the attorney/client privilege.
>
> 4.  State whether Hans Hoobermann or Edgar Ellison knew that he had provided instructions for the testing of the widgenometer.
>
> Objection: Plaintiff objects to this interrogatory on the grounds that it is ambiguous in that it is unclear to whom the pronoun "he" refers. It is also vague with regard to the information sought, and hence it will be impossible to formulate an intelligent response to this interrogatory as drafted.
>
> 5.  Identify all relevant notes.
>
> Objection: Plaintiff objects to this interrogatory on the grounds that it is vague. The term "relevant notes" is undefined; hence it is possible to determine neither what document or documents would constitute such a "note," nor to what subject the document or documents should be "relevant."

## PARALEGALERT!

Copies of both interrogatory requests and interrogatory responses must be sent to all parties pursuant to Rule 5 of the FRCP. In other words, you cannot send requests only to the party from whom you seek a response or send responses only to the party who filed the requests.

response is required), so too the responses must be sent to all parties (not just the party who requested the response).

As we noted in the last subsection, there is some variance in court-filing requirements. Some courts require that the responses be filed; others don't, unless there is some issue as to the adequacy of compliance. You must check the applicable rules. See, for example, sections (b) and (c) of our local rule in Figure 9–2.

Finally, suppose new information arises after the

**Figure 9–10  Sample of Signature Block and Verification for Interrogatory Responses**

> *Responses to interrogatories will generally set forth each interrogatory in turn, immediately followed by the corresponding answer or objection. At the conclusion, they will be executed under oath by the party attesting to the truth of the responses, followed by the standard attorney signature block, as follows:*
>
> The President of the plaintiff, *Widgets and Gizmos, Inc.*, namely Edgar Ellison, hereby affirms and states that he has read the foregoing "Responses to Interrogatories of *TapTapTap, Inc.*" and has determined that they are true and correct to the best of his knowledge.
>
> _____
> Edgar Ellison
>
> Subscribed and sworn to
> before me, this the 10th day
> of January, 1994.
>
> _____
> Ms. Nadine Nemeth
> Notary Public of the State of
> Exurbia
> Commission Expires:
>
> THE PLAINTIFF, *Widgets and Gizmos, Inc.*
>
> By: _____
> Samuel Superlawyer, Esq.
> Its attorney
> Lincoln & Hoover
> 123 Lincoln Street
> Metro City, Exurbia 12345
> Atty. Reg. #: 87654
> Phone: (901) 222-2222

interrogatory responses are filed, but before trial; is there a duty to supplement the responses? **Supplementation** is addressed in Rule 26(e) of the FRCP. As a general rule, once a party files a response that is "complete when made," that party "is under no duty to supplement the response to include information thereafter acquired . . . ." There are, however, several exceptions to this general rule. First, supplementation as to "the identity and location of persons having knowledge of discoverable matters," or the identity of an "expert witness" expected to testify, is required. Second, supplementation is required if the responding party learns that a response was incorrect when made, or is no longer true and failure to amend would constitute a "knowing concealment." Third, supplementation can be required by order of the court, agreement of the parties, local rules, or by requests for supplementation prior to trial.

You should note that some states *do* require supplementation. In such states, you must be sure to update responses at some reasonable time prior to trial. Particularly with regard to items relating to damages or other evidentiary issues, failure to supplement may prevent the introduction of the items in evidence at trial. In personal injury cases, for exam-

---

**PARALEGALERT!**

State court requirements for supplementation of discovery responses may be stricter than the FRCP. Be sure you follow the applicable provisions carefully; failure to supplement might hinder your supervising attorney's ability to introduce certain evidence at trial.

ple, medical bills often continue to accrue right up until trial; if you represent the plaintiff, and if supplementation is required, you should make sure to send copies of all such bills to the other side.

## 9–3 Requests for Production of Documents and Things or Entry Upon Land

In addition to filing interrogatories to obtain written answers to questions, parties also seek to obtain access to documents and other tangible items in the hands of other parties. This can be done by filing a **Request for Production of Documents and Things or Entry Upon Land,** authorized and governed by Rule 34 of the FRCP, which gives access to documents and things "which are in the possession, custody or control of the party upon whom the request is served . . . ."

Rule 34 actually authorizes what might be thought of as three separate discovery procedures. The first is the production of *documents*; the second is the production of *things*; the third is the permission to enter upon designated *land* in the possession of an opposing party for the purpose of inspecting, photographing, surveying, testing, or some other such purpose.

Although both the production of "things" and the entry upon land can be essential elements in many cases, by far the most significant discovery procedure authorized by Rule 34 is the request for production of documents. Why is production of documents so important? Because for most lawsuits, documents are needed to establish such matters as damages, the nature of legal relationships and communications between parties, details of events recorded in contemporaneous records, and other facts that bear on the trial. Simply stated, ours is a society that maintains most records in the form of documents. Furthermore, Rule 34 holds the term "documents" to include "writings, drawings, graphs, charts, photographs, phono-records, and other data compilations from which information can be obtained . . . ." This definition is broad enough to include a wide range of materials, including such things as computer records or videotapes. Our expanded notion of "documents" in the definitions section of Figure 9–5 (page 226) gives some idea of the breadth of coverage of the term, and hence the importance of this discovery device.

In a moment, we'll begin our discussion of drafting and responding to production requests. But first, let's talk about a key consideration in litigation: control of documents in large cases.

## PARALEGALERT!

Rule 34 of the FRCP actually authorizes three separate discovery procedures:

1. Production of documents
2. Production of "things"; and
3. Permission to enter upon designated land.

### Document Control

Documents are not living things, but inert pieces of paper. How can paper get out of control?

If you find yourself asking that question at this point, then you've never been involved in a lawsuit with high-volume production requests. Complex litigation involving multiple parties and complicated transactions can lead to mountains of relevant documents. Attempting to conquer these mountains can leave a paralegal or attorney feeling like an adventurer at the base of Mount Everest, with the peak invisible in the distant clouds. How will you ever get to the top? What are you going to do with these boxes of documents?

Implausible though it may at first seem, working on a case for several years can actually leave involved personnel with firsthand mastery over an incredible number of documents. But that sort of familiarity is a substantive challenge; it involves analysis and memory. We want to discuss something a little different here: *organization*.

For all but the simplest cases (and perhaps even in them), organization of documents is very important to the successful advocacy of your client's position. Since the contents and meaning of documents often have crucial impact on the result of a lawsuit, you must establish control over these documents. "Control" implies the need to track several things.

First, you must be aware of the *source* of a document. Source is, by definition, clear when you first receive a document (at least *your* source will be clear, although sometimes the client or a witness will give you a document without knowing where he or she got it). The time to organize by source, then, is the moment you first receive a document.

Second, you may want to categorize the document on some substantive basis. We'll call this organization by *purpose*. For example, in the Widgets and Gizmos, Inc. matter, you or your supervising attorney may want to gather together all documents that relate to the specifications of the widgenometers; or you may want to organize documents in chronological order; or you may want to separate documents based upon their relevance to various witnesses.

Although these means of organization may seem obvious, it is perhaps at this point that the breakdown of organization is most likely to occur. The problem is simple: there will almost certainly be conflicts between sources and purposes. In other words, your organization by purpose will likely disrupt your organization by source. And, indeed, organization by multiple purposes will disrupt the situation further. In the Widgets and Gizmos, Inc. matter, for example, there will likely be documents relating to specifications of the widgenometer taken from (1) the files of Hans Hoobermann, (2) the files of Edgar Ellison, (3) the files of other Widgets and Gizmos, Inc. employees, and (4) the production requests received from TapTapTap, Inc. Furthermore, the documents received from TapTapTap, Inc. may have been received in response to separate, distinct, and significantly differing production requests (each request, for example, may relate to documents generated during a separate and specific time interval, with the timing crucial to the impact of the documents on the contract negotiation).

**PARALEGALERT!**

Documents generally need to be organized both in terms of their *source* and their substantive *purpose* in the case. Confusion often results if the person in charge of document control allows organization by source to disrupt organization by purpose, or vice versa.

The problem, in essence, is this: in your enthusiasm to gather everything together by purpose, you might lose track of a particular document's source, and vice versa.

This purpose/source problem is by no means the only way documents can get confused; by failing to clearly identify source at the time of receipt, or by mixing up file folders, or by failing to refile correctly, or simply by being sloppy, you may cause document organization to break down. Since you will be a hardworking and conscientious paralegal, none of these other things will happen to you, of course. The interesting and troublesome thing about the purpose/source problem, however, is that it can happen to someone who is being absolutely conscientious. And it can happen so fast that it becomes serious before you even realize it; hence you must be on guard.

How, then, can organization be protected? There are several possible solutions, some more workable than others, depending on the circumstances of the case. The first option is to prepare a written index (see Figure 9–11) that lists each document individually, including all information necessary to differentiate it from any other (for example: invoice numbers for bills; dates of and parties to correspondence; dates and number of pages of contracts). Also included for each document will be the source (or multiple sources, if identical copies are received from more than one source), as well as the purpose (or purposes).

Sometimes there are so many substantially similar documents (as where a large volume of similar business records is produced) that such lists or indices may become difficult to manage. Under these circumstances, a second option is to employ some numbering system. "Bates-numbering" is a term that refers to use of the stamping devices produced by the Bates Manufacturing Co., which can be set to click automatically to the next consecutive number after each stamping action (these are useful for marking large numbers of documents with consecutive numbers). Note that such numbers are generally stamped on copies, rather than originals; original documents should not be tampered with, since they may be introduced as exhibits at trial.

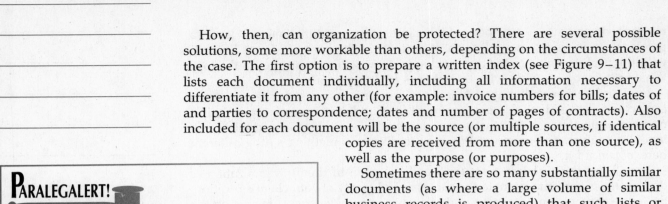

**P**ARALEGALERT!

When numbering documents for purposes of document control, stamp copies rather than originals. Originals should not be tampered with, since they may be introduced as exhibits at trial.

**Figure 9–11   Sample Written Index for Document Organization**

### Index of Documents of Widgets and Gizmos, Inc.

*Internal Memorandums*

| | | | | |
|---|---|---|---|---|
| Hoobermann to Rodriguez | January 15, 1992 | re: need for additional test on widgenometer | Source: Rodriguez file | Purpose: 3 |
| Ellison to Rodriguez | February 17, 1992 | re: Hoobermann memo | Source: Ellison file | Purpose: 3 |
| Rodriguez to Ellison | March 15, 1992 | re: negotiations on *TapTapTap, Inc.* contract | Source: Ellison file | Purpose: 2 |

*Correspondence*

| | | | | |
|---|---|---|---|---|
| Ellison to Tapman | May 15, 1992 | re: shipment of widgenometers | Source: Ellison file | Purpose: 1 |
| Tapman to Ellison | May 21, 1992 | re: reports of problems with widgenometers | Source: Ellison file | Purpose: 4 |
| Jinx Computers, Inc. to Tapman | June 4, 1992 | re: problems with widgenometer | Source: Production Request #4 | Purpose: 4 |

*Shipping documents*

| | | | | |
|---|---|---|---|---|
| Shipping invoice #1327 | April 3,1992 | re: shipment of 1500 widgenometers to *TapTapTap*, Inc. facility in California | Source: W&G Acct'g file | Purpose: 1 |
| Shipping invoice #1658 | May 1, 1992 | re: shipment of 650 widgenometers to *TapTapTap*, Inc. facility in California | Source: W&G Acct'g file | Purpose: 1 |

Purpose Key: 1/ Establish damages    2/ Specifications in contract    3/ Widgenometer development    4/ Potential liability

A typical format for organizing Bates-numbering is shown in Figure 9–12. Note that each page of each document is generally given a separate number. In this way the length of multiple-page documents is readily apparent. Indices would also generally be used in conjunction with a numbering system, perhaps identifying *categories* of documents rather than each individual document as we just described (again, refer to the format shown in Figure 9–12). Thus, indexing and numbering can be thought of as complements, rather than strictly as substitutes.

A third option, building on the first two, involves the cross-filing of multiple copies in separate file folders. For example, you may maintain one set of file folders organizing documents by source, and a second set organizing copies of these documents by purpose. For large numbers of documents, this system may grow unwieldy, unless the two groups of documents are coordinated by some indexing or numbering system. Thus, once again the various options we've discussed actually complement each other.

The fourth option results from the advances of the computer age. There are now computer programs that can greatly assist in document control. Because there are many different systems in use, we will not discuss the details of any specific software. But you should be familiar with a few general principles relevant to most computer programs.

First, you should be aware of the concept of "fields" for entering and later retrieving information. A field is a subset of data relating to the subject matter at hand. For documents, relevant fields might include the date of a document, the drafter, the person to whom it was sent, your source (or sources) for the document, a code relating to the subject matter (i.e., the purpose) of the document, and an indexing cross-reference for locating the hard copy of the document. After the pertinent information for each document has been entered into the system, the fields can be searched to identify, for example, all those documents that were drafted by a certain person, or all those documents that relate to the same subject matter, or that were obtained from the same source.

**Figure 9–12    Typical Format for *Bates-Numbering* Organization**

| **Widgets and Gizmos, Inc.**<br>**Documents: 000000 to 099999** | | **TapTapTap, Inc.**<br>**Documents: 100000 to 199999** | |
|---|---|---|---|
| Invoices: | 000001 to 009999 | Correspondence<br>from clients: | 100000 to 109999 |
| Correspondence: | 010000 to 019999 | Correspondence<br>with W & G: | 110000 to 119999 |
| Memoranda: | 020000 to 029999 | Memoranda: | 120000 to 129999 |
| Contract: | 030000 to 039999 | Miscellaneous<br>re negotiations: | 130000 to 139999 |
| Miscellaneous<br>re negotiations: | 040000 to 049999 | Miscellaneous<br>re specifications: | 140000 to 149999 |
| Miscellaneous<br>re specifications: | 050000 to 059999 | Miscellaneous<br>re damages: | 150000 to 159999 |
| Other: | 060000 to 099999 | Contract: | 160000 to 169999 |
| | | Other: | 170000 to 199999 |

Second, there are systems in which the document is entered in "full-text" form. Under such systems, the entire contents of a document are entered into the computer system, and can be accessed in several different ways. There will likely also be fields in a full-text system, so that documents can be searched in the same manner that we have just discussed. In addition, the full document itself, with a full-text system, can be recalled and reviewed in detail. Perhaps most innovative, a full-text system allows for the text of all documents to be searched for key terms; those passages found containing such key terms (for example, the name of a witness or reference to an important piece of evidence) can then be accessed. We consider full-text accessing further in our discussion of deposition transcripts in Section 9–4.

Computers are fast and accurate, and their expense is decreasing just as the sophistication of attorneys in their utilization is increasing. The number and variety of software programs on the market are also growing significantly. All these factors indicate that the role of computers in litigation will increase with time. At present, computerized litigation support is still most economically efficient for complex lawsuits involving large numbers of documents, but certain applications are often within reach for simple cases as well. Some courts have even begun experimenting with computerized filing of court documents. You can be sure that computers will be a big part of your future as a paralegal, whether you specialize in litigation or some other area. The more you learn about this amazing technology, the better prepared you will be.

Even with all the precautions and systems we've been discussing in this section, documents still have a way of getting mixed up if you're not careful. How easily this can happen is something that's hard to explain until it happens to you the first time. We hope, however, that this discussion will help you prevent a first time from ever occurring.

## Drafting Production Requests

Many of the considerations that apply to the drafting of interrogatories also apply to the drafting of production requests. Discussing the case with the client, studying the pleadings, reviewing your own file, looking at models or form books relating to similar factual contexts, using your own ingenuity—all these things are useful for formulating production requests as well. Because production requests are often prepared after interrogatory responses have been received, there is thus also another (perhaps the best) source for ideas: those very interrogatory responses. Interrogatories, as noted, are often used to uncover information as to categories or types of relevant documents in the possession of an opposing party, or even the existence of specific individual documents; you should thus use relevant interrogatory responses to assist in the drafting of production requests.

Certain categories of documents might be considered standard targets for production requests. Bills and invoices that support damages will be sought by the defendant; relevant contractual agreements and correspondence will be sought by both sides; if an injury case, the defendant will seek medical reports and other information pertaining to the injuries. Some of these items can be seen in Judith Johnson's request to Harry Hampton in Figure 9–13.

Production requests, like interrogatories, have a caption, designation, signature block, and certification. They also begin with an introductory paragraph, and often definitions. These are followed by numbered paragraphs identifying the items of which production is sought (see Figure 9–13).

**Figure 9-13   Production Request of Judith Johnson**

| | | |
|---|---|---|
| HARRY HAMPTON, | : | Superior Court |
| Plaintiff | : | State of Exurbia |
| v. | : | Judicial District<br>of |
| JUDITH JOHNSON and BUD'S | : | Metro County |
| AUTO SERVICE, | : | Civ. No. 93-0017 |
| | | March 10, 1994 |
| Defendants | : | |

### Request for Production from Judith Johnson to Harry Hampton

Pursuant to Rules 26 and 34 of the Rules of Procedure for the Superior Court of the State of Exurbia, the defendant Judith Johnson hereby requests that the plaintiff, Harry Hampton, produce and permit her to inspect and copy, within the deadline established in Rule 34(b), the documents identified below.

*Definitions*
1. "Documents" should be defined to include all writings or other media in which information is stored, including but not limited to correspondence, memorandums, invoices, charts, graphs, maps, specifications, technical drawings or illustrations, medical records of a medical professional or facility, x-rays, test results, laboratory reports, newspaper or other periodical articles, computer disks, audio or video tapes, any other electronic information storage or retrieval system, or any other source of written or stored information. Any copy of a document which has been altered or marked with notations or comments of any kind shall be considered to be a separate original.
2. "You" or "your" refers to the plaintiff, Harry Hampton.

*Production Requests*

Please produce for inspection and copying the following documents:

1. All documents in your possession which relate to the injuries you allege in paragraph 11 of the First Count of the Complaint, including but not limited to physician's office notes, hospital records, medical reports, physical therapy records, emergency room records, nurse's notes, x-ray reports, CAT scan results, bills or invoices setting forth the cost of treatment, or any other documents of any kind. This would include all documents relating to the allegations in paragraph 15 of the First Count of the Complaint.
2. Your federal income tax return for the year of the collision, 1992.
3. All wage statements or pay stubs covering the period from one month before the collision on April 15, 1992 to one month after you allege that you were able to return to work full-time.
4. All written statements in your possession regarding any of the events described in the Complaint, including but not limited to your own statements or witness statements, except for materials which are protected from disclosure by a privilege.
5. All invoices, work statements, billing statements, estimates, or other documents relating to any service or repair work performed on the 1990 Pontiac Grand Am vehicle described in the Complaint for the period from six months prior to the collision of April 15, 1992, including but not limited to the work performed by Bud's Auto Service on April 14, 1992.
6. All invoices, work statements, billing statements, estimates, or other documents relating to the repair work on the 1990 Pontiac Grand Am vehicle which you claim constitute an element of damages as a result of your allegations against Judith Johnson in the Complaint.
7. Any police reports in your possession.

Figure 9–13 **Production Request of Judith Johnson, continued**

8. All documents which establish or identify the damages related to the "enjoyable activities" which you allege, in paragraph 13 of the First Count of the Complaint, an inability to perform.
9. All photographs, videotapes, diagrams, or other graphic representations of the scene of the collision, prepared either at the time of the collision or at any other time.
10. All photographs, videotapes, diagrams, or other graphic representations of the injuries you allege in paragraph 11 of the Complaint.
11. All photographs, videotapes, diagrams, or other graphic representations of the damages to your 1990 Pontiac Grand Am which you allege in your Complaint.

THE DEFENDANT, JUDITH JOHNSON

By: _____
Shawn Schmidt, Esq.
Her attorney
Benson & Arnold
985 Cook Lane
Metro City, Exurbia 12345
Atty. Reg. #: 62622
Phone: (901) 666-0001

**Certificate of Service**

This is to certify that a copy of the foregoing was mailed, postage prepaid, this 10th day of March, 1994, to attorney Sam Superlawyer, Esq., Lincoln & Hoover, 123 Lincoln Street, Metro City, Exurbia, 12345.

_____
Shawn Schmidt, Esq.

---

### Paralegalert!

Although descriptions of documents sought in a Request for Production need not be perfectly precise (only "reasonable particularity" is required by Rule 34 of the FRCP), in the interest of minimizing ambiguity the drafter should be as precise as possible.

---

The description of a requested document need not be perfectly precise; according to Rule 34(b), the items requested shall be set forth "either by individual item or by category," and each item shall be described "with reasonable particularity." Although this provides the drafter with some latitude, keep in mind the need to minimize ambiguity; the bottom line is that the drafter must be as precise as possible. Rule 34(b) also states that the request should "state a reasonable time, place, and manner of making the inspection and performing the related acts"; this is usually satisfied by specifying, in the introductory paragraph of the request, that the production shall be made at the address of the office of the serving attorney, or "in a reasonable manner acceptable to both parties" (see Figure 9–13).

As with interrogatories, requests for production are served on all parties to the case, pursuant to Rule 5, although the requirements with regard to filing with the court may vary from one court to another.

### Responding to Production Requests

Preparing responses to production requests can be a minor task, or a major undertaking, or something in between, depending on the type of case involved.

The first step, as with interrogatories, is contacting the client to review the requests. A sample cover letter to Harry Hampton is seen in Figure 9–14.

Hampton (or any client) must be informed that he must make reasonably diligent and thorough efforts to locate documents that are responsive to the request. He must also be made aware of the broad definition of "documents": he must understand that such things as computer records, electronic video- or audiotapes, and other less obvious media also fit the definition, and hence must be considered. You can explain that you are objecting to certain of the responses, but it probably still makes sense for the client to make at least preliminary efforts to locate documents responsive to these objectionable requests as well: if the objection fails, for example, the documents will have to be produced; and even if it succeeds, you will probably want to review the documents for your own information. Perhaps the most important thing to impress upon the client is that, when in doubt about some aspect of the document search, he or she should contact you or your supervising attorney.

**Figure 9–14    Letter to Hampton Regarding Production Request from Johnson**

# Lincoln & Hoover
## Attorneys at Law

March 12, 1994

Mr. Harry Hampton
1001 Elm Street
Milltown, Exurbia 12344

Dear Mr. Hampton:

Enclosed you will find a copy of a Request for Production which we have received from the attorneys for Judith Johnson. Please review this document and call me by March 16, 1994.

In the meantime, please begin gathering together documents which are responsive to these requests. As you know, we already have much of this information in our file; you do not have to provide copies of documents you've already forwarded to us, but please call me if you have any questions. I will also begin organizing responses based upon the materials already in our possession.

You must make reasonably diligent and thorough efforts to locate documents; however, you are not expected to make extraordinary efforts to obtain documents not currently within your custody or control. We will discuss these points when you call me.

We will carefully review each request, and will file objections if necessary. In the meantime, however, you should continue your efforts to locate the documents, as we may want to review even those materials responsive to requests found to be objectionable.

Make sure to call me at any time if you have any questions about the contents of this letter, the production requests themselves, or your role in the gathering of materials. We will set up an appointment to further coordinate these responses in the very near future.

Very truly yours,

Paula Paralegal

Paralegals are often closely involved in the document production process. In major cases, this may involve on-site review of client files and records to identify documents that will have to be produced. You may spend significant periods of time working closely with the client or the client's employees searching for and evaluating relevant records.

Is there any general advice that can be given for such on-site review, or for initial review of bulk documents delivered to your office by the client? Since every case is different, specifics can vary greatly; thus, in the first instance you must look to your supervising attorney for guidance. As a general matter, your task is to (1) identify documents that have been requested, (2) eliminate irrelevant documents, and (3) bring to the attention of your supervising attorney any documents of whose importance or relevance you are unsure.

Having done this, you will then conduct further review of those documents which fulfill the requests of the other side, keeping on the lookout for any privileged matters or material that includes references to trade secrets or other items concerning which the client would like to maintain confidentiality. Such items should be discussed with your supervising attorney. He or she may file a Motion for Protective Order (see Section 9–7) to prevent or at least limit such discovery; if the documents are important, however, they will probably have to be produced. If produced, you should take care that any limitation put in place by a protective order is made absolutely clear, for example by stamping certain documents as "Confidential" ("Top Secret" is going a bit far, unless you work for the government!).

Rule 34(b) holds that the "party upon whom the request is served shall serve a written response within 30 days after the service of the request," or 45 days after service of the summons and complaint, whichever is later. This written response will state, "with respect to each item or category, that inspection and related activities will be permitted as requested, unless the request is objected to, in which event the reasons for objection shall be stated." As with interrogatories, the same basic objections apply: irrelevance; privileged materials; vagueness or ambiguity; or one or more of the reasons listed in Rule 26(b)(1) (look back at Figure 9–3, p. 224). The written response must be signed by an attorney, and delivery certified to all other parties.

Next comes the issue of the manner of production of the documents themselves. Rule 34 allows for the party serving the request (or a representative) to "inspect and copy" items not objected to; this implies the scheduling of a convenient time, and some access to a photocopying machine. As a practical matter, however, the parties usually agree to supply each other with copies of documents. If there are multiple parties, the usual procedure (though not required by the FRCP) is for each party to make available a set of copies for every other party who wishes to pay for the copying. This may, of course, vary in the particular case. Remember also that you must indicate which documents are responsive to which requests.

The manner of photocopying is an issue that bears some discussion. Remember our discussion of document control, and the problem of mixing up documents? In a case involving a large production response, the photocopying stage is a classic example of a context in which documents might be

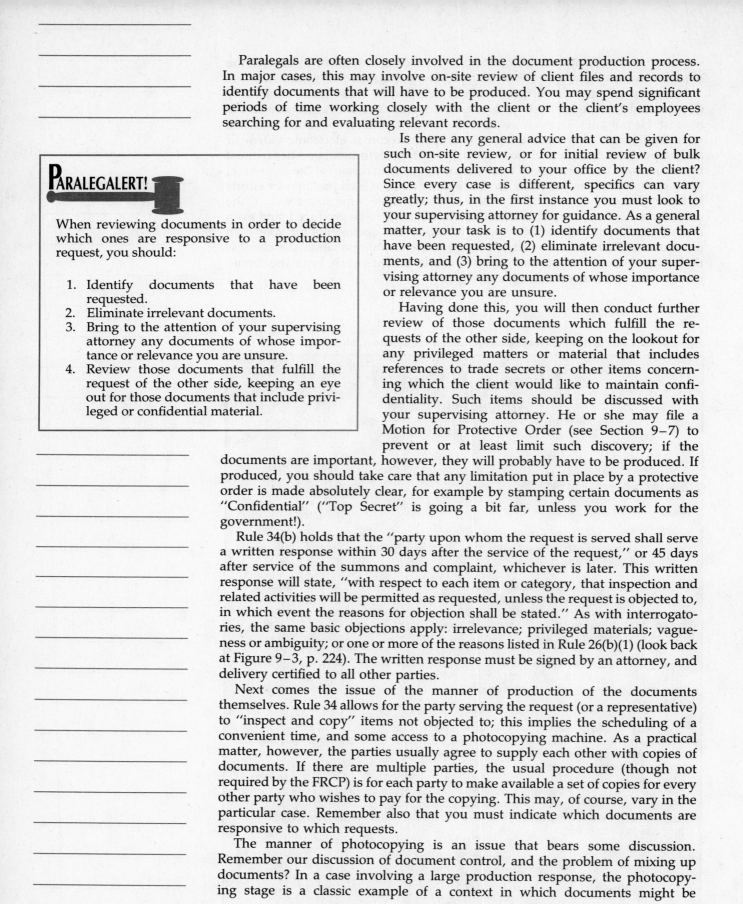

**PARALEGALERT!**

When reviewing documents in order to decide which ones are responsive to a production request, you should:

1. Identify documents that have been requested.
2. Eliminate irrelevant documents.
3. Bring to the attention of your supervising attorney any documents of whose importance or relevance you are unsure.
4. Review those documents that fulfill the request of the other side, keeping an eye out for those documents that include privileged or confidential material.

mixed up. Photocopying seems simple, but in a big case it requires significant organization. You must be careful to maintain control of the process: don't fall into the trap of trying to do too much at one time. Whether the actual copying is done by you yourself, or a secretary, or a commercial copying company, the possibility of disorder exists: guard against it. Commercial companies are usually dependable, and are often your best bet for high-volume copying or copying of oversize materials such as architectural drawings; nevertheless, make sure to provide them with a cover letter that includes precise instructions.

With regard to filing production responses with the court, the considerations are essentially the same as we discussed earlier regarding interrogatories. The bottom line is that the FRCP gives to the court some flexibility with regard to the filing of production materials, and many courts would rather not have boxes of documents taking up space in the courthouse. Review your local rules to determine the applicable provisions, and check with your supervising attorney if there is any doubt.

Finally, the issue of supplementation must be considered. What should you do if additional documents are discovered after you file the response? Again, our analysis matches that set forth with regard to interrogatories. Rule 26(e) of the FRCP has some requirements with regard to supplementation, but they are not excessive; the supplementation requirements of your state courts may be stricter. Under the FRCP, you must supplement if necessary to correct an earlier oversight, but newly generated documents (such as subsequent medical bills) do not necessarily have to be served to comply with an old production request. Nevertheless, be careful on this point; again, it is best to discuss the situation carefully with your supervising attorney.

## Production of "Things" and Entry Upon Land

Suppose your firm represents a client who was hit on the head with a golf ball while playing at a local country club. Based on your supervising attorney's investigation, a Complaint is served against the country club for its failure to maintain proper safety procedures with regard to a "blind spot" on the hole where the accident occurred.

It is possible that your firm will desire, under these circumstances, to inspect the actual scene of the accident. Your supervising attorney may want to walk along the hole, take measurements, snap photographs, and possibly even make a videotape of the premises.

Suppose further that, in response to an interrogatory that you served, the country club disclosed that it had in its possession the actual ball that struck your client's head. Your supervising attorney wants to look at this ball as well.

Under Rule 34 of the FRCP, both access to land and production of a "thing" such as a golf ball can be compelled. The request is made in a manner identical to requests for production of documents, which we have been discussing. The land to be inspected or the "thing" to be produced must be identified with "reasonable particularity" (which in our example would be easy: for example, the "tenth hole of the defendant country club" and "the golf ball that struck Mr. X, which you identified in your response to interrogatory #22"). In addition, the request must specify "a reasonable time, place, and manner of making" the inspection or production. The details would probably be worked out in advance of the request being filed, for the convenience of the parties involved.

What can be done with these "things" once they've been produced, or with land once permission to enter has been obtained? Under Rule 34(a), as to "things," a party can "inspect and copy, test, or sample any tangible things . . . ." With regard to land, the party is authorized to conduct "inspection and measuring, surveying, photographing, testing, or sampling . . . ."

### The Use of a *Subpoena* for Documents Held by a Nonparty Witness

*Subpoenas*, governed by Rule 45 of the FRCP, allow for court orders that can compel actions on the part of nonparty witnesses. We discuss the *subpoena* procedure in some detail in the next section. You should be aware, however, that *subpoenas* can be used, in a manner analogous to requests for production served on parties, with regard to documents held by nonparties. (See the 1991 amendments to Rules 34(c) and 45 of the FRCP.)

## 9–4   Depositions

A **deposition** is a procedure by which the sworn oral testimony of a party or nonparty witness is taken, prior to trial, in response to questions, with the questions, testimony, and other comments of the participants preserved in a verbatim **transcript.** The party or nonparty witness whose deposition is being taken is called the **deponent.** The individual recording the testimony and preparing the transcript is called a **court reporter** (see Figure 9–15).

Depositions are authorized and governed by Rules 27 to 32 of the FRCP. There are two broad categories of depositions: **depositions upon written questions** (Rule 31) and **depositions upon oral examination** (Rule 30). You should note, however, that depositions upon written questions are seen only

**Figure 9–15   Definitions of Some Deposition Concepts**

> *Deposition:* A procedure by which the sworn oral testimony of a party or non-party witness is taken, prior to trial, in response to questions, with the questions, testimony, and other comments of the participants preserved in a verbatim transcript.
>
> *Transcript:* A verbatim recitation of the words spoken by the participants in the deposition, recorded by the court reporter.
>
> *Deponent:* The person whose testimony is being taken.
>
> *Court Reporter:* The person who records the testimony, usually on a stenographic machine which records in a shorthand "code," later translated into a standard transcript.
>
> *Deposition Upon Written Questions:* Pursuant to Rule 31 of the FRCP, a deposition in which written questions, cross-questions, redirect-questions, and recross-questions are submitted in advance by involved counsel to the court reporter, who thereafter reads the questions to the deponent and records the verbatim responses.
>
> *Deposition Upon Oral Examination:* This type of deposition is by far the most common, involving direct on-the-spot questioning by involved attorneys, including follow-up questions.

rarely; we will say just a few words about them in the final subsection of this section.

Depositions upon oral examination (usually referred to simply as "depositions") are, in contrast, commonly seen. Witness testimony is an important element of most cases, and such depositions provide parties with a pretrial opportunity to question potential witnesses in person. The deponent in such a deposition answers, under oath, questions posed by one or more attorneys (or unrepresented parties). All parties or their attorneys are authorized to attend.

Depositions differ markedly from the other discovery devices. Interrogatories and document production, for example, involve, essentially, pieces of paper sent back and forth between the parties; a deposition involves live testimony, and, on occasion, real drama. Thus, the immediate surface difference between depositions and these other forms of discovery should be clear to you. But keep in mind that the differences actually go much deeper than mere appearances; depositions are indeed important for several reasons (see Figure 9–16), only one of which might be thought of as such a "surface" consideration.

The first importance of a deposition is that it gives counsel a chance to see a potential trial witness in action and to judge the witness's demeanor and ability to handle the pressure of questioning. Such factors will affect the witness's impact at trial, and they cannot be evaluated from written information provided by, for example, interrogatory responses.

The second reason that depositions are important is that they allow for the possibility of immediate **follow-up questions.** As we mentioned earlier, with interrogatories the potential for evasive answers is always present (which is why it is so important to draft unambiguous interrogatories). Certain important questions may, by their very nature, open the door to such evasion (as where there is inquiry into opinions or subtle nuances of the case, the so-called "soft facts" we mentioned in our discussion of interrogatories); these questions often lead to ineffective interrogatories. But in a deposition, with counsel asking questions constrained only by the minor limitations that the scope of discovery implies, evasive answers can be immediately investigated with follow-up questions, and the nuances of difficult areas explored. Counsel can inquire into the premises upon which a witness bases his or her suppositions; elicit clarification of fuzzy reasoning; and, if the questioning is skillful, resolve areas of uncertainty. A witness can be pinned-down on key points; and future testimony will be subject to impeachment if the story changes.

The third reason that depositions are important is that the deponent can be a witness who is not a party to the lawsuit. Depositions provide the only method

**Figure 9–16    Four Reasons Why Depositions are an Important Discovery Device**

(1) Counsel has a chance to see a potential trial witness in action, and to judge the witness's demeanor and ability to handle pressure.

(2) The recourse to immediate *follow-up questions* enables counsel to (a) inquire into the premises on which a witness bases his suppositions; (b) elicit clarification of fuzzy reasoning; and (c) resolve areas of uncertainty. A witness can be "pinned-down" on key points, and future testimony will be subject to impeachment if the story changes.

(3) Depositions can be taken not only of *parties*, but also of *non-party witnesses*.

(4) Depositions can be used to *preserve testimony* when a witness is "unavailable" (as defined by the court) for trial.

**PARALEGALERT!**

Nonparty witnesses can be compelled to testify in a deposition by the use of a subpoena; no other discovery device provides such direct access to nonparty witnesses.

by which a nonparty witness can be directly involved in the discovery process; as we will discuss, even if nonparty witnesses seek to avoid a deposition, they can be compelled to appear by *subpoena*. The one exception to this relates to expert testimony acquired or developed in anticipation of litigation; as you recall from the last section, and from Rule 26(b)(4) of the FRCP, depositions of experts cannot be compelled unless the court so orders upon motion, and fees for the testimony may be assessed to the party seeking the deposition.

A fourth reason why depositions are important involves their usefulness as a means of preserving testimony for use at trial. A witness who is dying, for example, or a witness who is beyond the *subpoena* power of the court where the trial will be held, can be deposed, and the transcript substituted for testimony at trial. Indeed, the FRCP and the rules of most states also provide for the preservation of a deposition on videotape.

Depositions are usually taken only of hostile or neutral witnesses. It is rare that you would take the deposition of your own client, for example, or of a friendly witness, unless there was a need to preserve the testimony for trial. The reason for this should be apparent: with regard to your client or a friendly witness, your supervising attorney will already have access to all the information in that person's possession; it can be obtained in an informal office conference, without the presence of opposing counsel. With regard to opposing parties or hostile (or neutral) witnesses, however, the deposition will be the only opportunity to obtain such testimony or information firsthand.

Our detailed investigation of the deposition begins with analysis of two concepts, the deposition notice and the *subpoena*; we then take you through the preliminaries, the deposition itself, and postdeposition procedure, and conclude with a brief passage regarding depositions upon written questions.

### Deposition Notices and Subpoenas

Suppose you've identified a person whose deposition should be taken by your supervising attorney; how is the deposition arranged? The deposition must be scheduled and the parties to the lawsuit notified. Sometimes discussion between attorneys is the first step in arranging a deposition, so that the participants can work together to avoid conflicts with previously scheduled events. At other times the deposition is scheduled without such discussions. Let's take a look at exactly how scheduling occurs.

A deposition is officially scheduled by the filing of a **Notice of Deposition.** A Notice of Deposition will identify the time and place of the deposition and the name and address of the person to be examined (Rule 30(b)(1)), and often the court reporter as well (see Figure 9–17). It will have a caption and signature block, and must be sent to all attorneys (or unrepresented parties) to the lawsuit. Rule 30(b)(1) also requires that the notice be "reasonable," which in essence implies that notice be given a reasonable period of time before the scheduled date of the deposition. No prior court approval is required before filing the notice, unless the deposition is scheduled prior to the expiration of 30 days after service of the summons and complaint; as a practical matter, depositions are not often taken so soon after commencement of the action. One of the main reasons that depositions are rarely taken so early in the process is that they often prove to be far more meaningful if conducted *after* responses to interrogatories and production requests have been received; the questioning can then inquire into the interrogatory responses and the documents produced.

**Figure 9–17   Deposition Notice of Edgar Ellison**

United States District Court
for the
District of Exurbia

WIDGETS AND GIZMOS, INC.                    :

    Plaintiff                              :          Civil Action No. 93-OWH-00543

    vs.                                    :
                           :          January 12, 1994
TAPTAPTAP, INC.                              :

    Defendant                              :

### Notice of Deposition of Edgar Ellison

PLEASE TAKE NOTICE that, pursuant to Rule 30 of the Federal Rules of Civil Procedure, the defendant *TapTapTap, Inc.* acting by and through its attorneys, Tiptop & Towe, will take the deposition of Edgar Ellison, President of the Plaintiff, *Widgets and Gizmos, Inc.*, of 888 Widget Street, Metro City, Exurbia, at 10:00 A.M. on the 20th day of February, 1994, and continuing from day to day thereafter, at the offices of Tiptop & Towe, 71 Ferguson Street, Metro City, Exurbia, before Laurel Redefer, a court reporter licensed in Exurbia and employed by the firm of Speedy Transcribers, Inc.

Pursuant to Rules 30 and 34 of the Federal Rules of Civil Procedure, the deponent shall produce at said time and place all the documents identified on the list attached hereto as Schedule A.

All parties and counsel to the above-captioned matter are invited to attend and participate in the examination.

THE DEFENDANT, TAPTAPTAP, INC.

By: _____
    Tim Tiptop, Esq.
    Its attorney
    Tiptop & Towe
    Metro City, Exurbia 12345
    Atty. Reg. #: 65488

### Certification of Service

This is to certify that a copy of the foregoing Notice of Deposition of Edgar Ellison was mailed, postage prepaid, this 12th day of January, 1994, to attorney Sam Superlawyer, Esq., Lincoln & Hoover, 123 Lincoln Street, Metro City, Exurbia, 12345.

_____
Tim Tiptop, Esq.

### Schedule A

1.  All correspondence between employees of *TapTapTap, Inc.* and *Widgets and Gizmos, Inc.* relating to the contract identified in paragraph 5 of the Complaint, including but not limited to correspondence regarding the negotiation of said contract and the specifications of the widgenometers identified in said contract.
2.  All internal memoranda of *Widgets and Gizmos, Inc.* relating to said contract, including but not limited to memoranda regarding the negotiation of said contract and the specifications of the widgenometers identified in said contract.
3.  All documents relating to the testing, development, analysis, preparation, and/or manufacture of the widgenometers produced by *Widgets and Gizmos, Inc.* and referred to in paragraph 4 of the Complaint.
4.  All documents relating to the damages claimed by the plaintiff, *Widgets and Gizmos, Inc.*, as a result of the allegations set forth in the Complaint.

The term "Notice of Deposition" has actually developed into a verb form as well: a party completing the necessary filing is said to have "noticed the deposition."

Deposition notices relating to depositions of parties can include requests for production under Rule 34 (see reference to Rule 34 in Rule 30(b)(5)) that require the deponent to bring "documents and tangible things" to the deposition. Such a request accompanies the deposition notice in Figure 9–17. Generally speaking, there will have been a previous request for production filed anyway, and the better practice is to make sure you have obtained and reviewed all relevant documents before the deposition. It can, however, be useful to have the deponent bring to the deposition the originals of documents of which you have only copies.

Under certain circumstances where a corporation or other organization is involved in a lawsuit, a party to the lawsuit may wish to depose some employee of the corporation who has knowledge of the matters at issue, but whose identity is not known. It is possible, under such circumstances, to notice the deposition of an unspecified person. Rule 30(b)(1) allows for a deposition notice that provides a "general description sufficient to identify the person or the particular class or group to which the person belongs." Of course, the better practice is to file, where possible, interrogatories that seek information as to the identity of corporate or other individuals who are likely prospects for a deposition.

When the deposition of a party is noticed, the party is automatically required to attend (unless a Motion for Protective Order is filed; more about that in Section 9–7). For depositions of nonparty witnesses, however, simply filing the deposition notice is not sufficient to compel attendance. The court has no jurisdiction over nonparty witnesses, because they are not involved in the lawsuit; and thus to compel attendance of such a witness, some method must be found to establish jurisdiction. The method used is the service of a *subpoena*. A *subpoena* is a document issued under authority of the court and served on a person to compel that person to appear at a certain place at a certain time. A *subpoena* can also compel the person to bring and produce certain documents or other items; if such a production request is included with the *subpoena*, it is called a *subpoena duces tecum*.

*Subpoenas* are governed by Rule 45 of the FRCP, which is relatively long and complicated. This rule was significantly modified in 1991; you should review it carefully. We will introduce five basic concepts pertaining to *subpoenas:* reach of the *subpoena* power of the court; issuance of the *subpoena;* preparation of the *subpoena;* service of the *subpoena;* and objection to the *subpoena* by the person to whom it is directed.

The "reach" of the *subpoena* power of the court means the geographical area within which the court has the authority to compel a nonparty to perform as required by the terms of the *subpoena*. It is analogous to the concept of *jurisdiction*, which we have addressed elsewhere; a court can only compel actions on the part of someone over whom it is authorized to exercise authority. Rule 45(b)(2) defines the physical region constituting the reach of the court's *subpoena* power as, basically, any place within the federal district, or outside the federal district if within 100 miles of the place of the deposition (a provision is also included that authorizes the application of a state statute of the state where the deposition is to be held, if the state statute authorizes statewide service; this would become relevant in geographically large states with multiple federal districts).

*Subpoenas* were, until recently, issued by the court. The 1991 amendments to the FRCP, however, have given broad authorization to attorneys to issue *subpoenas* themselves. Under Rule 45(a)(3), attorneys are now authorized to issue and sign a subpoena on behalf of "a court in which the attorney is authorized to practice," or in "a court in which a deposition or production is compelled by the *subpoena*, if the deposition or production pertains to an action pending in a court in which the attorney is authorized to practice." Translated into simpler English, this means two things. First, if your supervising attorney is authorized to practice in your local federal court (as he or she most likely will be), then he or she can issue *subpoenas* on behalf of that local court to persons within the federal district, or outside the district but within 100 miles of the place of the deposition. Second, since Rule 45(a)(2) requires that a *subpoena* for attendance at a deposition issue from the court "for the district designated by the notice of deposition as the district in which the deposition is to be taken," your supervising attorney is also authorized to issue *subpoenas* on behalf of the federal district in which the person to be served is located.

These rules may sound confusing. Indeed, they can be a bit intimidating, but if studied carefully they are actually quite logical. The main point here is that, if Widgets and Gizmos, Inc. needs to take the deposition of a nonparty witness far outside the state of Exurbia, the rules provide a means for doing so. When such a situation arises, you can review the particulars; and, of course, you will be working under the watchful eye of your supervising attorney.

This brings us to the preparation of the *subpoena*. An example of an executed *subpoena* for a witness in the Widgets and Gizmos, Inc. matter appears in Figure 9–18. Rule 45(a)(1)(A) through (D) requires that the *subpoena* include such things as the name of the court from which it is issued, the title of the action and court in which it is pending (which may be different from the court from which it is issued; if you don't understand how that can be, reread the last several paragraphs), the command to the person *subpoenaed* (including when and where the testimony or production is to be made), and the text of those provisions of Rule 45 that relate to the rights and obligations of the person *subpoenaed*. Note how these various requirements are met by our sample *subpoena* in Figure 9–18.

Next comes the issue of service of the *subpoena*. As noted earlier in this chapter, one of the reasons for seeking addresses of witnesses in interrogatory requests is that any future *subpoena* must be served in order to be enforced. Rule 45 requires that it be served by a "person who is not a party and is not less than 18 years of age." This could be a sheriff or a U.S. Marshal; it could also be a paralegal, or anyone who satisfies the requirement. Service is accomplished "by delivering a copy thereof to such person and, if the person's attendance is commanded, by tendering to that person the fees for one day's attendance and the mileage allowed by law" (Rule 45(b)(1)). The fee and mileage allowance are usually not substantial, but they are important; failure to include them can negate the effect of the *subpoena*, so be sure to check with your supervising attorney for the correct procedure on this point.

**P**ARALEGALERT!

Be prepared—even a paralegal can serve a *subpoena*.

A copy of the Notice of Deposition is often included with the *subpoena*, although this is not required.

Finally, the person *subpoenaed* has certain rights to object to the requirements set forth in the *subpoena*. Under Rule 45(c)(2)(B), a written objection to a production request within 14 days after service of a *subpoena* suspends the *subpoena's* requirements unless a Motion to Compel is granted. Rule 45(c)(3) authorizes a court to **quash** (i.e., suspend the requirements of) or modify a *subpoena* where the person *subpoenaed* is faced with excessive travel requirements or disclosure of trade secrets or other privileged information, or is otherwise unduly burdened. If your firm represents someone who has been *subpoenaed*, you should carefully review Rule 45.

*Subpoena* practice is not really as complicated as you may fear after reading this section, but the technicalities are important. We have provided you with a

Figure 9–18   Federal Subpoena in a Civil Case

# United States District Court

DISTRICT OF ____Exurbia____

Widgets & Gizmos, Inc.

V.

TapTapTap, Inc.

### SUBPOENA IN A CIVIL CASE

CASE NUMBER: 93-0WH-00543

TO: William Teller
  % Computerrific Corp.
  182 Main Street
  Elmville, Exurbia 12377

☐ YOU ARE COMMANDED to appear in the United States District Court at the place, date, and time specified below to testify in the above case.

| PLACE OF TESTIMONY | COURTROOM |
|---|---|
|  | DATE AND TIME |

☒ YOU ARE COMMANDED to appear at the place, date, and time specified below to testify at the taking of a deposition in the above case.

| PLACE OF DEPOSITION<br>The Offices of Lincoln & Hoover<br>123 Lincoln Street<br>Metro City, Exurbia 12345 | DATE AND TIME<br>January 15, 1994<br>10:00 a.m. |
|---|---|

☒ YOU ARE COMMANDED to produce and permit inspection and copying of the following documents or objects at the place, date, and time specified below (list documents or objects):

① Computer model A365 (serial #171723), manufactured by TapTapTap, Inc. which is allegedly defective.
② All documentation establishing or relating to damages resulting from said defective computer.

| PLACE<br>The Offices of Lincoln & Hoover<br>123 Lincoln Street<br>Metro City, Exurbia 12345 | DATE AND TIME<br>January 15, 1994<br>10:00 a.m. |
|---|---|

☐ YOU ARE COMMANDED to permit inspection of the following premises at the date and time specified below.

| PREMISES | DATE AND TIME |
|---|---|

Any organization not a party to this suit that is subpoenaed for the taking of a deposition shall designate one or more officers, directors, or managing agents, or other persons who consent to testify on its behalf, and may set forth, for each person designated, the matters on which the person will testify. Federal Rules of Civil Procedure, 30(b)(6).

| ISSUING OFFICER SIGNATURE AND TITLE (INDICATE IF ATTORNEY FOR PLAINTIFF OR DEFENDANT)<br>*Samuel Superlawyer, Esq.* Attorney for Plaintiff | DATE<br>January 2, 1994 |
|---|---|

ISSUING OFFICER'S NAME, ADDRESS AND PHONE NUMBER

Samuel Superlawyer, Esq.    123 Lincoln Street    (901) 222-2222
  Metro City, Exurbia 12345

(See Rule 45, Federal Rules of Civil Procedure, Parts C & D on Reverse)

**Figure 9–18    Federal Subpoena in a Civil Case, continued**

## PROOF OF SERVICE

| | DATE | PLACE |
|---|---|---|
| **SERVED** | | |

| SERVED ON (PRINT NAME) | MANNER OF SERVICE |
|---|---|
| SERVED BY (PRINT NAME) | TITLE |

## DECLARATION OF SERVER

I declare under penalty of perjury under the laws of the United States of America that the foregoing information contained in the Proof of Service is true and correct.

Executed on _____
DATE

SIGNATURE OF SERVER

ADDRESS OF SERVER

Rule 45, Federal Rules of Civil Procedure, Parts C & D:

(c) PROTECTION OF PERSONS SUBJECT TO SUBPOENAS.

(1)  A party or an attorney responsible for the issuance and service of a subpoena shall take reasonable steps to avoid imposing undue burden or expense on a person subject to that subpoena. The court on behalf of which the subpoena was issued shall enforce this duty and impose upon the party or attorney in breach of this duty an appropriate sanction, which may include, but is not limited to, lost earnings and a reasonable attorney's fee.

(2)(A)  A person commanded to produce and permit inspection and copying of designated books, papers, documents or tangible things, or inspection of premises need not appear in person at the place of production or inspection unless commanded to appear for deposition, hearing or trial.

(B)  Subject to paragraph (d)(2) of this rule, a person commanded to produce and permit inspection and copying may, within 14 days after service of the subpoena or before the time specified for compliance if such time is less than 14 days after service, serve upon the party or attorney designated in the subpoena written objection to inspection or copying of any or all of the designated materials or of the premises. If objection is made, the party serving the subpoena shall not be entitled to inspect and copy the materials or inspect the premises except pursuant to an order of the court by which the subpoena was issued. If objection has been made, the party serving the subpoena may, upon notice to the person commanded to produce, move at any time for an order to compel the production. Such an order to compel production shall protect any person who is not a party or an officer of a party from significant expense resulting from the inspection and copying commanded.

(3)(A)  On timely motion, the court by which a subpoena was issued shall quash or modify the subpoena if it

(i)  fails to allow reasonable time for compliance;
(ii)  requires a person who is not a party or an officer of a party to travel to a place more than 100 miles from the place where that person resides, is employed or regularly transacts business in person, except that, subject to the provisions of clause (c)(3)(B)(iii) of this rule, such a person may in order to attend trial be commanded to travel from any such place within the state in which the trial is held, or

(iii)  requires disclosure of privileged or other protected matter and no exception or waiver applies, or

(iv)  subjects a person to undue burden.

(B)  If a subpoena

(i)  requires disclosure of a trade secret or other confidential research, development, or commercial information, or

(ii)  requires disclosure of an unretained expert's opinion or information not describing specific events or occurrences in dispute and resulting from the expert's study made not at the request of any party, or

(iii)  requires a person who is not a party or an officer of a party to incur substantial expense to travel more than 100 miles to attend trial, the court may, to protect a person subject to or affected by the subpoena, quash or modify the subpoena or, if the party in whose behalf the subpoena is issued shows a substantial need for the testimony or material that cannot be otherwise met without undue hardship and assures that the person to whom the subpoena is addressed will be reasonably compensated, the court may order appearance or production only upon specified conditions.

(d)  DUTIES IN RESPONDING TO SUBPOENA.

(1)  A person responding to a subpoena to produce documents shall produce them as they are kept in the usual course of business or shall organize and label them to correspond with the categories in the demand.

(2)  When information subject to a subpoena is withheld on a claim that it is privileged or subject to protection as trial preparation materials, the claim shall be made expressly and shall be supported by a description of the nature of the documents, communications, or things not produced that is sufficient to enable the demanding party to contest the claim.

*Source:* Official Form for the United States District Court.

foundation; in actual practice, you should work closely with your supervising attorney and carefully review the rules, both federal and state.

## Deposition Preliminaries

Depositions require a great deal of preparation, much of which can be done by a paralegal.

The number of necessary tasks will be greater for the party that noticed the deposition than for other parties, since the noticing party must make the logistical arrangements. For example, a location for the deposition must be chosen. Often this will be a conference room in your own firm's offices; or, another firm's offices may be used for reasons of convenience. After discussing the situation with your supervising attorney, you should take the necessary steps to reserve the location.

If an out-of-town deposition is necessary, you must make travel arrangements, as well as identify and reserve a suitable location (such as a hotel conference room). Again, you can assist in making these arrangements after consultation with your supervising attorney.

Retaining a court reporter is obviously important. Your firm will likely have a list of reputable local reporting firms or freelance court reporters; you should be sure to obtain a definite commitment from a dependable reporter, and you may even want to make arrangements for an emergency backup. Maintaining cordial relationships with several reporting firms can prove of great importance in an emergency situation, where a scheduled reporter is unable to perform at the last minute. Great expense and confusion can be avoided if the deposition can still go forward with a substitute. For out-of-town depositions, the process can be a bit more complicated; you may need to consult the *Martindale-Hubbell Law Directory*, or contact firms in the area, to identify capable court reporters.

Minor logistical details of a deposition are important as well. Coffee or other refreshments, pads and pencils, and photocopy facilities should be available; even the number of chairs should be considered.

There is a provision in the rules allowing for videotaped or audiotaped depositions (see references to "non-stenographic recording" in Rule 30). If such alternative recordings are desired, special arrangements will have to be made. Some law firms are equipped to prepare such recordings themselves; many court-reporting firms also provide these services. You may be responsible to follow through on necessary details.

There are also substantive preparations that will have to be made. For a paralegal, the most important of these is probably identifying and preparing documents or other exhibits that will be used by your supervising attorney in the course of the deposition. You'll need to make copies of documents and ensure availability of other materials prior to the deposition. For documents, sufficient copies should be made such that all interested parties in attendance can have a copy (this is done as a courtesy, rather than as a requirement).

It's also important to prepare an outline of questions to be used during the actual deposition. Your supervising attorney will probably do most of this preparation him- or herself; but you may be called upon to assist. This preparation is similar to that for the witness interviews we discussed in Chapter 4; you must identify substantive areas of which the deponent has knowledge, including information on the various allegations in the pleadings (elements of the cause of action, defenses, damages, and the like).

When the deponent is your firm's client, you must be sure to notify the client quickly of the time and place of the deposition, and instruct him or her to begin organizing materials that are the subject of a related production request. You will need to spend time explaining the nature of a deposition, and preparing your client to testify (look back at the letter to Edgar Ellison in Figure 9–8, page 232). All relevant areas of testimony should be reviewed; an unprepared witness is a tremendous liability. Remember those "tough questions" we talked about in Chapter 4? The client will certainly face such tough questioning in a deposition, and he or she must be prepared.

Your supervising attorney will likely be integrally involved with preparing the client; but you may have an important role as well. You should note that "preparing" the client in no way implies that you are telling the deponent what to say; that would constitute unjustified interference with the judicial process, and is unethical. The deponent must tell the truth; indeed, one of your key instructions to the deponent should be *always* to tell the truth. By reviewing the facts of the case, however, and by instructing the deponent to listen carefully to questions and to think carefully before giving answers, you will minimize the possibility of inaccurate or confusing testimony (particularly with regard to dates and times) and maximize the chances for a successful and forthright deposition. A few other tips for the client-deponent are set forth in Figure 9–19.

Another consideration when your firm represents the deponent is the possibility of filing a Motion for Protective Order, which can limit the manner in which the deposition will proceed (or possibly even prevent it altogether). We discuss such motions further in Section 9–7.

### Conduct of Deposition Itself

As a paralegal, you are not authorized to conduct the questioning in a deposition; only an attorney can do that. But you may attend a deposition, and

**PARALEGALERT!**

When preparing a witness to testify, be sure to emphasize the importance of telling the truth!

**Figure 9–19  Some Tips for the Client-Deponent**

(1) Tell the truth!

(2) Answer only the question posed; don't volunteer information unless necessary to put a more "positive" spin on a "negative" response.

(3) Think carefully before you answer, and if there is anything you don't understand, don't answer until the confusion is eliminated.

(4) Remain calm. Your attorney is there to protect you if necessary, and you can request a recess at any time. Keep in mind, however, that because of the nature of the rules governing deposition procedure, there are a limited number of grounds on which we can justify objections.

(5) Opposing counsel may attempt to lull you into a false sense of security. Don't lose sight of the fact that this is an adversarial setting; thus while you should remain *calm*, that does not mean you should *relax*. You must maintain a high level of concentration at all times.

(6) Do not make assumptions. If anything is unclear to you, say so.

(7) If you are shown a document, take as much time as necessary to review and understand it. Don't allow yourself to be pressured.

you will certainly be working with transcripts, so you should have at least a general idea of the manner in which a deposition proceeds.

A deposition must proceed in the presence of a person who is "authorized to administer oaths" (Rule 28(a)). This person is often the court reporter, who swears in the deponent at the onset of the deposition. The attorneys present often begin by agreeing to certain stipulations with regard to the conduct of the deposition (authorized by Rule 29), such as an agreement not to challenge the qualifications or authority of the court reporter, or a waiver of the reading and signing of the deposition by the deponent (more about reading and signing later).

There is no judge present at a deposition; only the deponent, attorneys, the court reporter, and possibly paralegals or other parties. The questioning begins with the attorney who noticed the deposition. If objections are raised to any of the questions asked, the objections are noted for the record, but the deponent is expected to answer the question anyway (since there is no judge available to rule on the objection; see Rule 30(c)). If any party later seeks to introduce the answer at trial, the objection will then be considered by the judge before the testimony is allowed in evidence.

After the attorney who noticed the deposition completes his or her examination, other involved attorneys are allowed to cross-examine the witness.

The court reporter usually sits in front of a stenography machine, taking down all the words of all the participants. The record created by the stenography machine, which is in the form of a shorthand "code," will later be converted by the court reporter into the standard deposition transcript.

If a paralegal is in attendance at a deposition, he or she will likely have two major responsibilities. The first is to take notes on the questioning and testimony. A transcript will probably not be available for at least a few weeks (unless it is expedited, which we discuss in the next subsection). The notes will thus serve as a temporary record of the testimony. This can be particularly helpful where the deposition is lengthy; some depositions can last several days or longer, and it is often useful to review previous testimony even as the deposition is continuing.

The second task of the paralegal is to keep track of documents that will be needed in the course of the deposition. Just as with court testimony, documents utilized in a deposition are marked as exhibits; it is important to keep track of both those documents that have already been made exhibits, and those that will be introduced as exhibits by your supervising attorney at a later stage. If the number of documents is large, organization is very important (you may wish to review the discussion of document control). We discuss techniques for ensuring the ready availability of documents and exhibits for trial in Chapter 11; these same considerations are applicable in a deposition.

Rule 30(d) provides recourse to a bad-faith termination if a deposition degenerates in some fashion. Upon "a showing that the examination is being conducted in bad faith or in such manner as unreasonably to annoy, embarrass, or oppress the deponent or party," the court may limit the scope or manner of the deposition or terminate it altogether. If so terminated, it cannot be resumed without a further order of the court. As a practical matter, this sort of termination is not seen very often.

## Postdeposition Procedure

There are two aspects of postdeposition procedure that we will address: first, the transcript itself; second, the requirements surrounding the deponent's reading and signing of the transcript.

The transcript is, as stated, a verbatim recitation of questions, testimony, and other comments made while the deposition is being conducted. A sample page from the transcript of the deposition of Edgar Ellison is shown in Figure 9–20.

Transcripts can be fairly brief; in a case involving simple issues, the full transcript may be 60 pages or fewer (which, considering the double-spaced format, is shorter than it sounds). On the other end of the scale, a deposition in a complex matter might last several days and the transcript reach hundreds of pages, or more.

We referred earlier to something called an **expedited transcript.** Sometimes during a deposition that extends over several days, the attorneys involved seek daily transcripts so that they can carefully review the testimony that has been given. For such daily transcripts to be available, the court-reporting firm obviously has a difficult task, to be accomplished under heavy time pressure; hence expedited transcripts are often much more expensive than standard transcripts. Ordinarily, the delivery date of a transcript is at least two weeks after the deposition is completed.

In the last few years, a new transcript service has developed in conjunction with advances in computer technology. This is the transcript on computer disk, with the full-text search feature we spoke about in our discussion of document control. This new feature provides a valuable tool for deposition research, in that it enables counsel to quickly locate key terms that appear in the transcript. For example, suppose the deposition transcript of Edgar Ellison ran to 700 pages.

**Figure 9–20    Transcript Page from Edgar Ellison Deposition**

| Direct Examination by attorney Tim Tiptop (continued) | | |
|---|---|---|
| Question: | You received the Hoobermann memo-randum, which we've marked as defendant's Exhibit J, on January 28, 1992, is that correct? | 1 2 3 4 5 |
| Answer: | Yes. | 6 7 |
| Question: | Are you trained as an electrical engineer, Mr. Ellison? | 8 9 10 |
| Answer: | Yes, my undergraduate degree was in electrical engineering. | 11 12 13 |
| Question: | So you understood the reference in the memorandum, and I'm now quoting, quote, "Preliminary testing results indicate that there may be a correlation between the mean time between failure and the silicon composition of the aluminum chips on which we have etched the widgenometer circuit. In my opinion, more testing is needed." End quote. You understood that reference? | 14 15 16 17 18 19 20 21 22 23 24 |
| Answer: | I believe I had a reasonable understanding of what Hoobermann was implying. | 25 26 27 |
| Question: | And what, exactly, was that understanding? | 28 29 30 |

PAGE 31

That is a fairly lengthy document. Now suppose that several months after the deposition was concluded, Sam Superlawyer wants to review a passage in which Ellison discussed the memoranda generated by Hans Hoobermann, and asks you to locate the passage, since he can't remember exactly when it came up in the course of the deposition. Rather than hunting page-by-page through the entire transcript, you can place the disk in a compatible computer and search for the term "Hoobermann"; the computer program will then direct you to every reference to this name that appears in the deposition.

Full-text search is still not foolproof; if the court reporter, for example, misspelled "Hoobermann," the search may miss a reference. A sophisticated program might have some feature that minimizes such problems, but the point is that there is still great benefit to the "old-fashioned" method of deposition research: namely, the deposition digest. Let's talk about this concept for a moment.

A **deposition digest** is, in essence, a summary of the transcript, often prepared by a paralegal, which supplies faster access to general topics included in the deposition than does the full version. It highlights general subject matter of the deposition, with corresponding page references identifying where the subject matter was discussed. There are basically two types of deposition digest. One is keyed directly to the testimony in the sequence in which it was given; summaries are often provided on the right side of the digest page, and deposition references on the left (see Figure 9–21 for a sample page from a digest of the Ellison deposition). By reviewing the digest, a paralegal or supervising attorney can get a quick idea of where certain subject areas are covered in the transcript, then turn to the transcript itself for the details.

**Figure 9–21   Passage from Digest of Edgar Ellison Deposition Transcript**

| | Digest of Ellison Deposition—Page Three |
|---|---|
| 31 | Tiptop begins questioning Ellison on the Hoobermann memorandum. Ellison admits he received the memo on January 28, 1992. He admits he understood what Hoobermann was implying, but goes on to testify that, based upon his electrical engineering background and his first-hand analysis of the test results, he came to a reasoned judgment that Hoobermann was excessively cautious in his conclusions. Over the next several pages, Tiptop explores with Ellison the test results, probing for exact references which Ellison asserts support his, i.e. Ellison's, conclusion that Hoobermann was being overly cautious. |
| 42 | Tiptop then begins a series of questions on Ellison's memo to Rodriguez dated February 17, 1992. In particular, he questions him somewhat roughly on the passage in which Ellison suggests that the test results must be interpreted in light of the "needs of this corporation in the current business climate." Tiptop asked whether Ellison hadn't violated some duty to properly test the product regardless of the business considerations. Ellison held up fairly well, indicating that preliminary testing is not foolproof, and that the proper extent of testing cannot be evaluated in the absence of an analysis of cost. He contended that the testing conducted was reasonable. |
| 49 | Tiptop next asked Ellison about certain instructions which he gave to Rodriguez with regard to the negotiations with *TapTapTap, Inc.* over the specifications of the aluminum alloy |

The second kind of deposition digest is keyed to subject matter. For example, for each main topic the various deposition references would be listed (e.g., "References to Hans Hoobermann: pages 39–43, 71, 77–83, 126–139"). This type of digest is less commonly used; often, the sequential digest is prepared, and if a subject matter key is desired the information can be obtained from the sequential digest.

The extent of detail required in a digest is a matter for you to discuss with your supervising attorney. Sometimes the digest may be quite sketchy; other times quite detailed. It all depends on the personal preference of the attorney, and the nature of the case.

Finally we come to a consideration of the reading and signing of the deposition transcript. The witness has the opportunity to read and sign the deposition transcript (Rule 30(e)), indicating changes "in form or substance" that the witness desires to make. This process is, however, waivable, and such waiver often occurs. The official transcript is thereafter sealed in an envelope and filed with the court by the court reporter. The deposition can thereafter be used at trial, either for impeachment purposes, or as a substitute for live testimony, if the requirements of Rule 32 are satisfied. For the deposition to substitute for live testimony, the court must find that the witness has died in the interim, or is beyond the *subpoena* power of the court, or is unavailable for some similar reason.

## Depositions Upon Written Questions

As we mentioned at the beginning of this section, the second broad category of depositions, namely, depositions upon written questions, is rarely seen. To summarize the procedure briefly, such depositions are commenced by a Notice of Deposition, which is accompanied by a series of written questions to be asked of the deponent. In response, written "cross questions," "redirect questions," and "recross questions" may also be submitted by other parties prior to the scheduled date of the deposition. Attorneys need not be present at the deposition, except possibly for the attorney representing the deponent; Rule 31 neither requires nor forbids the attendance of counsel. Since the arrangements for the time and place of the deposition are made by the court reporter (i.e., the "officer" designated in the notice) and the witness-deponent, as a practical matter the attendance of attorneys would be difficult to arrange. At the arranged time and place, the written questions are put to the deponent by the court reporter, and the responses are recorded in a transcript in a manner identical to that of the oral deposition.

Perhaps the greatest shortcoming of the written deposition, as compared with the oral deposition, is the inability to frame on-the-spot follow-up questions. Another shortcoming is the inability to observe the demeanor of the deponent.

Under most circumstances, the other methods of discovery constitute more apt and effective means of obtaining information than the deposition upon written questions. One possible exception might involve a desire to obtain information from a nonparty witness at a distant location. Such a witness is subject only to the deposition method of discovery (or a *subpoena* of documents, as discussed previously). If the cost of sending an attorney to the distant location to ask questions orally is high, it might be more efficient to *subpoena* the witness for a deposition on written questions.

It is appropriate at this point to make a general point about obtaining information from nonparty witnesses. As we have discussed, the only official discovery method that applies to nonparty witnesses is the deposition. However, in Section 9–3, we discussed the usefulness of *subpoenas* for obtaining

**Figure 9–22    Obtaining Information from Parties and from Non-Parties**

|  | *From Party* | *From Non-Party Witness* |
|---|---|---|
| *Oral Testimony in Response to Oral Questioning* | Deposition upon oral examination | Deposition upon oral examination |
| *Answers to Written Questions* | Written responses to interrogatories; oral answers in deposition upon written questions | Oral answers in deposition upon written questions |
| *Production of Documents* | Request for production of documents | Subpoena duces tecum under Rule 45 of the FRCP |
| *Admission of Facts* | Request for admissions | An attempt can be made to elicit an admission in the context of a deposition |

pretrial production of documents in the hands of nonparty witnesses. The deposition on written questions is in some sense analogous to filing written interrogatories on a nonparty witness, with the key difference being that the answers are given orally rather than in writing. To some extent, written or oral depositions can also be used to obtain admissions from nonparty witnesses. Thus, you should keep in mind that, although the only official discovery device that can be used to compel nonparty witnesses to supply information is the deposition, the alternatives identified in Figure 9–22 provide somewhat analogous substitutes for every discovery method (except the request for medical examination).

## 9–5    Request for Medical Examination

Requests for medical examination are only necessary in cases in which physical or mental condition of the parties may be crucial: in medical malpractice cases, for example, or in personal injury lawsuits. In the Hampton case, for example, both Harry Hampton and Judith Johnson have alleged significant physical injuries; hence opposing parties would likely seek to examine and evaluate these injuries.

Rule 35 of the FRCP gives to a party the right to compel examination of another party (or a person "in the custody or under the legal control of a party," as where a parent has sued on behalf of an injured minor child). The examination must be conducted by a "suitably licensed or certified examiner" (see 1991 amendment to Rule 35 of the FRCP). The party seeking the examination would file a **Motion for Order Compelling Physical or Mental Examination;** the order will specify "the time, place, manner, conditions, and scope of the examination and the person or persons by whom it is to be made" (Rule 35(a)).

Rule 35 recognizes the need for all involved parties to obtain the results of the examination. Thus, whether the examining physician is expected to testify or not, the party examined has a right, under Rule 35(b), to review the "detailed written report of the examiner setting out the examiner's findings, including results of all tests made, diagnoses and conclusions . . . ." Once such a report has been delivered, the examining party is thereafter entitled to a report of any past or future examinations of the injured party relating to the same injuries.

These provisions are exceptions to the general rules regarding limited discovery of materials relating to expert witnesses.

You should note that the right to compel a physical or mental exam is often readily apparent from the facts of the case. That being true, the parties are often able to agree on the details of the examination without the need to file the motion. The rights created by Rule 35(b) with regard to the exchange of written medical reports also apply to examinations by agreement, unless the agreement "expressly provides otherwise" (Rule 35(b)(3)).

## 9–6 Request for Admissions

Although the discovery tools we have thus far discussed are useful for generating information, Rule 36 of the FRCP provides a discovery device that enables a party to do more than simply generate information. This device presents the parties with an opportunity to "conclusively establish" a fact for the purposes of trial. The device is called the **Request for Admissions,** and is authorized by Rule 36 of the FRCP.

The Request for Admissions is often the last discovery device resorted to by the parties. After interrogatories, production requests, and depositions have enabled the parties to develop a full picture of the facts and evidence that are relevant, each party is often in a position to pin down opponents on certain previously disputed points. By filing requests for admission, a party can force the opposing party to admit the truth of matters that are "within the scope of Rule 26(b)" including "statements or opinions of fact or of the application of law to fact, including the genuineness of any documents described in the request."

Although "statements or opinions of fact" and the "genuineness of any documents" are fairly straightforward categories, you may be wondering how one admits the "application of law to fact." An example contrasting this latter category with an admission of a simple fact is shown in Figure 9–23.

When seeking an admission as to the genuineness of a document, it is customary to attach a copy of the document to the request and inquire whether the copy is a "valid and accurate representation of the original," or some similar

**Figure 9–23    Comparison of Admission of "Fact" with Admission of "Application of Law to Fact"**

> *While a Request for Admission relating to a fact is a straightforward concept, an admission as to the application of law to fact is a somewhat more complicated concept. It seeks, in essence, an admission that a certain fact or facts not only exist, but have a definite legal implication. Consider the following examples:*
>
> **Request for Admission relating to a *fact*:**
>
> No members of the public were prevented by defendant Brown from entering the store owned by defendant Brown on June 15, 1994, between 2:00 P.M. and 3:00 P.M.
>
> **Request for Admission *applying law* to fact:**
>
> When plaintiff Jones entered the store of defendant Brown on June 15, 1994, at approximately 2:30 P.M., he had the legal status of a business invitee.

language. Follow-up requests can also be included, for example, requesting an admission as to who drafted the document, or when.

As with other discovery requests, the drafting of a request for admissions requires precision. The information about which an admission is sought should be absolutely clear and unambiguous from the language used. Remember, also, that it must be in the form of a *statement*, not a question.

Sometimes the previous information obtained through discovery may not be precise enough to draft a single request for admission that will conclusively establish the fact in question. Under such a circumstance, it is appropriate to draft several close alternatives, in an effort to force the opposing party to admit at least one (see, for example, Figure 9–24).

Responses to requests for admission are similar to the admissions and denials of the Answer. Good faith is required in preparing the response: "A denial shall fairly meet the substance of the requested admission, and when good faith requires that a party qualify an answer or deny only a part of the matter of which an admission is requested, the party shall specify so much of it as is true and qualify or deny the remainder." The resort to an assertion of insufficient knowledge is, however, somewhat more difficult when responding to a request for admission: "An answering party may not give lack of information or knowledge as a reason for failure to admit or deny unless the party states that the party has made reasonable inquiry and that the information known or readily obtainable by the party is insufficient to enable the party to admit or deny."

Unlike the responses seen in an Answer, a party can object to specific requests for admission. Objections might raise such issues as the ambiguity of the request, or the irrelevancy of the admission sought. The reason for the objection must be set forth in the response.

The effect of an admission, as we noted, is to conclusively establish the fact; this is, of course, an extremely significant effect. Thus, it is absolutely critical that procedures be followed and deadlines observed. Rule 36 holds as follows: "The matter is admitted unless, within 30 days after service of the request, or within such shorter or longer time as the court may allow, the party to whom the request is directed serves upon the party requesting admission a written answer or objection addressed to the matter, signed by the party or by the party's attorney . . . ." The only other exception to this deadline is that, if the requests are filed extremely early in the lawsuit, no response can be required "before the expiration of 45 days after service of the summons and complaint . . . ."

**Figure 9–24 Examples of "Close Alternative" Requests for Admission**

*Note how the following requests for admission differ only in the percentage identified. This technique can be used in an effort to "pin down" an opposing party on a disputed point.*

(1) Pursuant to the requirements of the contract between the parties identified in paragraph 5 of the Complaint, and the "specifications agreed upon in the negotiations" referenced in said contract, the minimum acceptable silicon content of the alloy used in the "aluminum chips" was **16%**.

(2) Pursuant to the requirements of the contract between the parties identified in paragraph 5 of the Complaint, and the "specifications agreed upon in the negotiations" referenced in said contract, the minimum acceptable silicon content of the alloy used in the "aluminum chips" was **14.5%**.

(3) Pursuant to the requirements of the contract between the parties identified in paragraph 5 of the Complaint, and the "specifications agreed upon in the negotiations" referenced in said contract, the minimum acceptable silicon content of the alloy used in the "aluminum chips" was **12.7%**.

As to format, once again a caption and signature block will be included, as well as certification.

Failure to admit a fact that is later proven by the party that sought the admission can subject a party to an order requiring payment of the "reasonable expenses incurred in making that proof," Rule 37(c) of the FRCP.

If a party is dissatisfied with the responses to a request for admission, a motion can be filed to determine the sufficiency of the response (see the last paragraph of Rule 36(a)).

## 9–7   Discovery Motions

The course of discovery is not always smooth. Despite the relatively clear-cut guidelines, and the general rule favoring liberal discovery, parties to a lawsuit often find themselves embroiled in disputes over the precise limits of the scope of discovery. This should not be entirely surprising, since discovery requests often seek to ferret out damaging information. If a party is able to obstruct the discovery efforts of an opposing party, then he may be able to prevent the disclosure of such damaging information.

Discovery procedures in most jurisdictions are designed to encourage the parties to work out their differences between themselves. There are often rules that *require* the parties to consult, either by phone or in a face-to-face conference, in an effort to resolve their differences before the court acts on any pending motions. Figure 9–2 (page 222) shows the local federal rule of Exurbia relating to discovery motions (sections (d) and (e)), requiring an affidavit of counsel attesting to efforts to resolve the dispute.

Despite such efforts, the parties will often be unable to work out their differences. If that is the case, the rules provide resort to several motions by which the parties can present the dispute to the court for resolution.

You have already been introduced to the **Motion for Protective Order,** to which we have referred in several preceding sections. Pursuant to the provisions of Rule 26(c) of the FRCP, the court is empowered to enter an order, upon motion of a party or a nonparty from whom discovery is sought (such as a nonparty deponent), that "justice requires to protect a party or person from annoyance, embarrassment, oppression, or undue burden or expense . . . ."

As a practical matter, such a Motion for Protective Order is not ordinarily filed when the discovery request can simply be met with an objection, as would be the case with certain interrogatories, production requests, or requests for admission. It is most often seen in two standard circumstances. First, with regard to scheduling of depositions, it is filed in place of an objection, since there is really no other way to "object" to this discovery device. Second, with regard to the other discovery devices, there are situations in which certain requests for sensitive material are not, in fact, objectionable, since the material or information sought falls within the scope of discovery, but are nevertheless sensitive (such as a discovery request that seeks to inquire into a party's trade secrets; or a request for marginally relevant documents that will be expensive to gather) and hence justify, at least in the eyes of the moving party,

**PARALEGALERT!**

As a practical matter, objections are filed to discovery requests that seek material outside the scope of discovery, or which are vague or otherwise defective; whereas a Motion for Protective Order is filed where objections are unavailable (for example, regarding scheduling of depositions) or if the material is within the scope of discovery but is nevertheless sensitive (for example, if it is confidential).

**Figure 9–25  Motion for Protective Order Regarding Ellison Deposition**

*[Note: A memorandum of law would be filed in support of this motion.]*

United States District Court
for the
District of Exurbia

WIDGETS AND GIZMOS, INC.

    Plaintiff

    vs.

TAPTAPTAP, INC.

    Defendant

Civil Action No. 93-OWH-00543

January 28, 1994

### Motion for Protective Order of Defendant *Widgets and Gizmos, Inc.* Regarding Deposition of Edgar Ellison

The plaintiff, *Widgets and Gizmos, Inc.*, hereby moves the court for a protective order under Rule 26 of the Federal Rules of Civil Procedure with regard to the deposition of Edgar Ellison currently scheduled to take place on February 20, 1994. In particular, the plaintiff seeks an order of this court limiting the ability of the defendant *TapTapTap, Inc.*, acting through its counsel, to inquire into information consisting of trade secrets or confidential and proprietary business information of the plaintiff, *Widgets and Gizmos, Inc.*

A memorandum of law has been filed this day, explaining the legal rationale justifying the entry of such an order.

A proposed order is set forth as Exhibit A hereto, identifying the relief which the plaintiff is seeking from this court on this motion.

THE PLAINTIFF, WIDGETS AND GIZMOS, INC.

By: _____
    Samuel Superlawyer, Esq.
    Its attorney
    Lincoln & Hoover
    Metro City, Exurbia 12345
    Atty. Reg. #: 87654

### Certificate of Service

This is to certify that a copy of the foregoing Motion for Protective Order was mailed, postage prepaid, this 28th day of January, 1994, to attorney Tim Tiptop, Esq., Tiptop and Towe, 71 Ferguson Street, Metro City, Exurbia, 12345.

_____
Sam Superlawyer, Esq.

### Exhibit A

### Proposed Order

In conducting questioning during the deposition of Edgar Ellison, the defendant, *TapTapTap, Inc.*, shall not inquire into any matters relating to trade secrets or confidential and proprietary business information of the plaintiff, *Widgets and Gizmos, Inc.* If defendant anticipates asking questions which arguably fall under this prohibition, and believes it must inquire into these areas in order to properly protect its interests in this action, it should submit to the court and to the plaintiff a statement briefly describing the areas into which inquiry is desired. After allowing oral argument in which both parties are given an opportunity to state their position on the issues presented, the court will thereafter render an order with regard to further inquiry into the various areas addressed.

The Court

ORAL ARGUMENT
IS REQUESTED

By: _____
    Judge

some protection by the court. An example of a Motion for Protective Order that fits both these "standard" circumstances is seen in Figure 9–25, filed by Edgar Ellison to protect the trade secrets of Widgets and Gizmos, Inc. from disclosure during his deposition.

When a Motion for Protective Order is filed, the court has numerous options with regard to modifying the discovery process, including an order that the requested discovery not be allowed (see Rule 26(c)); a list of these various options appears in Figure 9–26.

The Motion for Protective Order applies to a party trying to *prevent* discovery; what about a party whose efforts to *obtain* discovery responses are being thwarted? There will arise, for example, situations in which an opposing party has filed an objection to a discovery request, or simply failed to respond to a discovery request, or responded with an answer that is evasive or in some way incomplete. If a party is dissatisfied with the response of the other side to discovery requests, Rule 37 of the FRCP allows for a **Motion for Order Compelling Discovery** (also called a **Motion to Compel**) to be filed. The list of situations to which Rule 37 applies is fairly extensive and the text of the rule is lengthy. If a deponent fails to answer a question properly; if an interrogatory is objected to; if a production response is ignored; or for any other similar reason, the party seeking the discovery may file the Motion for Order Compelling Discovery. After deciding such a motion, the court "shall" (under Rule 37(a)(4)) award to the prevailing party any expenses (including attorney's fees) incurred on the motion, unless the losing party was "substantially justified" in its position.

You should note that, although under the FRCP objections are not argued directly, but only if they are referenced in a Motion to Compel, some state rules allow for the court to decide discovery objections directly.

If an order is entered by the court compelling a discovery response, and the party so ordered fails to obey the order, further **sanctions,** or penalties, may be imposed under Rule 37(b). The sanctions may include such things as an

**Figure 9–26  The Court's Options with Regard to a Protective Order**

> *A protective order "protects" against "annoyance, embarrassment, oppression, or undue burden or expense..." (Rule 26(c) of the FRCP) regarding discovery sought or a deposition to be taken. The court can enter one or more of the following orders (listed in Rule 26(c)):*
>
> (1) that the discovery not be had;
>
> (2) that the discovery may be had only on specified terms and conditions, including a designation of the time or place;
>
> (3) that the discovery may be had only by a method of discovery other than that selected by the party seeking discovery;
>
> (4) that certain matters not be inquired into, or that the scope of the discovery be limited to certain matters;
>
> (5) that discovery be conducted with no one present except persons designated by the court;
>
> (6) that a deposition after being sealed be opened only by order of the court;
>
> (7) that a trade secret or other confidential research, development, or commercial information not be disclosed or be disclosed only in a designated way; and/or
>
> (8) that the parties simultaneously file specified documents or information enclosed in sealed envelopes to be opened as directed by the court.

additional order that establishes, for the purposes of the action those matters or facts affected by the original order compelling discovery; or an order denying to the disobedient party further right to support or oppose designated claims or defenses; or an order of contempt of court; or several other specified sanctions.

## 9—8  Practical Considerations

In contrast to pleading and motion concepts, discovery rules and procedures are, for the most part, fairly straightforward and easily understandable. In some sense, then, practical considerations (as opposed to technical analyses) are of primary importance in properly conducting discovery. With that thought in mind, we leave you with several suggestions that we hope will prove useful.

First of all, remember that just because the concepts themselves are straightforward doesn't mean that discovery practice is "easy." Indeed, a great deal of work (and thought) goes into properly drafting and responding to discovery requests (which you should now recognize, having completed this chapter). Resist any temptation to dismiss the discovery stage as "routine"; you must be alert to the many angles and twists of your cases in order to draft requests properly, and you must be both thorough and thoughtful in avoiding the potential pitfalls of improper responses.

Second, complete your discovery tasks *early*. You may recall a similar consideration that we identified as one of the cardinal rules of investigation; many of the same justifications apply here. A deponent's recollection of events, for example, will be fresher if the deposition occurs soon after the events in question; one set of discovery responses may indicate a need for additional inquiry into new areas not previously recognized; it may take significant blocks of time to prepare large production responses, or to obtain answers to complicated interrogatories. All these factors point to the importance of early attention to discovery tasks.

Third, avoid time-consuming motion battles over the disclosure of information that will not be harmful to your client. This is a consideration that is perhaps more important for your supervising attorney to keep in mind, since he or she will be setting strategy; but you might actually be more familiar with the contents of documents in the early stages of discovery, and thus you can at least point out to your supervising attorney that the information which is responsive to certain arguably objectionable discovery requests will not, even if disclosed, do any damage to your client's position. If such is the case, it may not be worth the time and expense of arguing over objections.

Our fourth practical consideration follows from the third: keep in mind that expense is a relevant consideration in determining the extent to which discovery options should be pursued. Depositions, for example, are costly, and hence the number of depositions justified in a given case will be directly related to the amount in controversy. A million-dollar case will justify more extensive inquiry, for example, than a thousand-dollar case involving similar facts. Since the goal

---

**PARALEGALERT!**

Keep in mind the following practical considerations for discovery.

1.  Don't dismiss it as "routine"—*think*!

2.  Complete discovery tasks *early*!

3.  Don't fight unnecessary battles.

4.  Remember that expense is a relevant factor.

5.  Don't make frivolous requests and don't make evasive responses.

6.  Don't forget to review supplementation before trial.

of a lawsuit is generally to maximize the economic benefit to the client, you shouldn't waste the client's resources on unnecessary, duplicative, or excessively picayune discovery.

A fifth practical consideration relates to professional ethics: avoid drafting frivolous discovery requests, and avoid making evasive responses. You, your firm, and the client must act in good faith throughout the discovery process.

Finally, you must remember to review carefully all discovery responses (both those made by the other side and those of your own side) before trial. Although rules as to supplementation are not excessively strict under the FRCP, and vary among the state court systems, it is nevertheless always important that you make sure that you are in possession of all necessary information from the opposition, and further, that you have not failed to disclose any information which will prevent you from making necessary presentations of evidence at trial.

**Recent Developments**   Between the first and second printing of this book, the Supreme Court of the United States submitted to Congress amendments to the Federal Rules of Civil Procedure. Pursuant to Section 2074 of Title 28 of the United States Code, these amendments took effect on December 1, 1993.

The amendments include significant changes to the Rules pertinent to discovery, Rules 26-37. These changes include, among other things: an entirely new concept requiring disclosure of relevant information to opposing parties even before such information is requested; limitations on numbers of interrogatories (commonly found in local rules but not previously in the FRCP); limitations on the number and duration of depositions; less restrictive procedures for the taking of depositions by non-stenographic means; and revision of the sanction provisions to reflect the new provisions requiring disclosure even before a request has been made.

# SUMMARY

## 9-1

Discovery is the term applied to the rules, methods, and procedure by which the parties to a lawsuit are authorized to request and, by court order, compel the disclosure of information held by opposing parties (or, in some instances, nonparty witnesses). The scope of discovery is broad; any matter relevant, not privileged, and reasonably calculated to lead to the discovery of admissible evidence is generally discoverable. The client is closely involved in discovery practice; the paralegal has an important role as well.

## 9-2

Interrogatories are written questions posed by one party to another party (but not to nonparty witnesses) with regard to matters within the scope of allowable discovery. They are often the first discovery device used, because they are useful to "set the stage" for production requests and depositions. The requests you draft will be based on the pleadings, information obtained from the client, and forms and models; they will generally always include requests regarding such background information as relevant names and addresses, corporate information, relevant documents, names of witnesses, facts regarding damages, and information regarding experts. The information that can be sought regarding experts is limited to four categories identified in Rule 26 of the FRCP, and any discovery beyond these four categories requires a court order. Be sure to make your interrogatory requests absolutely unambiguous. The FRCP allows the courts some flexibility with regard to the setting of filing requirements; review your local rules. When responding to interrogatories, first contact the client. Make any relevant objections. Answer the questions fully and accurately, but generally avoid volunteering additional information. The client will have to sign the final version of the responses "under oath." Keep in mind the supplementation requirements of Rule 26 of the FRCP, and any applicable local rules or discovery orders.

## 9-3

Rule 34 of the FRCP authorizes three discovery procedures: production of documents; production of "things"; and permission to enter upon land. Document control is a very important aspect of litigation practice. It can be accomplished through the employment of such measures as written indices, numbering systems, cross-filing of multiple copies, and computerized systems. Ideas for production requests are generated in a manner similar to interrogatories; keep in mind, however, that responses to earlier interrogatories are an additional source of ideas for proper production requests. Documents sought need only be described with "reasonable particularity," but the descriptions should be as precise as possible. Paralegals often work closely with the client in preparing responses to the other side's production requests; be sure to inform the client of the need to be thorough, and check for privileged or confidential materials. Be careful when photocopying documents; this is often when they can get mixed up. Tangible "things" and land are subject to inspection and testing under Rule 34.

## 9-4

A deposition is a procedure by which the oral testimony of a party or nonparty witness is taken, prior to trial, in response to questions, with the questions, testimony, and other comments of the participants preserved in a verbatim transcript. Depositions are important because they (1) allow the witness's demeanor to be observed; (2) allow for follow-up questions; (3) can be used with nonparty witnesses; and (4) can be used to preserve testimony. Depositions are officially scheduled by the filing of a Notice of Deposition; for nonparty witnesses, a *subpoena* will also likely be necessary. *Subpoena* practice is governed by Rule 45 of the FRCP, which was amended in 1991 to allow attorneys to issue *subpoenas* directly. *Subpoenas* must be served upon the person to whom the command is directed. A *subpoena duces tecum* commands the person identified also to bring certain documents or materials to a specified place at a specified time. A person *subpoenaed* has certain rights to object to the *subpoena*; a court may act to quash it. Deposition preliminaries include reserving a suitable location, retaining a court reporter, organizing necessary documents, outlining relevant questions, and (if the deponent is your firm's client) preparing the client to testify truthfully. During the deposition itself, the witness will generally be sworn in by the court reporter, followed by questioning by all attorneys; no judge is present, so objections are recorded but not resolved. The paralegal will likely have two responsibilities: taking notes, and organizing exhibits and documents. After the deposition, the transcript will have to be digested, and the formalities of reading, correcting, and signing observed. Depositions upon written questions are a rarely seen alternative method for a deposition; generally, depositions will be conducted by oral questioning.

## 9–5

For cases in which the medical condition of a party is a relevant issue, Rule 35 of the FRCP gives to a party the right to compel the medical examination of an opposing party (or someone under the control of the opposing party). Rule 35 provides guidelines for the exchange of expert medical reports, which allows for more liberal discovery than the limitations of Rule 26, which concerns expert testimony in general.

## 9–6

A Request for Admissions enables a party to pin down an opposing party on certain factual statements, thereby "conclusively establishing" certain facts prior to trial. It is usually the last discovery device employed by a party, after the other discovery devices have developed a full and accurate picture of the facts of the matter. Matters to which requests for admission are appropriate include any matter "within the scope of Rule 26(b)" including "statements or opinions of fact or of the application of law to fact, including the genuineness of any documents described in the request" (Rule 35). Since the effect of an admission is to conclusively establish the fact, be sure to pay careful attention to deadlines; the request is considered admitted if not denied or objected to within the deadline.

## 9–7

A Motion for Protective Order is available to a party who wants to limit the other side's discovery rights in some fashion; Rule 26 of the FRCP provides to the court a wide range of options for dealing with such a motion. Discovery objections are generally filed when matters requested are outside the scope of allowable discovery, or are vague or otherwise defective. A Motion for Protective Order is filed where an objection is not a viable alternative (as with scheduling of a deposition) or where the request is within the scope of discovery but is nevertheless sensitive for some reason (such as confidentiality). If the efforts of a party to obtain discovery are being thwarted by objections or inadequate responses, that party may file a Motion for Order Compelling Discovery (also called a Motion to Compel). If the offending party fails to follow an order issued after such a motion, he or she is subject to sanctions.

## 9–8

There are several key practical considerations to keep in mind with regard to discovery. Don't dismiss discovery as "routine"—Think! Complete all your discovery tasks early. Don't fight unnecessary battles. Remember that expense is a relevant factor to keep in mind. Don't make frivolous requests, and don't make evasive responses. Finally, don't forget to review supplementation requirements before trial.

# REVIEW

## Key Terms

Before proceeding, review the key terms listed below to be sure you understand each one. If necessary, read over the corresponding section of the chapter. When you are ready to test your understanding, answer the Review Questions.

discovery
scope of discovery
attorney work-product
scheduling order
discovery conference
interrogatories
expert witnesses
objections
supplementation
Request for Production of Documents and Things or Entry Upon Land
deposition
transcript
deponent
court reporter
depositions upon written questions
depositions upon oral examination
follow-up questions
Notice of Deposition
*subpoena*
*subpoena duces tecum*
quash
expedited transcript
deposition digest
Motion for Order Compelling Physical or Mental Examination
Request for Admissions
Motion for Protective Order
Motion for Order Compelling Discovery
Motion to Compel
sanctions

## Questions for Review and Discussion

1. Define *discovery*.
2. Why is the scope of discovery described as "liberal?"
3. Why are interrogatories often the first discovery device utilized?
4. Explain how discovery methods are applied to information held by the opposing party's expert witnesses.
5. How are large volumes of documents kept under control?
6. What steps should a paralegal follow when reviewing a client's documents in preparation for making a discovery response?
7. Why are depositions important?
8. What is a *subpoena duces tecum*?
9. What are some of the tasks that a paralegal will perform with regard to a deposition?
10. Compare a Motion for Protective Order with a discovery objection.

## Activities

1. Go to your nearest law library and locate a collection of sample interrogatories. Ask the librarian for help, if necessary. Using the samples as a guideline, draft several interrogatories that Judith Johnson might serve upon Bud's Auto Service with regard to her cross-claim (these would relate to such things as the work performed on Hampton's car, including identification of mechanics; identification of invoices, work orders, or other written records; and description of the services performed). Spend some time simply looking through the collection of sample interrogatories to get some idea of the vast quantity of potential interrogatories in various typical case types.
2. Review your state court's rules regarding preparation and service of *subpoenas*.
3. If you have worked for a law firm or know any lawyers, try to obtain a copy of a deposition transcript. You may also be able to obtain one from your local clerk's office. Review the deposition, and prepare a digest covering at least 50 pages of testimony.

# CHAPTER 10   Resolution Before Trial: Dispositive Motions and Settlement

## OUTLINE

## COMMENTARY

The lawsuit between Widgets and Gizmos, Inc. and TapTapTap, Inc. is moving swiftly along. The pleadings are closed. Discovery, which involved an enormous volume of documents and great effort on your part, has been completed. Deposition transcripts have been received, reviewed, and carefully digested. A complete picture of the dispute has been developed.

The Hampton matter is likewise advancing. The evidence likely to be presented at trial has been reviewed and analyzed by all involved parties and attorneys; depositions have revealed the likely thrust of witness testimony, as well as the demeanor of the witnesses. All that remains in question is the ultimate decision; no one can predict with any certainty which way the jury will lean.

These two cases have reached a stage where resolution is imminent. Such resolution may result from a decision of the court on contested dispositive motions; it may result from settlement; or it may only result after the full playing out of the trial process (and even an appeal after that).

## OBJECTIVES

In this chapter you'll learn about motions that request that the court enter judgment in favor of the moving party, effectively ending the lawsuit before trial; you'll also learn about the settlement process. After completing this chapter, you'll be able to:

1. Explain what is meant by a dismissal with prejudice.
2. Identify the prerequisites for the entry of a default judgment by the clerk of the federal court.
3. Explain what a military affidavit is.
4. Describe how the facts are established on a Motion for Judgment on the Pleadings.
5. Identify the basic standard by which the court scrutinizes a Motion for Summary Judgment.
6. Explain what the court is seeking to determine when it investigates the facts on a Motion for Summary Judgment.
7. Identify the two basic methods by which the nonmoving party attacks a Motion for Summary Judgment.
8. Explain what is meant by partial summary judgment.
9. Provide a brief explanation of how an attorney arrives at a preliminary settlement value.
10. Explain how the parties officially conclude a lawsuit that has been settled.

## 10–1  Moving Toward Trial

In the last three chapters, we've talked about pleadings, motions attacking pleadings, multiparty practice, and discovery. These are all important components of something we've called the "pretrial process." You've learned how to define the issues, ensure that they are legitimate, and further ensure that all necessary claims and parties have been included in the lawsuit. You've also learned how to use the court system's official information-gathering process—discovery—in order to uncover a great deal of information about pending cases.

You would be ready, at this point, to learn about that aspect of the litigation process which we earlier described as its focus—namely, the trial—except for one thing: the great majority of lawsuits that are filed *never go to trial*. It is only in a minority of cases that a judgment is ultimately rendered by the trial court at the conclusion of the evidence. For the rest, something happens along the way to end the case without a trial.

In this chapter, we introduce you to some of the ways in which a case might be resolved before trial. In particular, we talk about dispositive motions (with an emphasis on the Motion for Summary Judgment) and settlement.

## 10–2  Dispositive Motions in General

In Chapter 7 we defined **dispositive motions** as motions that, if granted, constitute a final resolution of some aspect of the case, or possibly even the entire case. They "dispose" of the need for the trial court to further consider the issues resolved, hence the name *dispositive*. If allowed to stand, the granting of a dispositive motion might be appealed to a higher court, but the issues will not be considered further by the trial court.

In this section, we discuss several of these dispositive motions in more detail, having introduced them in Chapter 7. First, we briefly review the Motion to Dismiss in conjunction with the concept of dismissal in general. Then we discuss the procedure leading to a default judgment. Finally, we discuss the Motion for Judgment on the Pleadings under Rule 12 of the FRCP. This latter motion is actually seen only rarely, but it serves as a useful introduction to the concepts behind the Motion for Summary Judgment, a very important dispositive motion, seen often, which we will discuss in the next section.

### The Motion to Dismiss, and Dismissal in General

In Chapter 7 we discussed in some detail the Motion to Dismiss filed under Rule 12 of the FRCP. Such a motion is available to parties defending against claims for relief, usually defendants but sometimes plaintiffs defending a counterclaim (plaintiffs would never, however, file a "Motion to Dismiss the Answer," because the Answer is not a claim for relief). A Motion to Dismiss is based on one of the seven defenses identified in Rule 12(b), and is accompanied by a memorandum of law arguing that it be granted. The opposing party will thereafter file a memorandum in opposition. Finally, the court will hear oral argument, then render a decision determining whether dismissal is appropriate.

What does it mean when a case is dismissed? It means that the case, or the parts of the case affected by the motion, have been disposed of by the court; hence a Motion to Dismiss is a dispositive motion. Rule 41(b) notes:

> Unless the court in its order for dismissal otherwise specifies, a dismissal under this subdivision and any dismissal not provided for in this rule, other than a dismissal for lack of jurisdiction, for improper venue, or for failure to join a party under Rule 19, operates as an *adjudication upon the merits.* [emphasis supplied]

Thus, with the exceptions noted, a **dismissal** is an "adjudication upon the merits," meaning that it is considered to be a final resolution of the substantive questions presented.

It is important to note the language with which the quoted passage begins, authorizing the court to "otherwise" specify the effect of its ruling of dismissal. This language gives the court the right to modify the impact of a dismissal, so that it is something less than the final "adjudication on the merits" set forth in the rule. The court's right to specify "otherwise" the effect of the dismissal is actually utilized fairly often. It is not uncommon, for example, for a court to dismiss a complaint conditioned on the explicit right of the plaintiff to submit an amended complaint within a certain specified time limit, curing the defect that engendered the original Motion to Dismiss in the first place; after the refiling the court vacates the dismissal (a situation we touched on briefly in Chapter 7). Such a situation is often referred to as a **dismissal without prejudice** to the right of the party to assert the claim again at some future time. A **dismissal with prejudice,** on the contrary, denies the party asserting the claim the right to assert the same claim again at some future time; it does, in fact, constitute a final adjudication of the contested issues presented.

Finally, Rule 41(a) addresses something called a "voluntary dismissal." We'll talk further about voluntary dismissals in our discussion of settlement in Section 10–4.

### The Procedure for Obtaining a Default Judgment

In Chapter 7 we introduced you to the concept of default, and to Requests to the Clerk for Entry of Default filed under the FRCP. To refresh your recollection briefly, such a request is addressed to the clerk, usually accompanied by an affidavit from the moving attorney. When entered, the default constitutes, in essence, a recognition by the court that the party defaulted has failed to plead within a required deadline or otherwise to defend the lawsuit.

The entry of the default itself is only the beginning of the process. We have saved the ensuing analysis for this chapter, because it relates to a final disposition of the lawsuit: namely the **default judgment.** We will continue using the hypothetical example we began in Chapter 7, in which defendant TapTapTap, Inc. filed neither an appearance nor a responsive pleading within 20 days of the service of the complaint filed by Widgets and Gizmos, Inc. We showed you in that chapter how the default itself was obtained; the procedure for obtaining judgment based on the default is governed by Rule 55(b)(1) of the FRCP, which reads in pertinent part as follows:

> (b) Judgment. Judgment by default may be entered as follows:
> (1) By the Clerk. When the plaintiff's claim against a defendant is for a sum certain or for a sum which can by computation be made certain, the clerk upon request of the plaintiff and upon affidavit of the amount due shall enter judgment for that amount and costs against the defendant, if the defendant has been defaulted for failure to appear and is not an infant or incompetent person.

Let's consider the requirements of this rule one by one. The claim of Widgets and Gizmos, Inc. against TapTapTap, Inc. is indeed for a "sum certain," namely, the unpaid balance due for widgenometers (identified in paragraph 9 of the complaint as $750,000). An example of a sum that would *not* satisfy this "certainty" requirement would be, for example, the amount of damages for pain and suffering due to a physical injury, which can only be determined after evidence is presented to the court; such damages are not subject to a precise and certain computation.

Next, the default entered against TapTapTap, Inc. was indeed for failure to appear, so that requirement of the rule is satisfied as well. In addition, TapTapTap, Inc. is neither an "infant" nor an "incompetent person," so those provisions are also satisfied.

Having satisfied all these provisions, the next question that arises is: how does one then proceed to obtain the default judgment? Although the procedure is not spelled out in detail in the rule, the method followed almost universally requires the filing of two documents, and often a third. First is a **Request for Entry of Default Judgment,** shown in Figure 10–1. Note that the request in Figure 10–1 includes a proposed order; this is sometimes filed as a separate document. Second is an affidavit of the moving party (or, in the case of a corporate party, an officer of the corporation with knowledge of the events in question), which establishes the amount of the damages, and possibly also speaks to the other requirements of Rule 55(b)(1) (such as the noninfant status of the opposing party; see Figure 10–2). The third document is required only when the opposing party is an individual person; it is referred to as a **military affidavit.** Under section 520 of the Appendix to Title 50 of the United States Code, members of the military service are protected against the entry of default judgments while engaged in the service of their country. This requirement recognizes the sensitive and important nature of military service, and the difficulty of obtaining an assurance that an individual in the military was properly notified of the pendency of the suit. If these papers

## PARALEGALERT!

When filing for a default judgment against an individual, you must include an affidavit attesting to the fact that the party against whom the default was entered is not in the military service.

United States District Court
for the
District of Exurbia

WIDGETS AND GIZMOS, INC.     :

    Plaintiff     :     Civil Action No. 93-OWH-00543

    vs.     :

        :     December 10, 1993

TAPTAPTAP, INC.     :

    Defendant     :

        :

### Request for Entry of Default Judgment
### Against Defendant *TapTapTap, Inc.*

TO THE CLERK:

    The plaintiff, *Widgets and Gizmos, Inc.*, hereby requests that the clerk enter a judgment of default against the defendant, *TapTapTap, Inc.*, pursuant to the terms of Rule 55(b)(1) of the Federal Rules of Civil Procedure. The full amount of the claim and judgment requested (which is a sum certain as required by the applicable provisions of Rule 55(b)(1)) is $855,000.00, with interest continuing to accrue at the rate of $200.00 per day, as identified in the Affidavit of Edgar Ellison, filed on even date herewith. The plaintiff asserts that the defendant is a corporation, and hence not in the military service. The plaintiff further asserts that, since the defendant is a corporation, it can be characterized neither as an infant nor incompetent person as those terms are understood in the context of Rule 55(b)(1).

    WHEREFORE, the plaintiff respectfully requests that judgment be entered against the defendant, *TapTapTap, Inc.*, in the amount of $855,000.00, plus interest accruing at the daily rate of $200.00, and costs.

        THE PLAINTIFF, WIDGETS AND GIZMOS, INC.

    By: _____
        Samuel Superlawyer, Esq.
        Its attorney
        Lincoln & Hoover
        123 Lincoln Street
        Metro City, Exurbia 12345
        Atty. Reg. #: 87654
        Phone: (901) 222-2222

### Order

    The foregoing request having been presented to this court, and it appearing that (1) the defendant *TapTapTap, Inc.* has been defaulted for its failure to appear, (2) the defendant is neither in the military service, nor an infant, nor an incompetent person, and (3) the defendant is indebted to the plaintiff in the sum certain of $855,000.00 plus interest at the rate of $200.00 per day, it is hereby ORDERED:

    That judgment is entered in favor of the plaintiff, *Widgets and Gizmos, Inc.* and against the defendant, *TapTapTap, Inc.* in the above-referenced matter in the amount of $855,000.00, plus interest in the amount of $200.00 per day from _____, 1993 to the date of payment, plus costs in the amount of _____.

        The Court

    By: _____
    Clerk
    Date:

**Figure 10–2    Affidavit of Edgar Ellison in Support of Default Judgment**

United States District Court
for the
District of Exurbia

WIDGETS AND GIZMOS, INC.                      :

         Plaintiff                            :        Civil Action No. 93-OWH-00543

                 vs.                          :

                                              :        December 10, 1993

TAPTAPTAP, INC.                               :

         Defendant                            :

                                              :

### Affidavit of Edgar Ellison

The affiant, Edgar Ellison, being duly sworn, hereby deposes and says as follows:

1.  I am the President of *Widgets and Gizmos, Inc.*, the plaintiff in the above-captioned matter.

2.  I am over the age of eighteen years and understand the obligation of an oath.

3.  The principal amount of the debt owed by the defendant *TapTapTap, Inc.* to the plaintiff pursuant to the claim stated in the Complaint is the sum certain of $750,000.00

4.  The interest on said debt is, as of the date of this affidavit, $75,000.00.

5.  The interest continues to accrue on said debt at the rate of $200.00 per day.

6.  The attorney's fees incurred in this matter to date, which are an element of damages specifically identified in the contract attached as Exhibit A to the Complaint, are $30,000.00.

7.  The defendant, *TapTapTap, Inc.*, is a corporation and hence is not in the military service of the United States. As a corporation, defendant *TapTapTap, Inc.* is neither an incompetent person nor an infant.

                                        _____
                                        Edgar Ellison
                                        President
                                        *Widgets and Gizmos, Inc.*

Subscribed and sworn to before
me, this the _____ day
of _____, 1993.

_____
Ms. Nadine Nemeth
Notary Public of the State of
Exurbia
Commission expires:

have all been properly filed, and the prerequisites of Rule 55(b)(1) satisfied, the clerk will enter judgment.

Suppose the various prerequisites of Rule 55(b)(1) are *not* satisfied; suppose, for example, that the sum claimed is not "certain"; or that the default was entered for failure to file a required pleading within the applicable deadline, rather than for failure to appear; or that the defendant is an infant or an incompetent person. What then?

Under those circumstances, the default judgment procedure is governed by Rule 55(b)(2). Under that provision, the clerk is no longer empowered to enter the judgment; it must be done by the "court," meaning a judge. An **Application for Entry of Default Judgment** (similar to the Request for Entry of Default Judgment seen in Figure 10–1) will be filed; instead of directing it to the clerk, however, it is directed to the court. A military affidavit is again required (if the defendant is an individual person). If the default is for something other than failure to appear, written notice must be provided to the opposing party (or counsel) "at least 3 days prior to the hearing" on the application. Finally, the hearing conducted will include the admission of evidence on damages or the truth of any other "averment" that must be established.

The request for, and the application for, a default judgment can both be described as "dispositive." Once granted, a default judgment is theoretically final; it disposes of the need for the trial court to further consider any of the issues presented by the matter (of course, there might still be an appeal to a higher court; see also the discussion in the next paragraph regarding the "setting aside" of a default judgment).

As we noted in Chapter 7, all is not lost for a party after a default has been entered against him or her; the default can be set aside "for good cause shown." Under Rule 55(c), a default judgment, despite the apparent finality we just discussed, "may likewise" be set aside "in accordance with Rule 60(b)." The requirements of Rule 60(b) must be carefully observed. Several specific reasons for relieving a party from a final judgment are set forth in the rule, including such things as mistake, excusable neglect, or fraud; there is also a catch-all allowing for "any other reason justifying relief from the operation of the judgment." But don't be lulled into thinking the process is liberal; a Motion to Set Aside Judgment must be filed, and persuasive reasons cited before the court is likely to set aside a judgment. The deadline for filing such a motion must also be considered: "The motion shall be made within a reasonable time, and for reasons (1), (2), and (3) [which relate to mistake, inadvertence, excusable neglect, surprise, newly discovered evidence, and fraud] not more than one year after the judgment . . . was entered." The bottom line is that you should file such a motion at the earliest possible date; indeed, an even more important rule is never to allow defaults to enter in the first place.

State court procedures with regard to defaults and default judgments, as we noted in Chapter 7, can vary. Check your state's procedure on these points, including any rules or statutes that require the filing of a military affidavit.

> ### PARALEGALERT!
>
> The best rule to keep in mind with regard to defaults is to avoid allowing them to enter against the client. But if a default enters (or worse yet, a default *judgment*), file an Application to Set Aside Default (or Default Judgment) at the earliest possible date, set forth good reasons why the judgment should be set aside, and carefully review Rules 55 and 60(b) of the FRCP.

## Motion for Judgment on the Pleadings Under Rule 12

Rule 12(c) of the FRCP allows for something called a **Motion for Judgment on the Pleadings.** Such a motion is authorized after the "pleadings are closed but within such time as not to delay the trial. . . ." What such a motion essentially asserts is that the court can render a judgment in the case based on a review of the pleadings alone (and an accompanying memorandum of law), with no need for a trial or further factual inquiry.

As we noted earlier, this motion is not often seen, but it is worth discussing for some of the concepts it introduces. These concepts also apply to the analysis of the motion for summary judgment, which we address in the next section.

As a first step in learning these concepts, consider the following. In a broad sense, a lawsuit can be thought of as being essentially about two things: first, determining the facts that apply; and second, applying principles of law to those facts. We've addressed these two divergent concepts elsewhere in this text; at this point, you should be comfortable with the distinction between facts and law.

In a Motion for Judgment on the Pleadings, the moving party asserts (1) that the facts can be established by the pleadings alone, without further need for resolution by trial, and (2) that when these established facts are analyzed in light of the applicable principles of law, they are sufficient to justify the entry of judgment in favor of the moving party.

How are the facts "established" by the pleadings? For the purposes of the motion, the moving party must assume (1) that all the allegations of the other party are true, and (2) that only such of his or her own allegations as have been admitted by the other party are true.

Having established the facts in this manner, how is it shown that judgment is justified as a matter of law? A *memorandum of law* must be filed, showing that the application of legal principles to the facts as established leads to a conclusion that the moving party is entitled to judgment. We will talk more about such a memorandum of law in our discussion of summary judgment.

Taking into account the method just described for establishing the facts, there will arise only very limited contexts in which a Motion for Judgment on the Pleadings would likely be filed. First would be a context in which the allegations of the complaint, even if all true, fail to constitute a valid cause of action as a matter of law; in other words, they fail to state a claim on which relief can be granted. This context (and language) should be familiar to you; it also applies to a Motion to Dismiss under Rule 12(b)(6). Such a Motion to Dismiss (alleging failure to state a claim on which relief can be granted) can be filed immediately after the complaint is filed, before the pleadings are closed. A Motion for Judgment on the Pleadings, on the other hand, cannot be filed until *after* the pleadings are closed (see Rule 12(c)). Thus, defendants rarely file such a Motion for Judgment on the Pleadings, since they are able to exercise what is in essence the same right at an earlier stage of the litigation, through the filing of a Rule 12(b)(6) Motion to Dismiss. A defendant might be more likely to file a Motion for Judgment on the pleadings if an affirmative defense, such as an assertion of the statute of limitations, negates the enforceability of the cause of action asserted by the plaintiff, although even this might be asserted by a Rule 12(b)(6) motion.

A plaintiff is more likely to file a Motion for Judgment on the Pleadings, although even then an appropriate context does not, as a practical matter, arise in many cases. If a defendant has admitted all the allegations of the complaint, for example, or enough of them so that the cause of action asserted by the plaintiff is admitted as a matter of law, a Motion for Judgment on the Pleadings would be in order. Such would be unlikely if the complaint had only one count; the defendant in such a case would more likely have settled, rather than simply admitting liability in the answer (although it can happen, as where a defendant has no resources to offer in settlement). An appropriate context is more likely to occur if a defendant has admitted the allegations of the complaint but states an affirmative defense; if the affirmative defense as stated is legally insufficient, then the plaintiff would move for judgment on the pleadings, asserting defendant's failure to state a valid defense. Perhaps most likely of all is the context wherein a multicount complaint was filed, where the allegations of one count might be admitted but those of other counts denied (the Motion for Judgment on the Pleadings would then apply only to the count admitted).

In sum, perhaps the best way to think of the Motion for Judgment on the Pleadings is as follows. From the defendant's perspective, it authorizes essentially the same approach as a Rule 12(b)(6) Motion to Dismiss for failure to state a claim on which relief can be granted, and since such a Motion to Dismiss is a better alternative, the Motion for Judgment on the Pleadings is rarely filed by a defendant. For the plaintiff, the Motion for Judgment on the Pleadings is, in a sense, analogous to the Rule 12(b)(6) Motion to Dismiss, except that rather than asserting a failure to state a *claim* on which relief can be *granted*, it asserts that defendant has failed to state any *defense* on which relief can be *denied*.

As we have noted, the Motion for Judgment on the Pleadings is based on two things: that the facts can be established by the pleadings, and that, based on the application of legal principles to these facts, the moving party is entitled to judgment as a matter of law. Suppose that conclusive facts cannot be established merely by reviewing the pleadings, since an opposing party contests certain facts needed to justify the entry of judgment; does that mean there *must* be a trial? Not necessarily; let's turn now to an analysis of the Motion for Summary Judgment.

## 10–3  Summary Judgment

When a lawsuit begins, there is often disagreement and confusion between and among the parties regarding the facts. Allegations put forth by one party are often disputed by the opposing party. Once the motions attacking the pleadings have been resolved and the answer filed, some of this disagreement and confusion may be eradicated as certain claims or defenses are eliminated and certain facts admitted. Nevertheless, there usually remain sufficient well-pleaded claims for relief, and sufficient well-pleaded denials and defenses, so that the filing of a Motion for Judgment on the Pleadings is inappropriate. Contested issues of fact, in other words, still exist on the face of the pleadings.

As the pretrial process progresses, however, regardless of the contested allegations that remain in the pleadings, realistic questions as to the facts may begin to dissolve as the outlines of the case become apparent. Indeed, the discovery phase often leads to a relatively clear picture of the facts, as deposition testimony of witnesses, responses to requests for admission, production of significant documents, and other revelations resolve inconsistent allegations.

Sometimes the pretrial process is so successful in eliminating disagreement and confusion that the facts are virtually indisputable; there are no longer any legitimately "contested issues of fact." This may occur even though the pleadings, on their face, indicate that factual disputes still exist.

If the facts appear indisputable, a party can file a motion requesting the court to (1) accept this indisputable version of the facts, despite allegations of certain pleadings to the contrary, and (2) enter judgment in favor of the moving party on the remaining legal issues. The motion filed is called a **Motion for Summary Judgment.**

Summary judgment under the FRCP is governed by Rule 56. The basic standard by which the court scrutinizes a motion for summary judgment is contained in Rule 56(c): the motion and supporting materials must show "that there is no genuine issue as to any material fact and that the moving party is entitled to judgment as a matter of law."

**P**ARALEGALERT!

The standard governing motions for summary judgment is found in Rule 56 of the FRCP: "that there is no genuine issue as to any material fact and that the moving party is entitled to judgment as a matter of law."

Let's compare this to the Motion for Judgment on the Pleadings. In that motion, the facts are "established" by accepting as true everything alleged by the opposing party, as well as those allegations of the moving party that are admitted by the opposing party. In contrast, in the Motion for Summary Judgment the facts are "established" by a showing, through the attachment of exhibits, deposition transcripts, and the like, that there is no genuine controversy over material facts, despite allegations in the pleadings to the contrary.

Thus, the Motion for Judgment on the Pleadings and the Motion for Summary Judgment differ in the manner of their assertion that the facts are "established." They are similar, however, in that they both require an accompanying memorandum of law that applies legal principles to these "established" facts in order to demonstrate that the moving party is entitled to judgment "as a matter of law" (see Figure 10–3).

In some cases, the facts relating to the issue of liability may be indisputable, but there remains a contested issue of fact over the amount of damages. Is summary judgment precluded because of the presence of a "genuine issue of fact" on the damages question? No. Again, according to Rule 56(c): "A summary judgment . . . may be rendered on the issue of liability alone although there is a genuine issue as to the amount of damages."

Sometimes both parties assert that there remain no genuine issues of material fact, with each asserting a right to prevail based on the legal principles involved. Under these circumstances, they would file what are commonly known as **cross-motions for summary judgment;** such motions are really nothing more than separate and opposing motions for summary judgment. Sometimes these cross-motions assert inconsistent versions of the facts as "indisputable;" if each has evidence to back up its position, it would be unlikely that either would be granted, since the very inconsistency of the factual positions is just the sort of "contested" situation that requires resolution at trial. Sometimes the

**PARALEGALERT!**

Even though there remains a genuine issue of material fact as to the amount of damages, a party can nevertheless file a motion for summary judgment on the issue of liability.

Figure 10–3   Comparison of Motion for Judgment on the Pleadings with Motion for Summary Judgment

**Motion for Judgment on the Pleadings:**

A.  Establishes the facts by (1) accepting all the allegations contained in the pleadings of the opposing party, and (2) asserting only those allegations of the moving party which have been admitted by the opposing party.

B.  Based on these established facts, argues in a memorandum of law that the moving party is entitled to judgment as a matter of law.

**Motion for Summary Judgment:**

A.  Establishes facts by (1) identifying those areas where the allegations of the opposing parties are in agreement; and (2) demonstrating, as to those issues which appear from the pleadings to be contested, that the evidence indicates that there is *no genuine issue as to any material fact.*

B.  Based on these established facts, argues in a memorandum of law that the moving party is entitled to judgment as a matter of law.

*You will note that the two types of motion differ as to Characteristic A (i.e., the manner in which the facts are established), but are identical as to Characteristic B (the manner in which the moving party demonstrates an entitlement to judgment as a matter of law).*

cross-motions actually agree on the facts; if that is the case, they might be accompanied by a **stipulation of facts** signed by both parties, and the battle would be fought in memoranda of law that differ in their analysis of the impact of the applicable legal principles.

This is a good time to inject a key point regarding the nature of the court's inquiry into the underlying facts of the case as they affect the Motion for Summary Judgment. The court is not deciding contested issues of fact here, but rather determining whether any contested issues of fact exist. For example, if it is clear that some evidence supports one conclusion about an important fact, and other evidence supports a different conclusion, the court will not decide which evidence is more convincing. The court will, rather, deny the Motion for Summary Judgment on the grounds that there is, in fact, a genuine contested issue of fact that must be resolved at trial, making summary judgment inappropriate.

**PARALEGALERT!**

When considering the competing positions of the parties as to the facts underlying a Motion for Summary Judgment, the court is not weighing evidence to determine which version of the facts appears to be true, but rather seeking to determine whether a "genuine issue" exists as to a "material fact." If it does, it will be resolved at trial, not in the context of the Motion for Summary Judgment.

Yet another consideration to be kept in mind is the timing of the summary judgment motion. Rule 56 allows a plaintiff to file a motion for summary judgment "at any time after 20 days from the commencement of the action"; a defendant can file one "at any time." This technically authorizes the filing of a Motion for Summary Judgment at a very early stage of the litigation, even before the pleadings are closed. As a practical matter, however, such motions are often filed late in the pretrial process, after the pleadings have been closed and often after discovery has been completed. If such a motion were filed early in the process, before the opposing party has had a chance to investigate the facts of the case fully, the court can refuse to enter judgment, even if it appears justified based on the facts and arguments set forth in the motion and memorandum, until the opposing party is given the opportunity, by "affidavits to be obtained or depositions to be taken or discovery to be had," to further develop the facts (see Rule 56(f)).

One final general point to keep in mind with regard to the Motion for Summary Judgment is its relationship, under Rule 12, with situations in which a Rule 12(b)(6) Motion to Dismiss or Motion for Judgment on the Pleadings has been filed. With those two motions, matters outside the pleadings are not considered; but under identical language from Rules 12(b) and 12(c), if in the consideration of these motions "matters outside the pleadings are presented to and not excluded by the court, the motion shall be treated as one for summary judgment and disposed of as provided in Rule 56."

There are two aspects of the summary judgment procedure that we will address in more detail. They are drawn directly from the basic standard. First, we discuss the supporting materials that must be gathered in order to demonstrate that there is "no genuine issue as to any material fact"; second, we will discuss the preparation of the motion itself, as well as the memorandum of law filed to demonstrate that the moving party is entitled to judgment "as a matter of law."

## Gathering the Supporting Materials

Proving that there is no genuine issue as to any material fact requires a showing that the important facts in the case are no longer contested. This is done by including with the motion certain supporting materials that establish to the satisfaction of the court those facts that are alleged to be undisputed. Rule 56(c) indicates that the supporting materials include "the pleadings, depositions, answers to interrogatories, and admissions on file, together with the affidavits, if any . . . ."

The best place to start in gathering materials for the motion for summary judgment is by reviewing the pleadings. Matters on which the parties agree (for example, those allegations of the complaint that have been admitted) are no longer contested issues. These points can be asserted by the moving party as having been indisputably established.

Next, the moving party identifies those allegations on which the pleadings indicate that there remains a contested issue of fact. These may relate to such things as allegations of the complaint that have been denied, or other allegations contained in affirmative defenses. Here is where the gathering of materials in support of the motion becomes important. The moving party will be attempting to demonstrate that, despite the implication of the pleadings that there remains a "genuine issue of material fact" on these issues, in fact no real dispute exists, and the supporting materials establish the true and undisputed facts. An example of such a situation is shown in Figure 10–4.

The first source of supporting materials is found in the responses of the opposing party to any Requests for Admissions. These responses may resolve additional issues that appear to be contested on the face of the pleadings. As with admissions in pleadings, these admissions can be asserted by the moving party as having indisputably established certain facts.

After completing analysis of the pleadings and the Requests for Admissions, the task becomes somewhat more intricate. The party filing the motion must next demonstrate that those issues that remain contested, after taking into account the pleadings and Requests for Admissions, are in fact indisputable

**Figure 10–4  Example of Fact Requiring Supporting Materials Beyond the Pleadings in Order to Justify a Motion for Summary Judgment**

*Assume that the defendant in a relatively straightforward personal injury case arising out of a car accident is filing a motion for summary judgment.*

***Allegation of the Complaint:*** *"6. Defendant ran a red light at the intersection in which the accident occurred."*

***Response of the Answer:*** *"3. Paragraph 6 of the Complaint is denied."*

*Thus, based on the pleadings alone, a genuine issue of fact exists as to the issue of whether the defendant ran a red light. However, events subsequent to the pleadings have revealed the following:*

***Deposition of the plaintiff:*** *Plaintiff admitted under oath that he could not see the light facing the defendant, and further that he could not remember if his own light was green or red.*

***Deposition of the defendant:*** *Defendant swore under oath that the light facing him was green.*

***Deposition of an eyewitness:*** *The eyewitness swore under oath that the light facing the defendant was green.*

*The defendant would attach the relevant pages of deposition transcript to his motion for summary judgment, in order to demonstrate that, despite the allegation by plaintiff that the light facing defendant was red, there is absolutely no evidence to support any conclusion other than that the light facing the defendant was green. Hence there is no "genuine issue" as to this particular "material fact."*

based on the available evidence, regardless of whether the pleadings imply the existence of a continued factual dispute. As stated in Rule 56(c), the court considers, in addition to the pleadings and requests for admissions, the "depositions, answers to interrogatories, and . . . affidavits" submitted by the parties, in order to determine whether or not a "genuine issue as to any material fact" exists. By setting forth relevant passages from these various sources, the moving party will attempt to demonstrate that no real dispute exists over the true nature of the facts. Again, review Figure 10–4, which shows how a fact disputed in the pleadings can be shown to be indisputable in reality.

The next issue to consider is the affidavit. An *affidavit* is a sworn statement; there is no requirement under Rule 56 that an affidavit be filed by either the moving party or the opposing party. Nevertheless, affidavits are often prepared setting forth relevant facts, and often referencing relevant documents. Such an affidavit will usually be executed by your firm's client, or a key witness, or perhaps several affidavits from several key individuals will be filed. Under Rule 56(e), an affidavit "shall be made on personal knowledge, shall set forth such facts as would be admissible in evidence, and shall show affirmatively that the affiant is competent to testify to the matters stated therein." What this means, briefly stated, is that the affidavit should establish an evidentiary foundation (see Chapter 5) for the statements made therein, and the statements made and documents attached must themselves be admissible in evidence at trial. The oath under which an affidavit is executed must not be taken lightly, nor should questionable assertions be included; there are sanctions for affidavits made in "bad faith" or "solely for the purpose of delay" (Rule 56(g)). An example of a brief affidavit appears in Figure 10–5.

## PARALEGALERT!

An affidavit relating to a Motion for Summary Judgment must be made on personal knowledge, must set forth only such facts as would be admissible in evidence, and must show affirmatively that the affiant is competent to testify as to the matters stated therein.

Deposition transcripts and interrogatory responses are generally on file with the court and can be referenced, but it is often good practice to photocopy relevant passages and include them with your motion and memorandum, so that the court has everything it needs to refer to in one easily accessible location. This brings us to the final issue relating to the gathering of the materials: the manner in which these materials are presented to the court. As a general proposition, copies of the materials are attached as exhibits to the motion itself, or to the memorandum of law; affidavits are often filed individually. As a practical matter the volume of supporting materials will often be too large to attach physically to either the motion or the memorandum. If that is the case, the filing party will often prepare a separate appendix that includes all the various factual materials, and which can be referenced in the motion and/or memorandum.

Finally, we consider the manner in which the opposing party argues that there *is* a genuine issue of fact, making the Motion for Summary Judgment inappropriate. Under Rule 56(e), the adverse party "may not rest upon the mere allegations or denials of the adverse party's pleading, but . . . must set forth specific facts showing that there is a genuine issue for trial." Thus, the adverse party must also gather together supporting materials, this time with an eye toward demonstrating that there is, in fact, some genuine issue that needs to be resolved by trial. As we noted, the task is not to convince the court that a particular factual position is supported by the evidence, but only that a genuine issue exists over that position. What this implies for the party opposing the motion is simple: he or she need not prove the case, but only demonstrate to the satisfaction of the court that there is adequate evidence to demonstrate that the factual issue will need to be resolved at trial.

United States District Court
for the
District of Exurbia

WIDGETS AND GIZMOS, INC.

    Plaintiff                         Civil Action No. 93-OWH-00543

    vs.                               August 5, 1994

TAPTAPTAP, INC.

    Defendant

### Affidavit of Edgar Ellison in Support of
### Motion for Summary Judgment

The affiant, Edgar Ellison, being duly sworn, hereby deposes and says as follows:

1. I am the President of *Widgets and Gizmos, Inc.*, the plaintiff in the above-captioned matter.
2. I am over the age of eighteen years and understand the obligation of an oath.
3. In the course of my duties as President of *Widgets and Gizmos, Inc.*, I had occasion to enter into certain negotiations with Emily Tapman, President of *TapTapTap, Inc.*, the defendant in the above-captioned matter.
4. On or about April 21, 1991, I received the letter from Emily Tapman dated April 17, 1991, which is attached hereto as Exhibit A.
5. The letter discusses the specifications of the widgenometers which are the subject of the contract which is Exhibit A to the Complaint in this action.
6. In the letter, Emily Tapman indicates that "it is the expectation of *TapTapTap, Inc.* that the silicon content of the alloy used in the production of the widgenometers will not fall below 11%, but we do not demand that it exceed 15%."
7. This letter was the one and only communication received by the plaintiff, *Widgets and Gizmos, Inc.*, from the defendant, *TapTapTap, Inc.*, on the issue of the silicon content of the alloy during the period from April 15, 1991, through and including May 25, 1991.

 

                                  _____
                                  Edgar Ellison
                                  President
                                  *Widgets and Gizmos, Inc.*

Subscribed and sworn to before
me, this the _____ day
of _____, 1994.

_____
Ms. Nadine Nemeth
Notary Public for the State of Exurbia
Commission expires:

### Certificate of Service

This is to certify that a copy of the foregoing Affidavit of Edgar Ellison in Support of Motion for Summary Judgment was mailed, postage prepaid, this 5th day of August, 1994, to attorney Tim Tiptop, Esq., Tiptop and Towe, 71 Ferguson Street, Metro City, Exurbia 12345.

                                  _____
                                  Sam Superlawyer, Esq.

*Memo–States the facts of* [handwritten annotation]

Actually, the defending party has two methods of attacking the Motion for Summary Judgment: first, arguing that there is a genuine issue of fact that must be resolved at trial; second, if it cannot demonstrate that a contested issue of fact exists, arguing that the moving party is wrong on its interpretation of the law as it applies to the uncontested facts. This brings us to our consideration of the motion and memoranda.

## The Summary Judgment Motion and Memoranda

The actual Motion for Summary Judgment is a deceptively simple creature. An example is shown in Figure 10–6; as you can see, it does little more than allege the basic standard, namely, that there is no genuine issue as to any material fact and that the moving party is entitled to judgment as a matter of law.

The memorandum filed in support of the motion, however, is often quite lengthy. This memorandum has, essentially, two purposes. First, it must state the facts of the case, making reference to the various supporting materials to make clear that there is "no genuine issue as to any material fact." Second, it must demonstrate that, based on these undisputed facts, the moving party is entitled to judgment "as a matter of law." For the plaintiff, this would require a showing that the undisputed facts are sufficient to support the cause or causes of action alleged; for the defendant, this would require a showing that the undisputed facts are either inadequate to establish the cause or causes of action, or that there is a conclusive defense based on undisputed facts.

A word should be said about the drafter's approach to the statement of facts. Each fact alleged in the statement of facts should be referenced either to admissions in the pleadings, discovery responses, deposition transcripts, or other supporting materials. The reference can be made in the manner shown in the brief example drawn from a memorandum from the Widgets and Gizmos, Inc. case (see Figure 10–7). The purpose of these references is to make it clear to the court exactly how the moving party is establishing each fact; it may also be necessary to make references to supporting materials that refute the opposing side's version. As you can imagine, matching factual allegations with supporting materials can be a time-consuming task, involving extended searches through deposition transcripts, documents, interrogatories, pleadings, and such. Paralegals are often given such a task, since they often have a solid working familiarity with the discovery materials generated during the course of the lawsuit.

The legal arguments made in a memorandum supporting a Motion for Summary Judgment are often complex. They go to the heart of the substantive law that governs the dispute. If filed by the plaintiff, they will assert that causes of action have been established, whereas defenses have not; if filed by the defendant, they will assert that no cause of action has been established, and/or that the defenses raised defeat the claims. As a paralegal, your skills of legal research, analysis, and writing will come into play if you are given a role in the preparation of the memorandum itself.

Memoranda of law filed in opposition to motions for summary judgment, as noted, often attack the motion by two distinct methods. First, they challenge the assertion that the facts are undisputed; they attempt to demonstrate, by references to their own supporting materials, that there is, in fact, a genuine issue over certain material facts, hence it is premature to consider whether the moving party is entitled to judgment "as a matter of law." The

**PARALEGALERT!**

The party opposing a Motion for Summary Judgment generally attacks it in two ways: (1) asserting that there is, in fact, a genuine issue as to the material facts, and (2) asserting that, even if the facts are as the moving party asserts, the moving party is nevertheless not entitled to judgment as a matter of law.

**Figure 10–6  Motion for Summary Judgment**

United States District Court
for the
District of Exurbia

WIDGETS AND GIZMOS, INC.                          :

     Plaintiff                                       :            Civil Action No. 93-OWH-00543

     vs.                                             :            August 5, 1994

TAPTAPTAP, INC.                                   :

     Defendant                                       :

### Motion for Summary Judgment of Plaintiff
### *Widgets and Gizmos, Inc.*

The plaintiff, *Widgets and Gizmos, Inc.*, acting pursuant to Rule 56 of the Federal Rules of Civil Procedure, hereby moves the court for an order entering summary judgment against the defendant, *TapTapTap, Inc.*, on all issues presented by the Complaint and the Counterclaim. There are no genuine issues of material fact, and the plaintiff is entitled to this judgment as a matter of law. The plaintiff has filed a Memorandum of Law in support of this motion, together with the Affidavit of Edgar Ellison and an appendix containing supporting materials which are referenced in the memorandum.

THE PLAINTIFF, WIDGETS AND GIZMOS, INC.

By: _____
    Samuel Superlawyer, Esq.
    Its attorney
    Lincoln & Hoover
    123 Lincoln Street
    Metro City, Exurbia 12345
    Atty. Reg. #: 87654
    Phone: (901) 222-2222

### Order

The foregoing Motion for Summary Judgment having been heard, it is hereby
ORDERED:                                          GRANTED / DENIED

The Court

By _____
    Judge

### Certificate of Service

This is to certify that a copy of the foregoing was mailed, postage prepaid, this 5th day of August, 1994, to attorney Tim Tiptop, Esq., Tiptop and Towe, 71 Ferguson Street, Metro City, Exurbia 12345.

ORAL ARGUMENT                     _____
  IS REQUESTED                      Sam Superlawyer, Esq.

**Figure 10–7** Partial Statement of Facts from Memorandum of Law of *Widgets and Gizmos, Inc.* in Support of Motion for Summary Judgment

---

### Statement of Facts

After several years of research, the plaintiff *Widgets and Gizmos, Inc.* completed development of a computer component known as a widgenometer in December, 1990 (deposition of Edgar Ellison, page 67; deposition of Hans Hoobermann, pages 15–23). In early 1991, *Widgets and Gizmos, Inc.* began negotiations with *Tap Tap Tap, Inc.* under which widgenometers produced by *Widgets and Gizmos, Inc.* would be sold to *Tap Tap Tap, Inc.* (deposition of Ellison, pages 43–48; deposition of Emily Tapman, pages 17–31). At the conclusion of the negotiations, the parties entered into the contract which is referenced as Exhibit A to the Complaint (paragraph 5 of the Complaint, admitted by defendant in paragraph 4 of its Answer, Affirmative Defense and Counterclaim). Pursuant to the terms of that contract, the minimum silicon content of the alloy used in the production of the widgenometer was 14.5% (Request for Admission #11 from the responses of *Tap Tap Tap, Inc.* dated March 28, 1994). All tests performed to date have

---

"facts" segment of the opposition memorandum of law will thus emphasize those facts on which the opposition party asserts a different conclusion than the moving party. The second method is to assert that, if there is, indeed, no further genuine issue of material fact, then the moving party is nevertheless *not* entitled to judgment as a matter of law, because the allegedly uncontested facts do not support the moving party's legal conclusions. The legal arguments in an opposition memorandum will be no less complex than those in the moving party's memorandum; great care must be taken, because the stakes are high.

## Oral Argument and Partial Summary Judgment

Like any other contested motion, a Motion for Summary Judgment often involves oral argument before the court. You should be sure to include a request for oral argument on your moving papers, if required by your local rules, and be aware of any other applicable local provisions. The oral argument itself will, of course, be handled by your supervising attorney, but you might be asked to attend in order to assist in organizing and presenting documents or other supporting materials to the court.

The court may grant a motion for summary judgment, deny it, or grant it in part and deny it in part. Rule 56(d) allows for the court to specify in its ruling what areas remain in controversy, requiring further resolution at trial:

> If on motion under this rule judgment is not rendered upon the whole case . . . the court . . . shall if practicable ascertain what material facts exist without substantial controversy and what material facts are actually and in good faith controverted. It shall thereupon make an order specifying the facts that appear without substantial controversy, including the extent to which the amount of damages or other relief is not in controversy, and directing such further proceedings in the action as are just. Upon the trial of the action the facts so specified shall be deemed established . . . .

One possible result of a Motion for Summary Judgment might thus be a court order in which judgment is entered in favor of the plaintiff on one count of a complaint, in favor of a defendant on another count, and reserved for trial on a third count, with certain of the facts pertaining to the third count considered to be established. Where the judgment is rendered so as to affect only limited portions of the lawsuit, it is referred to as a **partial summary judgment.**

## 10–4   Settlement

**Settlement,** which is an agreement by adverse parties to resolve disputed issues on specified terms, can happen at any moment during the course of a dispute. It can happen at a very early stage, even before the parties involve their lawyers. It can happen before a lawsuit is filed. It can happen before the parties incur the expense of depositions, or of lengthy briefs on dispositive motions. Indeed, if resolution appears possible, it is often beneficial to everyone involved if agreement can be reached early in the process.

Nevertheless, many cases proceed through the investigation stage, the pleading process, the discovery phase, and even through dispositive motions without meaningful settlement discussions. This is not always the case, but it is often the case. There are probably two general reasons why this is so. First, if liability is fairly clear, the plaintiff may seek unrealistically high damages in the early stages of the matter, or may want to wait until the full extent of the damages (such as the potentially permanent nature of physical injuries) becomes clearer over time, whereas the defendant may see a benefit in avoiding payment of the ultimate and inevitable judgment for as long as possible. Second, if liability or damages are not clear, both sides may want to flush out the relevant facts and law before staking out bargaining positions.

Thus, we are discussing settlement at this stage of our text because it commonly occurs late in the process. Keep in mind, however, that the same issues generally apply at whatever stage settlement discussions occur.

### Establishing a Preliminary Settlement Value

Before your supervising attorney begins to negotiate a settlement, the matter must be carefully reviewed and reasonable figures discussed as to probable settlement range. Determining such reasonable figures can be a fairly elaborate process. Sometimes the equation requires an analysis of more than just dollar figures, as where one or both parties are seeking some form of equitable relief (*equitable* relief, you should recall from Chapter 1 and elsewhere in this text, involves nonmonetary damages, such as an injunction or specific performance of a contract), thereby further complicating matters.

Even monetary damages can pose problems. Special damages, such as invoices for car repair or unpaid invoices for widgenometers, are easily calculable; general damages, on the other hand, for such things as the long-term disability or the pain and suffering of Harry Hampton, or the loss of business "goodwill" of TapTapTap, Inc., cannot be calculated with certainty. Potential punitive damages may be even more difficult to estimate, since not only is the amount impossible to calculate with certainty, but there is also no assurance that a court will even allow such damages.

In a business litigation case such as the Widgets and Gizmos, Inc. matter, several factors enter into the analysis. The costs of continuing the litigation, such as attorney's fees, expert witness fees, and the lingering effect of litigation on a client's business interests, constitute a significant consideration. An estimate as to chances of success at trial, based on a careful and objective interpretation of both the applicable legal precedents and statutes and the anticipated evidence to be presented to the trier-of-fact, is also central. Finally, there may be some question as to whether a large judgment, even if won after trial, will ever be collected from an opposing party short on resources; under such circumstances, a lesser sum in settlement might be more attractive than the potential for a large, but uncollectible, court award.

In personal injury cases, collectibility is not usually an issue, since an insurance company is often involved on behalf of the defendant. Furthermore, the insurance interrogatories we discussed in the last chapter can be used to obtain the precise limits of insurance coverage. But some of the other factors we've discussed remain relevant: the client's personal financial condition; costs of trial; estimated chances for success.

When determining preliminary settlement value, some important factors include (1) reasonably estimated damages; (2) the impact of any non-monetary relief involved; (3) costs of continuing the litigation; (4) an estimate of success at trial based on an objective appraisal of the likely evidence and applicable legal precedents; and (5) if a plaintiff, the potential for collection after judgment (including the availability of insurance coverage).

The role of the paralegal in determining settlement value will be largely administrative. Gathering relevant documents, bills, and other information; doing background legal research; perhaps relaying information to and from the client—these are the likely tasks you will be performing. If the settlement proposal is to be submitted to the other side in some elaborate format, as is sometimes the case with large personal injury cases or complicated business litigation, you may have an important role in preparing relevant materials. Final substantive settlement positions will be established by your supervising attorney and the client.

## Negotiation

We'll be up-front with you—you're not going to be directly involved in the negotiating process. Since you are not authorized to represent a client (only an attorney can do that), you may not engage in the give-and-take with opposing parties that characterizes negotiation.

Nevertheless, you will likely be involved on at least the periphery of the negotiations, and you may well be involved in discussions with the client that relate to the status of negotiations, so you should have at least a basic understanding of the process.

To begin with, you should note that, like other aspects of litigation involving personal judgment, negotiation is in many ways more of an art than a science. Many books have been written detailing alternative techniques of resolving disputes. Often there is a psychological component to the suggested techniques: negotiations involve people, and people are influenced by their emotions and belief systems. Finally, there is no substitute for the experience of your supervising attorney in similar negotiations. We'll talk here about a few fairly concrete principles and leave it at that.

A useful approach to negotiating is to apply sufficient imagination to come up with proposals in which additional give-and-take can conceivably lead to something positive for everyone. In the context of business litigation, for example, there are often available many alternatives that can open the door to settlement, including such things as commitments on future business relationships or terms, or agreements to cooperate for the benefit of all involved parties. In the Widgets and Gizmos, Inc. matter, for example, the parties might agree to an adjusted price on future widgenometer purchases, an agreement to reestablish in a new contract the precise specifications of the widgenometers, an agreement to share costs incurred by dissatisfied customers, or an agreement to make cash payments in compensation for past and anticipated future damages. A settlement proposal incorporating these various elements might lead to a counter proposal that adjusts some elements in one party's favor in exchange for adjustments on other elements in another party's favor. At some point this give-and-take may lead to a result that all involved parties can agree to.

The most difficult negotiations are often in the personal injury context, in which the only significant issue is how much money the insurance company is willing to pay in compensation for the injuries sustained. The opportunity for a negotiation leading to "something positive for everyone" is limited. In such a situation, a gain for the plaintiff can only be a loss for the defendant, and vice versa, making negotiation difficult. Sometimes this can be minimized by the use of **structured settlements,** in which payments are spread out over time; a higher figure might then be acceptable, if it can be paid out at a later date, or in installments, rather than all at once. If liability and the extent of injuries are fairly clear, then experienced counsel may have reasonable beliefs as to anticipated court awards, making settlement more likely. But personal injury cases often settle late in the process.

Negotiations between the parties often stall on certain key points. When they do, it is often useful to turn to the court to assist in the negotiation process. We discuss this further in our section on pretrial conferences in Chapter 11.

Finally, there is one consideration to keep in mind that has both practical importance and a significant ethical aspect as well. You and your supervising attorney must remember that it is the client who has the final word on negotiations. The client may be relying on his or her lawyers to provide insight as to whether a settlement proposal is realistic, and to handle the details of the negotiation itself, but having been informed of the terms of a settlement proposal the client must make the final decision him- or herself. The client's wishes control: if he or she wants to settle a case that the attorneys recommend fighting, the case should settle; if he or she wants to take the risk of fighting a case in which the attorneys have recommended settlement, the case should continue. Furthermore, every settlement proposal submitted by the opposing party must be reported to the client; it is entirely inappropriate for a settlement proposal to be rejected (or accepted) out-of-hand by attorneys before consulting with the client.

# PARALEGALERT!

The client is absolutely and unequivocally central to the settlement negotiation. No settlement can be agreed upon without the client's express and informed approval, and every settlement proposal submitted by an opposing party *must* be sent to the client for consideration.

Suppose the parties are successful in their efforts to reach agreement; settlement is achieved! What happens next?

Two objectives must be accomplished. First, the terms of the settlement must be clearly identified in a document or documents, such that if they are violated by one party, the other party has the right to enforce the agreement. Second, the lawsuit must be officially terminated.

Sometimes the two objectives are accomplished by the same document. See, for example, the **Stipulated Judgment** (also sometimes called a **Consent Judgment**) filed in the Widgets and Gizmos, Inc. case in Figure 10–8. It identifies the terms of the settlement, and incorporates them into a judgment,

**Figure 10–8  Stipulated Judgment**

United States District Court
for the
District of Exurbia

WIDGETS AND GIZMOS, INC.                                :

    Plaintiff                                              :                    Civil Action No. 93-OWH-00543

    vs.                                                       :

TAPTAPTAP, INC.                                          :                    November 3, 1994

    Defendant                                          :

                                                                  :

### Stipulated Judgment

The parties to the above-captioned matter, namely the plaintiff *Widgets and Gizmos, Inc.* and the defendant *TapTapTap, Inc.*, hereby agree and stipulate to judgment in this matter on the following terms:

1.  The defendant, *TapTapTap, Inc.*, shall pay to the plaintiff, *Widgets and Gizmos, Inc.*, the amount of $375,000.00 within thirty days of the entry of this Judgment by the Court.

2.  The defendant, *TapTapTap, Inc.*, shall pay to the plaintiff, *Widgets and Gizmos, Inc.*, the additional amount of $125,000.00 within one year of the date of the entry of this Judgment by the Court.

3.  The plaintiff, *Widgets and Gizmos, Inc.*, agrees to replace certain widgenometers in the possession of the customers of *TapTapTap, Inc.* with new widgenometers utilizing alloys with a silicon content of at least 15.25%. The customers and serial numbers of the widgenometers are specifically identified in the list appearing hereto as Exhibit A.

4.  This judgment will resolve all claims regarding all widgenometers shipped to date.

5.  The parties will continue to abide by all terms of the contract made Exhibit A to the Complaint, except that all future widgenometers produced by *Widgets and Gizmos, Inc.* and supplied to *TapTapTap, Inc.* pursuant to this contract shall utilize an alloy having a silicon content of 15.25%.

THE PLAINTIFF, WIDGETS AND GIZMOS, INC.

By: _____
    Samuel Superlawyer, Esq.
    Its attorney
    Lincoln & Hoover
    123 Lincoln Street
    Metro City, Exurbia 12345
    Atty. Reg. #: 87654
    Phone: (901) 222-2222

By: _____
    Edgar Ellison
    President
    *Widgets and Gizmos, Inc.*

**Figure 10–8  Stipulated Judgment, continued**

THE DEFENDANT, TAPTAPTAP, INC.

By: _____
    Tim Tiptop, Esq.
    Its attorney
    Tiptop and Towe
    71 Ferguson Street
    Metro City, Exurbia 12345
    Atty. Reg. #: 65488
    Phone: (901) 333-3333

By: _____
    Emily Tapman
    President
    *TapTapTap, Inc.*

**Order**

The court hereby ORDERS that the foregoing Stipulated Judgment is entered as the Judgment of this court.

THE COURT

By: _____
          Judge
    Date:

which is then officially entered by the court, terminating the litigation in a manner equally as binding as a judgment entered after trial. When the parties having obligations under the Stipulated Judgment have satisfied those obligations (such as, in Figure 10–8, the cash payments to which TapTapTap, Inc. agreed, and the replacement of widgenometers to which Widgets and Gizmos, Inc. agreed), then the opposing party files with the court a **Satisfaction of Judgment** so indicating.

Another possibility is to prepare a separate **Settlement Agreement** outside the bounds of the litigation, which is then executed by both parties. Such a settlement agreement would look much like an ordinary contract; indeed, that is basically what a settlement agreement is. In the Widgets and Gizmos, Inc. case, a settlement agreement could include virtually the same terms as the Stipulated Judgment in Figure 10–8, except that they would be set forth in contract format.

If the settlement of the lawsuit involves something other than a Stipulated Judgment, then a question presents itself: what happens to the lawsuit? We touched on one possibility in our discussion of dismissal under Rule 41 of the FRCP: the **voluntary dismissal**. Under that rule, the parties can agree to a stipulation of dismissal of the action. Unless otherwise stated, such a dismissal is generally without prejudice to the action being brought again; often in the context of a settlement the parties will, however, specify that the dismissal is with prejudice and the action cannot be brought again. An example of a stipulation for dismissal with prejudice is seen in Figure 10–9.

Under the rules of some state court systems, a plaintiff is allowed to file a **withdrawal** of the action, which operates as a voluntary dismissal without prejudice. If a lawsuit is settled and a withdrawal filed, it is prudent to include among the settlement documents a **general release** executed by the plaintiff under which the plaintiff releases all future rights to bring an action against the defendant based upon prior events (an example of such a general release, as

**Figure 10–9   Voluntary Stipulation for Dismissal with Prejudice**

United States District Court
for the
District of Exurbia

WIDGETS AND GIZMOS, INC.                    :

      Plaintiff                                         :

           vs.                                        :

TAPTAPTAP, INC.                                   :

      Defendant                                       :

                                   Civil Action No. 93-OWH-00543

                                   November 3, 1994

### Stipulation for Dismissal with Prejudice

    The parties to the above-captioned matter, namely the plaintiff *Widgets and Gizmos, Inc.* and the defendant *TapTapTap, Inc.*, hereby agree and stipulate to dismiss this matter with prejudice, pursuant to Rule 41 of the Federal Rules of Civil Procedure.

THE PLAINTIFF, WIDGETS AND GIZMOS, INC.

By: _____
    Samuel Superlawyer, Esq.
    Its attorney
    Lincoln & Hoover
    123 Lincoln Street
    Metro City, Exurbia 12345
    Atty. Reg. #: 87654
    Phone: (901) 222-2222

By: _____
    Edgar Ellison
    President
    *Widgets and Gizmos, Inc.*

THE DEFENDANT, TAPTAPTAP, INC.

By: _____
    Tim Tiptop, Esq.
    Its attorney
    Tiptop and Towe
    71 Ferguson Street
    Metro City, Exurbia 12345
    Atty. Reg. #: 65488
    Phone: (901) 333-3333

By: _____
    Emily Tapman
    President
    *TapTapTap, Inc.*

executed by Judith Johnson under a hypothetical settlement with Harry Hampton, is seen in Figure 10–10). Such a general release negates the possibility that the plaintiff will be able to assert the same claim again. Another document that accomplishes basically the same purpose as a general release is called a **covenant not to sue.** With regard to both covenants not to sue and general

**Figure 10–10  General Release**

### General Release

In consideration of the sum of $35,000.00, paid to him this date by Judith Johnson, the receipt of which is acknowledged, Harry Hampton hereby releases and discharges the said Judith Johnson and her heirs and assigns from any and all claims or causes of action which he might now possess against the said Judith Johnson arising out of any matter occurring before August 15, 1995.

In particular, this General Release is intended to release and discharge the said Judith Johnson from any and all claims which Harry Hampton may have had arising from an automobile collision which occurred on April 15, 1992.

In witness whereof, we have entered our signatures this 15th day of August, 1995.

_____  Witness

_____  Witness

_____
Harry Hampton

The foregoing General Release was subscribed and sworn to by Harry Hampton in my presence, on this the 15th day of August, 1995.

_____
Ms. Nadine Nemeth
Notary Public of the
State of Exurbia
Commission Expires:

releases, keep in mind that it is generally important to make some reference on the face of the document to the consideration given, in order to make the rights obtained thereunder enforceable.

## 10–5  Practical Considerations

We have talked a great deal in this chapter about something called a "judgment," whether a default judgment, a judgment based on the pleadings, or a summary judgment. A judgment is, of course, the final ruling of the trial court disposing of the case. Even when such a final judgment is entered, the case may not, however, be over. There may be an appeal by the losing party, and there may be extensive efforts to collect the judgment by the victorious party (if the victorious party was pursuing, rather then defending, a claim for relief) through a process known as *execution*. In the next chapter, after discussing trials and the judgment that is entered after the completion of a trial, we address further both appeals and executions. For now, keep in mind that these concepts are equally relevant after the entry of summary (or other) judgment as they are after the entry of judgment at the conclusion of a full-scale trial.

# SUMMARY

## 10–1

The great majority of cases never go to trial. Most are resolved in some other manner before trial, by such things as dispositive motions or settlement.

## 10–2

Dispositive motions, if granted, constitute a final resolution of some aspect of a case, or possibly even the entire case. A dismissal is an adjudication upon the merits, unless it is a dismissal without prejudice to the right of the party dismissed to assert the underlying claim at some future time. A default judgment can be obtained from the clerk, if the requirements of Rule 55(b)(1) of the FRCP are met, or from the court, if the requirements of Rule 55(b)(2) are met. A Motion to Set Aside a Default Judgment is a sensitive matter; good reasons must be included. A Motion for Judgment on the Pleadings establishes the facts by assuming the nonmoving party's allegations to be true, and only such of the moving party's allegations as have been admitted by the nonmoving party. Having thus established the facts, the moving party then asserts that it is entitled to judgment as a matter of law.

## 10–3

If the facts appear indisputable based on the available evidence, despite allegations in the pleadings to the contrary, any party can file a Motion for Summary Judgment asserting that there is no genuine issue as to any material fact, and that the moving party is entitled to judgment as a matter of law. The facts under such a motion are established by the pleadings, depositions, answers to interrogatories, admissions on file, and affidavits. Opposing parties can simultaneously file cross-motions for summary judgment, sometimes based on a stipulation of facts. Affidavits filed in support of a Motion for Summary Judgment must be made on personal knowledge, relate to facts admissible in evidence, and establish that the affiant is competent to testify to matters stated therein. Memoranda in support of a Motion for Summary Judgment should carefully reference the sources from which the factual assertions are drawn. Opposition to a Motion for Summary Judgment can be based on (1) an assertion that there is, indeed, a genuine issue as to a material fact, and/or (2) that even if the facts are as the moving party asserts, the moving party is not entitled to judgment as a matter of law. The court is not weighing contrary evidence to reach a conclusion as to the true facts, but only determining whether a genuine issue of material fact exists. Summary judgment can be limited to only certain aspects of a case through the entry of a partial summary judgment.

## 10–4

Settlement often happens at a fairly late stage in the litigation process. Factors considered in determining preliminary settlement value include such things as estimated damages, impact of non-monetary relief sought, litigation costs, estimates of success at trial, and likelihood of collecting any judgment obtained. Paralegals are not involved directly in negotiations. Settlement documents include such things as stipulated judgments or voluntary dismissals, which can be used to conclude the litigation, and settlement agreements, releases, and covenants not to sue, which relate to the rights of the parties after the litigation is concluded.

## 10–5

Judgments are often followed by appeals or efforts by a plaintiff to execute on the judgment.

## Key Terms

Before proceeding, review the key terms listed below to be sure you understand each one. If necessary, read over the corresponding section of the chapter. When you are ready to test your understanding, answer the Review Questions.

dispositive motions
dismissal
dismissal without prejudice
dismissal with prejudice
default judgment
Request for Entry of Default Judgment
military affidavit
Application for Entry of Default Judgment
Motion for Judgment on the Pleadings
Motion for Summary Judgment
cross-motions for summary judgment
stipulation of facts
partial summary judgment
settlement
structured settlements
Stipulated Judgment
Consent Judgment
Satisfaction of Judgment
Settlement Agreement
voluntary dismissal
withdrawal
general release
covenant not to sue

## Questions for Review and Discussion

1. What is meant by a dismissal with prejudice?
2. What are the prerequisites for the entry of a default judgment by the clerk of the federal court?
3. What is a military affidavit?
4. How are the facts "established" on a Motion for Judgment on the Pleadings?
5. State the basic standard by which the court scrutinizes a Motion for Summary Judgment.
6. What is the court seeking to determine when it investigates the facts on a Motion for Summary Judgment?
7. What are the two basic methods by which the nonmoving party attacks a Motion for Summary Judgment?
8. What is meant by the term *partial summary judgment?*
9. How does an attorney arrive at a preliminary settlement value?
10. How do the parties officially conclude a lawsuit that has been settled?

## Activities

1. Identify the dispositive motions that apply in the courts of your state, and review the procedural requirements of each. Pay particular attention to the manner in which defaults are entered and default judgments obtained.
2. Contact your federal court clerk's office and ask whether you can obtain a calendar of motions scheduled to be heard. Find a scheduled motion for summary judgment on the calendar, and ask to see the memoranda and other supporting materials that were filed in support of the opposing positions on this motion. Review these materials, then attend the oral argument. This activity will be time-consuming, but if you follow through you will develop a good feel for the process.
3. Go to your local library and find some books about negotiating techniques. They will probably be found in the section relating to business. Read through these books, searching for principles that apply to negotiating the settlement of a lawsuit.

# CHAPTER 11  Trial and Appeal

## OUTLINE

## COMMENTARY

Settlement talks in the Widgets and Gizmos, Inc. matter have broken down. The final pretrial conference has been set for three weeks from today, with the trial itself to begin in 30 days. Sam Superlawyer has informed you that, although there may still be some efforts to resolve the dispute, serious preparations for trial must begin.

It looks as if the Harry Hampton matter will be going to trial as well. Although some tentative agreements have been reached between Hampton and Judith Johnson with regard to reasonable damage figures, the three parties have been unable to agree on a satisfactory division of responsibility for these damages. Bud's Auto Service is still claiming that it isn't liable for any of the damages, and Hampton and Johnson continue pointing fingers at each other. One last effort to settle will be made in a state court pretrial conference; if that fails, then it's on to the courthouse.

## OBJECTIVES

Though settlement is often beneficial, it is not always achieved. Cases sometimes proceed through the final pretrial conference, through trial preparations and trial, and even through appeal; the paralegal must have a working knowledge of these final steps in the litigation process. After completing Chapter 11, you will be able to:

1. Identify four types of pretrial conference.
2. List some of the considerations addressed in a final pretrial conference.
3. Explain what is meant by the term *voir dire.*
4. Explain the difference between a peremptory challenge and a challenge for cause.
5. Identify the standard burden of proof for a typical civil trial.
6. Explain the function of a Motion for Judgment as a Matter of Law.
7. Explain how and why a paralegal must monitor the scheduling of a trial.
8. Identify some of the considerations to keep in mind when preparing a witness to testify.
9. List some of the sections of a typical trial notebook, and explain the importance of each.
10. Explain what is meant by the record on appeal.

## 11–1   The Pretrial Conference

We begin this chapter with a discussion of the **pretrial conference.** A pretrial conference is a meeting occurring during the pretrial stage of a lawsuit involving (1) the judge assigned to the case, (2) the attorneys for each represented party, and (3) any unrepresented parties themselves. Pretrial conferences can vary from formalized affairs, conducted "on the record" in an open courtroom with a court reporter recording the proceedings, to informal meetings held in the judge's chambers with no record kept.

Some pretrial conferences actually occur quite early in the litigation process. This may lead you to wonder why we're discussing such conferences in this late chapter. The reason might be thought of as a "chicken and egg" problem. The matters that are discussed in an early pretrial conference often relate to deadlines and guidelines for such items as discovery and motions; thus, had we discussed such conferences earlier, you would not yet have had a meaningful understanding of these topics. In addition, one particularly important type of pretrial conference (which we will discuss later) is held just before trial, and thus is logically discussed at this late point in the text.

Under the FRCP, there are actually four types of pretrial conference. First is the discovery conference under Rule 26(f), which we discussed in Chapter 9. The other three types are defined by Rule 16; one is the pretrial "scheduling" conference under Rule 16(b) (which can incorporate the function of the discovery conference, among other things); the second might be called a pretrial "status" conference; the third is the final pretrial conference under Rule 16(d).

The broad purposes of every Rule 16 pretrial conference are set forth in Rule 16(a). They include:

1. Expediting the disposition of the action;
2. Establishing early and continuing control so that the case will not be protracted because of lack of management;
3. Discouraging wasteful pretrial activities;
4. Improving the quality of the trial through more thorough preparation; and
5. Facilitating the settlement of the case.

In general, then, the pretrial conference is intended to provide the judge, the attorneys, and any unrepresented parties with an opportunity to work together to plan an orderly and efficient progression of the case. The many specific topics appropriate for discussion in a Rule 16 pretrial conference are identified in Rule 16(c) and restated in Figure 11–1. Despite the fact that these topics are suitable for discussion in each of the three types of Rule 16 conferences we've identified, the focus of each type of conference is different. We examine these differences in the next three subsections, followed by a brief discussion of pretrial conferences under the various state court systems.

One final consideration to keep in mind is the preparation of the **pretrial memorandum.** This is a document submitted by each party to the court prior to a pretrial conference, addressing the issues to be discussed in the conference. There is no specific requirement under the FRCP that any such memorandum be submitted; some state courts and local federal rules, however, do require such memoranda. We discuss pretrial memoranda further in the subsections that follow.

**Figure 11–1    Subjects to Be Discussed at a Pretrial Conference under Rule 16 of the FRCP**

> *The following list of subjects appropriate for a pretrial conference is taken from Rule 16(c) of the FRCP.*
>
> (1) The formulation and simplification of the issues, including the elimination of frivolous claims or defenses.
>
> (2) The necessity or desirability of amendments to the pleadings.
>
> (3) The possibility of obtaining admissions of fact and of documents which will avoid unnecessary proof, stipulations regarding the authenticity of documents, and advance rulings from the court on the admissibility of evidence.
>
> (4) The avoidance of unnecessary proof and of cumulative evidence.
>
> (5) The identification of witnesses and documents, the need and schedule for filing and exchanging pretrial briefs, and the date or dates for further conferences and for trial.
>
> (6) The advisability of referring matters to a magistrate or master.
>
> (7) The possibility of settlement or the use of extrajudicial procedures to resolve the dispute.
>
> (8) The form and substance of the pretrial order.
>
> (9) The disposition of pending motions.
>
> (10) The need for adopting special procedures for managing potentially difficult or protracted actions that may involve complex issues, multiple parties, difficult legal questions, or unusual proof problems.
>
> (11) Such other matters as may aid in the disposition of the action.

## The Pretrial Scheduling Conference

The optional pretrial **scheduling conference,** if it is held, is the pretrial conference that occurs early in the process; indeed, under Rule 16(b), the entering of a **scheduling order** by the court subsequent to such a conference shall issue "in no event more than 120 days after filing of the complaint," so that the conference itself can be held no later than that date.

The purposes of a pretrial scheduling conference are set forth in Rule 16(b). Simply stated, the conference is designed to lead to a scheduling order that sets time limits for (1) joining parties, (2) amending pleadings, (3) filing and hearing motions, and (4) completing discovery. By setting specific deadlines for certain procedures or options that, in the absence of such an order, would ordinarily be available at any time before trial, the court and parties can ensure the reasonable movement of the case toward the earliest realistic trial date. Appropriate deadlines will vary with the complexity and nature of the factual and legal issues presented by the case. The scheduling order may also set dates for future pretrial conferences and even for the trial itself, and may address "any other matters appropriate in the circumstances of the case" (Rule 16(b)).

In attempting to formulate a reasonable schedule, the parties are, in essence, working together, along with the judge, to establish a framework in which all the elements of pretrial practice that we've discussed to this point can best proceed. This often involves a significant amount of cooperation among and between various parties. On occasion, where one or more parties may advocate an unrealistic deadline for a tactical purpose, there may arise disagreements. The court has the final word in setting pretrial scheduling orders, and will attempt to balance the interests of the parties with the need for an efficient judicial process. Furthermore, if circumstances change over time or deadlines originally set begin to appear unrealistic, the court will generally be liberal in amending the schedule to adjust to the legitimate needs of the parties.

Pretrial memoranda associated with a pretrial scheduling conference would probably be fairly brief, or not required at all. The contents might include nothing more than proposed deadlines for various steps, perhaps with accompanying reasons justifying the deadlines.

A court may issue a scheduling order on its own initiative, without a scheduling conference, pursuant to Rule 16(b). In some jurisdictions, or with some judges, a **standing pretrial scheduling order** is issued, which is applicable to all pending cases (see Figure 11–2), subject to modification where specific changes are necessary for an individual case. You and your supervising attorney must take care to determine, and then follow, the requirements of any applicable scheduling order.

## Pretrial Status Conferences

One or more pretrial **status conferences** subsequent to the 120-day deadline for the scheduling order are often useful. The term *status conference* is not specifically identified in Rule 16, but it is often applied to conferences held after a scheduling order has been entered, but before the final pretrial conference. In addition to dealing with any necessary or desired modifications of the scheduling order, such a conference allows the attorneys and the judge to review the progression of the case and plan its future course.

As a practical matter, periodic status conferences force attorneys to focus on a case that might otherwise languish until trial approaches. Judges often view status conferences as a means of prompting busy attorneys to take the necessary preliminary steps that can lead to settlement, or at least move the case more quickly toward trial. Some judges schedule such conferences on a regular and

**Figure 11–2 Standing Pretrial Scheduling Order**

United States District Court
for the
District of Exurbia

:

:

:

ALL CASES                                    As of January 15, 1991

:

:

:

**Standard Pretrial Scheduling Order**

TO: All Counsel and Parties in Civil Cases

1. As provided in Rule 16(b) of the FRCP, the Court hereby ORDERS that the parties adhere to the following deadlines and file the specified papers with the Clerk of the Court on or before the following dates:
   (a) All motions relating to joinder of parties, claims or remedies, class certification, and amendment of the pleadings: within 60 days after the filing of the Complaint.
   (b) All motions to dismiss based on the pleadings: within 90 days after the filing of the Complaint.
   (c) Completion of discovery: within eight months after the filing of the Complaint.
   (d) All motions for summary judgment: within ten months after the filing of the Complaint.

2. This order may be modified FOR CAUSE by a written stipulation signed by all parties, subject to the approval of the Court. In the absence of a stipulation of the parties, any party, FOR CAUSE, may apply to the Court for a modification of this order.

3. The Court, in its discretion or upon request of one or more of the parties, may at any time schedule the case for a pretrial status conference.

4. A copy of this order shall be served on the plaintiff by the Clerk upon the filing of the Complaint, and upon each defendant with the service of the Complaint and summons.

THE COURT

recurring basis every few months; other judges schedule them only as requested, or as needed.

Potential for settlement is often one of the key items addressed in a status conference. In the early stages of a case, settlement may be unlikely; but often, the closer a case moves to trial, the more likely it is that the case will be ripe for settlement talks. As we noted in Chapter 10, settlement talks between the parties often stall on certain key points. It can thus be extremely beneficial to involve the court in the negotiation process, and courts are generally open to providing such assistance. When negotiating in such a conference, the judge often encourages the parties to be candid with him or her in their confidential discussions, providing information to which the opposing party is not privy, so that the judge can develop a valid understanding of the case. Some judges are expert at using this confidential information to coax the parties toward reasonable bargaining positions that can lead to settlement.

The involvement of the paralegal in the preparation for a status conference may be significant. The file must always be reviewed in detail, including the status of the pleadings and discovery. Documents must be organized, sometimes evidence must be reviewed, and, to the extent that settlement discussions are anticipated, steps must be taken to establish a settlement value. The client will also be involved in the process, particularly with regard to settlement discussions. Often the court will require the client to be available, either in person or by telephone, for settlement discussions during a pretrial conference. You may be asked to inform the client of the need for such availability, and to coordinate any necessary arrangements (such as obtaining a phone number where the client can be reached during the conference).

**P**ARALEGALERT!

The client must often be available for a status conference, either in person or by phone.

The pretrial memorandum that might be filed prior to a status conference can take one of many forms, depending on the anticipated scope of the conference. If regularly scheduled status conferences are held throughout the pendency of a case, the need for a detailed memorandum at any one conference may be minimized. If only one status conference is held, or if a subject such as settlement is likely to be discussed, the need for a detailed memorandum increases.

## Final Pretrial Conference

The **final pretrial conference** is addressed by Rule 16(d). The "participants at any such conference shall formulate a plan for trial, including a program for facilitating the admission of evidence." At least one of the attorneys who will conduct the trial for each party, as well as each unrepresented party, is required to be in attendance. It is likely that the potential for settlement will still be a key topic for discussion, but as the likelihood for settlement dissolves, the focus of the conference shifts to the manner in which the trial will proceed. Identifying witnesses and exhibits, resolving potential evidentiary disputes (including those presented by motions *in limine*), stipulating to certain facts and documents so as to avoid unnecessary and time-consuming proof at trial, and organizing many other aspects of the trial are all appropriate topics for a final pretrial conference (see Figure 11–3).

The pretrial memorandum submitted prior to a final pretrial conference is likely to be detailed, addressing all the considerations in Figure 11–3. Although there may or may not be a joint filing in which both parties concur, there will likely be substantial coordination between the parties in the preparation of such memoranda, in that Rule 16(d) requires that they "shall formulate a plan for trial . . . ." In general, the parties will be identifying areas of agreement and areas where they have, in essence, agreed to disagree.

**P**ARALEGALERT!

The terms of a pretrial order are extremely important, since they can be modified only to prevent manifest injustice. Thus, any confusion or disagreement as to the appropriateness of the terms should be worked out at the final pretrial conference.

After the conference, and pursuant to Rule 16(d), a **final pretrial order** is issued "reciting the action taken" at the final pretrial conference (Rule 16(e)). The terms of such an order are often quite detailed, again taking into account the many factors listed in Figure 11–3, and are a critically important consider-

**Figure 11–3 Topics for Final Pretrial Conference**

*The following constitute some of the major considerations at the final pretrial conference envisioned by Rule 16(d) of the FRCP:*

(1) Potential for *stipulations* as to the following:
  (a) that the Court has *jurisdiction*, and that the *venue* is appropriate;
  (b) whether the trial is *jury* or *non-jury*;
  (c) that there are certain *uncontested facts*, which are then specifically identified;
  (d) that certain *documents* and *exhibits* can be admitted into evidence for certain purposes without objection; and
  (e) that the *qualification of experts* justify the anticipated expert testimony;

(2) Need for further *amendment to pleadings*.

(3) Estimate of anticipated *length of trial*.

(4) Alternative *dates for trial* (taking into account availability of witnesses, attorneys, parties, and the judge).

(5) *Relief sought* by the parties making claims for relief.

(6) Each side's *view of contested issues*.

(7) Resolution of *any outstanding motions*.

(8) Identification of *disputed issues of law* (substantive or procedural, including consideration of evidentiary issues presented by any Motion in Limine).

(9) Proposed *voir dire questions* for juror examination.

(10) Proposed *jury instructions* (which may be submitted, or for which a schedule of submission may be arranged).

(11) Assignment of specific *number or letter designation of exhibits*.

(12) Exchange of *copies of exhibits*.

(13) Lists of *witnesses*.

ation in preparing for trial. Once ordered, the terms "shall be modified only to prevent manifest injustice" (Rule 16(e)); thus, it is important that any confusion or disagreement as to the efficiency and justice of proposed terms be carefully addressed and resolved at the final pretrial conference.

## State Court Pretrial Conference

The rules, procedures, and practices relating to pretrial conferences in the various state court systems vary significantly. Some proceed pursuant to rules as formalized as Rule 16 of the FRCP; others are more informal, and often more dependent on the preferences and personal characteristics of the individual judge assigned. The pretrial memoranda required will likewise vary with the rules, the nature of the conference, and the judge involved. Ultimately, however, essentially the same considerations apply to state court pretrial conferences as to those in the federal courts. Preliminary scheduling considerations, the orderly progression of the case toward trial, the potential for settlement, and final preparations before trial are all relevant subjects for discussion. You should consult your state court rules to identify relevant procedures and practices.

## 11–2  A Basic Outline of the Trial

Before we begin to discuss trial preparation, it will be useful for you to have a broad overview of the course of a typical trial (see Figure 11–4). By developing some sense of the manner in which a trial unfolds in the courtroom, you can then put the importance and significance of trial preparation into its proper perspective. In this section we'll actually provide a basic outline of two types of trial: the **jury trial,** in which the jury is the trier-of-fact; and the **bench trial** (also called a **court trial** or a **nonjury trial**), in which the judge is the trier-of-fact. You should recall that we introduced you to these two types of trial in Chapter 1; you should also recall that, regardless of who the trier-of-fact is, it is always the judge who decides questions of law.

Before we launch into our discussion of these two types of trial, it will be useful to review briefly the physical layout of a courtroom (see Figure 11–5) and the identities of the various players. A typical courtroom has two tables, called **counsel tables,** one for the plaintiff's side and one for the defendant's side. The attorneys sit at these tables, sometimes with clients or paralegals as well; clients and paralegals might also sit in the gallery, which is usually behind the tables. As cases get more complicated, with multiple parties and claims, a larger courtroom with multiple counsel tables may be necessary.

At the front of the courtroom sits the judge, usually on a raised podium area known as the **bench.** He or she is in charge of the trial and the courtroom. Next to the bench is the **witness stand,** from which the witnesses will testify.

Judges are often assisted by one or more **law clerks.** These clerks are generally law students or recent law school graduates who work for the judge for a one-

**Figure 11–4  Course of Typical Jury and Bench Trials**

| Jury Trial | Bench Trial |
|---|---|
| (1) Final efforts to settle | (1) Final efforts to settle |
| (2) Jury selection | (2) Opening statement |
| (3) Opening statement | (3) Plaintiff's evidence |
| (4) Plaintiff's evidence | (4) Defendant's Motion for Judgment on Partial Findings |
| (5) Defendant's Motion for Judgment as a Matter of Law | (5) Defendant's evidence |
| (6) Defendant's evidence | (6) Plaintiff's Motion for Judgment on Partial Findings |
| (7) Plaintiff's Motion for Judgment as a Matter of Law | (7) Rebuttal |
| (8) Rebuttal | (8) Judgment |
| (9) Either party's Motion for Judgment as a Matter of Law | (9) Motion to Amend the Judgment |
| (10) Jury instructions given | (10) Motion for New Trial |
| (11) Jury deliberation | |
| (12) Verdict | |
| (13) Judgment | |
| (14) Renewal of any previous Motion for Judgment as a Matter of Law | |
| (15) Motion for New Trial | |

**Figure 11–5   Physical Layout of Typical Courtroom**

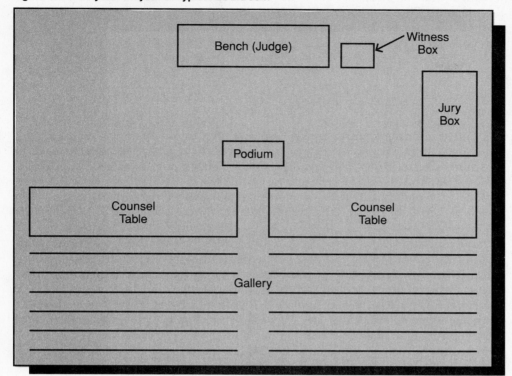

or two-year period to learn about the workings of the court from the inside. Clerks often handle the swearing-in of witnesses.

Most courtrooms have a **bailiff** or **sheriff,** whose role is to maintain order in the courtroom should a disruption occur. The bailiff or sheriff is often the person designated to announce that court is in session, usually in ceremonial fashion such as the following:

> Oyez! Oyez! Oyez! The United States District Court for the District of Exurbia is now in session. All persons having business herein shall state their names and purpose according to law. The Honorable Oliver Wendell Holmes, presiding.

The trial will generally be recorded by a **court reporter** using a stenographic transcribing machine (in a manner similar to the recording of a deposition, which we described in Chapter 9). The court reporter is an employee of the judicial system, and is automatically assigned to the trial. Thus, you generally do not have to make special arrangements to ensure his or her presence, as you did when arranging for a court reporter for a deposition. Some court systems utilize audiotaping systems for trials, rather than stenographic recording, and the person who runs the taping system is sometimes called a "monitor" rather than a court reporter.

To one side of the bench is the **jury box.** In a jury trial, this is where the jury sits; in a bench trial, it will be empty.

Sometimes there is a small podium in front of the counsel tables, from which counsel can address questions to the court or to witnesses. Attorneys are often free to move about the area in front of the bench during questioning, but some judges restrict this; your supervising attorney will follow the practices imposed by the relevant court or judge.

When the parties and their attorneys arrive at court at the appointed hour for trial (we discuss how this hour is determined in a later section), the judge may request that the attorneys come into his or her chambers for one last effort at settlement. Eleventh-hour settlements, when the reality of the impending trial hits home for both attorneys and clients, are not uncommon.

Let's turn now to our consideration of the two basic types of trial.

### Jury Trial

If settlement appears impossible, the next step in a jury trial is to select the members of the jury, called **jurors.** Jury selection and jury trials are governed by sections 1861 to 1878 of Title 28 of the United States Code, as well as by Rules 38, 39, 47, 48, 49, and 51 (among others) of the FRCP. Groups of potential jurors, called **jury panels,** are initially selected at random by the judicial system (see sections 1863 and 1866 of Title 28 for a detailed description of the process, which goes so far as to include the use of physical devices called "jury wheels" to ensure randomness). These potential jurors are citizens of the United States who have resided for at least one year in the district in which the court sits, and they are generally identified from such sources as motor vehicle registration lists, voter lists, or tax records. Once panels are selected and brought to court, a questioning process, called *voir dire,* is initiated by the court and attorneys involved in a specific case. The purpose of *voir dire* is to identify and exclude those jurors who might be biased in deciding the facts. Eeach attorney attempts to exclude jurors biased against his or her client, and hopes to seat a jury receptive to his or her client's arguments.

*Voir dire* procedures may vary from court to court and state to state. A few jurisdictions still allow for questioning of potential jurors individually, one by one, in civil cases; in most cases, however, the questions are posed to a full panel of as many as 15 or 20 or more potential jurors.

After the panel is brought into the courtroom, the judge begins by providing the prospective jurors with basic background information about the case. He or she then introduces the attorneys. The attorneys usually stand up to identify themselves, their clients, their law firm, and the witnesses who are expected to testify. At this point those jurors who indicate that they personally know any of the involved parties, attorneys, or witnesses (or even the judge) are generally excused from the case.

Then the questioning begins. Sometimes the attorneys are allowed to pose questions to the panel; sometimes the questions must be provided to the judge, who conducts the questioning. Under Rule 47 of the FRCP, the "court may permit the parties or their attorneys to conduct the examination of prospective jurors or may itself conduct the examination." If the federal court conducts the examination itself, it may allow the parties or their attorneys either to ask additional questions, or submit questions for the court to ask.

Jurors are selected by a process of elimination. A juror is eliminated if a valid *challenge* is exercised. There are two types of challenge (see Rule 47 of the FRCP and section 1870 of Title 28). The first type, called a **peremptory challenge,** gives to an attorney the power to disqualify a juror arbitrarily, without providing a reason. Each party is allowed a limited number of such peremptory challenges (three, under section 1870). The second type of challenge is called a **challenge for cause.** If a juror appears to be openly and blatantly biased, or turns out to have a close relationship to someone involved in the case or a proprietary interest in the outcome of the case, or lacks the capacity to perform the duties of a juror,

**P**ARALEGALERT!

Attorneys are authorized to exercise a specified number of arbitrary peremptory challenges, but only the judge can order a potential juror disqualified on a challenge for cause.

one or both attorneys can seek to have the juror's further participation ended on a challenge for cause. The court must be convinced that the circumstances justify the disqualification; only the court has the power to disqualify based on a challenge for cause. We speak further about the role of the paralegal in jury selection, and the use of these challenges, in Section 11–4.

The number of jurors varies from one jurisdiction to the next, even in the federal system (see Rule 48 of the FRCP, which was amended in 1991 to establish a maximum of 12 jurors and a minimum of 6). Local federal rules often control the issue. Although 12 jurors were commonly required in the past, the current trend is toward the 6-person jury. As a result of the 1991 amendments to the FRCP, the use of alternate jurors was ended in the federal courts. The result of this will likely be the use of juries slightly larger than the minimum required (for example, eight jurors where the minimum required is six) so that if a juror is excused under the new provision (Rule 47(c)) there will still be enough jurors remaining to render a valid decision. Many state court systems still allow for the use of alternate jurors; you should check your state's rules and practices on jury selection.

Eventually jury selection is complete. The next step in a jury trial is the **opening statement** of each attorney, in which they sketch out their respective views of the nature of the case, as well as brief summations of what the jury should expect to hear and see as the evidence is presented. The opening statement is not a context in which the attorneys will be arguing the merits of the case, but rather an opportunity for each to get the jury thinking about the case in a certain way beneficial to his or her client. Of course, each side gets a chance to make an opening statement, so different views of the case will be provided.

After the opening statements are completed, the presentation of evidence begins. The plaintiff's counsel goes first, calling witnesses and offering documents and exhibits into evidence; this is referred to as the "plaintiff's case-in-chief." As you will recall from our discussion in Chapter 5, the rules of evidence govern the presentation and admission of evidence. As you will also recall, witness examination involves **direct examination** by the attorney calling the witness, and **cross-examination** by the opposing attorneys. Since the plaintiff goes first, he or she conducts the initial direct examination, followed by the defendant's cross-examination. **Leading questions** are allowed on cross, but generally not on direct.

**Objections** to questions posed to witnesses, or to exhibits offered into evidence, are ruled on by the court. In federal court, if an evidentiary ruling goes against a party, no formal **exception** need be taken in order to preserve rights of appeal; in some state courts, however, exceptions to adverse rulings must still be stated on the record (if they are not so stated, the right to appeal the ruling is waived).

An important concept to keep in mind at trial is the **burden of proof.** Simply stated (although it is a concept that can be analyzed in some depth and complexity), the burden of proof is the requirement that one party or the other must provide a certain level of evidentiary support for a given issue; failure to do so leads to judgment in favor of the other party. The burden of proof is determined by researching the controlling law, found in judicial opinions and/or statutes.

Generally speaking, the burden of proof in a civil trial falls on the plaintiff (the defendant has the burden of proof in an affirmative defense), who must show by a **preponderance of the evidence** that his or her alleged facts are true. Roughly stated, this means that it is "more likely than not" that the alleged facts are true, based on the evidence presented. This does not mean that the party with the most evidence

**P**ARALEGALERT!

The *preponderance of the evidence* standard does not require that the party with the burden produce the most evidence, but rather the most persuasive evidence.

wins, but rather the party with the most persuasive evidence. For example, if one side produced 50 shaky witnesses and the other side produced one highly credible witness, the party producing only one witness could very possibly prevail under the preponderance of the evidence standard.

The burden of proof is sometimes more difficult to meet in civil cases involving serious allegations such as fraud or intentional wrongdoing. Under those circumstances, the plaintiff might be charged with providing **clear and convincing evidence,** or some similar and higher standard (for example, "clear and indubitable" or "compelling" evidence). You may be familiar with a still higher burden of proof used in criminal (but not civil) trials, where the prosecution's evidence must establish the accused's guilt "beyond a reasonable doubt." Civil cases do not impose such a high requirement, except in rare circumstances where some criminal behavior is alleged (as where, for example, a signature on a deed was allegedly forged; even then, the higher standard is not often imposed).

After the plaintiff's attorney has **rested** (meaning that he or she has completed presentation of the evidence), the defendant may make a motion arguing that the evidence presented by the plaintiff is insufficient to sustain a judgment, and the defendant is therefore entitled to judgment in his or her favor. In a jury trial, such a motion is referred to as a **Motion for Judgment as a Matter of Law,** under Rule 50 of the FRCP, which was amended in 1991. The motion may be granted against the plaintiff at this stage (since the plaintiff has rested and thus "has been fully heard" with respect to the contested issues, as required by Rule 50) if the defendant can show "that there is no legally sufficient evidentiary basis for a reasonable jury to have found for" the plaintiff.

If any such motion made by the defendant is denied, or if no such motion was made, the trial thereafter continues with the defendant now presenting his or her own evidence. This time, the defendant calls witnesses and conducts direct examination, and the plaintiff conducts cross-examination.

After the defendant has rested, the plaintiff might also file a Motion for Judgment as a Matter of Law. The plaintiff then proceeds with any **rebuttal** evidence, which should be limited to refuting the arguments raised by the defense, as opposed to introducing new matters supporting the claim. The defendant may thereafter rebut the rebuttal, and so on.

If multiple parties and multiple claims are involved, the order of presentation becomes more complicated. To the extent possible and logical, however, the basic concept of first allowing presentation by the party making a claim for relief, followed by presentation of the defense to that claim, is maintained.

At the conclusion of the presentation of evidence in a jury trial, either party may make a motion arguing that the evidence is clear and unambiguous and requires the entry of judgment against the other party as a matter of law, with no need for further deliberation by the jury. The appropriate motion is, once again, the Motion for Judgment as a Matter of Law under Rule 50 of the FRCP (as amended in 1991). This motion might be thought of as analogous to the Motion for Summary Judgment, in that it argues that, after the presentation of the evidence, there is "no legally sufficient evidentiary basis" for any conclusion other than the version of the facts asserted in the motion (similar to the standard for summary judgment in Rule 56, which requires the showing of "no genuine issue as to any material fact"). A Motion for Judgment as a Matter of Law "shall specify the judgment sought and the law and facts on which the moving party

**PARALEGALERT!**

If the plaintiff's attorney calls the witness, he or she conducts direct examination and the defendant's attorney conducts the cross-examination. If the defendant's attorney calls the witness, he or she conducts the direct examination and the plaintiff's attorney conducts the cross-examination. It is erroneous to assume that the plaintiff always conducts direct examination and the defendant cross-examination.

is entitled to the judgment" (Rule 50(a)(2)); it is hence likely to be accompanied by a memorandum of law. If the motion is granted, the case is over; if denied, the decision on the facts is turned over to the jury.

If the jury is to proceed with the finding of facts, the jurors must be provided with **jury instructions** intended to guide them in their deliberations (see Rule 51 of the FRCP; jury instructions are also discussed further in Section 11–3). Each side generally submits written proposed instructions. Outside the hearing of the jury, the judge will hear arguments from both sides regarding these proposed instructions, then make a decision as to what the appropriate instructions will be. Once the decision is made, the jury is recalled, informed of the instructions, and thereafter dispatched to the jury room to deliberate.

Jury deliberation can last only minutes, or it may take many days. On occasion agreement cannot be reached, creating a "hung jury" and the need for a new trial. In most cases, however, the jury eventually reaches a decision, called a **verdict.** Verdicts are governed by Rules 48 and 49 of the FRCP. Unless the parties stipulate otherwise, a verdict must be unanimous, and must be taken from a jury of at least six remaining members (see Rule 48, as amended in 1991). There are essentially three types of verdict (see Rule 49): a **special verdict,** in which the jury is asked to decide specific individual issues of fact, which are then incorporated into the judgment of the court; the **general verdict,** in which the jury identifies, in the simplest and most straightforward fashion, which party has won and the amount of any applicable damages (there would be no damage award if a noncounterclaiming defendant won); and the **general verdict with interrogatories,** in which the jury reaches the same general verdict just described, but also answers certain specific "interrogatories" about its findings with regard to specific, individual issues of fact. These interrogatories are not to be confused with the interrogatories used in the discovery process; those are entirely unrelated. If "one or more" of the interrogatory responses is "inconsistent with the general verdict," the judge can either enter judgment based on the interrogatory answers, or return the matter to the jury "for further consideration of its answers . . . ."

Following the decision of the jury, the court thereafter enters **judgment** in the case, officially incorporating the jury's decision. We discuss the concept of judgment further in a later section.

Either just before or shortly after the judgment is entered, the losing party has certain remaining motion options. If a Motion for Judgment as a Matter of Law was previously filed and denied, and the jury's verdict thereafter goes against the party that filed the motion, the Motion for Judgment as a Matter of Law is subject to being "renewed by service and filing not later than ten days after entry of judgment" (Rule 50(b)).

The renewal of a Motion for Judgment as a Matter of Law can also be joined with a **Motion for New Trial** under Rule 59 of the FRCP. The Motion for New Trial is filed if procedural irregularities or perceived shortcomings of the trial justify a new trial. The rule itself does not set forth the specific grounds that might require such a new trial, referencing only "any of the reasons for which new trials [or rehearings] have heretofore been granted." Juror misconduct, grossly inappropriate damages (either too high or too low), newly discovered evidence, or other similar reasons have all been used to justify new trials in the past. The new trial may relate to "all or any of the parties and on all or part of the issues," giving the court the authority to limit a new trial to only so many of the original contested issues as must be retried in order to do justice. The court is also authorized to grant a new trial on its own initiative, even without a motion having been filed, under Rule 59(d).

The 1991 amendments to the FRCP, which created the new Motion for Judgment as a Matter of Law under Rule 50, replaced two former motions that are still in use in many state courts. The former **Motion for Directed**

**Verdict** performed essentially the function now fulfilled by the Motion for Judgment as a Matter of Law made prior to the jury deliberation; the former **Motion for Judgment Notwithstanding the Verdict** (also called a **Motion for Judgment JNOV,** with the letters standing for a Latin phrase meaning "notwithstanding the verdict") performed, essentially, the function of the Motion for Judgment as a Matter of Law that is renewed under Rule 50(a) after the verdict comes in. You should review your state procedures to determine whether these two motions are still relevant in the trial practice of your state's courts.

Once any posttrial motions are resolved and a final judgment is rendered, two possible courses can follow. First, the losing party may seek to appeal the judgment, arguing to a higher court that the decision of the trial court is flawed and should be overturned. Second, the judgment may simply be allowed to stand. If the latter course is followed, and the losing party does not immediately pay the judgment in full, the issue of collecting the judgment thereafter becomes relevant. We discuss many of these matters as they relate to the practice of a paralegal further in the sections that follow.

## Bench Trial

A bench trial is similar to a jury trial, except that the judge, rather than a jury, decides the contested issues of fact. This is a circumstance that may well influence the manner in which the attorneys present their evidence, since judges are more experienced in analyzing and resolving factual disputes than are juries.

The *voir dire* process of jury selection is, obviously, dispensed with in a bench trial. Opening statements are sometimes dispensed with as well (since the judge is often familiar with the case), but in most cases they are retained.

Evidence will be presented by the parties in a bench trial, but no verdict is rendered, because there is no jury; the ultimate decision comes in the form of the judgment of the court. The court makes separate findings of fact and conclusions of law (see Rule 52(a) of the FRCP). Appeals are possible after bench trials, just as with jury trials; collection of the judgment may also become an issue. Thus, the parallels between a jury trial and a bench trial are fairly obvious, as are the differences.

There is one other key area in which the bench trial differs significantly from the jury trial: with regard to motions presented at the close of the plaintiff's case. The Motion for Judgment as a Matter of Law, which we discussed previously, applies only to jury trials. In a bench trial, at the close of the plaintiff's case, or any time after any party has been "fully heard" on a contested issue, the opposing party can make a **Motion for Judgment on Partial Findings** (see Rule 52(c) of the FRCP; this is a new motion created by the 1991 amendments and meant to be analogous to revised Rule 50(a) in the nonjury context). The court may grant this motion immediately, or "decline to render any judgment until the close of all the evidence" (Rule 52(c)).

Finally, within 10 days after judgment in a bench trial, a party can make a **Motion to Amend the Judgment** under Rule 52(b) (which may be combined with a Motion for New Trial under Rule 59).

---

**PARALEGALERT!**

Under the FRCP, the Motion for Judgment as a Matter of Law applies only to jury trials. In a bench trial, analogous functions are performed by the Motion for Judgment on Partial Findings and the Motion to Amend the Judgment.

---

## 11-3  Trial Preparation

There's an old saying among trial lawyers, that the cases you're best prepared to try are the ones you settle. Although you and your supervising attorneys should take care that all your cases are properly prepared, there's a message between the lines of that saying that bears further remark.

What the saying implies is this: when you're well prepared for trial, the other side will respect, possibly even fear, your level of readiness. Under such circumstances, the likelihood of settlement increases. It is enormously important that you understand this.

The most important factor in winning a trial is preparation. If you and your supervising attorney are shuffling desperately around at trial, hunting for missing documents, searching through undigested deposition transcripts, pacing the floor waiting for a witness who promised to testify but wasn't *subpoenaed*, you run the risk of alienating the judge, the jury, and even your own client. You must not let this happen; you must be prepared for trial.

What does trial preparation involve? It involves becoming the foremost authority on a highly specialized and individualized subject area—namely, the case about to be tried. It involves pulling together all the disparate elements we've been addressing throughout this book—facts and law, rules and procedures, personalities and practicalities. In general, you'll be coordinating the facts developed through investigation, the elements of the complaint, the defenses asserted, the documents obtained, the witnesses who will testify, the materials uncovered in discovery, both the issues resolved by the pleadings and requests for admission and those left contested, the legal issues presented, the specific evidence to be introduced, the pretrial order of the court, and the practical issues presented by the nature of the trial itself (for example, whether it is a jury trial or a bench trial), all in an effort to ensure a flawless presentation of the client's position in order to prevail.

In short, trial preparation means doing everything necessary (and ethical) to win!

**P**ARALEGALERT!

Trial preparation requires that you become the foremost authority on a highly specialized subject: the case about to be tried.

### Scheduling

We mentioned earlier that we would discuss how the "appointed hour for trial" is determined. One of the most maddening aspects of trial practice is lingering uncertainty over trial date. Although most courts work hard to provide attorneys with the "date certain" on which the trial will begin, they are often dealing with scores or even hundreds of cases approaching readiness for trial. These cases are tracked by the court on a **trial list** or **trial docket.** Some settle; some are postponed; some move on to trial. In trying to balance the interests of all involved parties with the need to maximize judicial efficiency, the court system is often placed in a scheduling dilemma: they have many cases approaching trial with no clear indication of which cases will actually end up being tried, with the additional problem of coordinating a finite number of judges and courtrooms.

As a result, the procedures in use in most court systems necessitate a certain amount of flexibility on the part of all involved parties and court personnel. It is often difficult to pin down the precise trial date until fairly late in the process: there may be many cases ahead of yours on the trial list and, for one reason or another, few may settle, tying up courtrooms and judges for an inordinate amount of time.

Thus the first consideration for pretrial preparation is monitoring the progression of your firm's case toward trial. If you are lucky enough to have a "date certain" set by the court early on, you can use this as the target date for your additional preparation. If not, you will have to stay abreast of the court's schedule. This requires (1) determining the scheduling procedures that are in place in the relevant court system, and (2) maintaining contact with the clerk's office or other relevant communication source (perhaps a courthouse phone recording, a local judicial newspaper, or lists posted in the courthouse). These monitoring tasks are often performed by a paralegal.

## PARALEGALERT!

An important step in trial preparation is determining when the trial will occur. If a date certain has been set, this is easy; if not, it requires (1) determining the relevant scheduling procedures, and (2) maintaining contact with the court.

Sometimes the date established for the trial by the court is inconvenient or problematic for some reason. A witness may have plans to be out of the country, for example, or your supervising attorney may be scheduled for another trial at the same time. Under such circumstances, a **continuance** may be requested; if authorized by the court, it postpones the date of the trial. If certain dates present problems, that fact should be brought to the court's attention at the earliest possible date. Many judges are unwilling to grant continuances at the last minute for trials that have been scheduled for some time, unless the problem that underlies the request for continuance has itself only recently arisen. The reason for this should be fairly obvious: many individual schedules must be coordinated when setting the date for a trial, including the court's trial docket. An ill-timed request for continuance can lead to great disruption for many parties, and might possibly cause a waste of judicial resources (for example, an empty courtroom that could have been used for the trial of another case).

## PARALEGALERT!

If a continuance is to be sought, it should be requested at the earliest possible date. To delay the request is to risk a denial of the continuance by the court.

### Review of Investigation and Discovery

The factual setting of your firm's cases is uncovered through investigation and the discovery process. As we have noted in earlier chapters, it is important to be thorough in your factual inquiries. Surprises at trial can be avoided, or at least minimized, by careful preparation. As the case advances closer to trial, you must review your factual preparation to be sure that (1) you were thorough in your initial efforts, and (2) any changed circumstances that have (or might have) developed since your initial efforts are accounted for. This may involve filing supplemental discovery requests and responses (if court-imposed deadlines are not violated), recontacting witnesses, reanalyzing discovery responses, making sure all depositions have been properly digested, and ensuring that all necessary documents have been obtained and organized.

Preparation for the trial of the factual aspects of your case involves, essentially, matching the proof you have developed with (1) the elements of the cause of action, (2) the damages alleged, and (3) the defenses raised. This is true whether your firm represents the plaintiff or the defendant; of course, your emphasis will be different depending on whom your firm represents. You will be working closely with your supervising attorney throughout this process.

## Organization of Documents

Organization of documents bears emphasis. As noted in Chapter 9, documents often play a central role in a lawsuit. In a contract dispute the importance is obvious; the documents that comprise, or are alleged to comprise, the contract must be interpreted by the parties and the court. But even in a personal injury suit, documents are often important: in the Hampton case, for example, such things as the work records of Bud's Auto Service, the police report pertaining to the accident, and the various medical bills and records detailing the damages all constitute vital evidence.

You should prepare sufficient copies of those documents that will be offered into evidence to be able to supply a copy to the judge and each counsel. Original documents to be offered as exhibits, with multiple copies for the other participants, can be organized using file folders, binder clips, or some other method preferred by your supervising attorney.

We spoke of document control at some length in Chapter 9, and the techniques that we addressed obviously retain their importance at trial. Sources and purposes of documents remain critically important considerations. In essence, you must develop a system that enables you to locate exactly what your supervising attorney needs exactly when he or she needs it. Events happen fast and furiously at trial; as a result, it is very important to keep at least one set of **working copies** of all relevant documents easily at hand, separate and distinct from your carefully organized originals. Perhaps the best way to maintain such working copies is in the context of a trial notebook, a concept we consider further in a moment. As we also discuss, the trial notebook (or any other system) may well include detailed summaries or indices of particularly lengthy documents, such as contracts or hospital reports running to 50 or 100 pages or more.

## Preparation of Exhibits

Particularly when your supervising attorney's trial presentation will be made in front of a jury, but even when it is made only to a judge, the manner in which facts are presented is important. It is often not enough merely to get the facts in front of the trier-of-fact; they must be presented with the proper emphasis. There is, indeed, a place for style in trial work, as well as substance.

A brief example will make the concept clearer. You may recall our discussion, in the context of explaining attorney work-product in Section 9–1, of certain tables that might be prepared summarizing vast quantities of business records. The information contained in the records can, if studied, speak for itself; but the summary tables may establish the point in a more emphatic and easily understandable manner.

Take the analysis one step further. If the table is a useful device, imagine how emphatically the point might be made if the table were taken to a graphics company and blown-up to poster size for display at trial on an easel. Such a display, set up before the jury, would capture their attention and underscore the importance of the information contained in the table. Suddenly it's not just another dry document; it's a prominent prop. This use of demonstrative evidence (recall our discussion of such evidence in Chapter 5) can be very helpful at trial.

Preparation of such a poster-size table, or similar exhibits constituting demonstrative evidence, often entails significant expense; hence the decision to proceed will not be made until trial is reasonably imminent. Another task similar to the preparation of demonstrative exhibits is arranging for expensive enlargements of relevant photographs. Finalizing such details before trial often falls to the paralegal.

Other physical exhibits (such as an allegedly defective widgenometer in the Widgets and Gizmos, Inc. case), which constitute *real evidence*, as opposed to demonstrative evidence (again, review our discussion in Chapter 5), are already in existence, so the pretrial preparation considerations differ slightly. With these exhibits, the issue is one of coordination and organization: efforts must be made to ensure that such exhibits are accounted for, and that they are properly dispatched to the court when they are needed for trial.

## Subpoenas of Witnesses

We addressed the procedures associated with *subpoenas* at length in Chapter 9. Rule 45 of the FRCP is a detailed and important source of the specifics of this procedure. *Subpoenas* are equally (if not more) important at trial as they are for depositions. If a necessary witness fails to appear to testify, and you have taken no steps to *subpoena* that witness, the court can simply pass over the omission and move on with the trial. It is the responsibility of your supervising attorney to make sure that his or her evidence is ready to be presented to the court at the appropriate time, and you will likely assist in the preparation of *subpoenas* to ensure the presence of witnesses.

Another consideration with regard to witnesses is simply to coordinate each witness's schedule with the anticipated court date, as well as the anticipated moment during the trial when the witness's testimony will be necessary. As a practical matter, witnesses generally have jobs or other commitments, and it is often difficult to keep their schedule clear for testifying at a moment's notice. For friendly witnesses, and even for hostile witnesses under *subpoena*, efforts must be made to inform the witness by phone or other means as to the approximate date and time when their testimony will be necessary. As the time grows closer, the precision with which this date and time can be estimated improves.

## Legal Research

As the trial approaches, the litigation case file will likely be filled with internal memoranda, memoranda of law on contested motions, photocopies of relevant judicial opinions and statutes, and assorted other research materials related to the key legal issues presented by the case. Questions regarding the elements of causes of actions asserted, the defenses raised, the damages allegedly incurred, and the impact of evidentiary rules will likely have been researched in detail. But further pretrial preparation is still necessary. This preparation will center on four specific areas.

First, efforts must be made to organize all the research already completed.

Second, all previous research must be updated. This will include such things as shepardizing and performing additional research from scratch, to see whether new cases can be uncovered and whether all previously cited cases are still in force. Statutes will have to be reviewed as well.

Third, new legal issues present themselves at trial. Standards regarding such things as posttrial motions might be researched in a preliminary (or possibly even in a detailed) manner as a contingency. Motions *in limine* may have to be researched and filed. Perhaps most importantly, jury instructions will have to be researched and prepared.

We should say a further word here about jury instructions. Jury instructions generally relate to legal conclusions that are to be drawn, should certain facts be found by the jury. Model jury instructions are often found in commercial publications that collect in one place many different types of jury instructions; they can also be drafted from scratch, taking into account the elements of the cause of action, the nature of a defense, and the substantive law surrounding and governing the issues in controversy. Although proposed jury instructions are often not submitted to the court until after the evidence has been presented, they should be analyzed and prepared in a "polished" draft form much earlier in the process. Indeed, some attorneys suggest that the best way to prepare for a trial is to draft jury instructions (and possibly a closing argument as well) first, then work backward to determine how best to present evidence and legal arguments at trial that will conform to these instructions (and closing argument) and lead to the desired verdict and judgment.

Finally, your supervising attorney may wish to file a **trial memorandum** at the commencement of the trial, setting forth your legal positions on various disputed issues. The court sometimes actually requires that such a memorandum be filed; you may be involved in the research and drafting of such a memorandum.

## Preparation of Client (and Other Witnesses) for Testimony

Your firm's client will likely be an important witness, and, because the client has much riding on the results of the trial, a very nervous one. Some clients are more calm than others, especially if they have more experience with litigation; in general, however, most people are not familiar with the "ins and outs" of a trial and must be prepared for what they will be facing.

Similarly, you will also be counting on the testimony of certain friendly witnesses, whose recounting of relevant events you anticipate will help the client's case. Such witnesses may be even more nervous, and less enthusiastic, than the client.

How do you prepare these witnesses for trial? It is likely that you will be working under the close direction of your supervising attorney in client and witness preparation, but a few general pointers are widely accepted. In general, there are three basic aspects to the preparation of a client or witness to testify: first, the review; second, the rehearsal; third, the final instructions (see Figure 11–6). Let's talk a moment about each.

Preparing a witness to testify provides the opportunity to *review* the matter with the witness. This is not the time for you or your supervising attorney to be learning what the witness has to say; this should have been known since early in the investigation process. Nor should this be the first time the witness has considered the issues presented; since you will be preparing presumably friendly witnesses (and your firm's client), they should have been approached earlier and should have some familiarity with the case and their role in it. In preparing the witness or client, then, you should first review any statements or deposition testimony they have given, along with exhibits and documents that are relevant to their testimony, review discovery responses, and review relevant portions of the pleadings; in general, review every relevant portion of the case.

**Figure 11–6 Preparation of Witness or Client to Testify**

> **(1) Review.** Review any prior statements, deposition testimony, relevant exhibits and documents, discovery responses, relevant portions of pleadings, and any other relevant materials. The witness or client will, of course, have studied these same materials at one or more times in the past.
>
> **(2) Rehearsal.** It is important to give the client or witness a preview of both the questions to be asked by your supervising attorney on direct examination, and the questions which are anticipated on opposing counsel's cross-examination. Do *not*, however, over-prepare; the appearance of having memorized a "script" can damage a witness's credibility.
>
> **(3) Final Instructions.** The witness or client should also be provided with several final instructions:
> - Listen carefully to the questions.
> - Answer only the questions asked.
> - If you don't understand the question, say so.
> - When an objection is made, don't answer until it is ruled upon.
> - Avoid phrases like, "To tell you the truth..."
> - Don't guess.
> - Always tell the *TRUTH!*

Next comes the *rehearsal* stage. A word of caution should be noted here. Although rehearsal is important, too much rehearsal can lead to testimony that seems memorized, and the appearance of having memorized a "script" can lead to skepticism on the part of the trier-of-fact. It is important to give the witness a good idea of the questions that will be asked by your supervising attorney on direct examination, since they are known and the responses will be used to establish certain points. It is also important to anticipate the probing questions that can be expected on cross-examination. There is a relatively fine line between adequate preparation and overpreparation. You must work at the close direction of your supervising attorney in rehearsing a witness's examination; indeed, it is likely that your supervising attorney will be closely involved in this aspect of the preparation.

The third aspect of witness preparation is the *final instructions*. These are similar to those given to a deponent: listen carefully to the questions; answer only the question asked; if you don't understand a question, ask for repetition or explanation; when an objection is made, wait until it is ruled on by the judge before proceeding; avoid beginning answers with phrases such as, "To tell you the truth . . ." (which imply that the witness has not been truthful in prior answers); don't guess; and always tell the truth.

## Trial Notebook

The **trial notebook** is an essential tool for most litigation attorneys, and assisting in its preparation will likely be an essential task for a litigation paralegal. In some ways, the trial notebook represents a summary of the entire case: both what has already occurred, and what is anticipated to occur through trial and beyond. A trial notebook is, in many ways, a microcosm of the entire litigation process.

The basic format for a trial notebook is the three-ring binder for $8\frac{1}{2} \times 11''$ paper (legal-size documents can be folded to fit or, better yet, photocopied at a reduced size on $8\frac{1}{2} \times 11''$ paper). The key characteristic of the trial notebook is the division into sections corresponding to different aspects of the case, or of the trial. The sections of a typical trial notebook are listed and explained in

**Figure 11–7   Sections in a Typical Trial Notebook**

*Each lawyer has his or her own personal preference with regard to trial prepa-
ration, including trial notebook format. The following is included for instructional purposes only; when preparing for trial, be sure to consult closely with
your supervising attorney. The following sections will often be included in a
typical trial notebook:*

**(1) Pleadings.** The final, operative version of all pleadings is essential. Earlier versions
which were filed but later replaced by amended pleadings are optional; in general, it is
best to have these in another file, but not in the trial notebook. Note also that, depending
on the complexity of the case and the pleadings, summaries of pleadings are often helpful (for example, a summary of a complex, multi-count complaint would quickly identify,
in shorthand fashion, the causes of action and major facts asserted).

**(2) Motions and Memoranda.** Major motions (such as a Motion to Dismiss or a Motion
for Summary Judgment), together with supporting memoranda and court rulings, often
supply useful discussions of certain of the legal issues presented in the case, and should
be included.

**(3) Investigation.** Certain basic information should be maintained in this, or a similarly-
titled, section: such things as phone numbers (for witnesses, other involved law firms,
the client, experts, the courthouse, a sheriff for service of subpoenas, etc.); FAX numbers which might be relevant; and mailing addresses.
   In addition, there may be aspects of your actual investigation of the case which do not
fit into any other category below (such as *Discovery Responses, Documents,* or *Exhibits*). An example might be the basic corporate information regarding an opposing party
obtained from the Secretary of the State. It may be useful to have some of these materials
readily available; if so, they should be maintained in this or a similarly-titled section.

**(4) Discovery Responses.** Discovery responses of reasonably convenient page-
length (for example, interrogatory responses or responses to request for admission)
should be kept at hand. Separate sections may be maintained for the responses of each
separate party. Depending on the extent of the production response, original documents
may be included as well. Where originals are too voluminous to include in the notebook,
summaries are useful.

**(5) Legal Research.** All relevant research memorandums would be included in this section, as well as photocopies of relevant judicial opinions and statutes.

**(6) Trial Memorandum.** Often a trial memorandum is filed at some point during a trial,
addressing disputed issues of law.

**(7) Jury Selection.** This section should contain voir dire questions and blank sheets or
charts for recording information obtained on each juror, as well as preliminary information supplied by the court.

**(8) Opening Statement.** Full text written out, along with notes or prompts which attorney will use when presenting argument.

**(9) Witnesses.** The contents of this section will vary with the attorney. Possible matters
to be included: background information on each witness (i.e., age, residence, employment, etc.); outline of anticipated testimony, including analysis of the key areas to
emphasize; outline of examination (direct or cross, depending on who will be calling the
witness; level of detail depends on level of experience of attorney); copies of subpoenas
served on witness, if any; digests of depositions or statements given, and possibly the
full draft of a statement if not too lengthy; copies or lists of documents relevant to the witness's testimony.

Figure 11–7. You should study Figure 11–7 carefully, because you may be asked
to assist in the preparation of a trial notebook.
   Your supervising attorney may begin preparing his or her trial notebook early
in the litigation process, possibly even before a lawsuit is commenced. This is
because, for many complicated cases, the level of organization provided by a
concise trial notebook is of great help at virtually every preliminary step of the

Figure 11–7 Sections in a Typical Trial Notebook, continued

**(10)  Documents.** Copies of all documents to be introduced into evidence, unless too voluminous. Summaries of key documents are very desirable. Any exhibit numbers or other designation assigned at the final pretrial conference should be indicated.

**(11)  Non-documentary Exhibits.** Lists or descriptions of non-documentary exhibits, together with identification of exhibit number or designation, if any, assigned at a final pretrial conference.

**(12)  Closing Argument.** Full text written out, along with notes or prompts which attorney will use when presenting argument. Extra space or blank sheets should be included for notes and comments based on the actual course of the trial, which might lead to some changes in the closing argument.

**(13)  Proposed Jury Instructions.** Initial draft of jury instructions, subject to review and revision during trial. Unlikely to be revised substantially; hence they should be prepared in a "polished" draft form.

**(14)  Trial Motions and Post-Trial Motions.** It may be useful to draft certain of the trial and post-trial motions ahead of time, such as the Motion for Judgment as a Matter of Law. If pre-drafted, drafts can be quickly finalized and filed when necessary.

litigation, not just at trial. The trial notebook expands as the case advances toward trial. Certain trial-related sections will not be finalized until right before the time of trial.

Not all attorneys use trial notebooks to organize their materials for trial; some use file folders or some other sorting and retrieval system. It is nevertheless worthwhile to study the various sections of the trial notebook identified in Figure 11–7, since any system of organization would be subdivided in an analogous manner.

## 11–4  Paralegal Responsibilities at Trial and Beyond

Were this a textbook intended for attorneys, or those studying to be attorneys, a section discussing trial responsibilities would be one of the most detailed and important sections of the book. Paralegals never try cases themselves, however, so this section is important not for specific hints as to how to win at trial, but rather for a broad understanding of a few key ways in which your assistance at trial can be helpful.

### Selecting the Jury

By virtue of the *voir dire* process of which we spoke earlier, attorneys can have significant impact on the composition of the jury. Selecting a jury has increasingly become a science, in which psychologists or other social scientists are sometimes hired to assist in identifying those potential jurors who project as favorable to a client, and those who project as hostile.

The role of a paralegal in this process will vary with both the firm and the specific case. If the client is prepared to expend significant resources, your jury selection duties may begin prior to trial with a review of lists of potential jurors obtained from the court, followed by background research on these jurors. Such preliminary research is limited by two factors: first, the willingness of the court system to provide access to these lists prior to trial (some court systems are more protective of this information than others); second, the ethical restrictions and statutory prohibitions regarding contact with jurors. Generally speaking, such intensive research is only justified in the rare case. If conducted, keep in mind both the guidelines established by your supervising attorney and the ethical and legal restrictions; you must not engage in jury-tampering.

In most jury trials, your first contact with the jury will be through information sheets or questionnaires provided by the court that identify certain key characteristics of each juror who will sit on a panel. The precise format of these sheets and questionnaires can vary greatly; a sample questionnaire is shown in Figure 11–8. Such information as age, spouse and children, residence, prior experience as a juror, occupation, and level of education attained are commonly shown on these sheets. Your role will likely be to assist your supervising attorney in matching the information on the sheets to the faces sitting on the jury panel. When the panel has a large number of potential jurors, it is important to maintain a level of organization with regard to information obtained on each individual juror. Your role will likely be to keep notes on each juror. An example of such notes relating to a fictitious juror appears in Figure 11–9.

You might also assist in the preparation of questions to be posed, either by the judge or by your supervising attorney, during the *voir dire* process. Some typical *voir dire* questions, and factors to consider in jury selection, are set forth in Figure 11–10.

Use of peremptory challenges involves tactical considerations. It is important for your supervising attorney to conserve his or her peremptory challenges if possible, so that he or she has at least one in reserve to bump a particularly problematic potential juror; part of your job may be to keep careful track of the attorney's use of these challenges, as well as the number of challenges that the other parties have remaining.

Your supervising attorney may also ultimately want to know your general impressions as to the suitability of each potential juror. The decision to accept or to challenge a potential juror is not an easy one. As a trained paralegal, your opinion counts.

## Opening Statements

An attorney's opening statement is a peculiarly personal performance, and your supervising attorney will likely take overarching responsibility for its preparation. Nevertheless, you may assist in preparing lists of areas to cover, or verifying facts or evidence to be cited, or serving as an audience as your supervising attorney works on perfecting his or her presentation.

## Presentation of Evidence

Once again, it will be your supervising attorney who conducts the presentation of evidence, not you. Nevertheless, your role can be important.

First of all, your supervising attorney cannot take notes while he or she is conducting questioning; thus, note taking during testimony is a useful role for the paralegal. Even when an opposing attorney is conducting questioning, your ability to take accurate notes can free up your supervising attorney to observe the witness's demeanor, and to focus on analyzing, rather than recording, the testimony.

Second, you can assist in the organization of documents and other exhibits. To the extent that your supervising attorney can count on your superior level of

Figure 11–8   Sample Juror Questionnaire

**MARK A "YES" OR "NO" BOX FOR EACH QUESTION**    YES    NO

1. ARE YOU A CITIZEN OF THE UNITED STATES?

2. ARE YOU 18 YEARS OF AGE OR OLDER? GIVE YOUR AGE

3. HAVE YOU LIVED FOR THE PAST FULL YEAR   IN THIS STATE,   IN THE SAME COUNTY?

IF "NO," SHOW UNDER REMARKS ON REVERSE THE NAMES OF OTHER COUNTIES OR STATES IN WHICH YOU LIVED DURING THE YEAR AND SHOW DATES.

4. DO YOU READ, WRITE, SPEAK AND UNDERSTAND THE ENGLISH LANGUAGE?

IF YOUR ANSWER TO NO. 5, 6 OR 7 IS "YES" PLEASE GIVE MORE INFORMATION ON REVERSE SIDE.

5. ARE ANY CHARGES NOW PENDING AGAINST YOU FOR A VIOLATION OF STATE OR FEDERAL LAW PUNISHABLE BY IMPRISONMENT FOR MORE THAN ONE YEAR?

6. HAVE YOU EVER BEEN CONVICTED, EITHER BY YOUR GUILTY OR NOLO CONTENDERE PLEA OR BY A COURT OR JURY TRIAL, OF A STATE OR FEDERAL CRIME FOR WHICH PUNISHMENT COULD HAVE BEEN MORE THAN ONE YEAR IN PRISON?

7. (IF ANSWER TO QUESTION #6 IS "YES") WERE YOUR CIVIL RIGHTS RESTORED? (IF "YES," EXPLAIN ON REVERSE SIDE.)

8. DO YOU HAVE ANY PHYSICAL OR MENTAL DISABILITY THAT WOULD INTERFERE WITH OR PREVENT YOU FROM SERVING AS A JUROR? (IF "YES," EXPLAIN UNDER REMARKS ON REVERSE)

9. PHONE    HOME    WORK (INCL. EXTENSION)

   AREA CODE   NUMBER    AREA CODE   NUMBER & EXT.

---

10. TO ASSIST IN ENSURING THAT ALL PEOPLE ARE REPRESENTED ON JURIES, PLEASE INDICATE WHICH OF THE FOLLOWING APPLIES TO YOU. NOTHING DISCLOSED WILL AFFECT YOUR SELECTION FOR JURY DUTY (SEE NOTE 10 ON REVERSE).

**RACE**

BLACK   AMERICAN INDIAN

WHITE   ASIAN

OTHER (SPECIFY)

Are you Hispanic?   Yes   No

12. **OCCUPATION** (SEE NOTE ON REVERSE SIDE)

ARE YOU NOW EMPLOYED?   NO   YES    YOUR USUAL OCCUPATION, TRADE OR BUSINESS

YOUR EMPLOYER'S NAME

BUSINESS OR EMPLOYER'S ADDRESS

11. SHOW THE EXTENT OF YOUR EDUCATION BY GIVING THE NUMBER OF YEARS COMPLETED ABOVE GRADE SCHOOL.

In High School

Above High School

Trade/Vocational School

15. I declare under penalty of perjury that all answers are true and correct to the best of my knowledge and belief.

SIGN HERE    MR    MRS    MISS    DATE

## NOTES REGARDING THE QUALIFICATION FORM

**Question 3 - RESIDENCE.** If you answered "NO," that you have not lived in the same state or same county for the past year, name the other states and counties where you lived, and give dates.

**Questions 5 and 6 - CRIMINAL RECORD.** If your answer to either question 5 or 6 is "YES," please show under "Remarks" a) date of the conviction (or date of pending charge), b) date of the offense, c) the sentence imposed (if a conviction), and d) the name of the court. One is disqualified from jury service only for criminal offenses punishable by imprisonment for more than one year, but it is the maximum penalty, and not the actual sentence, which controls.

**Question 8 - YOUR HEALTH.** If you claim a mental or physical disability please explain and give evidence of it either under "Remarks" section or by attaching a separate letter.

**NOTE -** Do not ask the court to call your doctor. Any doctor's statement you obtain regarding your physical condition must be sent to the court by you rather than by the doctor.

**Question 10 - RACE.** Federal law requires you as a prospective juror to indicate your race. This answer is required solely to avoid discrimination in juror selection and has absolutely no bearing on qualifications for jury service. By answering this question you help the federal court check and observe the juror selection process so that discrimination cannot occur. In this way the federal court can fulfill the policy of the United States which is to provide jurors who are randomly selected from a fair cross section of the community.

**Question 12 - OCCUPATION.** Federal law requires that you answer the questions about your occupation so that the Federal Courts may determine promptly whether you fall within an excuse or exemption category. (See Questions 13 & 14).

**Question 14 - GROUNDS FOR EXCUSE.** If you have indicated that you wish to be excused because you belong to one of the categories of persons that may be excused, please make sure you give, under "Remarks" such additional information as may be requested in the Instructions Letter where it describes the excuse category. For example, if you claim an excuse because you are "Over 70 Years of Age" you must show under "Remarks" the Month, Day and Year of your birth.

**Box Number 15 - YOUR SIGNATURE.** Be sure you have signed the questionnaire where indicated.

---

13. **EXEMPTIONS**    YES    NO

ARE YOU EMPLOYED ON A FULL TIME BASIS AS A:

PUBLIC OFFICIAL OF THE UNITED STATES, STATE, OR LOCAL GOVERNMENT WHO IS ELECTED TO PUBLIC OFFICE OR DIRECTLY APPOINTED BY ONE ELECTED TO OFFICE.

MEMBER OF ANY GOVERNMENTAL POLICE OR REGULAR FIRE DEPT. (NOT INCLUDING VOLUNTEER OR NON-GOVERNMENTAL DEPARTMENTS).

MEMBER IN ACTIVE SERVICE OF THE ARMED FORCES OF THE UNITED STATES.

14. **GROUNDS FOR REQUESTING EXCUSE**    14

PART 2 OF THE ATTACHED LETTER OF INSTRUCTIONS DESCRIBES CERTAIN CATEGORIES OF PERSONS WHO MAY BE EXCUSED BY THE COURT FROM SERVICE AS A JUROR. IF YOU ARE A PERSON IN ONE OF THESE CATEGORIES AND YOU WISH TO BE EXCUSED WRITE THE NUMBER OF YOUR CATEGORY HERE

OR, IF YOU WISH TO SERVE DO NOT SHOW ANYTHING HERE. PERSONS SHOWING A CATEGORY OF EXCUSE WHICH REQUIRES MORE INFORMATION MUST GIVE IT ON THE OTHER SIDE UNDER "REMARKS."

IF ANOTHER PERSON FILLED OUT THIS FORM PLEASE GIVE YOUR NAME AND ADDRESS ON THE OTHER SIDE OF FORM AND EXPLAIN THE REASON YOU GAVE ASSISTANCE

OFFICIAL USE ONLY

*Source: Federal Court Juror Qualification Questionnaire*

organization, he or she can concentrate on the content of exhibits, rather than searching frantically for them on the counsel table.

Third, if research issues arise during the course of the trial, or if your supervising attorney needs someone to make an independent investigation of some fact or issue that requires some legwork outside the courtroom, your availability will allow him or her to continue conducting the trial while you handle the research assignment or peripheral task.

Fourth, you can coordinate details, such as the whereabouts of a witness, phone calls to the office, or other miscellaneous matters that arise during the course of the trial. Your availability to handle these details allows your supervising attorney to concentrate full attention on the trial.

## Trial Motions and Posttrial Motions

We earlier identified such motions as the Motion for Judgment as a Matter of Law, the Motion for a New Trial, and the Motion for Judgment on Partial Findings. You may be called on during trial to assist in the drafting of these motions, as you might for any other motion during the pretrial process.

## The Judgment

As we noted earlier, the final decree of the court, resolving the contested issues of law and fact, is called a "judgment" (see Rule 54(a) of the FRCP). Under Rule 58 of the FRCP, every judgment "shall be set forth on a separate document." This written judgment then becomes effective when entered on the docket of the court, pursuant to Rules 58 and 79(a) of the FRCP. Two principal issues arise with regard to a judgment. First, who prepares and signs it? Second, what must it include?

The answers to these questions depend on the context in which the decision of the court was rendered. Under Rule 58 of the FRCP, where the decision in a jury trial was on a general verdict, or where the decision of the court in a bench trial allows recovery of a "sum certain" or denies all relief, the "clerk, unless the court otherwise orders, shall forthwith prepare, sign, and enter the judgment . . . ." In more theoretically complicated contexts, namely, where the decision in a jury trial was on a special verdict or a general verdict with interrogatories, or where the decision of the court in a bench trial allows some relief other than merely a sum certain, the "court shall promptly approve the form of the judgment, and the clerk shall thereafter enter it." This latter direction means that the judge, not the clerk, must sign these more theoretically complicated judgments.

Attorneys, under Rule 58, do not submit proposed judgments unless directed to do so by the court. Submission of proposed judgments by attorneys is, however, a fairly common practice in state courts. It is generally the prevailing party who will prepare a proposed judgment, since he has the incentive to do it quickly. Any proposed judgment so submitted does not, of course, take effect until officially acted upon in the appropriate manner by the court.

You may be asked to assist in the preparation of proposed judgments, and you will be referencing judgments in the context of appeals and collection matters (discussed later), so we next turn to a consideration of the text of a judgment. Simply stated, under Rule 54 of the FRCP the judgment should be sufficient to "grant the relief to which the party in whose favor it is rendered is entitled . . . ." As we noted in our discussion of bench trials in Section 11–2, the court's decision in a bench trial must include findings of fact and conclusions

Figure 11-9 Sample Notes Relating to a Potential Juror

John Doe

Back row
Seat 4

Age: 26

Occupation: Carpenter — owns his own business

Education: H. S. grad; one year of college

Married, 1 child

Currently suing a contractor who failed to pay on
    sub contract: frustrated with court delays

Says he might not understand complex contract
    but will try to be fair

Wore shirt + tie: demeanor respectful

Appears wishy-washy: unlikely to fight for his
    beliefs, although he indicated
    (with hesitation) that he would stand
    alone if necessary

of law. Such findings and conclusions will either be stated as part of the judgment or set forth separately.

As a general matter, all judgments, both for bench trials and jury trials, must resolve the factual and legal issues presented. The whole point of the judgment is that it should settle the outstanding issues, including the amount of monetary damages awarded. Nevertheless, the form of the judgment is often exceedingly

**Figure 11–10   Typical Questions and Considerations During Voir Dire Questioning**

> *The following areas of inquiry with regard to a potential juror are typical subjects of voir dire questioning:*
>
> (1)  Age
>
> (2)  Cultural background
>
> (3)  Marital status and children
>
> (4)  Occupation
>
> (5)  Residence for previous several years
>
> (6)  Level of education attained
>
> *The following are typical questions asked during voir dire questioning:*
>
> (1)  Are you personally acquainted with the judge or any of the parties or attorneys involved in this case?
>
> (2)  Can you follow the instructions given to you by the judge, even if you disagree with those instructions?
>
> (3)  Have you ever been involved in a lawsuit? If so, how does that affect your attitude towards this case?
>
> (4)  Have you ever served on a jury? If so, how does that affect your attitude toward this case?
>
> (5)  Having just heard a basic description of the nature of this case from the judge, is there anything in his description which prevents you from performing the function of a juror in a fair and impartial manner?
>
> (6)  If everyone else on the jury disagrees with your position, but you feel it is right, will you stand up for what you believe in?
>
> *The following are some considerations to keep in mind during voir dire questioning:*
>
> (1)  The basic attitude of the potential juror: Is he or she belligerent, attentive, curious, polite, or open-minded?
>
> (2)  The physical characteristics of the potential juror: Are the clothes sloppy? Does the grooming reflect an attitude of respect for the judicial process?
>
> (3)  .The "body language" of the potential juror: Does he or she slump and slouch? Recoil at a difficult question? Avoid eye contact when giving answers? Appear nervous when giving a suspect answer?

simple, with little more than an identification of the prevailing party and the damages awarded; complicated legal rationales and findings of fact are saved for written judicial opinions. For an example of a simple judgment following a general jury verdict, see the Judgment in the Widgets and Gizmos, Inc. matter that appears in Figure 11–11, which is based on Form 31 from the Table of Official Forms of the FRCP.

Sometimes a judgment may inaccurately reflect the actual result at trial. If a party seeks an amendment or correction of a clerical error in the text of a judgment, motions to such effect can be made under Rules 59(e) or 60.

You will note a reference in paragraph 2 of Figure 11–11 to the "costs" of the action, which were awarded to the defendant, TapTapTap, Inc., but with no corresponding reference to the amount of such costs. Costs are allowed to the prevailing party under Rule 54(d) of the FRCP, and are presented to the court in

**Figure 11–11 Judgment in the *Widgets and Gizmos, Inc.* Case**

United States District Court
for the
District of Exurbia

WIDGETS AND GIZMOS, INC.

    Plaintiff

       vs.

TAPTAPTAP, INC.

    Defendant

Civil Action No. 93-OWH-00543

December 15, 1994

### Judgment

This action came on trial before the Court and a jury, Honorable O.W. Holmes, District Judge, presiding, and the issues having been duly tried and the jury having duly rendered its verdict, it is hereby ORDERED, ADJUDGED, and DECREED that:

1. the plaintiff, *Widgets and Gizmos, Inc.*, shall take nothing from the defendant, *TapTapTap, Inc.*; and

2. the defendant, *TapTapTap, Inc.*, shall recover the sum of $125,000.00 from the plaintiff, *Widgets and Gizmos, Inc.*, plus its costs in this action as allowed by law.

Dated at Metro City, Exurbia, this 15th day of December, 1994.

_____
Clerk of Court

a document called a **Bill of Costs** (see Figure 11–12), which is thereafter approved by the clerk. Those items which constitute allowable costs are identified by statute or court rules (see, for example, sections 1911 to 1931 of Title 28 of the United States Code, and also review your local federal rules). Allowable costs include such things as filing fees, witness fees, and sheriff's fees for service of process. Recovery of attorney's fees (which can be quite high) is not a standard "cost," but is generally only allowable where authorized by statute or under other extraordinary circumstances.

## Collecting the Judgment

Winning a judgment for money damages does not necessarily mean that a check will soon be in the client's mailbox. Such a judgment is not a guarantee of payment, but rather only a certificate of the right to pursue the assets of the losing party so as to satisfy the judgment. Sometimes, as where an insurance company is involved and no appeal is taken, payment does, in fact, follow soon after judgment, with little associated hassle. But in many cases a party winning a judgment for damages must take steps to enforce that judgment against the losing party. The process of enforcing a judgment by obtaining title and possession of the losing party's assets is known as **execution.** The winning party

**Figure 11–12 Bill of Costs**

---

| **United States District Court** | DISTRICT |
|---|---|
| | DOCKET NO. |
| v. | |
| | MAGISTRATE CASE NO. |

Judgment having been entered in the above entitled action on _____
<br>date

against _____ the clerk is requested to tax the following as costs:

### BILL OF COSTS

Fees of the clerk ................................................................................ $_____

Fees for service of summons and complaint ............................ _____

Fees of the court reporter for all or any part of the transcript
necessarily obtained for use in the case ............................. _____

Fees and disbursements for printing ........................................ _____

Fees for witnesses (itemized on reverse side) ......................... _____

Fees for exemplification and copies of papers necessarily
obtained for use in case ........................................................ _____

Docket fees under 28 U.S.C. § 1923 ....................................... _____

Costs incident to taking of depositions .................................... _____

Costs as shown on Mandate of Court of Appeals .................... _____

Other costs (Please itemize) ..................................................... _____

_____

_____

_____

TOTAL $_____

SPECIAL NOTE: Attach to your bill an itemization and documentation for requested costs in all categories. Briefs should also be submitted supporting the necessity of the requested costs and citing cases supporting taxation of those costs.

### DECLARATION

I declare under penalty of perjury that the foregoing costs are correct and were necessarily incurred in this action and that the services for which fees have been charged were actually and necessarily performed. A copy hereof was this day mailed with postage fully prepaid thereon to:

SIGNATURE OF ATTORNEY _____

FOR: _____ DATE _____
<br>Name of claiming party

| Please take notice that I will appear before the clerk who will tax said costs on the following day and time: | DATE AND TIME |
|---|---|
| Costs are hereby taxed in the following amount and included in the judgment: | AMOUNT TAXED<br>$ |
| CLERK OF COURT | (BY) DEPUTY CLERK | DATE |

*Source:* Official Form of the United States District Court

---

seeking to enforce a judgment is called a **judgment creditor;** the losing party from whom payment is sought is called a **judgment debtor.** You may be involved in drafting documents or taking other steps to facilitate collection of a judgment, so let us review the relevant procedures.

Rule 69 of the FRCP holds that the legal "process" (i.e., the official document) for enforcement of a judgment shall be a **writ of execution.** Issuance of this writ by the court is thus an instrumental step in the execution procedure. The precise procedures that surround the issuance of this writ are not specifically defined under the FRCP, however; Rule 69 holds that execution procedures "shall be in accordance with the practice and procedure of the state in which the district court is held . . . ." Thus, the FRCP authorizes the use of analogous state court procedures, rather than any specific federal procedures; with only a few exceptions, there is no specific federal procedure for execution. Figure 11–13 shows an application for a Writ of Execution to be issued by the U.S. District Court for the District of Connecticut. Instructions to the sheriff and information as to exempt property of the judgment debtor, pursuant to the relevant provisions of state law, accompany processing of the writ. Because certain principles and practices are common to the execution procedures of most states, let us briefly consider a few relevant concepts.

Keep in mind that many state procedures call for a two-step procedure. First, certain forms or filings must be completed and submitted to the court, and court authorization of the execution procedure obtained. Second, after obtaining such court authorization, the judgment creditor generally must retain a sheriff or other authorized official who conducts the actual seizure of assets.

**Figure 11–13    Writ of Execution (Application)**

UNITED STATES DISTRICT COURT
DISTRICT OF CONNECTICUT

WRIT OF EXECUTION
(APPLICATION)

:

Plaintiff                                    :    Civil Action No.

v.                                           :

Defendant                                    :

:

:

ADDRESS OF COURT:                                          DATE OF JUDGMENT:

NAME OF JUDGMENT CREDITOR MAKING APPLICATION:

NAME OF JUDGMENT DEBTOR:

1. Amount of Judgment:
2. Amount of Costs:
3. Total Judgment and Costs:
4. Interest:
5. Total Paid on Account:
6. Total Unpaid Judgment:

SIGNED

_____                Date:
Attorney for Plaintiff
Name and Address
Tel. No.

*Source:* Official Form of the United States District Court, District of Connecticut

The seizure itself can take several forms. A **garnishment** is an execution on property owned by the judgment debtor but held by some third party. For example, a bank account might be garnished (the funds are owned by the judgment debtor, but held by the third-party bank); wages or salary are also subject to garnishment directly from the employer.

Execution on real estate can often be commenced by the placement of a **judgment lien** on the land records, which informs any prospective purchasers that there is an outstanding claim against the property. If the judgment is not otherwise satisfied, the judgment creditor can start a **foreclosure action** based on the judgment lien, and ultimately receive proceeds from the sale of the property up to the amount of the outstanding judgment.

Many states have laws that protect all creditors, including judgment creditors, against **fraudulent conveyances.** An example of a fraudulent conveyance might be a transfer of title to real property with a market value of one million dollars by a husband to his wife for, say, one thousand dollars, where a showing can be made that the transfer was for the purpose of defrauding creditors.

Sometimes the basic problem associated with collecting a judgment is locating assets owned by the judgment debtor. Thus, an important execution tool, authorized by Rule 69 of the FRCP, is **postjudgment discovery.** Rule 69 holds that a creditor "may obtain discovery from any person, including the judgment debtor, in the manner provided by these rules or in the manner provided by the practice of the state in which the district court is held." Thus, a judgment debtor can be examined under oath in a deposition, or can be forced to respond under oath to interrogatories, which inquire into the existence or availability of assets to satisfy a judgment. The questioning would inquire into such things as the judgment debtor's bank accounts, stocks and bonds, real estate, automobiles, personal possessions such as artwork, inheritances, rents and royalties, business records, and employment income.

Rule 64 of the FRCP authorizes "remedies providing for seizure of person or property for the purpose of securing satisfaction of the judgment ultimately to be entered in the action . . . ." These so-called "prejudgment remedies" authorize such things as the **attachment** of property or the filing of a *lis pendens* **notice** on the land records (which indicates to a title searcher that "litigation is pending"); they are not final seizures of property, but rather constitute steps taken to ensure that property will be available to satisfy any judgment ultimately rendered. Once again, the rule does not set out specific federal procedures for obtaining such prejudgment remedies, but rather authorizes their use "under the circumstances and in the manner provided by the law of the state in which the district court is held . . . ." As a general matter, the trend of the laws regarding prejudgment remedies is to make them more difficult to obtain.

The practices of the states vary significantly in the precise manner in which execution of a judgment proceeds, and the details of forms and procedures are often essential to complete an execution. You should review the laws of your state to determine the proper procedures for execution.

## 11–5 Appeals

The losing party at trial often has the right to appeal the decision of the trial court to a higher court. An **appeal** is a review of the actions of the trial court by a higher court. You will recall that in Chapter 1 we identified intermediate appellate courts and high courts as the courts in which appeals are pursued. Appellate practice, like the basic pretrial and trial practice we have been addressing throughout this text, is governed by precise rules that must be carefully followed.

Before we provide some background on the specifics of appellate practice, we need to remind you of a distinction we emphasized in Chapter 1. The purpose of an appeal is not to retry the facts of the case; only in the trial court does a trial take place. In the appellate courts, the actions of the trial court are reviewed with an eye to identifying any errors committed. Improper exclusions or admissions of evidence, incorrect application of the law to the facts found, conclusions of fact grossly inappropriate in light of the evidence admitted—these are the sorts of errors committed by the trial court that might justify an appellate **reversal** (which changes the judgment of the trial court) or a new trial.

Sometimes errors are committed that nevertheless do not, in the eyes of the appellate court, justify changing the ruling of the trial court. For example, a certain piece of evidence might have been wrongfully excluded, but, because other evidence was admitted that made the same point, the exclusion of this evidence is not seen as having had any significant impact on the result of the trial. The error of the trial court in excluding this evidence might thus be considered **harmless error** (see Rule 61 of the FRCP and section 2111 of Title 28 of the United States Code), and the appeal will be denied by the appellate court despite the error.

Appeals generally occur after the conclusion of a trial. Under section 1291 of Title 28 of the United States Code, the federal circuit courts of appeals "shall have jurisdiction of appeals from all *final decisions* of the district courts of the United States . . ." [emphasis supplied]. The idea behind postponing appeals until a final decision is made is that it would be inefficient, and indeed an administrative nightmare, to allow an immediate appeal every time a party or attorney disagreed with some action of the trial court. To allow, for example, an appeal every time an objection to the admission of evidence was overruled (or sustained, for that matter) would lead to trials that drag on almost indefinitely while one appeal after another is resolved in a higher court.

There are, however, a few limited appeals that can proceed before the trial is over. Such appeals are referred to as **interlocutory appeals.** *Interlocutory* means, in this context, "interim" or "preliminary." Under section 1292(a) of Title 28, interlocutory appeals can be made of nonfinal court orders relating to injunctions, appointment of receivers, and admiralty issues. Under 1292(b), appeal is also authorized for any other preliminary order in which the district court judge who issued the order "shall be of the opinion" that the order affects a "controlling question of law" and that "an immediate appeal from the order may materially advance the ultimate termination of the litigation." District judges are not often willing to indicate such an opinion, however, and even when they do the appellate court still retains the ultimate right to disagree and reject the appeal.

Whereas sections 1291 and 1292 of Title 28 of the United States Code authorize the appeals in the federal system, the details of federal appellate procedure are actually spelled out in two other places—the Federal Rules of Appellate Procedure (FRAP, also found in Title 28) and the various local rules for each of the appellate circuits (also found in Title 28). Both the FRAP and the local rules must be carefully consulted; you should keep in mind that the local rules can regulate appellate practice "in any manner not inconsistent with" the FRAP (see Rule 47 of the FRAP).

You should begin to study and master appellate terminology. The losing party at trial who files an appeal, whether originally the plaintiff or the defendant, is called an **appellant.** The other party is called the **appellee.**

Sometimes both parties appeal the ruling of the court; under this situation, the party appealing first is generally considered the appellant, and the other party is considered a **cross-appellant** (see, for example, the 1991 amendment to Rule 28(h) of the FRAP).

As we also noted in Chapter 1, the appellate court reviews the **record** of the trial to determine whether errors have been made. The record is made up of the pleadings, the transcript prepared by the court reporter, and all the evidence (documents and other exhibits) introduced by the parties. The appellate court does not simply review these materials in search of errors, however; the appealing party must identify the specific errors that it asserts constitute valid **grounds for appeal.**

For most appeals, a notice will be filed and possibly also a *bond* indemnifying the other side for costs incurred, if the appeal fails. The filing fee must be paid, and the record forwarded to the court. In some state court systems, a statement of the grounds for appeal must be filed, identifying the specific issues or errors that form the basis for the appeal. A briefing schedule will be established, and legal briefs filed by each party in support of its position. For most appeals the rules of the applicable jurisdiction will be precise on the required procedures; as we noted, it is important to follow the appropriate rules.

In the subsections that follow, we'll assume that Widgets and Gizmos, Inc. lost at trial and has decided to appeal, and we'll identify some of the key provisions of the FRAP that govern such an appeal. Keep in mind that additional facets of the rules not mentioned might become important in the individual case, and thus the rules themselves must always be specifically and carefully consulted. Also keep in mind that your state court's procedures may depart substantially from the federal requirements.

## Notice of Appeal

Under Rule 3 of the FRAP, an appeal of right under sections 1291 or 1292(a) of Title 28 of the United States Code is commenced by the filing of a **Notice of Appeal.** The format for the notice is simple (see Figure 11–14). There is no requirement that the grounds for the appeal be identified; such identification is saved, rather, for the brief. The notice is filed not directly with the appellate court, but rather with the district court clerk's office; the clerk thereafter forwards it to the other parties and to the court of appeals. The court of appeals then enters the appeal onto its docket under the provisions of Rule 12 of the FRAP. Applicable filing fees must be paid to the clerk of the district court (see Rule 3(e) of the FRAP). Deadlines for filing the notice are established in Rule 4 of the FRAP; the basic deadline is 30 days from the date of the entry of the judgment (see Rule 4(a)(1) of the FRAP), but there are certain circumstances entailing different deadlines. Hence you must carefully consult the rules (not to mention your supervising attorney) when questions arise.

Interlocutory appeals are commenced by a **Petition for Permission to Appeal** under Rule 5 of the FRAP (rather than by a Notice of Appeal), which must be filed with the court of appeals (not the

**PARALEGALERT!**

The Notice of Appeal is filed with the District Court, not the Court of Appeals.

**PARALEGALERT!**

The Petition for Permission to Appeal is filed with the Court of Appeals, not with the District Court (unlike the procedure for the Notice of Appeal).

**Figure 11–14  Notice of Appeal**

United States District Court
for the
District of Exurbia

WIDGETS AND GIZMOS, INC.

    Plaintiff

        vs.

TAPTAPTAP, INC.

    Defendant

Civil Action No. 93-OWH-00543

**Notice of Appeal**

Notice is hereby given that *Widgets and Gizmos, Inc.*, plaintiff above-named, hereby appeals to the United States Court of Appeals for the Second Circuit from the final judgment entered in this action on the 15th day of December, 1994.

THE PLAINTIFF, WIDGETS AND GIZMOS, INC.

By: _____
    Samuel Superlawyer, Esq.
    Its attorney
    Lincoln & Hoover
    123 Lincoln Street
    Metro City, Exurbia 12345
    Atty. Reg. #: 87654
    Phone: (901) 222-2222

*[Based on Form 1 from the Appendix of Forms to the Federal Rules of Appellate Procedure. Assume that the State of Exurbia is in the Second Circuit.]*

district court this time) within 10 days of the entry of the order appealed from, and copies must be served on all parties. Note also that the content of this petition (see Rule 5(b) of the FRAP) is significantly more detailed than the Notice of Appeal, requiring a "statement of facts," a "statement of the question itself" (i.e., the issue on which appeal is sought), and a statement as to why "an immediate appeal is justified."

## Bond

Rule 7 of the FRAP authorizes the district court to require the appellant to file a **bond** on appeal. The requirement may be imposed by local rule or may be specific to the individual case. The amount is left to the discretion of the court, but shall be adequate to cover the potential expense of those items identified in Rule 39 of the FRAP, relating to taxable costs (for example, the cost of multiple copies of briefs under Rule 39(c) or copies of the transcript under Rule 39(e)). The purpose of the bond is to protect the opposing party against the costs incurred, should the appeal fail.

## Record on Appeal

Rules 10 and 11 of the FRAP relate, respectively, to the composition of the record on appeal and the manner in which this record is supplied to the appellate court. The scope of the record, as defined by Rule 10, is wide-ranging—all "original papers and exhibits filed in the district court, the transcript of the proceedings, if any, and a certified copy of the docket entries prepared by the clerk of the district court . . . ." Under Rule 10(d), however, this wide-ranging scope can be narrowed to an abbreviated "statement of the case" upon agreement of the parties (subject to district court approval).

The transcript must be ordered by the appellant from the court reporter within ten days of the filing of the notice of appeal under Rule 10(b)(1). A partial transcript containing only those portions of the proceedings applicable to the appeal may be acceptable, but if the appellant orders such a partial transcript, he or she must file (within 10 days) a "statement of the issues" he or she intends to present on appeal, and must further serve the appellee with both a copy of this statement and a copy of the transcript order. Then the appellee can order any further portion of the transcript he or she deems necessary, or move the court for an order compelling the appellant to obtain this further transcript.

Rules 10(c) and 10(e) provide for situations where the record is incomplete, or where there is some dispute over exactly what constitutes the contents of the record. Disputes as to the appropriate content of the record are settled by the district court (i.e., the trial court, not the appellate court).

Rule 11(a) requires the appellant to "take any action necessary to enable the clerk to assemble and transmit the record," and requires that "a single record shall be submitted" to the court of appeals. Special arrangements may have to be made for bulky materials (Rule 11(b)). Rules 11(e) and (f) allow for parts of the record to be retained at the location of the District Court, which may often be more convenient for everyone involved. Finally, the transcript is to be supplied by the court reporter to the court of appeals within 30 days; if the court reporter cannot meet the deadline, an extension must be requested.

## Appellate Briefs

The heart of an appeal is the **appellate brief.** An appellate brief is an extensive and formal memorandum of law arguing the merits of the drafter's position on the appeal. There are actually four types of appellate brief: the **appellant's brief;** the **appellee's brief;** the **reply brief;** and the *amicus curiae* brief. The appellant's brief is filed first ( under Rule 31 of the FRAP, it must be filed within 40 days of the date on which the record is filed, although extensions are frequently granted). The appellee's brief is filed next, within 30 days after service of the appellant's brief. The reply brief, also filed by the appellant, responds to the arguments raised in the appellee's brief. The *amicus curiae* ("friend of the court") brief, under Rule 29 of the FRAP, is filed by a nonparty who asserts an interest in the subject matter of the case and whose participation has been consented to by all parties or by order of the court.

The basic format of a federal appellate brief includes several elements identified in Rule 28 of the FRAP. These include a table of contents; a table of cases, statutes, and authorities; a statement of the issues presented for review; a statement of the subject matter and appellate jurisdiction (a new requirement added by the FRAP amendments of 1991); a statement of the case; an argument; and a short conclusion stating the precise relief sought. Each of these elements is discussed in Figure 11–15.

**Figure 11–15  The Elements of an Appellate Brief**

*Table of Contents:* The various sections of the brief, with corresponding page numbers, are identified in the Table of Contents. This section is included in all briefs filed.

*Table of Cases, Statutes, and Authorities:* An appellate brief frames arguments based upon many judicial opinions, statutes, and other authorities such as treatises or articles in legal journals. The Table of Cases, Statutes, and Authorities collects the citations of these sources in one easily-referenced table. This section is included in all briefs filed.

*Statement of the Issues Presented for Review:* This section contains a concise statement of the grounds on which the appeal is based. This section is included in the appellant's brief; it can also appear in an appellee's brief if the appellee is "dissatisfied with the statement of the appellant" (Rule 28(b) of the FRAP). It is unnecessary to include this section in a reply brief, since the appellant (who files the reply brief) will have previously identified the issues in the appellant's brief.

*Statement of the Subject Matter and Appellate Jurisdiction:* This new section was added by the 1991 amendments to the FRAP. The statement must identify (1) the basis for subject matter jurisdiction in the district court or agency, with citation to applicable statutory provisions and relevant facts which establish jurisdiction, and (2) the basis for jurisdiction in the court of appeals, again referencing applicable statutes and relevant facts (including the filing dates which establish the timeliness of the appeal). The statement shall also indicate either (1) that the appeal is from a "final order or a final judgment" or (2) information establishing that the court has jurisdiction on some "other basis," i.e., interlocutory jurisdiction. According to the advisory committee notes to the 1991 amendment, it was intended to "aid the court of appeals in determining whether it has both federal subject matter and appellate jurisdiction." The section is mandatory in the appellant's brief, again optional for the appellee's brief (appearing only where the appellee is "dissatisfied" with the appellant's statement), and again unnecessary in the reply brief.

*Statement of the Case:* This section is analogous to the "Statement of Facts" in the memorandum of law supporting a Motion for Summary Judgment, which we discussed in an earlier chapter. A basic statement of the nature of the case, the course of proceedings, and the disposition of the case in the court below should be included, followed by a detailed recitation of the facts relevant to the issues presented on the appeal, with appropriate references to the record. This statement is once again optional in the appellee's brief and unnecessary in the reply brief.

*Argument:* This section is the heart of the appellate brief, containing the legal arguments of the filing party. It may be preceded by a summary of the argument. Citations to legal sources and references to the record should be included. This section is obviously included in all briefs filed.

*Conclusion:* Rule 28 calls for a "short conclusion stating the precise relief sought." This section is to be included in both appellant's and appellee's briefs, but is unnecessary in the reply brief.

## Oral Argument

Federal court appeals are generally decided by a **three-judge panel.** A party may suggest the appropriateness of an *in banc* hearing, in which all the judges of the appellate circuit together hear and decide the appeal; the deadline for such a request is "the date on which the appellee's brief is filed" (Rule 35(c)). The court may order such an *in banc* hearing, either after such a suggestion or on its own initiative (see Rule 35 of the FRAP), but *in banc* hearings are not common; Rule 35 indicates that they will ordinarily not be conducted unless "necessary to secure or maintain uniformity" of the court's decisions, or if the appeal "involves a question of exceptional importance."

**Oral argument** is allowed in most federal appeals, unless the local rules provide otherwise. The parties can waive oral argument under Rule 34(f), but even then the court may direct that the argument shall nevertheless proceed, despite the agreement.

It is not inconceivable that you will be in attendance at an appellate argument in a case on which you have worked, but practically speaking it is your supervising attorney on whom the focus of the argument falls. You may be involved in identifying beforehand the key points to emphasize during the actual argument, but even that will more often be a task for attorneys.

Since the appeal is a review of the trial court proceeding, rather than a separate trial, there will be no witnesses or other admissions of evidence. The entire substance of the appeal is thus embodied in the content of the briefs and the course of the oral argument.

## Decision of the Appellate Court and Subsequent Events

The decision of the appellate court usually comes in the form of a written opinion. The judgment is considered "entered" when noted in the docket by the clerk (see Rule 36 of the FRAP). A party dissatisfied with the judgment of the court can file a **Petition for Rehearing** under Rule 40, specifying the errors it purports exist in the decision. The filing must be made "within 14 days after entry of judgment," unless local rules hold otherwise. The petition can request an *in banc* rehearing, even if the original hearing was in front of a three-judge panel. Twenty-one days after entry of judgment is final, with no further petitions for rehearing pending, the court will issue a **mandate** pursuant to Rule 41, incorporating the judgment, the written opinion of the court, and any costs taxed.

Once the decision of the appellate court is final, review by the Supreme Court of the United States may be available. The procedures related to Supreme Court review are complex; if the issue arises, your supervising attorney will probably direct you to assist him or her in researching and reviewing both the Supreme Court rules of procedure, and sections 1251–1259 of Title 28 of the United States Code. You should note that relevant deadlines run from the date of entry of the final judgment of the appellate court, and not from the date of the mandate.

## 11–6  Practical Considerations

The importance of proper preparation for trial cannot be overemphasized. Although you and your supervising attorney will likely have toiled long hours on the tasks presented by the pretrial process, and though most of the groundwork will have been laid by the time of trial, there is simply no substitute for that last "big push" before trial when all the elements of the case are pulled together for trial.

Even if you have been absolutely thorough in every imaginable way throughout the process, you must nevertheless take the time to prepare yet again for trial. It is through the repetition, the review, the updating of research, the re-organization of documents, the renewed analysis of pleadings and motions, the detailed re-evaluation of discovery responses, and the thousand little steps that occur before trial that you and your supervising attorney will minimize potential pitfalls and develop the familiarity with the case that leads to the best possible result at trial.

**Recent Developments**   Between the first and second printing of this book, the Supreme Court of the United States submitted to Congress amendments to the Federal Rules of Civil Procedure and the Federal Rules of Appellate Procedure. Pursuant to Section 2074 of Title 28 of the United States Code, these amendments took effect on December 1, 1993.

The amendments include changes to Rules 16, 50, 52, 54, and 58 of the FRCP. Rule 16 has been modified to allow for a new deadline for the initial scheduling order, as well as to identify additional specific areas appropriate for discussion at a pretrial conference, and to clarify the court's authority to take appropriate actions and to require availability of a party during settlement discussions. Rules 50 and 52 have been clarified to indicate clearly that they may lead to judgments with respect to defenses, as well as claims. Rules 54 and 58 have been modified to account for an expanded procedure with regard to claims for attorneys' fees sought in conjunction with a judgment.

The FRAP have been amended to, among other things: specify more clearly the requirements relating to the identification of the appealing parties; eliminate some deadline pitfalls and/or ambiguities where post-trial motions have been filed; and require in the argument section of certain briefs a statement of the standard of review applicable to the appealable issues.

# SUMMARY

## 11–1

A pretrial conference is a meeting involving the judge, the attorneys, and any unrepresented parties to plan an orderly progression of the action. There are four types of pretrial conference under the FRCP: the discovery conference under Rule 26, and three types of Rule 16 conference. A pretrial scheduling conference, if held, occurs within the first 120 days after the complaint is filed and leads to a scheduling order setting deadlines for discovery, motions, and other pretrial steps. Status conferences monitor the progress of the case, and often involve settlement discussions. The final pretrial conference may also involve settlement discussions, but as settlement becomes unlikely the focus shifts to formulating a plan for trial, including facilitating the admission of evidence. Identification of witnesses and exhibits, stipulating to certain undisputed facts, and organizing other aspects of the trial are appropriate subjects of a final pretrial conference; the end result is the final pretrial order, which can be modified only to prevent manifest injustice. State court pretrials vary, but generally have the same purposes as those in the federal court.

## 11–2

A typical courtroom has two counsel tables, possibly a podium, the bench where the judge sits, a witness box, a jury box, and a gallery for the public. Courtroom principals include the judge, one or more law clerks, the court reporter, a bailiff or sheriff, jurors, the attorneys, paralegals, clients, and witnesses.

For a jury trial, jurors are selected from panels through the *voir dire* process, which involves questioning and challenges (peremptory and for cause). After a jury is selected, the attorneys make opening statements, then the plaintiff presents evidence. The rules of evidence control the presentation. The burden of proof the plaintiff must meet in a civil trial is generally the "preponderance of the evidence" standard. After the plaintiff's counsel has rested, defendant's counsel often makes a Motion for Judgment as a Matter of Law. If the motion is denied, the trial continues with the defendant presenting evidence. This is followed by rebuttal; then, before the case is submitted to the jury, either party can make a Motion for Judgment as a Matter of Law. The jury is thereafter provided jury instructions, begins deliberations, and eventually returns a verdict. The verdict is incorporated into the judgment of the court. After the verdict any Motions for Judgment as a Matter of Law may be renewed, and a Motion for New Trial might also be filed. In state court trials, the Motion for Directed Verdict and Motion for Judgment Notwithstanding the Verdict (JNOV) might still be applicable. After the posttrial motions are resolved, appeal might follow.

In a bench trial, there is no jury, so there is no verdict, only a judgment. Rather than Motions for Judgment as a Matter of Law, a party might file the analogous Motion for Judgment on Partial Findings or Motion to Amend the Judgment.

## 11–3

Trial preparation is extremely important. The scheduling of the trial must be tracked, unless the court sets a "date certain" for the trial. If the date set is inconvenient, a continuance can be requested. Facts should be reviewed to verify that initial investigation was thorough, and to account for recent developments. Elements, defenses, and damages must be matched with the related evidence. Documents must be organized, demonstrative exhibits prepared, and other exhibits organized. Witness *subpoenas* should be prepared and schedules coordinated. Prior research should be organized and updated, new legal issues researched, preliminary jury instructions drafted, and possibly a trial memorandum prepared. Clients and friendly witnesses should be prepared for testifying by reviewing relevant matters, rehearsing (but not over-rehearsing) the testimony, and receiving final instructions. The trial notebook is an essential tool for most litigators; it represents a microcosm of the entire case, with particular emphasis on the trial.

## 11–4

The paralegal's role in jury selection includes coordinating and organizing information received for each juror, drafting appropriate *voir dire* questions, and keeping track of peremptory challenges. Usually the supervising attorney drafts the opening statement, although the paralegal may assist in developing background information. As evidence is presented, the paralegal takes notes, organizes documents and other exhibits, performs last-minute research or investigation tasks, and coordinates details so that the supervising attorney can maintain full attention on the trial. You may be involved in the preparation of trial or posttrial motions. Judgments resolve the factual and legal issues presented by the case. Collecting a money judgment is not automatic; execution procedures involving garnishment, judgment liens, and other measures (including postjudgment discovery to locate assets of the judgment debtor) may be necessary.

## 11–5

In the federal courts, an appeal of right is commenced by filing a Notice of Appeal in the district court. An interlocutory appeal is commenced by filing a Petition for Permission to Appeal with the court of appeals. The record on appeal comprises all original papers and exhibits filed in the district court, the transcript of the trial, and a certified copy of the docket entries; the record can be abbreviated, however, subject to district court approval. Appellate briefs include several key sections that identify the issues presented on appeal, the arguments in favor of the filing party's position, and the authorities that support those arguments. The briefs and the oral argument constitute the substantive aspects of the appeal. Following the decision of the appellate court, the losing party may file a Petition for Rehearing or may seek review by the U.S. Supreme Court.

## 11–6

The importance of trial preparation cannot be overemphasized. The intensive review and reorganization before trial will minimize potential pitfalls and lead to the best possible result at trial.

## REVIEW

### Key Terms

Before proceeding, review the key terms listed below to be sure you understand each one. If necessary, read over the corresponding section of the chapter. When you are ready to test your understanding, answer the Review Questions.

pretrial conference
pretrial memorandum
scheduling conference
scheduling order
standing pretrial scheduling order
status conferences
final pretrial conference
final pretrial order
jury trial
bench trial

court trial
nonjury trial
counsel tables
bench
witness stand
law clerks
bailiff
sheriff
court reporter
jury box
jurors
jury panels
*voir dire*
peremptory challenge
challenge for cause
opening statement
direct examination
cross-examination

leading questions
objections
exception
burden of proof
preponderance of the evidence
clear and convincing evidence
rested
Motion for Judgment as a Matter of Law
rebuttal
jury instructions
verdict
special verdict
general verdict
general verdict with interrogatories
judgment
Motion for New Trial
Motion for Directed Verdict
Motion for Judgment Notwithstanding
 the Verdict
Motion for Judgment JNOV
Motion for Judgment on Partial Findings
Motion to Amend the Judgment
trial list
trial docket
continuance
working copies
trial memorandum
trial notebook
Bill of Costs
execution
judgment creditor
judgment debtor
writ of execution
garnishment
judgment lien
foreclosure action
fraudulent conveyances
postjudgment discovery
attachment
lis pendens notice
appeal
reversal
harmless error
interlocutory appeals
appellant
appellee
cross-appellant
record
grounds for appeal
Notice of Appeal
Petition for Permission to Appeal

bond
appellate brief
appellant's brief
appellee's brief
reply brief
*amicus curiae* brief
three-judge panel
in banc
oral argument
Petition for Rehearing
mandate

## Questions for Review and Discussion

1. What are the four types of pretrial conference under the FRCP?
2. What are some of the considerations addressed in a final pretrial conference?
3. What is meant by the term *voir dire*?
4. What is the difference between a peremptory challenge and a challenge for cause?
5. What is the standard burden of proof for a typical civil trial?
6. What is the function of a Motion for Judgment as a Matter of Law?
7. Why must the scheduling of a trial be monitored, and how is this done?
8. What are some of the considerations to be kept in mind when preparing a witness to testify?
9. List some of the sections of a typical trial notebook, and explain the importance of each.
10. What is meant by the record on appeal?

## Activities

1. Contact your local federal court clerk's office, and arrange to observe the selection of a jury for a trial.
2. Contact your local state court clerk's office, and arrange to observe a short bench trial from start to finish. The clerks should be able to identify a trial of the appropriate length.
3. Review your state's procedures regarding post-judgment discovery and execution on a judgment.

# CHAPTER 12 Administrative Hearings, Arbitration, and Alternative Dispute Resolution

## OUTLINE

## COMMENTARY

Let's go back in time. It's just a few days after Edgar Ellison originally came to your supervising attorney with information about the dispute between Widgets and Gizmos, Inc. and TapTapTap, Inc. No complaint has yet been filed; there has been only the exchange of some correspondence between your firm and attorneys for TapTapTap, Inc.

Sam Superlawyer calls you into his office for a brief conference. It seems an interesting proposal has been made by TapTapTap, Inc. In recognition of the fact that the dispute is unlikely to be resolved quickly, and mindful of the potential expense of a lawsuit, the attorneys for TapTapTap, Inc. have suggested submitting the matter to a private company, "Quick Resolutions, Inc.," which provides a forum in which parties can attempt to reach accord without incurring the expense of litigation in the courts. The staff of "Quick Resolutions, Inc." includes retired judges and experienced trial attorneys who have devised a streamlined system for the resolution of business disputes. Superlawyer asks you to look into this company and prepare a memo explaining the services they provide.

## OBJECTIVES

Throughout this book we have focused on the court system as the principal forum in which disputes are resolved. There are, however, other mechanisms and forums in which "litigation" (as we have defined it) takes place. After completing Chapter 12, you'll be able to:

1. Explain the function of an administrative agency.
2. Identify two sources for the text of federal regulations.
3. List four major areas of concern addressed by the federal Administrative Procedure Act (APA).
4. Explain the purpose of the rule-making provisions of the APA.
5. Explain what is meant by exhaustion of administrative remedies.
6. Explain what is meant by court-annexed arbitration.
7. Identify a set of rules commonly employed in private arbitration.
8. Explain what a mediator does.
9. Identify some factors that might induce parties to resolve their disputes through mediation.
10. List three qualities of a good mediator.

## 12–1  Administrative Hearings and Procedure

In Chapter 1 we defined "civil litigation" to include mechanisms for dispute resolution beyond the court system. Our text to this point, however, has been concerned with litigation in the courts. In this chapter we look at several nonjudicial forums for the adjudication of disputes, beginning with one of the most common and important of these: the **administrative hearing.**

To help you understand fully the nature of an administrative hearing, we begin our analysis one step further back—by introducing the concept of an **administrative agency.** Administrative agencies are governmental institutions established by statute and intended to implement stated legislative policy. The modern era of administrative agencies began in 1887 with the creation by Congress of the Interstate Commerce Commission (ICC); explosive growth in the number of federal administrative agencies, however, began in the 1930s. We focus in this section on the federal administrative structure; keep in mind that there are many state administrative agencies as well.

> **PARALEGALERT!**
>
> Although we have defined "civil litigation" broadly enough to include the nonjudicial forums discussed in this chapter, many people apply the term only to that dispute resolution which takes place in the courts.

The basic justification for the creation of administrative agencies is that certain activities or situations requiring government regulation are so complicated that it would be unwieldy to require the legislature to pass statutes to address every relevant detail; hence the legislature creates an administrative agency charged with the responsibility to pursue certain broadly stated objectives with regard to the activity or situation in question. The agency then develops more detailed and specific guidelines and procedures designed to achieve the broad objectives of the legislative mandate. The generic name given to the rules, regulations, guidelines, and procedures of administrative agencies is **administrative law.** Other examples of federal administrative agencies, besides the ICC, are the Environmental Protection Agency (EPA) and the Federal Communications Commission (FCC); as noted, there are also many state administrative agencies.

Administrative agencies have been described as embodying, in one institution, the functions of all three of our traditional governmental branches—legislative, executive, and judicial (see Figure 12–1). They pass rules and regulations, like a legislature; they execute and enforce these rules and

**Figure 12–1    The Functions of a Typical Administrative Agency**

> *An administrative agency embodies, in one institution, the functions of all three of our traditional governmental branches—legislative, executive, and judicial:*
>
> (1)  issuing rules and regulations, in the manner of a legislature;
>
> (2)  executing and enforcing these rules and regulations, in the manner of the executive branch; and
>
> (3)  adjudicating disputes, in the manner of the judicial branch.

regulations, like the executive branch; and they resolve disputes, like the judicial branch. The application (as well as the limits) of such broad powers must be carefully defined; indeed, in the 1940s, as the impact of federal administrative agencies grew, it became apparent that there was a need for certain standardized guidelines applicable to the practices of all federal agencies. Thus, in 1946 Congress passed the Administrative Procedure Act (APA), which is found in Title 5 of the United States Code. The most important provisions of that act, for our purposes, are found in sections 551 to 706 of Title 5, to which we will make frequent reference.

Before we begin our discussion of the APA, let's touch first on a fundamental (and practical) concern: where can a researcher (such as a paralegal) find the text of federal regulations issued by federal administrative agencies? The answer: in two places, the *Federal Register* and the *Code of Federal Regulations.* The *Federal Register*, a daily publication of the United States government, is the most immediate source of the text of administrative rules and regulations, both those that have merely been proposed and those that are newly adopted. Each day in the *Federal Register* will be found pages and pages of information regarding the administrative process, including full text of rules and required legal notices of certain agency activities. Most major law libraries have current copies of the *Federal Register;* you should inspect a few issues on your next research trip.

**PARALEGALERT!**

The text of both proposed rules and newly adopted rules is issued on a daily basis in the *Federal Register*; all those rules and regulations currently in force are published annually in the *Code of Federal Regulations*.

Because the *Federal Register* publishes the rules and regulations of a large number of agencies in, essentially, the chronological order of their issuance (irrespective of subject matter), and because it includes proposed regulations as well as those actually adopted, it is a cumbersome research tool. Virtually all the regulations that are in force are collected annually, however, in a multivolume publication called the *Code of Federal Regulations* (cited as C.F.R.). By checking the most recent C.F.R., and subsequent issues of the *Federal Register*, you can develop an accurate picture of the text of regulations currently in force. You should also take a few minutes, on your next law library visit, to review both the C.F.R. and sections 1501 et seq. of Title 44 of the United States Code, which establish the *Federal Register* and the *Code of Federal Regulations*.

Now on to our consideration of the APA. The APA addresses four major areas of concern: (1) access of the public to agency information; (2) agency rulemaking powers; (3) agency adjudication procedures; and (4) the right to appeal an adverse agency decision to the courts (see Figure 12–2). We look at each of these areas, then briefly consider administrative procedure in the state law context.

**Figure 12–2    Four Key Issues Addressed by the Administrative Process**

> (1)  Access of the public to agency information
>
> (2)  Agency rulemaking powers
>
> (3)  Agency adjudication procedures
>
> (4)  Right to appeal an adverse agency decision

## Access to Information

Agencies gather much information in performing their functions. Indeed, they are often charged with responsibility for conducting in-depth investigations of various problems or issues in their particular area of expertise. The public, not surprisingly, began demanding access to the information gathered and maintained by these agencies. The response of the federal government to these public demands can be found in three sections of the APA: section 552, frequently referred to as the Freedom of Information Act; section 552a, the Privacy Act of 1974; and section 552b, the Government in the Sunshine Act. These three acts give to citizens express access to information in the hands of federal administrative agencies, with certain exceptions related to national security, confidentiality, or proprietary business concerns.

The Freedom of Information Act (FOIA) is found in section 552 of the APA. It makes accessible to private individuals unpublished information held by the government, unless the information falls within one of nine exempt categories (including, as mentioned, such things as classified national security materials, trade secrets obtained from private parties, and certain law enforcement investigatory records). A request made under the FOIA is proper if it "reasonably describes" the materials sought (section 552(a)(3)), and fees may be charged for the direct costs of searching for, reviewing, and photocopying the materials (section 552(a)(4)).

The Privacy Act of 1974 is found in section 552a of the APA. It restricts the right of agencies to maintain extensive files on individuals unless such information is "relevant and necessary" to further a lawful purpose of the agency (section 552a(e)). It also provides to an individual, upon request, access to any file pertaining to him or her maintained by an agency (section 552a(d)). In addition, it restricts the right of an agency to divulge information about an individual to others (section 552a(b)).

The interplay between the right of access to information given by the FOIA and the ability of individuals to restrict access to such information if it pertains to them under the Privacy Act of 1974 can get complicated, despite the exception for FOIA matters found in section 552a(b)(2) of the Privacy Act of 1974. If such issues present themselves in a matter on which you are working, you will have to do further research and consult your supervising attorney.

The Government in the Sunshine Act is found in Section 552b of the APA. With specified exceptions, it holds that "every portion of every meeting of an agency shall be open to public observation." The term "meeting" is broadly defined in the statute (section 552b(a)(2)) so as to encourage open conduct of government affairs.

## Rulemaking

The basic federal statute relating to agency rule-making is section 553 of the APA. That statute provides for (1) required public notice of proposed rulemak-

## PARALEGALERT!

The rulemaking provisions of the APA are designed to provide for (1) public notice of proposed rulemaking, (2) public input into the content of rules, (3) public hearings on the content and adoption of rules, (4) publication of rules adopted, and (5) the right of the public to seek amendment or repeal of a rule.

## PARALEGALERT!

Most rulemaking hearings conducted under the APA are informal, and are referred to as "notice and comment" proceedings.

ing by an agency, (2) the opportunity for public input into such rulemaking, (3) public hearings regarding proposed rules, where required by statute, (4) publication of rules ultimately adopted, and (5) the right of the public to seek amendment or repeal of a rule.

Notice of proposed rulemaking is given in the *Federal Register* (see section 553(b) of the APA). A notice of proposed rulemaking that appears in the *Federal Register* includes (1) a statement of the time, place, and nature of any public rulemaking proceedings; (2) reference to the legal authority (often the authorizing statute) underlying the rule; and (3) the terms of the proposed rule or a description of the subjects and issues involved (see section 553(b)(3)).

Opportunity for public input into the rulemaking process is addressed in section 553(c) of the APA. Under that section, interested persons "shall" be given the opportunity to participate in the rulemaking process "through submission of written data, views, or arguments with or without opportunity for oral presentation." Where formal public hearings are required "by statute," such formal hearings must be held according to the terms of sections 556 and 557 of the APA (discussed in the next subsection). Most rulemaking hearings under the APA are conducted in a more informal manner, however. This informal manner, which is sometimes referred to as "notice and comment," involves public hearings where individuals may present their opinions or other information, but with no opportunity for cross-examination and no application of other formal rules of evidence.

Members of the public even have the opportunity to petition for the issuance of their own proposed rule, under section 553(e).

Publication of any substantive rule adopted "shall be made not less than 30 days before its effective date" (section 553(d)), and shall include a "concise general statement" of the "basis and purpose" of the rule (section 553(c).

Finally, after a rule is adopted, members of the public have the right to petition for the amendment or repeal of the rule (section 553(e)).

The foregoing provides you with a brief sketch of the rulemaking process. There are certain exceptions carved out in section 553 (for example, section 553 does not apply to matters involving "a military or foreign affairs function of the United States," section 553(a)(1)), and there may be other rules and procedures that apply in the specific instance (such as practices and guidelines specific to a given agency), so if you are faced with issues involving administrative rulemaking, you should be sure to conduct thorough research and consult with your supervising attorney.

## Administrative Adjudication

The need for a specific administrative adjudication procedure exists because the actions of administrative agencies affect the rights and property of citizens, sometimes substantially. Citizens are entitled, under the Constitution, to have such interests protected from any encroachment occurring without "due process of law"; hence a procedure must be provided that meets minimum due process requirements. The administrative adjudication procedures are set forth, essentially, in sections 554 to 557 of the APA. They establish the true "litigation" aspect of administrative law.

As noted in the previous section, certain rulemaking proceedings are required by statute to be conducted as formal adjudication hearings. Most formal adjudication hearings, however, are held not to further the general rulemaking function, but rather to resolve such matters as the issuance of licenses or the enforcement of regulations against specific individuals or organizations. Evidence on these matters is presented to, and evaluated by, the agency, and a decision is thereafter rendered.

**PARALEGALERT!**

Administrative adjudication procedures, which are the true "litigation" aspect of administrative law, are designed to satisfy the "due process" requirements of the U.S. Constitution.

The trier-of-fact and presiding officer in an administrative adjudication is often an **administrative law judge,** a quasi-judicial official appointed under section 3105 of Title 5. Under section 556(c), "employees presiding at hearings" (as noted, often administra-tive law judges) have the authority to (1) administer oaths, (2) issue subpoenas, (3) make evidentiary rulings, (4) allow depositions, (5) regulate the course of a hearing, and (6) make or recommend a decision, among other things.

In considering the adjudication function of an administrative agency, an immediate problem presents itself: the potential for conflict. As we noted earlier, an administrative agency embodies many governmental functions in one institution: it makes rules and enforces them, and in enforcing rules it acts as investigator, prosecutor, and judge. It is the confluence of these multiple functions that presents the potential for conflict. Section 554(d) of the APA thus explicitly holds (with just a few exceptions) that a person "engaged in the performance of investigative or prosecuting functions for an agency in a case may not, in that or a factually related case, participate or advise in the decision" resulting from an adjudication.

The procedures related to an administrative hearing are fairly straightforward. Parties are generally entitled to notice of the time and place of the hearing, the jurisdiction asserted by the agency, and the nature of the hearing and matters of fact and law at issue (section 554(b)). They are entitled to present evidence (section 554(c) and 556(d)) and may be represented by counsel or "other qualified representative," depending on the rules of the agency (section 555). It is thus possible that a paralegal might qualify to represent a party in an administrative hearing.

**PARALEGALERT!**

Under some circumstances, a paralegal may be authorized to represent a client at an administrative hearing.

The official rules of evidence do not apply at an agency hearing, although the presentation of evidence is by no means unrestricted. Evidence that is "irrelevant, immaterial, or unduly repetitious" may be excluded. Parties are authorized to submit oral or documentary evidence, rebuttal evidence, "and to conduct such cross-examination as may be required for a full and true disclosure of the facts" (section 556(d)).

The decision made by the administrative law judge is to be based on the record and is to be made within a reasonable time, including "prompt notice" of a denial of a written application or petition (section 555). As noted, hearings can range from enforcement adjudications directed against specifically identified regulation violators to general hearings regarding rulemaking at which inter-

## PARALEGALERT!

Although the official rules of evidence do not apply at an agency hearing, evidence that is "irrelevant, immaterial, or unduly repetitious" may be excluded by the administrative law judge or the presiding officer.

ested parties offer evidence. It is important for you to research all applicable rules when your work assignments involve a specific administrative hearing; this may include certain provisions outside the APA that are specific to the process in a given agency.

Under section 702 of Title 5, a "person suffering legal wrong because of agency action, or adversely affected or aggrieved by agency action . . ., is entitled to judicial review thereof." Thus, an administrative adjudication, though final and binding if judicial review is not sought, can also lead to litigation in the courts. Under section 703, the form of the judicial review is "the special statutory review proceeding" defined by the applicable statutes, or in the absence of such statutes, "any applicable form of legal action" in a court of "competent jurisdiction," usually a United States District Court.

A key concept relating to judicial review is the **exhaustion of administrative remedies.** Under section 704 of Title 5, only those agency actions that are made reviewable by statute or that constitute "final agency action" can be reviewed. What this means is that, if the applicable administrative action is reviewable within the administrative framework, and no statute specifically authorizes judicial review, then no judicial review may be had until the final review process within the administrative framework has been completed.

## PARALEGALERT!

Under the doctrine of "exhaustion of administrative remedies," only final agency actions are reviewable.

The civil action seeking judicial review is brought against "the United States, the agency by its official title, or the appropriate officer" (section 703). The court reviewing the appeal has the authority to compel the agency to take certain actions, or to set aside agency actions found to be arbitrary, capricious, an abuse of discretion, contrary to constitutional or statutory rights, unsupported by the evidence, or otherwise flawed (see section 706 of the APA). The court generally reviews the record of the administrative agency, rather than conducting a new hearing; it thus acts as an appellate court. On those occasions when the court starts from scratch and hears the evidence all over again, the proceeding is called a **trial** *de novo.*

Where necessary to prevent irreparable harm, or when justice so requires, both the agency itself and the reviewing court have the authority to postpone the effective date of actions taken by the agency, pending the conclusion of the judicial review proceedings (section 705 of the APA).

### State Law Administrative Procedure

Our focus in this section has been on administrative procedure as practiced in the federal system, under the APA. The states also have administrative agencies with many and varied procedural rules and requirements. Many of the states have adopted some version of the Model State Administrative Procedure Act (1981) of the Uniform Law Commissioners (found in Volume 15 of the *Uniform Laws Annotated*, West Publishing Co. (1990)).

Because the administrative and judicial systems of every state differ, the manner in which the model act has been adopted can vary substantially with regard to such details as notice requirements and procedures for judicial review. These details are important when pursuing a particular matter. In general, however, the theories and goals of the model state act are similar to the federal APA.

The 1981 revision of the model act was extensive, expanding the precision and particularity with which its provisions addressed various issues of administrative law. The former version (adopted in 1961) was more straightforward, along the lines of the APA.

Most states have provisions that regulate the four key areas of administrative law addressed by the APA: access to information; rulemaking; administrative adjudication; and judicial review. You should be sure to review your state's administrative procedure provisions, and compare them to both the corresponding sections of the model act and the APA.

## 12–2  Arbitration

**Arbitration** is a means of dispute resolution in which the neutral third party resolving contested issues is some person (called an **arbitrator**) or group of persons (called a **panel of arbitrators**) other than a judge and jury. Arbitration really encompasses two distinct areas of dispute resolution. The first is generally called **court-annexed arbitration** (other terms meaning essentially the same thing are **judicially linked arbitration** or **statutory arbitration**), in which the dispute is resolved under official statutes and procedural rules in some alternative manner but within the judicial system. The second is called **private arbitration,** in which the dispute is resolved outside the court system.

To the extent that "alternative dispute resolution" (sometimes called ADR) is defined as including any alternative to traditional litigation in the courts, both court-annexed and private arbitration fit the definition. Even if ADR is defined to include only private sector alternatives to the courts, private arbitration, at least, would still be considered "alternative dispute resolution." Nevertheless, we have chosen to discuss private and court-annexed arbitration in a section of their own for two reasons. First, since court-annexed arbitration is so closely related to the traditional judicial system, it is appropriate to consider it separately. Second, since private arbitration is a form of alternative dispute resolution with a long history, it provides a useful entrée into the discussion in the next section of more recent developments in the burgeoning field of alternative dispute resolution.

Let's begin with a consideration of court-annexed arbitration.

PARALEGALERT!

Private arbitration is really a method of alternative dispute resolution.

### Court-Annexed Arbitration

As noted, when considering alternatives to the traditional process of litigation in the courts, it is common to focus on those alternatives that have been developed in the private sector, and indeed, we introduce you to many such nongovernmental avenues to dispute resolution in the remainder of this chapter. In this subsection, however, we talk about a constructive development within the judicial system itself—court-annexed arbitration.

Beginning in the 1950s, many state court systems began developing, by court rules and by statute, mechanisms for the resolution of disputes within the judicial system but without (at least initially) the application of formal judicial procedures (such as the participation of a judge or jury, or the imposition of the formal rules of evidence). These mechanisms were established in recognition of the fact that the expense, the complexity, and the delays associated with a typical lawsuit often made it an unattractive means of resolving certain types of disputes, and that some official alternative might be of benefit. These various systems are often grouped together under the heading of court-annexed arbitration.

There is significant variety between and among the various court-annexed arbitration systems that have been adopted by the states. Some are little more than informal efforts to evaluate the competing positions of the parties and recommend a resolution; others are more formalized, involving presentation of evidence (which may or may not be governed by the offical rules of evidence) and the creation of a record. Some involve the rendering of a decision on both questions of fact and questions of law; others are limited to fact finding. Some are mandatory; some are voluntary.

As a result of this variety, it is somewhat difficult to generalize about court-annexed arbitration, but it is possible to identify a few key considerations to keep in mind when researching the details of a particular system (see Figure 12–3). First, you must determine the nature of the disputes to which the court-annexed arbitration will be addressed. There are often jurisdictional limits applied to the amount in dispute (for example, only those matters in which the amount in dispute is less than $15,000) or the subject matter of the dispute (for example, perhaps only contract cases).

Second, you must determine the identity of the arbitrator, who acts as the judge. Statutes and rules often allow for certain qualified and experienced attorneys (five years of active practice is a commonly applied cutoff) to perform as arbitrators. The use of such attorneys in this role often enables a court system to resolve pending matters much more expeditiously than would be possible with the limited number of full-fledged judges. You must also note the manner in which the final selection of an arbitrator is made; sometimes the arbitrator will be appointed by the court, sometimes selected from a list by agreement of the parties.

Third, you must identify the procedural requirements that govern the proceeding: Are the rules of evidence applicable? Is it merely fact-finding, or will questions of law be addressed? What are the pleading requirements? Discovery rights? Where will the hearings be held, in a courtroom or somewhere else? What form will the award take? All these things are important considerations,

**Figure 12–3  Factors to Consider When Analyzing a System of Court-Annexed Arbitration**

> (1) The nature of the disputes to which the court-annexed arbitration process is addressed (for example, jurisdictional limits as to subject matter or amount in dispute)
>
> (2) The identity and manner of selection of the arbitrator
>
> (3) Procedural requirements governing the process (for example, applicability of the rules of evidence, or applicability to both questions of fact and questions of law)
>
> (4) Nature of appeal process and penalty provisions

and the answers will be found in the statutes and rules establishing and defining the process.

Fourth, you must determine one final and very important procedural consideration that bears separate mention: the availability of, and requirements surrounding, appeal of the arbitrator's decision. You must identify time limits and comply with them. Many court-annexed arbitration decisions, if appealed (and if the decision on appeal is not more favorable to the appealing party than was the original arbitrator's award), lead to the imposition of a penalty (often the costs associated with either the arbitration or the appeal) on the appealing party. The purpose of this penalty is to provide a disincentive to a losing party to file a questionable appeal; such penalty provisions must be identified and evaluated prior to any appeal being filed.

Court-annexed arbitrations are by no means limited to state court systems. The federal courts began experimenting with court-annexed arbitration in 1978 (in pilot programs limited to the Eastern District of Pennsylvania, Northern District of California, and the District of Connecticut). In 1988 Congress enacted sections 651–658 of Title 28 of the United States Code, which represent an expanded five-year experiment in court-annexed arbitration taking place in 10 to 20 judicial districts. The specific rules applicable vary from one district to another; indeed, one of the purposes of the experiment is to evaluate the actual performance of various alternative rules. Section 655 offers to the involved parties a right to a trial *de novo* if they are not satisfied with the results of the arbitration, with penalty provisions similar to those described, but also requiring a showing of "bad faith" in taking the appeal (in effect making this only a light disincentive for those contemplating appeals).

Under the federal system, any civil action may be arbitrated if the parties so consent (section 652(a)(A)). Arbitration can be made compulsory if the amount in controversy is less than $100,000, exclusive of interest and costs (section 652(a)(B); the cap is $150,000 in certain other districts that had established a higher cap at the time section 652 was promulgated).

You should review both your state's court-annexed arbitration procedure (if you live in one of the majority of states that have such provisions), and sections 651–658 of Title 28 of the United States Code. In addition, if you live in one of the federal districts in which the arbitration experiment is proceeding, review your local federal rules regarding arbitration (if not, on your next trip to a law library review the local rules of one of those other districts in which the experiment is proceeding, such as rules 500–1 to 500–8 of the Northern District of California, or rule 300–9 of the Western District of Texas).

**PARALEGALERT!**

If the decision rendered in a court-annexed arbitration is appealed, and the decision on the appeal is not more favorable to the appealing party than was the original arbitrator's award, a penalty will often be imposed against the appealing party.

## Private Arbitration

As we noted above, private arbitration is really a form of alternative dispute resolution, a topic we explore further in the next section. Private arbitration provides an alternative to the judicial system, allowing the parties to resolve their dispute in some manner acceptable to all.

Private arbitrations of one sort or another have been used as an alternative to the judicial system for centuries. In the 1920s Congress recognized the value of such private dispute resolution by passing arbitration legislation (now found in sections 1–16 and 201–208 of Title 9 of the United States Code) that accomplishes (among other things) two objectives: (1) it provides for the recognition by the courts of the validity and enforceability of arbitration awards, and (2) it makes written agreements to arbitrate enforceable.

The first of these two objectives is straightforward. By providing for the recognition of an award by the courts, the legislation prevents a party losing at arbitration from getting a "second bite of the apple" by bringing the dispute to the court system.

The importance of the second objective is perhaps less immediately apparent but, upon closer inspection, no less significant. The legislation provides that a valid written agreement to arbitrate a dispute is binding on the parties, so that even if the claim could have been brought directly to the court in the absence of the agreement to arbitrate, the existence of the agreement to arbitrate forestalls any attempt by one of the parties to ignore the agreement and bring the case to court anyway (unless all parties agree to waive the agreement).

The trend in the federal courts has been to expand the enforceability of arbitration agreements, even into areas where in past years enforceability was questioned. In the area of securities law, for example, where for years arbitration clauses were often looked at askance by the courts, recent Supreme Court decisions have favored arbitration. In addition, the recently adopted section 16 of Title 9 has served to limit the ability of a party questioning the arbitrability of a dispute to appeal the decision of a United States District Court staying a court action and ordering arbitration to proceed; now such decision cannot generally be appealed until after the arbitration has been completed.

Many of the same concepts embodied in the federal legislation are also seen in state statutes (indeed, there were a few such state statutes in effect at the time the federal legislation was originally passed). You should review the statutes in your state that regulate private arbitration, and you should also take a look at the Uniform Arbitration Act (1955) of the Uniform Law Commissioners (found in Volume 7 of the *Uniform Laws Annotated,* West Publishing Co. (1985)).

Arbitration clauses themselves can be mandatory or voluntary at the option of the parties; they can call for arbitration that is binding or nonbinding; they can be drafted and included in a contract long before a dispute has arisen, or they can be drafted after a dispute has arisen as an alternative to litigation in the courts. Quite often, however, the events that lead to an arbitration follow a familiar pattern: a binding arbitration clause is placed in a contract, before any dispute has developed; the dispute develops; the parties thereafter proceed to arbitrate. What are some of the key considerations surrounding this pattern?

The first consideration involves the drafting of the contract clause. The parties generally identify the rules that will govern the arbitration—often by referencing the Commercial Arbitration Rules of the American Arbitration Association (AAA), which establish such things as the number of arbitrators (Rule 17), the procedure for setting the date and time of a hearing (Rule 21), the mode of presentation of evidence (usually at the discretion of the arbitrator, Rule 31), and the form of the award (in writing and signed by a majority of arbitrators, Rule 42). There are other sets of rules that are often referenced to cover specific types of disputes (for example, the Securities Arbitration Rules of the AAA; the Construction Industry Arbitration Rules of the AAA; the Code of Arbitration Procedure of the National Association of Securities Dealers, Inc.). Finally, the parties can modify the rules chosen in many different ways (for example, allocating the costs of the arbitration; identifying the laws that will govern the dispute; specifying the allowable scope and format of awards).

Other considerations to be kept in mind flow out of the ground rules ultimately agreed upon by the parties. The arbitrator (or arbitrators) must be selected; the scope of the issues that are arbitrable identified; the means of invoking the arbitration clause must be defined (usually by a written demand for arbitration); the place of the hearing (often the office of the arbitrator) must be set.

Recourse to arbitration is often beneficial in complicated areas where specific expertise on the part of the arbitrator is helpful. Construction contract disputes, for example, often present extremely complicated issues that can be foreign and confusing to judges and juries who lack the requisite expertise, and hence are often arbitrated by experts in the field. Patent and copyright disputes and labor/management disputes are other examples of complex matters in which arbitration is commonly used.

Professional sports have provided another high-profile arena for arbitration. In major league baseball, for example, salary disputes often go to arbitration, and such disputes provide a good example of the manner in which the parties to an arbitration can, by agreement, control and modify the procedure. The arbitrator in a baseball salary dispute does not independently determine a fair award after hearing the evidence. Rather, each side presents a figure, and the arbitrator must choose between the two figures presented; he or she has no authority to suggest or mandate some compromise figure.

## 12–3 Alternative Dispute Resolution

Much has been written about the "explosion" of litigation that has occurred in the United States. As a result of the great number of lawsuits filed each year, the courts have become overcrowded, with litigants often facing long delays (sometimes years) before trials can be scheduled. These delays add frustration and often additional expense to what is at best a difficult and expensive process.

As the level of frustration with traditional litigation has risen, interest in finding alternative methods by which disputes can be administered and resolved has increased. Arbitration is but one of many such methods that have been categorized under the generic name of **alternative dispute resolution.** Alternative dispute resolution is generally considered to include those forms or methods of dispute resolution to which disputing parties can avail themselves as an alternative to formal, governmental dispute resolution procedures such as litigation in the courts (see Figure 12–4 for a comparison of several methods of alternative dispute resolution).

**Figure 12–4  Comparison of Several Methods of Alternative Dispute Resolution**

*Conciliation:* The neutral third-party, who has *no authority* to issue a resolution of the dispute binding upon the parties, acts as a "go-between," shuttling information back and forth between parties who wish to avoid face-to-face negotiation.

*Mediation:* The neutral third-party (called a *mediator*), who *also* has no authority to issue a resolution of the dispute binding upon the parties, attempts, through participation in the face-to-face negotiations of the parties, to assist them in reaching an agreement which resolves their dispute.

*Private Arbitration:* The neutral third-party (called an *arbitrator*) is empowered to issue a resolution of the dispute *binding* upon the parties (unless the arbitration is some non-binding hybrid method of alternative dispute resolution).

*Mock Trial:* A "quasi-trial" often conducted with the assistance of a private dispute-resolution company, in which the parties are free to define the ground rules and are seeking a non-binding example of one possible outcome should the case go to an actual trial. Sometimes a single party will utilize a mock trial without the participation of the other side, as a means of preparing for an actual trial.

The growth and scholarly study of alternative dispute resolution is a relatively new and exciting phenomenon. We do not even pretend to be able to cover this field adequately in just a few pages. We can, however, introduce a few concepts that will provide an introduction. You should note that terminology associated with the many forms of alternative dispute resolution varies somewhat; the definitions we provide are, however, generally understood and accepted.

## Conciliation

**Conciliation** is a form of dispute resolution where the neutral third party serves as a "go-between," shuttling information back and forth between parties who wish to avoid face-to-face negotiation. Since the third party is generally not empowered to impose a binding resolution, this form of dispute resolution does not fit our definition of litigation. It can serve, however, to resolve a dispute before it escalates to a level requiring greater authority on the part of the third party. Although potentially useful, resort to conciliation is not common.

## Mediation

**Mediation** is a form of dispute resolution that also fails to fit precisely our definition of civil litigation, because once again the neutral third party who administers the dispute (in this case called a **mediator**) does not have the authority to issue a decision binding upon the disputants. Mediation can be defined as a process in which a neutral third party (i.e., the mediator) attempts, through participation in the face-to-face negotiation of the disputing parties, to assist these parties in reaching an agreement that resolves their dispute. Since the mediator has no authority over the parties, if the mediation fails the parties may eventually end up in court. Mediation is far more commonly seen than is conciliation.

What factors might induce parties to resort to mediation? Perhaps the most important factor is a mutual desire to minimize antagonism. For example, parties who are linked in some way (for example, management and a union in a labor dispute) often attempt to mediate their disputes, since they will have to coexist after the dispute is resolved. Hence all benefit from a resolution achieved in a relatively amicable manner. Interfamily disputes are likewise good candidates for mediation, for the same reason.

A second factor is a desire to keep costs low. Because mediation can be conducted in a relatively informal manner, it is often one of the least expensive methods for dispute resolution.

A third factor might be a desire to resolve a dispute quickly. Again, because of the informality, mediation can often resolve a matter fairly quickly.

There may be other considerations inducing parties to mediate. A desire to keep the dispute private is furthered by mediation (this goal is also fostered by private arbitration or other forms of private alternative dispute resolution). If the parties are unwilling to risk total defeat to achieve total victory (a prospect that is present where evidence is presented and a binding decision rendered), then mediation provides a useful alternative (in mediation, compromise is often achieved and, in any event, the parties cannot be bound until they agree to be bound).

### PARALEGALERT!

A mediator does not have the authority to render a resolution binding upon the disputants; rather, he or she attempts through participation in face-to-face negotiation to assist the parties in negotiating a settlement.

Ultimately, mediation can be thought of as an organized face-to-face settlement effort. Indeed, when a judge assists the parties in their settlement efforts at a pretrial conference, he or she is acting in a role analogous to a mediator. No rules of evidence apply to a mediation, because the mediator will not render a "decision"; but, as with any serious settlement conference or discussion, the parties will carefully prepare their arguments and positions ahead of time.

What qualities should you look for in choosing a mediator? Essentially, the best mediators are those who can combine three qualities: (1) the ability to deal with complex issues in a fair and reasoned manner; (2) the ability to assist the parties to do the same without engendering mutual animosity; and (3) the ability to formulate reasonable, workable, and persuasive compromises acceptable to the disputants. An example of a strategy that might be employed by a mediator is shown in Figure 12–5.

When the parties involved in a mediation come to an agreement, the terms of the agreement will have to be memorialized in some form of contract or settlement agreement. The considerations are similar to those that apply in the context of any settlement; releases of claims may be necessary, and the terms should be binding to the extent desired by the parties.

Mediation is an area that has gained broader application in the last 20 years. Community-based mediation systems have been developed nationwide, for example, utilizing mediation as a means of defusing conflicts before the results become counterproductive to all. You should check to see what mediation services and programs are available in your community.

Contractual clauses calling for mediation often suggest yet another form of alternative dispute resolution should the mediation fail, in an effort to resolve contractual disputes by applying a "graduated" progression of third-party input. For example, a contract might specify that, should a dispute develop between the parties, they will first attempt to settle the dispute in a "good faith" effort through the mediation process, and only then resort to arbitration or some other form of binding resolution.

## Mock Trial, Minitrial, and Other Private Sector Alternatives

Many companies (such as the fictional "Quick Resolutions, Inc." identified in the Commentary to this chapter) are springing up to offer private judging services and other made-to-order "private trial" processes, as well as arbitration, mediation, or other hybrid forms of dispute resolution. Entrepreneurs have recognized that there is a market for efficient dispute resolution among parties fed up with the delays and expense of litigation in the courts.

**Figure 12–5   Example of a Potential Mediation Strategy**

Assume that two equal partners in a partnership of long standing have decided that the time has come to dissolve their partnership. They want to end the relationship on an amicable basis, but are having difficulty determining what would constitute a fair distribution of the assets and liabilities of the partnership (which include such diverse elements as inventory, accounts payable, accounts receivable, cash-on-hand, building, and equipment).

Seeking to avoid litigation, they engage the services of a mediator. After spending time investigating the situation and identifying the issues, the mediator suggests the following: Partner A should prepare two packages, each representing what is, in his opinion, an equal one-half share of the partnership assets. Then Partner B should pick which of these two packages he wishes to take as his share.

Mock trials or minitrials can be conducted by these private companies, presided over by a qualified individual employed by the company. The parties are often free to define the rules that will govern such processes. They can establish through contractual agreements the applicability of the rules of evidence, the legal standards or precedents that will govern the issues presented for decision, and the enforceability of the result. In some cases the parties will agree beforehand that the results of such proceedings will be advisory only (hence the "mock" label), giving them a chance to see how the dispute may play out if allowed to proceed in the courts. Sometimes one party will submit to the mock trial process individually, presenting both sides of the case, simply to identify how a jury might view the evidence (in preparation for the actual trial).

The companies entering the dispute resolution field often hire former judges and litigation attorneys to add to their level of professionalism. Conference room facilities and other amenities are also often available.

The full extent to which these services may supplant more traditional means of dispute resolution remains to be seen. But it seems safe to say that, as litigation costs grow and the ability of the courts to handle the demands erodes, the private sector will continue to offer innovative alternatives to disgruntled disputants.

## 12−4   Practical Considerations

Litigation in the courts can be expensive and slow. Sometimes it cannot be avoided, as where one or both parties desire the establishment of a legal precedent, or where the parties cannot agree on an alternative forum. But if the issues presented by a dispute are such that some form of alternative dispute resolution is possible, avoiding the courts can often be beneficial to all involved.

This brings us to an important practical consideration with regard to some of the forums we've discussed in this chapter: the extent to which they present an option to disputants. A decision to submit an ongoing dispute to a private mediation service, for example, rather than going directly to the courts, is indeed an option that the disputants can exercise. The administrative adjudication process, however, is not an option that disputants can choose but is, rather, a mandatory forum distinguishable from the courts. Private arbitration may be mandatory (as where the agreement to arbitrate is embedded in a contract, and a statute makes the agreement enforceable); it may also, in the absence of such an agreement, be optional (in that the parties can choose to go to arbitration after a dispute arises). This practical consideration—namely, whether a particular alternative forum is mandatory or optional—will, of course, be essential to your (and your supervising attorney's) evaluation of the future course of a pending matter.

The alternative forums discussed in this chapter each present a wealth of complex and fascinating issues for study. Administrative law is an entire field of law unto itself, with many twists and turns on which multivolume treatises have been written. The contractual and other aspects of private arbitration present their own unique set of challenges. Alternative dispute resolution is a rapidly evolving area that is becoming more important all the time. Our survey represents no more than an abbreviated introduction to these subjects; further study is recommended.

# SUMMARY

## 12-1

An administrative agency is a governmental institution established by statute and intended to implement stated legislative policy in areas too complicated for direct statutory regulation. The Administrative Procedure Act (APA) was implemented by Congress to regulate the manner in which federal administrative agencies exercise their powers. The text of federal regulations is found in the *Federal Register* and the Code of Federal Regulations. Access to agency information is controlled by legislation such as the Freedom of Information Act. The rulemaking provisions of the APA are designed to provide for such things as public input into the rulemaking process and the publication of rules adopted. Administrative adjudication procedures constitute the true "litigation" aspect of administrative law; the trier-of-fact is often an administrative law judge, who exercises many quasi-judicial powers. The official rules of evidence do not apply at agency hearings, but evidence that is irrelevant, immaterial, or unduly repetitious may be excluded. Judicial review is available once administrative remedies are exhausted. State law administrative procedures are often patterned on the Model State Administrative Procedure Act.

## 12-2

Court-annexed arbitration is a generic term referring to efforts to resolve disputes within the judicial system but without (at least initially) the application of formal judicial procedures. Arbitrators in court-annexed arbitrations are often experienced attorneys. Procedures governing court-annexed arbitrations often vary significantly from one jurisdiction to the next. The federal judicial system is currently experimenting with court-annexed arbitration, in a program established in 28 U.S.C. 651–658. Private arbitration is really a form of alternative dispute resolution. Agreements to arbitrate are generally made enforceable by statute. The trend in the federal courts has been to expand the enforceability of such agreements, even into areas where enforceability was formerly questioned. The arbitration clause in a contract often references the Commercial Arbitration Rules of the American Arbitration Association. Recourse to arbitration is often beneficial in complicated areas where specific expertise on the part of the arbitrator is helpful.

## 12-3

Alternative dispute resolution is generally considered to include those forms or methods of dispute resolution to which disputing parties can avail themselves as an alternative to formal, governmental dispute resolution such as litigation in the courts. Conciliation involves a neutral "go-between" who shuttles information between parties who wish to avoid face-to-face negotiation; it is not often used. Mediation is a relatively common method of alternative dispute resolution, in which the mediator attempts, through participation in the face-to-face negotiation of the parties, to assist them in reaching an agreement resolving their dispute. The mediator has no authority to issue a decision binding on the disputants. A key factor inducing parties to mediate is a mutual desire to minimize antagonism, particularly where it is anticipated that a relationship will continue after the dispute is resolved (as in a family or labor/management context). Mediation agreements must generally be formalized by a contract. Many private companies are springing up to offer various types of alternative dispute resolution, including mock trials or other hybrids.

## 12-4

Among the various nonjudicial dispute-resolution mechanisms considered in this chapter, it is important to distinguish between those that are mandatory (such as the administrative law process) and those that offer disputants alternatives to commencing a lawsuit (such as private arbitration).

# REVIEW

## Key Terms

Before proceeding, review the key terms listed below to be sure you understand each one. If necessary, read over the corresponding section of the chapter. When you are ready to test your understanding, answer the Review Questions.

administrative hearing
administrative agency
administrative law
*Federal Register*
*Code of Federal Regulations*
administrative law judge
exhaustion of administrative remedies
trial *de novo*
arbitration
arbitrator
panel of arbitrators
court-annexed arbitration
judicially linked arbitration
statutory arbitration
private arbitration
alternative dispute resolution
conciliation
mediation
mediator

## Questions for Review and Discussion

1. What is the function of an administrative agency?
2. What are two sources for the text of federal regulations?
3. List four major areas of concern addressed by the federal Administrative Procedure Act (APA).
4. What purposes are furthered by the rulemaking provisions of the APA?
5. What is meant by exhaustion of administrative remedies?
6. What is court-annexed arbitration?
7. Identify a set of rules that are commonly employed in private arbitrations.
8. What does a mediator do?
9. List some factors that might induce parties to resolve their disputes through mediation.
10. List three qualities that are desirable in a mediator.

## Activities

1. Review the statutes that govern administrative procedure in your state. You should also determine how and where to locate the text of state regulations currently in force.
2. Check your state's statutes and court rules to determine whether there is a program of court-annexed arbitration.
3. Obtain from your local law library a copy of the Commercial Arbitration Rules of the American Arbitration Association and read them.

# GLOSSARY

**Abode service:**  Accomplished under the Federal Rules of Civil Procedure (FRCP) when process server leaves summons and complaint with competent person at defendant's place of residence.

**Administrative agency:**  Governmental institution established by statute and intended to implement stated legislative policy.

**Administrative hearing:**  Adjudication or rule-making hearing of an administrative agency.

**Administrative law:**  Generic name given to the rules, regulations, guidelines, and procedures of administrative agencies.

**Administrative law judge:**  The quasi-judicial presiding officer at a federal administrative hearing.

**Admissible:**  Appropriate to be admitted into evidence at trial.

**Admission:**  An acceptance of the truth of an allegation in a claim for relief; an acceptance of the truth of an assertion in a Request for Admission.

**Affirmative defense:**  A set of facts or a legal restriction that goes beyond the allegations of the complaint and that, if established to the satisfaction of the court, would constitute a valid defense even if the allegations of the complaint were true.

**Agent for service of process:**  The person designated by a corporation to accept service of process.

**Alternative dispute resolution:**  The various methods of private dispute resolution, such as mediation, conciliation, etc.

**Amended pleading:**  Under the FRCP, a pleading filed which alters the allegations and/or responses of an earlier pleading based upon something other than newly-occurring transactions.

**Amicus curiae brief:**  A brief filed in an appeal by an interested outside third party.

**Answer:**  The pleading filed by a defendant to respond to the allegations of the complaint, identify defenses, and state any additional relevant claims.

**Answer to Cross-claim:**  The response of a co-party to a cross-claim filed against it.

**Appeal:**  A review of the actions of a lower court by a higher court.

**Appearance:** A document often filed with the court by an attorney to establish representation of the client in a pending lawsuit.

**Appellant:** The party filing an appeal.

**Appellant's brief:** The brief filed by the appellant on appeal.

**Appellate brief:** A generic name for a brief filed on appeal (by appellant, appellee, or amicus curiae).

**Appellate jurisdiction:** The jurisdiction of a court to hear and decide an appeal of the actions of a lower court.

**Appellee:** The party against whom an appeal is filed.

**Appellee's brief:** The brief filed by an appellee on appeal.

**Application for Entry of Default Judgment:** Under the FRCP, filed after a default is entered, seeking entry by the judge of a judgment.

**Arbitration:** A means of dispute resolution in which the neutral third party is an arbitrator or panel of arbitrators whose decision is generally binding. Arbitration can be private or court-annexed.

**Arbitrator:** The neutral third-party decision maker in an arbitration, whether private or court-annexed.

**Associate Justices:** The eight justices of the United States Supreme Court other than the Chief Justice.

**Associates:** Salaried lawyers without ownership or "partner" status in a law firm, and without a decisive voice in firm management.

**Attachment:** A pre-judgment remedy providing for the seizure of property to satisfy a judgment which might ultimately be rendered in a pending civil action.

**Attorney work-product:** Materials prepared by an attorney in anticipation of litigation, to assist the attorney in pursuing his client's interests. Discoverable only upon a showing of substantial need and undue hardship.

**Authentication:** The process by which evidence is shown to actually *be* what the offering party claims it to be.

**Authorization forms:** Signed by the client to authorize release to his attorneys of confidential information (often medical or employment information).


**Bailiff:** The official charged with maintaining order in the courtroom.

**Bench:** Raised podium area at the front of a courtroom where a judge sits.

**Bench trial:** Non-jury trial in which the judge is the trier-of-fact (see also *court trial* and *non-jury trial*).

**Best Evidence Rule:** Requires that, if available, the *original* of a document must be offered into evidence, rather than a copy.

**Billable hour:** An hour in which tasks are performed by an attorney or paralegal on behalf of a specific client; the value of the time is then billed to the client.

**Billing subfile:** The subfile of a litigation case-file containing information related to the billing of the client by the firm for services rendered.

**Bond:** A payment or surety filed by an appellant to protect the opposing party against the costs incurred should the appeal fail.

**Brief:** A formal memorandum of law filed with a court setting forth legal arguments with citations to legal authorities, often including a statement of facts and possibly other sections as well.

**Burden of proof:** Basically, the requirement that one party or the other must provide a certain level of evidentiary support for a given issue; failure to so provide leads to judgment for the opposing party.

**Caption:** The informational area found at the top of pleadings, motions, and other documents filed with the court in a pending lawsuit.

**Cause of action:** A legal claim which, if proven, and if no successful defenses are raised, is sufficient to lead to judgment.

**Certificate of service:** Component of a pleading, motion, or other paper filed with the court in which the filing party certifies that a copy has been provided to all other parties.

**Chain of custody:** A thorough accounting of the whereabouts of a piece of evidence from the time obtained through the trial.

**Challenge for cause:** Used by counsel to attempt to disqualify a juror who is biased or who knows the parties, or is otherwise unfit to serve; the judge makes the final decision whether to disqualify.

**Chief Justice:** The presiding justice in the United States Supreme Court.

**Choice of forum:** When concurrent jurisdiction exists, the decision to be made as to the court in which to file a complaint.

**Circumstantial evidence:** Offered to prove a secondary fact from which the trier-of-fact must draw an inference to find the primary fact.

**Civil action:** A lawsuit.

**Civil action number:** The number assigned by the court to a lawsuit, for purposes of internal control (also called a *docket number*).

**Civil cover sheet:** Filed with the court along with a complaint, in order to provide the court with basic background information.

**Civil litigation:** The process by which the non-criminal disputes of opposing parties are administered by a neutral third party, where the neutral third party has the power to render a resolution of the dispute binding upon the disputants, and where the dispute centers upon the determination of the bounds of certain alleged rights, privileges, and/or obligations of the disputants.

**Class action:** Lawsuit in which a large number of parties act as a group, with their claims joined together and pursued by a "representative party"; the group (called a "class") can also be made up of defendants.

**Clear and convincing evidence:** A high burden of proof sometimes required in a civil case involving serious allegations, such as fraud.

**Clerk's office:** The office in a courthouse where pleadings are filed and other administrative tasks are performed.

**Code of Federal Regulations:** The annual publication of the federal government in which federal regulations in force are arranged by topic.

**Compensatory damages:** Money damages designed to reimburse the wronged party for the amount of the quantifiable damages (including special damages and general damages).

**Complaint:** The formal statement of a plaintiff's cause or causes of action seeking a legal or equitable remedy against one or more defendants, which when filed with the court and served upon the defendants in the required manner successfully commences a lawsuit.

**Compulsory counterclaim:** A claim by a party brought against an opposing party which arises out of the transaction that is the subject matter of the original claim; it must be filed, or is waived.

**Conciliation:** A form of alternative dispute resolution where the neutral third party ("conciliator") is a go-between for parties who wish no contact; the conciliator has no authority to render a binding resolution.

**Concurrent jurisdiction:** Exists where two courts (for example, state and federal) could potentially exercise jurisdiction over a dispute.

**Confidentiality:** The privacy maintained with regard to the client's situation, and the law firm's strategy, in a legal matter.

**Conflict of interest:** Arises when an attorney or paralegal has a vested interest of some sort which is against the client's interest.

**Conflict of laws:** Situation arising when it is not absolutely clear which laws apply to a dispute (for example, such a situation might arise in a dispute over a contract which was signed in one state but performed in another).

**Conflicts check:** Effort by a law firm to ensure that no conflict of interest exists before accepting a new case.

**Consent Judgment:** A judgment the terms of which have been agreed upon by the parties (also called a *stipulated judgment*).

**Consolidation:** Under the FRCP, the combining of Rule 12 motions.

**Contested:** Opposed, as where a motion engenders opposition.

**Contingent fee case:** Case where the fee charged by lawyers varies depending on the result in the case.

**Continuance:** Sought for the purpose of postponing a scheduled trial.

**Contract law:** That broad field of substantive law concerned with the interpretation and enforcement of contracts.

**Copies:** Photocopies (or carbon copies) of an original document; to be distinguished from *duplicates* (see also *duplicates*).

**Correspondence subfile:** A subfile of a litigation case-file that contains correspondence generated in the ordinary course of moving a case forward, but not correspondence with evidentiary value.

**Counsel tables:** Where opposing counsel (and sometimes clients and paralegals) sit in the courtroom during a trial.

**Count:** A single cause of action stated in a complaint, counterclaim, or the like.

**Counterclaim:** Claim filed by a party against an opposing party in a responsive pleading, usually by a defendant against a plaintiff.

**Court-annexed arbitration:** Alternative program that is part of the official judicial system, in which the presiding officer and decision maker (called the arbitrator) is someone other than a judge or jury.

**Court reporter:** In a deposition, a private individual who records the transcript; in a trial, an official employee who records the transcript.

**Court trial:** A trial in which there is no jury; the judge decides questions of fact (also called a *bench trial* or *non-jury trial*).

**Covenant not to sue:** An agreement prepared in conjunction with a settlement, negating the possibility that the signing party will again file suit on the same claim.

**Crimes:** Offenses against the public at large, prosecuted by the government.

**Criminal litigation:** Litigation involving the prosecution and punishment of crimes.

**Cross-appellant:** Party who, after the filing of an appeal by an opposing party, proceeds to appeal the same decision on other grounds.

**Cross-claim:** A claim for relief asserted against a co-party.

**Cross-examination:** Questioning by one who did not originally call the witness; follows direct examination.

**Cross-motions for summary judgment:** Competing motions for summary judgment filed by opposing sides in a lawsuit; sometimes submitted on stipulated facts.

**Damages:** Losses suffered by an injured party as a result of wrongful behavior by another.

**Deadlines:** Time by which an act must be completed, or else be waived.

**Declarant:** In the context of hearsay law, person who made an out-of-court statement.

**Default:** Under the FRCP, an official recognition by the court that a party against whom a claim has been raised has failed to plead or otherwise defend against the claim.

**Default judgment:** Judgment entered subsequent to, and based upon, a default.

**Defendant:** The party against whom a complaint raises a claim.

**Demonstrative evidence:** Physical evidence used to illustrate, demonstrate, or explain something relevant to a case, although it did not itself play a role in the case.

**Denial:** Disputing the truth of an allegation in a complaint, or of an assertion in a Request for Admission.

**Deponent:** Person who is examined at a deposition.

**Deposition:** Procedure by which the oral testimony of a party or non-party witness is taken, prior to trial, in response to questions, with the proceedings recorded in a transcript.

**Deposition digest:** Summary of deposition transcript prepared by a law firm for its internal use.

**Deposition upon oral examination:** Common form of deposition, where the examination is made up of oral questions; allows for follow-up questions.

**Deposition upon written questions:** Less common form of deposition, where examination is based upon written questions, with no opportunity for follow-up.

**Designation:** Identifies the purpose of a pleading or motion; often appears just below (or as a part of) the caption.

**Direct evidence:** Evidence as to a fact in dispute not requiring the trier-of-fact to draw an inference.

**Direct examination:** Questions posed by the attorney or party who calls a witness or who noticed a deposition.

**Discovery:** Rules, methods, and procedure by which the parties to a lawsuit are authorized to request (and, by seeking a court order, to compel) the disclosure of factual information held by opposing parties (or, in some instances, non-party witnesses).

**Discovery conference:** Meeting at which attorneys and judge work out a plan (followed by a corresponding court order) for the orderly progression of the discovery process.

**Discovery subfile:** Subfile to litigation case-file in which are filed materials related to the discovery process.

**Dismissal:** Order of the court disallowing further litigation of a complaint or other claim for relief, or some individual cause of action raised in a complaint or claim for relief.

**Dismissal without prejudice:** A dismissal that does not preclude the party asserting the claim dismissed from raising it again at a later time.

**Dismissal with prejudice:** A dismissal that precludes the party asserting the claim dismissed from raising it again at some later time.

**Dispositive motions:** Motions that, if granted, constitute a final resolution of some aspect of a case, or possibly even the entire case; the granting of such a motion might be appealed, but the issues involved will not be further considered by the trial court.

**Diversity jurisdiction:** Federal jurisdiction conferred by virtue of the diverse citizenship of the parties and the amount in controversy.

**Docket number:** See *civil action number.*

**Domestic relations law:** That broad field of substantive law dealing with marital status, child custody, and other circumstances of the family relationship.

**Duplicates:** Documents conformed with an original signature, as contrasted to *copies.*


**Elements:** Essential components of a cause of action.

**Equitable remedies:** Remedies that involve something other than money damages, such as an injunction.

**Exception:** Under some court rules, a brief statement made on the record at trial which preserves the right to appeal an adverse evidentiary ruling.

**Exclusive jurisdiction:** Jurisdiction of a court when no concurrent jurisdiction exists; such court is the only court empowered to hear that case.

**Execution:** Enforcing a judgment by obtaining possession and title of the losing party's assets.

**Exhaustion of administrative remedies:** Completing the final stage of the administrative adjudication process; prerequisite to judicial review.

**Exhibits:** Documents or physical evidence entered into evidence at trial, or marked at a deposition.

**Exhibits and original documents subfile:** Subfile of a litigation case-file in which are kept materials with evidentiary purpose.

**Expedited transcript:** Transcript received from court reporter on an accelerated schedule at additional expense.

**Expert witness:** Witness whose qualifications have been accepted by the court as sufficient to justify scientific, technical, or specialized opinion testimony on a relevant issue.


**Fact-pleading:** Strict requirement that all significant facts be pleaded; requires more detail than notice-pleading.

**Federal Register:** Daily publication of federal government containing information with regard to administrative agencies.

**Federal Rules of Civil Procedure:** The rules of procedure which govern civil practice in the federal courts (FRCP).

**Final pretrial conference:** Pretrial conference held just before trial, at which the participants formulate a plan for the orderly conduct of the trial.

**Final pretrial order:** Order entered by the judge subsequent to the final pretrial conference; under the FRCP, can be modified only to prevent "manifest injustice."

**Follow-up questions:** Available at a deposition upon oral examination; enable an examining attorney to explore the deponent's response.

**Form books:** Official or commercial compilations of model pleadings and motions.

**Foundation:** Background information establishing that a witness has knowledge sufficient to justify the testimony to come, or that a piece of physical evidence *is* what it is asserted to be.

**FRAP:** Abbreviation for Federal Rules of Appellate Procedure.

**Fraudulent conveyances:** Transfers of property for the purpose of defrauding creditors.

**FRCP:** Abbreviation for Federal Rules of Civil Procedure.


**Garnishment:** An execution on property owned by a judgment debtor but held by some third party.

**General appearance:** An appearance held to constitute an admission that the court has personal jurisdiction. (Most courts have eliminated this category of appearance; see also *special appearance.*)

**General damages:** Those compensatory damages that are not subject to precise calculation, such as damages for pain and suffering.

**General jurisdiction:** Applied to a court that is empowered to hear cases covering a broad spectrum of subject matters.

**General release:** A document by which a party releases all future rights to bring an action against another party based upon prior occurrences.

**General verdict:** Decision of a jury in which the decision identifies, in the most simple and straightforward fashion, which party has won and the amount of applicable damages (if any).

**General verdict with interrogatories:** General verdict augmented with responses of the jury to certain specific questions.

**Grounds for appeal:** The specific errors of the lower court that an appealing party asserts justify remedial action by the appellate court.


**Harmless error:** Error committed by a lower court that does not, in the view of the appellate court, justify any remedial action.

**Hearsay:** A statement made out-of-court but offered in the court to establish the truth of the facts contained in the statement.

**Hearsay Rule:** This rule holds that hearsay is inadmissible; there are, however, many exceptions.

**High court:** Highest court in a particular court system.

**Impeach:**  To discredit the testimony of a witness.

**Impleader:**  Third-party complaint practice (see *third-party complaint*).

**Inadmissible:**  Inappropriate to be admitted into evidence at trial.

**In banc:**  Before all the judges of an appellate circuit.

**In-hand service:**  Method by which a process server places a summons and complaint directly in the hands of a defendant.

**Initial client interview:**  The first interview of a client by a law firm at the beginning of a new matter.

***In rem* jurisdiction:**  Jurisdiction over a thing (such as land).

**Injunction:**  An order of the court that a party perform a certain act, or refrain from performing a certain act.

**Interlocutory appeal:**  An appeal occurring prior to judgment in the trial court; such appeals are authorized only under limited circumstances.

**Intermediate appellate court:**  In a typical court system, hears appeals from the trial court, and renders decisions which can be reviewed by the high court.

**Internal litigation case-file:**  Folder and contents of the file for any matter assigned to or handled by the litigation department.

**Interpleader:**  An action brought by a plaintiff to avoid the possibility of double or multiple liability (often involving a "stakeholder" situation).

**Interrogatories:**  (1) Written questions posed as part of the formal discovery process, by one party to another, and requiring written responses; (2) questions propounded to the jury to elicit a "general verdict with interrogatories."

**Intervention:**  Procedure by which an outside third party can participate in a pending lawsuit.

**Investigation:**  The gathering of facts in general, and more particularly the gathering of facts admissible in evidence.

**Investigation subfile:**  Subfile of a litigation case-file in which are maintained materials generated by, or relevant to, investigation.

**Irreparable harm:**  Injury suffered that cannot be compensated by money damages which are easily calculable or readily identifiable.

**Joinder:**  Combining of claims; combining of parties.

**Joinder of claims:**  Combining two or more claims in one lawsuit.

**Joinder of parties:**  The right of two or more plaintiffs to pursue common claims in one lawsuit; the right to file one lawsuit against two or more defendants.

**Judgment:**  The final decree of a court, resolving the contested issues of law and fact.

**Judgment by default:**  Final decree entered by the court based upon the entry of a prior default.

**Judgment creditor:**  One who is owed money under the terms of a judgment.

**Judgment debtor:**  One who owes money under the terms of a judgment.

**Judgment lien:**  An interest in property of a judgment debtor asserted subsequent to entry of judgment.

**Judicial branch:** The branch of government which is made up of the court system.

**Judicial review:** The right of the courts to determine the meaning of statutes and regulations, and to determine the constitutionality of the actions of the other branches of government (including the constitutionality of statutes passed).

**Jurisdiction:** The authority of a court to decide and administer cases.

**Jurisdictional statement:** Statement setting forth the jurisdictional basis for a lawsuit; required by the FRCP (and the rules of some states) to appear in a complaint.

**Jurors:** Members of the jury who decide questions of fact in jury trials.

**Jury box:** Where the jury sits in a courtroom.

**Jury demand:** Filed by a party who seeks a jury trial with regard to a disputed issue of fact.

**Jury instructions:** Guidelines submitted by the judge to the jury which must be followed by the jury as they conduct their deliberations and reach their conclusion.

**Jury panels:** A group of potential jurors from whom a jury is selected.

**Jury trial:** A trial in which the trier-of-fact is the jury.

**Justices:** The "judges" of a high court.


**Law clerk:** (1) Non-lawyer employee of a law firm (often a law student); (2) law students or recent law school graduates who work for a judge for a one- or two-year period.

**Lawsuit:** A civil action in which a plaintiff and defendant, and possibly other parties, litigate their dispute in the courts.

**Lay witness:** A non-expert witness.

**Leading question:** A question that suggests the answer as part of the question.

**Legal remedies:** Remedies that involve money damages.

**Legal research subfile:** Subfile of a litigation case-file containing legal research memoranda, copies of relevant statutes or judicial opinions, or other research materials.

**Limited jurisdiction:** Jurisdiction of a court empowered to hear only certain specified types of cases.

**Lis pendens notice:** Filed on the land records with regard to the property of a defendant, to notify the world that title to the property is subject to judgment in a pending lawsuit.

**Litigants:** Parties to litigation.

**Litigation:** The process by which the disputes of opposing parties are administered by a neutral third party, where the neutral third party has the power to render a resolution of the dispute binding upon the disputants.

**Litigation strategy:** The "big picture" view of a dispute which drives the decision-making processes of the party.

**Local rules:** Rules of an individual court in addition to those rules that apply throughout a court system (for example, each U.S. District Court has "local rules" in addition to the FRCP).

**Long-arm jurisdiction:**  Jurisdiction over an out-of-state defendant.

**Long-arm statute:**  Statute that establishes and defines long-arm jurisdiction.

**Mail notice:**  Service of process accomplished by mail.

**Mandate:**  Issued by federal Court of Appeals twenty-one days after the judgment of that court is entered; incorporates judgment, written opinion (if any), and costs.

**Materiality:**  The extent to which a fact to be proven is of consequence to the determination of a civil action.

**Mediation:**  Form of alternative dispute resolution in which the neutral third party (called a "mediator") assists the parties in their face-to-face negotiations, but has no power to bind the parties.

**Mediator:**  Neutral third party in a mediation.

**Medical report:**  A written evaluation of the medical situation of a patient prepared by a treating physician.

**Memorandum of law:**  (1) Written document filed with the court in support of a motion, referencing judicial opinions, statutes, or other applicable facts and law; (2) research memorandum prepared for internal firm use.

**Military affidavit:**  Required to show that a party against whom a default judgment is sought is not in the military service of the United States.

**Motion:**  A request to a court for an order of some sort.

**Motions and other court filings subfile:**  Subfile of a litigation case-file in which are placed documents filed with, or generated by, the court, other than pleadings or discovery material.

**Motion calendar:**  Proceeding at which many pending motions are heard by the court (also called a *motion day*); also applied to the document scheduling such a proceeding.

**Motion day:**  Proceeding at which many pending motions are heard by the court (also called *motion calendar*).

**Motion for Directed Verdict:**  Motion no longer used in federal court (but still in use in certain states) in which a party requests at trial that the judge compel a verdict in its favor.

**Motion for Extension of Time:**  Motion by which a party can request additional time, beyond a current deadline, to complete an act.

**Motion for Judgment as a Matter of Law:**  Pursuant to Rule 50 of the FRCP as amended in 1991, a motion made at a jury trial by which a party requests that the judge enter judgment in its favor.

**Motion for Judgment JNOV:**  Motion no longer used in federal court (but still in use in certain states) in which a party requests at trial that the court enter judgment in its favor despite the contrary verdict of the jury (also called a *Motion for Judgment Notwithstanding the Verdict*).

**Motion for Judgment Notwithstanding the Verdict:**  See *Motion for Judgment JNOV*.

**Motion for Judgment on Partial Findings:**  Motion created by 1991 amendments to Rule 52 of the FRCP, by which a party in a bench trial requests that judgment be entered in its favor after the opposing party has been fully heard.

**Motion for Judgment on the Pleadings:**  Under Rule 12(c) of the FRCP, a motion by which a party requests that judgment be entered in its favor based upon the application of legal analysis to the facts as established by the pleadings alone.

**Motion for More Definite Statement:** Under Rule 12(e) of the FRCP, a motion by which a party seeks correction of vague or ambiguous assertions in a previous pleading to which a response is required.

**Motion for New Trial:** A request for a new trial that, under the FRCP, must be served not later than 10 days after the entry of judgment.

**Motion for Order Compelling Discovery:** Under Rule 37 of the FRCP, a motion seeking an order that instructs the opposing party to comply with a previous discovery request (also called a *Motion to Compel*).

**Motion for Order Compelling Physical or Mental Examination:** Under Rule 35 of the FRCP, a motion seeking an order authorizing the physical examination of a party (or person in the custody or legal control of a party).

**Motion for Protective Order:** Under Rule 26(c) of the FRCP, a motion seeking an order limiting or regulating an opposing party's discovery rights.

**Motion for Sanctions:** (1) Under Rule 26(c) of the FRCP, a motion seeking an order imposing a penalty against an opposing party who has failed to obey an order compelling a discovery response; (2) a motion seeking an order imposing a penalty under Rule 11 of the FRCP (related to the obligation of an attorney to sign a pleading or other court document only after reasonable inquiry, and in good faith).

**Motion for Summary Judgment:** A motion seeking the entry of judgment in favor of the moving party as a result of there being no genuine issue of material fact, and the moving party being entitled to judgment as a matter of law.

**Motion *in Limine*:** A motion filed prior to trial seeking a preliminary ruling or order with regard to some issue of evidence expected to arise at trial.

**Motion to Amend the Judgment:** Under the FRCP, a motion filed not later than 10 days after entry of the judgment of the trial court, seeking modification of the judgment or the inclusion of some additional findings.

**Motion to Compel:** See *Motion for Order Compelling Discovery*.

**Motion to Dismiss:** A motion filed seeking the dismissal of one or more claims for relief; see, for example, Rules 12(b) and 41 of the FRCP.

**Motion to Strike:** Under Rule 12(f) of the FRCP, a motion seeking an order compelling the removal from a pleading of any insufficient defense or any redundant, immaterial, impertinent, or scandalous matter.

**Non-jury trial:** A bench trial, in which questions of fact are decided by a judge (see *bench trial* and *court trial*).

**Notice of Appeal:** In federal practice, filed by a party seeking an appeal by right (see Rule 3 of the Federal Rules of Appellate Procedure).

**Notice of Deposition:** Document provided to parties in a pending lawsuit that officially schedules a deposition and that identifies the deponent, place, and time of the deposition, etc.

**Notice of Hearing:** A document that may be required in order to schedule oral argument on a pending motion.

**Notice-pleading:** Requirement that pleading place opposing party on notice of the claim or defense; less strict than fact-pleading requirement.

**Numbered paragraphs:** The manner in which averments of claim or defense are set forth in a pleading, and in which statements are set forth in a motion.

**Objections:** Asserted in opposition to inappropriate questions posed to a witness, inadmissible materials offered into evidence, or inappropriate discovery requests.

**Of counsel:** An attorney affiliated with a firm in some way other than full-time employment, such as a retired (but still somewhat active) attorney, or an occasional advisor.

**Offer of Judgment:** Under Rule 68 of the FRCP, an official offer to settle a case made by a party defending a claim. If refused, there are certain potential repercussions for the party refusing. Under the laws of some states, a plaintiff may also file an offer of judgment.

**Office administrator:** Law firm employee who coordinates the hiring and management of staff (also called an *office manager*).

**Office manager:** See *office administrator.*

**Opening statement:** Statement made by counsel to the jury just prior to the presentation of evidence at trial.

**Opinion testimony:** Testimony by a witness as to his or her opinion with regard to a situation, as opposed to testimony with regard to a fact.

**Oral argument:** Formal argument by counsel to a judge in open court, as on a motion or on an appeal.

**Order:** A formal command of the court.

**Order of notice:** A command of the court that service of process be completed in some specified alternative manner.

**Original jurisdiction:** Empowers a court to hear a case from the filing of the complaint through the completion of the trial.

**Panel:** (1) A group of potential jurors; (2) a group of appellate judges; (3) a group of arbitrators.

**Panel of arbitrators:** A group of arbitrators acting together as the neutral third party deciding an arbitration.

**Partial summary judgment:** Summary judgment as to less than all the issues presented by a lawsuit.

**Parties:** Litigants or disputants.

**Partner:** One of the senior attorneys having ownership status and a voice in the management of a law firm.

**Pendent jurisdiction:** Jurisdiction of a court to hear all causes of action which exist between the parties as long as at least *one* of the causes of action justifies jurisdiction and all such causes of action would ordinarily be tried together.

**Peremptory challenge:** Used by a party to automatically disqualify a potential juror without stated reason; each party is entitled to only a limited number of peremptory challenges.

**Permanent injunction:** An injunction entering pursuant to a judgment after trial, of theoretically infinite duration.

**Permissive counterclaim:** A counterclaim which does not arise out of the transaction or occurrence identified in the complaint; if not raised, it is not waived.

**Permissive joinder:** Concept regulating the rights of multiple plaintiffs to join together in one action, or the rights of a plaintiff to sue multiple defendants in one action (see, for example, Rule 20 of the FRCP).

**Personal jurisdiction:** Authority of a court to exercise its powers over the specific parties involved in the case.

**Petition for Certiorari:** Filed by a party seeking review in the United States Supreme Court of an adverse decision of the lower federal courts, or of the state high courts.

**Petition for Permission to Appeal:** Filed in the federal courts by a party seeking to bring an interlocutory appeal.

**Petition for Rehearing:** Filed by a party seeking a reconsideration of the decision of a United States Court of Appeals.

**Physical evidence:** Non-testimonial evidence.

**Plaintiff:** The party who commences a lawsuit by filing a complaint.

**Pleading:** Any one of the documents listed in Rule 7(a) of the FRCP, each of which represents an assertion by a party as to that party's legal and factual positions on matters at issue, made in anticipation of trial, requiring resolution at trial, and immediately operative for the purpose of defining the matters at issue without any need of further court order. Note that certain states may identify certain other pleadings beyond those identified in Rule 7(a) of the FRCP.

**Pleadings subfile:** Subfile of litigation case-file in which pleadings are kept.

**Police report:** Document filed by investigating police officer with his police department with regard to his investigation of an accident.

**Postinterview memorandum:** The internal firm memorandum prepared at the conclusion of an initial client interview, setting forth the substance of the interview.

**Post-judgment discovery:** Procedures by which a judgment creditor can compel a judgment debtor to reveal the existence of assets available to satisfy the judgment.

**Prayer for relief:** The "wherefore clause" in a complaint or related pleading, in which the party filing the pleading sets forth the nature of the relief sought.

**Preliminary injunction:** Injunction obtained after a pretrial hearing which remains in force during the pendency of the action.

**Preponderance of the evidence:** Usual standard with regard to the burden of proof at a civil trial.

**Pretrial conference:** Under Rule 16 of the FRCP, a meeting prior to trial between and among the judge, the attorneys in a case, and any unrepresented parties, at which are discussed such things as the status of discovery and motions, scheduling issues, settlement, etc.

**Pretrial memorandum:** Document often required in conjunction with a pretrial conference, prepared by one or more of the parties and related to the issues to be addressed in the conference.

**Private arbitration:** A form of alternative dispute resolution, occurring outside the judicial system, in which a private arbitrator renders a binding decision.

**Privilege:** A right to prevent testimony as to certain past communications between certain individuals whose relationship fits into a protected category, such as husband/wife or attorney/client.

**Probative value:** The tendency of proffered evidence to make a material fact more or less probable.

***Pro bono:*** Performed without a fee, or for a reduced fee.

**Procedural rules:** Rules (such as the FRCP) that establish the manner in which a lawsuit is administered.

**Process:** The "package" of documents (usually the summons, complaint, and any other related documents) served on a defendant at the outset of a lawsuit.

**Process server:** A person (such as a sheriff) who delivers to the defendant the summons, complaint, and other related documents which constitute the "process" served at the outset of a lawsuit.

**Professional codes of ethics:** Canons or rules governing the actions of professionals (such as attorneys or, in a growing trend, paralegals) in the conduct of their profession.

**Property law:** That broad field of substantive law concerning interests related to land (known as "real property") and other tangible things (known as "personal property").

**Proposed order:** Accompanies a motion, identifying the order sought from the court.

***Pro se* appearance:** Appearance filed by a party who is not represented by an attorney.

***Pro se* party:** A party who is not represented by an attorney.

**Punitive damages:** Damages in excess of the amount necessary to compensate the injured party, intended to punish the wrongdoer or to discourage like behavior in the future.

**Quash:** To render a subpoena ineffective and unenforceable.

**Real evidence:** Physical evidence that played a direct role in the events at issue in a lawsuit.

**Rebuttal:** Evidence put on by the plaintiff after the defendant has finished presenting his case; limited to refuting arguments raised by the defendant.

**Record:** Pleadings, trial transcript, evidence, and other exhibits from the trial court which are filed with the appellate court on an appeal.

**Relevancy:** The tendency of evidence to make the existence of any fact that is of consequence to the determination of a lawsuit more probable or less probable than it would be without the evidence.

**Relief:** The legal or equitable remedy sought in a claim.

**Remand:** The order by which a higher court sends an appealed case back to the lower court for further action.

**Remedy:** A legal resolution to a problem.

**Removal:** The transfer of a case filed in state court to the federal court for the federal district in which the state court is located, provided there is concurrent jurisdiction and provided further that certain other statutory conditions are met.

**Reply brief:** The optional brief filed by an appellant in response to the appellee's brief.

**Reply to Affirmative Defenses:** Responsive pleading addressing an opposing party's affirmative defenses, required by some state procedural rules but only if *ordered* by a federal court (see Rule 7(a) of the FRCP).

**Reply to Counterclaim:** Pleading which represents essentially an "answer" to the claims raised in a counterclaim.

**Request for Admissions:** Discovery device by which a party can compel an opposing party to admit or deny the truth of certain facts, or certain statements applying law to fact.

**Request for Entry of Default Judgment:** Under Rule 55 of the FRCP, the document filed with the court seeking entry by the clerk of judgment based upon a default which has previously been entered.

**Request for oral argument:** Notation often required on the first page of a motion indicating whether oral argument is desired.

**Request for Production of Documents and Things or Entry Upon Land:** Under the FRCP, a discovery request seeking the right to inspect and copy documents, enter upon land, inspect and perform tests upon tangible things, etc.

**Rested:** Indication that a plaintiff or defendant has completed presentation of evidence.

**Retainer:** An amount paid in advance to an attorney by a client against which amounts are withdrawn as earned.

**Retainer letter:** A letter identifying billing arrangements between an attorney and a client, as well as the fact of representation.

**Return of Service:** The method by which a court is notified that a defendant has been served with a summons and complaint.

**Reversal:** Overturning the decision of a lower court.

**Revised pleading:** A term used in the practice of some state courts; can refer to an amended or supplemented pleading.

**Rule 12(b) Motion:** A motion filed asserting one of the seven defenses set forth in Rule 12(b) of the FRCP.

**Rule 12 Defense:** One of the seven defenses identified in Rule 12(b) of the FRCP.


**Sanctions:** Penalties imposed by the court, as where a pleading is signed in violation of Rule 11 of the FRCP, or where a party ignores an order compelling compliance with a discovery request.

**Satisfaction of Judgment:** A document filed with a court by a judgment creditor, indicating that the judgment debtor has paid off the judgment.

**Scheduling conference:** A pretrial conference under Rule 16(b) of the FRCP which establishes time limits for joining parties, amending pleadings, completing discovery, filing motions, etc.

**Scheduling order:** An order of the court pursuant to Rule 16 of the FRCP establishing time limits for joining parties, amending pleadings, completing discovery, filing motions, etc.

**Scope:** In witness examination, the breadth of the questioning of the previous questioner which limits the current questioner; for example, the allowable questions on cross-examination are limited to the *scope* of direct examination. (See also *scope of discovery*.)

**Scope of discovery:** The breadth of allowable discovery, as established by Rule 26 of the FRCP; generally described as liberal.

**Senior partner:** Law firm partner with higher status than an ordinary partner, exercising a more powerful voice in firm management or taking a larger share of the firm's profits.

**Service:** Delivery, as of a pleading or of the "process" which is delivered to the defendant at the outset of a lawsuit.

**Service of process:** Delivery to the defendant of the "package" which includes the summons and complaint, made by a process server or by mail at the outset of a lawsuit.

**Settlement:** Resolving a lawsuit or other dispute by agreement of the parties prior to the full playing-out of the litigation process.

**Settlement Agreement:** A document incorporating the terms on which disputing parties have agreed to resolve their dispute.

**Sheriff:** A public official who is often charged with responsibility for completing service of process, or of serving subpoenas; may also be called upon to maintain order in a courtroom.

**Signature block:** That portion of a pleading or motion that is signed by the attorney; often includes the attorney's address and phone number, the party represented, and possibly other information as well.

**Sole practitioner:** An attorney who practices alone, with no partners.

**Special appearance:** An appearance filed for the limited purpose of contesting jurisdiction. (Most courts have eliminated this category of appearance; see also *general appearance*.)

**Special damages:** Money damages which are capable of precise calculation.

**Special defense:** See *affirmative defense*.

**Special verdict:** Verdict in which the jury is asked to decide specific individual issues of fact, which are then incorporated into the judgment of the court.

**Specific performance:** An equitable remedy, requiring a party to perform the obligations of a contract; generally only applied where the object of the contract is "unique."

**Standing pretrial scheduling order:** A permanent order of the court applicable to all cases filed and relating to the timing of, and deadlines for, such things as discovery, amendments to pleadings, filing of motions, joining parties, etc.

**Status conference:** A pretrial conference occurring after the scheduling conference and before the final pretrial conference, designed to expedite the administration of the case and often focusing on the possibility of settlement.

**Statute of limitations:** The deadline, established by statute, by which a cause of action must be asserted in a lawsuit, or be lost forever.

**Stipulated Judgment:** A judgment the terms of which have been agreed upon by the parties (also called a *consent judgment*).

**Stipulation of facts:** A statement setting forth those facts which have been agreed upon by the parties.

**Structured settlement:** Settlement in which the amount of damages agreed upon is paid not in one lump sum, but in a series of installments over time.

**Subject matter jurisdiction:** Jurisdiction of a court over the type or category of dispute existing between the parties.

**Subpoena:** A document issued under the authority of the court and served upon a person, commanding that person to appear at a certain place at a certain time, usually at a deposition or trial (see also *subpoena duces tecum*).

**Subpoena duces tecum:** A subpoena that commands the person subpoenaed to produce certain documents and things at a certain place at a certain time.

**Substantive law:** The rules that govern the non-procedural issues presented to the court for decision.

**Summons:** Served with a complaint to summon the defendant to appear in court by a certain date, and to inform the defendant of the possibility of default if such appearance is not made.

**Supplemental pleading:** Under the FRCP, a pleading that modifies an earlier pleading based upon transactions or occurrences taking place *subsequent* to that earlier pleading.

**Supplementation:** Updating of previously-served discovery responses (see Rule 26(e) of the FRCP, for example).


**Temporary restraining order:** A form of injunctive relief which may be ordered by the court in an ex parte manner but which remains in force for only a very brief time (usually no more than ten days) until a hearing can be held; abbreviated "TRO."

**Theory of the case:** The litigation strategy formulated by a plaintiff.

**Theory of the defense:** The litigation strategy formulated by a defendant.

**Third party complaint:** A complaint filed by a party defending a claim against an outside third party who may be liable to the defending party for any judgment obtained on the original claim (also called *impleader*).

**Three-judge panel:** Group of judges assigned to decide a case heard in the U.S. Court of Appeals.

**Tickler system:** A method for deadline tracking in which empty slots in a receptacle correspond to future dates, with reminder forms inserted into relevant slots.

**Time sheets:** Forms used by most law firms on which attorneys and paralegals enter time spent working on various tasks, then identify the client to be billed for such time.

**Title of the action:** Names of the parties as they appear in the caption of a pleading or motion.

**TRO:** See *temporary restraining order*.

**Tort law:** That broad field of substantive law concerned with allegations of one party asserting that another party has wrongfully caused injury to person or property.

**Transcript:** A written verbatim recitation of a deposition or trial, prepared by a court reporter.

**Trial:** Proceeding in a lawsuit in which evidence is presented by the parties and ruled upon by the judge, after which a decision is made resolving the case. The trial is the focus of the entire process of litigation in the courts. (See also *bench trial; jury trial; non-jury trial; court trial*).

**Trial court:**   The court of original jurisdiction in which a lawsuit is first filed, and in which a trial will eventually be held unless the lawsuit is resolved prior to trial. Only in the trial court do trials take place.

**Trial *de novo*:**   A new trial begun from scratch, with no direct reliance on a previous record.

**Trial docket:**   The list of cases awaiting trial; impacts on the scheduling of cases for trial based upon length of docket and available courtrooms and judges (also called a *trial list*).

**Trial list:**   See *trial docket*.

**Trial memorandum:**   Memorandum of law sometimes requested from counsel (by the trial court judge) and relating to factual and legal questions at issue in the trial.

**Trial notebook:**   Notebook used by attorney at trial; it contains separate sections for easy access to pleadings, discovery materials, jury selection materials, witness information, model jury instructions, etc.

**Trier-of-fact:**   The entity charged with deciding questions of fact; in a bench trial the judge is the trier-of-fact, while in a jury trial the jury is the trier-of-fact.


**Uncontested:**   Unopposed, as a motion to which there is no opposition.

**United States Courts of Appeal:**   The intermediate appellate courts in the federal court system.

**United States District Courts:**   The trial courts in the federal court system.

**United States Supreme Court:**   The high court in the federal court system.


**Venue:**   Essentially, the geographical location in which a lawsuit proceeds.

**Verdict:**   The decision rendered by the jury with regard to questions of fact.

**Verification:**   A signature by the party making allegations attesting to their truth, as where a plaintiff signs a verified complaint.

**Verified complaint:**   A complaint where the truth of the allegations has been sworn to by the plaintiff, who then signs the complaint to that effect.

**Voir dire:**   The process by which potential jurors are questioned so as to identify potential bias or other incapacity.

**Voluntary dismissal:**   A dismissal under Rule 41 of the FRCP to which the party whose claim is dismissed agrees. Unless otherwise specified, such a voluntary dismissal is generally without prejudice to the claim being raised again.


**Waiver:**   Under Rule 12(g) and (h) of the FRCP, loss of the right to raise subsequent Rule 12 issues based upon the prior filing of a Rule 12 motion (or a pleading) which omitted such issues.

**Withdrawal:**   Under the rules of some state court systems, a document which has an effect similar to that of a voluntary dismissal without prejudice.

**Witness stand:**   Area in a courtroom where the witness submits to examination by the attorneys.

**Working copies:**   Copies made when working with documents, to avoid marking original documents.

**Writ of certiorari:** The writ issued by the Supreme Court of the United States indicating a willingness to review a decision for which review had been requested by a Petition for Certiorari.

**Writ of execution:** The official document required for the enforcement of a judgment for the payment of money (see, for example, Rule 69 of the FRCP).

# INDEX